Enjoy the "Pearls of Wisdom" that make this the finest of Practice textbooks!

TM   © ETC 2005

California
REAL ESTATE
PRACTICE

4th Edition

Walt Huber
Glendale College

Arlette Lyons, CRS, GRI
Mt. San Antonio College

Owner/Broker, Lyons & Associates, Inc.

COPYRIGHT 1974, 1981, 1988, 1994, 2005
Educational Textbook Company, Inc.
P. O. Box 3597
Covina, California 91722
(626)339-7733
(626)332-4744 (Fax)
www.etcbooks.com

Library of Congress Cataloging-in-Publication Data

California Real Estate Practice - Walt Huber and Arlette Lyons - 4th Edition

Summary: Covers all material in Real Estate Practice classes with special emphasis on California real estate procedures. Written in very clear and simple language, easy-to-read format with photographs, charts, and graphs. Includes glossary and index. Suitable for students, salespeople, brokers, and teachers seeking information about the practice of real estate in the day-to-day operations of a real estate brokerage. This textbook is designed to fulfill the course requirement necessary to take the California Real Estate Salesperson and Broker Exams.

1. Real estate business - California
2. Real property - California
    I. Walt Huber, II. Arlette Lyons
HD266. C2B644 2005
333.33

ISBN 0-916772-27-6

Preface

The 4th edition of *CALIFORNIA REAL ESTATE PRACTICE* is a real "jewel" of a book. The most significant improvement we've made is the addition of our new co-author, Arlette Lyons. Not only is she a well-respected and popular professor of real estate at Mt. San Antonio College, she is also a successful broker and owner of Lyons and Associates Realty, Inc. of West Covina, California. With over 20 years of experience as a teacher of Principles and Practice, and more than 25 licensees in her employ, Arlette has mentored literally hundreds of new agents—taking them from students to agents to brokers.

Based on her remarkable career, Arlette is uniquely qualified to share her "pearls of wisdom" with you, the reader. Her advice ranges from precious little gems like making an open house seem homier, to flawless diamonds like how to avoid liability due to easily overlooked loopholes in a sales contract. Thanks to her priceless contributions, every page of this book is a treasure trove of helpful information.

In addition to Arlette's gems, we "outshine" the competition by providing step-by-step instructions for filling out important real estate forms, including how to avoid common and costly mistakes. You'll also find numerous examples of "sample scripts" to help guide you through common dialogue scenarios you're sure to encounter in the listing and selling of real estate. In other words, we teach you how to apply the "principles" you've learned to the actual "practice" of real estate.

Let this be your treasure map in the quest for the riches of a rewarding career!

Authors Walt Huber and Arlette Lyons would like to express our appreciation to the professionals who helped make this text "solid gold." We couldn't have done it without the extraordinary efforts of Colleen Taber, our executive editor, and Rick Lee, our prepress and layout editor, as well as the editorial and proofreading skills of Linda Serra and Andrea Atkins. We're also grateful for the talented contributions of art director Phillip Dockter, and cover artist Melinda Winters.

A special thanks goes out to Professor Andrea Elizalde of Citrus College and attorney Steve Holohan for their helpful input. We also received helpful advice from Hank Greenberg of Golden Empire Mortgage, Inc., and escrow officer Debbie Aquila of Ford Escrow Services Company, Inc.

We appreciate the contributions of Charles Krackeler of Los Altos, California, whose radio show answers many real estate questions for many people, and Ignacio Gonzalez, planning consultant and professor in Ukiah, California.

Acknowledgments

This book contains the input of many prominent educators and real estate professionals. Their involvement as contributing advisors has made it possible for us to cover a wide range of material in detail and, at the same time, offer practical perspectives based upon their extensive classroom and industry experience. Their contributions were invaluable and merit our most sincere thanks.

R. Bryant
Allan Hancock College

J. DiRuscio
Allan Hancock College

R. Smith
American River College

Steve Sodergren
Antelope Valley College

Professor Ballman
Antelope Valley College

Joe Newton
Bakersfield College

Robin Sherman
Cabrillo College

Bruce Southstone, CRB, CRS
Cabrillo College

R. Gable
Canada College

John T. Martinez
Chabot College

Richard McCartney
Chabot College

John A. Culver
Chabot College

Robert Andersen
Chabot College

C. Weeks
Chabot College

J. Brooks
Chabot College

Earl H. Bond
Chaffey College

A. Turner
Chaffey College

J. O. Wright
Chaffey College

Frederick A. Henning
Citrus College

Fred Martinez
City College San Francisco

M. Zelaya
City College San Francisco

Hal Bouley
Coastline College

D. Ables
Coastline College

Corina D. Rollins
College of Marin

K. Fowler
College of Marin

Mark Jenkins
College of The Canyons

R. Vitale
College of The Canyons

Jeff Eddy
College of The Sequoias

Robert Morgan
Compton College

Ronald G. Rueb
Contra Costa College

Mike Hoey
Cosumnes River College

B. Mnichowicz
Cosumnes River College

Professor Ellerman
Cosumnes River College

Nick Zoumbos
Crafton Hills College

Don Blazej
Cuesta College

Professor Langager
Diablo Valley College

Dr. Elliott J. Dixon
East Los Angeles College

O. Vasquez Anderson
East Los Angeles College

Michael Botello, Esq.
El Camino College

Dr. Donna Grogan, GRI, CPM
El Camino College

Derf Fredericks
El Camino College

Charles Krackeler
Foothill College

John E. Roberto, CRS, GRI
Fresno City College

M. Saito
Fresno City College

Dr. Robert J. Bowers
Fullerton College

Charmaine Smith
Fullerton College

Andrea Elizalde
Glendale College

Karen Obuljen
Golden West College

Dino Vlachos
Golden West College

W. Gibson
Hartnell College

C. Storey
Imperial Valley College

Frank Pangborn
Irvine Valley College

John Shaw
Lassen Community College

Thomas Duffy
Los Angeles City College

M. Eisenberg
Los Angeles City College

Professor Maricich
Los Angeles Harbor College

Harold Lerner
Los Angeles Pierce College

L.G. Bellamy
Los Angeles Southwest College

Professor Taylor
Los Angeles Trade-Tech College

Patricia Moore
Los Medanos College

Ignacio Gonzalez
Mendocino College

Harvey Rafel
Merced College

Shirley Jones
Merced College

T. Gee
Merritt College

Edward L. Culbertson
MiraCosta College

Mike Daniels
MiraCosta College

Frank Diaz
Mission College

J.C. Bawiec
Modesto Junior College

T. Provance
Modesto Junior College

Becky D. Jones
Monterey Peninsula College

Mary Ann Zamel
Mt. San Antonio College

Glenn Vice
Mt. San Antonio College

R. Stephan
Mt. San Antonio College

Paul Guess
Mt. San Jacinto College

S. James
Mt. San Jacinto College

Heli Sairanen
Napa Valley College

G. Daum
Orange Coast College

Edwin Estes, Jr.
Palomar College

David Kemp
Palomar College

R. Graves
Palomar College

A. Carmello
Riverside Community College

William L. Nunally
Sacramento City College

Charles D. Brown
Sacramento City College

Paul Grutsis
San Bernardino Valley College

E. Delcoure
San Bernardino Valley College

Michael Durrett
San Bernardino Valley College

Dr. Shad Jefferies
San Diego Mesa College

S. Griger
San Diego Mesa College

D. Stone
San Joaquin Delta College

Janet Truscott
San Joaquin Delta College

R. Hall
San Jose City College

Gary Goldberg, Attorney
Santa Barbara City College

Steve Herndon
Santa Rosa Junior College

Jim Michaelson
Santa Rosa Junior College

Dr. Evelyn D. Winkel
Santiago Canyon College

William Rawlings
Santiago Canyon College

Kim Tyler
Shasta College

Marty Carrick
Shasta College

John Jurivich
Shasta College

M. Wurschmidt
Shasta College

Jo Middleton
Shasta College

Mike Walker
Sierra College

Allan Nuttall
Skyline College

Robert C. Cass
Southwestern College

Ronald E. Loncki
Southwestern College

J.R. Chantengco, CCIM, MBA
Southwestern College

Chris Grover
Victor Valley College

Professor Faz Elahi
West Los Angeles College

George H. Miller
West Valley College

Real Estate Specialists

Charles Ellis
Occidental College

James Short
San Diego State Univ.

Reginald Woolfolk
West Valley Occupational Cntr.

Lorraine Abrams
West Valley Occupational Cntr.

Evan Morris
North Valley Occupational Cntr.

Claudia Wagner
North Valley Occupational Cntr.

Table of Contents

CHAPTER 1: *The Salesperson*   1

  I. ENTER THE SALESPERSON (p. 1)
    A. First, Get the Support of Your Family (p. 1)
    B. Brokers Know When You Pass the Salesperson's Exam (p. 3)
  II. THE BROKER INTERVIEW (p. 5)
    A. How to Select Your Employing Broker (p. 5)
    B. The Appointment (p. 5)
  III. LARGE vs. SMALL OFFICES (p. 9)
  IV. EMPLOYEE-EMPLOYER RELATIONSHIP (p. 12)
    A. Independent Contractor Agreement Highlights (p. 12)
  V. PLANNING OBJECTIVES AND GOALS (p. 17)
    A. Sphere of Influence (p. 17)
    B. Daily Activities Schedule (p. 19)
    C. Soliciting (p. 19)
    D. Previewing (p. 19)
    E. Showing Properties (p. 21)
    F. Becoming an Expert (p. 21)
    G. Attributes of an Effective Salesperson (p. 22)
    H. Why Salespeople Fail (p. 24)
  VI. ENTER THE BROKER (p. 24)
    A. Agency Representation (p. 24)
    B. Directing and Supervising (p. 25)
    C. Cooperative Sales (p. 25)
    D. Commissions (p. 28)
  VII. THE BROKERAGE FIRM (p. 28)
    A. Getting Started in Business (p. 28)
    B. Forms of Business Ownership (p. 30)
  VIII. RECORD KEEPING (p. 32)
    A. Trust Fund Records (p. 32)
    B. Sales Records (Keep for Three Years) (p. 32)
  IX. CHAPTER SUMMARY (p. 35)
  X. KEY TERMS (p. 37)
  XI. CHAPTER 1 QUIZ (p. 38)

CHAPTER 2: *Prospecting* 41

I. PROSPECTING (p. 41)
  A. Sources of Listings and Sellers (p. 41)
  B. Open Houses (p. 46)
  C. Finding Buyers (p. 48)
  D. The Art of Developing Referrals (p. 51)
II. ADVERTISING AND PROMOTION (p. 55)
  A. Product Advertising (p. 57)
  B. Advertising Media (p. 57)
  C. Advertising Pointers (p. 62)
  D. Writing Effective Ads (AIDA) (p. 64)
  E. Budgeting for Advertising (p. 64)
  F. Evaluating Advertising Effectiveness (p. 66)
  G. A Word of Caution (p. 66)
III. CHAPTER SUMMARY (p. 68)
IV. KEY TERMS (p. 69)
V. CHAPTER 2 QUIZ (p. 70)

CHAPTER 3: *The Listing Agreement* 73

I. EMPLOYING AN AGENT (p. 73)
  A. Right to a Commission (p. 75)
  B. Types of Listings (p. 79)
II. AGENCY RELATIONSHIP DISCLOSURE ACT (p. 86)
  A. Single Agency (p. 87)
  B. Dual Agency (p. 87)
III. PREPARING FOR THE LISTING APPOINTMENT (p. 89)
  A. Meeting the Listing Prospect (p. 90)
  B. Research Procedures in Obtaining a Listing (p. 91)
IV. CLOSING THE SELLER (p. 92)
  A. Overcoming Objections to Listing (p. 93)
V. SERVICING LISTINGS (p. 99)
  A. Steps in Servicing a Listing (p. 100)
VI. CHAPTER SUMMARY (p. 105)
VII. KEY TERMS (p. 106)
VIII. CHAPTER 3 QUIZ (p. 107)

CHAPTER 4: Breakdown of the Listing Agreement 111

I. BREAKDOWN AND ANALYSIS OF THE LISTING AGREEMENT (p. 111)
II. COMPLETING THE LISTING KIT (p. 124)
III. THE BROKER'S ROLE IN REAL ESTATE APPRAISAL (p. 142)
    A. Helping Sellers Determine Listing Price (p. 142)
    B. Market Approach or Comparative Value (p. 144)
    C. Cost Approach to Valuation (p. 147)
    D. Capitalization Approach to Valuation (p. 148)
    E. Pitfalls in Accepting Overpriced Listings (p. 149)
    F. Licensed Appraisers (p. 149)
IV. CHAPTER SUMMARY (p. 151)
V. KEY TERMS (p. 153)
VI. CHAPTER 4 QUIZ (p. 154)

CHAPTER 5: Selling 157

I. THE AMERICAN DREAM (p. 157)
II. SHOPPING FOR A HOME (p. 159)
    A. Purchasing a Home: A General Discussion (p. 160)
    B. Some Advantages to Owning a Home (p. 162)
    C. Some Disadvantages to Owning a Home (p. 162)
    D. Budgeting for a Home (p. 163)
III. WHY BUYERS BUY (p. 164)
IV. TECHNIQUES OF SELLING (p. 165)
    A. Direct Contact Communications (Face-to-Face) (p. 165)
    B. Letter Communications (One-Way) (p. 167)
    C. Telephone Communications (Two-Way) (p. 168)
V. THE CRITICAL PATH OF SELLING (p. 179)
    A. Steps Involved in a Sale (p. 179)
VI. THE SALE (p. 193)
    A. Closing Techniques (p. 194)
    B. Overriding Objections (p. 196)
VII. CHAPTER SUMMARY (p. 199)
VIII. KEY TERMS (p. 201)
 IX. CHAPTER 5 QUIZ (p. 202)

CHAPTER 6:   *The Purchase Offer*   **205**

I. OVERVIEW OF THE PURCHASE CONTRACT (p. 205)
A. Why Purchase Contracts are Used (p. 205)
II. EVALUATION AND ANALYSIS OF THE PURCHASE CONTRACT (p. 208)
A. Interpretation of the Form (p. 217)
B. Filling Out the Form—A Breakdown (p. 217)
III. CHAPTER SUMMARY (p. 250)
IV. KEY TERMS (p. 251)
V. CHAPTER 6 QUIZ (p. 252)

CHAPTER 7:   *Additional Forms for the Purchase Contract*   **255**

I. FORMS SUPPLIED TO THE BUYER (p. 255)
II. CAR® REAL ESTATE DISCLOSURE SUMMARY CHART (p. 273)
III. CHAPTER SUMMARY (p. 286)
IV. KEY TERMS (p. 287)
V. CHAPTER 7 QUIZ (p. 288)

CHAPTER 8:   *Finance*   **291**

I. NATURE OF FINANCING (p. 291)
A. Introduction to the Financing Process (p. 291)
B. The Cost of Borrowing Money (p. 294)
II. INSTITUTIONAL (CONVENTIONAL) FINANCING (p. 296)
A. Mortgage Bankers (p. 296)
B. Savings Banks (p. 296)
C. Commercial Banks (p. 298)
D. Life Insurance Companies (p. 299)
E. Private Mortgage Insurance (PMI) (Provide a Valuable Service) (p. 299)
F. Fixed Rate Mortgages (p. 300)
G. Adjustable Rate Mortgages (ARMs) (p. 300)
H. Special Purpose Loans (p. 301)
III. THE SECONDARY MORTGAGE MARKET (p. 303)
A. Secondary Mortgage (Trust Deed) Market (p. 303)
B. Final Word on Conventional Loans (Risk—Without Government Backing) (p. 304)
IV. GOVERNMENT FINANCING (GOVERNMENT-BACKED LOANS) (p. 304)
A. Federal Housing Administration (FHA) (p. 305)
B. Veterans Administration (VA) (p. 309)
C. California Department of Veterans Affairs (Cal-Vet) (p. 311)
V. QUALIFYING THE BORROWER (p. 312)
A. The Loan Application (p. 312)
VI. NONINSTITUTIONAL FINANCING (p. 317)
A. Junior Loans (Secondary Financing) (p. 317)

B. All-Inclusive Trust Deed (AITD) (p. 319)
C. Contract of Sale (Land Contract) (p. 319)
D. All-Cash Transactions (p. 320)
VII. LOAN TAKEOVERS (p. 321)
A. "Assumption" vs. "Subject To" (p. 321)
VIII. LOAN BROKERAGE (p. 322)
A. Mortgage Loan Disclosure Statement (p. 322)
B. Business and Professions Code (Commissions and Other Requirements) (p. 326)
C. Usury Limitations (p. 326)
IX. CHAPTER SUMMARY (p. 327)
X. KEY TERMS (p. 329)
XI. CHAPTER 8 QUIZ (p. 331)

CHAPTER 9: Escrow

335

I. THE ESCROW PROCEDURE (p. 335)
A. Requirements of a Valid Escrow (p. 337)
B. Escrow Holder (p. 337)
C. Real Estate Brokers Can Conduct Escrows (p. 339)
II. HOW ESCROWS WORK (p. 339)
A. Fax Purchase Agreement to Escrow (p. 339)
B. Follow-Through Checklist (p. 339)
C. Opening Escrow (p. 343)
D. Escrow Rules (p. 343)
E. Who Selects the Escrow Company? (p. 344)
F. Escrow Instructions (p. 344)
G. Financing is an Important Aspect of the Escrow (p. 345)
H. Escrow Example (p. 345)
I. Closing Date is the Date of Recordation (p. 346)
III. PRORATION (p. 346)
A. 30 Days is the Basis for Proration (p. 349)
IV. TERMITES AND OTHER PROBLEMS (p. 349)
A. Structural Pest Control Certification Report (Report and Clearance) (p. 349)
B. Broker Maintains Pest Control Documentation (p. 350)
V. FIRE INSURANCE (p. 351)
A. Fire Insurance... A Must! (p. 351)
B. Fire Insurance Proration (p. 352)
VI. TITLE INSURANCE (p. 352)
A. Chain of Title (Recorded Public History) (p. 352)
B. Title Insurance (Has Four Functions) (p. 352)
C. Preliminary Title Report (Ordered First) (p. 353)
VII. TYPES OF TITLE INSURANCE POLICIES (p. 355)
A. California Land Title Association (CLTA) (Standard Coverage Policy) (p. 355)

B. American Land Title Association (ALTA)
(Extended Coverage Policy - Survey Included) (p. 360)
C. ALTA-R (One-to-Four Residential Units) (p. 361)
D. Who Pays Title Insurance Fees? (p. 362)
E. Title Insurance Disclosure (p. 362)

VIII. REAL ESTATE SETTLEMENT PROCEDURES ACT (RESPA) (p. 362)
IX. CALIFORNIA ESCROW ASSOCIATION (p. 363)
X. CHAPTER SUMMARY (p. 368)
XI. KEY TERMS (p. 370)
XII. CHAPTER 9 QUIZ (p. 371)

CHAPTER 10: Taxation

375

I. PROPERTY TAXES (p. 375)
A. Proposition 13 (p. 378)
B. Property Taxes Become a Specific Lien (p. 382)
C. Property Tax Time Table (p. 382)
D. Property Tax Proration Problem (p. 383)
E. Homeowner's Property Tax Exemption (p. 385)
F. Disabled and Senior Citizen's Property Tax Postponement (p. 386)
G. Veteran's Exemption (p. 386)
H. Tax Exempt Property (p. 386)
II. SPECIAL ASSESSMENT TAX (p. 387)
A. Improvement Bond Act of 1915 (p. 387)
B. Mello-Roos Community Facilities Act (p. 388)
III. DOCUMENTARY TRANSFER TAX (p. 388)
IV. GIFT AND ESTATE TAXES (p. 388)
A. Federal Gift Taxes (p. 388)
B. Federal Estate Tax (p. 390)
C. No State Gift and Inheritance Taxes (p. 390)
V. FEDERAL AND STATE INCOME TAXES (p. 390)
VI. INCOME TAX ASPECTS OF REAL ESTATE TRANSACTIONS (p. 391)
VII. TAXES ON PERSONAL RESIDENCE (p. 392)
A. Deduction of Interest (p. 393)
B. Deduction of Property Taxes (p. 393)
C. Deduction of Prepayment Penalties (p. 393)
D. Sale of a Residence (p. 394)
VIII. TAXES FOR INCOME PRODUCING PROPERTIES (p. 394)
A. Depreciation of Business Property (Federal and State) (p. 395)
B. Advantages of "Sale-Leaseback" (Buyer Gets to Depreciate New Building Cost) (p. 395)
IX. SALE OF REAL PROPERTY (p. 396)
A. Capital Assets (Gains and Losses) (p. 396)
B. Federal Income Tax Rates (p. 396)
C. Alternative Minimum Tax (AMT) (Must Calculate Taxes Twice) (p. 397)

D. Accounting for the Sale of Real Estate (Investment/Commercial) (p. 398)
X. INSTALLMENT SALES AND EXCHANGES (p. 398)
A. Installment Sales of Real Estate (p. 398)
B. Exchanges Tax-Deferred (Federal and State) (Section 1031 of the IRS Code) (p. 399)
XI. DEALER PROPERTY (p. 401)
XII. WE ARE NOW TAX COLLECTORS
(FEDERAL AND STATE INCOME TAX LAWS) (p. 402)
A. Federal Tax Collection Requirements and Exemptions (If a Foreigner) (p. 402)
B. State Tax Collection Requirements and Exemptions
   (If a Foreigner or Resident of Another State) (p. 403)
XIII. OTHER TAXES PAID BY BROKERS (p. 405)
A. Business License Taxes (City Taxes) (p. 405)
XIV. CHAPTER SUMMARY (p. 405)
XV. KEY TERMS (p. 406)
XVI. CHAPTER 10 QUIZ (p. 407)

CHAPTER 11: Investing   411

I. WHY INVEST IN REAL ESTATE? (p. 411)
A. Objectives (p. 411)
B. Capacity (p. 413)
C. Soundness (p. 413)
II. BENEFITS OF INVESTING (p. 414)
A. Tax Shelter (Ways to Reduce Gains) (p. 414)
B. Other Tax Benefits (p. 414)
C. Appreciation Potential (p. 414)
D. Hedge Against Inflation (p. 415)
E. Income (p. 415)
F. Interim Use (p. 415)
G. Stability (p. 415)
H. Control and Use (p. 416)
I. Refinancing (To Buy More Property) (p. 416)
J. Amenities (p. 416)
III. CHALLENGES TO REAL ESTATE INVESTING (p. 416)
A. Large Capital Outlay (p. 416)
B. Lack of Liquidity (p. 417)
C. Professional Property Management Needed (p. 417)
D. Potentially Unfavorable Financing (p. 417)
E. Personal Attachment (Affecting Profitability) (p. 418)
F. Miscellaneous Negative Factors (p. 418)
IV. FINANCING INCOME PROPERTIES (p. 418)
A. Sources of Financing (p. 418)
B. Available Funds (p. 420)
V. YOUR ROLE IN THE INVESTMENT PROCESS (p. 420)

A. Apartment Prospecting and Marketing (p. 420)
B. Investment Planning and Counseling (p. 422)
VI. RESIDENTIAL INCOME PROPERTIES (p. 423)
A. Property Analysis (Appraisal) (p. 423)
B. Analyzing the Rental Market (p. 428)
C. Study Area Characteristics (p. 429)
D. Characteristics of the Rental Market (p. 430)
VII. SYNDICATION (PURCHASE GROUP) (p. 431)
A. Definition (p. 431)
B. Brokerage Opportunities (p. 432)
C. Forms of Legal Organization (p. 432)
VIII. CHAPTER SUMMARY (p. 436)
IX. KEY TERMS (p. 438)
X. CHAPTER 11 QUIZ (p. 439)

CHAPTER 12: *Sale of a Business* 443

I. SMALL BUSINESS OPPORTUNITIES (p. 443)
II. SELLING A BUSINESS (p. 445)
A. Listing Agreement (p. 445)
B. Uniform Commercial Code (UCC) (p. 446)
C. Security Agreement and Financing Statement (p. 448)
D. Sales and Use Taxes (p. 450)
E. Bill of Sale (p. 451)
F. Assignment of Lease (p. 451)
III. VALUATION OF BUSINESS OPPORTUNITIES (p. 451)
IV. TAX CONSEQUENCES ON THE SALE OF BUSINESS OPPORTUNITIES (p. 453)
V. ALCOHOLIC BEVERAGE CONTROL ACT (p. 453)
VI. ANCILLARY ACTIVITIES AND SPECIALTY ROLES (p. 455)
A. Real Properties Securities Dealer (RPSD) (p. 455)
B. Notary Public Services (p. 456)
VII. PROPERTY MANAGEMENT ACTIVITIES (p. 457)
VIII. ESCROW ACTIVITIES (p. 457)
IX. LOAN BROKERAGE ACTIVITIES (p. 458)
X. SYNDICATION (p. 459)
XI. BROKERAGE OPPORTUNITIES IN PROBATE SALES (p. 459)
A. Mechanics of the Probate Sale (p. 460)
XII. STATE OF CALIFORNIA SALES OPPORTUNITIES (p. 463)
A. Board of Education Real Estate Sales (p. 463)
B. CALTRANS (p. 463)
C. Subdivision Sales Opportunities (p. 464)
D. Real Estate Investment Counselor (p. 466)
XIII. REAL ESTATE BROKERAGE—GENERAL VS. SPECIALIZATION (p. 467)
XIV. MANUFACTURED HOUSING AND THE LICENSEE (p. 469)

A. Mobile Home Parks (p. 469)

B. Opportunities (p. 470)

C. Mobile Home Dealer vs. Real Estate Broker (p. 470)

D. Marketing (p. 470)

E. Listing Manufactured Homes (p. 470)

F. Selling Manufactured Homes (p. 471)

XV. CHAPTER SUMMARY (p. 475)

XVI. KEY TERMS (p. 477)

XVII. CHAPTER 12 QUIZ (p. 478)

CHAPTER 13: Property Management   481

I. FAIR HOUSING LAWS (p. 481)

A. State Law - Unruh Civil Rights Act (p. 484)

B. State Law - California Fair Employment and Housing Act (FEHA) (p. 484)

C. State Law - Housing Financial Discrimination Act of 1977 (No Redlining) (p. 484)

D. Federal Law - Federal Civil Rights Act of 1968 (p. 485)

II. PROPERTY MANAGEMENT (p. 487)

A. Types of Properties (p. 488)

B. Types of Property Managers (p. 488)

C. Duties and Responsibilities of Property Managers (p. 490)

D. Landlord-Tenant Termination Laws (30- and 60-Day Notices) (p. 492)

E. Selection of Property Managers (p. 493)

F. Leasing and Tenant Selection (p. 499)

G. Accurate Record Keeping (A Must for Property Managers) (p. 509)

H. Common Interest Development (CID) Management (p. 512)

I. Prepaid Rental Listing Service (PRLS) (p. 515)

J. Improving Value Through Balanced Management (p. 516)

K. Rent Control (p. 518)

L. Low-Income Housing (p. 518)

M. Professional Associations for Managers (p. 518)

III. CHAPTER SUMMARY (p. 519)

IV. KEY TERMS (p. 522)

V. CHAPTER 13 QUIZ (p. 523)

CHAPTER 14: Real Estate Assistants   527

I. ASSISTING AS A CAREER (p. 527)

A. What is a Real Estate Assistant? (p. 529)

B. Why Become an Assistant? (p. 530)

II. WHO HIRES ASSISTANTS? (p. 532)

A. When Does an Agent Need an Assistant? (p. 532)

III. GETTING THE JOB DONE (p. 534)

A. Your Résumé (p. 534)

B. Interview Questions (p. 536)
C. The Job Offer (p. 537)
IV. WHAT DO ASSISTANTS DO? (p. 542)
A. Office Administration (p. 542)
B. Updating Data (p. 545)
C. Keeping and Assisting with Appointments (p. 546)
D. Staying in Touch with Your Agent's Clients (p. 546)
E. Technology (p. 547)
F. Notary Public (p. 548)
G. Escrow Coordinator (p. 552)
H. Follow-Up Details (p. 552)
V. CHAPTER SUMMARY (p. 553)
VI. KEY TERMS (p. 554)
VII. CHAPTER 14 QUIZ (p. 556)

CHAPTER 15: *Licensing, Ethics, and Associations* 559

I. DEPARTMENT OF REAL ESTATE (DRE) (p. 559)
II. REAL ESTATE LICENSE REQUIREMENTS (p. 561)
A. Who Must Have a License (p. 561)
B. When a License is Not Required (p. 562)
C. Obtaining the Salesperson's License (p. 562)
D. Obtaining the Broker's License (Renewable Four-Year License) (p. 569)
E. Renewal of License - Every Four Years (Salesperson and Broker) (p. 570)
F. Continuing Education (CE) Requirement
   (45 Hours Every Four Years to Renew Your License) (p. 570)
G. Prepaid Rental Listing Service (PRLS) License (p. 571)
III. REAL ESTATE LAW AND REGULATIONS (p. 572)
A. Real Estate Commissioner (Appointed by the Governor) (p. 572)
B. Enforcement of Real Estate Law (p. 573)
C. Hearings for License Violations (p. 573)
D. Licenses: Revoke, Restrict, Suspend (p. 574)
E. Real Estate Bulletin, and Other Bulletins (p. 574)
IV. COMMON REAL ESTATE LAW VIOLATIONS (p. 574)
A. Section 10176: Licensee Acting in a Licensee Capacity (p. 576)
B. Section 10177: Licensee Not Necessarily Acting as a Licensee (p. 576)
C. Regulations of the Commissioner (Found in the Administrative Code) (p. 576)
V. REAL ESTATE GENERAL FUND (p. 580)
VI. TRADE AND PROFESSIONAL ASSOCIATIONS (p. 580)
A. Local Real Estate Associations (p. 581)
B. California Association of Realtors® (CAR) (p. 581)
C. National Association of Realtors® (NAR) (p. 582)
D. Realtist Defined (p. 592)
E. National Association of Hispanic Real Estate Professionals (NAHREP) (p. 594)

    F. Asian Real Estate Association of America (AREAA) (p. 594)

    G. Independent Associations (p. 595)

    H. Other Associations (p. 595)

    I. Real Estate Instructor and Licensing Associations (p. 595)

    J. No Affiliation Necessary (p. 595)

  VII. CHAPTER SUMMARY (p. 597)

 VIII. KEY TERMS (p. 599)

   IX. CHAPTER 15 QUIZ (p. 600)

Appendix I: Policy Manual   **603**

Appendix II: Glossary   **607**

Index   **639**

Order Form: All the Great Books From ETC!   **652**

CHAPTER 1
The Salesperson
How to Get Started

I. Enter the Salesperson

You've worked long and hard to get through basic training and acquire your real estate salesperson's license, so now is the time to set your goals and focus on how to achieve them.

Always put your goals in writing and review and revise them at least once a year. Short-term and long-term goals are ideal. Where do you want to be in five years?

You need to know what your job description is, what is expected of you, and how to best perform the duties which will lead to a rewarding and successful career in real estate sales.

People will buy and sell real estate in all types of economies, both up and down.

Real estate is cyclical and the only constant is change.

A. FIRST, GET THE SUPPORT OF YOUR FAMILY

It's important to have the support of family members. Your time will not always be your own. You may have to show property on Sunday afternoon, or sit at an "Open

1

CHAPTER 1 OUTLINE

I. ENTER THE SALESPERSON (p. 1)
   A. First, Get the Support of Your Family (p. 1)
      1. You Should Have Six Months' Savings (p. 3)
   B. Brokers Know When You Pass the Salesperson's Exam (p. 3)

II. THE BROKER INTERVIEW (p. 5)
   A. How to Select Your Employing Broker (p. 5)
   B. The Appointment (p. 5)
      1. What Questions to Ask (p. 5)
         a. What are the Startup Costs? (p. 5)
         b. Who Pays for Expenses? (p. 5)
         c. What are the New Salesperson Requirements? (p. 6)
         d. What Training and Support Will I Receive? (p. 7)
         e. What is My Portion of the Commission? (p. 8)
         f. What are the Miscellaneous Benefits? (p. 8)
         g. Who Answers the Telephone? (p. 9)

III. LARGE vs. SMALL OFFICES (p. 9)

IV. EMPLOYEE-EMPLOYER RELATIONSHIP (p. 12)
   A. Independent Contractor Agreement Highlights (p. 12)

V. PLANNING OBJECTIVES AND GOALS (p. 17)
   A. Sphere of Influence (p. 17)
   B. Daily Activities Schedule (p. 19)
   C. Soliciting (p. 19)
   D. Previewing (p. 19)
      1. The Sales Kit (p. 19)
   E. Showing Properties (p. 21)
   F. Becoming an Expert (p. 21)
   G. Attributes of an Effective Salesperson (p. 22)
   H. Why Salespeople Fail (p. 24)

VI. ENTER THE BROKER (p. 24)
   A. Agency Representation (p. 24)
      1. Disclosure Regarding Agency Relationships (p. 24)
   B. Directing and Supervising (p. 25)
   C. Cooperative Sales (p. 25)
   D. Commissions (p. 28)

VII. THE BROKERAGE FIRM (p. 28)
   A. Getting Started in Business (p. 28)

      B. Forms of Business Ownership (p. 30)
         1. Sole Proprietorship (p. 30)
         2. Partnership (p. 30)
         3. Corporation (p. 31)
VIII. RECORD KEEPING (p. 32)
      A. Trust Fund Records (p. 32)
      B. Sales Records (Keep for Three Years) (p. 32)
         1. Listings (p. 34)
         2. Purchase Contracts and Commissions (p. 34)
IX. CHAPTER SUMMARY (p. 35)
X. KEY TERMS (p. 37)
XI. CHAPTER 1 QUIZ (p. 38)

House" on your listing, or some other agent's listing. Many real estate tasks demand evening performances, when clients are usually home, so your family meals will not always be a "planned gourmet event." Some creative adjustments will need to be made by all.

1. You Should Have Six Months' Savings

It is also extremely important to have saved a little nest egg to meet your financial obligations for approximately **six months**, as there is a lag time of at least two to three months prior to receiving your first commission. Your clients' needs should be your first priority, not your concerns about paying your bills.

If your expectations are realistic, you should be able to enjoy an adequate standard of living while building your new career and wealth.

B. BROKERS KNOW WHEN YOU PASS THE SALESPERSON'S EXAM

Because it's a matter of public record, when you pass the state real estate examination, you will be inundated by solicitations from various offices wanting to interview you. Some will be large franchises and some will be smaller independently owned offices. Therefore, finding a sponsoring broker—a real estate office in which to hang your license—may not be a problem, but selecting the right environment for you is one of the most important choices that you're going to make at this time.

Changing from one office to another is always expensive and emotional. Not only will you need to start anew, learn the office procedures, meet new associates, purchase new business cards, and other necessary advertising items to the industry, you'll also need to contact your whole sphere of influence to let all your contacts know of your move, and how to reach you. *SPHERE OF INFLUENCE is a list of prospects that an*

There are numerous local area "Association of Realtors®" that operate under the umbrella of the National Association of Realtors® (NAR) and the California Association of Realtors® (for an example, see **Figure 1-1**). These trade associations serve the same function to the real estate professional that Bar Associations do to lawyers and Medical Associations do to doctors. It is a voluntary membership and a force for good for the betterment of its practitioners and the public they serve. The Association may operate a Multiple Listing Service (MLS), wherein Realtors® place the property listings they have for sale for the benefit of the membership and their sellers. Agents are permitted to enter their listings electronically in the MLS through the Internet.

Figure 1-1

agent contacts in the hope they will become clients. These people are contacted on a regular basis. A sphere of influence can be a geographical farm of potential clients, a group of people with whom you share a common interest, friends, relatives, etc.

More importantly, while considering a move, it's hard for new real estate agents to be productive, as the eminent move drains time and energy away from clients' needs. So take your time and be wise in your selection of a sponsoring broker and office. We suggest you interview with at least three brokers.

Remember, you have one year after passing the licensing examination to pay for and obtain your salesperson's license and select your "sponsoring" broker.

II. The Broker Interview

A. HOW TO SELECT YOUR EMPLOYING BROKER

One good broker source is a personal referral from buyers or sellers who are pleased with the services rendered them. Successful agents work for brokers with good reputations—that's where you want to be, and with whom you want to be associated.

Your reputation as an agent is directly related to the reputation of the broker for whom you choose to work.

Observe the real estate signs and the newspaper advertising in the areas you plan to service. If one company overshadows all others, then you may want to interview with its broker or office manager.

Another way of locating a broker in good standing is to call the local Association of Realtors®. You may also want to get on the Internet and check out listings from various websites, check the various brokers' presence in the industry and how they represent themselves.

B. THE APPOINTMENT

You'll need to make an appointment for approximately one hour with the brokers of your choice, preferably at their place of business, so that you can form an opinion of their facilities and the other agents in the company. It's important to feel comfortable in your new environment. Naturally, you should dress in sensible business clothes, be punctual, and pleasant. These outer signs of **professionalism** are highly regarded by all industries. Remember, first impressions are important, and professionalism is what you are striving for.

You and the broker are interviewing each other.

1. What Questions to Ask

a. What are the Start-Up Costs?

Remember, you probably will be considered an independent contractor, and it's important to start off on the right foot. Some brokers charge a monthly desk and telephone fee. These can be minimal, such as $20 per month, all the way to thousands of dollars per month, depending on what's being offered in benefits and commission split.

b. Who Pays for Expenses?

You need to know what the broker pays for and what you are expected to pay:

1. Costs of signs, "For Sale" and "Open House" signs, flags, etc.
2. Cost of having signs put up and taken down
3. Multiple Listing input (Most inputs are computer generated)
4. Business cards
5. Stationary, literature, brochures
6. Newspaper and magazine advertisements
7. Telephone charges (including long distance)
8. Desk fees
9. Forms – The California Association of Realtors® offers WINForms® free to their members. *WINFORMS are constantly upgraded forms that can be downloaded from the Internet, saving time and expense and the use of outdated forms.*
10. Trade magazines
11. Local Chambers of Commerce membership
12. Yellow Page advertisement
13. Internet websites and E-mail addresses

c. What are the New Salesperson Requirements?

Brokers expect their agents to have a clean and operable car with adequate insurance to cover any mishap while showing property.

A four-door car is always preferable for showing clients around.

Professional liability insurance is a must. Most brokers carry **Error and Omission insurance**, which is usually paid for by the salesperson in conjunction with the broker. It can be paid yearly or on a per transaction basis. The cost of this professional liability insurance depends on the broker's claim history. As with most types of insurance, there usually is a deductible which can range from $1,000 to $10,000 per claim.

Error and Omission (liability) insurance protects real estate agents and their brokers against catastrophic lawsuits brought about by the public.

Will your broker contribute a reasonable amount should you be found liable in a lawsuit or arbitration judgment? Regulations require that all agents sign a contract with their brokers. See the CAR® **Independent Contractor Agreement (Between Broker and Associate-Licensee Contract) form** (**Figure 1-3**, later in the chapter).

Professionalism will lead to a successful real estate career. It entails a business-like demeanor and dress code, an appropriate vocabulary, showing expertise in real estate transactions, and, most importantly, a genuine caring for the clients' needs and goals.

www.lyonsandassociatesrltr.com

Lyons and Associates, Inc., Realtor

	Current Weather	Sunny 72	Hi 90° / Lo 60°
	More Detail	5-Day Forecast	Historical Weather

MAIN PAGE

FEATURED PROPERTY

OUR LISTINGS

SEARCH FOR HOMES

OPEN HOUSES

MORTGAGE CENTER

KNOW YOUR REALTORS
REAL ESTATE EXCELLENCE

Arlette Lyons, CRS, GRI - 1972 to PRESENT --
Independent real estate professional.
Lyons & Associates, Inc. Realtor, owned and managed by
Arlette Lyons is conveniently located in its own 5000 sq.ft.
building in the East San Gabriel Valley, in West Covina,
California right off the San Bernardino Freeway. The

Most offices have their own websites where their listings appear with links to other related sites of interest, such as Realtor.com. Promote your electronic addresses on all your advertisement and mail outs.

d. What Training and Support Will I Receive?

Some companies will send you to a school for a week or so. Others will have an in-house trainer teaching the forms and various closing techniques. Other firms will have a seasoned agent as a mentor checking with the new salespeople on a regular basis, answering their questions, making suggestions on how to improve their performances, and accompanying them on appointments.

Practicing on a client can prove expensive for all concerned. Don't let pride stand in the way of asking for guidance if you need it.

Additionally, there is a wealth of training at the local Association of Realtors® offered free, or for a very minimal fee, to their members. These classes and seminars address the multifaceted real estate industry's need for technical support and the constant legal changes brought on by this dynamic field.

e. What is My Portion of the Commission?

Commission splits are important, but not as important as it may at first appear. You need to know when and how your broker pays your commission. You must remember that not all agents are on the same commission split. Most seasoned agents with a good track record receive a higher percentage than a brand new untried agent. To encourage higher productivity, many brokers offer a bonus incentive after a certain amount of commission has been earned by the agent. This escalating type of commission benefits both the broker and the agents.

Remember: 90% commission of nothing is still nothing!

With a ***STRAIGHT COMMISSION***, *the broker does not charge a fee, but charges a commission based on a percentage of the selling price on a closed escrow transaction.* Hence, the compensation paid to a sales agent reflects the same method, on a shared basis, which varies widely from office to office.

A ***100% COMMISSION*** *refers to any commission payment arrangement between a real estate salesperson and the employing broker in which the salesperson handling a real estate transaction receives all (or nearly all) of the commission earned by the office.* In this case, the salesperson usually pays the broker a monthly desk fee and a proportionate share of the office expenses, such as advertising, clerical and secretarial, telephone and multiple listing services. Or the salesperson may pay for all expenses incurred in addition to a flat monthly fee, which may total more than $1,000 per month.

A real estate broker cannot use a 100% commission arrangement to evade his or her responsibility under the Real Estate Law to supervise salespeople. An agent can work for only one broker at a time, and cannot act independently of his or her broker. All fees and commissions are disbursed through the agent's broker.

The 100% commission plan is not appropriate for you as a new agent, for the obvious reason that you still have much to learn about the real estate business. You cannot be expected to pay an adequate and proportionate contribution to the company at such an early stage in your career.

f. What are the Miscellaneous Benefits?

Some brokers provide additional incentives to successful salespeople to assist them in attending educational seminars offered by local, state, and national boards of real estate. Real estate certificates and degrees are available through many community colleges and other educational institutions. The broker may also permit salespeople, or the more successful ones at least, to purchase their own residence without having to pay for a listing or a selling commission or at a drastically reduced commission. Whatever the final compensation plan arranged, you and your broker should avoid any misunderstanding by having the details carefully spelled out in writing in an Independent Contractor Agreement (see Figure 1-3).

It's important at this time to disclose your past work experiences, how much time and effort you plan to devote to all aspects of your real estate career, including ongoing education, as this may bring about a more favorable split. Let's remember that in order for an office to be successful, there must be a reasonable margin of profit for both the broker and the associates. Presenting a first class picture to the Industry and to the clients bears a cost which should not be overlooked. You may be asked at this time to fill out an **Application for Sales Associate (Figure 1-2)**.

The most important issue in the interview is to determine the integrity of the broker and the office and your level of comfort and harmony experienced while there.

g. Who Answers the Telephone?

Who answers the telephone in the office? This is an important issue as it determines how you'll prioritize your tasks and budget your time. (See "Floor Time" in Chapter 5.)

III. Large vs. Small Offices

As a new agent, you'll want to examine the size of the company for which you want to work. Keep in mind that a firm's growth potential may be the opposite of what you expect. A corporate-owned business may decide to remain small, while a sole proprietor may choose to go big, opening up a number of branch offices and hiring as many as 60 licensees and more to staff each.

Size invariably determines the types of technical and managerial problems that confront a firm, as well as training and opportunities provided to new employees.

In general, the small firm tends to remain flexible, thus better able to seize upon opportunities with no need to obtain corporate approval. Its activities are limited primarily to selling, however, unless there are several good listing agents in the company to increase its inventory.

The large firm, by contrast, is diversified, can develop capital more readily, is less flexible, and must carry a higher burden of overhead, including extensive training, with less accurate control of its resources.

Figure 1-2

APPLICATION FOR SALES ASSOCIATE
(All information held in confidence)

Date of application _____

Name _____ Social Security number _____

Address _____ City _____ Zip _____

How long at this address? _____ Telephone number ( ) _____

Are you over 18 years of age? _____ If employed, can you verify your legal right to work in the U.S.? _____

Referred to this firm by _____

FORMER RESIDENCE ADDRESSES
Show last 10 years, beginning with most recent address

Dates		
from	to	

GENERAL DATA

Are you familiar with the irregular hours and weekends you will be working? _____ And the irregular earnings? _____

Are these acceptable to you? _____ Do you have any family problems which might interfere with your work? _____

Indicate for how long you are in a position financially to sustain yourself:

☐ 3 months ☐ 6 months ☐ 1 year ☐ other _____

Will you devote full-time to a career in real estate? _____ What total annual earnings do you expect to receive from selling real estate? _____

Why do you want to join our organization? _____

Are you willing to abide by our rules and policies? _____

Are you willing to devote a reasonable time to learn the basics of the real estate business? _____ If employed by us, will you join the local Board of REALTORS®?

Have you ever been associated with us before? _____ Dates: _____ Positions: _____

Are you acquainted with any of our associates? _____ If so, list names: _____

When can you begin to work? _____

Bonding may be a condition of hire. Is there any reason that you cannot secure bond? ☐ Yes ☐ No

Have you ever been convicted of a felony, or within the last five years a misdemeanor which resulted in imprisonment? Such convictions will not necessarily disqualify applicant from the job applied for. _____

Enter here any additional information or comments which should be considered in evaluating your qualifications for this work _____

Do you have any physical defects which would interfere with your ability to perform the normal duties of a Sales Associate? _____

Person to be notified in case of emergency

Name _____

Address _____

Telephone _____

EDUCATION

Type of School	Name and address of school	Major	Highest grade completed
Preparatory, or high school:			
College:			
Other:			

What specific courses have you had in the real estate field? _____

REAL ESTATE EXPERIENCE
Complete this section only if you have had previous experience in selling real estate

Do you have a real estate salesman's license? _____ Broker's license? _____ Insurance license? _____
                                                number   number   number

License ever suspended? _____

Are you or have you been a member of a Board of REALTORS®? _____ Which Board? _____

Dates of membership: _____

With what region in this general vicinity are you most familiar? _____

Which territory do you prefer at this time? _____

In which of the following kinds of negotiations have you been most successful?

☐ Apartment Buildings ☐ Residential ☐ Industrial ☐ Farms ☐ Commercial ☐ Leasing ☐ Cooperatives ☐ Condominiums

List the individuals in our firm with whom you have had cooperative real estate transactions: _____

EMPLOYMENT RECORD

Beginning with present or most recent employer, account for all time during the last 10 years

Dates employed	Name of company and nature of business	Address and telephone	Job Title/Superior	Earnings	Reason for leaving
from					
to					
from					
to					
from					
to					
from					
to					

Are you employed at present?.................... May inquiries be made of your present or most recent employer at this time? ☐ Yes ☐ No

Who is most familiar with your work there?...

ORGANIZATIONAL ACTIVITIES

Please list job-related organizations, clubs, professional societies or other associations to which you belong. You may omit those which indicate your race, religious creed, color, national origin, ancestry, sex, or age.

Name of group	Type of organization such as business, social, or service	Location of activity	Offices held	Meetings per month

What are your hobbies?...

REFERENCES

List 4 persons willing to provide professional and/or character references (excluding relatives or previous employers).

Name	Telephone	Address	Occupation

AUTOMOBILE

Do you own a car?.................... Make.................... Year.................... How long have you driven a car?....................

Have you a driver's license?.................... Have you had an accident in the last three years?....................
(state and number)

If so, give details....................

NOTE: All Associates who use an automobile in connection with their work are required to carry automobile insurance for limits of not less than $50/100,000 bodily injury and $5,000 property damage. Your policy must be submitted to us for approval **before** you join the staff of this organization. We require an endorsement to the effect that the carrier will send to us a 5-day written notice of cancellation or material change and require that we be named co-insured.

I authorize investigation of all statements contained in this application. The statements and answers to all questions in this application are true and correct to the best of my knowledge. I understand that material misrepresentation or omission of facts called for is cause for dismissal.

....
Signature of applicant

(THIS SECTION FOR OFFICE USE ONLY)

Interview by:.................... Date:.................... Comments:....................

Date associated:.................... Office:.................... Date scheduled to begin:....................

Contract:.................... Date actually began:....................

APPROVED BY:.................... Date of approval of contract:....................

It can't hurt to ask about a company's long-range growth plans before deciding where you want to work.

IV. Employee-Employer Relationship

A salesperson who is actively engaged in professional real estate activities must be employed by a licensed real estate broker.

In California, most salespeople working under a broker are considered employees for the purposes of administration of the real estate law, even if they act as independent contractors for other purposes, such as income tax wage withholding, social security, or medicare coverage.

An **INDEPENDENT CONTRACTOR** *sells results rather than time, and his or her physical conduct is not subject to the control of another.* An **EMPLOYEE**, *on the other hand, works under the direct control (designated hours and breaks) and supervision of the employer.*

The Department of Real Estate considers a salesperson an employee of the broker for the administration of the real estate broker law, even if he or she is an independent contractor. This makes the broker responsible for the real estate activities of the salesperson.

In most real estate offices the salespeople are treated as independent contractors. They come and go at will, working no fixed hours and pay their own payroll taxes (federal and state income taxes, social security, medicare, unemployment insurance, and state disability insurance). More strictly supervised workers, such as secretaries and assistants, are generally considered employees.

A. INDEPENDENT CONTRACTOR AGREEMENT HIGHLIGHTS

Here are some highlighted sections of the Independent Contractor Agreement (Between Broker and Associate-Licensee) (**Figure 1-3**).

3. Independent Contractor Relationship. This paragraph establishes the associate licensee's status as an independent contractor "to the maximum extent permissible by law."

5. Proprietary Information and Files. This establishes that the broker owns all listings and other agreements; they are taken and performed in the broker's name.

(continued on page 16)

Figure 1-3

CALIFORNIA
ASSOCIATION
OF REALTORS®

INDEPENDENT CONTRACTOR AGREEMENT
(Between Broker and Associate-Licensee)

This Agreement, dated _____ is made between _____
_____ ("Broker") and
_____ ("Associate-Licensee").

In consideration of the covenants and representations contained in this Agreement, Broker and Associate-Licensee agree as follows:

1. **BROKER:** Broker represents that Broker is duly licensed as a real estate broker by the State of California, ☐ doing business as _____
_____ (firm name), ☐ a sole proprietorship, ☐ a partnership, ☐ a corporation.
Broker is a member of the _____
Association(s) of REALTORS®, and a subscriber to the _____ multiple
listing service(s). Broker shall keep Broker's license current during the term of this Agreement.

2. **ASSOCIATE-LICENSEE:** Associate-Licensee represents that, (a) he/she is duly licensed by the State of California as a ☐ real estate broker,
☐ real estate salesperson, and (b) he/she has not used any other names within the past five years, except _____
_____. Associate-Licensee shall keep his/her license current during
the term of this Agreement, including satisfying all applicable continuing education and provisional license requirements.

3. **INDEPENDENT CONTRACTOR RELATIONSHIP:**
    A. Broker and Associate-Licensee intend that, to the maximum extent permissible by law: **(i)** This Agreement does not constitute an employment agreement by either party; **(ii)** Broker and Associate-Licensee are independent contracting parties with respect to all services rendered under this Agreement; **(iii)** This Agreement shall not be construed as a partnership.
    B. Broker shall not: **(i)** restrict Associate-Licensee's activities to particular geographical areas or, **(ii)** dictate Associate-Licensee's activities with regard to hours, leads, open houses, opportunity or floor time, production, prospects, sales meetings, schedule, inventory, time off, vacation, or similar activities, except to the extent required by law.
    C. Associate-Licensee shall not be required to accept an assignment by Broker to service any particular current or prospective listing or parties.
    D. Except as required by law: **(i)** Associate-Licensee retains sole and absolute discretion and judgment in the methods, techniques, and procedures to be used in soliciting and obtaining listings, sales, exchanges, leases, rentals, or other transactions, and in carrying out Associate-Licensee's selling and soliciting activities, **(ii)** Associate-Licensee is under the control of Broker as to the results of Associate-Licensee's work only, and not as to the means by which those results are accomplished, **(iii)** Associate-Licensee has no authority to bind Broker by any promise or representation and **(iv)** Broker shall not be liable for any obligation or liability incurred by Associate-Licensee.
    E. Associate-Licensee's only remuneration shall be the compensation specified in paragraph 8.
    F. Associate-Licensee shall not be treated as an employee with respect to services performed as a real estate agent, for state and federal tax purposes.
    G. The fact the Broker may carry worker compensation insurance for Broker's own benefit and for the mutual benefit of Broker and licensees associated with Broker, including Associate-Licensee, shall not create an inference of employment.

4. **LICENSED ACTIVITY:** All listings of property, and all agreements, acts or actions for performance of licensed acts, which are taken or performed in connection with this Agreement, shall be taken and performed in the name of Broker. Associate-Licensee agrees to and does hereby contribute all right and title to such listings to Broker for the benefit and use of Broker, Associate-Licensee, and other licensees associated with Broker. Broker shall make available to Associate-Licensee, equally with other licensees associated with Broker, all current listings in Broker's office, except any listing which Broker may choose to place in the exclusive servicing of Associate-Licensee or one or more other specific licensees associated with Broker. Associate-Licensee shall provide and pay for all professional licenses, supplies, services, and other items required in connection with Associate-Licensee's activities under this Agreement, or any listing or transaction, without reimbursement from Broker except as required by law. Associate-Licensee shall work diligently and with his/her best efforts: **(a)** To sell, exchange, lease, or rent properties listed with Broker or other cooperating Brokers; **(b)** To solicit additional listings, clients, and customers; and **(c)** To otherwise promote the business of serving the public in real estate transactions to the end that Broker and Associate-Licensee may derive the greatest benefit possible, in accordance with law. Associate-Licensee shall not commit any unlawful act under federal, state or local law or regulation while conducting licensed activity. Associate-Licensee shall at all times be familiar, and comply, with all applicable federal, state and local laws, including, but not limited to, anti-discrimination laws and restrictions against the giving or accepting of a fee, or other thing of value, for the referral of business to title companies, escrow companies, home inspection companies, pest control companies and other settlement service providers pursuant to the California Business and Professions Code and the Real Estate Settlement Procedures Acts (RESPA). Broker shall make available for Associate-Licensee's use, along with other licensees associated with Broker, the facilities of the real estate office operated by Broker at _____
_____ and the facilities of any other office
locations made available by Broker pursuant to this Agreement.

Broker and Associate-Licensee acknowledge receipt of copy of this page, which constitutes Page 1 of _____ Pages.
Broker's Initials (_____) (_____)   Associate-Licensee's Initials (_____) (_____)

Published and Distributed by:
REAL ESTATE BUSINESS SERVICES, INC.
a subsidiary of the CALIFORNIA ASSOCIATION OF REALTORS®
525 South Virgil Avenue, Los Angeles, California 90020
PRINT DATE

REVISED 10/98

OFFICE USE ONLY
Reviewed by Broker
or Designee _____
Date _____

EQUAL HOUSING OPPORTUNITY

INDEPENDENT CONTRACTOR AGREEMENT (ICA-11 PAGE 1 OF 3)

5. **PROPRIETARY INFORMATION AND FILES: (a)** All files and documents pertaining to listings, leads and transactions are the property of Broker and shall be delivered to Broker by Associate-Licensee immediately upon request or termination of their relationship under this Agreement. **(b)** Associate-Licensee acknowledges that Broker's method of conducting business is a protected trade secret. **(c)** Associate-Licensee shall not use to his/her own advantage, or the advantage of any other person, business, or entity, except as specifically agreed in writing, either during Associate-Licensee's association with Broker, or thereafter, any information gained for or from the business, or files of Broker.

6. **SUPERVISION:** Associate-Licensee, within 24 hours (or ☐ _____) after preparing, signing, or receiving same, shall submit to Broker, or Broker's designated licensee: **(a)** All documents which may have a material effect upon the rights and duties of principals in a transaction, **(b)** Any documents or other items connected with a transaction pursuant to this Agreement in the possession of or available to Associate-Licensee and, **(c)** All documents associated with any real estate transaction in which Associate-Licensee is a principal.

7. **TRUST FUNDS:** All trust funds shall be handled in compliance with the Business and Professions Code, and other applicable laws.

8. **COMPENSATION:**

   A. **TO BROKER:** Compensation shall be charged to parties who enter into listing or other agreements for services requiring a real estate license:
   ☐ as shown in "Exhibit A" attached, which is incorporated as a part of this Agreement by reference, or
   ☐ as follows: _____
   _____
   Any deviation which is not approved in writing in advance by Broker, shall be (1) deducted from Associate-Licensee's compensation, if lower than the amount or rate approved above; and, (2) subject to Broker approval, if higher than the amount approved above. Any permanent change in commission schedule shall be disseminated by Broker to Associate-Licensee.

   B. **TO ASSOCIATE-LICENSEE:** Associate-Licensee shall receive a share of compensation actually collected by Broker, on listings or other agreements for services requiring a real estate license, which are solicited and obtained by Associate-Licensee, and on transactions of which Associate-Licensee's activities are the procuring cause, as follows:
   ☐ as shown in "Exhibit B" attached, which is incorporated as a part of this Agreement by reference, or
   ☐ other: _____
   _____

   C. **PARTNERS, TEAMS, AND AGREEMENTS WITH OTHER ASSOCIATE-LICENSEES IN OFFICE:** If Associate-Licensee and one or more other Associate-Licensees affiliated with Broker participate on the same side (either listing or selling) of a transaction, the commission allocated to their combined activities shall be divided by Broker and paid to them according to their written agreement. Broker shall have the right to withhold total compensation if there is a dispute between associate-licensees, or if there is no written agreement, or if no written agreement has been provided to Broker.

   D. **EXPENSES AND OFFSETS:** If Broker elects to advance funds to pay expenses or liabilities of Associate-Licensee, or for an advance payment of, or draw upon, future compensation, Broker may deduct the full amount advanced from compensation payable to Associate-Licensee on any transaction without notice. If Associate-Licensee's compensation is subject to a lien, garnishment or other restriction on payment, Broker shall charge Associate-Licensee a fee for complying with such restriction.

   E. **PAYMENT: (1)** All compensation collected by Broker and due to Associate-Licensee shall be paid to Associate-Licensee, after deduction of expenses and offsets, immediately or as soon thereafter as practicable, except as otherwise provided in this Agreement, or a separate written agreement between Broker and Associate-Licensee. **(2)** Compensation shall not be paid to Associate-Licensee until both the transaction and file are complete. **(3)** Broker is under no obligation to pursue collection of compensation from any person or entity responsible for payment. Associate-Licensee does not have the independent right to pursue collection of compensation for activities which require a real estate license which were done in the name of Broker. **(4)** Expenses which are incurred in the attempt to collect compensation shall be paid by Broker and Associate-Licensee in the same proportion as set forth for the division of compensation (paragraph 8(B)). **(5)** If there is a known or pending claim against Broker or Associate-Licensee on transactions for which Associate-Licensee has not yet been paid, Broker may withhold from compensation due Associate-Licensee on that transaction amounts for which Associate-Licensee could be responsible under paragraph 14, until such claim is resolved. **(6)** Associate-Licensee shall not be entitled to any advance payment from Broker upon future compensation.

   F. **UPON OR AFTER TERMINATION:** If this Agreement is terminated while Associate-Licensee has listings or pending transactions that require further work normally rendered by Associate-Licensee, Broker shall make arrangements with another associate-licensee to perform the required work, or Broker shall perform the work him/herself. The licensee performing the work shall be reasonably compensated for completing work on those listings or transactions, and such reasonable compensation shall be deducted from Associate-Licensee's share of compensation. Except for such offset, Associate-Licensee shall receive the compensation due as specified above.

9. **TERMINATION OF RELATIONSHIP:** Broker or Associate-Licensee may terminate their relationship under this Agreement at any time, with or without cause. After termination, Associate-Licensee shall not solicit **(a)** prospective or existing clients or customers based upon company-generated leads obtained during the time Associate-Licensee was affiliated with Broker, or **(b)** any principal with existing contractual obligations to Broker, or **(c)** any principal with a contractual transactional obligation for which Broker is entitled to be compensated. Even after termination, this Agreement shall govern all disputes and claims between Broker and Associate-Licensee connected with their relationship under this Agreement, including obligations and liabilities arising from existing and completed listings, transactions, and services.

Broker and Associate-Licensee acknowledge receipt of copy of this page, which constitutes Page 2 of _____ Pages.
Broker's Initials (_____) (_____)   Associate-Licensee's Initials (_____) (_____)

REVISED 10/98

Page 2 of ___ Pages.

PRINT DATE

INDEPENDENT CONTRACTOR AGREEMENT (ICA-11 PAGE 2 OF 3)

10. **DISPUTE RESOLUTION:**
   A. **Mediation:** Mediation is recommended as a method of resolving disputes arising out of this Agreement between Broker and Associate-Licensee.
   B. **Arbitration:** All disputes or claims between Associate-Licensee and other licensee(s) associated with Broker, or between Associate-Licensee and Broker, arising from or connected in any way with this Agreement, which cannot be adjusted between the parties involved, shall be submitted to the Association of REALTORS® of which all such disputing parties are members for arbitration pursuant to the provisions of its Bylaws, as may be amended from time to time, which are incorporated as a part of this Agreement by reference. If the Bylaws of the Association do not cover arbitration of the dispute, or if the Association declines jurisdiction over the dispute, then arbitration shall be pursuant to the rules of California law. The Federal Arbitration Act, Title 9, U.S. Code, Section 1, et seq., shall govern this Agreement.

11. **AUTOMOBILE:** Associate-Licensee shall maintain automobile insurance coverage for liability and property damage in the following amounts $_____/$_____. Broker shall be named as an additional insured party on Associate-Licensee's policies. A copy of the endorsement showing Broker as an additional insured shall be provided to Broker.

12. **PERSONAL ASSISTANTS:** Associate-Licensee may make use of a personal assistant, provided the following requirements are satisfied. Associate-Licensee shall have a written agreement with the personal assistant which establishes the terms and responsibilities of the parties to the employment agreement, including, but not limited to, compensation, supervision and compliance with applicable law. The agreement shall be subject to Broker's review and approval. Unless otherwise agreed, if the personal assistant has a real estate license, that license must be provided to the Broker. Both Associate-Licensee and personal assistant must sign any agreement that Broker has established for such purposes.

13. **OFFICE POLICY MANUAL:** If Broker's office policy manual, now or as modified in the future, conflicts with or differs from the terms of this Agreement, the terms of the office policy manual shall govern the relationship between Broker and Associate-Licensee.

14. **INDEMNITY AND HOLD HARMLESS:** Associate-Licensee agrees to indemnify, defend and hold Broker harmless from all claims, disputes, litigation, judgments, awards, costs and attorney's fees, arising from any action taken or omitted by Associate-Licensee, or others working through, or on behalf of Associate-Licensee in connection with services rendered. Any such claims or costs payable pursuant to this Agreement, are due as follows:
   ☐ Paid in full by Associate-Licensee, who hereby agrees to indemnify and hold harmless Broker for all such sums, or
   ☐ In the same ratio as the compensation split as it existed at the time the compensation was earned by Associate-Licensee
   ☐ Other: _____
   _____
   _____

   Payment from Associate-Licensee is due at the time Broker makes such payment and can be offset from any compensation due Associate-Licensee as above. Broker retains the authority to settle claims or disputes, whether or not Associate-Licensee consents to such settlement.

15. **ADDITIONAL PROVISIONS:** _____
   _____
   _____

16. **DEFINITIONS:** As used in this Agreement, the following terms have the meanings indicated:
   (A) "Listing" means an agreement with a property owner or other party to locate a buyer, exchange party, lessee, or other party to a transaction involving real property, a mobile home, or other property or transaction which may be brokered by a real estate licensee, or an agreement with a party to locate or negotiate for any such property or transaction.
   (B) "Compensation means compensation for acts requiring a real estate license, regardless of whether calculated as a percentage of transaction price, flat fee, hourly rate, or in any other manner.
   (C) "Transaction" means a sale, exchange, lease, or rental of real property, a business opportunity, or a manufactured home, which may lawfully be brokered by a real estate licensee.

17. **ATTORNEY FEES:** In any action, proceeding, or arbitration between Broker and Associate-Licensee arising from or related to this Agreement, the prevailing Broker or Associate-Licensee shall be entitled to reasonable attorney fees and costs.

18. **ENTIRE AGREEMENT; MODIFICATION:** All prior agreements between the parties concerning their relationship as Broker and Associate-Licensee are incorporated in this Agreement, which constitutes the entire contract. Its terms are intended by the parties as a final and complete expression of their agreement with respect to its subject matter, and may not be contradicted by evidence of any prior agreement or contemporaneous oral agreement. This Agreement may not be amended, modified, altered, or changed except by a further agreement in writing executed by Broker and Associate-Licensee.

Broker:

_____
(Brokerage firm name)

By _____
Its Broker/Office manager (circle one)

_____
(Print name)

_____
(Address)

_____
(City, State, Zip)

_____
(Telephone)   (Fax)

Associate-Licensee:

_____
(Signature)

_____
(Print name)

_____
(Address)

_____
(City, State, Zip)

_____
(Telephone)   (Fax)

REVISED 10/98

Page 3 of ___ Pages.

OFFICE USE ONLY
Reviewed by Broker
or Designee _____
Date _____

EQUAL HOUSING OPPORTUNITY

INDEPENDENT CONTRACTOR AGREEMENT (ICA-11 PAGE 3 OF 3)

6. Supervision. This paragraph focuses on the ways in which the broker will supervise the associate licensee's work, such as the licensee submitting, within 24 hours, certain documents to the broker for review—including documents connected with any transaction in which the associate licensee is a principal, whether or not the property is listed with the broker.

8A. Compensation. In this paragraph, brokers set forth their ordinary commission rates by filling in the blanks or attaching a commission schedule to the contract. Under California Law, all commissions are negotiable between the client and broker. The licensee must obtain the broker's permission to charge a different fee that does not match the broker's rate schedule.

8B. Compensation to Associate-Licensee. This paragraph provides that the licensee is entitled to a share of a commission only when the commission has actually been collected by the broker. The broker has a right to enforce payment, but is not obligated to sue the client or otherwise try to enforce the listing agreement. It is important to note that brokers who do not fight to uphold their licensees' rights will quickly lose their agents and their reputation as fair brokers.

8F. Commission Upon or After Termination. Both parties agree that the broker owes the licensee his or her share of the commission even if terminated with cause. If the licensee has not completed all work on the transaction prior to termination, the work must be finished by another licensee or the broker. Whoever does the work is entitled to a "reasonable compensation" which is offset from the terminated agent's share of the commission.

9. Termination of Relationship. Broker or Associate-Licensee can terminate the relationship at any time, with or without cause.

10A-B. Dispute Resolution. Both parties agree to submit to either mediation or arbitration if they cannot resolve their disputes.

14. Indemnity and Hold Harmless. This section concerns responsibility for liabilities or expenses the broker incurs as a result of the associate's handling of a transaction. Many brokers will check the first box leaving the agent with the full responsibility of the liability. Others may share the responsibility proportionately to the extent of their respective share of the commission earned.

The broker is required to carry worker's compensation and public liability insurance for salespeople (independent contractors) in the same way that they do for employees.

V. Planning Objectives and Goals

Now that you've carefully selected your office, it's important to set realistic goals; draw a blueprint and follow it. Without defining objectives or charting a course, you're like the sailor without a rudder, haphazardly navigating a sea of confusion. Knowing how much money you need to make per year helps you define your monthly and weekly goals. How many people must you usually contact prior to getting a listing appointment? How many showings do you normally make before writing an offer?

Plan your work and work your plan.

Ideally, goals ought to be in writing because they then have visual impact and are more readily examined and reviewed. Abstract and unreasonable goals will become more apparent if written. Certain real estate activities bring about better results than others. Knowing this, you can be selective and schedule daily business so as to save time and effort.

Write down your yearly goals and put them away in a drawer. Take them out periodically for review and updating.

A. SPHERE OF INFLUENCE

Immediately contact friends, relatives, past co-workers, trades and service people, and people in your geographical "farm" by letting them know the name of your firm, and how you can be contacted. A *FARM is a group of people within a geographical area with whom the agent stays in touch monthly, advising each property owner of all real estate activities throughout the year.* A personal note asking about family and pets is best, but a pre-printed form is also acceptable. Business cards should be included as well as E-mail address and information on your company's website. See a sample letter of introduction (**Figure 1-4**), which you will need to adjust based on the type of organization chosen.

There are many "spheres of influence." They could be clubs, church groups, your friends, your neighbors, or organizations to which you belong. The list should continually be adjusted and increased. All contacts should be meaningful to you. Naturally, these people also receive appropriate greetings during the holiday season.

Figure 1-4

I have great news for you!

I am now associated with

Lyons and Associates, Inc., Realtor

Our goal is to provide excellence

in real estate

If I can be of service to you.

please call anytime

2820 E. Garvey Avenue South, West Covina, CA 91791
(626) 331-0141 • FAX: (626) 331-9772

B. DAILY ACTIVITIES SCHEDULE

Prior to coming into the office, you should write out a schedule of your daily activities. Allow a certain amount of time to return phone calls, develop new leads, and answer correspondence. Review all new listings and edit out sold properties.

C. SOLICITING

Call on past clients, buyers, and sellers. Other sources are open house leads, walk-ins, referrals, door-to-door solicitations, cold calls, warm calls, "For sale by owners," and expired listings. *COLD CALLS are telephone calls to people you don't know. WARM CALLS are calls to people you already know and are usually more productive.* Always identify yourself as a salesperson when calling and ask if it's a convenient time to call. *EXPIRED LISTINGS are listings that did not sell within the contract period.* These are good sources of listings, as the owners are probably still motivated to sell.

Telephone neighbors to inform them about a new listing or sale by using a reverse directory. These do not need to be your own listings, as you should have access to this information through various channels. A *REVERSE DIRECTORY is a website or publication, similar to a phone book, where phone numbers are listed by address rather than name.*

Don't become attached to your desk, as it's only a place to keep your real estate tools. You're only truly productive when you're talking to someone who's willing and able to buy or sell!

D. PREVIEWING

New properties should be previewed (as well as reviewing older listings) on behalf of potential buyers and for your own information. There may be some important changes, such as condition and price reduction. It is important to let your buyers know that you preview many properties before selecting the best ones for their viewing. Naturally, you'll call the seller prior to previewing.

It pays to keep your clients continually informed of your activities on their behalf.

1. The Sales Kit

This is simply an inventory of items, or aids, that you may need in your daily real estate related activities. With them, you should be able to handle both the expected and the unexpected opportunities presented to you.

You should keep a briefcase in your mobile office (your car), containing all of those items that may have to be used in listing, selling, and prospecting activities. The list that follows can be added to, depending upon your own personality and special requirements (see **Figure 1-5**).

In short, all those items the you may need away from the office ought to be included in your attaché case or vehicle. Use the sales kit, especially the kit book, subtly to direct the prospect's attention to your services. Don't use your sales kit to lecture or argue; the pictures and references will speak for themselves. Keep it current and present your material in a persuasive way, adjusting it to the personality, intelligence, and needs of the client.

Figure 1-5   **Your Sales Kit**

1. Cell phone and charger.

2. Laptop computer.

3. Portable printer.

4. Kit book—a loose-leaf binder you show the client about your firm, the sales associates, marketing methods, photos of sold properties, list of properties sold by you and your company, letters of recommendation from satisfied clients, advertising examples, publicity items, etc. You should also include a résumé or personal bio sheet in your kit book.

5. Market Analysis software or forms (these are now almost exclusively done online).

6. Measuring tapes (although many agents now use the assessor's measurements).

7. Packet of forms (including Win-forms which can be downloaded from your laptop).

8. Multiple listing sheets.

9. Buyers Confidential Financial Status forms and Prequalification letter from lender.

10. Purchase Contract/Deposit Receipt forms.

11. Promissory note deposit pads.

12. Escrow closing worksheets for computing seller's net and buyer's closing costs.

13. Schedules of title insurance fees, escrow costs, documentary transfer tax, and recording charges.

14. Business cards and promotional literature.

15. Polaroid camera and film or digital camera.

16. Loan amortization schedule.

17. Flashlight.

18. Pen, pencil, scratch pads, and clipboard.

19. Appointment book or handheld palm device.

20. Signs and riders, including the necessary tools for securing the signs on the property, such as hammer, nuts and bolts, screwdriver, wrench, and pliers. (Or the business card of the company you hire to put up and maintain your signs!)

(continued)

---

21. Lock boxes.

22. Doorknob notices. (These notices have a variety of uses. One might say "Sorry I missed you. Please call me for some valuable information.")

Warning: doorknob notices can also alert burglars that the property is unoccupied!

23. Street maps and a Thomas Guide.
24. School bus and general bus routes.
25. Utility company addresses and rates.
26. Expense records for your buyer and seller.

Travel expenses cannot be deducted for driving between home and office (unless you preview a home on the way). Expenses begin where you meet your buyer/seller.

27. Promotional giveaways that advertise the broker, such as pot holders, rulers and yardsticks, telephone attachments, key rings, calendars, welcome mats, pens, mouse pads, etc.

E. SHOWING PROPERTIES

Remember that only "direct" personal contacts lead to sales.

Prior to showing properties, the buyer should be pre-qualified by at least one lender. This can be done at your office or at the buyer's home. Do not show more than five houses in any one showing. Have the buyers participate in the process by having them write their comments on a "Buyers' Comment Sheet," with their own rating (found in Chapter 5). Of course, you should also have a copy of all the properties being viewed for future reference. See Chapter 5 for more information on showing properties.

F. BECOMING AN EXPERT

You should create your own sphere of expertise by becoming knowledgeable in condo sales, new sales, probates, foreclosures, or property management. The more you know, the more confident you'll become, and this will be reflected in your attitude and conveyed to clients, who will appreciate working with a confident and knowledgeable agent.

There are many advanced Realtor® designations that indicate a higher degree of education and specialty. The Certified Residential Specialist (CRS) designation, for example, indicates a broker's advanced training and expertise.

G. ATTRIBUTES OF AN EFFECTIVE SALESPERSON

Successful salespeople, in general, find their jobs satisfying and rewarding, both emotionally, because of the satisfaction they get helping people buy and sell their homes, and career-wise, because of their financial reward. **Figure 1-6** lists some factors that lead salespeople to success.

Figure 1-6   **Factors That Lead To Success**

1. Ability to think critically and make sound judgment.

2. Interest in advancement toward higher financial rewards.

3. Ambition and the willingness to work hard and long hours to excel.

4. Appearance should be neat, clean, and in good taste; attractive carriage.

5. Appreciation for business received, graciousness.

6. Art of negotiating, being persuasive in buying and selling on behalf of one's clients.

7. A positive attitude toward job, colleagues, clients, employer and others.

8. A well-running, fairly new vehicle is essential to give the appearance of success, and for comfort and safety, because so much driving of clients is involved.

It's important to have clients in the car with you to get their overall impressions, except when there are young children involved. Young children require car seats and may increase your liability. Clients with children should follow in their own car. This is not the ideal situation, but it is the safest.

9. Good salespeople know they cannot operate in a vacuum, that they must belong to a team. Creating comradeship in various professional organizations and community betterment groups is a must. Genuine interest in the project is extremely important.

10. Building goodwill with contacts by sending thoughtful notes goes a long way.

11. Controlling one's actions in order to maximize productivity.

12. Consistency in completing details, even if it's dull paperwork.

13. Courtesy and respect for all others encourages the same attitude towards you.

14. Cultivation of good habits. Developing sales executive attitude.

15. Determination to succeed. There are costs involved in this, including time and energy.

16. Good salespeople know that they cannot last long in the business without keeping up with the latest information and changing technology. Take some computer classes and adult education classes, which are available through many community colleges.

17. Efficiency saves time. Time is well spent getting ready for the office and showings.

(continued)

---

18. Empathy for other people. Listen and put yourself in the other person's place.

19. Enthusiasm, energy, good health, and a positive attitude are contagious.

20. Ethics. The "golden rule" is never out of fashion. Be fair to all.

21. Evaluate the competition and learn from it. What is your competition doing? Learn from their successes and avoid their failures.

22. Experience. Learn to do better from past mistakes—yours and others.

23. Family. Having a well-balanced life, and moderation in all things. Do not put life on hold.

24. Positive goals should be in writing, reviewed and revised. Keep focused.

25. Honesty and integrity in all dealings. Salespeople who live up to their fiduciary relationships are trustworthy in the eyes of the public and their colleagues.

26. Initiative. Good salespeople are self-starters. They know that wasted time is wasted opportunity.

27. Keep your eyes open for new opportunities, read newspapers, and keep informed. There are many ways of structuring any transaction. Focus on the participants' needs and goals.

28. Patience to handle all the many small details and to handle clients' whims. Buyers and sellers do not transact real estate on a regular basis. Therefore, it is understandable that they may need explanations of every step of the selling process on a regular basis. It is a stressful time that can be made less so by your patience and understanding.

Sometimes it's your job to be a hand-holder.

29. Minimize your weaknesses and maximize your strengths. Examine the above list and work to increase the number of good attributes you already possess. Good habits can be created and developed.

Be persistent in establishing good habits. Keep them for seven days and they will become your own.

H. WHY SALESPEOPLE FAIL

Just as it's difficult to define success, it's also difficult to label the unsuccessful salesperson, because success varies with unpredictable market conditions, types of offices, and the social environment of each office. Every salesperson's approach may not be suitable for every type of sale. You must know your buyers and sellers just as an author must know his or her audience.

VI. Enter the Broker

While the majority of this text addresses your responsibilities as a salesperson, it eventually transitions into mainly broker's responsibilities. It's only natural, as a successful agent, that you'll eventually aspire to become a broker.

The broker, like the salesperson, acts as an intermediary, a catalyst, in bringing together buyers and sellers. You'll help others in the acquisition, listing, sale, leasing, exchanging, financing, and managing of real property. Some brokers just manage their office and supervise their salespeople, while others also get out there and sell. Some brokers don't want the responsibility of running their own offices, so they work for other brokers.

A. AGENCY REPRESENTATION

The listing agreement establishes a **FIDUCIARY RELATIONSHIP,** *meaning brokers owe a duty of the highest care and confidentiality to their principals (sellers), whose interest they promote even at the cost of some greater benefit to themselves.* Prior to entering into any real estate contracts, there must be full disclosure regarding agency relationships.

1. Disclosure Regarding Agency Relationships

Who the broker is representing (buyer, seller, or both) must be disclosed to all parties, in writing, prior to entering into a transaction. (See Chapter 3, Disclosure Regarding Real Estate Relationships form, Figure 3-4, page 88).

*When a broker represents more than one party, it is known as **DUAL AGENCY.*** This must also be disclosed in writing prior to entering into the transaction. Both your clients have the expectation of complete confidentiality.

It is unethical for a salesperson (as a broker's representative) to state that the "price is soft." Your obligation is to obtain the best possible price and terms for your client.

When two agents from the same office are representing both the buyer and the seller in one transaction, it is also considered a dual agency. This must be disclosed in writing prior to entering into a contract, although each agent may not know the other agent's client.

B. DIRECTING AND SUPERVISING

Included in this concept are the supervision and the administration of personnel, and the guidance the broker offers the staff in achieving planned objectives. The *POLICY MANUAL, found in many brokerage offices to handle recurring situations, is designed to give rules and policies for the staff in their relationships inside and outside the office sphere.* Policies may be outlined in a simple single-page statement, receipt of which is acknowledged by the agents, or an elaborate manuscript of many pages, depending upon the particular operation and its needs. An illustration of a policy manual is shown in **Appendix I** (back of book). In order for an operation to run smoothly, everyone in an office should adhere to a strict policy regarding the handling of files and clients.

The office must run as a well disciplined team.

As a broker/manager, you must provide leadership to your salespeople, who should not merely be hired and expected to learn the principles of salesmanship without direction. You should encourage questions, and be readily available to your staff.

A detailed *TRANSACTION FILE, which includes all property contracts, documents, and disclosures signed or initialed by the principals,* must be approved in writing by you, the broker, or your office manager. In an effort to coordinate these activities, you should use a checklist dated and initialed by you or your office manager, and the real estate agent. (**See Figure 1-7**.) See Chapter 14, "Real Estate Assistants," for more details concerning transaction files. No commission check is issued until the file is complete.

C. COOPERATIVE SALES

The showing and selling of listings, in practice, remain non-exclusive to a brokerage. In fact, most properties are not sold by the listing broker.

As often as not, properties are sold by a broker who is not the listing agent. **Compensation to the selling office is determined at the time the listing is taken and posted on the Multiple Listing form available to all MLS subscribers.** It is unethical to write an offer and renegotiate the commission paid to the selling office. Some brokers are good listing agents, while others excel strictly as selling agents. Both activities require creativity and salesmanship. While obtaining listings renews the office's inventory, it is also important to move them. See **Figure 1-8** for an example of a sample MLS listing showing the selling agent's compensation.

Obviously, a great deal of cooperation is needed for brokers to function smoothly in the marketing process. To show property listed by another broker, permission should first be obtained through the seller, if possible, by making a **showing appointment**. Should there be a cancellation, it goes without saying that the seller will be made aware of it.

Figure 1-7   **Transaction File**

Contracts & Disclosures	Seller	Buyer	Broker Initials
Agency - Seller and Buyer (both should be in file) **(AD)**	/	/	/
Listing w/Termite and Title Clauses stated on 2nd page. & Sellers Advisory **(LA & SA)**			
Transfer Disclosure (Do not qualify problems) **(TDS)**			
FRPTA/Fed. & Calif. Law (Seller/Buyer) **(SA)**	/	/	/
Smoke Detector and Water Heater **(SDS & WHS)**			
Horizontal Defective Furnaces (if applicable)			
Lead Base Paint Disclosure (housing blt. prior to 1978) **(FLD)**			
Res. Earthquake Booklet and receipt of same	/	/	/
Zone Disclosures appropriately signed: Natural Hazard, Mold, Database, Airport, etc.			
Supplemental Tax Disclosure			
Supplemental Statutory Contractual Disclosure. **(SSD)**			
Order sign up and send mail outs to neighborhood			
Sellers/Buyers Estimate Costs **(ESP/EBC)**			
Res. Purchase Agreement (All pages initialed including buyer's agency & Advisory) **(RPA-CA,AD & BIA)**			
Prequalification letter & Copy of Check			
Counters to Purchase Agreement & Multiple Offer (Item 7). **(CO)**			
Compensation to cooperating broker **(CCB)**			
Receipt from Escrow of Buyers' earnest money deposit within 3 days of acceptance			
Escrow Inst. & Prelim (Read both carefully)			
Appraisal (ordered and appointment made); provide comps			
Physical Inspection or Waiver (Do not Meddle)			
Termite Inspection and clearance to be **signed by buyers**			
Request for Repairs From Buyers **(RRI)**			
Response to Request for Repairs from Sellers			
Removal of Contingencies or Cancellation			
Home Warranty/Waiver (Watch the amount to be paid by seller)			
Walk Through or Waiver **(VP)**			
Check closing costs (Have escrow give you estimated proceed two days prior to close of escrow)			
Remove lock box and have sign taken down			
Report Sale to Association (otherwise you will be fined by the Board)			
Send mail outs to the neighbors and follow up			

Figure 1-8   # MLS Listing with Compensation

ARLETTE LYONS 4/26/2004 13:59 | Long Report - Residential
ML# C317326

Status: S	**Area:** 614	**County:** LA	**Price:** $ 398000*
Address: 535 S SAN JOSE AV		**Unit#:**	**TG#:** 599C6
City: CVN	**Zip:** 91723	**List Type/ Service Type:** ER/FS	**APN:** 8445-025-013
Cross Streets: W/BARRANCA, N/ROWLAND			**Lease?:** N
Type: SFR /D	**#Units:**	**SubDv/Trct:** /	
Bdr: 3	**Bath:** 2.00 /	**ASF:** 1689 / A	**View:** N
Model: /		**Zone:** CVR	

Features and Descriptions

DP / DY / FR / GA / HW / LL / LW / MF / MM / NC / PV / RA / / / / / / / / /

- Drapes/curtains
- Lot-level/flat
- Pool View
- Driveway
- Lot 6,500-9,999
- Rv Garage
- Freestanding
- Main Floor Bdrs
- Dir Garage Acc
- Mn Flr Mstr Bdr
- Home Warranty
- No Common Walls

LP Excl: STOVE IS RESERVED

Description: EXCELLENT MCINTYRE BUILT HOME POOL HOME IN SOUTH HILLS SCHOOL NEIGHBORHOOD. MASTER BEDROOM HAS ITS OWN FIREPLACE. TASTEFULLY DECORATED AND LANDSCAPED. SELLERS BOUGHT ANOTHER HOME AND BOTH ESCROWS TO CLOSE AS CONCURRENTLY AS POSSIBLE. R V. PARKING TOO! SELLERS RESERVE ALL SERVICES.

More: 2 Slide Show

Additional Property Information

Lot: 37 /	**TR#:** 17368	**LtSz:** 8111 / / A		**Acres:**
Termite: Y	**Horse:** N	**Flood Zone:**	**Add/Alt:** N	**Spec Stdy:**
Sch Dist: CVN	**El:** BARRANCA	**Jr:** SIERRA VIS	**HS:** SO.HILLS	**Year Built:** 1955
Assmnt: UN /	**FP:** Y , FR- / MB-	**Garage:** 2A/ /	**Yard:** Y	**Enclosed:** / /
Floors: CR/RF/WW/	**Gr Dr Op:**	**Remotes:**	**Office-Den:** N	**CnvtBdr:** N
Master Suite:	**Retreat:** N	**RV Space:** 10X20	**Sec Sys:**	**Formal Din Rm:** N
Dressing Area:	**Walk-In Closet:**	**Patio:** , / /	**Solar:** / /	**Eating Area:** FK/FR
Heat: FA/	**AC:** N/	**Pool:** Y, IG/	**Spa:** ,	**Sprnklr:**
Timer:	**Family Room:** Y	**Separate?:**	**R/O:**	**Appl:** G/ / / / /
Roof: CT / /	**Story:** A	**TV:**	**Living Room:** Y	**Entry:** Y
Laundry: /	**Dryer:**	**Softener:**	**220V:** /	**Bonus:** N
Wet Bar:	**Cable TV:**	**Intercom:**	**Water:** DIST	**Sewer:**

Financial Information

Points: 0	**Possession:** COE+3	**Terms:** CTNL/ / / / /
1st:	**Loan Type:**	**Interest:** %,
2nd:	**Loan Type:**	**Interest:** %,

Addtional Financial Information:

Land Fee/Lease: FEE	**Land Lse/Yr:** $	**Lease Expires:**	**Lease Renews:**
Lease Transfer: $	**Land Lse Purch:**	**Assn #1:** $ 0/mo	**Assn #2:** $ /mo

Office Information

SO Comp: 2.25	**Dual/Var Rate Comm:** N	**Occupant:** OWN / WITHHELD	
Occ Ph: xxx-xxx-xxxx	**LO:** 2072 / LYONS & ASSOC., INC.		**LO Ph:** 626-331-0141
LO Fax: 626-331-9772	**LA Public ID:** C20327	**LA:** ARLETTE LYONS	
LA Res: 626-332-2800	**Pager:**	**LA Cell:**	**LA Fax:**
Voice Mail: / 0		**LA Email:**	
Showing Instr: CF/ /	**Key Safe Type:** SM/	**Key Safe Location:** FD	
ListDt: 11/10/03 **ActDOM:** 74 **RcvDt:** 11/10/03 **ExpDt:** 02/12/04 **TrnDt:** 01/23/04 **Sign:**			

Office Comments:

MLS Information   **"SO Comp" refers to Selling Office Compensation.**

Photo Instruction: UPLOAD /	**Supplement:**
Free Internet Advertisement?: Y	**Show Address?:** Y

Pending And Comparable Information

PendDt: 12/11/03	**COE/End Date:** 01/14/04	**Sold Price:** $ 390000
Days On Market: 31	**SO:** 2072 / LYONS & ASSOC., INC.	
SA: ARLETTE LYONS		**SA Public ID:** C20327
Sold Terms:	**Financing:** CONV /	

Always leave a business card (usually in the kitchen) when showing a property. A smart listing agent should collect these cards regularly, get feedback from the showing agents, and share this information with the seller.

D. COMMISSIONS

Most brokers are paid acommission based on a percentage of the sales price they obtain on their transactions. In commercial and industrial transactions, the rate of commission is sometimes based on a **graduated scale**. For example, in the sale of a shopping center, you may be paid five percent on the first $500,000, three percent on the next $300,000, two percent on the next $200,000 and one percent on any amount over $1,000,000.

No matter which plan is being used, all commissions are negotiable between the seller and the listing broker, and determined when the listing agreement is signed, not when an offer is presented.

In some instances, brokers are able to command a fee for their services, similar to the lawyer who establishes the amount of the fee on the basis of the time involved, complexity of the case, economy, and other factors. This fee is usually paid by the person or firm that contracts for your broker's services, be it for the acquisition, disposition, exchange, or lease of property. It is important to stress that all commissions are negotiable between the parties and are regionally influenced.

VII. The Brokerage Firm

As a broker, you'll be heavily involved with the managerial functions of planning, organizing, directing, and controlling all aspects of your brokerage. These functions require a lot of time and energy. Because of these demanding and time-consuming tasks, not all brokers decide to open their own brokerages. Some work for other brokers and have more time to devote elsewhere. Nevertheless, as a salesperson, if you want to open your own office, you'll first have to become a broker.

A. GETTING STARTED IN BUSINESS

As a licensed salesperson with aspirations to open your own office, you will need to follow a course patterned along the following steps.

1. **Get licensed.** Obtain a real estate broker's license. (See Chapter 15 for licensing information.)

2. **Secure the necessary capital.** You should have sufficient capital to pay for the initial setup as well as all operative charges and expenses for the first year. In addition, you should have enough money to support your family for a period that will likely not show much profit. Most of the initial charges are non-recurring.

3. **Decide on a location.** The selected office site must be zoned for commercial use allowing for future expansion. It also should be readily accessible, close to a well-known and widely recognizable point of reference such as a major shopping center.

4. **Choose a building.** The building must be suitable for present needs and, like the site itself, one that will provide for expansion and convenience of office layout. For a general brokerage, it's wise to have broad exposure to traffic. Select a building close to the street with large windows for displays. The building should also provide for a reception area and a private "closing" room, which may double as a conference room.

5. **Obtain a business license.** Most cities require that anyone conducting a business obtain a permit from the city or county. If you're going to use a **fictitious firm name (FFN)**, a filing of the fictitious firm name is also required. This **"doing business as" (DBA)** is filed with the clerk of the county where the principal place of business is located. It is also necessary to give notice of the intended DBA by publishing the information in a newspaper of general circulation in the judicial district in which the business is headquartered for three weeks (21 days).

6. **Have a telephone system installed.** Usually a large deposit is required in order to obtain the initial installation of a business phone, unless you have had previous dealings or in some manner are able to satisfy the telephone company that the business is a good credit risk.

7. **Open a trust account and a regular business checking account.** Trust accounts are not required, but most brokers find them to be an appropriate depository for their clients' funds. (The maximum amount of personal funds a broker may keep in a trust fund is $200.)

8. **Order supplies.** This includes forms, business cards, and other items that are needed in the orderly conduct of the business.

9. **Arrange for newspaper credit.** Like the telephone, this item is high on the list of expenditures. Advertising is an absolute must for survival.

10. **Obtain office equipment.** This includes such items as computers, printers, fax machine, copier, typewriters, and file cabinets. Sometimes these can be leased if you need to conserve capital.

11. **Order signs.** These would be for the office building and others for your listings. Hire a company to install these.

12. **Hire a receptionist/secretary.** This may, of necessity, be on a part-time basis.

13. **Create a policy manual. (See Appendix I.)**

14. **Create a training program** for new licensees.

15. **Contract for other services.** Custodial or janitorial services need to be obtained.

16. **Establish connections with ancillary companies.** Such companies provide the essential supporting services. Among those you should call on are the local escrow, loan, title insurance, physical inspection, and termite companies.

17. **Join local, state, and national associations of Realtors®.** By joining, you will be allowed the use of the copyrighted designation Realtor® and enjoy the use of other services provided by virtually every local board.

18. **Announce the firm's establishment.** Send out letters to all those located in the area in which your brokerage is to operate. Advertise your opening in your local newspaper.

19. **Establish a website.** Hire a professional to design your website. The better your website looks, the better you look.

B. FORMS OF BUSINESS OWNERSHIP

As a new broker, you must decide what kind of organizational structure is best for your business. This varies with different circumstances. As conditions change, an entrepreneur will adapt accordingly, by changing from one form of ownership to another.

1. Sole Proprietorship

A *SOLE PROPRIETORSHIP is characterized by an office run by one owner solely responsible for all decisions.* The owner/manager type of organization may operate alone, but typically employs one or more salespeople. This type of real estate ownership once comprised the bulk of brokerage firms in California, but large corporations are quietly gaining on them. **One disadvantage is the unlimited liability on the part of the owner**. Another is the continuous personal supervision and attention that are required to assure success. The benefits include:

a. **All profits and expenses accrue to the owner.** (Some restrictions may apply due to insufficient capital and a limited ability to raise large sums of capital.)

b. **Ease and low cost of organization** with strict control on its operation. (There are salespeople, however, who prefer to work for larger organizations and the recognition they enjoy.)

c. **Secrecy and flexibility can be maintained**. The methods of doing business can be altered quickly to meet changes in competition, economic condition, and so on. The sole proprietorship can readily change to partnership or corporation if desired.

d. **Dissolution.** The business may be dissolved or discontinued with relative ease.

2. Partnership

Under the Uniform Partnership Act adopted by California, a *PARTNERSHIP is an association of two or more persons as co-owners of a business for profit.* Real estate partnerships are relatively few in number—about 10% of all firms. Both partners must be licensed brokers. Like a sole proprietorship, **a major disadvantage of this type of ownership is the unlimited liability of all partners**. Benefits include:

a. **Partners are taxed as individuals**, not as a partnership. There is no requirement for approval by the state.

b. **Relative freedom from government regulations.** (It is the least permanent form of business ownership, however, usually due to lack of resources to buy out deceased or withdrawing partner's interest.)

c. **Additional partners can be invited to join**, creating a new partnership should the firm want to expand. (Of course, this divided authority can cause managerial difficulties, making decisions more difficult to reach or resolve.)

d. **Retention of valuable salespeople** through new partnership offerings, can make a productive salesperson, who has obtained a broker's license, an owner.

e. **Check and balance system.** Each partner is liable for the others' actions, therefore developing a sense of responsibility in the success of the firm.

f. **Greater stability is** possible than with a sole proprietorship, because what is beneficial to the partnership is also beneficial to each of the various partners.

3. Corporation

A *CORPORATION is a legal "artificial being" that conducts business under its chartered name.* The number of real estate companies that are incorporated is growing. Most of these were motivated to incorporate for any of three reasons: income tax benefits, limited liability, and growth into a large-scale operation better suited to the corporate form. *Ownership in a corporation is evidenced by shares of STOCK.* Advantages and disadvantages include:

a. **Liability of the owners** is limited only to the amount of their investment, but cost of incorporation is relatively high, including incorporation and charter fees, records books, attorney fees, etc.

b. **Transfer of ownership** is easily facilitated by simple endorsement of the stock certificate. Some **disadvantages** are due to governmental requirements, such as filing of annual reports, decision making made by the board of directors, and various tax ramifications.

c. **Permanency.** Death, disability, or retirement of one of the owners does not lead to dissolution of the corporate entity. A corporation is said to have a perpetual existence.

d. **Tax benefits.** Recent tax legislation permits brokers *to combine into a corporation, but be taxed as a partnership called a SUBCHAPTER S CORPORATION.* (One disadvantage is that income taxes are paid first by the corporation and by the stockholders individually on the paid dividends, although at a lower rate.)

The Supreme Court has recently found sole proprietorships and partners in a brokerage personally liable for the torts (illegal acts) of salespeople working for that brokerage. Corporations, on the other hand, cannot be held personally liable for those acts.

VIII. Record Keeping

A. TRUST FUND RECORDS

All offices, regardless of size, are required to keep detailed records of client funds and other forms of deposit.

Brokers are not required to have a trust fund, but most do, especially if they are involved in property management. A columnar record of all trust funds received and paid out is required (**See Figure 1-9, CAR's® Trust Bank Account Record for All Trust Funds Deposited and Withdrawn**). Trust account funds must be placed in, or with, one of the following, within **three working days** of being received:

1. A neutral escrow depository, also known as the escrow company.
2. A trust fund account.
3. Given to the principal (seller).

It is so important that client funds be separate from the brokers' business and personal accounts that we recommend different banks be used for the trust fund accounts.

COMMINGLING *is the illegal mixing of the client's and broker's funds.* **CONVERSION** *is the illegal practice of misappropriation and using the client's money.*

In order not to be accused of commingling, brokers cannot put their personal funds in the trust account with the exception of $200 to cover bank services.

The law (**Section 10148, Business and Professional Code**) states that a real estate broker must retain for **three years** copies of all **listings, purchase contracts, canceled checks, trust records,** and any other documents executed in connection with any transaction for which a real estate broker license is required. Records for transactions involving loans under the real property loan law or security dealer transactions must be retained for **four years**. Upon notice, all records must be made available for inspection by auditors or other designated representatives of the Real Estate Commissioner.

B. SALES RECORDS (Keep for Three Years)

Keep your filing system uncomplicated; everyone in the office should know how to file properly.

Figure 1-9

CALIFORNIA
ASSOCIATION
OF REALTORS®

**TRUST BANK ACCOUNT RECORD FOR ALL TRUST FUNDS
DEPOSITED AND WITHDRAWN**

Broker: _____

Address: _____

DATE	DEPOSIT (Received From)	OR	WITHDRAWAL (Paid To)	AMOUNT	BALANCE
	Name: _____ ☐ check ☐ cash ☐ _____ For: _____		Name: _____ Check #_____ For: _____	$	$
	Name: _____ ☐ check ☐ cash ☐ _____ For: _____		Name: _____ Check #_____ For: _____	$	$
	Name: _____ ☐ check ☐ cash ☐ _____ For: _____		Name: _____ Check #_____ For: _____	$	$
	Name: _____ ☐ check ☐ cash ☐ _____ For: _____		Name: _____ Check #_____ For: _____	$	$
	Name: _____ ☐ check ☐ cash ☐ _____ For: _____		Name: _____ Check #_____ For: _____	$	$
	Name: _____ ☐ check ☐ cash ☐ _____ For: _____		Name: _____ Check #_____ For: _____	$	$
	Name: _____ ☐ check ☐ cash ☐ _____ For: _____		Name: _____ Check #_____ For: _____	$	$
	Name: _____ ☐ check ☐ cash ☐ _____ For: _____		Name: _____ Check #_____ For: _____	$	$
	Name: _____ ☐ check ☐ cash ☐ _____ For: _____		Name: _____ Check #_____ For: _____	$	$
	Name: _____ ☐ check ☐ cash ☐ _____ For: _____		Name: _____ Check #_____ For: _____	$	$

Published and Distributed by:
REAL ESTATE BUSINESS SERVICES, INC.
a subsidiary of the CALIFORNIA ASSOCIATION OF REALTORS®
525 South Virgil Avenue, Los Angeles, California 90020

PRINT DATE

REVISED 10/99

OFFICE USE ONLY
Reviewed by Broker
or Designee _____
Date _____

FORM TAA-11

One way to keep a filing system simple is to file the transactions chronologically (according to date), from opening of escrow, with a cross reference to the sellers and buyers. All contracts, even cancelled escrows and rejected offers, are kept in the transaction file along with all the executed disclosures. Agents are encouraged to keep a paper trail of all communications, faxes, e-mails, and telephone conversations during the escrow period. They are also encouraged to streamline their operation by discarding all duplications. The transaction files are kept for a minimum of **three years** in the office file cabinets. For more detailed filing information, see Chapter 14 (Real Estate Assistants).

All files must remain in the office. Agents should copy pertinent information for their own use out of the office.

1. Listings

Most multiple listing services are now computerized, and the office listing inventory is readily accessible to the broker and the salesperson. You can see at a glance all the active listings, the listings in escrow, and the closed sales.

Keep computer files the same way you would paper—simple and easy to access. Always backup computer files, periodically saving them to disk, CD, or DVD.

2. Purchase Contracts and Commissions

The sales contracts, as well as all rejected offers and cancelled escrows, must also be retained in the office for a minimum of **three years**. Commissions are paid through the escrow company from the sellers' proceeds to the broker, who in turn issues a check to the salesperson in a timely fashion, usually weekly. At this time, there are deductions for miscellaneous agreed-upon shared expenses. After having checked and initialed all contracts and disclosures necessary to close the transaction, the broker pays the salesperson his or her commission and the records are filed. There is no withholding for tax purposes by the broker.

All closed and pending sales must be reported to the local Association of Realtors® MLS, within a very short period, usually two days. If this rule is not adhered to, the agent and the broker may be heavily fined.

IX. CHAPTER SUMMARY

Always put your realistic goals in writing. Review and revise them at least once a year.

The support of family members and a monetary reserve (at least six month's savings) at the onset of any career is of utmost importance.

As a new licensee, you may be inundated by solicitations from various offices wanting to interview and hire you. Selecting the office with the right **working environment** is one of the most important decisions you will make. You should interview with at least three brokers.

You have **one year** after passing the licensing examination to pay for and obtain your salesperson's license and select your sponsoring broker.

You can locate potential sponsoring brokers by observing real estate signs and newspaper advertising, as well as checking local Associations of Realtors® and the Internet.

You should also know what the start-up costs are (six month's savings in bank), who pays for expenses, what training and support you can expect to receive. There are also various commission schedules of which you should be aware.

You'll want to examine the size of the company for which you want to work. Size invariably determines the types of technical and managerial problems which confront a firm, as well as training and opportunities provided to new employees.

Salespeople working under a broker are considered **employees** for the purposes of administration by the Department of Real Estate, even if the real estate office treats you as an **independent contractor** for other purposes (such as taxation).

After choosing your office, immediately contact friends, relatives, past co-workers, trades, and service people, who make up your **sphere of influence**. Become knowledgeable in condo sales, new sales, probates, foreclosures, and property management. Find your niche. The more you know, the more confident you'll become, and it'll show!

The listing agreement creates a **fiduciary relationship**, meaning listing brokers owe a duty of the highest care and confidentiality to the sellers. A broker may represent a seller, a buyer, or both, but that relationship must be disclosed to all parties, in writing, **prior** to entering a transaction.

A **policy manual** is designed to establish rules and policies for a brokerage's staff governing their relationships inside and outside the office (see **Appendix I**). A broker/manager must supervise his or her salespeople, who should not merely be hired and expected to learn principles of salesmanship without direction.

As often as not, properties are sold by a broker who is not the listing broker (**cooperative sales**). Always be sure to leave a business card when showing a property.

All **commissions are negotiable** at the time the listing is taken.

As a salesperson, if you want to open your own office, you'll first have to become a broker. There are a number of steps involved in opening an office, including securing the necessary capital and deciding on a location. You will also have to decide what form of business ownership is best suited for you, whether it is a **sole proprietorship**, a **partnership**, or a **corporation** (or **"S" corporation**).

All offices, regardless of size, are required to keep detailed records of clients' funds and other forms of deposit. Client funds **must be kept separate** from the broker's business and personal accounts.

A trust fund is limited to $200 of a broker's money. All clients' funds must be deposited within three business days of receipt or acceptance of offer.

Sales records must be kept for a minimum of **three years**.

X. KEY TERMS

100% Commission
Application for Sales Associate
Cold Calls
Compensation
Commingling
Conversion
Cooperative Sales
Corporation
Dual Agency
Employee
Error and Omission Insurance
Expired Listings
Farm
Fiduciary Relationship
Floor Time
Independent Contractor Agreement
Independent Contractor
Listings
Lock Boxes
Partnership
Previewing
Policy Manual
Sales Records
Sole Proprietorship
Sphere of Influence
Sponsoring Broker
Startup Costs
Stock
Straight Commission
Subchapter S corporation
Trust Fund Records
Warm Calls
WINForms®

XI. CHAPTER 1 QUIZ

1. After passing the licensing exam, the licensee has:
    a. six months to open his or her own office.
    b. eighteen months to select a sponsoring broker.
    c. one year to pay for and obtain the salesperson's license.
    d. none of the above

2. Which of the following is a way to find a sponsoring broker?
    a. Observe real estate signs.
    b. Check newspaper advertising in the areas you plan to service.
    c. Call the local Association of Realtors®.
    d. All of the above.

3. What is a "sphere of influence"?
    a. Central location of a telecommunication company
    b. People living outside an agent's city
    c. People living in an area that the agent "farms"
    d. Both b and c

4. A salesperson who is actively engaged in professional real estate activities:
    a. must have his or her own office.
    b. must be employed by a licensed real estate broker.
    c. must pay compensation directly to cooperating agents.
    d. none of the above.

5. A broker is required to have:
    a. a trust account.
    b. an accounting system (disbursement ledger).
    c. an escrow company.
    d. $300 of the broker's personal fund in the trust account.

6. The listing agreement can best be described as a(n):
    a. dual agency.
    b. deposit receipt.
    c. employment contract.
    d. offer to buy.

7. What is Broker's Error and Omission insurance?
    a. Insurance to protect the borrower against foreclosure
    b. Insurance to protect the seller against buyers' claims
    c. Insurance to protect the agent and broker against buyers' and seller's claims
    d. Buyers' protection against earthquake damages

8. In order to open his or her own office, a real estate agent must:
   a. obtain a broker's license.
   b. secure the necessary capital.
   c. decide on a location.
   d. all of the above.

9. What are cold calls?
   a. Contacting clients late at night.
   b. Contacting people the agent does not know.
   c. Contacting people the agent does know on a cold day.
   d. Returning calls for another agent.

10. All deposits from clients must be placed in a broker's trust fund, given to the principal, or placed in a neutral escrow depository:
   a. within one week.
   b. within 10 days.
   c. minus a small fee.
   d. within three working days.

ANSWERS: 1. c; 2. d; 3. c; 4. b; 5. b; 6. c; 7. c; 8. d; 9. b; 10. d

CHAPTER 2
Prospecting
How to Market, Advertise, and Promote

I. Prospecting

A. SOURCES OF LISTINGS AND SELLERS

Listings are the lifeblood of all real estate offices.

Without listings, the inquiries and opportunities to sell real estate dwindle dramatically. Below are some of the ways to solicit listings. You may think of others.

1. **Telephone contacts** with all clients on a monthly basis should be personal and also have pertinent information of interest to the homeowner. All potential clients should be contacted at least four times a year, one way or another.

2. **E-mail** is an excellent way to keep in touch with clients (with their permission). Make sure they have your personal E-mail address as well as the company website.

3. **Greeting cards** for, say, Valentine's Day, Fourth of July, and Thanksgiving are a nice way to stay in touch, rather than the traditional holiday cards that often get lost in the shuffle.

4. Send your clients a Competitive Market Analysis. The **COMPETITIVE MARKET ANALYSIS (CMA)** *is a tool to give the sellers a price range for their home by comparing*

CHAPTER 2 OUTLINE

I. PROSPECTING (p. 41)
A. Sources of Listings and Sellers (p. 41)
B. Open Houses (p. 46)
C. Finding Buyers (p. 48)
D. The Art of Developing Referrals (p. 51)
   1. Plan Your Strategy (p. 52)
   2. Sources of Referral Information (p. 52)
   3. Actually Getting the Client to Give You Referrals (p. 54)
   4. The Follow-Up (p. 55)

II. ADVERTISING AND PROMOTION (p. 55)
A. Product Advertising (p. 57)
B. Advertising Media (p. 57)
   1. Newspapers (p. 57)
   2. Magazines (p. 59)
   3. Telephone and City Directories (p. 59)
   4. Shopping Guides (p. 60)
   5. Signs (p. 60)
   6. Direct Mail (p. 60)
   7. Billboards and Other Outdoor Advertising (p. 60)
   8. Window Displays (p. 60)
   9. Radio and Television (p. 60)
   10. Bus, Car, Bench, and Taxi Signs (p. 61)
   11. Club and Institutional Newsletters (p. 61)
   12. Letterheads, Company Post Cards, Institutional Folders (p. 61)
   13. Giveaways (p. 61)
   14. Internet Sites (p. 61)
C. Advertising Pointers (p. 62)
D. Writing Effective Ads (AIDA) (p. 64)
E. Budgeting for Advertising (p. 64)
F. Evaluating Advertising Effectiveness (p. 66)
G. A Word of Caution (p. 66)
   1. Regulations of the Real Estate Commissioner (Regarding Advertising) (p. 67)

III. CHAPTER SUMMARY (p. 68)
IV. KEY TERMS (p. 69)
V. CHAPTER 2 QUIZ (p. 70)

the property to similar homes that have recently sold. Update the client's competitive market analysis (CMA) once a year for information and insurance purposes. The CMA should be thorough and attractive, with color pictures of the seller's home, which can be taken with a digital camera. It should include samples of your flyers from previous listings, post cards, copies of a recent advertisement, and a well-structured resume with your color picture. (See Chapter 5 for a detailed breakdown of a CMA.)

Remember, you only have one chance to make a good first impression!

5. A **personalized newsletter,** with your color picture on the front, is an excellent way of staying in touch (**See Figure 2-1**). Most contacts appreciate being kept informed about real estate activity in the neighborhood, as well as current interest rates. They will also welcome information about current legislation affecting taxes and investments.

Always offer something of value to your readers and they will be more likely to read and welcome your correspondence.

6. A **personal gift** showing your appreciation will impress your clients. Examples are pumpkins at Thanksgiving, chocolate kisses on Valentine's Day, a small American flag on Independence Day, and red candy during the Holidays. Find out what the clients like, and they will appreciate the thoughtfulness behind the gift more than its monetary value.

7. Gather information from your clients' statements of identification. A **STATEMENT OF IDENTIFICATION** *is a form used by title companies that is filled out by buyers and sellers to verify their identities.* This information can be used to send personal notes on kids' birthdays, anniversaries, etc. These should be handwritten and stamped rather than typed and metered through the stamp machine—make it personal!

> *Residents of your geographical farm should be kept in your database and contacted four to twelve times a year, through various means, including telephone, mail, and E-mail.*

8. **Geographical farms** are great to keep whole neighborhoods readily updated on real estate activities and values. A *GEOGRAPHICAL FARM consists of a neighborhood in which a real estate agent "cultivates" new clients, both sellers and buyers, by contacting its residents up to 12 times a year in order to update them on real estate activities and values.*

Figure 2-1

Sample Newsletter

Your REALTOR®

Arlette Lyons

*Call Me For All Your
Real Estate Needs*

REAL ESTATE Update

Increase Your Odds of Selling Quickly, Think Paint

By Michele Dawson

It can't be overstated - when it comes to buying a house, the first impression is everything. If you're selling or getting ready to sell in the coming months, one of the easiest and most dramatic ways to enhance that first impression is through paint.

Fresh paint makes your house look clean, bright, and inviting.

"Painting your house's exterior before you put it on the market give the biggest bang for your fix-up buck - if you use colors that conform with your neighborhood's decorating norm," says Eric Tyson and Ray Brown in their book "House Selling for Dummies (Hungry Minds Inc., 1999).

Agents agree that sellers shouldn't take curb appeal lightly, especially when so many buyers are doing their homework and looking at the exterior of houses before they even contact an agent.

Curb appeal is crucial. Buyers get a lot of information from the web now and I find that often they have already driven around with a list of addresses and have decided which ones they want to see, giving curb appeal a lot of weight.

The Rohm and Haas Paint Quality Institute, an educational resource for paint and paint-related coatings, offers the following tips for painting before selling:

• If nothing else, paint at least the door, door frame, and foyer or first room the would-be buyers will see.

• Use fresh, neutral colors. If you're painting the exterior, make sure the color blends in with the neighborhood. Opt for neutral whites, creams, or neutrals. The PQI says these colors appeal to the greatest number of people.

• Whether you paint yourself or hire someone, make sure all the prep work is done - washing all dirt away, and patching and repairing any necessary areas on the surface before it is painted.

• Paint railings, window frames, trim, and other accents to freshen up the exterior.

• Promote any recent painting in your ads, flyers and online descriptions of your house. Homeowners and buyers place a high value on the painted appearance of a home. Include the date the paint job was completed and the quality of paint that was used.

If you're thinking about going with a different color, the experts say you should consider the architecture of the home. You should also consider:

• What the house is made of. You can easily paint wood, brick, masonry, or aluminum siding. But if you have vinyl siding, it should only be painted the same color or a lighter color. Dark paint will absorb the heat and ultimately cause the vinyl to warp in the heat.

• The fixed colors - roof color, wood, masonry, and stone.

• The surroundings - houses and other buildings in the neighborhood.

And if you don't to paint the whole house, consider an eye-popper like the front door.

It is very important to have a home looking its best and that starts as soon as a buyer drives up to the home. One important tip is to paint the front door if you cannot paint the whole house. This brings a good feeling as you enter the house.

Another important tip is to get all your painting done before potential buyers view the house.

It is important to have all the repairs and paint done before going on the market. You need that "bam experience" from day one on the market. Anything less than bam and you're just helping the other homes in the neighborhood sell first.

Arlette Lyons, CRS
Tel: (626) 331-0141, Fax: (626) 331-9772
aalyons@aol.com
http://www.LyonsandAssociatesRltr.com

Lyons & Associates, Inc., Realtor
626-331-0141
2820 E. Garvey Avenue South
West Covina, CA 91791

9. Hold **Open Houses** and invite at least 25 neighbors up to four days prior to the event. Offering a drawing gift or lottery ticket to the invitees will help insure you'll get real names, telephone numbers, and addresses. Hand each potential buyer a packet with the flyer, your resume, and information about your website. This will not only gain you the sellers' goodwill, but the neighbors will know to call you when they are ready to sell. (See **Figure 2-2** for more information.)

10. Don't forget **absentee owners**! Absentee owners' names and addresses can be obtained from title companies. Owners may live in another state, in which case they appreciate all the more seeing how their properties look and how the neighborhood is faring. These owners can be gold mines of listing sources for you as an agent.

Send out-of-state owners a stamped, first class envelope with your personal name and return address, instead of a company envelope. A curious recipient will open the envelope to see what you have to say.

For tax purposes, be sure to review 1031 exchanges with these potential sellers. (See Chapter 11 for more information on 1031 exchanges.) Labels should not be used on this type of communication, and the correspondence should be addressed to the owner's name rather than "Property Owner." Metered mail should not be used.

11. **Probate attorneys** are another source of listings. They don't like to waste time, so you should be familiar with the probate and overbidding laws, as well as the streamlined disclosure laws for probate sales. Find out how they work and work with them.

Probate action takes place in superior court. There are general rules that govern the increase of any additional bids. For example, the first bid must be at least 10% of the first $10,000 and 5% of the remainder. At the discretion of the judge, subsequent bids may be for less depending on the value of the property.

12. **For Sale By Owners (FSBOs)** can lead to sales. For Sale By Owners (FSBOs) may think they don't need your services and therefore save themselves the commission. Understanding this, you can be very successful with this source of listings. If you supply them with several disclosures at a time and tell them to call you if they have questions, they will! Follow-up calls and additional disclosures will give you lots of opportunities to build rapport and appreciation from the sellers. Most FSBOs will need help filling out the Real Estate Transfer Disclosure Statement form. They will appreciate knowing where to have their

buyers pre-qualified, tips on how to write an ad and when is the best time to do so. See a sample of the Real Transfer Disclosure Statement form in Chapter 4.

13. **Foreclosures**, and those facing repossession are highly motivated sellers. They need help now! Don't hesitate to offer your services and a way out of their predicament.

14. **"Just Sold" and "Just Listed" cards** are a good way to keep your name in the public eye. You should be original and come up with a different format than what the competition is using. This is why it is important to know what the competition is doing, so you do it better!

15. **Expired listings**, particularly the ones that expired a year ago, may now be ready to sell. A hassle-free market analysis and a resume could go a long way in getting you, the agent, an appointment to meet with the sellers. If you can't meet with the sellers, then mail it, or better yet, drop it off at the property. The sellers may be reluctant to meet with a new agent when their old agent did not sell their house. You may want to suggest that a new and fresh approach is in order now.

Never criticize another agent in an attempt to get a listing for yourself.

16. **Extended Listing Relationships** should be cultivated. Stay in touch with buyers of your listed properties even if you didn't represent them in the transaction. A newsletter or a card may get that buyer to work with you when he or she is ready to sell and buy again. (**Never contact another agent's client while in escrow as you risk violating agency relationship.**)

B. OPEN HOUSES

An **OPEN HOUSE** *is a planned period of time during which a property for sale is held open for public viewing.*

An open house is an excellent prospecting tool for finding both sellers and buyers.

An organized and well presented open house assures potential clients that you're an agent with a sales plan, able to show their homes to the most prospective buyers and to their best advantage. When doing so, you'll meet people interested in the open house property, but even those who don't buy can become future clients. Aside from the merely curious, you'll encounter people who are at least contemplating buying a new home, which often means selling their current home.

Holding open houses can be beneficial to you, as an agent, for four basic reasons:

1. They expose your listings to the buying public and other agents who may not have previously seen your listings.

2. They demonstrate to your sellers how hard you're working for them to obtain the best price for their homes.

3. You get to meet potential buyers, as well as prospects who may need to sell their homes prior to purchasing another.

4. You get to meet the neighbors and build up your database of prospects.

You are in partnership with the sellers; the mutual goal is the sale of their property. You both must do your part and cooperate with each other for the best possible results. At the initial listing presentation, you will need to give the seller directions on the best ways to show a home. *Maximizing first impressions and preparing for showing and open houses is referred to as* **STAGING**.

One of the "tricks of the trade" when holding an open house includes baking a fresh batch of cookies in the oven—the delicious aroma is appealing, making the house seem "homier," plus you have cookies to offer your prospects!

Figure 2-2   **Open House Guidelines**

The following steps will insure a good response to the open house:

1. Place an open house sign on the property a week in advance, advising neighbors that the open house will be held on Saturday and/or Sunday from 1:00 to 5:00 pm.

2. Advertise the open house in the newspaper with easy driving instructions included.

3. Contact successful real estate agents and invite them to the open house.

4. Contact at least 25 neighbors and personally invite them to the open house. This can be done by telephone or with post cards.

5. Half an hour prior to the open house, visit the neighbors you have invited and remind them of the open house.

6. Place your open house signs in strategic locations to drive-by traffic near your open house. Always ask permission of the property owners beforehand. Although you won't be placing your signs directly on their lawn, it's always a good policy to be courteous. An annoyed property owner can easily destroy or remove your sign.

7. You will need a guest book to be signed by everyone entering the property.

A drawing for a lottery ticket encourages the visitors to accurately sign the guest book.

(continued)

8. If the house is large, there should be two agents on the premises.

9. It's a good idea to have only one group of visitors at a time go through the property.

You can place a sign on the door asking other visitors to wait for a few minutes while you finish showing the home.

10. Hand each visitor a flyer with at least one photograph of the property stating its square footage, lot size, room description and other amenities. It should also state when it was built, the school districts, and of course the price. On the reverse side of the flyer, you should have your resume or bio, complete with your picture.

11. It is important to leave the seller's home in neat condition, which means removing extra flyers, disposable coffee cups, miscellaneous trash, etc. Write them a note about the open house including information about how many people came through and thanking them for preparing their home.

12. Naturally, all visitors should be contacted and thanked for attending the open house. Get their feedback and offer your services to them. This is an excellent way of adding to your prospect database!

After the date for the open house has been set, remind the sellers that the house should be left in the best condition possible. Encourage them to remove as much clutter as possible, and to leave the property and the selling to you, the professional.

C. FINDING BUYERS

It has been said that "listings are in back of you; buyers are in front of you." Now that we've explored the sources of listings, we can concern ourselves with prospecting for buyers. There are unlimited ways of prospecting, and a limitless source of prospects. Some of these are presented here.

1. **For Sale By Owners (FSBOs)** offer a source for both listings and sales. You should recognize that not only is the owner seeking a sale of his or her residence, but that he or she will also need to find a suitable replacement property.

FSBOs represent a built-in seller and buyer combination. This is a particularly attractive source for the firm that offers a guaranteed sales plan.

A *GUARANTEED SALES PLAN* is an agreement by the company to purchase the property at a given price after the "holding period of the property"; that is, if it does not sell for more during the listing period.

2. **Owner ads** in newspapers are an obvious place to find people seeking to sell their properties. What's true about the FSBOs above is equally applicable here.

3. **Market ads** are often posted on supermarket bulletin boards. These postings can alert a shopper (and an agent/broker) to listing and selling opportunities. Within reason, you may occasionally place your card next to those owner ads, then follow through with a call or visit.

4. A **reverse phone directory** is an effective way to saturate a given area by calling owners and tenants. Through such "concentration prospecting," you will find an unlimited source of names, day in and day out—even in a relatively small community. The best times to call are midmorning, when the resident has an opportunity to unwind after sending the children off to school, and the early evening hours, before primetime television.

Keep abreast of current phone solicitation laws! You may be prohibited from contacting people on the federal "Do Not Call" list.

Most real estate offices have reverse phone directories or provide access to them online, whereby phone numbers are listed by addresses rather than names. Telephone solicitors use these to concentrate their efforts in a particular geographical area.

5. **Door knocking** is rarely used by salespeople because it's often considered distasteful, demeaning, and otherwise unpleasant. **Also, many communities have banned uninvited home solicitation.** Because many agents are hesitant to go door-to-door, this may be fertile ground for prospects with little or no competition.

You must seek out prospects. Cold canvassing, done consistently, is one way to reach those new prospects. A simple approach is "Mrs. Prospect, we have several people who are interested in buying in this neighborhood. Have you been thinking of selling? Do you know anyone who is?" Notice that you're not asking for a listing. If the reply is positive, then proceed to ask for an appointment to see the property and the owners together, perhaps that evening or the next. If your prospects hesitate to grant a "listing appointment," impress upon them that you cannot show the property without written consent. If necessary, give all the reasons why a verbal approval is without merit and ineffective.

The law of averages can work for you. Even the least aggressive request, couched in simple language, is bound to produce a two percent return. That is, two out of every 100 owners at any given time are receptive to the idea of selling and buying. Persistent effort can pay off in the end.

6. **Builders** represent a continuing source of business, if cultivated properly. Not only do they need a marketing specialist to sell their properties, but they can refer you to their clients who need licensed professionals for transactions like selling their homes prior to purchasing new ones.

You'll find builders more receptive in a slow market than in a seller's market.

7. **Open houses** may provide scores of people who are not necessarily genuine customers, but can alert you to bona fide potential buyers among the "looky-loos." As mentioned earlier in this chapter, an open house is an effective marketing vehicle for building up a list of prospects and obtaining name recognition.

Open houses offer an opportunity to find both potential buyers and sellers. They're a listing <u>and</u> a selling tool!

8. **Spheres of influence** are the salesperson's dream. You should cultivate a clientele, a reservoir of potential buyers, sellers, and investors, who are like "bird dogs" working on your behalf. Personnel managers, postal workers, union officials, and others who interact with many people can steer business your direction. When there are a half-dozen people referring business your way, you have a tried and true method of obtaining prospects.

Take good care of your clients, and your clients will take good care of you!

9. **Club and civic activities** provide an excellent source of customers. Real estate is a people business, so it's imperative that you expose yourself to the maximum number of people. The local Chamber of Commerce, Kiwanis, Rotary, Lions, Optimists, Elks, Toastmasters, and church groups are just a few of the many places you can find large numbers of people who may be sources of referrals, if not prospects themselves.

Be sincere! Join clubs that truly interest you.

10. **Former customers** may open a few doors and provide valuable leads, but you have to ask for them! Call on them, if only to get reacquainted from time to time. Ask them for a letter of recommendation; you may even write it yourself to save them time. Many salespeople remember their clientele by sending greeting cards throughout the year for birthdays, anniversaries, "saw you in the news" announcements, and so forth. **Do your research, as this approach may be restricted in some communities.**

11. **Rental wanted ads** in the newspaper classified section provide a daily source of prospects. Pointing out the advantages of ownership to people looking for a place to rent or lease may convince at least a small percentage that they should trade their rent receipts for home ownership.

Tenants are buying real estate—not for themselves, but their landlords. Why not point out the many advantages of home ownership, including tax advantages?

12. **Follow newspaper notices**. Newlyweds are excellent sources for buying, and divorcees for selling. Other announcements about promotions, obituaries, job transfers, condemnations, births, retirements, and so forth present situations where housing needs change.

13. **Prospects are all around you**. Talk real estate with whomever you come in contact, whether it be the service station attendant, police officer, friend, associate, carpenter, plumber, painter, salesperson and so on. Maintain a prospect file in a notebook which is readily available, preferably pocket-size for handy reference. Pass out business cards to everyone you meet.

> *Set a goal to give a calling card to ten new people each day, five days a week for 50 weeks. This will expose your name to 2,500 people a year. The law of averages shows a pay-off rate of at least one to two percent, or from 25 to 50 listings and sales annually. It pays to advertise yourself.*

Don't be a secret agent! Tell everyone you meet you're in real estate!

14. **Making the time to make the calls** for about one hour a day will definitely be rewarding. The calls you least like to make should be made first—get them out of the way. The best time for prospecting is when you're feeling your best. Focus on good objectives, the only ones that bring results—referrals, listings, and sales. A ready script that can easily be adapted to different situations is an excellent tool. The more people you contact, the better your chances of getting an appointment and then a listing or sale. You need to keep the momentum going, no matter how busy and hectic things get.

Following a strict daily routine is extremely important to your success!

D. THE ART OF DEVELOPING REFERRALS

To build clientele and achieve a high referral business, your buyers and sellers must be kept fully informed every step of the way in the escrow.

Goodwill is earned by making it known that you have the client's best interests in mind. But good intentions are not enough; you must be a doer. You'll be better (and more fondly) remembered if you explain to the client what you are doing each step of the way. Let them know when you order the termite report and credit report, when you check out the preliminary title report, submit the loan application, order an appraisal report, check out the documentation, get all the necessary final papers signed by all of the parties, etc.

Keep your client abreast of the progress of escrow. Know how long funding takes from the lender and plan accordingly.

You should also demonstrate interest beyond the close of escrow. You can do this by sending out monthly newsletters (Figure 2-1). You can help both buyers and sellers in their move by providing helpful information about such items as utility arrangements, address notification to publishers, and so on.

Helping buyers and sellers make the moving process less stressful will insure their gratitude and lead to repeat business and referrals. One way to do this is by providing them with a moving checklist (Figure 2-3) which covers many of the details often overlooked in the chaos of moving.

The art of developing referrals might be thought of as a four-step process, as outlined below.

1. Plan Your Strategy

a. Know your clients. You don't want to ask a less-than-satisfied client for a referral.

b. If possible, have a specific referral in mind (the FSBO down the street).

c. A good time to ask for leads is just (or soon) after you have done something for the client. One hand washes the other.

d. Bear in mind that often clients need to be asked to give a referral. There's nothing wrong with politely soliciting a referral.

e. Tell your clients what specific type of lead you're most interested in, like neighbors.

f. Remember that most people are flattered by a request for help. So ask your client to help you and your firm by giving you a referral.

g. Ask if there is anything you can do to improve your services.

Remember, if you ask for criticism, you're asking a client to find something wrong. Instead, consider asking about services they most appreciated.

2. Sources of Referral Information

a. Neighbors often know each other. The couple next door or near to your client may be a possible lead.

b. Let everyone you meet know that you are in the real estate business. Don't be stingy. You can't afford to be in real estate if you can't afford to give out business cards.

Figure 2-3   **MOVING CHECKLIST**

DO THE FOLLOWING BEFORE YOU LEAVE:

Put in an Address Change to:

1. Post office.
2. Credit cards.
3. Subscriptions (usually requires several weeks' notice).
4. Relatives and friends.

You can provide your clients with change of address cards courtesy of your company.

Bank, Savings Bank, Credit Union, etc.:

1. Transfer funds and open a checking account.
2. Establish credit references.

Insurance:

1. Notify life, health, fire, and automobile insurance companies of new location for coverages.

Utility Companies:

1. Gas, electricity, water, telephone, and fuel will need to be notified.
2. Have the utility company read the meter for final bill without turning off services! This can save a real estate agent showing the house in the dark, or a new homeowner spending a weekend without lights or air conditioning.
3. Obtain refunds on any deposits made.
4. Cancel your homeowner's insurance.

Medical, Dental, Prescription Histories:

1. Ask for referrals from your doctor and dentist.
2. Transfer prescriptions, eyeglasses, and X-rays.
3. Make sure you have birth records and medical records.

And Don't Forget To:

1. Empty and defrost the freezer and clean the refrigerator.
2. Clean rags or clothing before moving.
3. Wrap (or arrange to be wrapped) items for moving.
4. Check with your moving company about costs: insurance coverage, packing and unpacking, and method and time of expected payment. Also check on arrival day, and the various shipping papers.
5. Plan for transporting pets.

Check with the Better Business Bureau before hiring a moving company. There are many unscrupulous companies out there. Ask your agent for a referral.

(continued)

On Moving Day:

1. Carry cash or traveler's checks to pay the cost of moving services and for expenses in the new city until you make banking connections.
2. Carry jewelry and important documents or send by registered mail.
3. Leave old keys with your agent.

At Your New Address:

1. Double-check closets, drawers and shelves.
2. Check on services: telephone, gas, electricity, and water.
3. Check pilot lights: stove, water heater, and furnace.
4. Obtain a new driver's license (or update if move is within same state).
5. Register your car within 5 days after arrival in state or there may be a penalty.
6. Check procedure for registering children in school.

Other agents are excellent referral sources. Brokers with advanced designations, like CRS and GRI, are listed in a directory. Keep your information updated in all real estate referral publications. You will have to share a percentage of your commission if another agent gives you a referral that ends in a sale, but the reverse is true as well.

3. Actually Getting the Client to Give You Referrals

a. Some clients need only be asked.

b. Mention your brokerage's growth and tell them how your clients have helped you by referring new clients. Then ask them to do the same.

c. Tell your clients how you've enjoyed serving them. Explain that what you've done for them you'd like to do for their friends, customers, associates, suppliers, etc.

d. Mention a specific example of another client's helpful referral. Then, encourage this client to do the same.

e. Let your clients know about other services you offer, like refinancing notary, and property management.

f. Give your clients helpful referrals, such as reliable carpenters, electricians, and plumbers, and ask them to rate these tradespeople for your benefit.

g. Find helpful ways to make your client's decision to list with you less stressful. Provide them with helpful advice, like a moving check list (Figure 2-3). Your concern for their welfare will go a long way towards influencing them to recommend your services.

> *If your clients are moving to another area, look up competent agents in the CRS listing and refer them to your moving clients. Tell them to "reach out" to the referral broker with any questions they may have concerning their new neighborhood. Establishing this new relationship may add to that broker's referral database, and encourage him or her to reciprocate by referring clients to you.*

4. The Follow-Up

a. Always follow leads promptly.

b. Report back to your client as to what happened concerning the lead.

c. Thank your client for the referral.

d. If you're sure you have a worthwhile lead, you can ask your client to give the prospect a "heads up" to let them know you'll be contacting them.

e. If the lead turns out to be a long-term prospect, place it on your "sphere of influence" list, i.e., monthly contacts.

II. Advertising and Promotion

For many real estate offices, advertising is the only way to communicate their existence to potential buyers and sellers.

In spite of the importance and cost involved in advertising, many offices fail to give advertising the time and attention it deserves. The ads get routinely repeated, the job gets done mechanically, and the results may not be rewarding. Advertisements are often written and placed according to how other offices do it, instead of according to sound advertising principles that will motivate the reader to react, reach for the telephone, and contact you—the main purpose for the ad. If the advertisement does not reach the targeted audience or fails to convince prospects to respond, then your time and advertising dollars are wasted.

Remember: an advertisement is as much a listing tool as a selling tool.

Sellers watching the newspapers and trade magazines may be influenced for good or bad by an office's advertising method. Also, it should be noted that the best results are achieved when one person is put in charge of the advertising program. Agents, office managers, or trusted assistants and other persons in the office should give feedback and suggestions, but one person should be in charge. He or she should be responsible for

watching the cost, controlling the volume, scheduling advertising for the most effective exposure, compiling and interpreting sales data, evaluating the effectiveness of the advertising, and making sure that what actually needs to be done is, in fact, done. Putting one person in charge eliminates confusion and waste that can result from several people moving in conflicting directions.

Effective salespeople, the "high earners," will often place additional ads in publications, above and beyond the ads placed by the firm.

It is important to keep track of the results derived from advertising. If the ad works, then it can be repeated. If it doesn't, then it needs to be improved upon. To determine this, a **Traffic Sheet/Ad Call Log Book (see Figure 2-4)** should be used to keep track of which ads bring in which phone calls. It can illustrate your effectiveness as an agent as well.

There are also various free advertisement opportunities available to companies that regularly advertise in one medium. If you are overseeing the advertising, you should be on the lookout for good **public relation (PR)** opportunities. Take advantage of free press coverage to promote your firm, especially when someone in your organization has made some admirable social contribution that benefits the community, such as organizing or attending a philanthropic event. These articles are best written, and more credible, from a third person point of view.

Remember, writing good advertisements takes time. Be sure to set aside sufficient time to the actual task of designing the ad, reviewing it, and revising it.

Whenever an advertisement appears in any publication, as the listing agent, you or your assistant should send a copy to the seller and other clients. Don't be a secret agent. It pays to toot your own horn!

Figure 2-4

Traffic Sheet/Ad Call Log Book

Agent	Source	Property	Client's Name and Phone Number
A. L.	Homes & Land	500 San Jose	Mrs. Ben Buyer 555-5555 Needs 4 BR. & Covina schools.

A. PRODUCT ADVERTISING

Product advertising is meant to get the reader to purchase a particular item or service.

It gives the reader information about the benefits and specific features of a property. The advantages of owning property are always an effective selling point in an ad (see **Figure 2-5**).

Figure 2-5

Advantages to Owning Real Estate

There are many advantages to owning real estate, some of which are listed below and should be brought to the ad reader's attention:

1. Inflation protection – Equity build up
2. Small initial investment – Particularly if down payment requirements are low.
3. Provides necessity of life – Pride of home ownership
4. Higher return on investment
5. Loan security – Established fixed or adjusted interest rates
6. Establishes stability – Homeowners are considered stable
7. Security – No rent increase, no 30- or 60-day notice to quit
8. Forced savings as equity increases and prices escalate
9. Enduring resources – Real estate can be refinanced, money can be pulled out
10. Tax advantages – There are numerous deductions and write-offs available to homeowners.

B. ADVERTISING MEDIA

Advertising is more effective for selling a company than for selling an individual listing!

Knowing what and how to trigger a positive reaction from the reader is important, but now you need to select the best media for the advertisement. Generally speaking, the size of the company determines the scope and the variety of media to use. Each type of media must be expected to pay for itself in results, just as each property listed and sold must contribute to your firm's productivity.

1. Newspapers

For residential areas, the most favored media is newspaper advertising. Newspaper ads can be subdivided into classified, display, classified-display, institutional, and news releases.

a. Classified Advertising

Designed to advertise a specific property, classified ads enjoy high readership among those looking for low and medium-priced housing.

Classified ads are mostly designed for resale and rental properties.

b. Display Advertising

These ads are outside the classified section of the newspaper. Display advertising sells through the use of both words and graphic elements, such as pictures, drawings, and maps. For an example of display advertising, see **Figure 2-6**.

The main purpose of display advertising is to keep your firm's name before the public, and to attract sellers to list with the company.

Figure 2-6

Display Ad

c. Classified-Display Advertising

This is a hybrid of classified and display advertising. It is essentially a larger ad found in the classified section that uses larger type, illustrations, and spacing to create a strong impression and have greater impact.

Classified-display advertising is used by the brokerage office for listings, the advertising of new homes, developments, and high-priced properties.

d. Institutional Advertising

This is advertising in any medium (except brochures) that attempts to establish a firm's identity in the public's mind, as well as its reputation, and the services it offers.

Institutional advertising is intended to indirectly increase sales by enhancing a company's reputation and informing readers of its capabilities.

e. News Stories

News publicizing the achievements of a real estate firm or any of its staff is a great form of newspaper advertising. Not only is it free, it is, in many ways, more effective than paid advertising, because more credence is given to news stories. A reader is more likely to be impressed when the article reflects the knowledge, experience, and contributions of the real estate firm told from a third-person point of view.

News stories are similar to good public relations articles, except they focus more on "news worthy" events, like multi-million dollar sales. "PR" articles, on the other hand, are more often found in the society section of a newspaper and cover community and social events.

2. Magazines

Trade magazines, as well as general magazines, are an important advertising medium for any brokerage, although more costly than many other options.

A well-placed ad in an upscale local magazine is expensive, but may draw in well-to-do clients who can afford more expensive homes.

3. Telephone and City Directories

Your company's name in the telephone directory and the yellow pages is a must to facilitate maximum and convenient exposure. The yellow pages is a relatively expensive type of advertisement, but more than cost-effective.

While it costs money to advertise in a yellow page directory, it's delivered free to virtually every home in California. No matter what magazines or newspapers people subscribe to, it's practically guaranteed that they own a copy of the local area yellow pages.

4. Shopping Guides

Many supermarkets offer their customers free home-buyers' guides that advertise current real estate listings.

5. Signs

One of the most efficient, yet relatively inexpensive means of advertising, is your firm's own sign, prominently placed on a listed property. It should remain in place until the new owners move in, with riders attached, such as "In Escrow," "Sold," or "Bought." This is concrete proof that you and your firm get results.

6. Direct Mail

This form of advertising includes such items as postcards, letters, pamphlets, booklets, brochures, circulars, leaflets, and folders. The cost is relative, depending on the quality of the products, the frequency with which you update them, and the quantity you choose to mail out. Postcards, for example, are less expensive to print and mail than brochures.

As with all advertising, keep track of how many responses were generated by direct mail. Inquire as to which specific mail-out influenced your prospects, then increase that method.

7. Billboards and Other Outdoor Advertising

Freestanding signs along streets and large billboards on the outside of buildings are eye-catching. They also keep you and your firm in the public eye, and may, consciously or subconsciously, influence prospects to think of you when they're in need of a real estate professional.

8. Window Displays

When the advertising is large and accompanied with pictures of properties, the window displays in your office can be particularly effective. The window should not be cluttered—it should be neat and constantly updated. The more walk-by traffic, the more effective the window display.

9. Radio and Television

Only high cost limits the use of radio and TV as they are especially effective for the multi-office operation looking to promote the company.

Radio and television (including cable ads) reach a much larger audience than other advertising forms; they're a better outlet for promoting your firm and developing good public relations than for marketing specific properties. The cost may also be justified when you're representing a developer of tracts for homes or subdivisions.

10. Bus, Car, Bench, and Taxi Signs

Transit advertising can be productive in getting brief messages to the general public and keeping your name in the public eye.

11. Club and Institutional Newsletters

Brokers can get name recognition by advertising their firms in these publications.

12. Letterheads, Company Post Cards, Institutional Folders

These should be consistent and have your company logo, as well as all your other pertinent company information.

Lyons and Associates, Inc. incorporates a stylized blue lion's head in its logo. Over the years, this graphic has become highly recognizable in the community, assuring customers of the firm's stability and success.

13. Giveaways

Items imprinted with your company's logo, such as calendars, maps, notepads, pencils, pens, yardsticks, mouse pads, refrigerator magnets, and a variety of small household items are ways to keep your firm's name before the public.

The more useful the specialty item, the longer the prospect will keep it. The more visible the item, the more often it subconsciously reinforces your firm's presence.

14. Internet Sites

The Internet is the newest and one of the most important types of advertising media available to real estate companies. It is an arena "ripe for the picking" for companies looking to exploit many creative and unique advertising opportunities.

These sites have become much more technical, with links to other websites, such as those that can calculate mortgages and give school rating information. It must be stressed that your company's website should be professionally designed to attract prospective buyers and sellers. (See **Figure 2-7**.)

Figure 2-7   www.lyonsandassociatesrltr.com

It's important to constantly update your web page! If no one in your office has the expertise to do so, hire an assistant or a web consultant to regularly do this task.

C. ADVERTISING POINTERS

There are many points to keep in mind when planning and implementing an advertising program.

1. Be consistent. Advertising agencies are in agreement that it takes a long time before advertising makes an impact in the community. Select logo, typography, and slogans with care, as they will be around a long time.

The longer your logo and/or slogan is in the public eye, the more established and reliable your firm will appear to your community.

2. An advertising program must be thoroughly and carefully coordinated, every detail and step of a sales campaign supported at every point. All efforts should be totally integrated.

3. Base your advertising and sales campaigns on market research and buyer-reaction surveys.

Know your market potential and limitations.

4. Visit every property to be advertised, learning all you can about the listing before writing the ad. Take photographs for office, ads, and prospects.

5. Put the material in good order; write the ad from the buyer's viewpoint, not yours.

6. Use meaningful words and phrases, telling the story in as few words as possible. Use language that stirs the imagination and the emotions, but keep it simple. Keep all abbreviations to a minimum and don't use creative abbreviations that no one understands.

7. Decide on the audience for your ad; bear in mind the person who will be reading it. Use different appeals for different markets. Don't be concerned with crowds, but with individuals.

8. Write to inspire confidence, making the copy just long enough to tell your story. Don't oversell, and don't exaggerate.

Resist the temptation to overstate a home's appeal. A property should be at least as attractive when the buyer sees it as it is in the ad.

9. Include benefits; advertise not what the property is so much as what it will do for the buyer. "RELAX BY THE POOL" as a headline demonstrates what is referred to as "selling the sizzle, not the steak."

10. Furnish salespeople with the full facts about the advertising campaign so they're not in the dark when the telephones begin ringing. Train them to ask the right questions—get names and telephone numbers; encourage callers to come in and meet you.

Remember, the purpose of advertising is to meet the clients, to bring them into the office and build a rapport with them.

11. Make the most of all inquiries and prospect leads brought in by your ads and sales literature. This includes the proper use of the telephone. Illustrate the benefits of having a knowledgeable, thoughtful agent who knows callers' needs in order to find the right property for them.

12. Budget properly. About 10% to 15% of gross commissions earned is a safe amount to expend for advertising. Maintain cost records to measure the results of the advertising outlay.

In deciding which media to use, keep in mind that the objective is not automatically to reach the largest audience, but to reach the greatest number of potential buyers at the most economical cost.

D. WRITING EFFECTIVE ADS (AIDA)

A time-tested method used in writing ads is the AIDA formula.

AIDA stands for Attention, Interest, Desire, and Action.

Whatever type of advertisement is used, you, the writer, must:

1. **Attract Attention.** Use a clever heading or opening phrase. Use white space around margins, or bold type to emphasize key ideas or words that can be found in daily newspapers: WRITER'S RETREAT... DIRT CHEAP... DO IT YOURSELF... LOVE AT FIRST SIGHT... NO DOWN PAYMENT... ENCHANTMENT FOR SALE.

2. **Arouse Interest.** Get the readers to continue reading by maintaining interest and curiosity through a flood of ideas in the body of the ad. Invite readers to imagine enjoying the pool in the summertime, entertaining guests on the patio, or secluding themselves in a convertible den used as a study or library.

3. **Stimulate Desire.** Now that the reader's eye has been caught, the ad must continue with pictures or by words to paint a picture of the house, appealing to the senses and emotions. Tell the reader, in as few words as possible, what he or she wants to know. The language should be clear, concise, and understandable. Your firm's ads will inspire confidence if you consistently give just the facts and avoid exaggeration and overstatements.

4. **Compel Action.** The close of an effective ad stimulates immediate action, for example, "For inspection, Call XXX-XXXX now."

E. BUDGETING FOR ADVERTISING

No one makes money on properties that aren't selling. You can't sell a property without some form of advertising, and all advertising costs money.

> **In a very competitive market, you'll find that salespersons' commission splits are higher, resulting in brokers shifting some of the burden of advertising costs to their agents.**

The most successful brokers are the ones best able to divvy up their advertising dollars; you should know where your advertising dollars are best spent.

Learn from your successes and your mistakes. Put more money into advertising that has proven successful to you in the past and rethink the advertisement methods that aren't working for you. Advertising in and of itself will not sell the property. It's only a means by which to get your phones to ring. It takes a combination of factors and forces to produce a completed sale.

How should you budget for advertising? Of each dollar earned, the average real estate business allocates five to seven percent for sales promotion. Stated differently, of every dollar of gross income, about 1.5 cents is paid out in all forms of advertising and promotion. As to specific ways in which allocation is made (see **Figure 2-8**), pick one guideline to determine your advertising budget. If you find a method is not working for you, change it.

Send a copy of all advertising to your seller!

Figure 2-8

Guidelines for Budgeting for Advertising

The following is a list of methods brokerages use to calculate how much money to allocate for advertising:

1. So many dollars per month.

2. A percentage of gross income.

3. A stated amount per sales associate.

4. So many dollars per office each month.

5. A given amount per property listed, depending on the quality, type and length of listing, the commission potential, advertising "pull," and other factors.

6. A percentage of net commissions of the past period.

7. A percentage of anticipated sales or estimated profits.

8. A fixed or sustained figure per period, regardless of market conditions.

9. A variable amount, fluctuating with market conditions. For instance, some brokers advertise more during good times and less in bad spells. Others apply the opposite psychology: they advertise more heavily when business is slack, reducing the promotional outlay with a brisk market.

10. A figure based on tax considerations. For example, in a high volume/high earnings period, a broker in a high tax bracket tends to increase his or her advertising budget as the cost is used as a tax write-off.

11. Every spare dollar when just opening an office to get the firm's name before the public. Such concentrated advertising may be effective initially, but as any broker can testify, no one can afford to continue to do so indefinitely and still stay in business. Similarly, an extra heavy outlay may be budgeted for special sales campaigns or to seek out a new market.

F. EVALUATE ADVERTISING EFFECTIVENESS

If your advertising program is not producing the results you want, you must make some changes. In order to know the effectiveness of the advertising campaign, you must have an evaluating system whereby you can determine which ads work and which ads need help. Offices deal with this check and balance in various ways. One popular method is to have the telephone log maintained by the receptionist or floor person (Traffic Sheet/Ad Call Log Book—Figure 2-4—detailed earlier). Newspaper and magazine ads usually have a code number, making it easy for the person answering the telephone to know which property is involved.

> **Consider using the first three letters of the street name, combined with the listing agent's initials, as an advertising code. It makes referencing a property more effective for everyone in the office.**

Each call should be entered showing its source (signs, newspapers, yellow pages, mail outs) and which agent answered the inquiry. It's important to mention that any inquiry directly resulting from the efforts of another salesperson, such as a mail out, has to be referred to that particular agent, no matter who answers the telephone.

You should regularly examine the incoming call log book to determine the impact of any advertising campaign.

G. A WORD OF CAUTION

Advertising of real estate credit is under the jurisdiction of the Federal Trade Commission (FTC).

The Truth-in-Lending Act, or Regulation Z, a part of the federal Consumers Credit Protection Act of 1968, requires disclosure of credit costs as a percent as well as total finance charges. It is enforced by the Federal Trade Commission.

If any financing term is mentioned, the ad must also mention the annual percentage rate (APR).

1. Regulations of the Real Estate Commissioner (Regarding Advertising)

As covered in Chapter 15, the Real Estate Commissioner can adopt regulations that have the same force and intent as law. Regulations concerning advertising, for example, are covered in the following:

Article 9, Section 2770 – "Electronic Communication - Advertising and Dissemination of Information on the Internet." (b) Persons who advertise or disseminate information about services over the Internet, the World Wide Web, or similar electronic common carrier systems, **will not** be deemed to be engaged in the business, act in the capacity of, advertise or assume to act as a real estate broker within this state if any of the following apply:

(1) The advertisement or information involves a service but (A) is not directed to any particular person or customer located within the State of California, (B) is limited to general information about the services offered to customers or the public in general, and (C) includes the legend **"The services referred to herein are not available to persons located within the State of California."**

(2) The advertisement or information does not involve a service provided in connection with activity for which a real estate license is required.

(3) The advertisement or information is not being published, circulated or transmitted on behalf of another or others.

(c) A person who advertises or disseminates information with respect to providing a service is **not required to have a real estate broker license** if any of the following conditions apply:

(1) The person publishing, circulating, or transmitting the advertisement or disseminating the information is acting within the exemptions from the definition of real estate broker contained in Sections 10133 or 10133.1. of the Code;

(2) The services provided do not include any of the acts within the meaning of Sections 10131, 10131.1, 10131.2, 10131.3, 10131.4, 10131.45 and 10131.6 of the Code.

(3) (A) Prior to any direct electronic communication or any response or contact with a specific customer there is in place, barriers or other implemented policies and procedures, designed to ensure that prior to the response or contact, the person making it is appropriately licensed under the Real Estate Law or qualifies for an exemption from real estate broker licensure; and, (B) There is a legend in all advertising and information disseminated about services offered indicating whether the

person making the advertising or disseminating is a licensed California real estate broker. If the person is not a licensed California real estate broker, an additional legend shall be included which provides as follows: **"The services are not available to persons located within the State of California."**

Article 9, Section 2770.1. Advertising – "License Designation." Use of the terms broker, agent, Realtor, loan correspondent or the abbreviations bro., agt., or other similar terms or abbreviations, is deemed sufficient identification to fulfill the designation requirements of **Section 10140.6 of the Business and Professions Code**.

Use of the terms and abbreviations set forth above do not satisfy the requirements of Sections 10235.5 and 17539.4 of the Code.

III. CHAPTER SUMMARY

Listings are the lifeblood of all real estate offices. There are numerous ways to contact potential sellers, including telephone contacts, e-mail, greeting cards, newsletters, and many more. Listings may also come from expired listings, foreclosures, FSBOs, and **geographical farms** that consist of a neighborhood where agents cultivate new clients, regularly updating their real estate activities and values. **Open houses** are also an excellent way to prospect for both buyers and sellers.

It's important to get **referrals** to increase business. The more helpful an agent is both before and after a sale, the more likely a client is to give a positive referral. Other agents and brokers can also recommend your services, although you may have to share your commissions with them.

Effective advertising utilizes the the **AIDA formula**—Attention, Interest, Desire, and Action.

The purpose of advertising may be to sell a particular property, but more often than not, it is a tool to get potential clients into the office and build a relationship with them. **Newspaper ads** are the most commonly used forms of advertising. They include **classified**, **display**, **classified-display**, and **institutional advertising**, as well as **news stories** and **public relation (PR)** articles.

There are numerous other forms of advertising, including magazines, radio, and television, but one of the most cost-effective and widely used is the **yellow pages** of a phone directory.

The **Internet** is another advertising arena, limited only by your imagination and technical expertise. It's important to keep your company's website updated on a regular basis.

The effectiveness of advertising should be kept track of through the use of a **traffic sheet** or **ad call logbook**. The more successful the method, the larger the percentage of the advertising budget should be spent on that medium.

The **Federal Trade Commission (FTC)** enforces the **Truth-in-Lending Act (Regulation Z)** which regulates the advertising of real estate credit. If any financing term is used in an ad, the **annual percentage rate (APR)** must also be included. **Article 9** of the **Regulations of the Real Estate Commissioner** also establishes advertising guidelines and restrictions.

IV. KEY TERMS

Absentee Owners
Ad Call Log Book
AIDA Formula
Classified Advertising
Classified-Display Advertising
Competitive Market Analysis (CMA)
Direct Mail
Display Advertising
Federal Trade Commission (FTC)
For Sale By Owners (FSBOs)
Geographical Farm
Guaranteed Sales Plan
Institutional Advertising
News Stories
Open House
Personalized Newsletter
Product Advertising
Public Relations (PR)
Regulations of the Real Estate Commissioner
Staging
Sphere of Influence
Statement of Identification
Traffic Sheet
Window Displays

V. CHAPTER 2 QUIZ

1. A comparison of one property to similar recently sold properties is called a(n):
    a. cheat sheet.
    b. log book.
    c. competitive market analysis.
    d. none of the above.

2. A "geographical farm" is comprised of:
    a. a neighborhood of houses.
    b. the residents of a neighborhood.
    c. owners who may be contacted up to 12 times a year.
    d. all of the above.

3. Why are holding open houses beneficial to you as an agent?
    a. They expose your listing to the buying public and other agents who may not have previously seen your listing.
    b. They demonstrate to your sellers how hard you are working for them to obtain the best price for their home.
    c. You get to meet potential buyers as well as prospects who may need to sell prior to purchasing.
    d. All of the above.

4. Which groups should be included in your "sphere of influence"?
    a. Personnel managers
    b. Postal workers
    c. Union officials
    d. All of the above

5. The initials F.S.B.O. stand for:
    a. for sale by operator.
    b. for sale buyer's option.
    c. forced sale by owner.
    d. for sale by owner.

6. Giving the seller directions on the best ways to show a home by maximizing first impressions and preparing for showing and open houses is referred to as:
    a. orienting.
    b. prepping.
    c. staging.
    d. none of the above.

7. In general, the most effective media to use in the advertising of homes is:
    a. billboards.
    b. magazines.
    c. newspapers.
    d. none of the above.

8. The type of advertising that attempts to establish a firm's identity in the public's mind, as well as its reputation, and the services it offers is known as:

    a. institutional advertising.

    b. classified advertising.

    c. display advertising.

    d. classified-display advertising.

9. The time-tested model used in writing ads is the A-I-D-A formula, which stands for:

    a. always include disclaimers accurately.

    b. actual interest disclosed annually.

    c. artistic, illustrated, desirable, anticipation.

    d. attention, interest, desire, action.

10. When evaluating the effectiveness of the advertising campaign, the broker/manager should:

    a. send out surveys to clients.

    b. check the phone call log book/traffic sheet.

    c. ask other brokers what method works best for them.

    d. none of the above.

ANSWERS: 1. c; 2. d; 3. d; 4. d; 5. d; 6. c; 7. c; 8. c; 9. a; 10. b

CHAPTER 3
The Listing Agreement
How to Secure an Offer to Sell

I. Employing an Agent

A *LISTING is a contract by which a principal employs an agent (broker) to do certain things for the principal, usually selling his or her property.* It is often called a Residential Listing Agreement, and the most commonly used CAR® listing form is subtitled "Exclusive Authorization and Right to Sell." An agent holding a listing is always bound by the law of agency and owes certain duties to his or her principal. The buyer and seller, on the other hand, are two principals, yet not bound by the laws of agency.

An "agency" is the relationship between principal (usually a buyer or seller) and agent (salesperson/broker) wherein the agent is employed by the principal to do certain acts, like negotiating with third parties.

A listing, then, is a contract of employment, wherein a principal hires the services of an agent—a licensed real estate broker—to perform certain prescribed services. Usually these involve the selling (or exchanging) of real property of the owner/principal, but the definition can be much wider than this. On occasion, an agent may be employed to represent a potential buyer to purchase a certain (type of) property, to seek out and negotiate a rental or leasehold, or to represent a prospective borrower in obtaining a trust deed-backed loan. As an agent you may also be called upon to represent a principal in the purchase or sale of a business opportunity, and other services for which you are licensed.

CHAPTER 3 OUTLINE

I. EMPLOYING AN AGENT (p. 73)
   A. Right to a Commission (p. 75)
   B. Types of Listings (p. 79)
      1. Open Listing (p. 79)
      2. Exclusive Listing (p. 80)
         a. Exclusive Agency (p. 81)
         b. Exclusive Right to Sell (p. 82)
      3. Other Forms of Listings (p. 82)
         a. Net Listing (p. 82)
         b. Multiple Listing (Multiple Listing Service - MLS) (p. 83)
            1. MLS on the Internet (p. 84)
         c. Office Exclusive (p. 85)
      4. Buyer's Listing (Working for Buyer) (p. 85)
      5. Whom Does the Broker Represent? (p. 86)
II. AGENCY RELATIONSHIP DISCLOSURE ACT (p. 86)
   A. Single Agency (p. 87)
   B. Dual Agency (p. 87)
      1. Broker Relationship (p. 87)
III. PREPARING FOR THE LISTING APPOINTMENT (p. 89)
   A. Meeting the Listing Prospect (p. 90)
   B. Research Procedures in Obtaining a Listing (p. 91)
IV. CLOSING THE SELLER (p. 92)
   A. Overcoming Objections to Listing (p. 93)
V. SERVICING LISTINGS (p. 99)
   A. Steps in Servicing a Listing (p. 100)
      1. Lock Boxes (p. 100)
      2. Servicing the Listing—Weekly Summary (p. 101)
VI. CHAPTER SUMMARY (p. 105)
VII. KEY TERMS (p. 106)
VIII. CHAPTER 3 QUIZ (p. 107)

In California, as in almost all other states, employment contracts must be in writing to be enforceable. In real estate, the employment contract is the "listing agreement," but a signed disclosure of agency relationship is also required. Death of either the seller or broker terminates the listing contract.

Moreover, the listing agreement (employment contract) must be definite and complete in detail as to the terms of the broker's employment. (See **Figure 3-1**.) The **fiduciary obligation** owed the principals, discussed in earlier chapters, bears repeating here; in connection with the drafting of the listing agreement, as the licensee, you owe the highest duty of care, skill, and diligence in working for the best interests of your principal (client).

Listings are said to be the backbone of sales; that is, you must first be able to "sell the owners" on listing their property before you can sell a buyer a property.

Always give both buyer and seller a copy of any agreement when signed—it's the law. Couples who are considered "one legal person" receive one copy. If there are five couples, give five copies.

A. RIGHT TO A COMMISSION

The listing contract is basically a **bi-lateral (two party) contract** of employment for the purpose of finding a buyer. The agent is not employed to convey title.

The commission is therefore earned when you (the broker) have produced a buyer who is ready, willing, and able to purchase at the price and under the terms agreed to by both seller and buyer, whether or not escrow closes.

Occasionally the words ready, willing, and able become troublesome. In general, the words "ready and willing" mean that you must produce a buyer with a bona fide offer at a specified or accepted price and terms. The word "able" requires that you have a buyer financially capable of complying with the terms of the sale, including initial cash outlay and trust deed financing.

Once a contract has been fulfilled between the parties, the commission is deemed to be earned by the broker. Even if the seller refused to sign the purchaser's offer, he or she may be held liable to you, the broker, for a commission. Obviously the general rule is controlling only in the absence of any agreement to the contrary. Modification or variation can be made as the parties agree.

Similarly, a seller may be held liable to you, the broker, where, after both buyer and seller have signed a contract, the sale fails to close because of some fault of the seller. For instance, there may be a defective title, or failure to deliver the title, or the sellers may have changed their mind about selling, or be guilty of fraud, in which case you may still be entitled to the commission.

Figure 3-1

CALIFORNIA
ASSOCIATION
OF REALTORS®

RESIDENTIAL LISTING AGREEMENT
(Exclusive Authorization and Right to Sell)
(C.A.R. Form LA, Revised 10/02)

1. **EXCLUSIVE RIGHT TO SELL:** _____ ("Seller")
hereby employs and grants _____ ("Broker")
beginning (date) _____ and ending at 11:59 P.M. on (date) _____ ("Listing Period")
the exclusive and irrevocable right to sell or exchange the real property in the City of _____,
County of_____, California, described as: _____
_____ ("Property").

2. **ITEMS EXCLUDED AND INCLUDED:** Unless otherwise specified in a real estate purchase agreement, all fixtures and fittings that are attached to the Property are included, and personal property items are excluded, from the purchase price.
ADDITIONAL ITEMS EXCLUDED: _____.
ADDITIONAL ITEMS INCLUDED: _____.
Seller intends that the above items be excluded or included in offering the Property for sale, but understands that: **(i)** the purchase agreement supersedes any intention expressed above and will ultimately determine which items are excluded and included in the sale; and **(ii)** Broker is not responsible for and does not guarantee that the above exclusions and/or inclusions will be in the purchase agreement.

3. **LISTING PRICE AND TERMS:**
   A. The listing price shall be: _____
   _____ Dollars ($ _____).
   B. Additional Terms: _____
   _____.

4. **COMPENSATION TO BROKER:**
   Notice: The amount or rate of real estate commissions is not fixed by law. They are set by each Broker individually and may be negotiable between Seller and Broker (real estate commissions include all compensation and fees to Broker).
   A. Seller agrees to pay to Broker as compensation for services irrespective of agency relationship(s), either ☐ _____ percent of the listing price (or if a purchase agreement is entered into, of the purchase price), or ☐ $ _____,
   AND _____, as follows:
   (1) If Broker, Seller, cooperating broker, or any other person procures a buyer(s) who offers to purchase the Property on the above price and terms, or on any price and terms acceptable to Seller during the Listing Period, or any extension.
   (2) If Seller, within _____ calendar days after the end of the Listing Period or any extension, enters into a contract to sell, convey, lease or otherwise transfer the Property to anyone ("Prospective Buyer") or that person's related entity: **(i)** who physically entered and was shown the Property during the Listing Period or any extension by Broker or a cooperating broker; or **(ii)** for whom Broker or any cooperating broker submitted to Seller a signed, written offer to acquire, lease, exchange or obtain an option on the Property. Seller, however, shall have no obligation to Broker under paragraph 4A(2) unless, not later than **3 calendar days** after the end of the Listing Period or any extension, Broker has given Seller a written notice of the names of such Prospective Buyers.
   (3) If, without Broker's prior written consent, the Property is withdrawn from sale, conveyed, leased, rented, otherwise transferred, or made unmarketable by a voluntary act of Seller during the Listing Period, or any extension.
   B. If completion of the sale is prevented by a party to the transaction other than Seller, then compensation due under paragraph 4A shall be payable only if and when Seller collects damages by suit, arbitration, settlement or otherwise, and then in an amount equal to the lesser of one-half of the damages recovered or the above compensation, after first deducting title and escrow expenses and the expenses of collection, if any.
   C. In addition, Seller agrees to pay Broker: _____.
   D. **(1)** Broker is authorized to cooperate with and compensate brokers participating through the multiple listing service(s) ("MLS"): **(i)** in any manner; **OR (ii)** (if checked) by offering MLS brokers: either ☐ _____ percent of the purchase price, or ☐ $ _____.
   (2) Broker is authorized to cooperate with and compensate brokers operating outside the MLS in any manner.
   E. Seller hereby irrevocably assigns to Broker the above compensation from Seller's funds and proceeds in escrow. Broker may submit this agreement, as instructions to compensate Broker pursuant to paragraph 4A, to any escrow regarding the Property involving Seller and a buyer, Prospective Buyer or other transferee.
   F. **(1)** Seller represents that Seller has not previously entered into a listing agreement with another broker regarding the Property, unless specified as follows: _____.
   (2) Seller warrants that Seller has no obligation to pay compensation to any other broker regarding the Property unless the Property is transferred to any of the following individuals or entities: _____.
   (3) If the Property is sold to anyone listed above during the time Seller is obligated to compensate another broker: **(i)** Broker is not entitled to compensation under this agreement; and **(ii)** Broker is not obligated to represent Seller in such transaction.

LA REVISED 10/02 (PAGE 1 OF 3)   Print Date

Seller acknowledges receipt of a copy of this page.
Seller's Initials (_____)(_____)

Reviewed by _____ Date _____

EQUAL HOUSING OPPORTUNITY

RESIDENTIAL LISTING AGREEMENT-EXCLUSIVE (LA PAGE 1 OF 3)

This (along with the Seller Advisory and seller's net proceeds) is one of the few forms in the seller's "listing kit" that the buyer will not receive a copy of.

Property Address: _____ Date: _____

5. **OWNERSHIP, TITLE AND AUTHORITY:** Seller warrants that: **(i)** Seller is the owner of the Property; **(ii)** no other persons or entities have title to the Property; and **(iii)** Seller has the authority to both execute this agreement and sell the Property. Exceptions to ownership, title and authority are as follows: _____.

6. **MULTIPLE LISTING SERVICE:** Information about this listing will (or ☐ will not) be provided to the MLS of Broker's selection. All terms of the transaction, including financing, if applicable, will be provided to the selected MLS for publication, dissemination and use by persons and entities on terms approved by the MLS. Seller authorizes Broker to comply with all applicable MLS rules. MLS rules allow MLS data to be made available by the MLS to additional Internet sites unless Broker gives the MLS instructions to the contrary.

7. **SELLER REPRESENTATIONS:** Seller represents that, unless otherwise specified in writing, Seller is unaware of: **(i)** any Notice of Default recorded against the Property; **(ii)** any delinquent amounts due under any loan secured by, or other obligation affecting, the Property; **(iii)** any bankruptcy, insolvency or similar proceeding affecting the Property; **(iv)** any litigation, arbitration, administrative action, government investigation or other pending or threatened action that affects or may affect the Property or Seller's ability to transfer it; and **(v)** any current, pending or proposed special assessments affecting the Property. Seller shall promptly notify Broker in writing if Seller becomes aware of any of these items during the Listing Period or any extension thereof.

8. **BROKER'S AND SELLER'S DUTIES:** Broker agrees to exercise reasonable effort and due diligence to achieve the purposes of this agreement. Unless Seller gives Broker written instructions to the contrary, Broker is authorized to order reports and disclosures as appropriate or necessary and advertise and market the Property by any method and in any medium selected by Broker, including MLS and the Internet, and, to the extent permitted by these media, control the dissemination of the information submitted to any medium. Seller agrees to consider offers presented by Broker, and to act in good faith to accomplish the sale of the Property by, among other things, making the Property available for showing at reasonable times and referring to Broker all inquiries of any party interested in the Property. Seller is responsible for determining at what price to list and sell the Property. **Seller further agrees to indemnify, defend and hold Broker harmless from all claims, disputes, litigation, judgments and attorney fees arising from any incorrect information supplied by Seller, or from any material facts that Seller knows but fails to disclose.**

9. **DEPOSIT:** Broker is authorized to accept and hold on Seller's behalf any deposits to be applied toward the purchase price.

10. **AGENCY RELATIONSHIPS:**
    A. **Disclosure:** If the Property includes residential property with one-to-four dwelling units, Seller shall receive a "Disclosure Regarding Agency Relationships" form prior to entering into this agreement.
    B. **Seller Representation:** Broker shall represent Seller in any resulting transaction, except as specified in paragraph 4F.
    C. **Possible Dual Agency With Buyer:** Depending upon the circumstances, it may be necessary or appropriate for Broker to act as an agent for both Seller and buyer, exchange party, or one or more additional parties ("Buyer"). Broker shall, as soon as practicable, disclose to Seller any election to act as a dual agent representing both Seller and Buyer. If a Buyer is procured directly by Broker or an associate licensee in Broker's firm, Seller hereby consents to Broker acting as a dual agent for Seller and such Buyer. In the event of an exchange, Seller hereby consents to Broker collecting compensation from additional parties for services rendered, provided there is disclosure to all parties of such agency and compensation. Seller understands and agrees that: **(i)** Broker, without the prior written consent of Seller, will not disclose to Buyer that Seller is willing to sell the Property at a price less than the listing price; **(ii)** Broker, without the prior written consent of Buyer, will not disclose to Seller that Buyer is willing to pay a price greater than the offered price; and **(iii)** except for (i) and (ii) above, a dual agent is obligated to disclose known facts materially affecting the value or desirability of the Property to both parties.
    D. **Other Sellers:** Seller understands that Broker may have or obtain listings on other properties, and that potential buyers may consider, make offers on, or purchase through Broker, property the same as or similar to Seller's Property. Seller consents to Broker's representation of sellers and buyers of other properties before, during and after the end of this agreement.
    E. **Confirmation:** If the Property includes residential property with one-to-four dwelling units, Broker shall confirm the agency relationship described above, or as modified, in writing, prior to or concurrent with Seller's execution of a purchase agreement.

11. **SECURITY AND INSURANCE:** Broker is not responsible for loss of or damage to personal or real property, or person, whether attributable to use of a keysafe/lockbox, a showing of the Property, or otherwise. Third parties, including, but not limited to, appraisers, inspectors, brokers and prospective buyers, may have access to, and take videos and photographs of, the interior of the Property. Seller agrees: **(i)** to take reasonable precautions to safeguard and protect valuables that might be accessible during showings of the Property; and **(ii)** to obtain insurance to protect against these risks. Broker does not maintain insurance to protect Seller.

12. **KEYSAFE/LOCKBOX:** A keysafe/lockbox is designed to hold a key to the Property to permit access to the Property by Broker, cooperating brokers, MLS participants, their authorized licensees and representatives, authorized inspectors, and accompanied prospective buyers. Broker, cooperating brokers, MLS and Associations/Boards of REALTORS® are **not** insurers against injury, theft, loss, vandalism or damage attributed to the use of a keysafe/lockbox. Seller does (or if checked ☐ does not) authorize Broker to install a keysafe/lockbox. If Seller does not occupy the Property, Seller shall be responsible for obtaining occupant(s)' written permission for use of a keysafe/lockbox.

13. **SIGN:** Seller does (or if checked ☐ does not) authorize Broker to install a FOR SALE/SOLD sign on the Property.

14. **EQUAL HOUSING OPPORTUNITY:** The Property is offered in compliance with federal, state and local anti-discrimination laws.

15. **ATTORNEY FEES:** In any action, proceeding or arbitration between Seller and Broker regarding the obligation to pay compensation under this agreement, the prevailing Seller or Broker shall be entitled to reasonable attorney fees and costs from the non-prevailing Seller or Broker, except as provided in paragraph 19A.

16. **ADDITIONAL TERMS:** _____
    _____
    _____

17. **MANAGEMENT APPROVAL:** If an associate licensee in Broker's office (salesperson or broker-associate) enters into this agreement on Broker's behalf, and Broker or Manager does not approve of its terms, Broker or Manager has the right to cancel this agreement, in writing, within 5 days after its execution.

18. **SUCCESSORS AND ASSIGNS:** This agreement shall be binding upon Seller and Seller's successors and assigns.

Seller acknowledges receipt of a copy of this page.
Seller's Initials (_____)(_____)

Reviewed by _____ Date _____

LA REVISED 10/02 (PAGE 2 OF 3)

EQUAL HOUSING OPPORTUNITY

RESIDENTIAL LISTING AGREEMENT-EXCLUSIVE (LA PAGE 2 OF 3)

Property Address: _____ Date: _____

19. DISPUTE RESOLUTION:

A. MEDIATION: Seller and Broker agree to mediate any dispute or claim arising between them out of this agreement, or any resulting transaction, before resorting to arbitration or court action, subject to paragraph 19B(2) below. Paragraph 19B(2) below applies whether or not the arbitration provision is initialed. Mediation fees, if any, shall be divided equally among the parties involved. If, for any dispute or claim to which this paragraph applies, any party commences an action without first attempting to resolve the matter through mediation, or refuses to mediate after a request has been made, then that party shall not be entitled to recover attorney fees, even if they would otherwise be available to that party in any such action. THIS MEDIATION PROVISION APPLIES WHETHER OR NOT THE ARBITRATION PROVISION IS INITIALED.

B. ARBITRATION OF DISPUTES: (1) Seller and Broker agree that any dispute or claim in Law or equity arising between them regarding the obligation to pay compensation under this agreement, which is not settled through mediation, shall be decided by neutral, binding arbitration, including and subject to paragraph 19B(2) below. The arbitrator shall be a retired judge or justice, or an attorney with at least 5 years of residential real estate law experience, unless the parties mutually agree to a different arbitrator, who shall render an award in accordance with substantive California Law. The parties shall have the right to discovery in accordance with Code of Civil Procedure §1283.05. In all other respects, the arbitration shall be conducted in accordance with Title 9 of Part III of the California Code of Civil Procedure. Judgment upon the award of the arbitrator(s) may be entered in any court having jurisdiction. Interpretation of this agreement to arbitrate shall be governed by the Federal Arbitration Act.

(2) EXCLUSIONS FROM MEDIATION AND ARBITRATION: The following matters are excluded from mediation and arbitration hereunder: **(i)** a judicial or non-judicial foreclosure or other action or proceeding to enforce a deed of trust, mortgage, or installment land sale contract as defined in Civil Code §2985; **(ii)** an unlawful detainer action; **(iii)** the filing or enforcement of a mechanic's lien; and **(iv)** any matter that is within the jurisdiction of a probate, small claims, or bankruptcy court. The filing of a court action to enable the recording of a notice of pending action, for order of attachment, receivership, injunction, or other provisional remedies, shall not constitute a waiver of the mediation and arbitration provisions.

"NOTICE: BY INITIALING IN THE SPACE BELOW YOU ARE AGREEING TO HAVE ANY DISPUTE ARISING OUT OF THE MATTERS INCLUDED IN THE 'ARBITRATION OF DISPUTES' PROVISION DECIDED BY NEUTRAL ARBITRATION AS PROVIDED BY CALIFORNIA LAW AND YOU ARE GIVING UP ANY RIGHTS YOU MIGHT POSSESS TO HAVE THE DISPUTE LITIGATED IN A COURT OR JURY TRIAL. BY INITIALING IN THE SPACE BELOW YOU ARE GIVING UP YOUR JUDICIAL RIGHTS TO DISCOVERY AND APPEAL, UNLESS THOSE RIGHTS ARE SPECIFICALLY INCLUDED IN THE 'ARBITRATION OF DISPUTES' PROVISION. IF YOU REFUSE TO SUBMIT TO ARBITRATION AFTER AGREEING TO THIS PROVISION, YOU MAY BE COMPELLED TO ARBITRATE UNDER THE AUTHORITY OF THE CALIFORNIA CODE OF CIVIL PROCEDURE. YOUR AGREEMENT TO THIS ARBITRATION PROVISION IS VOLUNTARY."

"WE HAVE READ AND UNDERSTAND THE FOREGOING AND AGREE TO SUBMIT DISPUTES ARISING OUT OF THE MATTERS INCLUDED IN THE 'ARBITRATION OF DISPUTES' PROVISION TO NEUTRAL ARBITRATION."

Seller's Initials _____ / _____   Broker's Initials _____ / _____

20. ENTIRE CONTRACT: All prior discussions, negotiations and agreements between the parties concerning the subject matter of this agreement are superseded by this agreement, which constitutes the entire contract and a complete and exclusive expression of their agreement, and may not be contradicted by evidence of any prior agreement or contemporaneous oral agreement. If any provision of this agreement is held to be ineffective or invalid, the remaining provisions will nevertheless be given full force and effect. This agreement and any supplement, addendum or modification, including any photocopy or facsimile, may be executed in counterparts.

By signing below, Seller acknowledges that Seller has read, understands, accepts and has received a copy of this agreement.

Seller _____ Date _____

Address _____ City _____ State _____ Zip _____

Telephone _____ Fax _____ E-mail _____

Seller _____ Date _____

Address _____ City _____ State _____ Zip _____

Telephone _____ Fax _____ E-mail _____

Real Estate Broker (Firm) _____

By (Agent) _____ Date _____

Address _____ City _____ State _____ Zip _____

Telephone _____ Fax _____ E-mail _____

THIS FORM HAS BEEN APPROVED BY THE CALIFORNIA ASSOCIATION OF REALTORS® (C.A.R.). NO REPRESENTATION IS MADE AS TO THE LEGAL VALIDITY OR ADEQUACY OF ANY PROVISION IN ANY SPECIFIC TRANSACTION. A REAL ESTATE BROKER IS THE PERSON QUALIFIED TO ADVISE ON REAL ESTATE TRANSACTIONS. IF YOU DESIRE LEGAL OR TAX ADVICE, CONSULT AN APPROPRIATE PROFESSIONAL.

This form is available for use by the entire real estate industry. It is not intended to identify the user as a REALTOR®. REALTOR® is a registered collective membership mark which may be used only by members of the NATIONAL ASSOCIATION OF REALTORS® who subscribe to its Code of Ethics.

SURE TRAC — The System for Success™

Published by the
California Association of REALTORS®

EQUAL HOUSING OPPORTUNITY

LA REVISED 10/02 (PAGE 3 OF 3)

Reviewed by _____ Date _____

RESIDENTIAL LISTING AGREEMENT-EXCLUSIVE (LA PAGE 3 OF 3)

B. TYPES OF LISTINGS

Contrary to popular belief, there are essentially only **two main types of listings**—the exclusive and the open. All the others are either variations of these basic two or methods of marketing the property or compensating the agent.

1. Open Listing

An *OPEN LISTING is a written contract authorizing one or more brokers (and their salespeople) to act as agent in the sale of the principal's property.*

An open listing functions as shown in **Figure 3-2**; in this case, the owners have appointed four brokers to represent them. ("S" represents salespeople.)

Figure 3-2

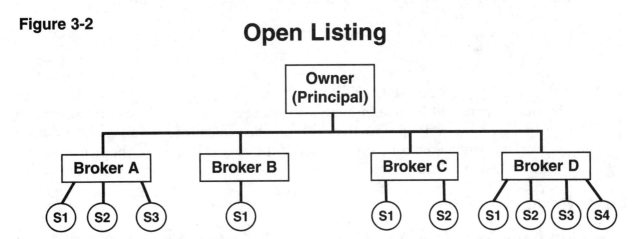

Open Listing

All four brokers, in turn, may have one or more salespeople working for them, represented by the circle S. Usually no time limit is specified for the work in an open listing; the owners may withdraw the property from the market whenever they wish. Sale of the property cancels all outstanding listings; it is not necessary to notify each agent. The commission is earned by the broker who is the first to find a buyer ready, willing, and able to meet the terms of the listing, or whose offer is accepted by the seller. **If the owners themselves sell the property, they are not liable for commission to the listing agents**.

An open listing is little better than no listing at all, and is not placed on the MLS.

Sometimes brokers take on such listings only when they can't obtain them on an exclusive basis. Consequently, they tend to store them in their "pockets" (not share with other brokers) until a buyer comes along, or if they already have a "pocket" buyer in mind. A *POCKET BUYER is prepared to buy a property before that property is actually listed with a broker*. Meanwhile, the brokers usually expend little or no effort and money in marketing the properties. Some of these listings may be

verbal only, however, until reduced to writing, no commission is enforceable. The use of the open listing is confined largely to people who do not want to be committed to any one broker or to owners who desire the exposure but want to reserve the right to sell.

Open listings are often used for vacant land.

Builders, subdividers, and developers will often utilize this type of listing when they can negotiate a reduced commission from the broker. This is often where "pocket buyers" come in. For example, a couple who is looking to buy into a condominium complex before it's even completed may be considered pocket buyers. Other frequent users are executors and administrators of estates, attorneys, trustees, and owners of industrial and commercial properties.

Open listings are the least desirable form of listings—one reason being that they don't benefit from the exposure of a multiple listing service.

You should be able to see how disadvantageous the open listing is. The broker obviously spends little time, money, and energy on such a listing, because such efforts are so often nonproductive. The owners also lose because there are no aggressive, sustained efforts on the part of the agents to sell for them, in contrast to the exclusive listing.

2. Exclusive Listing

An **EXCLUSIVE LISTING** *employs a particular broker, named in the contract, to represent the owner/principal exclusively*, as illustrated in **Figure 3-3**. Despite the fact that only one broker is shown, in practice it is very likely that a licensee other than the listing broker will end up selling the property. Cooperation among brokers is the rule, rather than the exception. Cooperative sales are an accepted way of life among licensees. In fact, scarcely half of all exclusives are sold by the listing agent, with the other half by "outsiders," that is, other brokers. A **COOPERATING BROKER** *is a non-listing broker with whom the listing broker must share a commission if he or she sells a property.*

An exclusive listing, posted on an MLS, encourages participation in the sale by numerous brokers, resulting in the most exposure and the highest possible selling price. Cooperating brokers then share the commission, as agreed.

The two major categories of the exclusive listing are discussed below. Both must be for a definite time period. Unless a specified termination date is stated in the agreement, you, as a licensee, may become subject to disciplinary action under California Real Estate Law.

Figure 3-3

Exclusive Listing

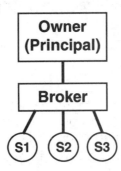

As an additional protection afforded the public, copies of exclusive listing agreements, as well as any other contracts, must be given to the person signing at the time the signature is obtained.

a. Exclusive Agency

THE EXCLUSIVE AGENCY LISTING is a listing providing that one agent has the right to be the only person, other than the owner, to sell a property during a specified period. The owner, however, has the right to independently sell the property without paying a commission to the listing broker. Therefore, the drawback of an exclusive agency listing is that the broker is, or could be, in competition with the owner for the sale.

An exclusive agency listing may be placed with an MLS, and the commission shared with any procuring broker.

Frequently, the exclusive agency is created by a provision in the agreement stating that the owner will pay a commission or fee to the listing broker if the property is sold either by the broker or by any other person during the term of the employment, including any extensions thereof.

Most brokers with an exclusive agency listing will insist that an owner quote the same asking price as the broker.

Carefully document every showing and provide the names of your (and any other broker's) prospects to the seller. This will keep a seller from dealing directly with your buyer and leaving you out of the commission.

b. Exclusive Right to Sell

Eliminating the pitfalls of the agency listing, the *EXCLUSIVE RIGHT TO SELL LISTING entitles the broker to commissions on all sales during the life of his or her agreement with the owner, even when the owners themselves sell the property.*

The "exclusive right to sell" is the most desirable listing from the broker's point of view.

Because you, as the listing broker, will reap the benefit of a commission regardless of who sells, you and your office will expend its full energies in the marketing of the property.

Because, as the listing broker, you are entitled to a commission without regard to whether or not you were the procuring or proximate cause, misunderstandings are greatly alleviated, if not eliminated altogether.

This type of listing often contains a section referred to as a *SAFETY CLAUSE, which is a negotiated period (any agreed to time period) after the termination of the listing in which the listing broker may still be entitled to a commission if the property is sold to a buyer who was shown the property during the listing period.* To protect yourself, you must furnish the owner/seller with a list of persons to whom you, or any cooperating broker, have shown the property during the listing period. If the owner or another broker sells the property to someone on the list within the protected period (usually 90 days), as the original listing broker, you should be entitled to a commission.

3. Other Forms of Listings

Two other forms of listings used in California are the net and multiple listings. They are lumped in this manner because neither is truly a listing type. They are, rather, variations of the basic two and represent methods of compensation or marketing. They not only include elements of either the open or exclusive listings, but also the method by which the broker is to be compensated or the authorization to cooperate with other agent/brokers.

a. Net Listing

Here, the compensation is not definitely determined, but a *NET LISTING provides that the agent is to retain all money received in excess of a predetermined net price to the owner.* For example, if the owner stipulates that he or she wants no less than $375,000 out of the deal, and you find a buyer for $390,000, your compensation is the difference—$15,000. The terms of the listing might require that the owner is to get no less than a fixed amount after all expenses of sale (other than brokerage) and after paying off all existing liens and encumbrances.

While the net listing is acceptable in California, it frequently gives rise to charges of misrepresentation or fraud and, therefore, is discouraged.

As the agent, you must disclose the full amount of your compensation before the owners bind themselves to accepting an offer. A violation of this real estate law (Section 10176(g) of the Business and Professions Code) constitutes grounds for revocation or suspension of the license.

With this type of listing it's imperative that you, as the broker, explain, in writing, the exact meaning of a net listing, so there is no confusion about any earned compensation.

The net listing may be either exclusive or nonexclusive. Thus, we see that there is no pure net listing type of agreement without combining it under either the open, exclusive agency, or exclusive right listing contracts.

b. Multiple Listing (Multiple Listing Service - MLS)

A **MULTIPLE LISTING** *is not really a listing as such, but a real estate listing service organized and administered by a group of brokers.* Almost all local real estate boards and independents find it mutually beneficial to charge a fee and group together, creating a broader market for the inventory of listings, which collectively is much larger. An example of the multiple arrangements appears in **Figure 3-4**.

A Multiple Listing Service (MLS) is an association of real estate brokers that provides a pooling of listings, recent sales, and the sharing of commissions on a regular basis.

As the diagram shows, the owner gives the listing to a broker, usually (though not necessarily) on an exclusive basis, authorizing him or her to distribute a right to sell to members of the MLS (as the multiple listing service is popularly designated).

Ordinarily, if you are the broker who secures the multiple listing, you exercise control over any negotiations and other rights incident to the listing. If you, as the listing broker, sell the property, you are entitled to the entire commission. On the other hand, if a member other than the original listing broker sells the property, the commission is divided between the two brokers in accordance with the terms pre-negotiated in the listing contract between the seller and broker.

Figure 3-4

Multiple Listing

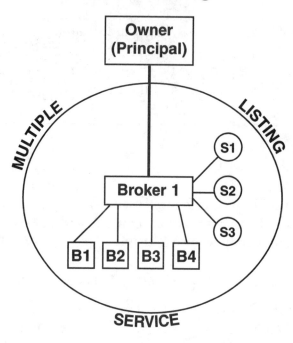

For the broker, the assurance of a more concentrated marketing effort provides a greater chance for a faster sale at top price, hence an easier and larger commission.

Because of the large number of licensees accessing an MLS, the property gains the advantage of wide exposure.

1. MLS on the Internet

Gone are the days of phone book size confidential MLS books. No longer do real estate agents have to wait for weekly publications to update property inventory. Now a click of a mouse is all it takes to access the most up-to-date MLS information, seven days a week, twenty-four hours a day. All Multiple Listing Services are on the Internet and member interactive, allowing retrieval and input from MLS participants.

All pending and sold properties must be updated on an MLS within 48 hours or the association will fine the listing office/agent.

Internet MLS postings include all the pertinent information about a property found on a listing agreement, plus additional information essential to agents who intend to show and sell the property. This information includes some basics like location, price, physical description, school district, and sewer

Occasionally, clients will make an offer through their own agent after you show them the property. You have done the work, but the other agent reaps the benefits. Always inquire from prospective buyers if they are working with another agent.

hookup information, as well as the location and type of lock box. It also lists contact information, like whether to contact the seller or the listing agent, delineates the commission split, and any other caveats attached to the selling of the property. The fact that the seller has a biting dog, for example, is a piece of valuable information you might find on an MLS posting.

c. Office Exclusive

In the sale of a residence, the most common marketing practice is to give an "exclusive right to sell" to a member of a multiple listing service, wherein each of the members is deemed to be a cooperating agent. This is, of course, done with approval of the owner. If such consent is not given, an *OFFICE EXCLUSIVE is generally obtained, that is, the listing agent, along with members of the same firm only, are given permission to show and to submit offers.* Of course, where a bona fide offer to purchase is obtained, it would be unreasonable and unrealistic for a seller to refuse to negotiate with an outside selling agent. Nevertheless, the owner may require that all offers be submitted exclusively through the listing office.

4. Buyer's Listing (Working for Buyer)

May a broker represent a buyer, or even both parties to a transaction? Yes. In the case of a *DUAL AGENCY, the law provides that a broker may act as agent for both parties to a transaction and can collect compensation from them if there is full disclosure to both, and each agrees to the arrangement.* Agency relationships and commission agreements, then, are not restricted solely to sellers.

The CAR® form, "Exclusive Authorization to Acquire Property (Buyer/Broker Compensation Contract) can be used to create an agency relationship and commission agreement whereby the buyer pays the commission. It contains a provision for separate compensation to be paid if the agent is successful in obtaining an option on the property that the buyer fails to exercise. Compensation can be based upon commissions, consultation fees, per diem charges, or any combination thereof.

5. Whom Does the Broker Represent?

Brokers are ordinarily agents of the parties who first employ them. By law, a listing broker is the agent of the seller of the property in every instance.

There are, however, many complicating factors in applying the law of agency to real estate brokerage transactions. The problem is not one of determining whose agent the broker is, with reference to the transaction as a whole, but of determining on whose behalf the broker is acting as to each particular aspect of the matter. For example, a listing broker who accepts a deposit toward purchase from an offeror holds the deposit as agent for the offeror until there is an acceptance of the offer by the seller.

The cooperating or selling broker in a transaction is usually considered an agent of the buyer. Even if the cooperating broker is not legally the agent of the seller, he or she has an obligation to deal fairly and honestly with all parties.

If, without the knowledge and consent of the principal (seller), the listing broker acts for the prospective buyer, the principal may, when discovering this fact, declare the contract void. This is true even though the transaction is a good one for the seller and even though the buyer acts in good faith and was unaware of the double agency.

Although brokers owe the utmost duty and loyalty to those who first employ them, their agency role is unique: brokers must deal fairly and honestly with both their clients and their customers/buyers at all times.

> **Be careful! When representing the seller, you should avoid discussing financial terms with a buyer or you may be inadvertently creating a dual agency that you have not disclosed.**

II. Agency Relationship Disclosure Act

Listing and selling agents are required to provide both buyers and sellers with specified written and oral agency disclosures. The law applies to all transactions involving one-to-four residential units or manufactured homes.

A written agency disclosure must be delivered to the seller prior to the signing of the listing contract. A copy of the buyers's agency disclosure must accompany all buyers' offers to the seller. As a licensee, you're also required to orally disclose to the buyer and seller whether you're acting as seller's agent, buyer's agent, or dual agent. The agency relationship must thereafter be confirmed in written form when a contract to purchase or lease is drafted. **Figure 3-5** is the CAR® Disclosure Regarding Real Estate Agency Relationships form which can be used to accomplish this disclosure. Additionally, this confirmation is included in the CAR® purchase contract.

All parties to the transaction must have a copy of both the buyer's and the seller's signed real estate agency relationship disclosure form.

The disclosure form or letter must set forth the agency relationship between buyers and sellers and you, the licensee, based upon your relationship to the buyer and/or seller. Only one of two agency relationships is possible.

A. SINGLE AGENCY

As a licensee, you are an agent for one party alone, representing **either the seller or the buyer**, but not both. Here the principal (seller or buyer) must specifically authorize you to perform acts on his or her behalf.

B. DUAL AGENCY

In this case you, the licensee, represent **both the buying and selling parties**. Being in the delicate position of representing both parties you must be completely neutral to avoid a conflict of interest. You may be privy to personal information you can't divulge to the other party, such as a seller's willingness to accept less for a home, or a buyer's intent to offer more. Because an agent by law is a fiduciary, you must be undivided in your loyalty to both parties, representing their interests equally. This task requires a certain amount of diplomacy but it has some real advantages for you as an agent, not the least of which is complete control and knowledge of all pertinent information of the transaction from start to finish.

If either party can prove that some material fact was not clearly disclosed, you may have breached your required fiduciary duty.

For self-protection, you must inform both parties of your dual representation, obtain consent from both parties, and disclose all relevant facts to each. (See Figure 3-5.)

1. Broker Relationship

It is important to remember that by definition and in practice, as a salesperson, you are an agent for the broker.

All listings you obtain are taken in the name of the broker, not your own. Hence, the broker is the agent of the sellers, even if the broker has never met the sellers, because when you took the listing you were acting on behalf of the broker. By the same token, when you write an offer for a buyer, you are also representing your broker in that transaction.

Figure 3-5

CALIFORNIA
ASSOCIATION
OF REALTORS®

DISCLOSURE REGARDING
REAL ESTATE AGENCY RELATIONSHIPS
(As required by the Civil Code)
(C.A.R. Form AD-11, Revised 10/01)

When you enter into a discussion with a real estate agent regarding a real estate transaction, you should from the outset understand what type of agency relationship or representation you wish to have with the agent in the transaction.

SELLER'S AGENT
A Seller's agent under a listing agreement with the Seller acts as the agent for the Seller only. A Seller's agent or a subagent of that agent has the following affirmative obligations:
To the Seller:
    A Fiduciary duty of utmost care, integrity, honesty, and loyalty in dealings with the Seller.
To the Buyer and the Seller:
    (a) Diligent exercise of reasonable skill and care in performance of the agent's duties.
    (b) A duty of honest and fair dealing and good faith.
    (c) A duty to disclose all facts known to the agent materially affecting the value or desirability of the property that are not known to, or within the diligent attention and observation of, the parties.

An agent is not obligated to reveal to either party any confidential information obtained from the other party that does not involve the affirmative duties set forth above.

BUYER'S AGENT
A selling agent can, with a Buyer's consent, agree to act as agent for the Buyer only. In these situations, the agent is not the Seller's agent, even if by agreement the agent may receive compensation for services rendered, either in full or in part from the Seller. An agent acting only for a Buyer has the following affirmative obligations:
To the Buyer:
    A fiduciary duty of utmost care, integrity, honesty, and loyalty in dealings with the Buyer.
To the Buyer and the Seller:
    (a) Diligent exercise of reasonable skill and care in performance of the agent's duties.
    (b) A duty of honest and fair dealing and good faith.
    (c) A duty to disclose all facts known to the agent materially affecting the value or desirability of the property that are not known to, or within the diligent attention and observation of, the parties.

An agent is not obligated to reveal to either party any confidential information obtained from the other party that does not involve the affirmative duties set forth above.

AGENT REPRESENTING BOTH SELLER AND BUYER
A real estate agent, either acting directly or through one or more associate licensees, can legally be the agent of both the Seller and the Buyer in a transaction, but only with the knowledge and consent of both the Seller and the Buyer.

In a dual agency situation, the agent has the following affirmative obligations to both the Seller and the Buyer:
    (a) A fiduciary duty of utmost care, integrity, honesty and loyalty in the dealings with either the Seller or the Buyer.
    (b) Other duties to the Seller and the Buyer as stated above in their respective sections.

In representing both Seller and Buyer, the agent may not, without the express permission of the respective party, disclose to the other party that the Seller will accept a price less than the listing price or that the Buyer will pay a price greater than the price offered.

The above duties of the agent in a real estate transaction do not relieve a Seller or Buyer from the responsibility to protect his or her own interests. You should carefully read all agreements to assure that they adequately express your understanding of the transaction. A real estate agent is a person qualified to advise about real estate. If legal or tax advice is desired, consult a competent professional.

Throughout your real property transaction you may receive more than one disclosure form, depending upon the number of agents assisting in the transaction. The law requires each agent with whom you have more than a casual relationship to present you with this disclosure form. You should read its contents each time it is presented to you, considering the relationship between you and the real estate agent in your specific transaction.

This disclosure form includes the provisions of Sections 2079.13 to 2079.24, inclusive, of the Civil Code set forth on the reverse hereof. Read it carefully.

I/WE ACKNOWLEDGE RECEIPT OF A COPY OF THIS DISCLOSURE.

BUYER/SELLER _____ Date _____ Time _____ AM/PM

BUYER/SELLER _____ Date _____ Time _____ AM/PM

AGENT _____ By _____ Date _____
         (Please Print)   (Associate-Licensee or Broker Signature)

THIS FORM SHALL BE PROVIDED AND ACKNOWLEDGED AS FOLLOWS (Civil Code §2079.14):
•When the listing brokerage company also represents the Buyer, the Listing Agent shall give one AD-11 form to the Seller and one to the Buyer.
•When Buyer and Seller are represented by different brokerage companies, then the Listing Agent shall give one AD-11 form to the Seller and the Buyer's Agent shall give one AD-11 form to the Buyer and one AD-11 form to the Seller.

SEE REVERSE SIDE FOR FURTHER INFORMATION

R E B S I N C Published and Distributed by:
REAL ESTATE BUSINESS SERVICES, INC.
a subsidiary of the CALIFORNIA ASSOCIATION OF REALTORS®
525 South Virgil Avenue, Los Angeles, California 90020

Reviewed by _____

Broker or Designee _____ Date _____

EQUAL HOUSING OPPORTUNITY

AD-11 REVISED 10/01 (PAGE 1 OF 1)   Print Date

DISCLOSURE REGARDING REAL ESTATE AGENCY RELATIONSHIPS (AD-11 PAGE 1 OF 1)

If you leave the employ of a broker, your listings are owned by your broker and stay with that broker.

III. Preparing for the Listing Appointment

The real estate transaction begins even before the listing interview. A **LISTING INTERVIEW** *is an appointment with a prospective seller with the intent of persuading that seller to list a property with a particular broker at a reasonable price.* You will need to do a market analysis of the area before you call upon the owner with whom you've made an appointment. This research is an absolute must if you're to obtain a saleable listing, that is, one that is accepted on the market as being competitive.

Overpriced listings are not much better than no listings at all. Once salespeople know a property is overpriced, it can take months before they will show it again.

As will be seen, the time involved in research can be greatly reduced if you have access to current files, which might be kept in the office, or to other brokers' comparative files. You can also subscribe to various services, such as the multiple listing service in the community, or to agencies that provide sales and other data.

Now, imagine yourself planning to conduct a listing interview. Drive through the area before visiting with the prospective sellers. You'll want to check "just sold" properties in the vicinity of the subject property; determine the type of sale, whether VA, FHA, or conventional; check other brokers' current listings, in addition to those recently expired; determine what For Sale By Owner signs are in the area, and be prepared to answer why owners are selling without benefit of a broker. Further, you'll want to get a good feel of the area by observing its appearance, preferably during daylight, finally driving up to the house to determine its **curb appeal.**

"Curb appeal" refers to how a house appears to a passerby, compared to the rest of the neighborhood.

You may want to complete as much of the listing form as possible before leaving your office. It helps to get down on paper many supporting facts and figures, thus conserving valuable time at the listing interview. You'll also impress the owners with your competency and efficiency. You may even compute the **SELLER'S PROCEEDS**, *that is, calculate how much (cash) the sellers will receive after payment of all liens and expenses, based upon a predetermined fair market value established through your research.*

You should, of course, arrive at the appointed time. To be late may cause you to lose a client's confidence even before you start. If it's a daytime appointment, you may want to arrive a few minutes early to take a Polaroid or digital picture of at least the front of the house. This shows the owners that you are interested in them, and proves to be a quick icebreaker.

Remember, first impressions are the most lasting.

A. MEETING THE LISTING PROSPECT

Knock on the door or ring the bell, then step back a few feet, awaiting the owner's response, meanwhile observing outside features for future use. When the door is opened, introduce yourself in a friendly way, showing that you are happy to meet them. Give them your card as you greet them. Once in, start the conversation on a positive note, finding some feature of the home that you can compliment, such as its cheerful atmosphere or attractive decorating. This should be sincere because sellers see through forced compliments.

Ask to see the house and grounds, finding subjects of common interest as you preview the premises. At some time you might inquire about their plans for relocating after the home is sold. This will aid you in finding out their true motives for selling, thus helping to direct your efforts more effectively. For instance, if the husband is being transferred or offered a better position by a competing employer, the sellers are highly motivated. They are likely to be more reasonable in setting the final listing price, supported by market data, which you will present to show the probable selling price. In contrast, the speculator who is simply interested in seeing what kind of profit can be obtained by placing his or her home on the market is going to be a hard bargainer. In the latter case, a long listing period is in order, and the ultimate listing price may be excessively high.

Where the listing interview should take place is a matter of preference, although the kitchen area usually provides the best atmosphere for a number of reasons. It's more informal, relaxed, and away from such distractions as television and stereo. A table is available where you can write without undue concern for scratching fine wood finish; a plug is usually accessible for your laptop computer and portable printer, beverages can be served without worrying about spillage; and everyone can gather around, making it easier to see your calculations, paper work, brochures, and computer screen.

Maintain a positive frame of mind throughout the interview. Assume from the very beginning that you will be listing and selling the property. Choose emphatic statements. "Once our sign is up...." "When we get our buyer...." "As we progress in the marketing process ...."

Get the owners involved as you emphasize "we" and "our" problems and solutions. Invite their interest in a partnership designed to solve their needs.

Even the negative features of the property can be brought up in a way that does not offend the sellers. You can always place the blame on the prospective buyer. Rather than direct criticism, allude to what the typical buyer might say. For example, if the house needs a paint job, you might say, "Mr. and Mrs. Owner, I'm a little concerned that buyers may remark on the number of paint chips and cracks on the house." In this way you are suggesting that something be done to help show the property at its best.

B. RESEARCH PROCEDURES IN OBTAINING A LISTING

Most agents use title companies to obtain the legal description, lot size, zoning, and surrounding streets in the same tract as the subject property.

Check out ownership from a title company, getting the owner's name, purchase date, and purchase price, which can be computed in many cases from the documentary transfer tax paid.

Transfer tax paid is based on $1.10 per thousand on full price paid.

Check out comparable sales, obtainable from closed escrow files maintained in the broker's office and title company data. These show how many homes in the area were sold, at what price and terms they sold, and those that did not sell (most probably because they were overpriced). Adjoining streets should be included in the study in addition to the street on which the subject property is located. If you belong to a multiple listing service, their up-to-date information is readily available to you, compiled in multiple summary sheets. Finally, viewing the homes on the market in the area can help you formulate a better picture of the market.

"Comparables" are properties that have closed escrow and are similar to the subject property in size and amenities, and located within one mile of said property.

Check out other sources of technical data—agencies that answer questions about items that buyers and other brokers are likely to ask. The following city, county, or state agencies are available to help you, since often a simple telephone call is all that's necessary to obtain the kind of information you seek.

Building and Safety Department – to check on certificate of occupancy for improvements made, and to check on building permits. It is important to note that most real estate attorneys recommend that securing building permits should be a buyer's prerogative.

Always let the buyer check on permits to limit your liability!

City or County Planning Departments – to check on existing and proposed zoning and to check on applications for zone changes, yard variances, conditional use permits, and so on. Cases are on file at the planning desks, and copies of their contents can usually be obtained. You need to give the physical location of the

property, since planning departments don't necessarily work by legal descriptions or popular street addresses. For example, state that the property is located on the south side of Morrison Street, between Ranchito and Murietta streets, measured as so many feet from major intersections.

Engineering Departments – to check on existing and proposed sewers, connections thereto, assessment bonds, acreage fees, public works projects, and so on. Be prepared with the street address and legal description. For complicated lot splits, or flag lots (lots shaped like flags), or legal boundary descriptions, a personal visit to obtain the information is recommended.

Bureau of Assessments – to check for any street, sewer, or lighting bonds against a property, or to check for the payoff on same. The bond number or legal description is needed. Payoff amounts can make the difference between your seller accepting a particular offer or not.

The seller can pay off assessment bonds or the buyer can assume them—as long as they are disclosed.

Division of Highways – for information regarding adopted or proposed freeway routes. Address inquiries to the public information counter, where you'll need to furnish the name of the freeway on which you want data, major cross streets on either side of the subject property, and the legal description.

Board of Education – to obtain new and old boundaries for elementary and high school districts, this city, county, or unified board is helpful. All you need to furnish is the street address and the type of school you're calling about.

IV. Closing the Seller

There is no distinct point in time that you start or stop the close, since all of the activities leading to the owners' signatures on the listing agreement form constitute one continuous sales process. If you remain confident and positive throughout, demonstrating that you can do the job of selling the property at a favorable price and under desirable terms, the owner is bound to react favorably.

A planned presentation should be made, using visual aids as much as possible. These include the excellent brochures and listing books which many companies provide. If your firm does not furnish such tools, the various realty boards and some outside firms do.

Sellers are pleasantly surprised when you bring them a picture of their property on the cover of your Competitive Market Analysis (CMA).

The market data your research has produced will not only be important to help in the close, but also critical in establishing the listing price at which the property should sell. Unfortunately, some agents, in order to get the listing, will inflate the asking price.

If you're going to get things done, you'll have to toot your own horn. Tell the prospects about yourself and your accomplishments in the field. Furnish information about your firm, using material that gives a short history of the company, including its achievements in marketing. Show listing and sales volume records, point out the many extras offered by the company and yourself, and explain the post-listing services to help persuade the owner to list with your company, and with you. Letters of recommendation from past clients are important at this stage of the presentation.

> *As a method of gaining consent, ask if you can use a lock box and display a sign on the property.*

Throughout the interview, listen carefully, anticipate any objections, and respond appropriately to questions. As each of the questions or objections is answered, you move nearer and nearer to the final close. A common technique that works well is the assumed consent. With the listing form (and pen) in front of you throughout the interview, at appropriate times you write and get agreement on minor points, such as the way in which title is held, the zip code or area code, and whether any assessments exist. Another technique that works well is to ask, "Would you prefer a 30-day or two-month escrow?" "Do you have a particular escrow company (or termite company, title company, etc.), or shall we use ours?" "Is it best to call for showing appointments in the morning, or are afternoons better?"

Should you want to plunge headlong into the business at hand, you might ask straightforwardly, "Mr. Seller, if you and I can get together on price and terms, can we place the property on the market tonight?"

A. OVERCOMING OBJECTIONS TO LISTING

It is rare indeed that anyone phones and asks that you come right out to take a listing, few or no questions asked. After all, you must realize that you're dealing with the largest single asset that the seller possesses. Listing property is selling at its most creative and a highly competitive game. You will be confronted with many questions and objections, and you must be ready and able to tactfully respond to and overcome these land mines if you are to successfully accomplish your mission. Listed below are a number of objections that are commonly made and some suggested responses.

Objection 1: "Saving the commission." "Why should we pay you a big commission when we can sell it ourselves?" This is perhaps the single most important reason why owners won't list, even if they don't state it this way. Many

replies can be made to this, all of them dramatizing the benefits which accrue to the owners if they list with you, for example, marketing know-how, saving time, avoiding legal entanglements, negotiations and specialization, financing, peace of mind, and so forth.

Responses to Objection 1:

(1) First, the chief reason you should not sell it yourself and save the commission is that, in reality, you aren't really saving the commission. Technically, while you, the seller, pay the commission, in practice it's always the buyer who pays it—and who saves it— if it's eliminated, since your price reflects a net figure to him.

(2) By not listing, you attract the very buyer who is trying to put the commission in his pocket. He knows that you have the commission cushion, that the asking price is not firm. He has many homes to choose from, but you have only your house to sell. He can force a compromise because you're not paying a commission.

(3) If you try to sell your house below the market price, you avoid paying the commission but you'll be on call day and night. You'll have to pay for all your own signs and advertising. You'll have to deal with all the problems, inconveniences, hazards, headaches, and legalities that go with selling a house, including the various disclosures and release of contingencies. Are you really saving anything? Is it really worth it?

(4) How good can your position be during negotiations? Do you think the buyer regards you as an impartial, disinterested party to the deal? Do you have the technical know-how to write a sound, binding contract that will stand up in court? We, in the business, are in a more neutral position than the buyer and seller. We're in a position to follow through and keep the deal hot, which you, as the seller, can't do for fear of appearing overanxious.

Mrs. Seller, you should be aware that the buyer who sees a For Sale By Owner sign is frequently the hardest bargainer in the business of real estate sales. The market today is competitive. It's tough and it's tricky. The buyers are sharp and they're shopping around. Because of their access to the Internet, buyers may have spent weeks, if not months, researching properties themselves. This may eliminate some of the man hours an agent would have dedicated to narrowing down a buyer's preferences. On the other hand, these "seasoned" shoppers are tough customers, particularly for FSBOs. They're expecting a bargain in exchange for all their legwork. Perhaps having done the work of an agent, they feel entitled to the commission a bonafide salesperson would have earned for the same efforts.

Since buyers are frequently hesitant about discussing their true objections (they can be noncommittal and even distrusting with a seller), this same feeling is apt to exist in direct negotiations when it comes to the all-important matter of price. I'm sure you'll be meticulously honest in your representations regarding the property. No matter how honest you are, prospects are naturally suspicious because they realize that this is the only home you have to sell, and if you allow them to walk out of the house, you've lost a deal. Whereas with our services, the buyers know that even if they don't like the house, we won't have lost a buyer but will be in a position to show them other properties.

(5) Mr. Owner, perhaps you haven't considered the difficulties involved in real estate financing. Are you prepared to answer all the questions about financing that a buyer might ask? Can you qualify a buyer? The GI buyer? Do you have access to the latest financial quotes and to a lender willing to qualify your buyer?

Do you know what terms of financing you can obtain with 80 percent or 90 percent or more financing? What do you know of second trust deeds? Do you know how to obtain a request for notice of default or an alienation clause or an acceleration clause? Could you show the buyer how to obtain the best type of financing with minimum cost to him? We have lenders who can answer all these questions and many others like them immediately. Our jobs depend on it.

(6) Selling a home is a 24-hour job, seven days a week. Are you and your wife going to stay around the house every day, including weekends? Buyers could show up at any time, and if you are not around when they phone or stop by, you may have lost them. Your salesperson is on the job all the time. If we find an interested party for the property, we're always available to follow up and stay in contact.

(7) When you list, we bring the right type of buyers to your home, after first qualifying them. As you may have already discovered, people answering owner ads and signs generally fall into four classifications. First there are the lookers, who are merely curiosity seekers, and the "tire kickers," who spend their weekends gallivanting from one open house to another. The second group is the bargain hunters. These people know the market; they have seen what is available, and are hunting down the unsuspecting, weary sellers who in a moment of weakness or discouragement practically give away their property just to get the whole thing over with. The third group consists of the dangerous elements of society who commit crimes in the household opened up to them through "For

Sale" signs and ads. They have been known to rob the house, and to commit crimes of violence—the kind that make headlines.

The fourth group consists of serious-minded shoppers who are aware that the proper place to find what they want is through the efforts of the professional salesperson or broker. They tell us what they want, where they want it, the down payment they can handle, the financing, and so on. We screen the lookers from the buyers, so that only qualified prospects are shown your home. Since we know what they're seeking, we can emphasize the advantages of your property as the answer to their housing needs. Aren't peace of mind and the security of a solid deal worth the commission to you?

(8) Planning the sale of a home is work for a specialist. Do you know which papers are most effective for your type of property? I know plenty of sellers who wasted hundreds of dollars in advertising and still had to turn their properties over to a real estate office to get them sold.

(9) We have a large advertising budget handled by an advertising expert who is trained to write ads that attract a wide variety of buyers. From the buyers who then come into our office we are able to qualify the right buyer for your property. Don't waste your money on advertising, Mr. Seller. Let our trained specialists get results!

Once I've taken the listing on your home, I'll be glad to keep you posted on any advertising and promotion activities directed toward your property. I like to send copies of these ads to my clients so that they can see for themselves, and then discuss the ad responses with my clientele.

Objection 2: "I want to think it over." When sellers say this, it's because they do not fully understand, or you have failed to satisfactorily answer questions or objections, or because of fear of the unknown. It's best to ask specifically what they want to think over. Go over the listing agreement, reviewing point by point, getting agreement on each item, that is, the financing, personal property included, taxes, size of lot and rooms. The listing should contain facts, not fiction, and the review is the golden opportunity to get the owner's commitment so that differences and doubts can be satisfactorily resolved. Maybe the owners are afraid of strangers, parting with a key, or having a sign on the lawn. By persistent questioning you could find out what is troubling them.

Responses to Objection 2:

Is there something that I have not made clear or explained thoroughly? Is it the price? Terms? Down payment? Let's think this over together. There's something that is preventing your making a decision. Let's discuss that first.

If you don't list now, you may lose potential buyers who are ready to buy now. While you're thinking it over, your neighbor could be selling his home to your buyers.

In the meantime, interest rates may be going up. Most people put things off to their loss. If we hurry, we can meet the newspaper deadline.

Objection 3: "I want to buy a new (replacement) house before I sell." This objection presents a golden opportunity for the broker who is active in guaranteed trade-in plans or who has dealt with contingent sales. Again emphasize the "we" in the problem-solving process. Get your buyers and yourself into the action.

Responses to Objection 3:

My company has an excellent guaranteed sales program that eliminates any risk or worry for you, Mr. Seller. Now the only problem we face is to find you the home that you're looking for. What exactly are your looking for?

We have a plan where you can purchase another home subject to the sale of your property. By selling before buying, you can be assured of a specific amount of equity that can be applied as a down payment on the replacement house.

You're in a poor bargaining position if you buy before you sell. Would you want someone to purchase your house in the hopes that maybe he could sell his? If you make your offer without a contingency, you could end up in double jeopardy, with two home mortgages to pay. You may end up selling in desperation, at a distressed price, and sustaining a loss.

Do you have $5,000 cash for a deposit on another home? Would you be willing to lose your deposit if your house doesn't sell?

If we were to find the home of your choice, will you buy with no contingency on the sale of yours? If there's no contingency on your home, would you be willing to sacrifice your property to make the deal?

Objection 4: "I have a friend in the business." With so many licenses outstanding in California, the typical owner is bound to know someone with a license. You should never attempt to belittle or downgrade the competitor, suggesting instead that his or her friend can participate in the sales effort in a number of ways. First, through membership in the multiple listing service. Second, though you may have the listing, through MLS, the friend could also show the property to any qualified buyer and share in the commission. Most important of all, stress again the many benefits and services your firm offers to get the job done effectively.

Responses to Objection 4:

> *I'm sure your friend is well qualified, but it might be difficult for him to be completely objective about your property, just as it is difficult for many of us to be impartial about our own homes. Your friend may be reluctant to discuss sensitive issues with you, or you may not wish for him to know all about your financial affairs. He might not wish to hurt your feelings, for instance, by suggesting how you could improve the salability of the property. He may be hesitant about telling you some of the objections raised by prospective buyers that could prove helpful in the marketing.*

Objection 5: "I don't want to sign a listing." This type of objection suggests that the owner doesn't mind if you expend efforts to sell, in which case you can then haggle over the compensation, but this seller won't list. Here you will need to explain the adverse consequences of taking a verbal or pocket listing and the many benefits to the owner of signing an exclusive, discussed in the early part of this chapter. You may also categorically state that it is office procedure to have all contracts in writing to avoid misunderstandings.

Responses to Objection 5:

> *When a broker accepts an exclusive, a strong fiduciary relationship is created, which obligates him to expend the maximum time and effort on the seller's behalf. With an exclusive, we must provide many more services, including expensive advertising.*

> *The legal pitfalls are so numerous without a written contract that we could not justify working on your property. Your house could not be advertised or merchandised properly.*

> *You are giving a verbal offer to sell. Do you want verbal offers to buy? I think you'll agree, Mr. Seller, that it just doesn't make sense for a buyer to tie up a deposit on a house where the sellers are not committed to negotiate in earnest.*

Objection 6: "We'll only give you a 30-day listing." Many people don't want to tie up their property for long periods of time, so this objection is a reasonable one. Anticipating this, an effective salesperson tries for a six-month listing, knowing it is easier to compromise to, say, a three-month listing. If you're doing a good job explaining the many services your company offers, and devote time to explaining the market, the sellers will be more understanding of the need to give the broker sufficient time to expose the property to the maximum number of qualified buyers at the best possible price.

Responses to Objection 6:

We need time to map our merchandising campaign, including processing, advertising, getting our mailers, caravanning, pitching to other brokers, and all the other things necessary to get it sold. Surveys show that it takes an average of 60 days to sell the typical house in today's market.

In a 30-day listing period there are four weekends, representing only eight days in which your property can be effectively shown and sold. Eight days just isn't enough time to reach the largest number of people in order to get the job done.

Objection 7: "Other brokers can get my price." Here we have the seller who is prepared to list, but who wants to do so only at his or her price, that is, one that is well above market. The best tool is the competitive market analysis (CMA), detailed in Chapter 5. Without reliable data, you may end up with a listing that takes up much time, expense, and energy, but with no results.

Responses to Objection 7:

Anyone with a license can list your property. But, do you really want to just list, or do you want to sell? Many brokers sign up a listing at any price, and then bring down the price later. False promises are not in line with our company's policy. We list to sell.

V. Servicing Listings

Service sells listings.

It's up to you to retain the harmonious relationship you set up in the listing appointments, making the seller a partner in the selling process. Explain what the seller can do to help sell, what is going to happen, and what to do, including what to do when strangers come.

Keeping in constant touch with your seller helps build confidence in your abilities. It's important to getting price reductions, extensions, changes in terms, and other concessions that might be necessary to get the property sold. Moreover, the sellers listen to an agent/broker who is in close contact, which can be particularly helpful when presenting an offer.

Keeping in touch on a regular basis helps to keep lines of communication open, avoiding any problems that might arise. You are afforded opportunities to let your clients know what you're doing to earn the agreed upon commission. All too often the owner who is not aware of the total services he or she is receiving may begrudge paying you a commission merely for spending an hour or two showing potential buyers the home. When you are working hard at selling, you should not hide this fact from your principal. A weekly or monthly written report stating all your activities is very effective.

> ***It's a good idea to have a duplicate key made and kept in the office for later inspections or should something happen to the original key.***

You should likewise keep in touch with others who have shown the property, since this helps uncover possible problem areas. For example, needed repairs might be suggested to help in the sale as well as in the appraisal and showing. Even the payment to the contractor may be arranged on terms. He may forgo part or all of the payments until close of escrow if the owners are strapped for funds. Such payments can be assigned directly from the escrow proceeds, thus assuring the contractor that funds are forthcoming.

A. STEPS IN SERVICING A LISTING

1. Have owners/sellers sign the listing agreement (give them a copy).

2. Enter the listing and a summary information sheet into the multiple listing service via the Internet (unless an "office only" exclusive is given).

3. Get keys.

4. Install lock box.

5. Order "For Sale" signs and riders. *RIDERS are supplemental attachments to signs (like "Three Bedrooms").*

6. Place signs at the front of the property.

1. Lock Boxes

LOCK BOXES contain the property's keys, and have greatly facilitated the showing process.

Lock boxes, made of sturdy material, are available through the local Association of Realtors®. These contain the keys to the property. Most of the time, they are placed on the front door.

Lock boxes have come a long way from the little metal container that use to sit on top of the front door. Now, most of them are electronic marvels that can chronologically read the code number of anyone entering the premises via the lock box. They are safer than ever before, but the code should be changed frequently to reduce the risk of someone inadvertently obtaining your secret code. Programmers or keys should never be loaned to anyone.

When finished with a showing, it is imperative that all doors be locked, that the lights be turned off, and that the key be replaced into the lock box. Reminders on stand-up cards placed in strategic positions throughout the house will remind other agents to follow your instructions and also focus on points of interest they may have overlooked.

2. Servicing the Listing—Weekly Summary

Sellers should be told what to expect and be prepared for visits by representatives of your office, interoffice, and multiple service offices. You should discuss with the sellers what to do when prospects show up without a salesperson (call to make arrangements for listing broker to show). You should advise the seller to demand a card from every caller, and to save each. You should explain the sequence of activity during and after the listing is processed. Finally, you should set up the owners for an offer before leaving their home and be available at all times for consultation.

Outlined below is a weekly summary of what you, as an agent, might do to service the listing property, from the moment of taking the listing to final sale and escrow.

Week 1: Send a thank-you letter to your new clients. Use language that is warm and friendly such as illustrated in **Figure 3-6**. Set up a listing file. Obtain a preliminary title report. Obtain necessary loan information and commitments, with respect to existing as well as new financing. Make up attractive, accurate information (setup) sheets for distribution to local real estate offices. Pitch listings to other brokers at their offices and multiple listing meetings. Enter the listing with pictures in the Internet and office website.

Contact seller after caravans, discussing the comments and reactions of those previewing the property. Make up complete and legible ad information sheets.

Where there is a second trust deed loan on the property, contact holder for possible discounting and complete upddate on the status of the loan.

April 26, 2004

Mr. & Mrs. A. Seller
1000 E. Main Street
Anytown, CA 10000

Dear Mr. and Mrs. Seller:

First of all, I want to thank you for listing your lovely home with Lyons and Associates. Please be assured that you will be kept informed of any and all real estate activities, not only on your home, but in your area.

I will be sending you copies of all our ads, and I will be contacting you at least on a weekly basis to evaluate the quality of our showings.

Should you have any question, suggestion or request, please do not hesitate to contact me; I am as near as your telephone.

Best regards,

Arlette A. Lyons, CRS, GRI
Owner-Broker

2820 E. GARVEY AVENUE SOUTH, WEST COVINA, CA 91791 • (626) 331-0141 • FAX: (626) 331-9772

Week 2: Call on the owners of the homes surrounding the subject property, asking if they would like to participate in choosing their new neighbor—a good source for additional listings as well as letting these neighbors see how hard you're working for the seller. Check to see if the sign is up, including name and other riders. Visit the owners, discuss and review information and ad sheets, problems, recommended changes, objections raised by lookers, and so forth. Also call on agents who have shown the property and get their feedback, thanking them for working on your listing.

Week 3: Visit the property again. Keep owners informed of market activity, including what sold, at what price and terms, price cuts, and the like. Recommend changes that may affect showing and desirability, such as landscaping, painting, minor repairs, or correcting unsightly conditions. Discuss loan commitments—if low, a price reduction may be indicated, especially if an FHA or VA appraisal was made. Mail advertising setup sheets with ad copy, with appropriate comments each time it is advertised.

Week 4: Continue to show clippings of any ads. Call sellers to discuss office and other brokers' activities. Show or send sellers copies of new listings or sales of comparable properties in the vicinity. Show them what you have done to promote the sale. Ask them what they in turn can do to make the listing more attractive and saleable. Continue to plug the listing to other offices. If still unsold by the end of the week, have a "30-day letter" sent by your manager or broker, summarizing the efforts to date and a suggestion that perhaps the listing price can be reduced at this time, terms liberalized, or listing extended, along with any other unique recommendations. The letter, coming from a third party, usually has considerable impact and produces better results. Sellers certainly are bound to better appreciate the interest of the firm when they receive a letter from your sales manager or broker.

Week 5: Check with broker or manager to determine response, if any, from owner. Visit the seller; review all aspects of the listing. Check to see if recommended improvements were made. Pick up cards and send sheets to cooperating agents. Poll each, transmitting opinions and comments to owner. Pitch listing at multiple meetings, and distribute information sheets.

Week 6: Visit the owner and reevaluate price and terms in light of latest sales data. Suggest that adjustments in price and terms are advisable based on neutral feedback from cooperating brokers and broker or manager's review.

Week 7: Review the entire picture with your clients. Show them what has been done to promote a sale, including advertising, direct mailings, door-to-door and telephone canvassing and your many personal efforts. Emphasize that since the property has not sold despite intensive merchandising efforts, changes are definitely needed to make it saleable. Be gentle but firm in asking for price reduction and in other things that must be done to solve the problem. Support arguments for these requests by using comparable sales, property analysis, properties listed and shown, ads, and comments of others. If a sale is to take place, resistance must be removed: does the seller really want to sell? A 60-day letter from your manager or employing broker should be sent out,

should the property not be sold by the end of two months. If permission to place a sign was not given before, it should be obtained now.

Week 8: Again, check with broker or manager to obtain response to the 60-day letter, if any. Again pitch the listing to both new and seasoned salespeople. Revive their enthusiasm. Obtain opinions after they have re-caravanned and discuss them with seller.

Week 9: Get an extension, if necessary. If financial concessions are being sought, approach the owner about obtaining a price reduction. Present the seller with information on activities, including ads, tear sheets, and cards. Show that despite the abundance of clients and calls, something must be wrong with the terms, price or condition.

Week 10: Call seller and review new comparables to push again for price and/or terms adjustments. Discuss new listings and the comments and criticisms of buyers and other brokers ("OBs"). If the house is vacant, sign-in sheets can be placed in the house for salespeople to sign whenever they show the property. Naturally, all agents are to leave their business card in the property. Advising the seller on how to increase the number of showings is especially appreciated by out-of-area sellers.

Week 11 to end of listing: Unless the original listing period exceeded three months, the twelfth and thirteenth weeks are bringing the end of your involvement with the subject listing. If no extension has been obtained, it is crucial that you get one now, so that your time, money, and energies won't have been in vain. Renew efforts to get help from cooperating brokers, and discuss the listing with active, top salespeople in the area. Visit the property regularly, making certain it is maintained appealingly, resolving any problems, and furnishing news of interest that may affect the property.

Take the listing file on every visit, to expedite explanations of what has been and is being done in the sellers' behalf. At every opportunity, pinpoint reasons for failure to sell; recommend changes each time. **Communication must be made weekly,** or as often as possible, to arrive at a satisfactory resolution to the problem. Before the expiration of the listing period, another letter from your broker/manager should be sent, containing information similar to that sent in the earlier letters, each time, however, stressing greater urgency.

If you and your broker have been diligent and conscientious in your pursuits, a sale usually results. What you do at this point, and the follow-up services offered through the escrow, is taken up in subsequent chapters.

VI. CHAPTER SUMMARY

A listing is a contract of employment, wherein a principal hires the services of an agent (licensed real estate broker) to perform certain prescribed services, usually selling. An **agency** is the relationship between a principal and an agent.

In California, **employment contracts** (listings) are required to be in writing to be enforceable.

Listings are the "backbone" of sales; an agent must be able to sell the seller on the listing before the agent can sell prospective buyers.

An **open listing** is a written contract that allows one or more brokers to act as agent in the sale of the principal's property. In reality, an open listing is little better than no listing at all.

An **exclusive listing** employs a broker, named in the contract, to represent the owner/principal exclusively. There are two categories of exclusive listings. The **exclusive agency listing** provides that only one agent has the right to sell a property. The drawback to this form of listing is that the broker could be in competition with the owner for the sale. The **exclusive right to sell** entitles the broker to commissions on all sales, during the life of the agreement, even if the owners themselves sell the property.

Two variations of the basic listings are net listing and the multiple listing. A **net listing** allows the agent to retain all money received in excess of a predetermined net price to the owner. A **multiple listing** is not really a listing as such, but a real estate service organized and administered by a group of brokers (a **multiple listing service - MLS**).

A broker may represent a buyer or even both parties to a transaction. When both parties are represented, it is known as **dual agency**. Such an arrangement is legal only if full disclosure is made to both parties to a transaction and they are in agreement.

Listing and selling agents are required to provide both buyers and sellers (of one-to-four residential units and manufactured homes) with specified written and oral disclosures through the **agency relationship disclosure** form.

There are many reasons for listing with a qualified broker, the most important being to employ a real estate marketing specialist who is knowledgeable in the rules and regulations of real estate transactions.

A commission is earned by the agent when all the terms of a listing or buying contract have been fulfilled.

VII. KEY TERMS

Agency
Agency Disclosure Act
Buyer's Listing
Competitive Market Analysis (CMA)
Cooperating Broker
Dual Agency
Exclusive Agency
Exclusive Listing
Exclusive Right to Sell
Listing
Listing Interview
Multiple Listing Service (MLS)
Net Listing
Office Exclusive
Open Listing
Pocket Buyer
Safety Clause
Seller's Proceeds
Single Agency Riders

VIII. CHAPTER QUIZ

1. Realtor Kelly lists a home held in community property with only the husband's signature on the listing agreement. Kelly's listing would generally be considered:
   - a. enforceable against the wife but not against the husband.
   - b. enforceable against the husband but not against the wife.
   - c. enforceable, but poor business practice.
   - d. not enforceable at all.

2. In California, a listing agreement:
   - a. is an employment contract.
   - b. must be in writing to be enforceable.
   - c. is both a and b.
   - d. is neither a nor b.

3. Although agents ordinarily represent owners and sellers, they may be employed occasionally to represent buyers in:
   - a. negotiating leaseholds.
   - b. obtaining mortgage loans.
   - c. purchasing business opportunities.
   - d. all of the foregoing activities.

4. The type of listing in which the owners would be held liable for a commission even if they themselves sold the property is called a(n):
   - a. exclusive agency listing.
   - b. exclusive right to sell listing.
   - c. multiple listing.
   - d. open listing.

5. The listing which is most likely to give rise to charges of misrepresentation or fraud is the:
   - a. multiple.
   - b. open.
   - c. net.
   - d. exclusive.

6. A "pocket buyer" refers to a buyer:
   - a. with deep pockets, meaning lots of money.
   - b. who is prepared to buy a property before it's listed with a broker.
   - c. who is a friend or relative of the broker.
   - d. all of the above.

7. A "safety clause" is usually found in which type of listing?
   - a. Exclusive agency listing
   - b. Exclusive right to sell listing
   - c. Net listing
   - d. Multiple listing

8. If you leave the employ of a broker and go to work for another broker:

   a. your listings stay with your old broker.

   b. your listings are your own, and go with you to your new brokerage.

   c. you must split your commissions between your old and new broker.

   d. none of the above.

9. A commission is earned by the broker when all terms of the contract have been fulfilled and he or she has produced a buyer who is:

   a. ready to buy.

   b. able to buy.

   c. willing to buy.

   d. all of the above.

10. How a house appears when compared to the rest of the neighborhood is called:

   a. landscape lookability.

   b. curb appeal.

   c. comparative shopping rating.

   d. paint and plaster appeal.

ANSWERS: 1. d; 2. c; 3. d; 4. b; 5. c; 6. b; 7. b; 8. a; 9. d; 10. b

SUNSET BROKERS

Scott Chapin

http://www.bankhomes.com

00/493-4357

CHAPTER 4
Breakdown of the Listing Agreement
How to Fill Out an Offer to Sell

I. Breakdown and Analysis of Listing Agreements

Because the listing agreement is usually the first in a series of contracts and documents used in the sale of real property, you must completely understand the form and fill it in accurately and explicitly, leaving no room for doubt.

> *A well-defined contract will eliminate potential disagreements and misunderstandings that can lead to a client's loss of confidence and, ultimately, your commission.*

An improperly drafted agreement may be indicative of an incompetent agent. If it can be demonstrated that you have violated your agency or fiduciary responsibility, it may lead to suspension of your license. In order to eliminate the possibility of poorly drawn contracts, the Real Estate Commissioner requires that all agreements prepared by salespeople be approved by their designated broker or office manager within a reasonable time.

Each section of the CAR® Residential Listing Agreement (Exclusive Authorization and Right to Sell) form is discussed in the following paragraphs, numbered and labeled to correspond with the paragraphs in the CAR form for our evaluation. (To see the entire

CHAPTER 4 OUTLINE

I. **BREAKDOWN AND ANALYSIS OF THE LISTING AGREEMENT (p. 111)**
II. **COMPLETING THE LISTING KIT (p. 124)**
III. **THE BROKER'S ROLE IN REAL ESTATE APPRAISAL (p. 142)**
    A. Helping Sellers Determine Listing Price (p. 142)
    B. Market Approach or Comparative Value (p. 144)
        1. Competitive Market Analysis (CMA) (p. 144)
    C. Cost Approach to Valuation (p. 147)
    D. Capitalization Approach to Valuation (p. 148)
    E. Pitfalls in Accepting Overpriced Listings (p. 149)
    F. Licensed Appraisers (p. 149)
IV. **CHAPTER SUMMARY (p. 151)**
V. **KEY TERMS (p. 153)**
VI. **CHAPTER 4 QUIZ (p. 154)**

form, refer back to **Figure 3-1.**) There are a wide variety of similar forms in use. While the specific language may differ in each, they all have the same basic intent: to create an agency relationship between the licensee and the owner whose property is being listed and to establish the basis for compensation, which under the Statute of Frauds must be in writing. Moreover, when properly drafted, a commission may be earned upon an offer to purchase on the exact price and terms shown in the listing, even if the seller does not choose to accept the buyer's offer.

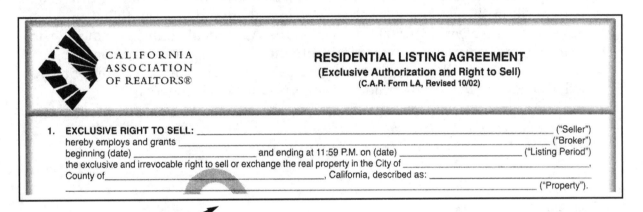

PAGE 1 OF 3

1. **Exclusive Right to Sell:** The name or names of the seller are entered on the first line. Then, the name of the broker (not the agent, who signs the form at the end of the contract), followed by the beginning and ending date of the contract (an average of three to six months) concluding at 11:59 P.M. of the last day. The city and county is then identified, followed by the unique street address of the property.

2. **Items Excluded and Included:** The form specifies that all fixtures and fittings that are attached to the property are included, and personal property items are excluded from the purchase price. This is the opportunity to fill in any "Additional Items Excluded and Included" in the listing. This does not preclude a buyer from asking for excluded items when making an offer, which may or may not be accepted by the seller.

In a listing agreement, any handwritten instructions take precedence over any preprinted instructions.

 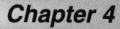

---

3. **LISTING PRICE AND TERMS:**
   A. The listing price shall be: _____
   _____ Dollars ($ _____).
   B. Additional Terms: _____
   _____.

---

3. **Listing Price and Terms:** This is the price at which the property is offered. In section (A) you fill in the amount (e.g., three hundred thousand dollars) followed by the numerical equivalent ($300,000). In section (B), Additional Terms, you include any financing terms such as down payment amount, all cash, loan assumption, subject to existing loan, and seller carry-back. If your seller is offering a loan assumption you will also need to include the amount and terms of the existing loan.

Unless terms are specified, sellers are not obligated to pay a commission when they refuse a full price offer, unless the offer is for all cash.

---

4. **COMPENSATION TO BROKER:**
   Notice: The amount or rate of real estate commissions is not fixed by law. They are set by each Broker individually and may be negotiable between Seller and Broker (real estate commissions include all compensation and fees to Broker).

---

4. **Compensation to Broker:** The compensation paid to brokers is always decided by mutual agreement between principal and agent. Contrary to popular belief, commission rates are not set by law, nor is the amount or percentage that can be negotiated regulated by law.

A. Seller agrees to pay to Broker as compensation for services irrespective of agency relationship(s), either ☐ _____ percent of the listing price (or if a purchase agreement is entered into, of the purchase price), or ☐ $ _____, AND _____, as follows:

(1) If Broker, Seller, cooperating broker, or any other person procures a buyer(s) who offers to purchase the Property on the above price and terms, or on any price and terms acceptable to Seller during the Listing Period, or any extension.

(2) If Seller, within _____ calendar days after the end of the Listing Period or any extension, enters into a contract to sell, convey, lease or otherwise transfer the Property to anyone ("Prospective Buyer") or that person's related entity: **(i)** who physically entered and was shown the Property during the Listing Period or any extension by Broker or a cooperating broker; or **(ii)** for whom Broker or any cooperating broker submitted to Seller a signed, written offer to acquire, lease, exchange or obtain an option on the Property. Seller, however, shall have no obligation to Broker under paragraph 4A(2) unless, not later than **3 calendar days** after the end of the Listing Period or any extension, Broker has given Seller a written notice of the names of such Prospective Buyers.

(3) If, without Broker's prior written consent, the Property is withdrawn from sale, conveyed, leased, rented, otherwise transferred, or made unmarketable by a voluntary act of Seller during the Listing Period, or any extension.

4(A) Fill in either the percentage of the selling price (preferable) or a specific amount. A percentage is preferable because it is automatically adjusted depending on the actual selling price.

(1) This simply states that the seller will pay a commission to the broker if he or she (or any cooperative brokers) sell the property during the listing or extension period.

(2) **THIS IS A SAFETY CLAUSE, NOT TO BE CONFUSED WITH THE LISTING PERIOD.** As the listing broker, you and the seller agree to a specific time period (180 days for example) after the termination of a listing in which the listing broker may still be entitled to a commission. To protect themselves, brokers must furnish the owners/sellers with a written notice including the names of prospects to whom they (and any other cooperating licensees) have shown the property or for whom they made an offer, during the listing period. If the owner **OR A NEW LISTING BROKER** sells the property to anyone on the list, which must be provided to the seller within **3 calendar days of the expiration of the listing**, you, as the original broker, may be entitled to a commission.

(3) This states that if the property is made unmarketable by any voluntary act of the seller during the listing period, the broker is entitled to his or her commission.

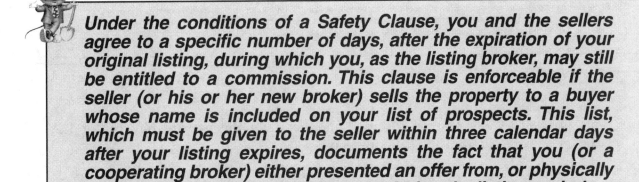

Under the conditions of a Safety Clause, you and the sellers agree to a specific number of days, after the expiration of your original listing, during which you, as the listing broker, may still be entitled to a commission. This clause is enforceable if the seller (or his or her new broker) sells the property to a buyer whose name is included on your list of prospects. This list, which must be given to the seller within three calendar days after your listing expires, documents the fact that you (or a cooperating broker) either presented an offer from, or physically entered the property with the buyer during the listing period.

B. If completion of the sale is prevented by a party to the transaction other than Seller, then compensation due under paragraph 4A shall be payable only if and when Seller collects damages by suit, arbitration, settlement or otherwise, and then in an amount equal to the lesser of one-half of the damages recovered or the above compensation, after first deducting title and escrow expenses and the expenses of collection, if any.

C. In addition, Seller agrees to pay Broker: _____.

4(B) This provides that if completion of the sale is prevented by a party other than the seller, then the total commission is to be the lesser of the commission due under section 4A, or one half of the damages recovered by the seller after deducting expenses.

4(C) This provides for any additional compensation due the broker such as MLS fees, advertising expenses, administration fees, etc. Some brokers do not charge this fee.

D. **(1)** Broker is authorized to cooperate with and compensate brokers participating through the multiple listing service(s) ("MLS"): **(i)** in any manner; **OR (ii)** (if checked) by offering MLS brokers: either ☐ _____ percent of the purchase price, or ☐ $ _____.
(2) Broker is authorized to cooperate with and compensate brokers operating outside the MLS in any manner.

4D (1) This is where the seller authorizes the broker to enter the listing in a multiple listing service thereby cooperating with other participating brokers. The amount of compensation that will be paid to the cooperating broker is entered as either a percentage or a flat fee. This amount is determined by the listing broker but approved by the seller.

4D (2) This indicates that the broker may cooperate with and compensate non-MLS members.

E. Seller hereby irrevocably assigns to Broker the above compensation from Seller's funds and proceeds in escrow. Broker may submit this agreement, as instructions to compensate Broker pursuant to paragraph 4A, to any escrow regarding the Property involving Seller and a buyer, Prospective Buyer or other transferee.

4E This is the broker's request for the seller to have the escrow pay his or her commission directly from the sale proceeds.

F. **(1)** Seller represents that Seller has not previously entered into a listing agreement with another broker regarding the Property, unless specified as follows: _____.

(2) Seller warrants that Seller has no obligation to pay compensation to any other broker regarding the Property unless the Property is transferred to any of the following individuals or entities: _____
_____

(3) If the Property is sold to anyone listed above during the time Seller is obligated to compensate another broker: **(i)** Broker is not entitled to compensation under this agreement; and **(ii)** Broker is not obligated to represent Seller in such transaction.

4F (1) This is where the seller would indicate if he or she has any previous agreement with another broker.

4F (2) This is where the seller indicates the list of names referred to in the above safety clause 4A(2), which would entitle a previous broker to the commission for the sale of the property.

4F (3) This indicates that the current broker will not be compensated if the property is sold to anyone on that list, and is released from any contractual obligation to the seller.

Seller acknowledges receipt of a copy of this page.
Seller's Initials (_____)(_____)

Reviewed by _____ Date _____

EQUAL HOUSING OPPORTUNITY

Seller's and Reviewer's Initials: The bottoms of pages 1, 2, and 3 must be initialed by the Seller. The bottoms of all three pages must be initialed by the broker or designated agent.

The Safety Clause not only protects your right to earn a commission as an original listing broker, but also protects you, as a secondary broker, from entering into a contract with a seller who is already obligated to another broker. By paying special attention to this clause, you may avoid spending a lot of time and energy on a sale only to find out, after the fact, that another broker is entitled to the commission. You should ask the seller directly if he or she has, or did have, a previous listing agreement. If the answer is yes, you should stress to your seller the importance of filling out the new Safety Clause honestly, including the list of previous prospects. If it turns out that you were mislead, either intentionally or unintentionally, the broker with a legitimate previous claim is still entitled to a commission. You may, however, have grounds to sue the seller for your lost compensation.

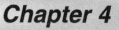

Property Address: _____ Date: _____

Property Address and Date: The address of the listed property and the date the listing form is being completed must be entered at the top of pages 2 and 3.

5. **OWNERSHIP, TITLE AND AUTHORITY:** Seller warrants that: **(i)** Seller is the owner of the Property; **(ii)** no other persons or entities have title to the Property; and **(iii)** Seller has the authority to both execute this agreement and sell the Property. Exceptions to ownership, title and authority are as follows: _____.

5. Ownership, Title, and Authority: This is where a seller acknowledges that he or she is authorized to convey the property. The fill-in portion asks for exceptions, hence the answer should be NONE.

6. **MULTIPLE LISTING SERVICE:** Information about this listing will (or ☐ will not) be provided to the MLS of Broker's selection. All terms of the transaction, including financing, if applicable, will be provided to the selected MLS for publication, dissemination and use by persons and entities on terms approved by the MLS. Seller authorizes Broker to comply with all applicable MLS rules. MLS rules allow MLS data to be made available by the MLS to additional Internet sites unless Broker gives the MLS instructions to the contrary.

6. Multiple Listing Service: This sections discloses to the sellers that the agent is a member of the local Board of Realtors' Multiple Listing Service, and that the information obtained in the listing agreement will be furnished to members of the MLS. Further, by virtue of their membership in the MLS, those agents may become cooperative agents. **Checking the box indicates a seller's refusal to be entered in the MLS.**

7. **SELLER REPRESENTATIONS:** Seller represents that, unless otherwise specified in writing, Seller is unaware of: **(i)** any Notice of Default recorded against the Property; **(ii)** any delinquent amounts due under any loan secured by, or other obligation affecting, the Property; **(iii)** any bankruptcy, insolvency or similar proceeding affecting the Property; **(iv)** any litigation, arbitration, administrative action, government investigation or other pending or threatened action that affects or may affect the Property or Seller's ability to transfer it; and **(v)** any current, pending or proposed special assessments affecting the Property. Seller shall promptly notify Broker in writing if Seller becomes aware of any of these items during the Listing Period or any extension thereof.

7. Seller Representations: This section indicates that the seller, unless otherwise specified in writing, is unaware of any financial, legal or physical reasons that would negatively affect the legal transfer of the property. This protects the broker from liability for damages.

8. **BROKER'S AND SELLER'S DUTIES:** Broker agrees to exercise reasonable effort and due diligence to achieve the purposes of this agreement. Unless Seller gives Broker written instructions to the contrary, Broker is authorized to order reports and disclosures as appropriate or necessary and advertise and market the Property by any method and in any medium selected by Broker, including MLS and the Internet, and, to the extent permitted by these media, control the dissemination of the information submitted to any medium. Seller agrees to consider offers presented by Broker, and to act in good faith to accomplish the sale of the Property by, among other things, making the Property available for showing at reasonable times and referring to Broker all inquiries of any party interested in the Property. Seller is responsible for determining at what price to list and sell the Property. **Seller further agrees to indemnify, defend and hold Broker harmless from all claims, disputes, litigation, judgments and attorney fees arising from any incorrect information supplied by Seller, or from any material facts that Seller knows but fails to disclose.**

8. Broker's and Seller's Duties: The Broker is to use due diligence to market the property in the best manner possible. This also gives authorization to the Broker, unless otherwise instructed by the sellers in writing, to order all necessary disclosures. The Seller must notify the Broker immediately should there be anticipated legal problems in conveying the property. Furthermore, the Seller is to make the property fully available for showing and takes full responsibility for all information he or she provides to the Broker, and agrees to indemnify the Broker from all claims arising from any incorrect information supplied.

9. **DEPOSIT:** Broker is authorized to accept and hold on Seller's behalf any deposits to be applied toward the purchase price.

9. Deposit: This is the authorization for the broker to accept and hold any deposits on the Seller's behalf to be applied toward the purchase price.

10. **AGENCY RELATIONSHIPS:**
   A. **Disclosure:** If the Property includes residential property with one-to-four dwelling units, Seller shall receive a "Disclosure Regarding Agency Relationships" form prior to entering into this agreement.
   B. **Seller Representation:** Broker shall represent Seller in any resulting transaction, except as specified in paragraph 4F.
   C. **Possible Dual Agency With Buyer:** Depending upon the circumstances, it may be necessary or appropriate for Broker to act as an agent for both Seller and buyer, exchange party, or one or more additional parties ("Buyer"). Broker shall, as soon as practicable, disclose to Seller any election to act as a dual agent representing both Seller and Buyer. If a Buyer is procured directly by Broker or an associate licensee in Broker's firm, Seller hereby consents to Broker acting as a dual agent for Seller and such Buyer. In the event of an exchange, Seller hereby consents to Broker collecting compensation from additional parties for services rendered, provided there is disclosure to all parties of such agency and compensation. Seller understands and agrees that: **(i)** Broker, without the prior written consent of Seller, will not disclose to Buyer that Seller is willing to sell the Property at a price less than the listing price; **(ii)** Broker, without the prior written consent of Buyer, will not disclose to Seller that Buyer is willing to pay a price greater than the offered price; and **(iii)** except for (i) and (ii) above, a dual agent is obligated to disclose known facts materially affecting the value or desirability of the Property to both parties.

10 (A) Agency Relationships: All agency disclosure forms must be signed prior to entering into the contract.

10 (B) Seller Representation: The Broker shall represent the Seller in any resulting transaction, except as specified in paragraph 4F (Names of Reserved Parties).

10 (C) Possible Dual Agency With Buyer: This addresses the possibility of the Broker representing both the Buyer and Seller and the need for full disclosure of said relationship. Also, as a dual agent, the Broker is obligated to disclose known facts materially affecting the value and desirability of the property to both parties.

> **D.** **Other Sellers:** Seller understands that Broker may have or obtain listings on other properties, and that potential buyers may consider, make offers on, or purchase through Broker, property the same as or similar to Seller's Property. Seller consents to Broker's representation of sellers and buyers of other properties before, during and after the end of this agreement.
>
> **E.** **Confirmation:** If the Property includes residential property with one-to-four dwelling units, Broker shall confirm the agency relationship described above, or as modified, in writing, prior to or concurrent with Seller's execution of a purchase agreement.

10 (D) Other Sellers: The Seller is made aware that the Broker may be listing other similar properties and as such the Broker may be representing the buyers purchasing these properties while directly involved in the sale of the Seller's property

10 (E) Confirmation: The appropriate agency relationship shall be confirmed prior to or concurrent with the Seller's execution of a purchase agreement.

> **11.** **SECURITY AND INSURANCE:** Broker is not responsible for loss of or damage to personal or real property, or person, whether attributable to use of a keysafe/lockbox, a showing of the Property, or otherwise. Third parties, including, but not limited to, appraisers, inspectors, brokers and prospective buyers, may have access to, and take videos and photographs of, the interior of the Property. Seller agrees: **(i)** to take reasonable precautions to safeguard and protect valuables that might be accessible during showings of the Property; and **(ii)** to obtain insurance to protect against these risks. Broker does not maintain insurance to protect Seller.

11. Security and Insurance: The Broker is not responsible for loss or damage to the property. The Seller must take reasonable steps to safeguard any valuables that might be accessible during showings of the Property. The Seller is advised to obtain insurance to cover these risks.

> **12.** **KEYSAFE/LOCKBOX:** A keysafe/lockbox is designed to hold a key to the Property to permit access to the Property by Broker, cooperating brokers, MLS participants, their authorized licensees and representatives, authorized inspectors, and accompanied prospective buyers. Broker, cooperating brokers, MLS and Associations/Boards of REALTORS® are **not** insurers against injury, theft, loss, vandalism or damage attributed to the use of a keysafe/lockbox. Seller does (or if checked ☐ does not) authorize Broker to install a keysafe/lockbox. If Seller does not occupy the Property, Seller shall be responsible for obtaining occupant(s)' written permission for use of a keysafe/lockbox.

12. Key Safe/Lockbox: This section gives a definition of a lockbox, which contains a key to permit access to the property to cooperating Brokers and other representatives in the sales transaction. The seller is made aware that these entities are not insured against injury, theft, loss, vandalism or damage attributed to the use of a key safe/lockbox.

13. SIGN: Seller does (or if checked ☐ does not) authorize Broker to install a FOR SALE/SOLD sign on the Property.
14. EQUAL HOUSING OPPORTUNITY: The Property is offered in compliance with federal, state and local anti-discrimination laws.

13. Sign: The Seller agrees or doesn't agree to have a sign placed on property. **Checking this box means that the seller does not agree.**

14. Equal Housing Opportunity: The property is offered in compliance with all laws adhering to anti-discrimination regulations.

15. ATTORNEY FEES: In any action, proceeding or arbitration between Seller and Broker regarding the obligation to pay compensation under this agreement, the prevailing Seller or Broker shall be entitled to reasonable attorney fees and costs from the non-prevailing Seller or Broker, except as provided in paragraph 19A.

15. Attorney Fees: States that any litigation between the Seller and the Broker regarding the obligation to pay compensation, the prevailing party shall be entitled to reasonable attorney costs, except as provided in paragraph 19A.

16. ADDITIONAL TERMS: _____

16. Additional Terms: This is an excellent place to insert additional terms not covered above, such as the sellers paying for termite clearance and title insurance.

17. MANAGEMENT APPROVAL: If an associate licensee in Broker's office (salesperson or broker-associate) enters into this agreement on Broker's behalf, and Broker or Manager does not approve of its terms, Broker or Manager has the right to cancel this agreement, in writing, within 5 days after its execution.
18. SUCCESSORS AND ASSIGNS: This agreement shall be binding upon Seller and Seller's successors and assigns.

17. Management Approval: Within five days from execution of this agreement, the Broker or Manager may disapprove this contract.

18. Successors and Assigns: This agreement is binding on the Seller and the Seller's successors and assignees.

Never give legal or tax advice to your principals, unless you are an attorney or CPA.

---

19. DISPUTE RESOLUTION:

A. MEDIATION: Seller and Broker agree to mediate any dispute or claim arising between them out of this agreement, or any resulting transaction, before resorting to arbitration or court action, subject to paragraph 19B(2) below. Paragraph 19B(2) below applies whether or not the arbitration provision is initialed. Mediation fees, if any, shall be divided equally among the parties involved. If, for any dispute or claim to which this paragraph applies, any party commences an action without first attempting to resolve the matter through mediation, or refuses to mediate after a request has been made, then that party shall not be entitled to recover attorney fees, even if they would otherwise be available to that party in any such action. THIS MEDIATION PROVISION APPLIES WHETHER OR NOT THE ARBITRATION PROVISION IS INITIALED.

---

19. Dispute Resolution

19 (A) Mediation: This explains that the Seller and the Broker will mediate any dispute arising from this agreement or any resulting transaction before resorting to arbitration.

B. ARBITRATION OF DISPUTES: (1) Seller and Broker agree that any dispute or claim in Law or equity arising between them regarding the obligation to pay compensation under this agreement, which is not settled through mediation, shall be decided by neutral, binding arbitration, including and subject to paragraph 19B(2) below. The arbitrator shall be a retired judge or justice, or an attorney with at least 5 years of residential real estate law experience, unless the parties mutually agree to a different arbitrator, who shall render an award in accordance with substantive California Law. The parties shall have the right to discovery in accordance with Code of Civil Procedure §1283.05. In all other respects, the arbitration shall be conducted in accordance with Title 9 of Part III of the California Code of Civil Procedure. Judgment upon the award of the arbitrator(s) may be entered in any court having jurisdiction. Interpretation of this agreement to arbitrate shall be governed by the Federal Arbitration Act.

(2) EXCLUSIONS FROM MEDIATION AND ARBITRATION: The following matters are excluded from mediation and arbitration hereunder: **(i)** a judicial or non-judicial foreclosure or other action or proceeding to enforce a deed of trust, mortgage, or installment land sale contract as defined in Civil Code §2985; **(ii)** an unlawful detainer action; **(iii)** the filing or enforcement of a mechanic's lien; and **(iv)** any matter that is within the jurisdiction of a probate, small claims, or bankruptcy court. The filing of a court action to enable the recording of a notice of pending action, for order of attachment, receivership, injunction, or other provisional remedies, shall not constitute a waiver of the mediation and arbitration provisions.

"NOTICE: BY INITIALING IN THE SPACE BELOW YOU ARE AGREEING TO HAVE ANY DISPUTE ARISING OUT OF THE MATTERS INCLUDED IN THE 'ARBITRATION OF DISPUTES' PROVISION DECIDED BY NEUTRAL ARBITRATION AS PROVIDED BY CALIFORNIA LAW AND YOU ARE GIVING UP ANY RIGHTS YOU MIGHT POSSESS TO HAVE THE DISPUTE LITIGATED IN A COURT OR JURY TRIAL. BY INITIALING IN THE SPACE BELOW YOU ARE GIVING UP YOUR JUDICIAL RIGHTS TO DISCOVERY AND APPEAL, UNLESS THOSE RIGHTS ARE SPECIFICALLY INCLUDED IN THE 'ARBITRATION OF DISPUTES' PROVISION. IF YOU REFUSE TO SUBMIT TO ARBITRATION AFTER AGREEING TO THIS PROVISION, YOU MAY BE COMPELLED TO ARBITRATE UNDER THE AUTHORITY OF THE CALIFORNIA CODE OF CIVIL PROCEDURE. YOUR AGREEMENT TO THIS ARBITRATION PROVISION IS VOLUNTARY."

"WE HAVE READ AND UNDERSTAND THE FOREGOING AND AGREE TO SUBMIT DISPUTES ARISING OUT OF THE MATTERS INCLUDED IN THE 'ARBITRATION OF DISPUTES' PROVISION TO NEUTRAL ARBITRATION."

Seller's Initials _____ / _____   Broker's Initials _____ / _____

---

19 (B) Arbitration of Disputes: This is an explanation of arbitration between the Seller and the Broker. In order to come into effect, both parties must initial it. Do not give advice on how to handle this clause, as this would call for you, the agent, to give legal advice.

Have the sellers read the clause and suggest that, if they are unsure on how to proceed, they should consult their legal adviser.

20. ENTIRE CONTRACT: All prior discussions, negotiations and agreements between the parties concerning the subject matter of this agreement are superseded by this agreement, which constitutes the entire contract and a complete and exclusive expression of their agreement, and may not be contradicted by evidence of any prior agreement or contemporaneous oral agreement. If any provision of this agreement is held to be ineffective or invalid, the remaining provisions will nevertheless be given full force and effect. This agreement and any supplement, addendum or modification, including any photocopy or facsimile, may be executed in counterparts.

By signing below, Seller acknowledges that Seller has read, understands, accepts and has received a copy of this agreement.

Seller _____ Date _____
Address _____ City _____ State _____ Zip _____
Telephone _____ Fax _____ E-mail _____

Seller _____ Date _____
Address _____ City _____ State _____ Zip _____
Telephone _____ Fax _____ E-mail _____

Real Estate Broker (Firm) _____
By (Agent) _____ Date _____
Address _____ City _____ State _____ Zip _____
Telephone _____ Fax _____ E-mail _____

20. Entire Contract: This contract supercedes all prior discussions, negotiations and agreements between the Seller and Broker.

All sellers sign the listing contract and date it entering their address and pertinent information. As the real estate agent, you enter the firm name, then sign it directly underneath (as a representative of the brokerage firm) including all pertinent information, such as fax number and e-mail address.

Under Section 10142 of the Real Estate Law, the agent is required to give a copy of the listing agreement to his or her principal (all signing parties) at the time the signature is obtained.

The owners' signatures constitute acknowledgment that they received a copy as of the date indicated. In the event they were to protest that they did not know what the contract contained, or what it meant, the agent can refute such allegations, unless of course the contract was indeed signed as a result of a broker's fraudulent representations.

If the owner is married, the signatures of both spouses should be obtained, even if the property is held in the name of one alone. Despite the apparent ownership by one alone, under the community property laws of California, the buyer may find it impossible to sue for specific performance unless both spouses have signed.

II. Completing the Listing Kit

Once the Listing Agreement has been properly filled out, you will need to supply your seller with additional information, including disclosures and forms to be filled out. These are all part of a listing kit. A *LISTING KIT is the packet of forms an agent provides to the seller when taking a listing.*

Fortunately, the California Association of Realtors® has come up with standardized forms to make fulfilling the sellers' listing requirements easier and more uniform. The following is a list of CAR forms that you should include in the listing kit:

1. Residential Listing Agreement (LA) (Complete form - see Chapter 3, **Figure 3-1**) with Seller's Advisory (SA) (**Figure 4-1**) (Buyer does not receive a copy of this form.)

2. Disclosure Regarding Real Estate Agency Relationships (AD-11) (**Figure 4-2**)

3. Seller's Affidavit of Nonforeign Status and/or California Withholding Exemption (AS) (**Figure 4-3**)

4. Transfer Disclosure Statement (TDS) (**Figure 4-4**)

5. Supplemental Statutory and Contractual Disclosures (SSD) (**Figure 4-5**)

6. Smoke Detector Statement of Compliance (SDS) (**Figure 4-6**)

7. Water Heater Statement of Compliance (WHS) (**Figure 4-7**)

8. Lead-Based Paint and Lead-Based Paint Hazards Disclosure, Acknowledgement and Addendum (FLD) (**Figure 4-8**)

9. Natural Hazards Disclosure Statement (NHD) (**Figure 4-9**) and *Combined Hazards Book* (**Figure 4-10**)

10. Estimated Seller's Proceeds form (ESP) (**Figure 4-11**) (Buyer does not receive a copy of this form.)

11. Notice to Buyers and Sellers - Defective Furnaces in California (**Figure 4-12**)

12. Home Warranty Application or Waiver (**Figure 4-13**)

You should advise the sellers to have the utilities read off their names to avoid a shut down that may cause water heater damage from sediment clogging up the system. Of course, the buyers should be given the names of all the utilities and the appropriate numbers so that they may follow up the sellers' request with their own.

Figure 4-1

CALIFORNIA
ASSOCIATION
OF REALTORS®

Seller's Advisory
(C.A.R. Form SA, Revised 10/01)

Property Address: _____ ("Property")

1. **INTRODUCTION:** Selling property in California is a process that involves many steps. From start to finish, it could take anywhere from a few weeks to many months, depending upon the condition of your Property, local market conditions and other factors. You have already taken an important first step by listing your Property for sale with a licensed real estate broker. Your broker will help guide you through the process and may refer you to other professionals as needed. This advisory addresses many things you may need to think about and do as you market your Property. Some of these things are requirements imposed upon you, either by law or the listing or sale contract. Others are simply practical matters that may arise during the process. Please read this document carefully and, if you have any questions, ask your broker for help.

2. **DISCLOSURES:**

   A. **General Disclosure Duties:** You must affirmatively disclose to the buyer, in writing, any and all known facts that materially affect the value or desirability of your Property. You must disclose these facts whether or not asked about such matters by the buyer, any broker, or anyone else. This duty to disclose applies even if the buyer agrees to purchase your Property in its present condition without requiring you to make any repairs. If the Property you are selling is a residence with one to four units, your broker also has a duty to conduct a reasonably competent and diligent visual inspection of the accessible areas and to disclose to a buyer all adverse material facts that the inspection reveals. If your broker discovers something that could indicate a problem, your broker must advise the buyer.

   B. **Statutory Duties** (For one-to-four Residential Units):

   (1) You must timely prepare and deliver to the buyer, among other things, a Real Estate Transfer Disclosure Statement ("TDS"), and a Natural Hazard Disclosure Statement ("NHD"). You have a legal obligation to honestly and completely fill out the TDS form in its entirety. (Many local entities or organizations have their own supplement to the TDS that you may also be asked to complete.) The NHD is a statement indicating whether your Property is in certain designated flood, fire or earthquake/seismic hazard zones. Third-party professional companies can help you with this task.

   (2) Depending upon the age and type of construction of your Property, you may also be required to provide and, in certain cases you can receive limited legal protection by providing, the buyer with booklets titled "The Homeowner's Guide to Earthquake Safety," "The Commercial Property Owner's Guide to Earthquake Safety," "Protect Your Family From Lead in Your Home" and "Environmental Hazards: A Guide For Homeowners and Buyers." Some of these booklets may be packaged together for your convenience. The earthquake guides ask you to answer specific questions about your Property's structure and preparedness for an earthquake. If you are required to supply the booklet about lead, you will also be required to disclose to the buyer any known lead-based paint and lead-based paint hazards on a separate form. The environmental hazards guide informs the buyer of common environmental hazards that may be found in properties.

   (3) If you know that your property is: (i) located within one mile of a former military ordnance location; or (ii) in or affected by a zone or district allowing manufacturing, commercial or airport use, you must disclose this to the buyer. You are also required to make a good faith effort to obtain and deliver to the buyer a disclosure notice from the appropriate local agency(ies) about any special tax levied on your Property pursuant to the Mello-Roos Community Facilities Act.

   (4) If the TDS, NHD, or lead, military ordnance, commercial zone or Mello-Roos disclosures are provided to a buyer after you accept that buyer's offer, the buyer will have 3 days after delivery (or 5 days if mailed) to terminate the offer, which is why it is extremely important to complete these disclosures as soon as possible. There are certain exemptions from these statutory requirements. However, if you have actual knowledge of any of these items, you may still be required to make a disclosure as the items can be considered material facts.

   C. **Death and Other Disclosures:** Many buyers consider death on real property to be a material fact in the purchase of property. In some situations, it is advisable to disclose that a death occurred or the manner of death. However, California Civil Code Section 1710.2 provides that <u>you have no disclosure duty</u> "where the death has occurred more than three years prior to the date the transferee offers to purchase, lease, or rent the real property, or [regardless of the date of occurrence] that an occupant of that property was afflicted with, or died from, Human T-Lymphotropic Virus Type III/Lymphadenopathy-Associated Virus." This law does not "immunize an owner or his or her agent from making an intentional misrepresentation in response to a direct inquiry from a transferee or a prospective transferee of real property, concerning deaths on the real property."

   D. **Condominiums and Other Common Interest Subdivisions:** If the Property is a condominium, townhouse, or other property in a common interest subdivision, you must provide to the buyer copies of the governing documents, the most recent financial statements distributed, and other documents required by law or contract. If you do not have a current version of these documents, you can request them from the management of your homeowners' association. To avoid delays, you are encouraged to obtain these documents as soon as possible, even if you have not yet entered into a purchase agreement to sell your Property.

The copyright laws of the United States (Title 17 U.S. Code) forbid the unauthorized reproduction of this form, or any portion thereof, by photocopy machine or any other means, including facsimile or computerized formats. Copyright © 1991-2001, CALIFORNIA ASSOCIATION OF REALTORS®, INC. ALL RIGHTS RESERVED.

SA-11 REVISED 10/01 (PAGE 1 of 2)   Print Date

Seller acknowledges receipt of a copy of this page.

Seller's Initials (_____)(_____)

Reviewed by _____
Broker or Designee _____ Date _____

EQUAL HOUSING
OPPORTUNITY

SELLER'S ADVISORY (SA-11 PAGE 1 OF 2)

This (along with the Listing Agreement) is one of the few forms in the "listing kit" that the buyer will not receive a copy of.

Property Address: _____ Date: _____

3. CONTRACT TERMS AND LEGAL REQUIREMENTS:

A. Contract Terms and Conditions: A buyer may request, as part of the contract for the sale of your Property, that you pay for repairs to the Property and other items. Your decision on whether or not to comply with a buyer's requests may affect your ability to sell your Property at a specified price.

B. Withholding Taxes: Under federal and California tax laws, a buyer is required to withhold a portion of the purchase price from your sale proceeds for tax purposes unless you sign an affidavit of non-foreign status and California residency, or some other exemption applies and is documented.

C. Prohibition Against Discrimination: Discriminatory conduct in the sale of real property against individuals belonging to legally protected classes is a violation of the law.

D. Government Retrofit Standards: Unless exempt, you must comply with government retrofit standards, including, but not limited to, installing operable smoke detectors, bracing water heaters, and providing the buyer with corresponding written statements of compliance. Some city and county governments may impose additional retrofit standards, including, but not limited to, installing low-flow toilets and showerheads, gas shut-off valves, tempered glass, and barriers around swimming pools and spas. You should consult with the appropriate governmental agencies, inspectors, and other professionals to determine the retrofit standards for your Property, the extent to which your Property complies with such standards, and the costs, if any, of compliance.

E. Legal, Tax and Other Implications: Selling your Property may have legal, tax, insurance, title or other implications. You should consult an appropriate professional for advice on these matters.

4. MARKETING CONSIDERATIONS:

A. Pre-Sale Considerations: You should consider doing what you can to prepare your Property for sale, such as correcting any defects or other problems. Many people are not aware of defects in or problems with their own Property. One way to make yourself aware is to obtain professional home inspections prior to sale, both generally, and for wood destroying pests and organisms, such as termites. By doing this, you then have an opportunity to make repairs before your Property is offered for sale, which may enhance its marketability. Keep in mind, however, that any problems revealed by such inspection reports should be disclosed to the buyer (see "Disclosures" in paragraph 2 above). This is true even if the buyer gets his/her own inspections covering the same area. Obtaining inspection reports may also assist you during contract negotiations with the buyer. For example, if a pest control report has both a primary and secondary recommendation for clearance, you may want to specify in the purchase agreement those recommendations, if any, for which you are going to pay.

B. Post-Sale Protections: It is often helpful to provide the buyer with, among other things, a home protection/warranty plan for the Property. These plans will generally cover problems, not deemed to be pre-existing, that occur after your sale is completed. In the event something does go wrong after the sale, and it is covered by the plan, the buyer may be able to resolve the concern by contacting the home protection company.

C. Safety Precautions: Advertising and marketing your Property for sale, including, but not limited to, holding open houses, placing a keysafe/lockbox, erecting FOR SALE signs, and disseminating photographs, video tapes, and virtual tours of the premises, may jeopardize your personal safety and that of your Property. You are strongly encouraged to maintain insurance, and to take any and all possible precautions and safeguards to protect yourself, other occupants, visitors, your Property, and your belongings, including cash, jewelry, drugs, firearms and other valuables located on the Property against injury, theft, loss, vandalism, damage, and other harm.

D. Expenses: You are advised that you, not the Broker, are responsible for the fees and costs, if any, to comply with your duties and obligations to the buyer of your Property.

5. OTHER ITEMS: _____
_____
_____
_____

Seller has read and understands this Advisory. By signing below, Seller acknowledges receipt of a copy of this document.

Seller _____ Date _____

Print Name _____

Seller _____ Date _____

Print Name _____

Real Estate Broker _____ By _____
(Agent)

Address _____ City _____ State _____ Zip _____

Telephone _____ Fax _____ E-mail _____

THIS FORM HAS BEEN APPROVED BY THE CALIFORNIA ASSOCIATION OF REALTORS® (C.A.R.). NO REPRESENTATION IS MADE AS TO THE LEGAL VALIDITY OR ADEQUACY OF ANY PROVISION IN ANY SPECIFIC TRANSACTION. A REAL ESTATE BROKER IS THE PERSON QUALIFIED TO ADVISE ON REAL ESTATE TRANSACTIONS. IF YOU DESIRE LEGAL OR TAX ADVICE, CONSULT AN APPROPRIATE PROFESSIONAL.

This form is available for use by the entire real estate industry. It is not intended to identify the user as a REALTOR®. REALTOR® is a registered collective membership mark which may be used only by members of the NATIONAL ASSOCIATION OF REALTORS® who subscribe to its Code of Ethics.

Published and Distributed by:
REAL ESTATE BUSINESS SERVICES, INC.
a subsidiary of the CALIFORNIA ASSOCIATION OF REALTORS®
525 South Virgil Avenue, Los Angeles, California 90020

Reviewed by _____

Broker or Designee _____ Date _____

SA-11 REVISED 10/01 (PAGE 2 of 2)

SELLER'S ADVISORY (SA-11 PAGE 2 OF 2)

Figure 4-2

CALIFORNIA ASSOCIATION OF REALTORS®

DISCLOSURE REGARDING REAL ESTATE AGENCY RELATIONSHIPS
(As required by the Civil Code)
(C.A.R. Form AD-11, Revised 10/01)

When you enter into a discussion with a real estate agent regarding a real estate transaction, you should from the outset understand what type of agency relationship or representation you wish to have with the agent in the transaction.

SELLER'S AGENT

A Seller's agent under a listing agreement with the Seller acts as the agent for the Seller only. A Seller's agent or a subagent of that agent has the following affirmative obligations:

To the Seller:
A Fiduciary duty of utmost care, integrity, honesty, and loyalty in dealings with the Seller.

To the Buyer and the Seller:
(a) Diligent exercise of reasonable skill and care in performance of the agent's duties.
(b) A duty of honest and fair dealing and good faith.
(c) A duty to disclose all facts known to the agent materially affecting the value or desirability of the property that are not known to, or within the diligent attention and observation of, the parties.

An agent is not obligated to reveal to either party any confidential information obtained from the other party that does not involve the affirmative duties set forth above.

BUYER'S AGENT

A selling agent can, with a Buyer's consent, agree to act as agent for the Buyer only. In these situations, the agent is not the Seller's agent, even if by agreement the agent may receive compensation for services rendered, either in full or in part from the Seller. An agent acting only for a Buyer has the following affirmative obligations:

To the Buyer:
A fiduciary duty of utmost care, integrity, honesty, and loyalty in dealings with the Buyer.

To the Buyer and the Seller:
(a) Diligent exercise of reasonable skill and care in performance of the agent's duties.
(b) A duty of honest and fair dealing and good faith.
(c) A duty to disclose all facts known to the agent materially affecting the value or desirability of the property that are not known to, or within the diligent attention and observation of, the parties.

An agent is not obligated to reveal to either party any confidential information obtained from the other party that does not involve the affirmative duties set forth above.

AGENT REPRESENTING BOTH SELLER AND BUYER

A real estate agent, either acting directly or through one or more associate licensees, can legally be the agent of both the Seller and the Buyer in a transaction, but only with the knowledge and consent of both the Seller and the Buyer.

In a dual agency situation, the agent has the following affirmative obligations to both the Seller and the Buyer:
(a) A fiduciary duty of utmost care, integrity, honesty and loyalty in the dealings with either the Seller or the Buyer.
(b) Other duties to the Seller and the Buyer as stated above in their respective sections.

In representing both Seller and Buyer, the agent may not, without the express permission of the respective party, disclose to the other party that the Seller will accept a price less than the listing price or that the Buyer will pay a price greater than the price offered.

The above duties of the agent in a real estate transaction do not relieve a Seller or Buyer from the responsibility to protect his or her own interests. You should carefully read all agreements to assure that they adequately express your understanding of the transaction. A real estate agent is a person qualified to advise about real estate. If legal or tax advice is desired, consult a competent professional.

Throughout your real property transaction you may receive more than one disclosure form, depending upon the number of agents assisting in the transaction. The law requires each agent with whom you have more than a casual relationship to present you with this disclosure form. You should read its contents each time it is presented to you, considering the relationship between you and the real estate agent in your specific transaction.

This disclosure form includes the provisions of Sections 2079.13 to 2079.24, inclusive, of the Civil Code set forth on the reverse hereof. Read it carefully.

I/WE ACKNOWLEDGE RECEIPT OF A COPY OF THIS DISCLOSURE.

BUYER/SELLER _____ Date _____ Time _____ AM/PM

BUYER/SELLER _____ Date _____ Time _____ AM/PM

AGENT _____ By _____ Date _____
     (Please Print)   (Associate-Licensee or Broker Signature)

THIS FORM SHALL BE PROVIDED AND ACKNOWLEDGED AS FOLLOWS (Civil Code §2079.14):
• When the listing brokerage company also represents the Buyer, the Listing Agent shall give one AD-11 form to the Seller and one to the Buyer.
• When Buyer and Seller are represented by different brokerage companies, then the Listing Agent shall give one AD-11 form to the Seller and the Buyer's Agent shall give one AD-11 form to the Buyer and one AD-11 form to the Seller.

SEE REVERSE SIDE FOR FURTHER INFORMATION

Published and Distributed by:
REAL ESTATE BUSINESS SERVICES, INC.
a subsidiary of the CALIFORNIA ASSOCIATION OF REALTORS®
525 South Virgil Avenue, Los Angeles, California 90020

Reviewed by _____
Broker or Designee _____ Date _____

AD-11 REVISED 10/01 (PAGE 1 OF 1)   Print Date

DISCLOSURE REGARDING REAL ESTATE AGENCY RELATIONSHIPS (AD-11 PAGE 1 OF 1)

Make sure this is filled out and signed prior to entering into any contract.

Figure 4-3

CALIFORNIA
ASSOCIATION
OF REALTORS®

**SELLER'S AFFIDAVIT OF NONFOREIGN STATUS
AND/OR CALIFORNIA WITHHOLDING EXEMPTION**
FOREIGN INVESTMENT IN REAL PROPERTY TAX ACT (FIRPTA)
AND CALIFORNIA WITHHOLDING LAW
(Use a separate form for each Transferor)
(C.A.R. Form AS, Revised 1/03)

USE ONLY FOR ESCROWS CLOSING ON OR AFTER JANUARY 1, 2003

Internal Revenue Code ("IRC") Section 1445 provides that a transferee of a U.S. real property interest must withhold tax if the transferor is a "foreign person." California Revenue and Taxation Code Section 18662 provides that a transferee of a California real property interest must withhold tax if the transferor: **(i)** is an individual (unless certain exemptions apply); or **(ii)** is any entity other than an individual ("Entity") if the transferor's proceeds will be disbursed to a financial intermediary of the transferor, or to the transferor with a last known street address outside of California. California Revenue and Taxation Code Section 18662 includes additional provisions for corporations.

I understand that this affidavit may be disclosed to the Internal Revenue Service and to the California Franchise Tax Board by the transferee, and that any false statement I have made herein (if an Entity Transferor, on behalf of the Transferor) may result in a fine, imprisonment or both.

1. **PROPERTY ADDRESS** (the address of the property being transferred):
    _____

2. **TRANSFEROR'S INFORMATION:**
    Full Name _____
    Telephone No. _____
    Address _____
    (Use HOME address for individual transferors. Use OFFICE address for Entities: corporations, partnerships, limited liability companies, trusts and estates.)
    Social Security No., Federal Employer Identification No., or California Corporation No. _____

3. **AUTHORITY TO SIGN:** If this document is signed on behalf of an Entity Transferor, THE UNDERSIGNED INDIVIDUAL DECLARES THAT HE/SHE HAS AUTHORITY TO SIGN THIS DOCUMENT ON BEHALF OF THE TRANSFEROR.

4. **FEDERAL LAW:** I, the undersigned individual, declare under penalty of perjury that, for the reason checked below, if any, I am exempt (or if signed on behalf of an Entity Transferor, the Entity is exempt) from the federal withholding law (FIRPTA):
    ☐ (For individual Transferors) I am not a nonresident alien for purposes of U.S. income taxation.
    ☐ (For corporation, partnership, limited liability company, trust, and estate Transferors) The Transferor is not a foreign corporation, foreign partnership, foreign limited liability company, foreign trust, or foreign estate, as those term are defined in the Internal Revenue Code and Income Tax Regulations.

5. **CALIFORNIA LAW:** I, the undersigned individual, declare under penalty of perjury that, for the reason checked below, if any, I am exempt (or if signed on behalf of an Entity Transferor, the Entity is exempt) from the California withholding law:
    ☐ The total sale price for the property is $100,000 or less.
    For individual or revocable/grantor trust Transferors only:
    ☐ The property being transferred is in California and was my principal residence within the meaning of IRC Section 121.
    ☐ The property is being, or will be, exchanged for property of like kind within the meaning of IRC Section 1031.
    ☐ The property has been compulsorily or involuntarily converted (within the meaning of IRC1033) and I intend to acquire property similar or related in service or use to be eligible for non-recognition of gain for California income tax purposes under IRC Section 1033.
    ☐ The transaction will result in a loss for California income tax purposes.
    For Entity Transferors only:
    ☐ (For corporation Transferors) The Transferor is a corporation qualified to do business in California, or has a permanent place of business in California at the address shown in paragraph 2 ("Transferor's Information").
    ☐ (For limited liability company ("LLC") or partnership Transferors) The Transferor is an LLC or partnership and recorded title to the property being transferred is in the name of the LLC or partnership and the LLC or partnership will file a California tax return to report the sale and withhold on foreign and domestic nonresident partners as required.
    ☐ (For irrevocable trust Transferors) The Transferor is an irrevocable trust with at least one trustee who is a California resident and the trust will file a California tax return to report the sale and withhold when distributing California source taxable income to nonresident beneficiaries as required.
    ☐ (For estate Transferors) The Transferor is an estate of a decedent who was a California resident at the time of his/her death and the estate will file a California tax return to report the sale and withhold when distributing California source taxable income to nonresident beneficiaries as required.
    ☐ (For tax-exempt Entity and nonprofit organization Transferors) The Transferor is exempt from tax under California or federal law.

By_____ Date _____
(Transferor's Signature) (Indicate if you are signing as the grantor of a revocable/grantor trust.)

_____   _____
Typed or printed name   Title (If signed on behalf of entity Transferor)

SURE TRAC
The System for Success™

Published by the
California Association of REALTORS®

Reviewed by _____ Date _____

EQUAL HOUSING OPPORTUNITY

AS REVISED 1/03 (PAGE 1 OF 1) Print Date

SELLER'S AFFIDAVIT OF NONFOREIGN STATUS AND/OR CALIFORNIA WITHHOLDING EXEMPTION (AS PAGE 1 OF 1)

(Often referred to as FRPTA). If all the seller's answers are "no" on this form, there's a good possibility of a tax liability. Advise your seller to consult a tax advisor! Also, make sure the buyer gets a copy of this (as he or she may be responsible for the seller's taxes)!

Figure 4-4

CALIFORNIA ASSOCIATION OF REALTORS®

REAL ESTATE TRANSFER DISCLOSURE STATEMENT
(CALIFORNIA CIVIL CODE §1102, ET SEQ.)
(C.A.R. Form TDS, Revised 10/03)

THIS DISCLOSURE STATEMENT CONCERNS THE REAL PROPERTY SITUATED IN THE CITY OF _____
_____, COUNTY OF _____, STATE OF CALIFORNIA,
DESCRIBED AS _____.

THIS STATEMENT IS A DISCLOSURE OF THE CONDITION OF THE ABOVE DESCRIBED PROPERTY IN COMPLIANCE WITH SECTION 1102 OF THE CIVIL CODE AS OF (date) _____. IT IS NOT A WARRANTY OF ANY KIND BY THE SELLER(S) OR ANY AGENT(S) REPRESENTING ANY PRINCIPAL(S) IN THIS TRANSACTION, AND IS NOT A SUBSTITUTE FOR ANY INSPECTIONS OR WARRANTIES THE PRINCIPAL(S) MAY WISH TO OBTAIN.

I. COORDINATION WITH OTHER DISCLOSURE FORMS

This Real Estate Transfer Disclosure Statement is made pursuant to Section 1102 of the Civil Code. Other statutes require disclosures, depending upon the details of the particular real estate transaction (for example: special study zone and purchase-money liens on residential property).

Substituted Disclosures: The following disclosures and other disclosures required by law, including the Natural Hazard Disclosure Report/Statement that may include airport annoyances, earthquake, fire, flood, or special assessment information, have or will be made in connection with this real estate transfer, and are intended to satisfy the disclosure obligations on this form, where the subject matter is the same:

☐ Inspection reports completed pursuant to the contract of sale or receipt for deposit.
☐ Additional inspection reports or disclosures: _____
_____

II. SELLER'S INFORMATION

The Seller discloses the following information with the knowledge that even though this is not a warranty, prospective Buyers may rely on this information in deciding whether and on what terms to purchase the subject property. Seller hereby authorizes any agent(s) representing any principal(s) in this transaction to provide a copy of this statement to any person or entity in connection with any actual or anticipated sale of the property.

THE FOLLOWING ARE REPRESENTATIONS MADE BY THE SELLER(S) AND ARE NOT THE REPRESENTATIONS OF THE AGENT(S), IF ANY. THIS INFORMATION IS A DISCLOSURE AND IS NOT INTENDED TO BE PART OF ANY CONTRACT BETWEEN THE BUYER AND SELLER.

Seller ☐ is ☐ is not occupying the property.

A. The subject property has the items checked below (read across):

☐ Range	☐ Oven	☐ Microwave
☐ Dishwasher	☐ Trash Compactor	☐ Garbage Disposal
☐ Washer/Dryer Hookups		☐ Rain Gutters
☐ Burglar Alarms	☐ Smoke Detector(s)	☐ Fire Alarm
☐ TV Antenna	☐ Satellite Dish	☐ Intercom
☐ Central Heating	☐ Central Air Conditioning	☐ Evaporator Cooler(s)
☐ Wall/Window Air Conditioning	☐ Sprinklers	☐ Public Sewer System
☐ Septic Tank	☐ Sump Pump	☐ Water Softener
☐ Patio/Decking	☐ Built-in Barbecue	☐ Gazebo
☐ Sauna		
☐ Hot Tub	☐ Pool	☐ Spa
☐ Locking Safety Cover*	☐ Child Resistant Barrier*	☐ Locking Safety Cover*
☐ Security Gate(s)	☐ Automatic Garage Door Opener(s)*	☐ Number Remote Controls _____
Garage: ☐ Attached	☐ Not Attached	☐ Carport
Pool/Spa Heater: ☐ Gas	☐ Solar	☐ Electric
Water Heater: ☐ Gas	☐ Water Heater Anchored, Braced, or Strapped*	
Water Supply: ☐ City	☐ Well	☐ Private Utility or
Gas Supply: ☐ Utility	☐ Bottled	Other _____
☐ Window Screens	☐ Window Security Bars ☐ Quick Release Mechanism on Bedroom Windows*	

Exhaust Fan(s) in _____ 220 Volt Wiring in _____ Fireplace(s) in _____
☐ Gas Starter _____ ☐ Roof(s): Type: _____ Age: _____ (approx.)
☐ Other: _____
Are there, to the best of your (Seller's) knowledge, any of the above that are not in operating condition? ☐ Yes ☐ No. If yes, then describe. (Attach additional sheets if necessary): _____
_____

(*see footnote on page 2)

The copyright laws of the United States (Title 17 U.S. Code) forbid the unauthorized reproduction of this form, or any portion thereof, by photocopy machine or any other means, including facsimile or computerized formats. Copyright © 1991-2003, CALIFORNIA ASSOCIATION OF REALTORS®, INC. ALL RIGHTS RESERVED.
TDS REVISED 10/03 (PAGE 1 OF 3) Print Date

Buyer's Initials (_____)(_____)
Seller's Initials (_____)(_____)

Reviewed by _____ Date _____

EQUAL HOUSING OPPORTUNITY

REAL ESTATE TRANSFER DISCLOSURE STATEMENT (TDS PAGE 1 OF 3)

When in doubt, DISCLOSE! Agents must make notes on this form. Be careful of "descriptive" words like "small" cracks. Just say cracks!

Property Address: _____ Date: _____

B. Are you (Seller) aware of any significant defects/malfunctions in any of the following? ☐ Yes ☐ No. If yes, check appropriate space(s) below.

☐ Interior Walls ☐ Ceilings ☐ Floors ☐ Exterior Walls ☐ Insulation ☐ Roof(s) ☐ Windows ☐ Doors ☐ Foundation ☐ Slab(s)
☐ Driveways ☐ Sidewalks ☐ Walls/Fences ☐ Electrical Systems ☐ Plumbing/Sewers/Septics ☐ Other Structural Components

(Describe: _____
_____
_____)

If any of the above is checked, explain. (Attach additional sheets if necessary.): _____
_____
_____
_____

*This garage door opener or child resistant pool barrier may not be in compliance with the safety standards relating to automatic reversing devices as set forth in Chapter 12.5 (commencing with Section 19890) of Part 3 of Division 13 of, or with the pool safety standards of Article 2.5 (commencing with Section 115920) of Chapter 5 of Part 10 of Division 104 of, the Health and Safety Code. The water heater may not be anchored, braced, or strapped in accordance with Section 19211 of the Health and Safety Code. Window security bars may not have quick release mechanisms in compliance with the 1995 edition of the California Building Standards Code.

C. Are you (Seller) aware of any of the following:

1. Substances, materials, or products which may be an environmental hazard such as, but not limited to, asbestos, formaldehyde, radon gas, lead-based paint, mold, fuel or chemical storage tanks, and contaminated soil or water on the subject property . . . . ☐ Yes ☐ No
2. Features of the property shared in common with adjoining landowners, such as walls, fences, and driveways, whose use or responsibility for maintenance may have an effect on the subject property . . . . ☐ Yes ☐ No
3. Any encroachments, easements or similar matters that may affect your interest in the subject property . . . . ☐ Yes ☐ No
4. Room additions, structural modifications, or other alterations or repairs made without necessary permits . . . . ☐ Yes ☐ No
5. Room additions, structural modifications, or other alterations or repairs not in compliance with building codes . . . ☐ Yes ☐ No
6. Fill (compacted or otherwise) on the property or any portion thereof . . . . ☐ Yes ☐ No
7. Any settling from any cause, or slippage, sliding, or other soil problems . . . . ☐ Yes ☐ No
8. Flooding, drainage or grading problems . . . . ☐ Yes ☐ No
9. Major damage to the property or any of the structures from fire, earthquake, floods, or landslides . . . . ☐ Yes ☐ No
10. Any zoning violations, nonconforming uses, violations of "setback" requirements . . . . ☐ Yes ☐ No
11. Neighborhood noise problems or other nuisances . . . . ☐ Yes ☐ No
12. CC&R's or other deed restrictions or obligations . . . . ☐ Yes ☐ No
13. Homeowners' Association which has any authority over the subject property . . . . ☐ Yes ☐ No
14. Any "common area" (facilities such as pools, tennis courts, walkways, or other areas co-owned in undivided interest with others) . . . . ☐ Yes ☐ No
15. Any notices of abatement or citations against the property . . . . ☐ Yes ☐ No
16. Any lawsuits by or against the Seller threatening to or affecting this real property, including any lawsuits alleging a defect or deficiency in this real property or "common areas" (facilities such as pools, tennis courts, walkways, or other areas co-owned in undivided interest with others) . . . . ☐ Yes ☐ No

If the answer to any of these is yes, explain. (Attach additional sheets if necessary.): _____
_____
_____
_____

Seller certifies that the information herein is true and correct to the best of the Seller's knowledge as of the date signed by the Seller.

Seller_____ Date _____

Seller_____ Date _____

Buyer's Initials (_____)(_____)
Seller's Initials (_____)(_____)

TDS REVISED 10/03 (PAGE 2 OF 3)

Reviewed by _____ Date _____

REAL ESTATE TRANSFER DISCLOSURE STATEMENT (TDS PAGE 2 OF 3)

Property Address: _____ Date: _____

III. AGENT'S INSPECTION DISCLOSURE
(To be completed only if the Seller is represented by an agent in this transaction.)

THE UNDERSIGNED, BASED ON THE ABOVE INQUIRY OF THE SELLER(S) AS TO THE CONDITION OF THE PROPERTY AND BASED ON A REASONABLY COMPETENT AND DILIGENT VISUAL INSPECTION OF THE ACCESSIBLE AREAS OF THE PROPERTY IN CONJUNCTION WITH THAT INQUIRY, STATES THE FOLLOWING:

☐ Agent notes no items for disclosure.

☐ Agent notes the following items: _____

_____

_____

_____

_____

Agent (Broker Representing Seller) _____ By _____ Date _____
       (Please Print)   (Associate Licensee or Broker Signature)

IV. AGENT'S INSPECTION DISCLOSURE
(To be completed only if the agent who has obtained the offer is other than the agent above.)

THE UNDERSIGNED, BASED ON A REASONABLY COMPETENT AND DILIGENT VISUAL INSPECTION OF THE ACCESSIBLE AREAS OF THE PROPERTY, STATES THE FOLLOWING:

☐ Agent notes no items for disclosure.

☐ Agent notes the following items: _____

_____

_____

_____

_____

Agent (Broker Obtaining the Offer) _____ By _____ Date _____
       (Please Print)   (Associate Licensee or Broker Signature)

V. BUYER(S) AND SELLER(S) MAY WISH TO OBTAIN PROFESSIONAL ADVICE AND/OR INSPECTIONS OF THE PROPERTY AND TO PROVIDE FOR APPROPRIATE PROVISIONS IN A CONTRACT BETWEEN BUYER AND SELLER(S) WITH RESPECT TO ANY ADVICE/INSPECTIONS/DEFECTS.

I/WE ACKNOWLEDGE RECEIPT OF A COPY OF THIS STATEMENT.

Seller _____ Date _____ Buyer _____ Date _____

Seller _____ Date _____ Buyer _____ Date _____

Agent (Broker Representing Seller) _____ By _____ Date _____
       (Please Print)   (Associate Licensee or Broker Signature)

Agent (Broker Obtaining the Offer) _____ By _____ Date _____
       (Please Print)   (Associate Licensee or Broker Signature)

SECTION 1102.3 OF THE CIVIL CODE PROVIDES A BUYER WITH THE RIGHT TO RESCIND A PURCHASE CONTRACT FOR AT LEAST THREE DAYS AFTER THE DELIVERY OF THIS DISCLOSURE IF DELIVERY OCCURS AFTER THE SIGNING OF AN OFFER TO PURCHASE. IF YOU WISH TO RESCIND THE CONTRACT, YOU MUST ACT WITHIN THE PRESCRIBED PERIOD.

A REAL ESTATE BROKER IS QUALIFIED TO ADVISE ON REAL ESTATE. IF YOU DESIRE LEGAL ADVICE, CONSULT YOUR ATTORNEY.

SURE TRAC
The System for Success™

Published by the
California Association of REALTORS®

Reviewed by _____ Date _____

EQUAL HOUSING OPPORTUNITY

TDS REVISED 10/03 (PAGE 3 OF 3)

REAL ESTATE TRANSFER DISCLOSURE STATEMENT (TDS PAGE 3 OF 3)

Figure 4-5

CALIFORNIA
ASSOCIATION
OF REALTORS®

**SUPPLEMENTAL STATUTORY
AND CONTRACTUAL DISCLOSURES**
(C.A.R. Form SSD, Revised 4/03)

1. Seller makes the following disclosures with regard to the real property or manufactured home described as _____, Assessor's Parcel No. _____, situated in _____, County of _____, California, ("Property").

2. **THE FOLLOWING ARE REPRESENTATIONS MADE BY THE SELLER AND ARE NOT THE REPRESENTATIONS OF THE AGENT(S), IF ANY. THIS DISCLOSURE STATEMENT IS NOT A WARRANTY OF ANY KIND BY THE SELLER OR ANY AGENT(S) AND IS NOT A SUBSTITUTE FOR ANY INSPECTIONS OR WARRANTIES THE PRINCIPAL(S) MAY WISH TO OBTAIN. A REAL ESTATE BROKER IS QUALIFIED TO ADVISE ON REAL ESTATE TRANSACTIONS. IF SELLER OR BUYER DESIRE LEGAL ADVICE, CONSULT AN ATTORNEY.**

3. Are you (Seller) aware of any of the following? (Explain any "yes" answers below)
   A. Whether the Property is a condominium or located in a planned unit development or other common interest subdivision . . . . ☐ Yes ☐ No
   B. Insurance claims affecting the Property within the past 5 years . . . . ☐ Yes ☐ No
   C. Matters affecting title to the Property . . . . ☐ Yes ☐ No
   D. Within the last 3 years, the death of an occupant of the Property upon the Property . . . . ☐ Yes ☐ No
   E. The following disclosures (E(1-4)) are made based upon Seller's knowledge or (☐ if checked) will not be made on this form and instead will be made on an independent third-party report:
      (1) Whether the Property is **located in** a zone or district allowing manufacturing . . . . ☐ Yes ☐ No
      (2) Whether the Property is **located in** a zone or district allowing commercial use . . . . ☐ Yes ☐ No
      (3) Whether the Property is **located in** a zone or district allowing airport use . . . . ☐ Yes ☐ No
      (4) Whether the Property is **located within** 1 mile of a former federal or state ordnance location . . . . ☐ Yes ☐ No
          (In general, an area once used for military training purposes that may contain potentially explosive munitions.)
   F. Whether the Property is **affected by** a zone or district allowing manufacturing, commercial or airport use . ☐ Yes ☐ No
   G. The release of an illegal controlled substance on or beneath the Property . . . . ☐ Yes ☐ No
   H. Material facts or defects affecting the Property not otherwise disclosed to Buyer . . . . ☐ Yes ☐ No
   Explanation or ☐ (if checked) see attached _____
   _____
   _____
   _____
   _____
   _____
   _____
   _____

4. Seller represents that the information herein is true and correct to the best of Seller's knowledge as of the date signed by Seller. Seller hereby authorizes any agent(s) representing any principal(s) in this transaction to provide a copy of this statement to any person or entity in connection with any actual or anticipated sale of the Property.
   Seller _____ Date _____
   Seller _____ Date _____

5. By signing below, Buyer acknowledges Buyer has read, understands, accepts and has received a copy of this **Supplemental Statutory and Contractual Disclosures** form.
   Buyer _____ Date _____
   Buyer _____ Date _____
   Agent (Broker Representing Seller) _____
   By _____ Date _____
   (Associate-Licensee or Broker Signature)
   Agent (Broker Obtaining the Offer) _____
   By _____ Date _____
   (Associate-Licensee or Broker Signature)

SURE TRAC
The System for Success™

Published by the
California Association of REALTORS®

SSD REVISED 4/03 (PAGE 1 OF 1) PRINT DATE

Reviewed by _____ Date _____

EQUAL HOUSING OPPORTUNITY

SUPPLEMENTAL STATUTORY AND CONTRACTUAL DISCLOSURES (SSD PAGE 1 OF 1)

Because the homeowners often are not qualified to answer these questions with any certainty, many hire outside vendors to fulfill this disclosure. A third party report is a fairly inexpensive way to minimize a seller's liability.

A military "ordnance" location (not the same spelling as ordinance!) is land once used for military training purposes that may contain potentially explosive munitions!

Figure 4-6

CALIFORNIA ASSOCIATION OF REALTORS®

SMOKE DETECTOR STATEMENT OF COMPLIANCE
As required by California State Health and Safety Code §13113.8(b)

Property Address: _____

1. **STATE LAW:** California law requires that every single-family dwelling and factory built housing unit sold on or after January 1, 1986, must have an operable smoke detector, approved and listed by the State Fire Marshal, installed in accordance with the State Fire Marshal's regulations. (Health and Safety Code §13113.8)

2. **LOCAL REQUIREMENTS:** Some local ordinances impose more stringent smoke detector requirements than does California law. Therefore, it is important to check with local city or county building and safety departments regarding the applicable smoke detector requirements for your property.

3. **TRANSFEROR'S WRITTEN STATEMENT:** California Health and Safety Code §13113.8(b) requires every transferor of any real property containing a single-family dwelling, whether the transfer is made by sale, exchange, or real property sales contract (installment sales contract), to deliver to the transferee a written statement indicating that the transferor is in compliance with California state law concerning smoke detectors.

4. **EXCEPTIONS:** Exceptions to the state law are generally the same as the exceptions to the Transfer Disclosure Laws.

5. **CERTIFICATION:** Seller represents that the Property, as of the close of escrow, will be in compliance with Health and Safety Code §13113.8 by having operable smoke detector(s) approved and listed by the State Fire Marshal installed in accordance with State Fire Marshal's regulations and in accordance with applicable local ordinance(s).

Seller _____ Date _____
       (Signature)   (Print Name)

Seller _____ Date _____
       (Signature)   (Print Name)

The undersigned hereby acknowledges receipt of a copy of this document.

Buyer _____ Date _____
       (Signature)   (Print Name)

Buyer _____ Date _____
       (Signature)   (Print Name)

Published and Distributed by:
REAL ESTATE BUSINESS SERVICES, INC.
a subsidiary of the CALIFORNIA ASSOCIATION OF REALTORS®
525 South Virgil Avenue, Los Angeles, California 90020
PRINT DATE

REVISED 4/99

OFFICE USE ONLY
Reviewed by Broker or Designee _____
Date _____

EQUAL HOUSING OPPORTUNITY

FORM SDS-11

Mandatory Disclosure. Most cities require at least one smoke detector per bedroom. Don't take your seller's word that they exist or are operational—check for yourself with a visual inspection.

Figure 4-7

CALIFORNIA
ASSOCIATION
OF REALTORS®

WATER HEATER STATEMENT OF COMPLIANCE
Water Heater Bracing, Anchoring, or Strapping
As required by California Health and Safety Code §19211

Property Address: _____

1. **STATE LAW:** California law requires that all new and replacement water heaters and existing residential water heaters be braced, anchored, or strapped to resist falling or horizontal displacement due to earthquake motion. (Health and Safety Code §19211)

2. **LOCAL REQUIREMENTS:** Some local ordinances impose more stringent water heater bracing, anchoring, or strapping requirements than does California law. Therefore, it is important to check with local city or county building and safety departments regarding the applicable water heater bracing, anchoring, or strapping requirements for your property.

3. **TRANSFEROR'S WRITTEN STATEMENT:** California Health and Safety Code §19211 requires the seller of any real property containing a water heater to certify, in writing, that the seller is in compliance with California state law.

4. **EXCEPTIONS: There are no exceptions to the state law.**

5. **CERTIFICATION:** Seller represents that the Property, as of the close of escrow, will be in compliance with Health and Safety Code §19211 by having water heaters braced, anchored, or strapped in place, in accordance with those requirements.

Seller _____ Date _____
      (Signature)   (Print Name)

Seller _____ Date _____
      (Signature)   (Print Name)

The undersigned hereby acknowledges receipt of a copy of this document.

Buyer _____ Date _____
      (Signature)   (Print Name)

Buyer _____ Date _____
      (Signature)   (Print Name)

Published and Distributed by:
REAL ESTATE BUSINESS SERVICES, INC.
a subsidiary of the CALIFORNIA ASSOCIATION OF REALTORS®
525 South Virgil Avenue, Los Angeles, California 90020

REVISED 4/99

OFFICE USE ONLY
Reviewed by Broker
or Designee _____
Date _____

EQUAL HOUSING OPPORTUNITY

PRINT DATE

FORM WHS-11

Mandatory Disclosure. Water heaters are usually required to be secured by two straps—check with city ordinances, and do a visual inspection.

Figure 4-8

CALIFORNIA
ASSOCIATION
OF REALTORS®

**LEAD-BASED PAINT AND LEAD-BASED PAINT HAZARDS
DISCLOSURE, ACKNOWLEDGMENT AND ADDENDUM
For Pre-1978 Housing Sales, Leases, or Rentals**
(C.A.R. Form FLD, Revised 1/03)

The following terms and conditions are hereby incorporated in and made a part of the: ☐ California Residential Purchase Agreement, ☐ Residential Lease or Month-to-Month Rental Agreement, or ☐ other: _____
_____,dated _____, on property known
_____ ("Property")
as: _____
in which _____ is referred to as Buyer or Tenant
and _____ is referred to as Seller or Landlord.

LEAD WARNING STATEMENT (SALE OR PURCHASE) Every purchaser of any interest in residential real property on which a residential dwelling was built prior to 1978 is notified that such property may present exposure to lead from lead-based paint that may place young children at risk of developing lead poisoning. Lead poisoning in young children may produce permanent neurological damage, including learning disabilities, reduced intelligent quotient, behavioral problems and impaired memory. Lead poisoning also poses a particular risk to pregnant women. The seller of any interest in residential real property is required to provide the buyer with any information on lead-based paint hazards from risk assessments or inspections in the seller's possession and notify the buyer of any known lead-based paint hazards. A risk assessment or inspection for possible lead-based paint hazards is recommended prior to purchase.

LEAD WARNING STATEMENT (LEASE OR RENTAL) Housing built before 1978 may contain lead-based paint. Lead from paint, paint chips and dust can pose health hazards if not managed properly. Lead exposure is especially harmful to young children and pregnant women. Before renting pre-1978 housing, lessors must disclose the presence of lead-based paint and/or lead-based paint hazards in the dwelling. Lessees must also receive federally approved pamphlet on lead poisoning prevention.

1. SELLER'S OR LANDLORD'S DISCLOSURE

I (we) have no knowledge of lead-based paint and/or lead-based paint hazards in the housing other than the following:
_____
_____
_____
_____

I (we) have no reports or records pertaining to lead-based paint and/or lead-based paint hazards in the housing other than the following, which, previously or as an attachment to this addendum have been provided to Buyer or Tenant:
_____
_____
_____

I (we), previously or as an attachment to this addendum, have provided Buyer or Tenant with the pamphlet "Protect Your Family From Lead In Your Home" or an equivalent pamphlet approved for use in the State such as "The Homeowner's Guide to Environmental Hazards and Earthquake Safety."

For Sales Transactions Only: Buyer has 10 days, unless otherwise agreed in the real estate purchase contract, to conduct a risk assessment or inspection for the presence of lead-based paint and/or lead-based paint hazards.

I (we) have reviewed the information above and certify, to the best of my (our) knowledge, that the information provided is true and correct.

_____   _____
Seller or Landlord   Date

_____   _____
Seller or Landlord   Date

FLD REVISED 1/03 (PAGE 1 OF 2) Print Date

Buyer's Initials (_____)(_____)
Seller's Initials (_____)(_____)

Reviewed by _____ Date _____

EQUAL HOUSING OPPORTUNITY

LEAD-BASED PAINT AND LEAD-BASED PAINT HAZARDS DISCLOSURE (FLD-11 PAGE 1 OF 2)

Must be filled out whether or not seller knows of any lead-based paint used on the property.

Property Address: _____ Date _____

2. LISTING AGENT'S ACKNOWLEDGMENT

Agent has informed Seller or Landlord of Seller's or Landlord's obligations under §42 U.S.C. 4852d and is aware of Agent's responsibility to ensure compliance.

I have reviewed the information above and certify, to the best of my knowledge, that the information provided is true and correct.

_____   By _____

Agent (Broker representing Seller)Please Print   Associate-Licensee or Broker Signature   Date

3. BUYER'S OR TENANT'S ACKNOWLEDGMENT

I (we) have received copies of all information listed, if any, in 1 above and the pamphlet "Protect Your Family From Lead In Your Home" or an equivalent pamphlet approved for use in the State such as "The Homeowner's Guide to Environmental Hazards and Earthquake Safety." **If delivery of any of the disclosures or pamphlet referenced in paragraph 1 above occurs after Acceptance of an offer to purchase, Buyer has a right to cancel pursuant to the purchase contract. If you wish to cancel, you must act within the prescribed period.**

<u>For Sales Transactions Only:</u> Buyer acknowledges the right for 10 days, unless otherwise agreed in the real estate purchase contract, to conduct a risk assessment or inspection for the presence of lead-based paint and/or lead-based paint hazards; OR, (if checked) ☐ Buyer waives the right to conduct a risk assessment or inspection for the presence of lead-based paint and/or lead-based paint hazards.

I (we) have reviewed the information above and certify, to the best of my (our) knowledge, that the information provided is true and correct.

_____   _____

Buyer or Tenant   Date   Buyer or Tenant   Date

4. COOPERATING AGENT'S ACKNOWLEDGMENT

Agent has informed Seller or Landlord, through the Listing Agent if the property is listed, of Seller's or Landlord's obligations under §42 USC 4852d and is aware of Agent's responsibility to ensure compliance.

I have reviewed the information above and certify, to the best of my knowledge, that the information provided is true and correct.

_____   By _____

Agent (Broker obtaining the Offer)   Associate-Licensee or Broker Signature   Date

SURE TRAC
The System for Success™

Published by the
California Association of REALTORS®

FLD REVISED 1/03 (PAGE 2 OF 2)

Reviewed by _____ Date _____

EQUAL HOUSING OPPORTUNITY

LEAD-BASED PAINT AND LEAD-BASED PAINT HAZARDS DISCLOSURE (FLD-11 PAGE 2 OF 2)

Figure 4-9

CALIFORNIA ASSOCIATION OF REALTORS®

NATURAL HAZARD DISCLOSURE STATEMENT
(C.A.R. Form NHD, Revised 10/99)

This statement applies to the following property: _____

The transferor and his or her agent(s) disclose the following information with the knowledge that even though this is not a warranty, prospective transferees may rely on this information in deciding whether and on what terms to purchase the subject property. Transferor hereby authorizes any agent(s) representing any principal(s) in this action to provide a copy of this statement to any person or entity in connection with any actual or anticipated sale of the property.

The following are representations made by the transferor and his or her agent(s) based on their knowledge and maps drawn by the state and federal governments. This information is a disclosure and is not intended to be part of any contract between the transferee and transferor.

THIS REAL PROPERTY LIES WITHIN THE FOLLOWING HAZARDOUS AREA(S): (Check the answer which applies.)

A SPECIAL FLOOD HAZARD AREA (Any type Zone "A" or "V") designated by the Federal Emergency Management Agency.

Yes _____ No _____ Do not know and information not available from local jurisdiction _____

AN AREA OF POTENTIAL FLOODING shown on a dam failure inundation map pursuant to Section 8589.5 of the Government Code.

Yes _____ No _____ Do not know and information not available from local jurisdiction _____

A VERY HIGH FIRE HAZARD SEVERITY ZONE pursuant to Section 51178 or 51179 of the Government Code. The owner of this property is subject to the maintenance requirements of Section 51182 of the Government Code.

Yes _____ No _____

A WILDLAND AREA THAT MAY CONTAIN SUBSTANTIAL FOREST FIRE RISKS AND HAZARDS pursuant to Section 4125 of the Public Resources Code. The owner of this property is subject to the maintenance requirements of Section 4291 of the Public Resources Code. Additionally, it is not the state's responsibility to provide fire protection services to any building or structure located within the wildlands unless the Department of Forestry and Fire Protection has entered into a cooperative agreement with a local agency for those purposes pursuant to Section 4142 of the Public Resources Code.

Yes _____ No _____

AN EARTHQUAKE FAULT ZONE pursuant to Section 2622 of the Public Resources Code.

Yes _____ No _____

A SEISMIC HAZARD ZONE pursuant to Section 2696 of the Public Resources Code.

Yes (Landslide Zone) _____

No _____ Map not yet released by state _____

Yes (Liquefaction Zone) _____

THESE HAZARDS MAY LIMIT YOUR ABILITY TO DEVELOP THE REAL PROPERTY, TO OBTAIN INSURANCE, OR TO RECEIVE ASSISTANCE AFTER A DISASTER.

THE MAPS ON WHICH THESE DISCLOSURES ARE BASED ESTIMATE WHERE NATURAL HAZARDS EXIST. THEY ARE NOT DEFINITIVE INDICATORS OF WHETHER OR NOT A PROPERTY WILL BE AFFECTED BY A NATURAL DISASTER. TRANSFEREE(S) AND TRANSFEROR(S) MAY WISH TO OBTAIN PROFESSIONAL ADVICE REGARDING THOSE HAZARDS AND OTHER HAZARDS THAT MAY AFFECT THE PROPERTY.

> The information in this box is not part of the statutory form.
> ☐ (if checked) The representations made in this form are based upon information provided by an independent third-party report provided as a substituted disclosure pursuant to California Civil Code §1103.4. Neither the seller nor the seller's agent (1) has independently verified the information contained in this form and the report or (2) is personally aware of any errors or inaccuracies in the information contained on this form.

Transferor represents that the information herein is true and correct to the best of the transferor's knowledge as of the date signed by the transferor.

Signature of Transferor _____ Date _____

Agent represents that the information herein is true and correct to the best of the agent's knowledge as of the date signed by the agent.

Signature of Agent _____ Date _____

Signature of Agent _____ Date _____

Transferee represents that he or she has read and understands this document.

Signature of Transferee _____ Date _____

SURE TRAC The System for Success™

Published by the California Association of REALTORS®

Reviewed by _____ Date _____

EQUAL HOUSING OPPORTUNITY

NHD REVISED 10/99 (PAGE 1 OF 1) Print Date

NATURAL HAZARD DISCLOSURE STATEMENT (NHD PAGE 1 OF 1)

Combined Hazards Book (Figure 4-10) includes Residential Environmental Hazards (Toxic Mold Update) and Lead-based paint information, as well as a Homeowners Guide to Earthquake Safety (includes Gas Shutoff Valve Update).

Figure 4-10

CALIFORNIA ASSOCIATION OF REALTORS®

Combined Hazards Book

- *Residential Environmental Hazards (Includes Toxic Mold Update)*
- *"Protect Your Family From Lead" Booklet*
- *Homeowners Guide to Earthquake Safety (Includes Gas Shutoff Valve Update)*

Seller signs acknowledgement of receiving book which goes into an agent's file. A copy is given to the buyer to sign when he or she makes an offer. Seller also fills out the form on Earthquake Hazards Report found in the booklet.

Figure 4-11

CALIFORNIA
ASSOCIATION
OF REALTORS®

ESTIMATED SELLER'S PROCEEDS

SELLER _____ DATE _____
PROPERTY ADDRESS _____
This estimate is based on costs associated with _____ type of financing.
PROJECTED CLOSING DATE _____ ESTIMATED SELLING PRICE $ _____

ESTIMATED COSTS: **ENCUMBRANCES** (Approximate):

Escrow Fee	$ _____	First Trust Deed	$ _____
Drawing, Recording, Notary	_____	Second Trust Deed	_____
Title Insurance Policy	_____	Bonds, Liens	_____
Documentary Transfer Tax:		Other Encumbrances	_____
County	_____	**TOTAL:**	$ _____
City	_____	**GROSS EQUITY:**	$ _____
Transfer Tax	_____	**APPROXIMATE CREDITS:**	
Prepayment Penalty	_____	Prorated Taxes	$ _____
Bene/Demand Fee	_____	Prorated Insurance	_____
Prorated Interest (all loans)	_____	Impound Accounts	_____
Reconveyance Deed	_____	Other: _____	_____
Misc. Lender Fees	_____	Other: _____	_____
Appraisal Fee	_____	**TOTAL:**	$ _____
VA/FHA Discount ____ Points	_____	**RECAP:**	
Preparation of Documents	_____	**ESTIMATED SELLING PRICE:**	$ _____
Misc. VA/FHA Fees	_____	**LESS:**	
Prorated Taxes	_____	Total Encumbrances	- _____
Structural Pest Control Inspection	_____	Estimated Costs	- _____
Structural Pest Control Repairs	_____	Sub-Total	$ _____
Other Required Repairs	_____	**PLUS:**	
Natural Hazard Disclosure Report	_____	Approximate Credits	+ _____
Home Protection Policy	_____	**ESTIMATED SELLER'S PROCEEDS:**	$ _____
Brokerage Fee	_____	**LESS:**	
Buyer's Closing Costs	_____	Purchase Money Note	- _____
Security Deposits	_____	(If carried by Seller)	
Prorated Rents	_____	**PLUS:**	
Administrative/Transaction Fee	_____	Proceeds From Sale of	
Other Fees/Costs:		Purchase Money Note	+ _____
_____	_____	**ESTIMATED SELLER'S CASH PROCEEDS:** $	_____
_____	_____		
_____	_____		

ESTIMATED TOTAL COSTS: $ _____

This estimate, based upon the above projected selling price, type of financing and projected closing date, has been prepared to assist the Seller in computing his/her costs and proceeds. Lenders, title companies and escrow holders will vary in their charges. Expenses will also vary depending upon any required repairs, differences in unpaid loan balances, bond assessments, other liens, impound account, if any, and other items. Therefore, these figures cannot be guaranteed by the Broker or his/her representatives. All estimates and information are from sources believed reliable but not guaranteed.

I have read the above figures and acknowledge receipt of a copy of this form.   Real Estate Broker (Firm) _____

Presented by _____

SELLER _____ Date _____   Address _____
SELLER _____ Date _____   Phone _____

Published and Distributed by:
REAL ESTATE BUSINESS SERVICES, INC.
a subsidiary of the CALIFORNIA ASSOCIATION OF REALTORS®
525 South Virgil Avenue, Los Angeles, California 90020

Reviewed by _____
Broker or Designee _____ Date _____

REVISION DATE 10/2000 Print Date
ESP-11 (PAGE 1 OF 1)

ESTIMATED SELLER'S PROCEEDS (ESP-11 PAGE 1 OF 1)

Most sellers forget that they're making mortgage payments in arrears (January's payment is for December), and may therefore be responsible for up to one month's payment at the time of closing. It's important to include a thirty-day interest payment under the estimated cost column.

This form is one of the few in the listing kit that the buyer DOES NOT receive a copy of!

Figure 4-12

Notice to Buyers and Sellers
Defective Furnaces in California

The CSPA has issued the following warning regarding defective furnaces in the State of California. As a result of this warning, Lyons and Associates, Inc., Realtor urges all clients to have a licensed heating contractor inspect the furnace in the home that they are selling or purchasing to determine if the furnace falls into the category described in the warning below.

The U.S Consumer Product Safety Commission (CPSC) is warning consumer in California that certain gas-fired, horizontal forced-air furnaces manufactured by Consolidated Industries (formerly Premier Furnace Co.) present a substantial risk of fire. There have been thirty reports of fires and damages to homes associated with these furnaces, as well as failures of burners and heat exchanges that can lead to fires. The furnaces were installed exclusively in California.

Consolidated manufactured approximately 190,000 of those furnaces from 1983-1994 under various brand names. Most of the furnaces were manufactured under the Premier/Consolidated labels. All of the furnaces can be identified by the fact that they are equipped with steel control rods installed above the burners. These steel rods were required to satisfy California air quality regulations for nitrous oxide emissions.

Many of these furnaces are still in use. Normally, the furnaces are installed in attics, although some may be installed in crawl spaces. The Commission is warning consumers to have their gas-fired furnaces inspected by a licensed heating contractor to determine they are subject to this safety alert. The contractor also should determine whether the burners and/or heat exchangers of units are damaged, or whether wood under or near the furnace shows signs of damages, such as charring blackening. If this is the case, the furnace should be replaced immediately or repaired.

Because Consolidated is currently in bankruptcy, the availability of repair parts is, at this time, unresolved. However, there is an ongoing private litigation which could enable consumers to recover at least some of their out-of-pocket expenses for replacement or repair of the furnaces.

We hereby acknowledge receipt of this form. We have read and understood the above warning and the recommendations that a licensed contractor inspect the furnace of the home we are currently selling or purchasing. We hold Lyons and Associates, its agents, and employees, harmless of any and all liability regarding the safely of the furnace located at:

_____.

_____	_____	_____	_____
Seller	Date	Buyer	Date
_____	_____	_____	_____
Seller	Date	Buyer	Date

Lyons & Associates, Inc., Realtor
2820 E. Garvey Avenue South
West Covina, CA 91791
*Business: (626) 331-0141 * Fax: (626) 331-9772*

This is a "broker-created" form. This type of horizontal attic furnace has been known to cause fires in the past and buyers will probably want it replaced. It is one example of a disclosure brokers may choose to include in the listing kit to mitigate their liability. Different areas may dictate the necessity for different forms.

Figure 4-13

A home warranty protects the buyer (for up to one year) from failure of built-ins like stove and dishwasher, as well as big ticket items like roofing, plumbing and electrical.

Although negotiable, the home warranty is often paid for by the seller as an incentive to the buyer. If the seller refuses to pay for this protection, always offer it to the buyer. If neither is interested, it's necessary for them to sign a waiver stating that the warranty's options were explained and that they declined coverage. Anybody can pay for home warranties—even brokers who want to offer incentives to their clients.

III. The Broker's Role in Real Estate Appraisal

Helping a seller determine a home's selling price is the key to getting the seller to set a reasonable listing price.

Just as financing is the key to the typical real estate transaction, valuation may be viewed as the foundation of real estate. If you're looking for an extensive treatment of appraisal, you'll find many excellent texts on the subject through The National Association of Independent Fee Appraisers (NAIFA), local realty boards, colleges, and libraries. **We suggest you read *Real Estate Appraisal*, by Walt Huber, Levin P. Messick, IFAC, and William Pivar, available through Educational Textbook Company (See back of book).**

A. HELPING SELLERS DETERMINE LISTING PRICE

Market value is sometimes referred to as "exchange value" or "value in exchange." It is the value of property as determined by sales in the open market. The Federal Register, V55, Washington, D.C., offers the following definition:

"The most probable price which a property should bring in a competitive and open market under all conditions requisite to a fair sale, the buyer and seller each acting prudently and knowledgeably, and assuming the price is not affected by undue stimulus. Implicit in this definition is the consummation of a sale as of a specified date and the passing of title from seller to buyer under conditions whereby:

1. *the buyer and seller are typically motivated;*

2. *both parties are well informed or well advised, and acting in what they consider their best interests;*

3. *a reasonable time is allowed for exposure in the open market (listing periods);*

4. *payment is made in terms of cash in United States dollars or in terms of financial arrangements comparable thereto; and*

5. *the price represent the normal consideration for the property sold unaffected by special or creative financing or sales concessions granted by anyone associated with the sale."*

In other words, **MARKET VALUE** *refers to the amount of cash (or cash equivalent) that is most likely to be paid for a property on a given date in a fair and reasonable open market sale.*

A property well listed is a property half sold.

Indeed, much of the listing interview will be concerned with price, since it is unlikely that the seller will arbitrarily accept the suggestion of a sales price without discussion and persuasion. The seller will say something like, "This other salesperson said I could get $380,000," where the house, in this case, is unlikely to go for more than $350,000. As a professional knowledgeable in comparable sales prices, your response should let the seller know that buyers are not usually inclined to pay more than what they would have to pay for a similar property.

As a fiduciary, you owe it to your principal to obtain the best market price, but you also owe it to yourself to get the listing at a saleable price.

Most sellers are misinformed about the market, choosing to believe that because of the excellent condition of the carpets and drapes, for example, they should get considerably more. This so-called "subjective value" holds little if any credence in the objective marketplace, where in the final analysis the value is established by what buyers are willing to pay in the sale of a property. Sellers usually ask for a much higher selling price than they could ever hope to get. They rely on reputed sales, attained from hearsay, where, for example, neighbors may have claimed to have sold their homes for higher figures than advertised. The remaining neighbors may be lulled into a false sense of security, believing their property to be worth more than it is.

It's up to you to research the market and come up with a saleable price, or market value, derived from reliable source, usually a MLS.

There are several approaches to valuation, the most acceptable of which is referred to as the **MARKET DATA** *or* **COMPARATIVE APPROACH**, *where value is indicated by recent sales of comparable properties in the market*. This approach is the most appropriate, and often used to set the listing price. The second method, called the **COST APPROACH**, *calculates the current cost of replacing or reproducing the improvement less depreciation, and adds the value of the land, which is never depreciated*. The third, useful only in income-producing properties, is the **NET INCOME** *or* **CAPITALIZATION APPROACH**, *which capitalizes the net earnings by an appropriate rate*.

Although the last two approaches are important in the appraisal process, and indeed may be the only ones used when no market data is available, the comparative approach is the most valid and reliable for establishing value in the residential market.

We dwell principally on this approach to value since it is here that you, the licensee, will be best equipped to arrive at a realistic probable selling price of the majority of your listings. We also examine the cost and capitalization approaches, but recommend that you take one or more courses in appraisal to fully understand these methods.

The market data approach is based on the assumption that both buyer and seller are fully informed as to the property and its uses; the state of the market for the particular type of property; each is willing to buy and to sell without undue pressure, that is, neither is compelled to buy or to sell; and that the property has been exposed in the open market for a reasonable period of time (the listing period).

B. MARKET DATA APPROACH OR COMPARATIVE VALUE

Comparing the potential listing with similar properties of the same type and class, which have sold recently or are currently on the market, produces an estimate of value under the market data approach.

Unfortunately, depending on a full market data appraisal has its limitations. For example: 1) there may be no recent sales with which to compare; 2) no two properties are exactly alike, even if the only difference is location; 3) differences exist in depreciation, maintenance, use, and occupancy; 4) it's hard to compare amenities because of the hard to define nature of views, topography, or the direction the house faces; 5) there may be motivations behind sales that influenced the price; and 6) the decor and appliances contained within each vary a good deal. Thus, adjustments must be made depending on the degree of variation: the more decisions and judgments the evaluator (appraiser) must make, the greater the potential error in accurately comparing values.

The comparative approach is the most reliable expression of value because it represents the reactions of informed buyers and sellers.

1. Competitive Market Analysis (CMA)

Real estate salespeople depend on the simplicity and availability of information necessary for a competitive market analysis over the complexity and cost of a full appraisal.

The most effective tool at your disposal is the competitive market analysis (CMA) form. All computer-generated CMAs differ slightly, but in general contain the information you'll find on **Figure 4-14.** It is relatively easy to complete, the information is readily obtainable and quite often pictures of the comparables are available—making it simple but convincing in presentation. You can present data in logical sequence and develop an accurate and current portrayal of what buyers will pay for property in the subject area.

Information needed to complete the form is most often secured from the multiple listing summaries available to subscribers on the Internet. Information can also be obtained from company files, other brokers specializing in the area, county records, appraisers, and title companies.

It is important to select only properties comparable to the subject property.

The more similar they are, the more readily sellers will accept the data, and the more likely they will be to accept your advice and counsel on listing price.

Figure 4-14

COMPETITIVE MARKET ANALYSIS

PROPERTY ADDRESS 13515 Tennis Lane, Van Nuys DATE ______

~~PROPERTY DESCRIPTION~~

~~FOR SALE NOW~~

Property	BD rms	Ba	FR/Den	Reported Sq. Ft.	Other	Existing Loans – First: Reported Balance	First: Rate	First: Type	Second: Reported Balance	Second: Rate	Second: Type	List Price	Days on Mkt	New Financing – Seller May Carry: Amount	Rate	Term	Other Terms & Comments
13431 Tennis	3	1¾		1450	FK	121,021	9 3/4	Conv				199,950	59				10% c/L, C/NL
13404 Sunshine	2	1½	D	1350		126,258	10 1/8	Conv				197,900	33				37,000 C/NL
13501 Humor	3	1¾	FR	1400		118,918	10	Conv				189,900	12				10% c/L, VA
13612 Smile	4	1¾	CD	1600		129,866	9 7/8	Conv				185,900	44				20% C/NL
4901 Spring	4	1½		1500		95,784	10	VA	4,916	12 1/2	Equity	199,000	19				20,000 c/NL
13598 Mellow	3	1¾	CD	1450		117,033	9 1/2	ARM				200,000	4	20,000	10½	5	53,000 c/L, VA, FH

REPORTED SOLD LAST 6 MONTHS

Property	BD rms	Ba	FR/Den	Reported Sq. Ft.	Other	First: Reported Balance	First: Rate	First: Type	Second: Reported Balance	Second: Rate	Second: Type	List Price	Days on Mkt	Sale Price	Financing	Date Sold	Other Terms & Comments
13543 Tennis	3	1½		1450	FK	106,486	10	Conv				185,900	9	192,000	20% c/NL	11/15/87	
13546 Tennis	3	1¾		1450		118,322	10	VA	16,390	12	Home Improvement	186,900	27	185,000	FHA	10/1/88	
13613 Tennis	3	1		1400		100,962	9 3/4	ARM				182,850	32	180,000	AITD	9/11/87	30 yrs, due in 10
4915 Ocean	4	1¾	CD	1450		121,680	9 1/2	ARM				183,900	18	181,000	C/NL	8/14/87	
13802 Mellow	3	1		1400		34,820	10	Conv				181,900	12	178,000	C/NL	7/14/87	
13647 Sunshine	3	1½	CD	1400		107,238	10	Conv				184,000	21	175,000	VA	12/18/87	
13507 [illegible]	4	1½		1430		116,000	9 7/8	Conv				199,500	41	185,500	C/EL	4/1/87	

REPORTED EXPIRED LAST 12 MONTHS

Property	BD rms	Ba	FR/Den	Reported Sq. Ft.	Other	First: Reported Balance	First: Rate	First: Type	Second: Reported Balance	Second: Rate	Second: Type	List Price	Days on Mkt	Amount	Rate	Term	Other Terms & Comments
4924 Ocean 1	2	1	D	1300		104,224						185,900	90				All cash
4954 Ocean	2	1	Add rm	1300		93,362						186,900	120	C/EL	12%	20	
4950 Care Free	3	1		1350		100,906			10,000	11	Int only	189,900	60	C/NL			
4902 Care Free	4	1¾	CD	1450		114,240						199,000	30	20,000			
13130 Tennis	3	1¾	CD	1400		97,538						188,000	90	Submit			
13911 Mellow	4	1½		1400		99,224						189,500	30	C/EL	12½%	15	

GENERAL COMMENTS:
Centrally located to complete shopping facilities, schools, large playroom, pool
Drawbacks: no A/C, unrepaired damages in pool area

COMPANY CBA Realtors / Rubicon Realty
AGENT Nick Carmiglia
PHONE ______

PROBABLE MARKETING RANGE $ 188,000 to 200,000

Information reported herein is based upon published reports or matters of public record. No representation is made or intended that this information is accurate or complete. Financing information may not reflect specific loan terms.

The undersigned acknowledge receipt of a copy.

William Pearll Date ______

______ Date ______

Moreover, the more comparable the data offered, the more valid and reliable your probable selling price will be.

A basic CMA may be divided into three broad sections. The first section, **"For Sale Now,"** contains current listings, representing asking prices. It shows the current competition. Of course, the amounts sellers would like to receive cannot necessarily be regarded as market value; they are a clue to valuation. ("For Sale Now" or "Currently on the Market" suggest the **upper value** of the property, above which few, if any, prospects would actually pay). Note the information includes the address of the listed properties; the number of bathrooms, which for greater accuracy ought to be broken down into full baths (one that includes tub and shower), three-quarter baths (one containing a stall shower, no tub), and half-baths (containing only bowl and sink). It should also address whether the house has a den or family room, the amount of square footage in the house and lot; and other improvements.

Properties "For Sale Now" on a CMA often have inflated asking prices that very few buyers actually expect to pay.

The list price entered and the number of days the property has been exposed on the market are important factors to consider, because they will help you explain to potential sellers the probable value of their homes.

If a property has been on the market for, say, 59 days but the average listing sells in 30 days, it's obvious that the property is overpriced. Other factors could account for the slowness in selling, of course, but the root causes of most slow sales are price, terms, and condition. Now is the time to suggest the seller reduce the price, secure more generous terms, or both.

Another section lists similar properties that have sold recently. **"Reported Sold Past 6 Months"** indicates current pricing and the probable top market price. Here we show not the asking price, but what the sellers actually accepted.

There should be a minimum of three properties in each category. If there is not enough data, then you should increase the time frame to eight or nine months. You may even extend the location up to one mile from the subject property.

In addition to the information called for under current listings, the date sold and the amount for which it sold is also included.

How much the similar property sold for and the terms under which it sold have the most impact on what the subject property is worth and how it can best be marketed.

The **"Reported Expired Past 12 Months"** section shows those properties which, once listed, failed to sell. These unsold properties might be called "rejected prices," because no sale took place after they had been exposed on the market for as long as four months. The acid test of a good listing is its successful sale.

Listings that do not sell are those listed at a price that buyers would not pay.

Another category in the CMA is the **PENDING LISTING**. *These properties are presently in escrow and only the listing price is made available, rather than the selling price.* It is important to include these because they show the length of time it took to open escrow and the mere fact that they did sell.

Perhaps this analysis of the Competitive Market Analysis has convinced you of the many benefits of the well-listed property. Moreover, the listing agent may very well end up losing the listing to a competitor.

C. COST APPROACH TO VALUATION

We have already demonstrated that the comparative or market data approach is usually the most valid and reliable in appraising single-family dwellings. However, what if no current data is available? Suppose there were no recent sales, current listings, or expired listings. Suppose that the subject house is in a young housing tract, where no sales have yet taken place and where reliance on the original selling prices is not valid because of varying and sometimes substantial changes that take place in new housing tracts in the early years. Under such circumstances, the market data approach cannot be used effectively or, if used, it should be supplemented by the cost approach.

To arrive at a value using the cost approach, a licensed appraiser estimates the current costs of reproducing or replacing the existing improvements. From this figure, they subtract the estimated accrued depreciation from all causes, such as from an older roof, furnace, or water heater. Finally, they add the depreciated value of the improvements to the estimated land value, established through the comparative approach. Under the economic principle of substitution, the value of a property tends to coincide with the value indicated by the actions of informed buyers in the market for comparable properties; the cost of producing through new construction a desirable substitute or replacement property usually sets the upper limit of value.

The value indicated through the cost approach is valid if the reproduction cost has been calculated accurately, if the depreciation from all causes has been correctly estimated, and if the value of the land is sound. Because of the serious limitations of the cost approach, the appraiser must correlate the data arrived at in all three basic approaches and apply skills and judgment in arriving at a final value estimate. Correlation is not averaging. One approach usually carries more weight than the other two approaches.

D. CAPITALIZATION APPROACH TO VALUATION

Though the thrust of this section is the single-family dwelling, the subject of the net income approach to value should at least be introduced.

In using the capitalization or income approach, the appraiser is concerned with the present worth of future benefits of an income-producing property. This is measured by the net income generated after deduction for all operating costs from the gross leases. In other words, by use of a proper rate of capitalization, determined through the marketplace, estimated future net rental income is converted into a specific sum of present value.

The steps involved in establishing a value based upon this approach are as follows:

First, the gross annual rental income is determined, adjusted for vacancy. Second, all costs of operation are deducted: management fees, insurance, property taxes, utility expenses, maintenance and repairs, janitorial and gardening expenses, refuse collection, licenses, and so on. Third, an appropriate capitalization rate, or present worth factor, is determined from the marketplace. Last, the net income is divided by the cap rate to establish the estimated value of the property. The **CAP RATE** *is a percentage obtained by dividing the sales prices of similar properties by their net incomes.* The higher the cap rate, the lower the appraised value.

While establishing the quantity and quality of the income and expenses is not impossible, the role of the appraiser in deriving the proper rate of capitalization is extremely complex, requiring great skill and keen judgment. A variation of even 1 percent can make an immense difference in the final outcome. For example, a net income of $28,800 capitalized at 9 percent will show $28,000 ÷ .09 or $320,000 indicated value. If capitalized at 8 percent, on the other hand, the same property will suddenly increase in value to $360,000. Though each increased by 12.5 percent, the dollar difference can be very significant, enough to inhibit many investors from paying, in this case, more than $320,000.

The most difficult problem confronting the appraiser is how to determine the appropriate capitalization rate. This rate depends on the particular type of property being considered, risks involved, market conditions, age of the property, requirements of the investor, cost of money, the expected holding period (again, the present worth of future benefits), the costs of forgoing the earnings that equity money could be earning in a safe investment such as an insured savings account, income tax considerations, and many other variables.

Some generalizations can be made about cap rates, nonetheless. Since the capitalization rate reflects the risk involved in a given investment, the greater the risk, the higher the rate will be. Conversely, the lower the risk, the lower the rate. Similarly, the older the property, the larger the cap rate should be, reflecting the larger risks accompanying such properties. By contrast, the rate can be expected to be lower for newer buildings, where the exposure is less.

As you can see, the cost and income approaches to value are very complex, therefore best left to licensed appraisal professionals.

E. PITFALLS IN ACCEPTING OVERPRICED LISTINGS

Do not take a listing when it is overpriced by a relatively large margin, that is, when its probability of selling is negligible. In a sellers' market, some agents will take a listing at any price, hoping to get it reduced during the life of the listing, as well as benefitting from sign value.

Extenuating circumstances, such as a favored client with whom you have other dealings, past or present, may lead you to exercise discretion. However, you should generally reject a listing when the owner is not serious about selling, when he or she is uncooperative and unreasonable.

If you must take a listing at a higher price, inform the sellers that you may need to be back in a month or so to adjust the price. Explain that now is the time to price right. You can otherwise justify taking an overpriced listing only if the price is within reason, if the seller has an urgent reason for selling, or when you are not sure of the value. In short, do not accept any listing wherein you cannot live up to your agency responsibility to perform satisfactorily on behalf of the principal.

Overpriced properties are stigmatized by market-savvy brokers who won't waste their time showing them! Houses on the market for too long, even once the price has been reduced, may now be perceived by buyers as having something wrong with them.

F. LICENSED APPRAISERS

A caveat should be observed by all practitioners: As a real estate agent, you should not hold yourself out as a licensed appraiser, unless, of course, you are. California allows sales agents to make unverified or informal appraisals, such as the competitive market analysis, but professional appraisers, whose work is vital for lending, expert testimony in legal proceedings, or taxation matters, must be licensed by the California Office of Real Estate Appraisers.

 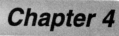
As a real estate licensee, you must limit your appraisal activities to market studies or market sales analysis.

IV. CHAPTER SUMMARY

A well-defined listing agreement will eliminate potential disagreements and misunderstandings, and help you earn your commission. The CAR® form for taking a listing is called the Residential Listing Agreement (Exclusive Authorization and Right to Sell).

The broker's name, not the agent's, is used in Section One of the form.

In a listing agreement, any handwritten instructions supersede any preprinted instructions.

Unless terms are specified, sellers are not obligated to pay a commission when they refuse a full price offer, unless the offer is for all cash.

Compensation paid to brokers is always decided by mutual agreement between principal and agent. There are no commission rates set by law.

Do not confuse the safety clause with the listing period. The agent and seller agree in a safety clause to a specific time period after termination of a listing in which the listing broker may still be entitled to a commission. Brokers must furnish the owners with a written notice of all the names of prospects to whom the property was shown during that period, either by the broker or a cooperating broker. If the owner, or a new listing broker sells the property to anyone on the list, the original broker may be entitled to a commission.

The bottom of pages one, two, and three must be initialed by the seller and the broker (or designated agent).

Remember, if the box is checked in the Multiple Listing Service [Section (6)], that means the seller is REFUSING to be entered into the MLS.

Never give legal or tax advice to your principals, unless you are an attorney or tax advisor, as it increases your liability.

An agent is required to give a copy of the listing agreement to his or her principal (all signing parties) at the time the signature is obtained.

A listing kit is comprised of several forms that complete the listing process, including The Listing, Disclosure Regarding Real Estate Agency Relationships, Seller's Affidavit of Nonforeign Status, Transfer Disclosure Statement, and Supplemental Statutory and Contractual Disclosures.

The Disclosures included in the kit also cover smoke detectors, water heaters, lead-based paint, natural hazards, and defective furnace notices.

Finally, an Estimated Seller's Proceeds form is included, and a Home Warranty Application or Waiver. If the seller refuses home warranty protection, always offer it to the buyer.

A military ordnance location (not spelled ordinance) is land used for military training purposes that may contain potentially explosive munitions.

Market value refers to the amount of cash (or cash equivalent) that is most likely to be paid for a property on a given date in a fair and reasonable open market sale.

There are several approaches to valuation, including the most commonly-used Market Data or Comparative Approach, where value is indicated by recent sales of comparable properties in the market. The Cost Approach is also used for residential property, and the Net Income or Capitalization Approach for income-producing properties.

A Competitive Market Analysis (CMA) can be compiled by a real estate salesperson, and does not require the expertise of an appraiser. A basic CMA has three sections, including properties "For Sale Now," which suggest an upper value of a property. The second section is "Reported Sold Past 6 Months," indicating current pricing and probable top market price, and finally "Reported Expired Past 12 Months," which shows houses that listed but failed to sell. A pending listing is still in escrow and only the listing price is available, not the selling price.

It's best not to accept overpriced listings, as they are harder to sell, even after the price has been reduced.

Real estate licensees are not appraisers. They must limit there appraisal activities to market studies or market sales analysis.

V. KEY TERMS

Capitalization Approach
Certified Appraisals
Combined Hazards Book
Comparative Approach
Competitive Market Analysis
Cost Approach
Defective Furnace Disclosure
Disclosure Regarding Agency Relationships
Estimated Seller's Proceeds
Exclusive Right to Sell
Home Warranty Application and Waiver
Lead-Based Paint Disclosure
Listing Period
Market Data Approach
Market Value
Military Ordnance
Net Income Approach
Residential Listing Agreement
Safety Clause
Seller's Affidavit of Nonforeign Status
Smoke Detector Statement of Compliance
Supplemental Statutory and Contractual Disclosures
Three Approaches to Value
Transfer Disclosure Statement
Water Heater Statement of Compliance

VI. CHAPTER 4 QUIZ

1. Which of the following is true concerning listing agreements?
    a. Handwritten instructions supersede preprinted instructions.
    b. Preprinted instructions supersede handwritten instructions.
    c. Handwritten and preprinted instructions have equal weight.
    d. None of the above.

2. An agent is required to give a copy of the listing agreement to his or her principal:
    a. at the time an offer is presented.
    b. at the time the signature is obtained.
    c. when the principal pays the commission.
    d. all of the above.

3. Which of the following is not a CAR form, but generated by the broker?
    a. Disclosure Regarding Agency Relationship
    b. Smoke Detector Statement of Compliance
    c. Defective Furnace Disclosure Form
    d. All of the above

4. Which form in the (seller's) Listing Kit does the buyer NOT get a copy of?
    a. Estimated Seller's Proceeds
    b. Residential Listing Agreement
    c. Water Heater Statement of Compliance
    d. The buyer sees neither a nor b

5. Land used for military training purposes that may contain potentially explosive munitions are called:
    a. dumping grounds.
    b. military ordnance locations.
    c. military ordinance locations.
    d. none of the above.

6. The amount of cash or cash equivalent that is most likely to be paid for a property on a given date in a fair and reasonable open market transaction is referred to as:
    a. market value.
    b. fair guess value.
    c. gross value.
    d. net value.

7. What type of valuation approach involves calculating the current cost of replacing or reproducing the improvement, less depreciation, and adding the value of the land?
    a. Comparative approach
    b. Cost approach
    c. Capitalization approach
    d. All of the above

8. Which of the following can provide information needed to complete a Competitive Market Analysis?
   a. Multiple listing summaries
   b. Other brokers
   c. County records
   d. All of the above

9. Lead-based paint disclosure is necessary for homes built:
   a. before 1978.
   b. before 1988.
   c. after 1978.
   d. all of the above.

10. Which of the following is TRUE concerning appraisals in California?
    a. Sales agents are allowed to make professional appraisals.
    b. Sales agents are allowed to make informal appraisals only.
    c. Professional appraisers need not be licensed.
    d. All of the above.

ANSWERS: 1. a; 2. b; 3. c; 4. d; 5. b; 6. a; 7. b; 8. d; 9. a; 10. b

CHAPTER 5
Selling
How to Find the Right Buyer for the Right House

I. The American Dream

We stated at the outset that this book is about general brokerage, which mainly consists of the listing and selling of homes. This chapter deals with characteristics of single-family dwellings, pointing out the advantages and disadvantages in purchasing a house or condo, in other words a home. We include home-buying factors, a checklist for the home shopper, and selling techniques. The purpose of this chapter is to improve your performance in helping buyers realize the "American dream" of home ownership.

As a real estate practitioner, you need to know as much about buying and selling properties as possible, understanding not only the obvious **benefits and rewards**, but also the drawbacks and risks associated with home ownership. You also need to know all aspects of the real estate business in order to more effectively assist your clientele, including anticipating and answering objections. Buyers and sellers look to you to be their guide.

Think of yourself as a navigator: you should guide your clients through the selling and buying process with a good map and a solid strategy.

CHAPTER 5 OUTLINE

I. THE AMERICAN DREAM (p. 157)

II. SHOPPING FOR A HOME (p. 159)

    A. Purchasing a Home: A General Discussion (p. 160)

        1. New Homes (p. 160)

        2. Older Homes (p. 160)

    B. Some Advantages to Owning a Home (p. 162)

    C. Some Disadvantages to Owning a Home (p. 162)

    D. Budgeting for a Home (p. 163)

III. WHY BUYERS BUY (p. 164)

IV. TECHNIQUES OF SELLING (p. 165)

    A. Direct Contact Communications (Face-to-Face) (p. 165)

    B. Letter Communications (One-Way) (p. 167)

    C. Telephone Communications (Two-Way) (p. 168)

        1. Proper Use of the Phone (p. 169)

        2. Incoming Call Register (p. 169)

        3. Answering Ad Calls (p. 171)

          a. When a Neighbor Calls (p. 172)

        4. From Phone Call to Appointment (p. 172)

        5. The Switch Sheet (p. 177)

        6. The Caravan (p. 179)

V. THE CRITICAL PATH OF SELLING (p. 179)

    A. Steps Involved in a Sale (p. 179)

        1. The Pre-Approach (p. 179)

        2. The Initial Contact or Greeting (p. 182)

        3. Counseling Buyers (p. 183)

          a. Credit Rules of Thumb (The Three C's) (p. 184)

          b. Types of Buyers (p. 185)

        4. The Sales Kit (p. 185)

        5. Planning the Showing (p. 188)

          a. Planning the Approach (The Buyer Comment Sheet) (p. 188)

          b. Planning the Actual Showing (p. 188)

        6. The Showing (p. 190)

          a. Feng Shui (p. 190)

        7. The Close (p. 193)

VI. THE SALE (p. 193)

    A. Closing Techniques (p. 194)

        1. Want Technique (p. 194)

        2. Assumptive Technique (p. 194)

        3. Alternative of Choice Technique (p. 194)

        4. Narrative Technique (p. 195)

        5. Opportunity Lost Technique (p. 195)

        6. Minimize the Difference Technique (p. 195)

      7. Negative-Yes Technique (p. 195)
      8. Yes-But Technique (p. 195)
      9. Yes and No Itemizing Technique (p. 195)
      10. Call-Back Technique (p. 196)
    B. Overriding Objections (p. 196)
  VII. CHAPTER SUMMARY (p. 199)
  VIII. KEY TERMS (p. 201)
   IX. CHAPTER 5 QUIZ (p. 202)

II. Shopping for a Home

For most buyers, purchasing a home is the most important financial decision they will ever make, and becomes the largest asset they will ever own as the loan is paid off.

When shopping for a loan, buyers ask themselves many questions. Are they buying the right type of house? Are they buying too much or not enough? Are they stretching their resources far enough to prevent another move within a short period of time?

Most property owners move on the average of every six to eight years.

You need to anticipate these concerns and address them before they ever come up. You have to be mindful of the characteristics of all forms of housing. The variety seems endless: the custom-built house, the subdivision home, the condominium, town house, or the growth of manufactured housing. You need to know and understand what to look for in selecting the house for yourself or for your client, realizing that price and terms are very significant, but by no means the only considerations.

Buyers should realistically select the area in which they want to purchase, which may not necessarily be the one in which they would prefer to live. For the first-time home buyer, that first house is often the one that will make it possible to eventually buy his or her dream home—a step in the right direction.

Schools are very important to a family, and you should know the various school district boundaries, and verify the information prior to crystallizing an offer. Commuting distance to work is another important issue you should prioritize.

It's extremely important to know exactly where school district lines are drawn. One side of a street may be in a more desirable school district than the opposite side, where houses sell for less money.

A. PURCHASING A HOME: A GENERAL DISCUSSION

The buyers, especially if they are first-time buyers, will have lots of questions regarding their home purchase. It's a good time to get to know them. They may want a large lot, or perhaps this is not that important to them, even a detriment. When looking at a model home, remind your client that it's expensively decorated for display purposes only, and that any upgrades will be added to the price of their house. Additionally, landscaping and window coverings are costs to be concerned with.

1. New Homes

New homes offer the advantages of modern, up-to-date design, construction, plumbing, electrical fixtures, wall and floor outlets, and built-ins, especially in the kitchen. They are more attractive in and out, have a greater useful economic life, and provide more efficient heating and cooling equipment. Moreover, new homes command larger and longer loans than older houses. Yet, many buyers believe that newer homes are not as well built as the older ones. Finally, land values are more likely to increase as the area builds up.

2. Older Homes

The older homes, or "re-sales," offer many advantages over the brand new ones. They are generally located in proven, fully-developed and established areas. There is often better public transportation and more shopping choices and schools, and they are closer to employment centers and central business districts. There is a wider variety of choices. The house has been physically "shaken down," in other words, faulty construction, structural defects, and settling problems are evident, corrected, or demonstrated to be non-existent. Whether or not a house is a "lemon" may not readily be apparent in the new house. Buyers can see exactly what they are getting in an older house and in the neighborhood. Landscaping, sprinklers, fencing, and patio, and many other expenditures that confront the typical new home buyer are already in existence. Finally, more house per square foot can be obtained for the price, with bargain prices often available for "fixer-uppers."

Any repairs made within the last five years must be disclosed to the buyer.

It's important to get a professional inspection (as a condition in the contract) on all real estate purchases, including new houses. This costs around $350, depending on the size of the property and the scope of the inspection. It's usually paid for by the buyer, who gets the report, with a copy going to the seller. Later, sellers being presented with the buyers' "wish list" for repairs, may decide to do some of the repairs (or none), at which time the transaction may be rescinded—buyers get their deposit back, and sellers get to put their property back on the market.

The shoppers for the used or older home look for the same things as the new home buyer, plus many more that are connected with the physical structure itself. Oversized hallways and kitchens, along with high ceilings, also mean extra fuel bills and maintenance. As a salesperson trying to sell an older home, you may be faced with many problems. There may be termite and dry-rot damage, cracked foundations or walls, chipped masonry, worn-out or obsolete electrical wiring, faulty heating and air conditioning, corroded plumbing, and a variety of other problems, including improperly built add-ons.

Additions made without the proper permits can be a source of problems when selling a property. Most buyers want to be reassured that the home they are purchasing is built up to current codes. Additionally, should there be a fire, the insurance company may deny full coverage because of the non-permitted additions or alterations.

The floor plan and design of older homes may suffer from obsolescence. *FUNCTIONAL OBSOLESCENCE is the loss of value due to adverse factors within a structure that affect the marketability of the property.* It could be a single-car garage, a wall furnace, no bath off the master bedroom, inefficient layout, or utility.

Exterior signs of decay include unsightly, neglected properties, larger houses divided into small apartments or room rentals, and many absentee owners renting to tenants, resulting in a transient quality that affects neighborhood status. Business and industry has a tendency to encroach upon the fringes, if not the core. Sociological problems also are more prevalent, evidenced by vandalism and crime in the decaying community.

ECONOMIC or SOCIAL OBSOLESCENCE is any loss of value due to conditions outside of the property itself (external). These are not considered "curable"—they are beyond the control of the property owner.

It's obvious that maintenance and repair costs might be significantly higher on an older home. The cost of refurbishing, renovating, or remodeling may more than offset the assumed advantages of lower price and other benefits.

The cost of upgrading a fixer-upper may over-improve the property to the extent that the purchaser may not be able to recover the investment.

B. SOME ADVANTAGES TO OWNING A HOME

1. **Possible appreciation**. Property values in California have historically increased throughout the years. Although, at times, there has been some flattening of the market, real estate values return and provide an edge against inflation.

2. **Tax benefits**. These benefits are considerable because interest paid and property taxes are deductible items for owner-occupied properties. The tax forgiveness for owner-occupied properties upon resale (up to $500,000) is a boon for the owner.

At the time of this publication, there is capital gains tax for the sale of a home up to $250,000 for singles and $500,000 for married people who file a joint return. To qualify, the home must have been the principal residence for a minimum of two years during the last five years prior to the sale. At least one spouse must be the owner during this time, but both spouses must have lived there for the two-year period.

3. **Equity buildup**. This is forced savings because each monthly housing payment partially repays the loan. In contrast, the residential tenant gets rent receipts in lieu of a tax deduction and equity buildup.

4. **Cash flow**. Should the owner-residents decide to convert the property to a rental, they may do so, and then are permitted additional tax benefits, such as depreciation.

C. SOME DISADVANTAGES TO OWNING A HOME

1. **Loss of Value**. Improvements ultimately wear out or lose value through functional, economic and social obsolescence.

2. **Upkeep and maintenance**. Some people, included the aged, who find it too burdensome to maintain a home, find that renting is less demanding.

3. **Liquidity**. A home investment is not very flexible due to the length of time needed to dispose of it. Even in a sellers' market, transfer of title does not formally take place until all of the terms and conditions of the sale have been complied with. A thirty day escrow is usually the shortest time necessary to close a transaction.

4. Foreclosure. There is always the possibility of losing a major investment through foreclosure for nonpayment of taxes and mortgage payments.

D. BUDGETING FOR A HOME

An important question all potential buyers must ask themselves is: How much should I pay for a house? The answer depends on many variables. Personal debt must first be taken into consideration. Many present day lenders realize that a borrower who is debt free is able to afford higher monthly payments than one who has maxed out his or her credit cards and is heavily in debt. Recently, there has been a move toward the use of a 3.5 to 1 multiplier, meaning that monthly housing payments should not exceed 30% of the borrower's gross monthly income. When you include personal debt in addition to the house payment, 38% of a buyer's gross income is usually the maximum.

Monthly Housing Payment
(Principal + Interest + Monthly Taxes and Insurance + Homeowner Assoc.) =
25% to 30% Gross Monthly Income

Monthly Housing Payment + Long-Term Monthly Debts =
33% to 38% Gross Monthly Income

Obviously, it is vital for you to be aware of these ratios in order to qualify buyers and not show them property priced above their means. This is a **big mistake** in any transaction which will cause the buyer embarrassment and a waste of time for all parties to the transaction—sellers, buyers, and agents.

When first meeting a client, you should explain that because of the various loans now available to buyers, which can be customized to their unique requirements, it is to their benefit to be prequalified by a lender who has the information on the best loans available—**leave this task to the professionals.**

Give your buyers the names of at least two lenders with whom you have successfully worked. Offer to make the appointment for them, or they can meet in your office at their convenience. Explain how important it is for buyers to be prequalified when presenting an offer and, as usual, ask your buyers for their feedback regarding these lenders.

All things being equal, the seller will choose a qualified buyer over an unknown quantity. Being **qualified** is an excellent benefit that the buyers should be made aware of, especially in a hot sellers' market where multiple offers are often received.

Not being prequalified can easily cost them their dream home. You should aim to have your buyers prequalified prior to showing properties.

In a "hot sellers' market," you often receive several offers on the same property. The seller naturally will consider only the better ones, and having a qualified buyer is one of these valid considerations.

Self-employed individuals quite often have difficulty qualifying for a loan. Lenders usually require these types of buyers to furnish at least two years tax returns with their loan applications. Again, because lenders have many ways of servicing borrowers, they have different loans for different folks.

If the buyers don't make an effort to be pre-qualified, it shows a lack of motivation or lack of good credit.

III. Why Buyers Buy

In correlating the purchase price and financing terms with the buyer's income and debt obligations, it was found that the typical purchaser paid more for a house than the rules of thumb suggested. Purchasers spent closer to four times their annual income for a house and budgeted almost 35 percent and more for housing expenses. You can draw your own conclusions concerning the reasons for such attitudes. Home buyers buy with **emotion rather than from an investment point of view**—they place their furniture in the various rooms; they imagine their quiet time in the den; they see themselves entertaining their family and friends in the family room around a cheerful fireplace.

It is interesting to note that 40% of buyers move less than five miles from their old location, and one out of every ten relocates within a mile. It stands to reason, then, that neighborhood must be uppermost in buyers' minds, with perhaps need for more space the prime motive for moving.

Buyers often keep buying the same type of house they already own. You should visit the buyers at their present home and take notice of their style of living in order to eliminate showing houses that don't fit their lifestyle. Buyers will be impressed by your intuitive knowledge and thoughtfulness concerning their needs.

People don't buy houses; they buy benefits.

As for selection of the house ultimately purchased, about 20 percent of the reasons given are **special features**—views, fireplaces, landscaping, number of baths and bedrooms, adequate closet space, expandable floor plan, large kitchen, and so on.

> **The busiest time of year for buying and selling is June and July when parents are free to investigate the housing market while children are not in school. For most people, February is a breathing period, following the heavy spending outlay at Christmas, while March is the time to get ready for tax deadlines in April. Nevertheless, people buy and sell real estate all year long.**

Among those buyers who shopped with licensees, most bought through them, yet over half went to more than one firm before buying.

IV. Techniques of Selling

Selling is communicating, therefore, in order to sell effectively you must be able to communicate effectively. It's important to remember that communication is a two-way process.

When interacting with clients, listening is just as important as talking!

We communicate most effectively with those who share our common interests, cultural background, income, and education. Young salespeople, for example, may be more successful when selling to their own age group, because they can communicate best with their own peers. This is not a hardfast rule, however, as communication skills vary from person to person. It's essential to know your client and speak appropriately. The more well-rounded you are, the more clients will be able to relate to you.

Don't try to impress a prospect with vocabulary or slang you're unfamiliar with.

In order to be most effective, you should communicate on more than one level. It's always helpful to include aids, like charts, photos, and graphs, as well as actually involving your clients in the decision-making process.

A. DIRECT CONTACT COMMUNICATIONS (Face-to-Face)

The most effective two-way communication occurs in a face-to-face situation. Inaccuracies and misunderstandings can be resolved by observing the instructions accompanying messages or by questioning the other party. This ability to react to the entire communication and to adjust behavior accordingly is called feedback.

Chapter 5

Soliciting business on a direct-contact basis is more effective than by telephone or mail.

The second most effective communication occurs in a two-way but not face-to-face situation. An example is the telephone call. Feedback is possible, but you don't have the benefit of nonverbal assists.

The least effective communication is one-way, such as a letter. At this level, neither immediate feedback nor the identification of accompanying nonverbal cues is possible.

The closer you get to the prospect, the better your chances for a sale.

Sending a letter to a prospect is fine, so long as it's a pre-approach letter. To be effective, however, you must call for an appointment. Although the telephone is an indispensible device, no one can list or sell real estate by phone. It is merely a tool through which you make arrangements to meet personally with your prospects.

If you want prospects to remember you, your company, and your properties, get them as involved in the sales process as possible.

For example, when you're on a listing appointment, getting the prospects to respond with a "yes" to questions puts them in a favorable frame of mind. Having them follow the listing contract with you, line by line, and getting agreement on each item helps to smooth communications. Better still, hand them a pad and pencil and directly involve them in the process. Not only will it be easier for them to understand in the present, but it will lessen the chance of problems arising later.

Repeating or summarizing important points can be an effective method of emphasizing the things you want the prospect to remember.

Your message should be delivered in a clear, articulate, and enthusiastic manner. Remember, it's not so much what you say, but how you say it. Voice inflection, facial expressions, and body language all contribute to the overall impression you leave with a prospect. Even with the best intentions, you can fail to persuade a prospect because of the way you express yourself.

Keep your voice calm. Qualify your opinions and avoid off-color remarks, jokes, and personal terms of endearment like "hon" or "sweetie." The use of the word "we" helps to involve both the salesperson and the prospects.

You should attempt to express, not impress. Look as good as you sound. Even a smile reflects an interest in the listener. Look the prospect in the eye as he or she speaks and listen. This habit tends to hold attention and establish trust. Avoid distracting mannerisms, both the verbal and nonverbal varieties. You don't have to be a toastmaster to recognize the irritating sound effects of *ah, er, ahm, eh;* be careful in your use of such expressions as *I mean, well, you know, now, to be honest, it's like* and *ok.* If you're at a loss for words, say nothing. Salespeople have been accused, perhaps justifiably, of talking too much and not listening enough.

Remember, you were given two ears and one mouth; therefore, you should listen twice as much as you speak.

B. LETTER COMMUNICATIONS (One-Way)

As the least effective mode of communication, the letter should be used principally as a pre-conditioner.

Use it to offer the prospects your services, suggesting that they call you for help or state that you will call them for something. In other words, use the letter to let the client know that you will follow through by telephone or in person. As such, the letter is a potentially powerful tool in the communications channel.

A well-organized letter is similar to the well-organized ad that we discussed in Chapter 3. You will want to state the purpose of the letter, the benefits being offered, your qualifications as an agent, and an invitation to call you. The format of the letter should be similar to the ad, using the A-I-D-A approach.

A-I-D-A stands for Attention, Interest, Desire and Action.

Suppose, for example, that you have the listing at 743 So. Fircroft Avenue, Covina, and you want to interest the neighbors in the property. See **Figure 5-1** for a sample of how such a letter can be drafted. Notice that it attracts attention at the outset-the address spelled out across from the heading immediately alerts the receiver that a neighbor's property is singled out for something. You can spark their interest, because who isn't at least curious about what's happening around his or her property? If the neighbors themselves desire another home or know someone who does, the letter may arouse this desire. Finally, you have invited action by asking the recipient to call or write for further information.

An unsolicited letter from a real estate agency might get tossed in the trash unopened, but nobody throws out a postcard without at least turning it over to see what it says. Be sure to include a photograph of the property on the postcard! It's also less expensive in that you can print two cards per page and the postage costs less for postcards than letters.

Figure 5-1

Lyons and Associates, Inc., Realtor

REAL ESTATE EXCELLENCE

(Date)

Re: 743 South Fircroft Avenue

Dear _____:

We have just listed 743 South Fircroft Avenue in your neighborhood. This is a beautiful 3 bedroom, family room, 2 bath home listed for $325,000.

We are very excited about this property, and I will be glad to show it to you or to your friends or relatives interested in moving to your area, giving you a chance to choose your new neighbors.

It is also important to know property values in your own area; in view of this I will keep you posted on the price of this home when it sells. If you are considering selling your home or buying a home, I welcome the opportunity of meeting with you and discussing how I can be of service to you in getting top price for your current home and finding your new home. Please call or E-mail me.

Best Regards,

Arlette Lyons, CRS, GRI
Owner-Broker
aalyons@aol.com - http://LyonsandAssociatesRltr.com

2820 E. GARVEY AVENUE SOUTH, WEST COVINA, CA 91791 • (626) 331-0141 • FAX: (626) 331-9772

In order to address letters personally to the owners adjacent to your listing, check with your favorite title company. Always address letters personally, never to "Occupant."

C. TELEPHONE COMMUNICATIONS (Two-Way)

If used properly, the telephone can open more doors and result in more sales because it leads to direct contact and saves time. You can reach far more prospects through efficient use of this instrument than you can contact by door-to-door solicitation. It eliminates call-backs (further calls on the same prospect), fixes the hour of appointment, and is appreciated by the busy prospect. Despite all these benefits, it is too often abused.

Used improperly, the telephone will cost the firm many dollars, sales, listings, and good will. Check the Federal "Do Not Call" regulations before using the phone to solicit business.

1. Proper Use of the Phone

Before telephoning, you should **organize** your schedule to make as many calls as possible at one session. Plan in advance what you're going to say. At all times have your material on hand—lists, pencil and pad, calendar, and appointment book, incoming call registers, ad switch sheets, and so on.

When making calls, be **natural**, use your normal speaking voice, and talk to the person on the other end as if he or she were sitting across the desk from you. Be clear in your enunciation and diction and simple in your language. A smile helps, and a sincere, pleasant ring in your voice may get you another listing or selling interview.

You should be **positive**. Avoid being apologetic or timid. Speak with firmness and authority, as if you expect the prospect to say yes.

Of course, no one can sell real estate on the telephone, so it's important to be brief. Stay on the line only long enough to sell the interview, that is, to make an appointment.

Learn how to be a **good listener**. When you do speak, get in step with the caller: talk slowly to slow talkers and fast to fast talkers. Use exciting words and phrases. Use the caller's name from time to time. Leave a good impression, even if the other person is not interested in your proposal: "It was delightful talking to you, Mrs. Prospect."

Finally, **practice** does make perfect. You should learn and constantly review good telephone techniques, practicing them on your spouse or fellow salespeople, preferably taping them for playback. Learn the prospect's most common objections, many of which will be raised later, and develop effective, practical answers to them.

If you believe in yourself, your product, and your company, your sincerity will come through. As a real estate salesperson you do, after all, have a valuable service to offer.

2. Incoming Call Register

We've discussed the general guiding principles of good telephone usage, with emphasis on outgoing calls. When the telephone rings in the office, greet the caller with "Lyons Realty, good morning (afternoon, evening), may I help you?" Vary the greeting at holidays with Happy Holidays, Happy New Year (Easter,

Thanksgiving, Fourth). By injecting the firm name first, you've assured the caller that he or she dialed correctly. By keeping the greeting short, you allow customers more time to speak, which is, after all, why they are calling. Your name should be de-emphasized in the greeting. After establishing a friendly relationship, you can give the caller your name in a way much more likely to be remembered.

One of the most effective time-saving tools you and your broker have to handle telephone calls is the Incoming Call Register. The Incoming Call Register provides the salesperson with a series of questions to ask the caller, and furnishes a handy record of calls for follow-up now or later. (See **Figure 5-2.**)

Figure 5-2

FILE REF. _____

Incoming Call Register

GOALS: 1. Create a Favorable Image

2. Make an appointment as soon as possible

REMINDER QUESTIONS: Name?   Address?   Phone No.?   What area preferred?   What type home?   What price range?   How many in family?   Ages?   What area of employment?   Will you sell present home?   Any special requirements?   Would you like list of available homes in preferred area?   What is convenient time for appointment?

Ad Reference _____ Date _____

Address of Home in Ad _____

Name of Caller _____

Address _____ Phone _____

Area Desired _____

Special Requirements _____

Type of Home _____ Price Range _____

Type or Place of Employment _____

Family Information _____

Now Owns or Rents _____

♦ Date and Time of Appointment _____

Comments _____

_____

Follow up _____

_____

_____

Because most incoming calls will be from people who saw an ad in the newspaper, a sign on the property, or the like, it's a wise policy for your real estate firm to retain the completed forms after the sales associates are through with them. Your company may wish to evaluate the responses to ads, assess the outcome of inquiries, and use those which did not sell for later call-backs.

Record keeping is essential for controlling revenue and expenses and follow-up.

Knowing which ads are pulling in callers, how many calls are needed to produce each sale, and the telephone effectiveness of the salespeople—during and outside of floor time—assists the broker in planning, directing, and controlling operations of the office and sales staff.

FLOORTIME *is the time assigned to an agent to answer the company phone.* Any new customers who don't ask for an associate by name become his or her prospect.

3. Answering Ad Calls

You, or your staff should always be prepared for incoming calls, answering as soon as the phone rings. Nothing turns off a caller faster than to have the telephone ring six or eight times before receiving a response. Because many prospects are calling in order to eliminate some of the advertised properties, a slow response to their call may eliminate that property from their list altogether, and you'll have lost a chance for a sale before you even began.

People like to talk to a live person rather than a machine with a variety of options.

Advertising frequently accounts for the major item of expense in the typical general brokerage office, so the broker can ill afford to lose any calls. Advertising dollars go down the drain whenever the salesperson carelessly allows the phone to ring so long that the caller hangs up.

If the call is for someone who is not in the office, carefully jot down the name and number of the caller and ask about the nature of the call. You may be able to assist the caller. After you hang up, call the salesperson for whom the message was intended if timing is important.

Sales associates ought to leave word of where they can be contacted and when they expect to return, or make clear under what conditions their cell phone number can be given out.

On the other hand, if the salesperson is in the office but is tied up at the moment, inform the caller that the agent is detained but will call right back, or ask whether the party will hold for a few moments. However, never leave someone hanging on the phone indefinitely. Frequently inform the caller that the salesperson is still busy. Otherwise the caller may hang up, just as he or she would have had the phone been allowed to ring too long.

Always ask permission before putting someone on hold!

Preparation for calls also means knowing the inventory. As the salesperson with floor duty (meaning it's your turn to stay in the office and answer the phones) you should inspect every new listing as well as review old listings in order to be familiar with any property people may call about.

To respond with, "I'm happy you called on this particular one—it's a sure winner," will not come off sincerely if you're unable to answer a few basic questions about the property.

You should always check the sold sheets to be sure the property is still available.

a. When a Neighbor Calls

A large number of ad calls emanate from people who just want to learn the listing price of a property. Look at these callers as opportunities for new business! They may be toying with the idea of selling their homes and are attempting to get a feel for market prices. Obtain their names and telephone numbers, which they should be eager to provide if they really want some information. Ask if they're familiar with the neighborhood in which the house is located. If they are, tell them what a good buy the house they're calling on is, and add that you wish you had two more like it in the neighborhood.

When neighbors call about the listing price of a property, don't assume they're just being nosy. Offer to drop by a free market analysis of their home's value—you may gain a new listing!

A significant number of buyers purchase homes within a half-mile radius of their present address!

Most callers will respond honestly to a friendly but direct question, so there's no harm in simply asking them if they live in the neighborhood. If the answer is yes, ask if they are considering selling their own property.

4. From Phone Call to Appointment

The telephone should primarily be used as a vehicle to secure an appointment. Real estate cannot be sold or listed by phone.

Callers ask many questions about ads and signs and raise many objections to meeting an agent in person when they merely want information. To become a successful agent or broker, you need to be aware of these roadblocks and be prepared to overcome them, even if it takes memorizing sets of responses.

It will pay off if you have ready answers to the below-mentioned questions. Make up your mind that the next time prospects ask for an address you will convince them they'll be better served if they visit your office and elect you as their official house hunter.

Some of the questions you will be asked to address are listed below.

a. *What is the size (location, down payment, price, style, etc.)?*

Answer #1 – "What kind of footage (location, down payment, price, house) are you looking for?" Your basic purpose is to get an appointment with the caller, so try not to give out too much information before actually agreeing to meet.

Answer #2 – If you don't know the answer, say, "I don't have the answer to that, Mr. Caller, but I'll be happy to look it up for you." He'll have to give you his phone number for you to call him back. Follow through.

Answer #3 – Answer the question, but follow it with a request for action. "Perhaps you'd like to see it this afternoon, or would tomorrow be better?" commonly brings the conversation to an early conclusion. Such "final alternatives" give the caller a choice about when to make the appointment (for showing or an interview for listing).

A gimmick used by many real estate professionals, is the "answer a question with a question" technique. While it does encourage callers to give out information, it can also be seen as evasive and annoying. Be careful not to over-use the technique.

b. *Where's this property located?*

Answer #1 – "This property is located in (give general area, not the specific address). Are you familiar with this area?" If the answer is no, offer the advantages of the neighborhood, good school districts, safe neighborhoods, etc., and offer to take them on a tour of the area.

Answer #2 – If your prospects express a dislike of that area, offer to show them around the improvements in the neighborhood, or ask what areas they do like and offer to show them properties in that area.

c. *We'd like to drive by the property.*

Answer #1 – "It's always a good idea to see the exterior of a home as well as the neighborhood. I'll be available to answer any questions you may have about the property. If you're going to be driving by anyway, I'd be happy to meet you and show you the inside as well."

d. *Will they sell on a GI or FHA?*

Answer #1 – "That's a possibility. (Or I'm sorry it's not, but) I can help put you in touch with a couple of great lenders who are really flexible and know all the available options. Tell me when you're available to drop by and we'll contact some lenders and get you prequalified over the Internet or on the phone."

e. What is the price of the home?

Answer #1 – De-emphasize price. Sell the house and it's advantages, not the price.

Answer #2 – Tell them the price and add a question or a positive comment.   "They're asking (amount). Is this about the price range you had in mind?" Or "They're asking (amount). At that price it's not going to last long."

> **Stress that prequalifying for loans helps buyers to narrow down their searches, and prequalifying letters give them leverage with sellers.**

Answer questions honestly, but include a little something extra (the sizzle). Tell your clients the price of the home, but add that it's a lot of house for the money, or that you don't often find such a great view at that price.

f. I don't have time to look with you.

Answer #1 – "I understand your frustration. Buying a home is an important decision, one that requires a lot of time. I have printed information on several homes, and my professional guidance can save you time and money. I'll be happy to send this information to you, Ms. Caller. What's your address and phone number?"

Answer #2 – If a caller is hesitant to give out an address, ask for an email address or fax number. You can send information, including pictures of properties to his or her fax machine or computer and respect the desire for privacy.

Many buyers are not aware that you can give them information on other agent's listings. Offer to look up other companies' listings and save them time and legwork!

g. I want a (modern/rustic, etc.). Is this modern?

Answer #1 – "I've found that people describe homes in different ways. How would you describe modern?" Help them narrow down what they're looking for—by modern, do they mean updated or do they mean built after a certain year? Offer to help them find the type of house they're looking for!

Answer #2 – Of course, if it is the style they've said they want, tell them so, then close for the appointment.

h. *I prefer not to give my name. I don't want to be hounded.*

Answer #1 – "I can appreciate your feelings. We're both busy people, and I promise not to waste your time, however, new listings are being processed daily, and exceptional homes don't remain on the market long. Would you be offended if I call you about a particularly good buy?" If they still don't want to give you their phone number or name, don't push. Ask for a fax or e-mail address so you can send them information and photos of those exceptional properties.

Use your switch sheet! If a house isn't right for them, let the callers know you have other listings that do fit the bill.

i. *I'll call you back rather than give my name and telephone number.*

Answer #1 – Don't push it. Respect your prospects' wishes. Ask if it would be less intrusive to e-mail or fax them with information.

Be sure to offer prospects your cell phone number so you can be reached at a moment's notice. It not only shows that you're eager to be of assistance, but you're sharing some of your personal information.

j. *I only want information. I have my own broker.*

Answer #1 – "We do cooperate with other brokers, Mr. or Ms. Caller, and we appreciate their cooperation. Perhaps you can have your broker give me a call."

k. *How big is the living room?*

Answer #1 – "Real estate agents no longer measure rooms (it's too easy to make mistakes). But I saw the home, and the open floor plan makes it appear very spacious for the size of the house. Why don't you take my cell phone number and give me a call when you decide to see it for yourselves?"

Real estate agents no longer give out dimensions of interior spaces. There is too much room for error and mistakes were grounds for lawsuits.

l. What's the size of the lot?

Answer #1 – Give them the dimensions (it's usually on the MLS printout anyway). Always follow up with a positive remark, like "that's enough room for a pool; plus it has about six fruit trees. I'm surprised it hasn't sold already. Do you have time to meet me today to look at it for yourself?

m. What's the down payment?

Answer #1 – "Down payments are usually pretty flexible. Do you expect to use the proceeds from the sale of your current house as a down payment?" If the answer is yes, tell them "I'd be happy to give you a market analysis on the value of your home so you'll know what you can expect to have in the way of finances."

n. What's the address?

The answer to this question usually depends on the policy of the brokerage for which you work, the policies you decide to make as a broker, or the specific wishes of your sellers.

Answer #1 – If your brokerage policy allows you to disclose addresses, ask for a name and call back number before giving out the address. Assure your caller that it's a safety measure, as you're sure they would understand your precautions before giving out their address should they be in the seller's position. Suggest you show them the property in person.

Answer #2 – If your brokerage policy discourages giving out addresses, ask about which house your caller is inquiring. "We have three of them in the same category but in various locations." Ask for the description of the property and call back number, then check your switch sheet, and call them back with a list of properties that fit their search.

Answer #3 – If your seller requests that you don't give out the address, inform the caller of your seller's instructions. "However, I'm sure they'll agree to let me show you the house with very short notice."

If you suggest other listings or don't give out the address for a homeowner that doesn't object to drive-by shoppers, you run the risk of alienating and losing that client.

Answer #4 – "Since my office is centrally located, you can save yourself a lot of time by seeing the homes with me and telling me what you like or don't like about each of them. Then, I'll really be able to help you find the right home for you and your needs." The prospect who's been getting nothing but addresses from other brokers can be the best kind of prospect.

5. The Switch Sheet

Callers rarely end up buying the properties about which they originally call. Moreover, many advertised homes may sell before the caller inquires about them. Therefore, it's important to be prepared at all times to show similar properties. For this purpose a series of "switch sheets" should be made up in advance; these sheets show the address, price, and so forth as illustrated in **Figure 5-3.**

Figure 5-3

Switch Sheet

Ad Heading: *Covina Charmer*   Property: *743 So. Fircroft Ave., Covina $325,000*

Other Properties	Listing No.	Price and room description
1. 834 Shasta, Covina	C20324	$335,000 3 BR, FR & pool
2. 656 Meadow Road	C56713	$317,500 2 BR, den
3. 754 Calvados Street	C059304	$320,000 3 BR, Covina schools

Agent taking floor time should be fully prepared for receiving ad calls. Not only should the agent know what is being advertised, what signs are out, but they should have other properties to discuss with the caller.

Remind your callers that by allowing you to look up all the ads they're interested in, they'll have to make fewer phone calls and, more importantly, will only give out their phone number to one agent.

A "switch sheet" is a quick reference list of properties within a similar price range, school district, size, etc. Computers greatly simplify and speed up this task.

Using switch sheets helps get appointments. They allow you to consider alternative listings before coming under the pressure of an actual call. When there are many calls, and you're the salesperson on the floor, you may not have time to think clearly enough to maintain buyer interest unless you do some homework in advance. Prepare before the calls roll in, and you'll make a more favorable impression on the caller.

Being prepared allows you to be more helpful from the very first phone call and gives you an advantage over less organized agents a caller may have previously contacted.

Often the newspaper ad about which the prospect is calling is still running, although the property has been sold. You might say, "I'm sorry, the other home was just sold, but we have a new listing that may be just what you're looking for. Let's hurry and get in right away—it may not last." Enthusiasm will pay off, especially in light of the speed with which the first property was sold. In any event, the ad switch sheet will expedite the selling process. You may also add that sometimes escrows fall through and offer to keep them posted.

An independent or smaller brokerage may not have other properties that fit the bill, but you can always remind a caller of your services. Remind the caller that your brokerage is a member of a multiple listing service, so you have access to many other listings. Ask them to bring a paper with their choices circled, and offer to check out all the houses together. Then, pin down a specific appointment.

If you can't get the appointment, offer to give them information on the circled ads—immediately look up the properties in the MLS and call them back with that information.

The remaining time is devoted to relatively nonproductive activities, such as traveling, waiting for interviews, running down data, preparing reports, and handling mountains of office details, which is why so many successful brokers are hiring professional assistants. (See Chapter 14 for more information regarding real estate assistants.) With or without an assistant, you should always organize your time and talents effectively. Devote time to pre-call planning and specific pre-approach analysis to improve your face-to-face selling.

To maximize the results of selling time, you should develop a lively, intelligent sales presentation. This presentation is a series of short, snappy, logical reasons why a prospect should use your services. It shouldn't, however, sound canned or prearranged.

There is no such thing as "canned talk," only a "canned salesperson" delivering the talk.

Breathe life into your presentation. Make it sound sincere and convincing each time you deliver it. If delivered in a routine manner, the presentation will sound scripted (canned) and be ineffectual. Although the presentation may seem repetitious to you, remember it's new to the prospect. If you're enthusiastic, the prospect will get fired up too.

Like courtesy, enthusiasm is contagious.

The pre-approach to selling, then, includes memorizing "pat" answers to typical questions, familiarity with the properties about which buyers will call and the best routes to the properties, as well as the most effective ways to show property.

In short, selling real estate involves preparation. This means being prepared at all times, for the expected as well as the unexpected.

As a competent salesperson, you should know how potential buyers initiate action. For example, studies show that typical buyers who check out local newspapers will look first at the back of the paper. Second, buyers mark the ads in which they're interested. Third, they make a decision to call about ads that appeal to them, those that offer what they want. Because buyers call for information, your efficient use of the telephone is vital. Fourth, buyers go to an office. Which office they choose depends in large measure on the ability of the salesperson who answered the call.

Once in the office, the question should no longer be whether prospects will buy, but when.

When buyer's call about an ad, find out why that particular property appealed to them. Buyers will often respond with something like: "I saw a house with the

most beautiful den (yard, dining room, etc.)." The appropriately rehearsed approach to this type of caller is: "Mr. Caller, I have many houses that may interest you. I know how valuable your time is, but I'll match my time with yours. Tell you what I'll do. Why not let me take you and Mrs. Caller out with no pressure to buy? I'd like to show you three or four homes and invite you to critique them. After that, I'll be able to tell what it is you like and dislike."

Determine your callers' "hot buttons," the things they find important. Don't sell price, size, or, for that matter, house. "Sell the interview."

Terminate the call with the usual close, "Can you be ready for previewing this morning, or would mid-afternoon be better?"

In light of the dangerous times in which we live, agents rarely pick up clients anymore. It's safer to ask them to meet you at your office, or have them follow you in your car. After establishing a relationship, it's a good idea to visit clients' homes to get a feel for how they live.

Get prospective buyers to commit to an appointment and agree to come to your office at a specific time, rather than just agreeing to "drop by."

2. The Initial Contact or Greeting

Wherever you have the interview, be on time. It's best to encourage prospective buyers to come to your office, rather than to meet with you at their home or at the property site, for safety issues and because you can more effectively control the situation there.

After greeting the buyers, cement the relationship with a warm, firm handshake. Offering a beverage is one of many ways to put your clients at ease. Build confidence by showing your knowledge and interest in them. To make a sale, you must satisfy the buyer's needs. These needs can be summarized into four broad classifications:

a. **The need for trust.** Buyers need to have complete confidence in your firm. If you believe in your company and product you can honestly say, "It's to your advantage, Mr. Prospect, to work with my brokerage because we have your best interest at heart."

b. **The need for information.** You must be knowledgeable and have the ability to communicate information accurately. This means knowing the neighborhood, market conditions, legal aspects, and so forth.

c. The need for advice. In your role of counselor and problem solver, you must be familiar with all aspects of real estate. You should have an understanding of human nature so you'll be able to react to the buyer's problems with empathy.

d. The need for financing. Because the typical family will invest the bulk of their savings and other assets in a home, you must know the kinds of financing plans available, the costs, and so on. You should also have a list of lenders to recommend and/or websites where buyers can be prequalified.

3. Counseling Buyers

Before prospects purchase a home, they must have the financial ability, desire, and intent to buy.

The process of rectifying a buyer's needs and desires with the reality of their financial capacity is called COUNSELING or QUALIFYING THE BUYER.

Determine what your buyers can afford and what they can buy for that amount. Whenever possible, avoid showing properties until after you've counseled your buyers.

Always try to prequalify a prospect before showing a property. It can save you and your client time and energy, not to mention saving your clients embarrassment and disappointment if they can't afford a particular property.

Find out why your prospects want to buy, what their needs are, and how these needs can be realistically met.

You will, no doubt, encounter prospects who are reluctant to get prequalified by a lender, particularly in the early stages of the house-hunting process. Rather than alienate or turn away potential buyers, you should keep in mind that first-time buyers, in particular, will probably be unfamiliar with real estate protocol. They may be "lender shy" only because the process feels like too much commitment too soon. Assure them that prequalification doesn't obligate them in any way to purchase or bind them to a lender.

If prospects refuse to be prequalified, you can give them a ballpark figure of how much they'll need to make in order to afford a particular price range.

A few simple leading questions can help you assess a "lender shy" buyer's psychological and financial capacity to buy.

>   1. *How soon do you want (or have) to buy?*

>   2. *How much of your savings have you designated for a down payment?*

>   3. *If I show you something you like, are you in a position to make an independent decision today?*

>   4. *Do you own your own home? If so, do you have to use the equity from your present house in order to buy another home?*

If the buyer owns, but doesn't have to sell first, you can respond with, "Mr. and Mrs. Prospect, I'm glad you don't have to sell first, but, because we're in a sellers' market (if this is currently the case), the house may sell higher today than it will next month. Right now, we have lots of clients who are looking to buy, so I'm confident we can sell your home rapidly."

If the answer is no, ask, "Why are you buying?" Determine how much desire the buyer has to purchase. Then, point out all the advantages of home ownership. "How long have you been looking?" is a question that helps to ascertain the strength of desire to buy. A buyer who's willing to come to your office, for example, indicates a strong desire.

Note that each of these questions is carefully worded to obtain important information without appearing to pry into buyers' private lives. To ask how much they've saved for a down payment may really be asking them to reveal their total savings. Be diplomatic. When asked how much money they have for a down payment, most people hesitate before giving a direct (and therefore candid) answer. If the question is asked in a sincere manner and a somewhat matter-of-fact tone of voice, as if the information is routine, the earnest buyer is more likely to answer honestly. Once you've determined a buyer's sincerity and basic financial potential for homeownership, see Chapter 8 for details concerning prequalifying.

Statistics reveal that buying a house is the largest single purchase most people will make in their lifetime, and that nearly all of their savings will be used in the initial purchase.

a. Credit Rules of Thumb (The Three C's)

Qualifying buyers must include the evaluation of their credit by the institutional lender who will be asked to make a loan commitment. Chapter 8 covers what lenders look for before they commit themselves to a long-term loan. The willingness of creditors to lend money against later payments is based upon the so-called three C's of Credit—Character, Capacity, and Capital.

1. **Character** – means how a person has handled past debt obligations.

2. **Capacity** – means how much debt a borrower can comfortably handle.

3. **Capital** – means current available assets of the borrower.

b. Types of Buyers

Seven basic types of buyers have been identified that you should recognize and deal with accordingly.

1. **The Selfish buyer** wants a special deal—better than anyone else's.

2. **The Friendly buyer** is optimistic, energetic, will give you his name right away and will ask for yours, and is excited and enthusiastic about every property you show. It can, however, be difficult to pin this buyer down on any one property.

3. **The Worrier** is pessimistic and concerned about numerous problems. This buyer is afraid he or she won't like the neighbors, is concerned that prices will come down, or fears that a bar will be erected next door. Such buyers need constant reassurance.

4. **The Shy type** is often artistic or intellectual and may take a while to start talking. He or she is a good listener, but can be easily overpowered. Most particularly, don't get too personal. Be somewhat standoffish with this type.

5. **The Belligerent type** must save face at all costs. These types need to win every argument; in fact, don't argue with these buyers at all—if you win the argument, you risk losing them.

6. **The Detail-Minded type** is often an engineer, lawyer, or accountant. These people usually expect to have their questions answered specifically. If you don't know an answer, don't approximate. Assure them you'll find out the answer and get back to them—then do it. Make liberal use of charts and grafts.

7. **The Highly Controlled** buyer loves tradition, lives by a strict code of rules, will not deviate, and likes nothing new. Treat this type conservatively and avoid getting personal. Assure them of the stability and respectability of the neighborhood, school districts, and your firm.

4. The Sales Kit

As a salesperson who has mastered the subject of human nature, and understand needs and motivation, you cannot be truly effective without a good sales kit. This is simply an inventory of items, or aids, that you may need in your daily real

estate related activities. With them you should be able to handle both the expected and the unexpected.

You should keep a briefcase in your mobile office (your car), containing all of those items that may have to be used in listing, selling, and prospecting activities. The list that follows can be added to, depending upon your own personality and special requirements.

In short, any items you may need away from the office ought to be included in your attaché case or vehicle. Use the sales kit, especially the kit book, subtly to direct the prospect's attention to your services. Don't use your sales kit to lecture or argue; the pictures and references will speak for themselves. Keep it current and present your material in a persuasive way, adjusting it to the personality, intelligence, and needs of the client.

The Following are Sales Kit Suggestions:

1. Cell phone and charger.
2. Notebook computer.
3. Portable printer.
4. Kit book—a loose-leaf binder you show the buyer about your firm, the sales associates, marketing methods, photos of sold properties, list of properties sold by you and your company, letters of recommendation from satisfied clients, advertising examples, publicity items, etc.

You should also include a résumé or personal bio sheet in your kit book.

5. Market Analysis software or forms (these are now almost exclusively done online).
6. Measuring tape.
7. Packet of forms (including WinForms® which can be downloaded from your notebook computer).
8. Multiple listing sheets.
9. Buyers Confidential Financial Status forms and Prequalification letter from lender.
10. Purchase Contract/Deposit Receipt forms.
11. Promissory note deposit pads.
12. Escrow closing worksheets for computing seller's and buyer's net closing costs.

(continued)

13. Schedules of title insurance fees, escrow costs, documentary transfer tax, and recording charges.

14. Business cards and promotional literature.

15. Polaroid camera and film or digital camera.

16. Loan amortization schedule.

17. Flashlight.

18. Pen, pencil, scratch pads, and clipboard.

19. Appointment book or PDA.

20. Signs and riders, and the necessary tools for securing the signs on the property, including hammer, nuts and bolts, screwdriver, wrench and pliers. (Or the business card of the company you hire to put up and maintain your signs!)

21. Lock boxes and keys.

22. Doorknob notices. These notices have a variety of uses. One might say "Sorry I missed you. Please call me for some valuable information."

Warning: doorknob notices can also alert burglars that the property is unoccupied when the notices remain on the property for any length of time.

23. Street maps and a Thomas Bros. Guide.

24. School bus and general bus routes.

25. Utility company addresses and rates.

26. Expense records.

Travel expenses cannot be deducted for driving between home and office (unless you preview a home on the way). Expenses begin where you meet your buyer/seller.

27. Promotional giveaways that advertise the broker, such as pot holders, rulers and yardsticks, telephone attachments, key rings, calendars, welcome mats, pens, mouse pads, etc.

5. Planning the Showing

Observe the following three steps before showing properties:

1. Plan the most effective approach;

2. Plan the showing (i.e., in what order you will expose the features of each property); and

3. Plan which advantages to emphasize. "Sell the sizzle, not the steak" means selling the benefits, not the house. It's not uncommon to hear a high producer claim he or she "sold a buyer the swimming pool, and threw in the house to boot."

Often prospects, worn out from looking at so many properties, appear to be incapable of making decisions. There is, in fact, a certain amount of inborn sales resistance in all of us. It's up to you to help them relax. Convince them that you really care for them, that you're concerned about their needs, and that you regard their concerns as important. Assure them that they're under no pressure and that "cold feet" are normal.

Avoid overwhelming your prospects by showing them too many properties at once, which can lead to sensory overload.

a. Planning the Approach (The Buyer Comment Sheet)

You should select three or four properties—rarely visit more at one time—to show a client. Visit each property first, make an appointment with the owners to show, and map out the most effective route. This means drawing a tour or downloading a map of the neighborhood. Mark parks, schools, convenient shopping, and points of interest. Generate the same amount of enthusiasm for the area (more house for the money or less money for the house) as the prospects had for the house they called about from the ad. (See Buyer Comment Sheet, **Figure 5-5**.)

b. Planning the Actual Showing

Know in advance what you want to emphasize about a property. If you're planning to save the best for last, map out the route accordingly. While some agents choose to drive into the driveway to give the prospects the feeling of "arriving home," others choose to pull up on the opposite side of the street to show them the "curb appeal." If the potential buyers like the looks of the house, it's appropriate for you to walk up to the front entry first and greet the owners. On the other hand, if a prospect declines to see the inside of a house based on the impression he or she gets from the exterior of the property, drive away, and use your mobile phone to call the owners and notify them that you will not be stopping by after all.

Figure 5-5

Buyer Comment Sheet

Barbara Buyer   # 1
2760 E Hillside Dr,

List Price:	**$ 898,000**		Poor (1)	Average (2)	Good (3)	Excellent (4)

Bedrooms: 5   Baths: 4.00   Showing Appeal: ☐   ☐   ☐   ☐

Sq. Feet: 3,879   Lot Size: 25155   Overall Condition: ☐   ☐   ☐   ☐

COMMENTS: _____

_____

_____

Elementary School: _____   **Junior High:** _____

High School: _____   **College:** _____

Barbara Buyer   # 2
1533 S Fairway Knolls Rd,

List Price:	**$ 849,000**		Poor (1)	Average (2)	Good (3)	Excellent (4)

Bedrooms: 5   Baths: 3.75   Showing Appeal: ☐   ☐   ☐   ☐

Sq. Feet: 3,800   Lot Size: 18891   Overall Condition: ☐   ☐   ☐   ☐

COMMENTS: _____

_____

_____

Elementary School: _____   **Junior High:** _____

High School: _____   **College:** _____

Barbara Buyer   # 3
3013 E Hillside Dr,

List Price:	**$ 699,888**		Poor (1)	Average (2)	Good (3)	Excellent (4)

Bedrooms: 4   Baths: 3.00   Showing Appeal: ☐   ☐   ☐   ☐

Sq. Feet: 2,844   Lot Size: 40218   Overall Condition: ☐   ☐   ☐   ☐

COMMENTS: _____

_____

_____

Elementary School: _____   **Junior High:** _____

High School: _____   **College:** _____

Information deemed to be reliable although not guaranteed.

If you do show a property, it's best to ask the sellers not to be present.

Spare the homeowner's feelings. If a buyer decides not to look inside a house based on its outside appearance, tell the seller that your clients have "chosen to go another direction" and assure them you'll soon call with other interested buyers.

6. The Showing

Once you've determined a client's needs and desires, you'll be better informed as to what features of a property you emphasize. Very few homes will completely fulfill a buyer's wish list of features, so it's important to draw attention to those elements that really do appeal to their tastes. (In Chapter 2, we discussed "staging" open houses; the same holds true here.) If the kitchen is dark or outdated, draw your client's attention back to the living room with the attractive fireplace. If it's winter, make sure to light a warm, inviting fire; if it's summer, light candles in the fireplace to give the impression of a fire, warm and glowing without the heat.

If your homeowner doesn't own one, you should consider investing in an inexpensive wrought iron candle holder made specifically for fireplaces. They hold several fat candles and, when lit, give the appearance of a comforting fire in the hearth without the heat or the mess.

Find the most appealing room in the house to make your strongest pitch for the sale. Different buyers will have different tastes, so pay attention to the signals they send out. A couple with a child, for example, will no doubt find consider a large den with built-in cabinets for storage more important than a formal living room. Sensitivity to your buyers' preferences reassures them that you're invested in their best interests and not just in trying to earn a commission.

It's imperative that you stay with the buyers while they tour the house, even if they ask for privacy. It's one thing to give them space and opportunity for private conversation, it's another to open the homeowner to thievery or invasion of privacy. Don't sell the "soft market," implying that a seller will accept less than the listed price. Avoid the temptation to take advantage of a seller's anxiety to sell. Sell the virtues of the property itself, not the virtues of the price, unless, of course, the price is such a bargain that it shouldn't be passed up. Keep in mind that a savvy buyer will know that if a property is very underpriced, it probably would have sold the moment the listing appeared.

Don't rush buyers. Give them as long as they need to inspect the property. Generally, the longer they stay, the greater their interest, particularly if they're "placing" their furniture in the room.

Assume that the prospects like the house. Ask them point blank if they do. If not, ask them what it is that they don't like. You can assure them that this is not, after all, your house, and that they can be candid with you, as you have other homes you can show them. On the other hand, if they say they like it, start to close!

a. Feng Shui

We have been stressing throughout this book the importance of knowing your clients. As such, it's important to acknowledge that California has a large Asian population; and is continuing to experience a strong influx from this growing cultural group. If you have clients from China, Korea, Vietnam, or Japan, it's likely you will encounter some who adhere to Feng Shui.

Feng Shui (pronounced "Fung Shway") means "wind and water" and its main purpose is to align an environment so as to live in harmony and balance with nature.

The proper siting of a building on the property, its architectural design, and its interior layout are all influenced by a balance between the dark, female, and passive "yin" and the light, male, and active "yang." The ideal environment balances both yin and yang, which are expressed through five elements: wood, fire, earth, metal and water.

There are many nuances to Feng Shui, but in terms of real estate, negatives and positives are often no different from any other "desirable" or "undesirable" features in a home. For example, a busy street, unless controlled by landscape, is a negative in any homebuyer's language. Furniture placement that prevents a door from opening or closing properly, or a table in the midst of a natural walkway is considered a negative factor, as it interrupts the "flow" of a house. In Feng Shui, the flow that's interrupted is called "ch'i."

Ch'i is the "breath," or "life force" of Feng Shui.

It is also important to remember that not all Asians practice Feng Shui, and to assume that they do may offend this growing group of buyers and sellers, resulting in lost opportunities. Also, many non-Asians in the U.S. (particularly in California) are adhering to a reformed version of Feng Shui, and builders, contractors and interior designers are paying more and more attention to the demands of these clients from the earliest stages of development.

1. Preferred Feng Shui Factors

1. Houses with the front door facing south.

2. Higher elevation, rather than valleys.

3. A property backed on the north by a mountain or hills.

4. A back yard slightly larger than the front yard.

5. House centered on the lot.

6. Healthy trees, birds, fish and fishponds.

7. Mirrors (except in bedrooms), crystals, interior screens, and hanging chimes.

8. Wooden, double-solid door entrances (that are not directly lined up with rear doors or windows).

9. Side or back facing garages.

10. Fish tanks.

11. Dining room close to the kitchen. The kitchen should be well lit with the cooking area not too close to the sink, preferably located in the south of the house, but not the southwest.

12. Five, eight, and nine are lucky numbers.

13. Red implies happiness and warmth. Gold and yellow represent wealth and longevity. Green represents tranquility. Blue is not recommended with white, while black and red is considered a lucky combination.

2. Negative Feng Shui Factors

1. Stagnant water.

2. One-way streets flowing away from the house.

3. Houses at the end of a cul-de-sac street or at a T-intersection.

4. A death in the house.

5. Proximity to a cemetery or garbage dumps.

6. Large tree or pole blocking the front door.

7. Straight pathway to front door.

8. West facing windows, or windows facing onto a busy street.

9. Staircase facing the front door, or starting right by the master bedroom.

10. Heavy beams.

11. Harsh colors.

12. Two or three doors in a row or bedroom doors should not be facing each other.

13. Children's bedroom over a garage.

14. Sharp angle of furniture pointing towards doors.

Demonstrating a tactful knowledge of Feng Shui (without a direct inquiry as to your client's belief system) will make you appear more knowledgeable and show that you have given another community the respect of researching some of their needs and preferences. As always, be sensitive to your particular client and act accordingly. For a deeper understanding, you may want to attend some seminars and read books on this important subject.

7. The Close

CLOSING means getting the offer to buy. The close should never be a sudden transition, as if it were a separate and distinct entity apart from the entire selling process. If the rest of the presentation has been persuasive and complete (all the necessary points and arguments included), the close should take place calmly and naturally. Don't pressure the prospect into signing, or problems may arise later, even before escrow opens.

Close the sale politely, but firmly.

VI. The Sale

"A sale is made in the presentation—it's only lost in the close."

There are a number of closing questions you can ask to confirm that the buyers are "sold"; for example, "How do you want to take title?" Your best ammunition, of course, are the prospects' past remarks. If they ask how soon they can move in, start writing the offer. Answering the question with a question can also be effective. "Will the sellers carry back a second?" can be answered with, "How much of a second would you like for the seller to take back?" Or state in a positive tone, as you begin to fill in the purchase offer, "Let's submit an offer right now, Mr. and Mrs. Buyer, to find out just how receptive the sellers are to helping finance the transaction."

Sometimes you need to be direct and actually ask your client to buy.

Never allow prospects access to personal or valuable property. Don't allow children to enter the property unless accompanied by both you and the parents. Insist that children stay with their parents—never leave them unattended.

Some prospects, such as the shy or highly controlled types, won't buy unless asked. So ask them to buy! If they say no, sell them again, reviewing those things that were apparently not clear the first time. If they express concern that the home may not meet their needs, or what they really want is beyond their ability to pay, remind them that half a loaf of bread is better than none. In other words, "If you wait 'til you can afford a $400,000 house, you lose the benefits and pleasures of living in a $350,000 house in the meantime. Besides, this house will probably increase in value while you're living in it. Think of it as an investment that will eventually help you afford the house of your dreams."

A. CLOSING TECHNIQUES

How many times do you take "no" for an answer before accepting it as a final rejection? There is no absolute rule, but clearly, you should use as many different types of persuasion as you can muster. Always focus attention on the buyers' needs and incorporate them in the closing argument. For every argument your buyer has against buying a property, you need to have a better one in favor of buying.

Either you convince the prospects to buy or the prospects convince you they're not going to buy.

1. Want Technique

The closing question (or "want" technique) can be used as a closer: "Will the sellers include the patio furniture (pool equipment, appliances, etc.)?" Your response should also be in the form of a question: "Would you like them to include the furniture?" Questions like this from buyers indicate that they may be ready to buy, and narrowing down what fixtures come with a property assumes an intent to buy.

2. Assumptive Technique

A second way to close is the assumed consent or order-blank close. You're assuming that the prospects will buy, and you begin to fill in the purchase offer by asking for information on minor points: "What is your correct address (phone number, full name, etc.)?" After completing the form, simply turn it around and say, "Would you approve this for me, please?" A word of caution though: this technique may seem too pushy to some clients. You should see some indication of a prospect's intent to buy before starting this technique.

3. Alternative of Choice Technique

A third close technique is the "alternative of choice." "Which do you prefer, to go conventional or FHA?" A variation, the "final alternative" approach, offers the prospect a major and a minor alternate choice: "Do you want to meet the seller's listing price or should we make a lower offer first?"

4. Narrative Technique

A fourth close is the "third-party story." You tell a story about how one of your clients lost an opportunity because of delay. "The value of the house continued to rise while they 'shopped around,' and someone else snatched it up. They wound up spending $30,000 more for a nearly identical house in that neighborhood six months later." This tactic works particularly well with the Worrier and the Selfish Buyer.

5. Opportunity Lost Technique

A fifth close, "don't miss the opportunity" or "buy before someone else" argument is effective with the Bargain Hunter. When the seller has just reduced the price, let the prospect know. Make him or her aware that no one else knows yet, but tomorrow everyone will, and it'll sell fast: "Let's place your bid in now, before everybody else does!" By not taking action now, the buyer, in effect, makes it possible for someone else to buy the property at the reduced price.

6. Minimize the Difference Technique

A sixth close is the "dollar difference" argument. Where price is a factor, the difference between, say, a $350,000 and $370,000 trust deed is only $131 more a month at seven percent interest on the average loan: "You don't want to lose this home over less than $131, do you?"

7. Negative-Yes Technique

"Negative-yes" is the seventh close: "Just to clarify my thinking, what is it that you object to? Is it the size, the location, the price?" Each time that he or she answers no, you have a yes answer. In effect, the prospects are actually negating their own objections.

8. Yes-But Technique

The eighth close, the "yes-but" technique, has been around for a long time. When you hear an objection, you turn it around, so that what started as a negative argument is converted into a positive one, i.e., the decision to buy. Examples: "The property is too close to the freeway." "I agree with that, Mr. and Mrs. Prospect, but have you considered how much less city travel will be required, and the time saved in getting to work?" A variation of this approach involves the empathetic remark, "I know how you feel, Mr. and Mrs. Prospect, others have expressed the same sentiments, and now those same buyers are finding that they underestimated the benefits of living nearer to where they work."

9. Yes and No Itemizing Technique

Ben Franklin's "yes and no" technique is the ninth close. It works well with the undecided, particularly the Detail-Minded and the Worrier. Give your prospects

a pen and paper and ask them to draw two columns, one headed yes, and the other no. Have them list all the pros in the first column and the arguments against buying (cons) in the second. The buyers weigh the pros and cons and make an intelligent decision based on the outcome. Gently, but firmly, guide them along in weighing the consequences, letting them know you support their decision, particularly if it is to purchase!

10. Call-Back Technique

A tenth, but by no means last method, is the call back. When you've finished at least one session, return later to your prospect with the call-back: "I'm very sorry, but the last time I was here I failed to tell you something that I believe you'll find interesting and valuable." Then give the buyer the whole presentation again: "As you'll recall..." and add an important point or two.

There is no limit to ingenuity. The creative salesperson establishes a program of self-analysis and self-improvement. Every day, as an imaginative salesperson, you should try to learn new selling points, set up a work pattern for more efficiently covering current clients, and for uncovering new ones. You should also attend seminars and read books on listings, selling, and other real estate topics, so as to be constantly aware of new developments in this dynamic field.

B. OVERRIDING OBJECTIONS

We've discussed overriding objections over the telephone in order to get a name and/or appointment. But you can expect to encounter many objections from buyers in day-to-day selling activities as well. Some of the more common ones are listed below along with some suggested responses. Handle objections judiciously. You may represent the seller in a typical transaction, but you also have a position of trust with the buyer and the public. Overselling can be perilous, leading to problems with a reluctant buyer. Don't allow your client to become a victim of a high-pressure sales campaign.

---

1. I'll go in my car.

Answer #1. "Don't you think you would have a better opportunity to look the neighborhood and community over if I drove? Besides, it is easier than me giving you directions."

Answer #2. "Why not come with me? It is too easy to get lost if we go in two cars."

2. My! What a dirty house!

Answer #1. "Yes, but look at the price! You can decorate to your own tastes and save money!"

---

3. The bedrooms are too small; it doesn't have central air, etc.

Answer #1. "Homes that are priced at this level naturally don't have the added features of more expensive homes, but you should think of this as your starter house. Investing in this property now will help you buy your dream home later."

Answer # 2. Point out how clever furniture arrangements will overcome room size, or the availability of inexpensive window air conditioners for houses without central air.

4. The house is priced too high.

Answer #1. "I can see why it would appear that way, but it is under the market, as you can see by the neighborhood comps. Everything today seems high. Compare your income today against one or two years ago."

Answer #2. "I understand how you feel. That's why we make our offers subject to obtaining the appraisal at sales price."

5. I can make the payments now, but maybe not later.

Answer #1. "Under this plan of financing, your payments will automatically drop in a few short years. Or you can always sell it and recover. Remember, you can't sell or borrow money on those rent receipts."

Answer #2. "Whether you rent or own, you can't escape that obligation, even if you do get into a stretch of hard times or lose your job. While you're employed, you should insure yourself against such an eventuality by saving money and buying a home now."

6. I should have a three-bedroom.

Answer #1. "This is an excellent buy for a two-bedroom. With a small expenditure at your own convenience, you could add another bedroom, and the total outlay for the house would be much less than any similar three-bedroom home in this locality."

Answer #2. "You can use the equity you build up from this house to eventually buy that three-bedroom home."

7. I don't like tract houses.

Answer #1. "Unfortunately, custom built homes are more expensive and the neighborhoods can be more unstable than those in established tracts."

Answer #2. "You're much better off buying a tract home today as practically all new construction is FHA-inspected, and must pass rigid inspections."

8. The payments are too high.

Answer #1. "Lenders guidelines say that 35% of your income is an appropriate amount to earmark for house payments. Then too, interest costs and property taxes are deductible each year from your income tax return."

Answer #2. "Let's compare payments on a trust deed to rent payments."

9. I'll look around.

Answer #1. "That's fine, but why not let me show you around and we'll both look. If you see something you like, it's possible that I can get it for you or something similar to it. I'd appreciate helping you."

Answer #2. "That's certainly one thing to do if you haven't already done so. By the way, how long have you been looking around? You know our company has been 'looking around for values' for many years, I'm sure we can be of some assistance."

10. I have another house in mind.

Answer #1. "That's fine. What is it like (size, location, cost, etc.)? It's possible that I haven't shown you what you want. What do you say we both go look at it?"

Answer #2. "Terrific! Once I've seen it, I'll have a much better idea of what it is that really appeals to you. Since you're still looking, I assume something about it has made you hesitate. Tell me what misgivings you have about the property, and maybe I can show you another place that fits your likes and addresses your needs."

11. I'll make a less than full price offer.

Answer #1. "I'd be glad to structure your offer on reasonable terms, but when we listed this house we listed it at a fair price. But, if we can get it for you for less, we'll do our best."

Answer #2. "If it's too low, I'm afraid it may not be acceptable. Some sellers may get insulted by low offers, assume you're not serious about buying, and refuse to counter offer."

12. We want to think it over.

Answer #1. "We all know people who passed up an opportunity to buy a good piece of real estate because they hesitated too long. Right now is the time to make decisions as far as property is concerned."

Answer #2. "Obviously you wouldn't need to think it over unless you were interested. Let me show you other properties, since you're not sold on this one."

Answer #3. "While we're still together and the facts are fresh in your mind, why not take a moment to think it over now? You're in a better position to judge the merits and benefits of the deal now than you will be even one hour from now. What haven't I made clear? How can I help you make this decision?"

As prospects will undoubtedly stop at other open houses, give them extra business cards. Remind them to notify the open house agent that they are working with you.

VII. CHAPTER SUMMARY

For most buyers, buying a home is the most important financial decision they will ever make—and it can be the biggest asset over time as well. Most property owners move on an average of every six to eight years.

It's important to know where school district lines are drawn—a slight miscalculation can result in a lost sale, or a lawsuit.

Additions must be up to current codes, or insurance companies may deny full coverage in the event of a mishap, like a fire. Get a professional inspection (as a condition of the contract) on all real estate purchases. This is usually paid for by the buyer, with a copy going to the seller. The seller can make all of the repairs requested by the buyer, some of them, or none of them. Until the requested repairs are done, the offer can be rescinded, with the deposit returned to the buyers.

Functional obsolescence is the loss of value due to adverse factors WITHIN a structure that affect the marketability of the property, like a single-car garage. Economic or social obsolescence is any loss of value due to conditions OUTSIDE of the property, and are considered "incurable."

Some of the advantages of homeownership include possible appreciation, tax benefits, equity buildup, and cash flow. There is no capital gains tax ($250,000 for singles and $500,000 for married) if the house sold is a principal residence and the sellers have lived there for a minimum of two years during the last five years prior to sale.

When budgeting for a home, buyers housing payments should not exceed 25% to 30% of their gross monthly income. When personal debt is included with the house payment, the max should be no more than 33% to 38%. Try to get potential buyers prequalified whenever possible.

Selling is communicating, and the most effective way to communicate is through direct contact, or face-to-face. If that's not possible, the next best thing is by telephone. Listening is an important skill, both in person and on the phone. Keep track of all incoming calls with an incoming call register or log book. Use the phone to make appointments, and get that face-to-face contact.

Letters, the least effective form of communication, should be used to precondition a customer—prior to a phone call or meeting. When writing a letter, use the advertising technique of AIDA—attention, interest, desire and action. Consider sending out postcards (with a photo) instead of letters, as they are less expensive and get read more often.

When asked about a listing on the phone, it's best to find out as much about a caller as possible. Find out what he or she is looking for, what they can afford, what school district they prefer, etc. Answer questions honestly, but strive to get an appointment to show a property whenever possible. Don't forget to inform a caller that your firm can look up information on other agents' listings—saving them the time and legwork. Using a switch sheet can steer a customer to other, similar properties.

An office caravan is a weekly outing where all available salespeople preview all the newest brokerage listings and other company listings. After caravaning, agents fill out an agent comment sheet describing and rating those properties.

Buyer's needs include four categories: the need for trust, information, advice, and financing.

Before buying a home, they must have financial ability, desire, and intent to buy.

Pre-qualifying a client is coordinating a buyer's needs with their actual financial capacity. Lenders look for the "C's" of credit: character, capacity, and capital.

Every salesperson should have a sales kit, including the listing, selling, and prospecting tools needed in real estate. A few of the items included in the kit should be a cell phone, a notebook or handheld computer, market analysis software or forms, purchase contract or deposit receipt forms, and more.

Don't overwhelm buyers by showing them too many properties at once. Help them to keep track of what they've seen with a buyer comment sheet. It's best to ask the owners not to be present during a showing. Feng shui is just one way to make sure your clients see a home to its best advantage. Feng shui is the aligning of the environment so as to live in harmony and balance with nature. Many buyers of all nationalities adhere to these theories.

In the case of showing homes, closing means getting the offer to buy. There are many techniques used to close the deal, all of which involve finessing a client towards making that final decision to buy. Some techniques are more aggressive than others; it's up to you to determine the best route to take when nudging a client toward such a decision. This is true for overcoming their objections as well. Your integrity and professionalism during "the close" will determine whether you get the sale.

VIII. KEY TERMS

Agent's Comment Sheet
AIDA
Buyer Comment Sheet
Capacity
Capital
Character
Closing
Counseling
Direct Contact Communication
Economic Obsolescence
Feng Shui
Floortime
Functional Obsolescence
Incoming Call Register
Office Caravan
One-Way Communication
Pre-Approach
Prequalifying
Sales Kit
Selling Techniques
Switch Sheet
Two-Way Communication

IX. CHAPTER 5 QUIZ

1. The loss of value due to conditions outside of the property is considered:
    a. functional obsolescence and curable.
    b. economic obsolescence and incurable.
    c. economic obsolescence and curable.
    d. none of the above.

2. The most effective communication usually occurs:
    a. by way of telephone calls.
    b. through letters.
    c. face-to-face.
    d. none of the above.

3. When selling an older home, it's important to remember that disclosure must be made to the buyers of any repairs made within the last:
    a. three years.
    b. five years.
    c. ten years.
    d. fifteen years.

4. Which of the following would be considered a disadvantage of owning a home?
    a. Appreciation
    b. Upkeep and maintenance
    c. Equity buildup
    d. All of the above

5. The time assigned to a salesperson to answer the company telephones is referred to as:
    a. facetime.
    b. phonetime.
    c. floortime.
    d. downtime.

6. A quick reference list of alternative listings within a similar price range, school district, size, etc., is called a(n):
    a. switch sheet.
    b. cheat sheet.
    c. incoming call register.
    d. all of the above.

7. An office caravan consists of:
    a. a group of MLS cooperating brokers who visit each others offices weekly.
    b. a weekly outing by office salespersons to preview new brokerage listings.
    c. a weekly visit to the car wash by all brokerage personnel.
    d. a brokerage that operates out of a mobile home rather than a traditional office.

8. The process of rectifying buyers' needs and desires with the reality of their financial capacity is called:
    a. qualifying buyers.
    b. counseling buyers.
    c. both a and b.
    d. neither a nor b.

9. Which of the following in NOT one of the three C's of credit?
    a. Character
    b. Capacity
    c. Capital
    d. Citizenship

10. The term "feng shui" literally means:
    a. for sale.
    b. air and earth.
    c. wind and water.
    d. none of the above.

ANSWERS: 1. b; 2. c; 3. b; 4. b; 5. c; 6. a; 7. b; 8. c; 9. d; 10. c

CHAPTER 6
The Purchase Offer
How to Fill Out the Residential Purchase Contract

I. Overview of the Purchase Contract

A. WHY PURCHASE CONTRACTS ARE USED

Most transactions for the purchase and sale of real estate begin with a written contract between the buyer and seller. An initial question might be, "Why bother with writing up a long contract and getting everyone to sign it?" Why not have the buyers give the sellers the money and the sellers give the buyers the deed? The sellers could then move out and the buyers could move in, the sale would be accomplished and everyone would be happy. After all, when you buy most other things, such as groceries or even furniture, you generally just pay cash, write a check, or give the seller your credit card, the merchandise is given to you, and you leave.

In a real estate transaction, however, questions relating to financing, possession, the condition of title, the possibility that persons other than the seller might have liens or other interests in the property, and arrangements for conveying possession and title must be addressed.

In a typical purchase, buyers don't have the available cash to buy the house. They must either make arrangements to borrow the money (from a bank or other lender)

CHAPTER 6 OUTLINE

I. OVERVIEW OF THE PURCHASE CONTRACT (p. 205)
   A. Why Purchase Contracts are Used (p. 205)

II. EVALUATION AND ANALYSIS OF THE PURCHASE CONTRACT (p. 208)
   A. Interpretation of the Form (p. 217)
   B. Filling Out the Form—A Breakdown (p. 217)
      1. Offer (p. 219)
      2. Financing (p. 219)
      3. Closing and Occupancy (p. 224)
      4. Allocation of Costs (p. 226)
      5. Statutory Disclosures (Including Lead-Based Paint Hazard Disclosures) and Cancellation Rights (p. 228)
      6. Condominium/Planned Unit Development Disclosures (p. 230)
      7. Conditions Affecting Property (p. 231)
      8. Items Included and Excluded (p. 232)
      9. Buyer's Investigation of Property and Matters Affecting Property (p. 232)
     10. Repairs (p. 233)
     11. Buyer Indemnity and Seller Protection for Entry Upon Property (p. 233)
     12. Title and Vesting (p. 234)
     13. Sale of Buyer's Property (p. 234)
     14. Time Periods; Waiver of Contingencies; Cancellation Rights (p. 235)
     15. Final Verification of Condition (p. 237)
     16. Liquidated Damages (p. 238)
     17. Dispute Resolution (p. 238)
     18. Prorations of Property Taxes and Other Items (p. 240)
     19. Withholding Taxes (p. 240)
     20. Multiple Listing Agreement (p. 241)
     21. Equal Housing Opportunity (p. 241)
     22. Attorney Fees (p. 241)
     23. Selection of Service Provider (p. 241)
     24. Time of Essence; Entire Contract; Changes (p. 242)
     25. Other Terms and Conditions (p. 242)
     26. Definitions (p. 243)
     27. Agency (p. 244)
     28. Joint Escrow Instructions (p. 245)
     29. Broker Compensation from Buyer (p. 246)
     30. Terms and Conditions of Offer (p. 246)
     31. Expiration of Offer (p. 247)
     32. Broker Compensation from Seller (p. 247)
     33. Acceptance of Offer (p. 248)

III. CHAPTER SUMMARY (p. 250)
IV. KEY TERMS (p. 251)
V. CHAPTER 6 QUIZ (p. 252)

or convince the seller to finance the transaction through some type of delayed payment plan. If the buyers intend to borrow the money from an outside source, time will be required to obtain lender's approval. This process, which may involve an appraisal and inspection of the property, a credit report on the borrowers, confirmation of the borrower's assets and employment information, and obtaining mortgage insurance can easily be a matter of weeks, not days. The buyers need some way to keep the sellers obligated to sell on the agreed terms during the time it takes them to arrange the financing. The buyers don't want to borrow the money unless they're sure they'll be able to buy the house when they get the loan.

Also, in most cases, the buyers don't want to be forced to buy the house (or lose their down payment or other deposit) if they're unable to arrange the type of financing they want. This means that there must be some sort of agreement between the buyers and the sellers which releases the buyers from an obligation to buy and allows them a refund of their deposit if they cannot obtain the intended financing after a good faith effort.

Another concern for the buyers is that, at the time they decide to buy the house, they usually don't know whether the seller really owns it or not. Questions regarding title to land are anything but simple. Even if the seller has legal title to the property, there may be encumbrances on the property (such as easements across it which interfere with the buyer's use or judgment, tax, or other liens against the property). This particular aspect of the transaction is handled in most states in one of two ways: an abstract of title or a title insurance policy.

In California, it is customary to arrange to have a title insurance company conduct a title search, prepare a preliminary report, and issue a policy of title insurance.

A real estate transaction is usually a pretty complicated affair in addition to the fact that, for most people, a large amount of money is involved. Financing must be arranged, title searched, existing liens (such as the seller's mortgage or assessments for local improvements) must be paid off or an agreement reached for the buyer to assume them, fire insurance must be obtained, and there are often a number of other matters which must be handled prior to the time the buyer pays the price and the seller delivers title and possession. During the time that both parties are performing their respective tasks, they both want to keep the other side obligated to perform. The buyer doesn't want to spend several hundred dollars in appraisal, credit report, and other financing-related fees, only to find out that the seller no longer wants to sell the house. The seller doesn't want to take the house off the market, and spend several hundred dollars to search title or provide a title insurance policy, only to find out the buyer no longer wants to buy the house.

It is, therefore, mutually advantageous that an enforceable contract to buy and sell the property be entered. These agreements are commonly known by a number of names in different states, such as "purchase and sale agreement," "earnest money agreement," "deposit receipt," "binder," and others. In California, "deposit receipt" has been the most widely used term, although "purchase contract" is gaining popularity among real estate professionals.

The most common real estate purchase contract used in California is the CAR form entitled "California Residential Purchase Agreement and Joint Escrow Instructions."

Although many buyers and sellers are under the mistaken impression that these forms are merely non-binding preliminary agreements, most forms make some indication that a binding contract is intended. With the CAR Purchase Agreement form, this information is located on page 8 (see **pages 216 and 248** of this chapter, "Confirmation of Acceptance").

II. Evaluation and Analysis of the Purchase Contract

Writing the offer is a vital step in the art of bringing the buyers and sellers together, and care should be taken to word it in simple but concise language.

The Department of Real Estate has often stated that the deposit receipt is the most important document in a real estate transaction; the broker's responsibilities in completing the purchase contract accurately and unambiguously cannot be overemphasized.

There is no required contract to use for this purpose, but most agreements for the purchase of real estate in California use some variation of the deposit receipt form, incorporating both the receipt for the consideration given the broker, and the terms of the offer. As mentioned earlier, CAR's **California Residential Purchase Agreement and Joint Escrow Instructions** (see **Figure 6-1**) is a practical and frequently used form. This form is used in most simple transactions, including the sale of single-family one-to-four unit residential dwellings.

What was called the "Deposit Receipt" is now usually referred to as the "Purchase Contract."

Figure 6-1

CALIFORNIA
ASSOCIATION
OF REALTORS®

CALIFORNIA
RESIDENTIAL PURCHASE AGREEMENT
AND JOINT ESCROW INSTRUCTIONS
For Use With Single Family Residential Property — Attached or Detached
(C.A.R. Form RPA-CA, Revised 10/02)

Date _JUNE 14, 2003_, at _Costa Mesa_, California.
1. **OFFER:**
   A. **THIS IS AN OFFER FROM** _Walter and Debbie Buyer_ ("Buyer").
   B. **THE REAL PROPERTY TO BE ACQUIRED** is described as _264 Beach Lane_
   _____, Assessor's Parcel No. _____, situated in
   Costa Mesa, County of _Orange_, California, ("Property").
   C. **THE PURCHASE PRICE** offered is _Eight Hundred Thousand_ ___ no/100 ___
   _____ Dollars $ _800,000_.
   D. **CLOSE OF ESCROW** shall occur on _____ (date)(or X _90_ Days After Acceptance).
2. **FINANCE TERMS:** Obtaining the loans below **is a contingency** of this Agreement unless: (i) either 2K or 2L is checked below; or
   (ii) otherwise agreed in writing. Buyer shall act diligently and in good faith to obtain the designated loans. Obtaining deposit, down
   payment and closing costs **is not a contingency.** Buyer represents that funds will be good when deposited with Escrow Holder.
   A. **INITIAL DEPOSIT:** Buyer has given a deposit in the amount of ....$ _10,000_
   to the agent submitting the offer (or to ☐ _____), by personal check
   (or ☐ _____), made payable to _ABC Escrow_,
   which shall be held uncashed until Acceptance and then deposited within 3 business days after
   Acceptance (or ☐ _____), with
   Escrow Holder, (or ☐ into Broker's trust account).
   B. **INCREASED DEPOSIT:** Buyer shall deposit with Escrow Holder an increased deposit in the amount of ...$ _____
   within _____ **Days** After Acceptance, or ☐ _____.
   C. **FIRST LOAN IN THE AMOUNT OF** ....$ _640,000_
   (1) NEW First Deed of Trust in favor of lender, encumbering the Property, securing a note payable at
   maximum interest of _8_ % fixed rate, or _____ % initial adjustable rate with a maximum
   interest rate of _____%, balance due in _____ years, amortized over _30_ years. Buyer
   shall pay loan fees/points not to exceed _2_. (These terms apply whether the designated loan
   is conventional, FHA or VA.)
   (2) ☐ FHA ☐ VA: (The following terms only apply to the FHA or VA loan that is checked.)
   Seller shall pay _____% discount points. Seller shall pay other fees not allowed to be paid by
   Buyer, ☐ not to exceed $_____. Seller shall pay the cost of lender required Repairs
   (including those for wood destroying pest) not otherwise provided for in this Agreement, ☐ not to
   exceed $ _____. (Actual loan amount may increase if mortgage insurance premiums,
   funding fees or closing costs are financed.)
   D. **ADDITIONAL FINANCING TERMS:** ☐ Seller financing, (C.A.R. Form SFA); ☐ secondary financing, ...$ _____
   (C.A.R. Form PAA, paragraph 4A); ☐ assumed financing (C.A.R. Form PAA, paragraph 4B)
   _____
   _____
   E. **BALANCE OF PURCHASE PRICE** (not including costs of obtaining loans and other closing costs) in the amount of ...$ _150,000_
   to be deposited with Escrow Holder within sufficient time to close escrow.
   F. **PURCHASE PRICE (TOTAL):** ....$ _800,000_
   G. **LOAN APPLICATIONS:** Within 7 (or ☐ _____) **Days** After Acceptance, Buyer shall provide Seller a letter from lender or
   mortgage loan broker stating that, based on a review of Buyer's written application and credit report, Buyer is prequalified or
   preapproved for the NEW loan specified in 2C above.
   H. **VERIFICATION OF DOWN PAYMENT AND CLOSING COSTS:** Buyer (or Buyer's lender or loan broker pursuant to 2G) shall, within
   7 (or ☐ _____) **Days** After Acceptance, provide Seller written verification of Buyer's down payment and closing costs.
   I. **LOAN CONTINGENCY REMOVAL:** (i) Within 17 (or ☐ _____) **Days** After Acceptance, Buyer shall, as specified in paragraph
   14, remove the loan contingency or cancel this Agreement; **OR** (ii) (if checked) ☐ the loan contingency shall remain in effect
   until the designated loans are funded.
   J. **APPRAISAL CONTINGENCY AND REMOVAL:** This Agreement is (**OR**, if checked, ☐ is NOT) contingent upon the Property
   appraising at no less than the specified purchase price. Buyer shall, as specified in paragraph 14, remove the appraisal
   contingency or cancel this Agreement when the loan contingency is removed (or, if checked, ☐ within 17 (or ☐ _____) **Days**
   After Acceptance).
   K. ☐ **NO LOAN CONTINGENCY** (If checked): Obtaining any loan in paragraphs 2C, 2D or elsewhere in this Agreement is NOT
   a contingency of this Agreement. If Buyer does not obtain the loan and as a result Buyer does not purchase the Property, Seller
   may be entitled to Buyer's deposit or other legal remedies.
   L. ☐ **ALL CASH OFFER** (If checked): No loan is needed to purchase the Property. Buyer shall, within 7 (or ☐ _____) **Days** After Acceptance,
   provide Seller written verification of sufficient funds to close this transaction.
3. **CLOSING AND OCCUPANCY:**
   A. Buyer intends (or ☐ does not intend) to occupy the Property as Buyer's primary residence.
   B. **Seller-occupied or vacant property:** Occupancy shall be delivered to Buyer at _11_ AM/PM, X on the date of Close Of
   Escrow; ☐ on _____; or ☐ no later than _____ **Days** After Close Of Escrow. (C.A.R. Form PAA, paragraph 2.) If
   transfer of title and occupancy do not occur at the same time, Buyer and Seller are advised to: **(i)** enter into a written occupancy
   agreement; and **(ii)** consult with their insurance and legal advisors.

The copyright laws of the United States (Title 17 U.S. Code) forbid the unauthorized
reproduction of this form, or any portion thereof, by photocopy machine or any other
means, including facsimile or computerized formats. Copyright © 1991-2002,
CALIFORNIA ASSOCIATION OF REALTORS®, INC. ALL RIGHTS RESERVED.
RPA-CA REVISED 10/02 (PAGE 1 OF 8) Print Date

Buyer's Initials (_WB_)(_DB_)
Seller's Initials (_TA._)(_mp._)
Reviewed by _JR_ Date _6/14/03_

EQUAL HOUSING
OPPORTUNITY

CALIFORNIA RESIDENTIAL PURCHASE AGREEMENT (RPA-CA PAGE 1 OF 8)

---

*When writing an offer for your client, do not suggest how to take title; this is best
left to an attorney or an accountant. Have the check for earnest money deposit made
out to your company's trust account, as you do not know which escrow company
will be agreed upon. You can have it endorsed to the selected escrow company at a
later date (within 3 working days from acceptance). It is also a good idea to use a
blue ink when signing all documents which will easily differentiate the original from
the copy. Some lenders insist on having the original Purchase Agreement.*

C. **Tenant-occupied property: (i) Property shall be vacant** at least 5 (or ☐ _____) **Days** Prior to Close Of Escrow, unless otherwise agreed in writing. **Note to Seller: If you are unable to deliver Property vacant in accordance with rent control and other applicable Law, you may be in breach of this Agreement.**

  OR (ii) (if checked) ☐ **Tenant to remain in possession.** The attached addendum is incorporated into this Agreement (C.A.R. Form PAA, paragraph 3.);

  OR (iii) (if checked) ☐ **This Agreement is contingent** upon Buyer and Seller entering into a written agreement regarding occupancy of the Property within the time specified in paragraph 14. If no written agreement is reached within this time, either Buyer or Seller may cancel this Agreement in writing.

D. At Close Of Escrow, Seller assigns to Buyer any assignable warranty rights for items included in the sale and shall provide any available Copies of such warranties. Brokers cannot and will not determine the assignability of any warranties.

E. At Close Of Escrow, unless otherwise agreed in writing, Seller shall provide keys and/or means to operate all locks, mailboxes, security systems, alarms and garage door openers. If Property is a condominium or located in a common interest subdivision, Buyer may be required to pay a deposit to the Homeowners' Association ("HOA") to obtain keys to accessible HOA facilities.

4. **ALLOCATION OF COSTS (If checked):** Unless otherwise specified here, this paragraph only determines who is to pay for the report, inspection, test or service mentioned. If not specified here or elsewhere in this Agreement, the determination of who is to pay for any work recommended or identified by any such report, inspection, test or service shall be by the method specified in paragraph 14.

  A. **WOOD DESTROYING PEST INSPECTION:**
    (1) ☐ Buyer ☒ Seller shall pay for an inspection and report for wood destroying pests and organisms ("Report") which shall be prepared by _BUG-R-GONE_ , a registered structural pest control company. The Report shall cover the accessible areas of the main building and attached structures and, if checked: ☐ detached garages and carports, ☐ detached decks, ☐ the following other structures or areas _____. The Report shall not include roof coverings. If Property is a condominium or located in a common interest subdivision, the Report shall include only the separate interest and any exclusive-use areas being transferred and shall not include common areas, unless otherwise agreed. Water tests of shower pans on upper level units may not be performed without consent of the owners of property below the shower.

  OR (2) ☐ (If checked) The attached addendum (C.A.R. Form WPA) regarding wood destroying pest inspection and allocation of cost is incorporated into this Agreement.

  B. **OTHER INSPECTIONS AND REPORTS:**
    (1) ☐ Buyer ☐ Seller shall pay to have septic or private sewage disposal systems inspected _____.
    (2) ☐ Buyer ☐ Seller shall pay to have domestic wells tested for water potability and productivity _____.
    (3) ☐ Buyer ☐ Seller shall pay for a natural hazard zone disclosure report prepared by _____.
    (4) ☐ Buyer ☐ Seller shall pay for the following inspection or report _____.
    (5) ☐ Buyer ☐ Seller shall pay for the following inspection or report _____.

  C. **GOVERNMENT REQUIREMENTS AND RETROFIT:**
    (1) ☐ Buyer ☒ Seller shall pay for smoke detector installation and/or water heater bracing, if required by Law. Prior to Close Of Escrow, Seller shall provide Buyer a written statement of compliance in accordance with state and local Law, unless exempt.
    (2) ☐ Buyer ☐ Seller shall pay the cost of compliance with any other minimum mandatory government retrofit standards, inspections and reports if required as a condition of closing escrow under any Law. _____.

  D. **ESCROW AND TITLE:**
    (1) ☒ Buyer ☒ Seller shall pay escrow fee _50%/50%_
    Escrow Holder shall be _ABC Escrow_ .
    (2) ☒ Buyer ☐ Seller shall pay for **owner's** title insurance policy specified in paragraph 12 _____.
    Owner's title policy to be issued by _____.
    (Buyer shall pay for any title insurance policy insuring Buyer's **lender**, unless otherwise agreed in writing.)

  E. **OTHER COSTS:**
    (1) ☐ Buyer ☐ Seller shall pay County transfer tax or transfer fee _____.
    (2) ☐ Buyer ☐ Seller shall pay City transfer tax or transfer fee _____.
    (3) ☐ Buyer ☐ Seller shall pay HOA transfer fee _____.
    (4) ☐ Buyer ☐ Seller shall pay HOA document preparation fees _____.
    (5) ☐ Buyer ☐ Seller shall pay the cost, not to exceed $ _____, of a one-year home warranty plan, issued by _____ with the following optional coverage: _____.
    (6) ☐ Buyer ☐ Seller shall pay for _____.
    (7) ☐ Buyer ☐ Seller shall pay for _____.

5. **STATUTORY DISCLOSURES (INCLUDING LEAD-BASED PAINT HAZARD DISCLOSURES) AND CANCELLATION RIGHTS:**
  A. **(1)** Seller shall, within the time specified in paragraph 14, deliver to Buyer, if required by Law: (i) Federal Lead-Based Paint Disclosures and pamphlet ("Lead Disclosures"); and (ii) disclosures or notices required by sections 1102 et. seq. and 1103 et. seq. of the California Civil Code ("Statutory Disclosures"). Statutory Disclosures include, but are not limited to, a Real Estate Transfer Disclosure Statement ("TDS"), Natural Hazard Disclosure Statement ("NHD"), notice or actual knowledge of release of illegal controlled substance, notice of special tax and/or assessments (or, if allowed, substantially equivalent notice regarding the Mello-Roos Community Facilities Act and Improvement Bond Act of 1915) and, if Seller has actual knowledge, an industrial use and military ordnance location disclosure (C.A.R. Form SSD).
    (2) Buyer shall, within the time specified in paragraph 14, return Signed Copies of the Statutory and Lead Disclosures to Seller.
    (3) In the event Seller, prior to Close Of Escrow, becomes aware of adverse conditions materially affecting the Property, or any material inaccuracy in disclosures, information or representations previously provided to Buyer of which Buyer is otherwise unaware, Seller shall promptly provide a subsequent or amended disclosure or notice, in writing, covering those items. **However, a subsequent or amended disclosure shall not be required for conditions and material inaccuracies disclosed in reports ordered and paid for by Buyer.**

Buyer's Initials (_WB_)(_DB_)
Seller's Initials (_TP._)(_up._)

RPA-CA REVISED 10/02 (PAGE 2 OF 8)

Reviewed by _SK_ Date _6/14/03_

CALIFORNIA RESIDENTIAL PURCHASE AGREEMENT (RPA-CA PAGE 2 OF 8)

EQUAL HOUSING OPPORTUNITY

Prior to writing the offer, you may also create a market analysis for the buyer, similar to the seller's. This gives the buyer a better understanding of the property's value and he or she can then be in a better position to make a "reasonable" offer that can be accepted or countered by the seller.

Property Address: 264 Beach Lane, Costa Mesa, CA 92627   Date: JUNE 14, 2003

(4) If any disclosure or notice specified in 5A(1), or subsequent or amended disclosure or notice is delivered to Buyer after the offer is Signed, Buyer shall have the right to cancel this Agreement within **3 Days** After delivery in person, or **5 Days** After delivery by deposit in the mail, by giving written notice of cancellation to Seller or Seller's agent. (Lead Disclosures sent by mail must be sent certified mail or better.)

(5) Note to Buyer and Seller: Waiver of Statutory and Lead Disclosures is prohibited by Law.

B. **NATURAL AND ENVIRONMENTAL HAZARDS:** Within the time specified in paragraph 14, Seller shall, if required by Law: **(i)** deliver to Buyer earthquake guides (and questionnaire) and environmental hazards booklet; **(ii)** even if exempt from the obligation to provide a NHD, disclose if the Property is located in a Special Flood Hazard Area; Potential Flooding (Inundation) Area; Very High Fire Hazard Zone; State Fire Responsibility Area; Earthquake Fault Zone; Seismic Hazard Zone; and **(iii)** disclose any other zone as required by Law and provide any other information required for those zones.

C. **DATA BASE DISCLOSURE:** NOTICE: The California Department of Justice, sheriff's departments, police departments serving jurisdictions of 200,000 or more and many other local law enforcement authorities maintain for public access a data base of the locations of persons required to register pursuant to paragraph (1) of subdivision (a) of Section 290.4 of the Penal Code. The data base is updated on a quarterly basis and a source of information about the presence of these individuals in any neighborhood. The Department of Justice also maintains a Sex Offender Identification Line through which inquiries about individuals may be made. This is a "900" telephone service. Callers must have specific information about individuals they are checking. Information regarding neighborhoods is not available through the "900" telephone service.

6. **CONDOMINIUM/PLANNED UNIT DEVELOPMENT DISCLOSURES:**
A. **SELLER HAS: 7 (or ☐ _____) Days** After Acceptance to disclose to Buyer whether the Property is a condominium, or is located in a planned unit development or other common interest subdivision.

B. If the Property is a condominium or is located in a planned unit development or other common interest subdivision, Seller has **3 (or ☐ _____) Days** After Acceptance to request from the HOA (C.A.R. Form HOA): **(i)** Copies of any documents required by Law; **(ii)** disclosure of any pending or anticipated claim or litigation by or against the HOA; **(iii)** a statement containing the location and number of designated parking and storage spaces; **(iv)** Copies of the most recent 12 months of HOA minutes for regular and special meetings; and **(v)** the names and contact information of all HOAs governing the Property (collectively, "CI Disclosures"). Seller shall itemize and deliver to Buyer all CI Disclosures received from the HOA and any CI Disclosures in Seller's possession. Buyer's approval of CI Disclosures is a contingency of this Agreement as specified in paragraph 14.

7. **CONDITIONS AFFECTING PROPERTY:**
A. Unless otherwise agreed: **(i) the Property is sold (a) in its PRESENT physical condition as of the date of Acceptance and (b) subject to Buyer's Investigation rights; (ii)** the Property, including pool, spa, landscaping and grounds, is to be maintained in substantially the same condition as on the date of Acceptance; and **(iii)** all debris and personal property not included in the sale shall be removed by Close Of Escrow.

B. **SELLER SHALL,** within the time specified in paragraph 14, **DISCLOSE KNOWN MATERIAL FACTS AND DEFECTS** affecting the Property, including known insurance claims within the past five years, **AND MAKE OTHER DISCLOSURES REQUIRED BY LAW.**

C. **NOTE TO BUYER:** You are strongly advised to conduct investigations of the entire Property in order to determine its present condition since Seller may not be aware of all defects affecting the Property or other factors that you consider important. Property improvements may not be built according to code, in compliance with current Law, or have had permits issued.

D. **NOTE TO SELLER:** Buyer has the right to inspect the Property and, as specified in paragraph 14, based upon information discovered in those inspections: **(i)** cancel this Agreement; or **(ii)** request that you make Repairs or take other action.

8. **ITEMS INCLUDED AND EXCLUDED:**
A. **NOTE TO BUYER AND SELLER:** Items listed as included or excluded in the MLS, flyers or marketing materials are **not** included in the purchase price or excluded from the sale unless specified in 8B or C.

B. **ITEMS INCLUDED IN SALE:**
(1) All EXISTING fixtures and fittings that are attached to the Property;
(2) Existing electrical, mechanical, lighting, plumbing and heating fixtures, ceiling fans, fireplace inserts, gas logs and grates, solar systems, built-in appliances, window and door screens, awnings, shutters, window coverings, attached floor coverings, television antennas, satellite dishes, private integrated telephone systems, air coolers/conditioners, pool/spa equipment, garage door openers/remote controls, mailbox, in-ground landscaping, trees/shrubs, water softeners, water purifiers, security systems/alarms;
(3) The following items: _____
_____
(4) Seller represents that all items included in the purchase price, unless otherwise specified, are owned by Seller.
(5) All items included shall be transferred free of liens and without Seller warranty.

C. **ITEMS EXCLUDED FROM SALE:** _____
_____

9. **BUYER'S INVESTIGATION OF PROPERTY AND MATTERS AFFECTING PROPERTY:**
A. Buyer's acceptance of the condition of, and any other matter affecting the Property, is a contingency of this Agreement as specified in this paragraph and paragraph 14. Within the time specified in paragraph 14, Buyer shall have the right, at Buyer's expense unless otherwise agreed, to conduct inspections, investigations, tests, surveys and other studies ("Buyer Investigations"), including, but not limited to, the right to: **(i)** inspect for lead-based paint and other lead-based paint hazards; **(ii)** inspect for wood destroying pests and organisms; **(iii)** review the registered sex offender database; **(iv)** confirm the insurability of Buyer and the Property; and **(v)** satisfy Buyer as to any matter specified in the attached Buyer's Inspection Advisory (C.A.R. Form BIA). Without Seller's prior written consent, Buyer shall neither make nor cause to be made: **(i)** invasive or destructive Buyer's Investigations; or **(ii)** inspections by any governmental building or zoning inspector or government employee, unless required by Law.

B. Buyer shall complete Buyer Investigations and, as specified in paragraph 14, remove the contingency or cancel the Agreement. Buyer shall give Seller, at no cost, complete Copies of all Buyer Investigation reports obtained by Buyer. Seller shall make the Property available for all Buyer Investigations. Seller shall have water, gas, electricity and all operable pilot lights on for Buyer's Investigations and through the date possession is made available to Buyer.

Buyer's Initials (WB)(DB)
Seller's Initials (TP.)(yp.)

Reviewed by SR Date 6/14/03

RPA-CA REVISED 10/02 (PAGE 3 OF 8)

CALIFORNIA RESIDENTIAL PURCHASE AGREEMENT (RPA-CA PAGE 3 OF 8)

10. **REPAIRS:** Repairs shall be completed prior to final verification of condition unless otherwise agreed in writing. Repairs to be performed at Seller's expense may be performed by Seller or through others, provided that the work complies with applicable Law, including governmental permit, inspection and approval requirements. Repairs shall be performed in a good, skillful manner with materials of quality and appearance comparable to existing materials. It is understood that exact restoration of appearance or cosmetic items following all Repairs may not be possible. Seller shall: **(i)** obtain receipts for Repairs performed by others; **(ii)** prepare a written statement indicating the Repairs performed by Seller and the date of such Repairs; and **(iii)** provide Copies of receipts and statements to Buyer prior to final verification of condition.

11. **BUYER INDEMNITY AND SELLER PROTECTION FOR ENTRY UPON PROPERTY:** Buyer shall: **(i)** keep the Property free and clear of liens; **(ii)** Repair all damage arising from Buyer Investigations; and **(iii)** indemnify and hold Seller harmless from all resulting liability, claims, demands, damages and costs. Buyer shall carry, or Buyer shall require anyone acting on Buyer's behalf to carry, policies of liability, workers' compensation and other applicable insurance, defending and protecting Seller from liability for any injuries to persons or property occurring during any Buyer Investigations or work done on the Property at Buyer's direction prior to Close Of Escrow. Seller is advised that certain protections may be afforded Seller by recording a "Notice of Non-responsibility" (C.A.R. Form NNR) for Buyer Investigations and work done on the Property at Buyer's direction. Buyer's obligations under this paragraph shall survive the termination of this Agreement.

12. **TITLE AND VESTING:**
  A. Within the time specified in paragraph 14, Buyer shall be provided a current preliminary (title) report, which is only an offer by the title insurer to issue a policy of title insurance and may not contain every item affecting title. Buyer's review of the preliminary report and any other matters which may affect title are a contingency of this Agreement as specified in paragraph 14.
  B. Title is taken in its present condition subject to all encumbrances, easements, covenants, conditions, restrictions, rights and other matters, whether of record or not, as of the date of Acceptance except: **(i)** monetary liens of record unless Buyer is assuming those obligations or taking the Property subject to those obligations; and **(ii)** those matters which Seller has agreed to remove in writing.
  C. Within the time specified in paragraph 14, Seller has a duty to disclose to Buyer all matters known to Seller affecting title, whether of record or not.
  D. At Close Of Escrow, Buyer shall receive a grant deed conveying title (or, for stock cooperative or long-term lease, an assignment of stock certificate or of Seller's leasehold interest), including oil, mineral and water rights if currently owned by Seller. Title shall vest as designated in Buyer's supplemental escrow instructions. THE MANNER OF TAKING TITLE MAY HAVE SIGNIFICANT LEGAL AND TAX CONSEQUENCES. CONSULT AN APPROPRIATE PROFESSIONAL.
  E. Buyer shall receive a CLTA/ALTA Homeowner's Policy of Title Insurance. A title company, at Buyer's request, can provide information about the availability, desirability, coverage, and cost of various title insurance coverages and endorsements. If Buyer desires title coverage other than that required by this paragraph, Buyer shall instruct Escrow Holder in writing and pay any increase in cost.

13. **SALE OF BUYER'S PROPERTY:**
  A. This Agreement is NOT contingent upon the sale of any property owned by Buyer.
  OR B. ☐ (If checked): The attached addendum (C.A.R. Form COP) regarding the contingency for the sale of property owned by Buyer is incorporated into this Agreement.

14. **TIME PERIODS; REMOVAL OF CONTINGENCIES; CANCELLATION RIGHTS: The following time periods may only be extended, altered, modified or changed by mutual written agreement. Any removal of contingencies or cancellation under this paragraph must be in writing (C.A.R. Form RRCR).**
  A. SELLER HAS: 7 (or ☐ _____ **) Days** After Acceptance to deliver to Buyer all reports, disclosures and information for which Seller is responsible under paragraphs 4, 5A and B, 6A, 7B and 12.
  B. (1) BUYER HAS: 17 (or ☐ _____ **) Days** After Acceptance, unless otherwise agreed in writing, to:
    (i) complete all Buyer Investigations; approve all disclosures, reports and other applicable information, which Buyer receives from Seller; and approve all matters affecting the Property (including lead-based paint and lead-based paint hazards as well as other information specified in paragraph 5 and insurability of Buyer and the Property); and
    (ii) return to Seller Signed Copies of Statutory and Lead Disclosures delivered by Seller in accordance with paragraph 5A.
    (2) Within the time specified in 14B(1), Buyer may request that Seller make repairs or take any other action regarding the Property. Seller has no obligation to agree to or respond to Buyer's requests. (C.A.R. Form RR)
    (3) By the end of the time specified in 14B(1) (or 2I for loan contingency or 2J for appraisal contingency), Buyer shall, in writing, remove the applicable contingency (C.A.R. Form RRCR) or cancel this Agreement. However, if the following inspections, reports or disclosures are not made within the time specified in 14A, then Buyer has **5 (or** ☐ _____ **) Days** after receipt of any such items, or the time specified in 14B(1), whichever is later, to remove the applicable contingency or cancel this Agreement in writing: **(i)** government-mandated inspections or reports required as a condition of closing; or **(ii)** Common Interest Disclosures pursuant to paragraph 6B.
  C. CONTINUATION OF CONTINGENCY OR CONTRACTUAL OBLIGATION; SELLER RIGHT TO CANCEL:
    (1) Seller right to Cancel; Buyer Contingencies: Seller, after first giving Buyer a Notice to Buyer to Perform (as specified below), may cancel this Agreement in writing and authorize return of Buyer's deposit if, by the time specified in this Agreement, Buyer does not remove in writing the applicable contingency or cancel this Agreement. Once all contingencies have been removed, failure of either Buyer or Seller to close escrow on time may be a breach of this Agreement.
    (2) Continuation of Contingency: Even after the expiration of the time specified in 14B(1), Buyer retains the right to make requests to Seller, remove in writing the applicable contingency or cancel this Agreement until Seller cancels pursuant to 14C(1). Once Seller receives Buyer's written removal of all contingencies, Seller may not cancel this Agreement pursuant to 14C(1).
    (3) Seller right to Cancel; Buyer Contract Obligations: Seller, after first giving Buyer a Notice to Buyer to Perform (as specified below), may cancel this Agreement in writing and authorize return of Buyer's deposit for any of the following reasons: **(i)** if Buyer fails to deposit funds as required by 2A or 2B; **(ii)** if the funds deposited pursuant to 2A or 2B are not good when deposited; **(iii)** if Buyer fails to provide a letter as required by 2G; **(iv)** if Buyer fails to provide verification as required by 2H or 2L; **(v)** if Seller reasonably disapproves of the verification provided by 2H or 2L; **(vi)** if Buyer fails to return Statutory and Lead Disclosures as required by paragraph 5A(2); or **(vii)** if Buyer fails to sign or initial a separate liquidated damage form for an increased deposit as required by paragraph 16. **Seller is not required to give Buyer a Notice to Perform regarding Close of Escrow.**
    (4) Notice To Buyer To Perform: The Notice to Buyer to Perform (C.A.R. Form NBP) shall: **(i)** be in writing; **(ii)** be signed by Seller; and **(iii)** give Buyer at least **24 (or** ☐ _____ **)** hours (or until the time specified in the applicable paragraph, whichever occurs last) to take the applicable action. A Notice to Buyer to Perform may not be given any earlier than **2 Days** Prior to the expiration of the applicable time for Buyer to remove a contingency or cancel this Agreement or meet a 14C(3) obligation.

Buyer's Initials (WB)(OB)
Seller's Initials (T.P.)(yp.)

Reviewed by _____ Date 6/14/03

Property Address: _264 Beach Lane, Costa Mesa, CA 92627_ Date: _JUNE 14, 2003_

D. EFFECT OF BUYER'S REMOVAL OF CONTINGENCIES : If Buyer removes, in writing, any contingency or cancellation rights, unless otherwise specified in a separate written agreement between Buyer and Seller, Buyer shall conclusively be deemed to have: **(i)** completed all Buyer Investigations, and review of reports and other applicable information and disclosures pertaining to that contingency or cancellation right; **(ii)** elected to proceed with the transaction; and **(iii)** assumed all liability, responsibility and expense for Repairs or corrections pertaining to that contingency or cancellation right, or for inability to obtain financing.

E. EFFECT OF CANCELLATION ON DEPOSITS: If Buyer or Seller gives written notice of cancellation pursuant to rights duly exercised under the terms of this Agreement, Buyer and Seller agree to Sign mutual instructions to cancel the sale and escrow and release deposits, less fees and costs, to the party entitled to the funds. Fees and costs may be payable to service providers and vendors for services and products provided during escrow. **Release of funds will require mutual Signed release instructions from Buyer and Seller, judicial decision or arbitration award. A party may be subject to a civil penalty of up to $1,000 for refusal to sign such instructions if no good faith dispute exists as to who is entitled to the deposited funds (Civil Code §1057.3).**

15. FINAL VERIFICATION OF CONDITION: Buyer shall have the right to make a final inspection of the Property within **5 (or _____) Days** Prior to Close Of Escrow, NOT AS A CONTINGENCY OF THE SALE, but solely to confirm: **(i)** the Property is maintained pursuant to paragraph 7A; **(ii)** Repairs have been completed as agreed; and **(iii)** Seller has complied with Seller's other obligations under this Agreement.

16. LIQUIDATED DAMAGES: If Buyer fails to complete this purchase because of Buyer's default, Seller shall retain, as liquidated damages, the deposit actually paid. If the Property is a dwelling with no more than four units, one of which Buyer intends to occupy, then the amount retained shall be no more than 3% of the purchase price. Any excess shall be returned to Buyer. Release of funds will require mutual, Signed release instructions from both Buyer and Seller, judicial decision or arbitration award.
BUYER AND SELLER SHALL SIGN A SEPARATE LIQUIDATED DAMAGES PROVISION FOR ANY INCREASED DEPOSIT. (C.A.R. FORM RID)

Buyer's Initials _WB_ _DB_	Seller's Initials _TA_ _vp_

17. DISPUTE RESOLUTION:
A. MEDIATION: Buyer and Seller agree to mediate any dispute or claim arising between them out of this Agreement, or any resulting transaction, before resorting to arbitration or court action. Paragraphs 17B(2) and (3) below apply whether or not the Arbitration provision is initialed. Mediation fees, if any, shall be divided equally among the parties involved. If, for any dispute or claim to which this paragraph applies, any party commences an action without first attempting to resolve the matter through mediation, or refuses to mediate after a request has been made, then that party shall not be entitled to recover attorney fees, even if they would otherwise be available to that party in any such action. THIS MEDIATION PROVISION APPLIES WHETHER OR NOT THE ARBITRATION PROVISION IS INITIALED

B. ARBITRATION OF DISPUTES: (1) Buyer and Seller agree that any dispute or claim in Law or equity arising between them out of this Agreement or any resulting transaction, which is not settled through mediation, shall be decided by neutral, binding arbitration, including and subject to paragraphs 17B(2) and (3) below. The arbitrator shall be a retired judge or justice, or an attorney with at least 5 years of residential real estate Law experience, unless the parties mutually agree to a different arbitrator, who shall render an award in accordance with substantive California Law. The parties shall have the right to discovery in accordance with California Code of Civil Procedure §1283.05. In all other respects, the arbitration shall be conducted in accordance with Title 9 of Part III of the California Code of Civil Procedure. Judgment upon the award of the arbitrator(s) may be entered into any court having jurisdiction. Interpretation of this agreement to arbitrate shall be governed by the Federal Arbitration Act.
(2) EXCLUSIONS FROM MEDIATION AND ARBITRATION: The following matters are excluded from mediation and arbitration: **(i)** a judicial or non-judicial foreclosure or other action or proceeding to enforce a deed of trust, mortgage or installment land sale contract as defined in California Civil Code §2985; **(ii)** an unlawful detainer action; **(iii)** the filing or enforcement of a mechanic's lien; and **(iv)** any matter that is within the jurisdiction of a probate, small claims or bankruptcy court. The filing of a court action to enable the recording of a notice of pending action, for order of attachment, receivership, injunction, or other provisional remedies, shall not constitute a waiver of the mediation and arbitration provisions.
(3) BROKERS: Buyer and Seller agree to mediate and arbitrate disputes or claims involving either or both Brokers, consistent with 17 A and B, provided either or both Brokers shall have agreed to such mediation or arbitration prior to, or within a reasonable time after, the dispute or claim is presented to Brokers. Any election by either or both Brokers to participate in mediation or arbitration shall not result in Brokers being deemed parties to the Agreement.

"NOTICE: BY INITIALING IN THE SPACE BELOW YOU ARE AGREEING TO HAVE ANY DISPUTE ARISING OUT OF THE MATTERS INCLUDED IN THE 'ARBITRATION OF DISPUTES' PROVISION DECIDED BY NEUTRAL ARBITRATION AS PROVIDED BY CALIFORNIA LAW AND YOU ARE GIVING UP ANY RIGHTS YOU MIGHT POSSESS TO HAVE THE DISPUTE LITIGATED IN A COURT OR JURY TRIAL. BY INITIALING IN THE SPACE BELOW YOU ARE GIVING UP YOUR JUDICIAL RIGHTS TO DISCOVERY AND APPEAL, UNLESS THOSE RIGHTS ARE SPECIFICALLY INCLUDED IN THE 'ARBITRATION OF DISPUTES' PROVISION. IF YOU REFUSE TO SUBMIT TO ARBITRATION AFTER AGREEING TO THIS PROVISION, YOU MAY BE COMPELLED TO ARBITRATE UNDER THE AUTHORITY OF THE CALIFORNIA CODE OF CIVIL PROCEDURE. YOUR AGREEMENT TO THIS ARBITRATION PROVISION IS VOLUNTARY."

"WE HAVE READ AND UNDERSTAND THE FOREGOING AND AGREE TO SUBMIT DISPUTES ARISING OUT OF THE MATTERS INCLUDED IN THE 'ARBITRATION OF DISPUTES' PROVISION TO NEUTRAL ARBITRATION."

Buyer's Initials _WB_ _DB_	Seller's Initials _TA_ _vp_

Buyer's Initials (_WB_)(_DB_)
Seller's Initials (_TA_)(_vp._)

Reviewed by _JL_ Date _6/14/03_

RPA-CA REVISED 10/02 (PAGE 5 OF 8)

EQUAL HOUSING OPPORTUNITY

CALIFORNIA RESIDENTIAL PURCHASE AGREEMENT (RPA-CA PAGE 5 OF 8)

Property Address: 264 Beach Lane, Costa Mesa, CA 92627   Date: June 14, 2003

18. **PRORATIONS OF PROPERTY TAXES AND OTHER ITEMS:** Unless otherwise agreed in writing, the following items shall be PAID CURRENT and prorated between Buyer and Seller as of Close Of Escrow: real property taxes and assessments, interest, rents, HOA regular, special, and emergency dues and assessments imposed prior to Close Of Escrow, premiums on insurance assumed by Buyer, payments on bonds and assessments assumed by Buyer, and payments on Mello-Roos and other Special Assessment District bonds and assessments that are now a lien. The following items shall be assumed by Buyer WITHOUT CREDIT toward the purchase price: prorated payments on Mello-Roos and other Special Assessment District bonds and assessments and HOA special assessments that are now a lien but not yet due. Property will be reassessed upon change of ownership. Any supplemental tax bills shall be paid as follows: **(i)** for periods after Close Of Escrow, by Buyer; and **(ii)** for periods prior to Close Of Escrow, by Seller. TAX BILLS ISSUED AFTER CLOSE OF ESCROW SHALL BE HANDLED DIRECTLY BETWEEN BUYER AND SELLER. Prorations shall be made based on a 30-day month.

19. **WITHHOLDING TAXES:** Seller and Buyer agree to execute any instrument, affidavit, statement or instruction reasonably necessary to comply with federal (FIRPTA) and California withholding Law, if required (C.A.R. Forms AS and AB).

20. **MULTIPLE LISTING SERVICE ("MLS"):** Brokers are authorized to report to the MLS a pending sale and, upon Close Of Escrow, the terms of this transaction to be published and disseminated to persons and entities authorized to use the information on terms approved by the MLS.

21. **EQUAL HOUSING OPPORTUNITY:** The Property is sold in compliance with federal, state and local anti-discrimination Laws.

22. **ATTORNEY FEES:** In any action, proceeding, or arbitration between Buyer and Seller arising out of this Agreement, the prevailing Buyer or Seller shall be entitled to reasonable attorney fees and costs from the non-prevailing Buyer or Seller, except as provided in paragraph 17A.

23. **SELECTION OF SERVICE PROVIDERS:** If Brokers refer Buyer or Seller to persons, vendors, or service or product providers ("Providers"), Brokers do not guarantee the performance of any Providers. Buyer and Seller may select ANY Providers of their own choosing.

24. **TIME OF ESSENCE; ENTIRE CONTRACT; CHANGES:** Time is of the essence. All understandings between the parties are incorporated in this Agreement. Its terms are intended by the parties as a final, complete and exclusive expression of their Agreement with respect to its subject matter, and may not be contradicted by evidence of any prior agreement or contemporaneous oral agreement. If any provision of this Agreement is held to be ineffective or invalid, the remaining provisions will nevertheless be given full force and effect. **Neither this Agreement nor any provision in it may be extended, amended, modified, altered or changed, except in writing Signed by Buyer and Seller.**

25. **OTHER TERMS AND CONDITIONS,** including attached supplements:
   A. ☑ Buyer's Inspection Advisory (C.A.R. Form BIA)
   B. ☐ Purchase Agreement Addendum (C.A.R. Form PAA paragraph numbers: _____)
   C. _____
      _____
      _____

26. **DEFINITIONS:** As used in this Agreement:
   A. **"Acceptance"** means the time the offer or final counter offer is accepted in writing by a party and is delivered to and personally received by the other party or that party's authorized agent in accordance with the terms of this offer or a final counter offer.
   B. **"Agreement"** means the terms and conditions of this accepted California Residential Purchase Agreement and any accepted counter offers and addenda.
   C. **"C.A.R. Form"** means the specific form referenced or another comparable form agreed to by the parties.
   D. **"Close Of Escrow"** means the date the grant deed, or other evidence of transfer of title, is recorded. If the scheduled close of escrow falls on a Saturday, Sunday or legal holiday, then close of escrow shall be the next business day after the scheduled close of escrow date.
   E. **"Copy"** means copy by any means including photocopy, NCR, facsimile and electronic.
   F. **"Days"** means calendar days, unless otherwise required by Law.
   G. **"Days After"** means the specified number of calendar days after the occurrence of the event specified, not counting the calendar date on which the specified event occurs, and ending at 11:59PM on the final day.
   H. **"Days Prior"** means the specified number of calendar days before the occurrence of the event specified, not counting the calendar date on which the specified event is scheduled to occur.
   I. **"Electronic Copy" or "Electronic Signature"** means, as applicable, an electronic copy or signature complying with California Law. Buyer and Seller agree that electronic means will not be used by either party to modify or alter the content or integrity of this Agreement without the knowledge and consent of the other.
   J. **"Law"** means any law, code, statute, ordinance, regulation, rule or order, which is adopted by a controlling city, county, state or federal legislative, judicial or executive body or agency.
   K. **"Notice to Buyer to Perform"** means a document (C.A.R. Form NBP), which shall be in writing and Signed by Seller and shall give Buyer at least 24 hours **(or as otherwise specified in paragraph 14C(4))** to remove a contingency or perform as applicable.
   L. **"Repairs"** means any repairs (including pest control), alterations, replacements, modifications or retrofitting of the Property provided for under this Agreement.
   M. **"Signed"** means either a handwritten or electronic signature on an original document, Copy or any counterpart.
   N. **Singular and Plural** terms each include the other, when appropriate.

Buyer's Initials (WB)(DB)
Seller's Initials (TP.)(yp.)
Reviewed by ___ Date 6/14/03

RPA-CA REVISED 10/02 (PAGE 6 OF 8)

CALIFORNIA RESIDENTIAL PURCHASE AGREEMENT (RPA-CA PAGE 6 OF 8)

Property Address: _264 Beach Lane, Costa Mesa, CA 92627_ Date: _JUNE 14, 2003_

27. AGENCY:

A. DISCLOSURE: Buyer and Seller each acknowledge prior receipt of C.A.R. Form AD "Disclosure Regarding Real Estate Agency Relationships."

B. POTENTIALLY COMPETING BUYERS AND SELLERS: Buyer and Seller each acknowledge receipt of a disclosure of the possibility of multiple representation by the Broker representing that principal. This disclosure may be part of a listing agreement, buyer-broker agreement or separate document (C.A.R. Form DA). Buyer understands that Broker representing Buyer may also represent other potential buyers, who may consider, make offers on or ultimately acquire the Property. Seller understands that Broker representing Seller may also represent other sellers with competing properties of interest to this Buyer.

C. CONFIRMATION: The following agency relationships are hereby confirmed for this transaction:
Listing Agent _Sail Realty_ (Print Firm Name) is the agent of (check one): X the Seller exclusively; or ☐ both the Buyer and Seller.
Selling Agent _Ramos Realty_ (Print Firm Name) (if not same as Listing Agent) is the agent of (check one): X the Buyer exclusively; or ☐ the Seller exclusively; or ☐ both the Buyer and Seller. Real Estate Brokers are not parties to the Agreement between Buyer and Seller.

28. JOINT ESCROW INSTRUCTIONS TO ESCROW HOLDER:

A. **The following paragraphs, or applicable portions thereof, of this Agreement constitute the joint escrow instructions of Buyer and Seller to Escrow Holder,** which Escrow Holder is to use along with any related counter offers and addenda, and any additional mutual instructions to close the escrow: 1, 2, 4, 12, 13B, 14E, 18, 19, 24, 25B and C, 26, 28, 29, 32A, 33 and paragraph D of the section titled Real Estate Brokers on page 8. If a Copy of the separate compensation agreement(s) provided for in paragraph 29 or 32A, or paragraph D of the section titled Real Estate Brokers on page 8 is deposited with Escrow Holder by Broker, Escrow Holder shall accept such agreement(s) and pay out from Buyer's or Seller's funds, or both, as applicable, the Broker's compensation provided for in such agreement(s). The terms and conditions of this Agreement not set forth in the specified paragraphs are additional matters for the information of Escrow Holder, but about which Escrow Holder need not be concerned. Buyer and Seller will receive Escrow Holder's general provisions directly from Escrow Holder and will execute such provisions upon Escrow Holder's request. To the extent the general provisions are inconsistent or conflict with this Agreement, the general provisions will control as to the duties and obligations of Escrow Holder only. Buyer and Seller will execute additional instructions, documents and forms provided by Escrow Holder that are reasonably necessary to close escrow.

B. A Copy of this Agreement shall be delivered to Escrow Holder within **3** business days after Acceptance (or ☐ _____). Buyer and Seller authorize Escrow Holder to accept and rely on Copies and Signatures as defined in this Agreement as originals, to open escrow and for other purposes of escrow. The validity of this Agreement as between Buyer and Seller is not affected by whether or when Escrow Holder Signs this Agreement.

C. Brokers are a party to the escrow for the sole purpose of compensation pursuant to paragraphs 29, 32A and paragraph D of the section titled Real Estate Brokers on page 8. Buyer and Seller irrevocably assign to Brokers compensation specified in paragraphs 29 and 32A, respectively, and irrevocably instruct Escrow Holder to disburse those funds to Brokers at Close Of Escrow or pursuant to any other mutually executed cancellation agreement. Compensation instructions can be amended or revoked only with the written consent of Brokers. Escrow Holder shall immediately notify Brokers: **(i)** if Buyer's initial or any additional deposit is not made pursuant to this Agreement, or is not good at time of deposit with Escrow Holder; or **(ii)** if Buyer and Seller instruct Escrow Holder to cancel escrow.

D. A Copy of any amendment that affects any paragraph of this Agreement for which Escrow Holder is responsible shall be delivered to Escrow Holder within **2** business days after mutual execution of the amendment.

29. BROKER COMPENSATION FROM BUYER:
If applicable, upon Close Of Escrow, **Buyer** agrees to pay compensation to Broker as specified in a separate written agreement between Buyer and Broker.

30. TERMS AND CONDITIONS OF OFFER:
This is an offer to purchase the Property on the above terms and conditions. All paragraphs with spaces for initials by Buyer and Seller are incorporated in this Agreement only if initialed by all parties. If at least one but not all parties initial, a counter offer is required until agreement is reached. Seller has the right to continue to offer the Property for sale and to accept any other offer at any time prior to notification of Acceptance. Buyer has read and acknowledges receipt of a Copy of the offer and agrees to the above confirmation of agency relationships. If this offer is accepted and Buyer subsequently defaults, Buyer may be responsible for payment of Brokers' compensation. This Agreement and any supplement, addendum or modification, including any Copy, may be Signed in two or more counterparts, all of which shall constitute one and the same writing.

Buyer's Initials (_WB_)(_QB_)
Seller's Initials (_TP_)(_yp_)

Reviewed by _JR_ Date _6/14/03_

EQUAL HOUSING OPPORTUNITY

CALIFORNIA RESIDENTIAL PURCHASE AGREEMENT (RPA-CA PAGE 7 OF 8)

Property Address: 264 Beach Lane, Costa Mesa, CA 92627   Date: JUNE 14, 2003

31. EXPIRATION OF OFFER: This offer shall be deemed revoked and the deposit shall be returned unless the offer is Signed by Seller and a Copy of the Signed offer is personally received by Buyer, or by _____, who is authorized to receive it by 5:00 PM on the third calendar day after this offer is signed by Buyer (or, if checked) ☐ by _____ (date), at _____ AM/PM).

Date JUNE 14, 2003   Date JUNE 14, 2003
BUYER _Walti Buyer_____   BUYER _Debbie Buyer_____
_Walter Buyer_____   _Debbie Buyer_____
(Print name) 700 Boat Lane, Malibu del Rey, CA 90292 (Print name)
(Address)

32. BROKER COMPENSATION FROM SELLER:
   A. Upon Close Of Escrow, **Seller** agrees to pay compensation to Broker as specified in a separate written agreement between Seller and Broker.
   B. If escrow does not close, compensation is payable as specified in that separate written agreement.
33. ACCEPTANCE OF OFFER: Seller warrants that Seller is the owner of the Property, or has the authority to execute this Agreement. Seller accepts the above offer, agrees to sell the Property on the above terms and conditions, and agrees to the above confirmation of agency relationships. Seller has read and acknowledges receipt of a Copy of this Agreement, and authorizes Broker to deliver a Signed Copy to Buyer.
   ☐ (If checked) **SUBJECT TO ATTACHED COUNTER OFFER, DATED** _____.

Date JUNE 15, 2003   Date JUNE 15, 2003
SELLER _Tony Seller_____   SELLER _Yolanda Seller_____
_TONY SELLER_____   _YOLANDA SELLER_____
(Print name)   (Print name)
264 Beach Lane, Costa Mesa, CA 92627
(Address)

(WB DB)   **CONFIRMATION OF ACCEPTANCE:** A Copy of Signed Acceptance was personally received by Buyer or Buyer's authorized
(Initials)   agent on (date) 6/15/03 _____ at __3__ AM/PM. A binding Agreement is created when a Copy of Signed Acceptance is personally received by Buyer or Buyer's authorized agent whether or not confirmed in this document. Completion of this confirmation is not legally required in order to create a binding Agreement; it is solely intended to evidence the date that Confirmation of Acceptance has occurred.

REAL ESTATE BROKERS:
A. Real Estate Brokers are not parties to the Agreement between Buyer and Seller.
B. Agency relationships are confirmed as stated in paragraph 27.
C. If specified in paragraph 2A, Agent who submitted the offer for Buyer acknowledges receipt of deposit.
D. **COOPERATING BROKER COMPENSATION:** Listing Broker agrees to pay Cooperating Broker (**Selling Firm**) and Cooperating Broker agrees to accept, out of Listing Broker's proceeds in escrow: **(i)** the amount specified in the MLS, provided Cooperating Broker is a Participant of the MLS in which the Property is offered for sale or a reciprocal MLS; or **(ii)** ☐ (if checked) the amount specified in a separate written agreement (C.A.R. Form CBC) between Listing Broker and Cooperating Broker.

Real Estate Broker (Selling Firm) Ramos Realty
By _Joseph Ramos_____   Date 6/14/03
Address 777 Newport Blvd.   City Newport Beach   State CA   Zip 92663
Telephone 714-647-0000   Fax 714-647-0001   E-mail jr@ramosrealty.com

Real Estate Broker (Listing Firm) Sail Realty
By _Carmen Caro_____   Date 6/15/03
Address 227 Harbor Blvd.   City Costa Mesa   State CA   Zip 92627
Telephone 714-626-2828   Fax 714-646-2829   E-mail carmen@sailreal.com

ESCROW HOLDER ACKNOWLEDGMENT:
Escrow Holder acknowledges receipt of a Copy of this Agreement, (if checked, ☐ a deposit in the amount of $ _____),
counter offer numbers _____ and _____
_____, and agrees to act as Escrow Holder subject to paragraph 28 of this Agreement, any supplemental escrow instructions and the terms of Escrow Holder's general provisions.

Escrow Holder is advised that the date of Confirmation of Acceptance of the Agreement as between Buyer and Seller is _____

Escrow Holder _____   Escrow # _____
By _____   Date _____
Address _____
Phone/Fax/E-mail _____
Escrow Holder is licensed by the California Department of ☐ Corporations, ☐ Insurance, ☐ Real Estate. License # _____

THIS FORM HAS BEEN APPROVED BY THE CALIFORNIA ASSOCIATION OF REALTORS® (C.A.R.). NO REPRESENTATION IS MADE AS TO THE LEGAL VALIDITY OR ADEQUACY OF ANY PROVISION IN ANY SPECIFIC TRANSACTION. A REAL ESTATE BROKER IS THE PERSON QUALIFIED TO ADVISE ON REAL ESTATE TRANSACTIONS. IF YOU DESIRE LEGAL OR TAX ADVICE, CONSULT AN APPROPRIATE PROFESSIONAL.
This form is available for use by the entire real estate industry. It is not intended to identify the user as a REALTOR. REALTOR® is a registered collective membership mark which may be used only by members of the NATIONAL ASSOCIATION OF REALTORS® who subscribe to its Code of Ethics.

SURE TRAC   Published by the
The System for Success™   California Association of REALTORS®

Reviewed by ____ Date 6/14/03   EQUAL HOUSING OPPORTUNITY

RPA-CA REVISED 10/02 (PAGE 8 OF 8)

CALIFORNIA RESIDENTIAL PURCHASE AGREEMENT   (RPA-CA PAGE 8 OF 8)

216

A. INTERPRETATION OF THE FORM

When using a printed form, you must be entirely familiar with it and understand the importance of what you insert in its blanks.

The written or typed word supersedes the printed word if there is a contradiction.

Where there are inconsistencies between general provisions and specific provisions, the specific provisions ordinarily qualify the meaning of the general provisions.

The blanks in the contract must be filled in correctly. What goes into them must express the understanding of the parties to the contract. You should strive for simplicity without leaving out essentials. It is more important that the terms be understood by the parties than by those who are versed in real estate parlance (e.g., attorneys).

At the same time, much contract drafting in simple real estate transactions is repetitive. Standard, trustworthy clauses can be adapted to the special situation and will, more often than not, create complete, final easily understandable contracts.

Use the form itself as a checklist for a contract that is complete in all important respects. Delete printed sentences or paragraphs that are not applicable and have the changes dated and initialed.

Go over the finished product with the clients. In difficult or unusual situations, consult a more experienced person for assistance in completing contractual provisions.

Strive for simplicity! It's essential that both buyer and seller understand the terms of the agreement!

A contract is similar to a blueprint. The parties, their advisers, the lenders, and escrow holders look to the contract just as the builder looks to the drawings and specifications. Without a proper contract incorporating the desires of the parties, there are certain to be problems before closing, and sometimes, after. The more complete the contract, the easier and smoother the road to completion of the sale.

B. FILLING OUT THE FORM—A BREAKDOWN

The following is a step-by-step guide for filling out the purchase contract.

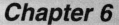

CALIFORNIA
ASSOCIATION
OF REALTORS®

**CALIFORNIA
RESIDENTIAL PURCHASE AGREEMENT
AND JOINT ESCROW INSTRUCTIONS**
For Use With Single Family Residential Property — Attached or Detached
(C.A.R. Form RPA-CA, Revised 10/02)

TITLE

PAGE 1 OF 8

"California" – the form may be used throughout this state.

"Joint Escrow Instructions" – the form includes Buyer and Seller's instruction to escrow holder for one-to-four residential units.

Date _JUNE 14, 2003_____, at _Costa Mesa_____, California.

DATE

Do not use numbers to denote the date, use actual months. "1/2/03" could mean January 2, 2003 in the United States, but February 1, 2003 in European countries.

"Date" – the date of preparation that is usually the date the Buyer signs the offer and earnest money is received. Note, however, that the key date is the **date of final acceptance** by the Buyer, which must be personally communicated. The date of acceptance is the date from which all the dates specified in the form are counted.

The word **"at"** means the city where the document is drafted, not where the property is located.

```
1.  OFFER:
    A.  THIS IS AN OFFER FROM  Walter and Debbie Buyer                          ("Buyer").
    B.  THE REAL PROPERTY TO BE ACQUIRED is described as  264 Beach Lane
                                         , Assessor's Parcel No. _____ , situated in
        ___Costa Mesc,_____ County of  Orange      , California, ("Property").
    C.  THE PURCHASE PRICE offered is  Eight Hundred Thousand ———— no/100 ———
        _____ Dollars $  800,000——
    D.  CLOSE OF ESCROW shall occur on _____ (date)(or X 90 Days After Acceptance).
```

1. OFFER

A. **Offer/Buyers** – Identifies document as an offer from a named Buyer which may be accepted by the named Seller to create a binding contract.

B. **Real Property to be Acquired** – Describes property by address, legal description, and assessor's parcel number.

C. **Purchase Price** – Price Buyer offers to pay. Does not include closing costs, insurance premiums, or any required funding fees.

D. **Close of Escrow** – May choose either of two dates: (1) specific date, or (2) a date a number of days after offer is accepted.

```
2.  FINANCE TERMS: Obtaining the loans below is a contingency of this Agreement unless: (i) either 2K or 2L is checked below; or
    (ii) otherwise agreed in writing. Buyer shall act diligently and in good faith to obtain the designated loans. Obtaining deposit, down
    payment and closing costs is not a contingency.  Buyer represents that funds will be good when deposited with Escrow Holder.
```

2. FINANCING

Obtaining specified loans is a contingency of the agreement, unless it is an all cash offer, or it is specified that obtaining the loan is not a contingency. If that contingency fails, the Buyer need not perform and is not liable for breach of contract, therefore getting the deposit back, less any expenses already incurred.

Obtaining deposit, down payment, closing costs, and the Buyer's promise that funds will be good, are not contingencies. If any of these are not obtained, the contract may be considered breached, and the Seller entitled to legal remedies or cancellation of the sale.

 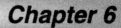

> A. **INITIAL DEPOSIT:** Buyer has given a deposit in the amount of . . . .$ *10,000*
> to the agent submitting the offer (or to ☐ _____), by personal check
> (or ☐ _____), made payable to *ABC Escrow* _____ ,
> which shall be held uncashed until Acceptance and then deposited within **3** business days after
> Acceptance (or ☐ _____), with
> Escrow Holder, (or ☐ into Broker's trust account).

A. Initial Deposit – The deposit is given to the agent submitting the offer, or agent's name inserted on blank line. The payee of the check is indicated on the blank line, usually a broker or title or escrow officer. **The amount is written in numbers in the right hand column.**

Funds received must be disposed of within three business days after acceptance of offer according to the directions, unless instructed otherwise in writing. Commingling is prohibited, and may subject broker to disciplinary action.

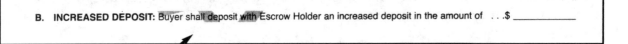

> B. **INCREASED DEPOSIT:** Buyer shall deposit with Escrow Holder an increased deposit in the amount of . . .$ _____

B. Increased Deposit – A separate receipt for increased deposit, at the time that it is paid, in order for the increased deposit to be included in the amount of liquidated damages. *LIQUIDATED DAMAGES are the sum of money, agreed to in advance and stated in the contract, that will be paid for not fulfilling a clause or condition in the contract.* The Buyer signs or initials the liquidated damages provision at the same time that it is paid. **Write the amount in the column to the right.**

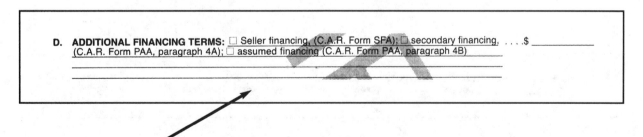

C. **FIRST LOAN IN THE AMOUNT OF** . . . .$ *640,000*
   (1) NEW First Deed of Trust in favor of lender, encumbering the Property, securing a note payable at
   maximum interest of _____*8*___% fixed rate, or _____% initial adjustable rate with a maximum
   interest rate of _____%, balance due in _____ years, amortized over ___*30*___ years. Buyer
   shall pay loan fees/points not to exceed ___*2*____. (These terms apply whether the designated loan
   is conventional, FHA or VA.)
   (2) ☐ FHA ☐ VA: (The following terms only apply to the FHA or VA loan that is checked.)
   Seller shall pay _____% discount points. Seller shall pay other fees not allowed to be paid by
   Buyer, ☐ not to exceed $_____. Seller shall pay the cost of lender required Repairs
   (including those for wood destroying pest) not otherwise provided for in this Agreement, ☐ not to
   exceed $ _____. (Actual loan amount may increase if mortgage insurance premiums,
   funding fees or closing costs are financed.)

C. First loan in the amount of – New loans can be either conventional or FHA/VA loans.

Subparagraph 1 deals only with conventional loans. Set forth terms specifically, not generally. If fixed rate and adjustable rate information are both filled in, Buyer is obligated to complete transaction with whatever of those two options is obtainable from the lender. Only fill in type of rate Buyer chooses.

Subparagraph 2 deals only with FHA/VA loans. Paragraph requires Seller to insert points percentage, if he or she agrees to pay them. Seller also must pay: (a) other fees not allowed to be paid by the Buyer, up to a pre-agreed amount, inserted on blank line; and (b) lender required repairs, up to a pre-agreed amount, inserted on blank line. **Write the amount in the column to the right**.

D. **ADDITIONAL FINANCING TERMS:** ☐ Seller financing, (C.A.R. Form SFA); ☐ secondary financing, ...$ _____
   (C.A.R. Form PAA, paragraph 4A); ☐ assumed financing (C.A.R. Form PAA, paragraph 4B)
   _____
   _____

D. Additional Financing Terms – **This paragraph relates only to financing**. Seller financing requires a **seller-financing addendum**. Secondary financing and assumption also require an addendum (e.g., C.A.R. Form PAA). Check the appropriate block and attach the addendum to the agreement. **Write the amount in the column to the right**.

 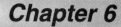

E. **BALANCE OF PURCHASE PRICE** (not including costs of obtaining loans and other closing costs) in the amount of . . .$ *150,000*
to be deposited with Escrow Holder within sufficient time to close escrow.
F. **PURCHASE PRICE (TOTAL):** .... $ *800,000*

E. Balance of Purchase Price – The balance of purchase price will be deposited with escrow holder within sufficient time to close. **Write the amount in the column to the right**.

F. Total Purchase Price – Add the amounts of the right hand columns in Sections 2A-E and **write in the column to the right**.

G. **LOAN APPLICATIONS:** Within 7 (or ☐ _____) **Days** After Acceptance, Buyer shall provide Seller a letter from lender or mortgage loan broker stating that, based on a review of Buyer's written application and credit report, Buyer is prequalified or preapproved for the NEW loan specified in 2C above.

G. Loan Applications – If the Buyer does not provide the letter from a lender showing the Buyer is either pre-qualified or pre-approved **within 7 days after acceptance**, or the number of days inserted on the blank line, the Seller may cancel the agreement.

H. **VERIFICATION OF DOWN PAYMENT AND CLOSING COSTS:** Buyer (or Buyer's lender or loan broker pursuant to 2G) shall, within 7 (or ☐ _____) **Days** After Acceptance, provide Seller written verification of Buyer's down payment and closing costs.

H. Verification of Down Payment and Closing Costs – To avoid the possibility that the Buyer will be unable to obtain the required down payment and closing costs before the close of escrow, the Buyer may be required to verify the down payment and closing costs within **7 days after acceptance**, or a number of days inserted on the blank line.

I. **LOAN CONTINGENCY REMOVAL: (i)** Within 17 (or ☐ _____) **Days** After Acceptance, Buyer shall, as specified in paragraph 14, remove the loan contingency or cancel this Agreement; **OR (ii)** (if checked) ☐ the loan contingency shall remain in effect until the designated loans are funded.

J. **APPRAISAL CONTINGENCY AND REMOVAL:** This Agreement is **(OR,** if checked, ☐ is NOT) contingent upon the Property appraising at no less than the specified purchase price. Buyer shall, as specified in paragraph 14, remove the appraisal contingency or cancel this Agreement when the loan contingency is removed (or, if checked, ☐ within **17 (or** ☐ _____ **) Days** After Acceptance).

K. ☐ **NO LOAN CONTINGENCY** (If checked): Obtaining any loan in paragraphs 2C, 2D or elsewhere in this Agreement is NOT a contingency of this Agreement. If Buyer does not obtain the loan and as a result Buyer does not purchase the Property, Seller may be entitled to Buyer's deposit or other legal remedies.

I. Loan Contingency Removal – The financing contingency is effective until it is removed **within 17 days after acceptance**, or the number of days inserted on the blank line, or until the loan is actually funded (if that block is checked).

J. Appraisal Contingency and Removal – Even if a lender is willing to lend the amount specified in Paragraph 2C, the Buyer is not obligated to purchase if the property appraises at less than the purchase price in Paragraph 2F. **The Buyer may check a box and opt out of this contingency.**

It's important to remember that if the Buyer is applying for an 80% loan and the appraisal does not come in at or above the specified purchase price, the Buyer will probably be released from further obligation.

K. No Loan Contingency – The parties may agree to check the block in this paragraph to state that obtaining a loan is not a contingency. If so, the Buyer agrees to complete the transaction even if the lender does not fund the loan, and is in breach of the agreement if he does not complete it. **Must be checked to apply.**

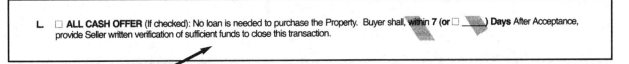

L. ☐ **ALL CASH OFFER** (If checked): No loan is needed to purchase the Property. Buyer shall, within 7 (or ☐ _____) **Days** After Acceptance, provide Seller written verification of sufficient funds to close this transaction.

L. All Cash Offer – A Buyer must give written verification of funds necessary to close **within 7 days after acceptance** or the number of days inserted on the blank line. If the verification is not provided or not approved by the Seller, the Seller may cancel the agreement.

---

3. CLOSING AND OCCUPANCY:

    A. Buyer intends (or ☐ does not intend) to occupy the Property as Buyer's primary residence.

    B. **Seller-occupied or vacant property:** Occupancy shall be delivered to Buyer at ___11__ AM/PM, X on the date of Close Of Escrow; ☐ on _____; or ☐ no later than _____ **Days** After Close Of Escrow. (C.A.R. Form PAA, paragraph 2.) If transfer of title and occupancy do not occur at the same time, Buyer and Seller are advised to: **(i)** enter into a written occupancy agreement; and **(ii)** consult with their insurance and legal advisors.

---

3. CLOSING AND OCCUPANCY

A. Buyer Occupancy – Whether the Buyer intends to occupy the property is important to matters such as liquidated damages, loan qualification, rate, and terms. Block should be checked.

"CE + 3" means the Buyer will take possession 3 days after the close of escrow.

B. Seller-Occupied or Vacant Property – Occupancy is to be delivered to the Buyer at the time specified on the close of escrow, or some other specified date. If the Buyer moves in before the close of escrow, the parties should enter into a written agreement to document that separate legal relationship, and consult with their insurance and legal advisors respecting insurance and risk of loss if property is damaged during that period. Applicable addendums include: "Residential Lease Agreement after Sale" or "Interim Occupancy Agreement" (C.A.R. Forms RLAS or IOA-11), or "Purchase Agreement Addendum" (if for less than 30 days, C.A.R. Forms PAA, paragraph 2, "Seller to Remain in Possession after Close of Escrow").

Buyer's Initials (WB)(DB)
Seller's Initials (TA)(mp.)
Reviewed by _JR_ Date 6/14/03

EQUAL HOUSING OPPORTUNITY

BUYER'S AND SELLER'S INITIALS/SELLING BROKER'S INITIALS

Pages one through seven of the Residential Purchase Agreement require the Buyer's and Seller's initials at the bottom of the page, which means the Buyers and Sellers have read the agreement, **but not necessarily accepted it**.

Pages one through eight require the Selling Broker's or Manager's initials at the bottom of the page and the date to show that he or she has reviewed the document.

Property Address: _264 Beach Lane, Costa Mesa, CA 92627_   Date: _JUNE 14, 2003_

PROPERTY ADDRESS AND DATE

Pages 1 through 8 of the Residential Purchase Agreement require the property address and the date to be filled in at the top of the page.

C. **Tenant-occupied property: (i) Property shall be vacant** at least **5 (or ☐ _____) Days** Prior to Close Of Escrow, unless otherwise agreed in writing. **Note to Seller: If you are unable to deliver Property vacant in accordance with rent control and other applicable Law, you may be in breach of this Agreement.**

OR (ii) (if checked) ☐ **Tenant to remain in possession.** The attached addendum is incorporated into this Agreement (C.A.R. Form PAA, paragraph 3.);

OR (iii) (if checked) ☐ **This Agreement is contingent** upon Buyer and Seller entering into a written agreement regarding occupancy of the Property within the time specified in paragraph 14. If no written agreement is reached within this time, either Buyer or Seller may cancel this Agreement in writing.

C. Tenant - Occupied Property – Seller is responsible to deliver the property vacant, unless otherwise agreed, so that the Buyer can inspect the property before the close of escrow. If not possible or practicable, the Buyer and Seller may check the following options: **Tenant to Remain in Possession** (Use C.A.R. Form PAA, and check paragraph 3), or, if the Buyer and Seller have not agreed, **This Agreement is contingent**, to permit the parties to come to an agreement about possession of the tenant, or either may cancel the sales agreement (**in writing**) if no agreement is made.

It's important to remember that a tenant with a valid lease may remain in possession after the sale.

D. At Close Of Escrow, Seller assigns to Buyer any assignable warranty rights for items included in the sale and shall provide any available Copies of such warranties. Brokers cannot and will not determine the assignability of any warranties.

E. At Close Of Escrow, unless otherwise agreed in writing, Seller shall provide keys and/or means to operate all locks, mailboxes, security systems, alarms and garage door openers. If Property is a condominium or located in a common interest subdivision, Buyer may be required to pay a deposit to the Homeowners' Association ("HOA") to obtain keys to accessible HOA facilities.

D. Warranties – Warranties of third parties are automatically assigned by the contract on close of escrow. Seller provides Buyer with the warranty documentation.

E. Keys – Seller delivers keys and means of opening all locks at time of possession.

4. **ALLOCATION OF COSTS** (If checked): Unless otherwise specified here, this paragraph only determines who is to pay for the report, inspection, test or service mentioned. If not specified here or elsewhere in this Agreement, the determination of who is to pay for any work recommended or identified by any such report, inspection, test or service shall be by the method specified in paragraph 14.

A. **WOOD DESTROYING PEST INSPECTION:**

(1) ☐ Buyer ☒ Seller shall pay for an inspection and report for wood destroying pests and organisms ("Report") which shall be prepared by _____BUG-R-GONE_____, a registered structural pest control company. The Report shall cover the accessible areas of the main building and attached structures and, if checked: ☐ detached garages and carports, ☐ detached decks, ☐ the following other structures or areas _____ _____. The Report shall not include roof coverings. If Property is a condominium or located in a common interest subdivision, the Report shall include only the separate interest and any exclusive-use areas being transferred and shall not include common areas, unless otherwise agreed. Water tests of shower pans on upper level units may not be performed without consent of the owners of property below the shower.

OR (2) ☐ (If checked) The attached addendum (C.A.R. Form WPA) regarding wood destroying pest inspection and allocation of cost is incorporated into this Agreement.

4. ALLOCATION OF COSTS

Remember that termite clearance is not mandated by law—it's a lender's requirement. Who pays for the inspection is negotiable.

A1 and A2 – Wood Destroying Pest Inspection – The parties identify which of them is responsible to pay for inspection of wood destroying pests and which company is to prepare the report. **The report covers accessible areas of the main building and attached structures**. If other areas, including inaccessible areas, are to be inspected, the appropriate block should be checked or areas specified.

Section A1 is actual termite infestation and (in Southern California) is usually paid for by the Seller. **Section A2** is conditions that exist that may allow for termite infestation. In Southern California, the Buyer usually pays for this.

B. **OTHER INSPECTIONS AND REPORTS:**

(1) ☐ Buyer ☐ Seller shall pay to have septic or private sewage disposal systems inspected _____.
(2) ☐ Buyer ☐ Seller shall pay to have domestic wells tested for water potability and productivity _____.
(3) ☐ Buyer ☐ Seller shall pay for a natural hazard zone disclosure report prepared by _____.
(4) ☐ Buyer ☐ Seller shall pay for the following inspection or report _____.
(5) ☐ Buyer ☐ Seller shall pay for the following inspection or report _____.

B1-B5 – Other Inspections and Reports – This paragraph identifies who will pay for other reports such as earthquake fault, seismic, flood and fire zones, or other specified inspection reports.

C. GOVERNMENT REQUIREMENTS AND RETROFIT:
(1) ☐ Buyer ☒ Seller shall pay for smoke detector installation and/or water heater bracing, if required by Law. Prior to Close Of Escrow, Seller shall provide Buyer a written statement of compliance in accordance with state and local Law, unless exempt.
(2) ☐ Buyer ☐ Seller shall pay the cost of compliance with any other minimum mandatory government retrofit standards, inspections and reports if required as a condition of closing escrow under any Law. _____.

C1 and C2 – Government Requirements and Retrofit – The parties may negotiate who has to pay for compliance with smoke detector installation, water heater bracing, and any other retrofits required any governmental agency. **Seller must deliver a statement of compliance with such requirements to the Buyer.**

D. ESCROW AND TITLE:
(1) ☒ Buyer ☒ Seller shall pay escrow fee *50% / 50%* _____.
Escrow Holder shall be *ABC Escrow* _____.
(2) ☒ Buyer ☐ Seller shall pay for **owner's** title insurance policy specified in paragraph 12 _____.
Owner's title policy to be issued by _____.
(Buyer shall pay for any title insurance policy insuring Buyer's **lender**, unless otherwise agreed in writing.)

D1 and D2 – Escrow and Title Costs – The parties decide who is to pay for the title policy and escrow fee, which includes the "bare" escrow fee only, and who will be the provider. **Seller, however, must pay entire escrow fee for VA transactions.**

E. OTHER COSTS:
(1) ☐ Buyer ☐ Seller shall pay County transfer tax or transfer fee _____.
(2) ☐ Buyer ☐ Seller shall pay City transfer tax or transfer fee _____.
(3) ☐ Buyer ☐ Seller shall pay HOA transfer fee _____.
(4) ☐ Buyer ☐ Seller shall pay HOA document preparation fees _____.
(5) ☐ Buyer ☐ Seller shall pay the cost, not to exceed $ _____, of a one-year home warranty plan, issued by _____
with the following optional coverage: _____.
(6) ☐ Buyer ☐ Seller shall pay for _____.
(7) ☐ Buyer ☐ Seller shall pay for _____.

E1-E7 – Other Costs – The parties decide who will pay the fees for the enumerated costs, and any other cost items.

Some home warranties carry additional insurance covering Seller's liabilities in case of a lawsuit by the Buyer.

> 5. **STATUTORY DISCLOSURES (INCLUDING LEAD-BASED PAINT HAZARD DISCLOSURES) AND CANCELLATION RIGHTS:**
>   A. (1) Seller shall, within the time specified in paragraph 14, deliver to Buyer, if required by Law: (i) Federal Lead-Based Paint Disclosures and pamphlet ("Lead Disclosures"); and (ii) disclosures or notices required by sections 1102 et. seq. and 1103 et. seq. of the California Civil Code ("Statutory Disclosures"). Statutory Disclosures include, but are not limited to, a Real Estate Transfer Disclosure Statement ("TDS"), Natural Hazard Disclosure Statement ("NHD"), notice or actual knowledge of release of illegal controlled substance, notice of special tax and/or assessments (or, if allowed, substantially equivalent notice regarding the Mello-Roos Community Facilities Act and Improvement Bond Act of 1915) and, if Seller has actual knowledge, an industrial use and military ordnance location disclosure (C.A.R. Form SSD).
>   (2) Buyer shall, within the time specified in paragraph 14, return Signed Copies of the Statutory and Lead Disclosures to Seller.
>   (3) In the event Seller, prior to Close Of Escrow, becomes aware of adverse conditions materially affecting the Property, or any material inaccuracy in disclosures, information or representations previously provided to Buyer of which Buyer is otherwise unaware, Seller shall promptly provide a subsequent or amended disclosure or notice, in writing, covering those items. **However, a subsequent or amended disclosure shall not be required for conditions and material inaccuracies disclosed in reports ordered and paid for by Buyer.**

5. STATUTORY DISCLOSURES (INCLUDING LEAD-BASED PAINT HAZARD DISCLOSURES) AND CANCELLATION RIGHTS

A1 – This paragraph summarizes the statutory disclosure requirements for Seller to deliver two mandated forms: **(1)** the **Transfer Disclosure Statement**, and **(2)** a **Natural Hazards Disclosure**. It also summarizes the requirement to obtain a disclosure notice from the taxing authorities if the property is in a **Mello-Roos District**, or subject to an assessment under the **Improvement Bond Act of 1915**.

Neither the Transfer Disclosure Statement nor the Natural Hazard Disclosure forms are warranties or part of the contract.

If the Seller has actual knowledge, he or she must disclose to the Buyer if: (a) there has been a release of illegal substances on the property, (b) if the property is in or affected by an industrial use zone (manufacturing, commercial, or airport use), or located within one mile of a former military ordnance location.

The Seller must also provide the Buyer with a Lead-Based Paint notice as an attachment to the contract if the residential property was constructed before 1978.

Also, "local option" disclosures are required in some areas, and must be provided on the statutory format under Civil Code § 1102. Those local option disclosures trigger a 3-5 day rescission period.

A2 – By the terms of the contract, the Buyer must return the signed statutory and lead disclosures to the Seller within the time specified in **Paragraph 14**.

A3 – The Seller must give the Buyer an amended written disclosure if the Seller becomes aware of any adverse material condition before the close of escrow of which the Buyer is not aware.

> **(4)** If any disclosure or notice specified in 5A(1), or subsequent or amended disclosure or notice is delivered to Buyer after the offer is Signed, Buyer shall have the right to cancel this Agreement within **3 Days** After delivery in person, or **5 Days** After delivery by deposit in the mail, by giving written notice of cancellation to Seller or Seller's agent. (Lead Disclosures sent by mail must be sent certified mail or better.)
>
> **(5) Note to Buyer and Seller: Waiver of Statutory and Lead Disclosures is prohibited by Law.**

A4 – The buyer has a right of cancellation **within 3 days of personal delivery** of the Transfer Disclosure Statement, Natural Hazard Disclosure, and Lead-Based Disclosure or amended disclosure, or **5 days after mailing**, if given to the Buyer after acceptance of the contract. **Therefore, it's important to have all disclosures acknowledged as promptly as possible.** If given before acceptance, there is no cancellation period.

A5 – Statutory and lead disclosures by law cannot be waived by either the Buyer or the Seller.

> **B. NATURAL AND ENVIRONMENTAL HAZARDS:** Within the time specified in paragraph 14, Seller shall, if required by Law: **(i)** deliver to Buyer earthquake guides (and questionnaire) and environmental hazards booklet; **(ii)** even if exempt from the obligation to provide a NHD, disclose if the Property is located in a Special Flood Hazard Area; Potential Flooding (Inundation) Area; Very High Fire Hazard Zone; State Fire Responsibility Area; Earthquake Fault Zone; Seismic Hazard Zone; and **(iii)** disclose any other zone as required by Law and provide any other information required for those zones.

B. Natural and Environmental Hazards – The Seller must provide to the Buyer the natural hazard disclosures specified in Paragraph 5 within the time specified in Paragraph 14. The Natural Hazard Disclosure form is required to be used to make six natural hazard zone disclosures:

1. **Earthquake Fault Zone** (Seller must complete questionnaire page of *The Homeowner's Guide to Earthquake Safety* booklet and give it to the Buyer, but no additional information need be given);

2. **Seismic Hazard Zones**;

3. **State Fire Responsibility Z Disclosures** (Seller must inform Buyer that the state has no responsibility to provide fire protection services to any building unless an agreement is reached with local fire fighting agency);

4. **Very High Fire Severity Zones** (subject to high fire risks, which may require maintaining firebreaks, clearing brush, etc.);

5. **Flood Z A** (designated by the Federal Emergency Management Agency [FEMA]; flood insurance usually required); and

6. **Inundation Zones** (subject to flooding if dam fails).

 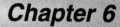

However, both the Seller and the broker must disclose known structural defects and earthquake hazards on the property.

If the Seller and broker deliver a copy of the *Environmental Hazard Booklet* (which discusses environmental hazards such as asbestos, formaldehyde, hazardous waste, household hazardous waste, lead, mold, and radon), they need not provide additional information, unless they have actual knowledge about the presence of those items on the property.

C. DATA BASE DISCLOSURE: NOTICE: The California Department of Justice, sheriff's departments, police departments serving jurisdictions of 200,000 or more and many other local law enforcement authorities maintain for public access a data base of the locations of persons required to register pursuant to paragraph (1) of subdivision (a) of Section 290.4 of the Penal Code. The data base is updated on a quarterly basis and a source of information about the presence of these individuals in any neighborhood. The Department of Justice also maintains a Sex Offender Identification Line through which inquiries about individuals may be made. This is a "900" telephone service. Callers must have specific information about individuals they are checking. Information regarding neighborhoods is not available through the "900" telephone service.

C. Data Base Disclosure

C. Data Base Disclosure – Statute requires the seller to inform the Buyer that information is available regarding the location of registered sexual offenders from law enforcement officials.

Forms and Disclosures listed in this purchase contract can be found in Chapter 7 of this textbook.

---

6. CONDOMINIUM/PLANNED UNIT DEVELOPMENT DISCLOSURES:
   A. **SELLER HAS: 7 (or ☐ _____) Days** After Acceptance to disclose to Buyer whether the Property is a condominium, or is located in a planned unit development or other common interest subdivision.
   B. If the Property is a condominium or is located in a planned unit development or other common interest subdivision, Seller has **3 (or ☐ _____) Days** After Acceptance to request from the HOA (C.A.R. Form HOA): **(i)** Copies of any documents required by Law; **(ii)** disclosure of any pending or anticipated claim or litigation by or against the HOA; **(iii)** a statement containing the location and number of designated parking and storage spaces; **(iv)** Copies of the most recent 12 months of HOA minutes for regular and special meetings; and **(v)** the names and contact information of all HOAs governing the Property (collectively, "CI Disclosures"). Seller shall itemize and deliver to Buyer all CI Disclosures received from the HOA and any CI Disclosures in Seller's possession. Buyer's approval of CI Disclosures is a contingency of this Agreement as specified in paragraph 14.

---

6. CONDOMINIUM/PLANNED UNIT DEVELOPMENT DISCLOSURES

This paragraph informs the Buyer, within a specified number of days after acceptance, that the property is part of a development where property is shared in common with other owners and is subject to certain common rules.

Seller must, within a specified number of days after acceptance, request from the Home Owners Association and provide to the Buyer certain contractually specified documents.

7. **CONDITIONS AFFECTING PROPERTY:**

 A. Unless otherwise agreed: (i) the Property is sold (a) in its PRESENT physical condition as of the date of Acceptance and (b) subject to Buyer's Investigation rights; (ii) the Property, including pool, spa, landscaping and grounds, is to be maintained in substantially the same condition as on the date of Acceptance; and (iii) all debris and personal property not included in the sale shall be removed by Close Of Escrow.

 B. SELLER SHALL, within the time specified in paragraph 14, DISCLOSE KNOWN MATERIAL FACTS AND DEFECTS affecting the Property, including known insurance claims within the past five years, AND MAKE OTHER DISCLOSURES REQUIRED BY LAW.

 C. NOTE TO BUYER: You are strongly advised to conduct investigations of the entire Property in order to determine its present condition since Seller may not be aware of all defects affecting the Property or other factors that you consider important. Property improvements may not be built according to code, in compliance with current Law, or have had permits issued.

 D. NOTE TO SELLER: Buyer has the right to inspect the Property and, as specified in paragraph 14, based upon information discovered in those inspections: (i) cancel this Agreement; or (ii) request that you make Repairs or take other action.

7. CONDITIONS AFFECTING PROPERTY

The property is to be transferred in substantially the same condition as on the date of the acceptance of the offer.

The Seller must also disclose known adverse material facts, including known insurance claims affecting the property, within the time specified in Paragraph 14.

The Buyer is admonished to conduct his or her own investigation of the property for all defect, because the property is sold without any warranties.

After inspecting the property, the Buyer, under Paragraph 14 of the agreement, may either: (1) cancel the agreement, or (2) request the Seller to make repairs or take other action.

8. ITEMS INCLUDED AND EXCLUDED:

A. NOTE TO BUYER AND SELLER: Items listed as included or excluded in the MLS, flyers or marketing materials are **not** included in the purchase price or excluded from the sale unless specified in 8B or C.

B. ITEMS INCLUDED IN SALE:

(1) All EXISTING fixtures and fittings that are attached to the Property;

(2) Existing electrical, mechanical, lighting, plumbing and heating fixtures, ceiling fans, fireplace inserts, gas logs and grates, solar systems, built-in appliances, window and door screens, awnings, shutters, window coverings, attached floor coverings, television antennas, satellite dishes, private integrated telephone systems, air coolers/conditioners, pool/spa equipment, garage door openers/remote controls, mailbox, in-ground landscaping, trees/shrubs, water softeners, water purifiers, security systems/alarms;

(3) The following items: _____

_____.

(4) Seller represents that all items included in the purchase price, unless otherwise specified, are owned by Seller.

(5) All items included shall be transferred free of liens and without Seller warranty.

C. ITEMS EXCLUDED FROM SALE: _____

_____.

8. ITEMS INCLUDED AND EXCLUDED

A. Note to Buyer and Seller – The contract alone determines what is or is not included in the sale of the property.

B. Items Included in Sale – The sale includes all existing attached fixtures and fittings. Certain items are listed, and others may be specified. All items are free of liens, and without warranty.

C. Items Excluded from Sale – The Seller and the Buyer may specify items excluded from the sale.

9. BUYER'S INVESTIGATION OF PROPERTY AND MATTERS AFFECTING PROPERTY:

A. Buyer's acceptance of the condition of, and any other matter affecting the Property, is a contingency of this Agreement as specified in this paragraph and paragraph 14. Within the time specified in paragraph 14, Buyer shall have the right, at Buyer's expense unless otherwise agreed, to conduct inspections, investigations, tests, surveys and other studies ("Buyer Investigations"), including, but not limited to, the right to: **(i)** inspect for lead-based paint and other lead-based paint hazards; **(ii)** inspect for wood destroying pests and organisms; **(iii)** review the registered sex offender database; **(iv)** confirm the insurability of Buyer and the Property; and **(v)** satisfy Buyer as to any matter specified in the attached Buyer's Inspection Advisory (C.A.R. Form BIA). Without Seller's prior written consent, Buyer shall neither make nor cause to be made: **(i)** invasive or destructive Buyer's Investigations; or **(ii)** inspections by any governmental building or zoning inspector or government employee, unless required by Law.

B. Buyer shall complete Buyer Investigations and, as specified in paragraph 14, remove the contingency or cancel the Agreement. Buyer shall give Seller, at no cost, complete Copies of all Buyer Investigation reports obtained by Buyer. Seller shall make the Property available for all Buyer Investigations. Seller shall have water, gas, electricity and all operable pilot lights on for Buyer's Investigations and through the date possession is made available to Buyer.

9. BUYER'S INVESTIGATION OF PROPERTY AND MATTERS AFFECTING PROPERTY

The Buyer's acceptance of the condition of the property or other matters affecting the property is a contingency of the agreement. Under paragraph 14, the Buyer, at his own expense unless otherwise agreed, has a specified period of time in which to conduct an investigation of the property including the specified types of investigations.

The Buyer then either removes the contingency or cancels the agreement within the time specified in paragraph 14. The Buyer will also provide the Seller with copies of any investigation reports at no cost.

> **10. REPAIRS:** Repairs shall be completed prior to final verification of condition unless otherwise agreed in writing. Repairs to be performed at Seller's expense may be performed by Seller or through others, provided that the work complies with applicable Law, including governmental permit, inspection and approval requirements. Repairs shall be performed in a good, skillful manner with materials of quality and appearance comparable to existing materials. It is understood that exact restoration of appearance or cosmetic items following all Repairs may not be possible. Seller shall: **(i)** obtain receipts for Repairs performed by others; **(ii)** prepare a written statement indicating the Repairs performed by Seller and the date of such Repairs; and **(iii)** provide Copies of receipts and statements to Buyer prior to final verification of condition.

10. REPAIRS

Repairs, if any, must be done with permits and in compliance with building codes and completed before the Buyer's final verification of condition of the property. Seller must obtain repair receipts, and prepare a written statement of performed repairs and dates for the Buyer.

> **11. BUYER INDEMNITY AND SELLER PROTECTION FOR ENTRY UPON PROPERTY:** Buyer shall: **(i)** keep the Property free and clear of liens; **(ii)** Repair all damage arising from Buyer Investigations; and **(iii)** indemnify and hold Seller harmless from all resulting liability, claims, demands, damages and costs. Buyer shall carry, or Buyer shall require anyone acting on Buyer's behalf to carry, policies of liability, workers' compensation and other applicable insurance, defending and protecting Seller from liability for any injuries to persons or property occurring during any Buyer Investigations or work done on the Property at Buyer's direction prior to Close Of Escrow. Seller is advised that certain protections may be afforded Seller by recording a "Notice of Non-responsibility" (C.A.R. Form NNR) for Buyer Investigations and work done on the Property at Buyer's direction. Buyer's obligations under this paragraph shall survive the termination of this Agreement.

11. BUYER INDEMNITY AND SELLER PROTECTION FOR ENTRY UPON PROPERTY

The Buyer must assure the Seller that the Seller will not be harmed as a result of the Buyer's investigations. Assurances include the Buyer will: (1) keep property free and clear of liens; (2) repair all damage arising from his investigations; and (3) indemnify and hold the Seller harmless for any damage or claims.

Seller may protect himself or herself by, among other things, recording a **"Notice of Non-Responsibility."**

12. TITLE AND VESTING:
  A. Within the time specified in paragraph 14, Buyer shall be provided a current preliminary (title) report, which is only an offer by the title insurer to issue a policy of title insurance and may not contain every item affecting title. Buyer's review of the preliminary report and any other matters which may affect title are a contingency of this Agreement as specified in paragraph 14.
  B. Title is taken in its present condition subject to all encumbrances, easements, covenants, conditions, restrictions, rights and other matters, whether of record or not, as of the date of Acceptance except: **(i)** monetary liens of record unless Buyer is assuming those obligations or taking the Property subject to those obligations; and **(ii)** those matters which Seller has agreed to remove in writing.
  C. Within the time specified in paragraph 14, Seller has a duty to disclose to Buyer all matters known to Seller affecting title, whether of record or not.
  D. At Close Of Escrow, Buyer shall receive a grant deed conveying title (or, for stock cooperative or long-term lease, an assignment of stock certificate or of Seller's leasehold interest), including oil, mineral and water rights if currently owned by Seller. Title shall vest as designated in Buyer's supplemental escrow instructions. THE MANNER OF TAKING TITLE MAY HAVE SIGNIFICANT LEGAL AND TAX CONSEQUENCES. CONSULT AN APPROPRIATE PROFESSIONAL.
  E. Buyer shall receive a CLTA/ALTA Homeowner's Policy of Title Insurance. A title company, at Buyer's request, can provide information about the availability, desirability, coverage, and cost of various title insurance coverages and endorsements. If Buyer desires title coverage other than that required by this paragraph, Buyer shall instruct Escrow Holder in writing and pay any increase in cost.

12. TITLE AND VESTING

A. The Buyer has the amount of time specified in paragraph 14 to review the preliminary title report and notify the seller of any corrective action.

B. The Buyer takes title in its present condition subject to all liens and encumbrances as of the date of acceptance, whether of record or not, except: (1) monetary lien of record unless assumed by the Buyer or taken by the Buyer subject to them, and (2) matters to which the Seller has agreed to remove.

C. Seller must disclose to Buyer all matters affecting title, whether of record or not, that are known to Seller.

D. Usually, the Buyer will be given a grant deed by the seller at close of escrow. Buyer's escrow shall designate vesting.

As an agent, you should never advise how to take title. For more information on the methods of taking title (vesting), see Chapter 9.

E. This paragraph provides that a Buyer will receive a CLTA/ALTA Homeowner's Policy of Title Insurance.

13. SALE OF BUYER'S PROPERTY:
  A. This Agreement is NOT contingent upon the sale of any property owned by Buyer.
  OR B. ☐ (If checked): The attached addendum (C.A.R. Form COP) regarding the contingency for the sale of property owned by Buyer is incorporated into this Agreement.

13. SALE OF BUYER'S PROPERTY

Unless paragraph 13B is checked, the sale of Buyer's property is **not a contingency** of the agreement and, therefore, will not be a loophole for the Buyer to get out of the contract. If it is a contingency, a separate addendum must be attached to the agreement.

14. **TIME PERIODS; REMOVAL OF CONTINGENCIES; CANCELLATION RIGHTS:** The following time periods may only be extended, altered, modified or changed by mutual written agreement. Any removal of contingencies or cancellation under this paragraph must be in writing (C.A.R. Form RRCR).
   A. **SELLER HAS: 7 (or ☐ _____) Days** After Acceptance to deliver to Buyer all reports, disclosures and information for which Seller is responsible under paragraphs 4, 5A and B, 6A, 7B and 12.
   B. (1) **BUYER HAS: 17 (or ☐ _____) Days** After Acceptance, unless otherwise agreed in writing, to:
      (i) complete all Buyer Investigations; approve all disclosures, reports and other applicable information, which Buyer receives from Seller; and approve all matters affecting the Property (including lead-based paint and lead-based paint hazards as well as other information specified in paragraph 5 and insurability of Buyer and the Property); and
      (ii) return to Seller Signed Copies of Statutory and Lead Disclosures delivered by Seller in accordance with paragraph 5A.
      (2) Within the time specified in 14B(1), Buyer may request that Seller make repairs or take any other action regarding the Property. Seller has no obligation to agree to or respond to Buyer's requests. (C.A.R. Form RR)
      (3) By the end of the time specified in 14B(1) (or 2I for loan contingency or 2J for appraisal contingency), Buyer shall, in writing, remove the applicable contingency (C.A.R. Form RRCR) or cancel this Agreement. However, if the following inspections, reports or disclosures are not made within the time specified in 14A, then Buyer has 5 (or ☐ _____) **Days** after receipt of any such items, or the time specified in 14B(1), whichever is later, to remove the applicable contingency or cancel this Agreement in writing: **(i)** government-mandated inspections or reports required as a condition of closing; or **(ii)** Common Interest Disclosures pursuant to paragraph 6B.

14. TIME PERIODS; WAIVER OF CONTINGENCIES; CANCELLATION RIGHTS

The time period for each contingency, which run from the date of acceptance of the agreement, are specified in the applicable paragraph and set forth for both the Seller and Buyer.

A. Seller Time Periods – The Seller must deliver within **7 days, or the specified number of days,** all reports and disclosures for which he is responsible under paragraphs 4 (Allocation of costs), 5A and B (Seller's statutory disclosures), 6A (Condominium or Planned Unit disclosures), 7B (Seller disclosure of known material facts) and 12 (Title and Vesting).

B. Buyer Time Periods – The Buyer must, **within 17 days, or the specified number of days,**:

(1) complete all investigations and review of reports, insurability investigations, and return copies of signed statutory disclosures.

(2) request Seller to make repairs. But the Seller may opt not to make them.

(3) in writing, either remove the contingency or cancel the agreement. However, if the Seller does not deliver mandated disclosures which are a condition to closing, the Buyer has **5 days after receipt of such notice, in writing,** to either remove the contingency or cancel the agreement.

C. **CONTINUATION OF CONTINGENCY OR CONTRACTUAL OBLIGATION; SELLER RIGHT TO CANCEL:**
(1) **Seller right to Cancel; Buyer Contingencies:** Seller, after first giving Buyer a Notice to Buyer to Perform (as specified below), may cancel this Agreement in writing and authorize return of Buyer's deposit if, by the time specified in this Agreement, Buyer does not remove in writing the applicable contingency or cancel this Agreement. Once all contingencies have been removed, failure of either Buyer or Seller to close escrow on time may be a breach of this Agreement.
(2) **Continuation of Contingency:** Even after the expiration of the time specified in 14B(1), Buyer retains the right to make requests to Seller, remove in writing the applicable contingency or cancel this Agreement until Seller cancels pursuant to 14C(1). Once Seller receives Buyer's written removal of all contingencies, Seller may not cancel this Agreement pursuant to 14C(1).
(3) **Seller right to Cancel; Buyer Contract Obligations:** Seller, after first giving Buyer a Notice to Buyer to Perform (as specified below), may cancel this Agreement in writing and authorize return of Buyer's deposit for any of the following reasons: **(i)** if Buyer fails to deposit funds as required by 2A or 2B; **(ii)** if the funds deposited pursuant to 2A or 2B are not good when deposited; **(iii)** if Buyer fails to provide a letter as required by 2G; **(iv)** if Buyer fails to provide verification as required by 2H or 2L; **(v)** if Seller reasonably disapproves of the verification provided by 2H or 2L; **(vi)** if Buyer fails to return Statutory and Lead Disclosures as required by paragraph 5A(2); or **(vii)** if Buyer fails to sign or initial a separate liquidated damage form for an increased deposit as required by paragraph 16. **Seller is not required to give Buyer a Notice to Perform regarding Close of Escrow.**
(4) **Notice To Buyer To Perform:** The Notice to Buyer to Perform (C.A.R. Form NBP) shall: **(i)** be in writing; **(ii)** be signed by Seller; and **(iii)** give Buyer at least **24** (or ☐ _____) hours (or until the time specified in the applicable paragraph, whichever occurs last) to take the applicable action. A Notice to Buyer to Perform may not be given any earlier than **2 Days** Prior to the expiration of the applicable time for Buyer to remove a contingency or cancel this Agreement or meet a 14C(3) obligation.

C. Continuation of Contingency or Contractual Obligation; Seller Right to Cancel

(1) Seller Right to Cancel; Buyer Contingencies – After first giving the Buyer a Notice to Buyer to Perform, the Seller may cancel the agreement and return the deposit if the Buyer does not remove the contingencies or cancel the agreement within the time period specified in paragraph 14B.

(2) Continuation of Contingency – Buyer retains the right to make requests of Seller, remove contingencies, or cancel agreement until Seller exercises cancellation rights—even after expiration of time periods provided in paragraph 14B(1).

(3) Seller Right to Cancel; Buyer Contract Obligation – After giving the Buyer a Notice to Buyer to Perform, Seller may cancel the agreement in writing and return the Buyer's deposit for reasons including:

(i) Buyer failing to deposit required funds (paragraph 2A or B);

(ii) Deposited funds not good when deposited (paragraph 2A or B);

(iii) Buyer failing to provide prequalification and pre-approval letter from lender (paragraph 2G);

(iv) Buyer failing to provide deposit or cash fund verification (paragraph 2H or L);

(v) Seller reasonably disapproving of deposit or cash fund verification (paragraph 2H or L);

(vi) Buyer failing to return Statutory Lead Disclosures (paragraph 5A);

(vii) Buyer failing to sign or initial a separate liquidation damage form for an increased deposit (paragraph 16.) **Liquidated damage may be increased by an additional deposit not to exceed 3%.**

(4) Notice to Buyer to Perform – The Seller's written and signed Notice to Buyer to Perform may be given within 24 hours, or a time specified in Paragraph 14B(1), and no earlier than 2 days before the applicable time for the Buyer to remove a contingency or cancel the agreement expires.

> **D. EFFECT OF BUYER'S REMOVAL OF CONTINGENCIES :** If Buyer removes, in writing, any contingency or cancellation rights, unless otherwise specified in a separate written agreement between Buyer and Seller, Buyer shall conclusively be deemed to have: **(i)** completed all Buyer Investigations, and review of reports and other applicable information and disclosures pertaining to that contingency or cancellation right; **(ii)** elected to proceed with the transaction; and **(iii)** assumed all liability, responsibility and expense for Repairs or corrections pertaining to that contingency or cancellation right, or for inability to obtain financing.
>
> **E. EFFECT OF CANCELLATION ON DEPOSITS:** If Buyer or Seller gives written notice of cancellation pursuant to rights duly exercised under the terms of this Agreement, Buyer and Seller agree to Sign mutual instructions to cancel the sale and escrow and release deposits, less fees and costs, to the party entitled to the funds. Fees and costs may be payable to service providers and vendors for services and products provided during escrow. **Release of funds will require mutual Signed release instructions from Buyer and Seller, judicial decision or arbitration award. A party may be subject to a civil penalty of up to $1,000 for refusal to sign such instructions if no good faith dispute exists as to who is entitled to the deposited funds (Civil Code §1057.3).**

D. Effect of Buyer's Removal of Contingencies – If Buyer removes, in writing, any contingency or cancellation rights, Buyer will conclusively be deemed to have: (i) completed all that needed to be done pertaining to the contingency or cancellation; (ii) elected to proceed with the transaction; and (iii) assumed all responsibility for completing the transaction.

E. Effect of Cancellation on Deposits – If the agreement is cancelled, the Buyer and Seller agree that the Buyer's deposit, less costs and fees, shall be returned. A notice of cancellation signed by the Buyer and the Seller will be provided to the escrow holder to release the deposit (it's never automatic).

> **15. FINAL VERIFICATION OF CONDITION:** Buyer shall have the right to make a final inspection of the Property within **5 (or _____) Days** Prior to Close Of Escrow, NOT AS A CONTINGENCY OF THE SALE, but solely to confirm: **(i)** the Property is maintained pursuant to paragraph 7A; **(ii)** Repairs have been completed as agreed; and **(iii)** Seller has complied with Seller's other obligations under this Agreement.

15. FINAL VERIFICATION OF CONDITION

This paragraph authorizes a "final walk-through" for the Buyer, within a specified number of days before close of escrow, to verify condition of property is as agreed and that Seller has complied with repair duties and other obligations.

16. **LIQUIDATED DAMAGES:** If Buyer fails to complete this purchase because of Buyer's default, Seller shall retain, as liquidated damages, the deposit actually paid. If the Property is a dwelling with no more than four units, one of which Buyer intends to occupy, then the amount retained shall be no more than 3% of the purchase price. Any excess shall be returned to Buyer. Release of funds will require mutual, Signed release instructions from both Buyer and Seller, judicial decision or arbitration award.
BUYER AND SELLER SHALL SIGN A SEPARATE LIQUIDATED DAMAGES PROVISION FOR ANY INCREASED DEPOSIT. (C.A.R. FORM RID)

Buyer's Initials	_WB OB_	Seller's Initials	_TJ. yp_

16. LIQUIDATED DAMAGES

This paragraph provides the amount of money that the Buyer agrees to pay the Seller if the Buyer breaches the agreement. It limits the amount to which the seller is entitled. The remedy is the amount of the deposit, up to 3% of the purchase price, if the property is a one-to-four unit dwelling, one of which was to be occupied by the Buyer. If not, the liquidated damages are for a reasonable amount of the deposit. **Buyers and Sellers must initial this section where indicated in order for this clause to apply.**

17. **DISPUTE RESOLUTION:**
   A. **MEDIATION:** Buyer and Seller agree to mediate any dispute or claim arising between them out of this Agreement, or any resulting transaction, before resorting to arbitration or court action. Paragraphs 17B(2) and (3) below apply whether or not the Arbitration provision is initialed. Mediation fees, if any, shall be divided equally among the parties involved. If, for any dispute or claim to which this paragraph applies, any party commences an action without first attempting to resolve the matter through mediation, or refuses to mediate after a request has been made, then that party shall not be entitled to recover attorney fees, even if they would otherwise be available to that party in any such action. THIS MEDIATION PROVISION APPLIES WHETHER OR NOT THE ARBITRATION PROVISION IS INITIALED.

17. DISPUTE RESOLUTION

A. **Mediation** – Under this mandatory provision, the Buyer and Seller agree to mediation by a neutral mediator to attempt to resolve any disputes. If mediation is not attempted by a party before filing an arbitration or court action, that party will not be entitled to be awarded legal fees, even if they are the prevailing party.

B. ARBITRATION OF DISPUTES: (1) Buyer and Seller agree that any dispute or claim in Law or equity arising between them out of this Agreement or any resulting transaction, which is not settled through mediation, shall be decided by neutral, binding arbitration, including and subject to paragraphs 17B(2) and (3) below. The arbitrator shall be a retired judge or justice, or an attorney with at least 5 years of residential real estate Law experience, unless the parties mutually agree to a different arbitrator, who shall render an award in accordance with substantive California Law. The parties shall have the right to discovery in accordance with California Code of Civil Procedure §1283.05. In all other respects, the arbitration shall be conducted in accordance with Title 9 of Part III of the California Code of Civil Procedure. Judgment upon the award of the arbitrator(s) may be entered into any court having jurisdiction. Interpretation of this agreement to arbitrate shall be governed by the Federal Arbitration Act.

(2) EXCLUSIONS FROM MEDIATION AND ARBITRATION: The following matters are excluded from mediation and arbitration: **(i)** a judicial or non-judicial foreclosure or other action or proceeding to enforce a deed of trust, mortgage or installment land sale contract as defined in California Civil Code §2985; **(ii)** an unlawful detainer action; **(iii)** the filing or enforcement of a mechanic's lien; and **(iv)** any matter that is within the jurisdiction of a probate, small claims or bankruptcy court. The filing of a court action to enable the recording of a notice of pending action, for order of attachment, receivership, injunction, or other provisional remedies, shall not constitute a waiver of the mediation and arbitration provisions.

(3) BROKERS: Buyer and Seller agree to mediate and arbitrate disputes or claims involving either or both Brokers, consistent with 17 A and B, provided either or both Brokers shall have agreed to such mediation or arbitration prior to, or within a reasonable time after, the dispute or claim is presented to Brokers. Any election by either or both Brokers to participate in mediation or arbitration shall not result in Brokers being deemed parties to the Agreement.

"NOTICE: BY INITIALING IN THE SPACE BELOW YOU ARE AGREEING TO HAVE ANY DISPUTE ARISING OUT OF THE MATTERS INCLUDED IN THE 'ARBITRATION OF DISPUTES' PROVISION DECIDED BY NEUTRAL ARBITRATION AS PROVIDED BY CALIFORNIA LAW AND YOU ARE GIVING UP ANY RIGHTS YOU MIGHT POSSESS TO HAVE THE DISPUTE LITIGATED IN A COURT OR JURY TRIAL. BY INITIALING IN THE SPACE BELOW YOU ARE GIVING UP YOUR JUDICIAL RIGHTS TO DISCOVERY AND APPEAL, UNLESS THOSE RIGHTS ARE SPECIFICALLY INCLUDED IN THE 'ARBITRATION OF DISPUTES' PROVISION. IF YOU REFUSE TO SUBMIT TO ARBITRATION AFTER AGREEING TO THIS PROVISION, YOU MAY BE COMPELLED TO ARBITRATE UNDER THE AUTHORITY OF THE CALIFORNIA CODE OF CIVIL PROCEDURE. YOUR AGREEMENT TO THIS ARBITRATION PROVISION IS VOLUNTARY."

"WE HAVE READ AND UNDERSTAND THE FOREGOING AND AGREE TO SUBMIT DISPUTES ARISING OUT OF THE MATTERS INCLUDED IN THE 'ARBITRATION OF DISPUTES' PROVISION TO NEUTRAL ARBITRATION."

Buyer's Initials _WB / DB_   Seller's Initials _TL / _____

B. Arbitration of Disputes – This paragraph must be initialed by both the Buyer and Seller to be included in the agreement. By initialing this contract provision, the parties are agreeing in advance to arbitrate arising out of their agreement. If Sellers are not agreeable to this clause, they must incorporate this in a counter offer.

Subparagraph (1) sets forth the terms of the arbitration agreement, including the right to discovery. Although the mediation is non-binding, the arbitration will result in a binding decision made by a neutral arbitrator, with no appeal rights.

Subparagraph (2) sets forth the matters which are excluded from mediation and arbitration.

Subparagraph (3) sets forth the agreement of the Buyer and Seller to mediate and arbitrate claims involving the broker(s), if they agree within a reasonable time after the claim is made.

The broker should not advise either the Seller or the Buyer whether to initial the arbitration provision in paragraph 17B. Never give legal or tax advice.

18. PRORATIONS OF PROPERTY TAXES AND OTHER ITEMS: Unless otherwise agreed in writing, the following items shall be PAID CURRENT and prorated between Buyer and Seller as of Close Of Escrow: real property taxes and assessments, interest, rents, HOA regular, special, and emergency dues and assessments imposed prior to Close Of Escrow, premiums on insurance assumed by Buyer, payments on bonds and assessments assumed by Buyer, and payments on Mello-Roos and other Special Assessment District bonds and assessments that are now a lien. The following items shall be assumed by Buyer WITHOUT CREDIT toward the purchase price: prorated payments on Mello-Roos and other Special Assessment District bonds and assessments and HOA special assessments that are now a lien but not yet due. Property will be reassessed upon change of ownership. Any supplemental tax bills shall be paid as follows: **(i)** for periods after Close Of Escrow, by Buyer; and **(ii)** for periods prior to Close Of Escrow, by Seller. TAX BILLS ISSUED AFTER CLOSE OF ESCROW SHALL BE HANDLED DIRECTLY BETWEEN BUYER AND SELLER. Prorations shall be made based on a 30-day month.

18. PRORATIONS OF PROPERTY TAXES AND OTHER ITEMS

Prorated items shall be paid current by the Seller and assumed by the Buyer as of the close of escrow. The Mello-Roos and other Special Assessments District Bonds and assessments and Home Owners Association (HOA) special assessments not yet due, but a lien, do not constitute a credit toward the purchase price.

19. WITHHOLDING TAXES: Seller and Buyer agree to execute any instrument, affidavit, statement or instruction reasonably necessary to comply with federal (FIRPTA) and California withholding Law, if required (C.A.R. Forms AS and AB).

19. WITHHOLDING TAXES

The two tax withholding laws that affect the transfer of all real property are:

(1) Buyer is responsible under Federal law for withholding 10% of the Seller's gross selling price if the Seller is a "foreign person" as defined by the Foreign Investment in Real Property Tax Act (FIRPTA). Buyer is responsible for the amount of the tax. But the broker is responsible for the failure to withhold taxes.

(2) 3.33% of the gross selling price must be withheld under California law, on all non-personal residences, if the seller's last known address is outside of California or if the Seller's proceeds are being paid to a financial intermediary. The Buyer is responsible for withholding the funds if he or she is notified by the escrow holder of the requirement to withhold. If not notified, the escrow holder is liable for the actual amount of the tax due.

---

20. MULTIPLE LISTING SERVICE ("MLS"): Brokers are authorized to report to the MLS a pending sale and, upon Close Of Escrow, the terms of this transaction to be published and disseminated to persons and entities authorized to use the information on terms approved by the MLS.

21. EQUAL HOUSING OPPORTUNITY: The Property is sold in compliance with federal, state and local anti-discrimination Laws.

22. ATTORNEY FEES: In any action, proceeding, or arbitration between Buyer and Seller arising out of this Agreement, the prevailing Buyer or Seller shall be entitled to reasonable attorney fees and costs from the non-prevailing Buyer or Seller, except as provided in paragraph 17A.

23. SELECTION OF SERVICE PROVIDERS: If Brokers refer Buyer or Seller to persons, vendors, or service or product providers ("Providers"), Brokers do not guarantee the performance of any Providers. Buyer and Seller may select ANY Providers of their own choosing.

---

20. MULTIPLE LISTING AGREEMENT

The parties authorized to disseminate the price, terms, and financing to authorized persons and entities.

21. EQUAL HOUSING OPPORTUNITY

It is illegal to discriminate on the basis of race, color, religion, sex, handicap, familial status, or national origin under both Federal and California law.

22. ATTORNEY FEES

This paragraph relates to disputes between only the Buyer and the Seller. Under this paragraph, the prevailing party is entitled to attorney's fees from the non-prevailing party in any arbitration or court action. **If a party initiates an arbitration or court action without first attempting to mediate the dispute under paragraph 17A, that party is not entitled to attorney's fees even if he or she is the prevailing party.**

23. SELECTION OF SERVICE PROVIDER

Service providers may be selected by the Seller and the Buyer, but the broker does not guarantee their performance.

> **24. TIME OF ESSENCE; ENTIRE CONTRACT; CHANGES:** Time is of the essence. All understandings between the parties are incorporated in this Agreement. Its terms are intended by the parties as a final, complete and exclusive expression of their Agreement with respect to its subject matter, and may not be contradicted by evidence of any prior agreement or contemporaneous oral agreement. If any provision of this Agreement is held to be ineffective or invalid, the remaining provisions will nevertheless be given full force and effect. **Neither this Agreement nor any provision in it may be extended, amended, modified, altered or changed, except in writing Signed by Buyer and Seller.**

24. TIME OF ESSENCE; ENTIRE CONTRACT; CHANGES

The Buyer and Seller agree that any act must take place on the time and date stated in the agreement. Any changes to the agreement must be in writing. Evidence of any prior oral agreements may not be used to contradict the written terms of this agreement.

This agreement incorporates all prior oral and written agreements.

> **25. OTHER TERMS AND CONDITIONS,** including attached supplements:
> A. ☑ Buyer's Inspection Advisory (C.A.R. Form BIA)
> B. ☐ Purchase Agreement Addendum (C.A.R. Form PAA paragraph numbers: _____)
> C. _____
> _____
> _____

25. OTHER TERMS AND CONDITIONS

Additional provisions to this agreement must be in writing, and should be set forth here or on written attachments. Two additional terms, the Buyer's Inspection Advisory (C.A.R. form BIA) and the Purchase Agreement Addendum (C.A.R. form PAA) may be checked to supplement the agreement. The paragraph number of the Purchase Agreement Addendum should be filled in. Both documents, if applicable, should be attached to the agreement.

Add "Seller to provide termite clearance report," otherwise the broker may end up paying for termite eradication.

26. DEFINITIONS: As used in this Agreement:

A. **"Acceptance"** means the time the offer or final counter offer is accepted in writing by a party and is delivered to and personally received by the other party or that party's authorized agent in accordance with the terms of this offer or a final counter offer.

B. **"Agreement"** means the terms and conditions of this accepted California Residential Purchase Agreement and any accepted counter offers and addenda.

C. **"C.A.R. Form"** means the specific form referenced or another comparable form agreed to by the parties.

D. **"Close Of Escrow"** means the date the grant deed, or other evidence of transfer of title, is recorded. If the scheduled close of escrow falls on a Saturday, Sunday or legal holiday, then close of escrow shall be the next business day after the scheduled close of escrow date.

E. **"Copy"** means copy by any means including photocopy, NCR, facsimile and electronic.

F. **"Days"** means calendar days, unless otherwise required by Law.

G. **"Days After"** means the specified number of calendar days after the occurrence of the event specified, not counting the calendar date on which the specified event occurs, and ending at 11:59PM on the final day.

H. **"Days Prior"** means the specified number of calendar days before the occurrence of the event specified, not counting the calendar date on which the specified event is scheduled to occur.

I. **"Electronic Copy" or "Electronic Signature"** means, as applicable, an electronic copy or signature complying with California Law. Buyer and Seller agree that electronic means will not be used by either party to modify or alter the content or integrity of this Agreement without the knowledge and consent of the other.

J. **"Law"** means any law, code, statute, ordinance, regulation, rule or order, which is adopted by a controlling city, county, state or federal legislative, judicial or executive body or agency.

K. **"Notice to Buyer to Perform"** means a document (C.A.R. Form NBP), which shall be in writing and Signed by Seller and shall give Buyer at least 24 hours **(or as otherwise specified in paragraph 14C(4))** to remove a contingency or perform as applicable.

L. **"Repairs"** means any repairs (including pest control), alterations, replacements, modifications or retrofitting of the Property provided for under this Agreement.

M. **"Signed"** means either a handwritten or electronic signature on an original document, Copy or any counterpart.

N. **Singular and Plural** terms each include the other, when appropriate.

26. DEFINITIONS

This paragraph defines certain terms for the purpose of the agreement. For purposes of calendaring time periods, the definitions of "Days," "Day after," and "Days prior" should be reviewed.

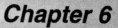
27. AGENCY:

    A. DISCLOSURE: Buyer and Seller each acknowledge prior receipt of C.A.R. Form AD "Disclosure Regarding Real Estate Agency Relationships."

    B. POTENTIALLY COMPETING BUYERS AND SELLERS: Buyer and Seller each acknowledge receipt of a disclosure of the possibility of multiple representation by the Broker representing that principal. This disclosure may be part of a listing agreement, buyer-broker agreement or separate document (C.A.R. Form DA). Buyer understands that Broker representing Buyer may also represent other potential buyers, who may consider, make offers on or ultimately acquire the Property. Seller understands that Broker representing Seller may also represent other sellers with competing properties of interest to this Buyer.

    C. CONFIRMATION: The following agency relationships are hereby confirmed for this transaction:
Listing Agent _*Sail Realty*_____ (Print Firm Name) is the agent of (check one): ☒ the Seller exclusively; or ☐ both the Buyer and Seller.
Selling Agent _*Ramos Realty*_____(Print Firm Name) (if not same as Listing Agent) is the agent of (check one): ☒ the Buyer exclusively; or ☐ the Seller exclusively; or ☐ both the Buyer and Seller. Real Estate Brokers are not parties to the Agreement between Buyer and Seller.

27. AGENCY

  A. Disclosure – The Buyer and the Seller acknowledge in this paragraph prior receipt of the form Disclosure Regarding Real Estate Agency Relationships (C.A.R. Form DA-11). This form is required to be presented to:

    (1) the Seller before taking a listing;
    (2) the Buyer before signing a contract to purchase; and
    (3) the Seller before presenting the offer (if the selling agent is not also the listing agent).

  B. Potentially Competing Buyers and Sellers – In this paragraph, both the Seller and the Buyer are advised of and consent to the fact that the broker of either the Seller or the Buyer might compete with the Buyer and the Seller for the property being purchased. Buyer's broker may represent other buyers of the property, and Seller's broker may represent sellers of competing properties.

  C. Confirmation – This confirmation of the agency relationship of listing and selling agents, which is required under Civil Code § 2079.17, needs to be signed concurrent with the execution of the Purchase Agreement.

  If this paragraph is not filled in at the time the Purchase Agreement is executed, then a written counter offer and a confirmation on a statutory form must be attached to the counter offer.

  Note well: The selling broker, who wrote this offer, must sign and present a disclosure to the Seller before presenting this offer, even if the listing broker already gave the Seller a written disclosure.

28. JOINT ESCROW INSTRUCTIONS TO ESCROW HOLDER:

A. The following paragraphs, or applicable portions thereof, of this Agreement constitute the joint escrow instructions of Buyer and Seller to Escrow Holder, which Escrow Holder is to use along with any related counter offers and addenda, and any additional mutual instructions to close the escrow: 1, 2, 4, 12, 13B, 14E, 18, 19, 24, 25B and C, 26, 28, 29, 32A, 33 and paragraph D of the section titled Real Estate Brokers on page 8. If a Copy of the separate compensation agreement(s) provided for in paragraph 29 or 32A, or paragraph D of the section titled Real Estate Brokers on page 8 is deposited with Escrow Holder by Broker, Escrow Holder shall accept such agreement(s) and pay out from Buyer's or Seller's funds, or both, as applicable, the Broker's compensation provided for in such agreement(s). The terms and conditions of this Agreement not set forth in the specified paragraphs are additional matters for the information of Escrow Holder, but about which Escrow Holder need not be concerned. Buyer and Seller will receive Escrow Holder's general provisions directly from Escrow Holder and will execute such provisions upon Escrow Holder's request. To the extent the general provisions are inconsistent or conflict with this Agreement, the general provisions will control as to the duties and obligations of Escrow Holder only. Buyer and Seller will execute additional instructions, documents and forms provided by Escrow Holder that are reasonably necessary to close escrow.

B. A Copy of this Agreement shall be delivered to Escrow Holder within **3** business days after Acceptance (or ☐ _____). Buyer and Seller authorize Escrow Holder to accept and rely on Copies and Signatures as defined in this Agreement as originals, to open escrow and for other purposes of escrow. The validity of this Agreement as between Buyer and Seller is not affected by whether or when Escrow Holder Signs this Agreement.

C. Brokers are a party to the escrow for the sole purpose of compensation pursuant to paragraphs 29, 32A and paragraph D of the section titled Real Estate Brokers on page 8. Buyer and Seller irrevocably assign to Brokers compensation specified in paragraphs 29 and 32A, respectively, and irrevocably instruct Escrow Holder to disburse those funds to Brokers at Close Of Escrow or pursuant to any other mutually executed cancellation agreement. Compensation instructions can be amended or revoked only with the written consent of Brokers. Escrow Holder shall immediately notify Brokers: **(I)** if Buyer's initial or any additional deposit is not made pursuant to this Agreement, or is not good at time of deposit with Escrow Holder; or **(II)** if Buyer and Seller instruct Escrow Holder to cancel escrow.

D. A Copy of any amendment that affects any paragraph of this Agreement for which Escrow Holder is responsible shall be delivered to Escrow Holder within **2** business days after mutual execution of the amendment.

28. JOINT ESCROW INSTRUCTIONS

A. This paragraph specifies which portions of the purchase agreement constitute instructions from the Buyer and Seller to the escrow holder. The escrow holder will disburse broker's compensation under separate compensation agreements provided for in paragraphs 29 or 32A and the Real Estate Broker section of the agreement.

B. The parties agree to deliver the agreement to the escrow within 3 business days, unless otherwise specified. The agreement is valid whether or when the escrow holder signs the agreement.

C. Brokers are parties to the agreement solely for compensation purposes. Buyer and Seller agree to irrevocably assign the compensation that is provided in the agreement to the brokers and irrevocably instruct the escrow holder to disburse those funds at the close of escrow, or under a mutually executed cancellation agreement.

D. The Buyer and Seller agree to provide the escrow holder with a copy of any written amendment affecting any paragraph of the agreement that is also an escrow instruction within 2 business days after it is executed.

29. **BROKER COMPENSATION FROM BUYER:** If applicable, upon Close Of Escrow, **Buyer** agrees to pay compensation to Broker as specified in a separate written agreement between Buyer and Broker.

29. BROKER COMPENSATION FROM BUYER

Under this paragraph, if the Buyer has a separate compensation agreement with the Buyer's broker, compensation will be paid at the close of escrow.

30. **TERMS AND CONDITIONS OF OFFER:**
This is an offer to purchase the Property on the above terms and conditions. All paragraphs with spaces for initials by Buyer and Seller are incorporated in this Agreement only if initialed by all parties. If at least one but not all parties initial, a counter offer is required until agreement is reached. Seller has the right to continue to offer the Property for sale and to accept any other offer at any time prior to notification of Acceptance. Buyer has read and acknowledges receipt of a Copy of the offer and agrees to the above confirmation of agency relationships. If this offer is accepted and Buyer subsequently defaults, Buyer may be responsible for payment of Brokers' compensation. This Agreement and any supplement, addendum or modification, including any Copy, may be Signed in two or more counterparts, all of which shall constitute one and the same writing.

30. TERMS AND CONDITIONS OF OFFER

This paragraph provides that the agreement is an offer to purchase property on the terms and conditions set forth in the agreement.

The terms of paragraphs with spaces for initials by both the Buyer and the Seller are incorporated into the agreement only if initialed by all parties. If all parties have not initialed those paragraphs, a counter offer is required because a party has not accepted the offer exactly as written.

31. EXPIRATION OF OFFER: This offer shall be deemed revoked and the deposit shall be returned unless the offer is Signed by Seller and a Copy of the Signed offer is personally received by Buyer, or by _____, who is authorized to receive it by 5:00 PM on the third calendar day after this offer is signed by Buyer (or, if checked) ☐ by _____ (date), at _____ AM/PM).

Date _JUNE 14, 2003_____   Date _JUNE 14, 2003_____

BUYER _Walti Buyer_____   BUYER _Debbie Buyer_____

Walter Buyer   _Debbie Buyer_
(Print name)   **(Print name)**
100 Boat Lane, Marina del Rey, CA 90292
(Address)

31. EXPIRATION OF OFFER

This provision specifies who is authorized to receive the Seller's acceptance on behalf of the Buyer, and how long the offer will remain open. It specifies that the Buyer (or authorized person) must personally receive the acceptance by a certain time and date.

32. BROKER COMPENSATION FROM SELLER:
   A. Upon Close Of Escrow, **Seller** agrees to pay compensation to Broker as specified in a separate written agreement between Seller and Broker.
   B. If escrow does not close, compensation is payable as specified in that separate written agreement.

32. BROKER COMPENSATION FROM SELLER

The Seller agrees to pay the broker compensation specified in a separate, written agreement. And if escrow doesn't close, the broker is paid the compensation specified in the separate, written agreement. Most brokers do not get paid until escrow closes.

33. ACCEPTANCE OF OFFER: Seller warrants that Seller is the owner of the Property, or has the authority to execute this Agreement. Seller accepts the above offer, agrees to sell the Property on the above terms and conditions, and agrees to the above confirmation of agency relationships. Seller has read and acknowledges receipt of a Copy of this Agreement, and authorizes Broker to deliver a Signed Copy to Buyer.

☐ (If checked) **SUBJECT TO ATTACHED COUNTER OFFER, DATED** _____.

Date _JUNE 15, 2003_   Date _JUNE 15, 2003_

SELLER _Tony Seller_   SELLER _Yolanda Seller_

TONY SELLER   _YOLANDA SELLER_

(Print name)   **(Print name)**

264 Beach Lane, Costa Mesa, CA 92627

(Address)

(_WP DB_) **CONFIRMATION OF ACCEPTANCE:** A Copy of Signed Acceptance was personally received by Buyer or Buyer's authorized
(Initials) agent on (date) _6/15/03_ at __3__ AM/PM. **A binding Agreement is created when a Copy of Signed Acceptance is personally received by Buyer or Buyer's authorized agent whether or not confirmed in this document. Completion of this confirmation is not legally required in order to create a binding Agreement; it is solely intended to evidence the date that Confirmation of Acceptance has occurred.**

33. ACCEPTANCE OF OFFER

The Seller warrants that he or she has authority to sell the property, agrees to the confirmation of agency relationships set forth in paragraph 27C, and authorizes the broker to deliver the signed contract to the Buyer to create a valid acceptance.

A. Seller's Signature Section – The Seller acknowledges the following by signing the agreement:

    (1) Acceptance of the exact terms and conditions of the offer
    (2) Agreement to sell the property
    (3) Agreement with the agency confirmation
    (4) Agreement to pay the identified broker the amount of compensation for services set forth in a separate, written agreement

B. Confirmation of Acceptance – A contract is formed when the Seller's acceptance is personally received by the Buyer or the Buyer's authorized agent. This paragraph provides written evidence of the date of acceptance.

REAL ESTATE BROKERS:
A. **Real Estate Brokers are not parties to the Agreement between Buyer and Seller.**
B. **Agency relationships are confirmed as stated in paragraph 27.**
C. If specified in paragraph 2A, Agent who submitted the offer for Buyer acknowledges receipt of deposit.
D. **COOPERATING BROKER COMPENSATION:** Listing Broker agrees to pay Cooperating Broker **(Selling Firm)** and Cooperating Broker agrees to accept, out of Listing Broker's proceeds in escrow: **(i)** the amount specified in the MLS, provided Cooperating Broker is a Participant of the MLS in which the Property is offered for sale or a reciprocal MLS; or **(ii)** ☐ (if checked) the amount specified in a separate written agreement (C.A.R. Form CBC) between Listing Broker and Cooperating Broker.

Real Estate Broker (Selling Firm) _Ramos Realty_
By _Joseph Ramos_   Date _6/14/03_
Address _777 Newport Blvd._   City _Newport Beach_   State _CA_   Zip _92663_
Telephone _714-647-0000_   Fax _714-647-0001_   E-mail _jr@ramosrealty.com_

Real Estate Broker (Listing Firm) _Sail Realty_
By _Carmen Caro_   Date _6/15/03_
Address _227 Harbor Blvd._   City _Costa Mesa_   State _CA_   Zip _92627_
Telephone _714-626-2828_   Fax _714-646-2829_   E-mail _carmen@sailreal.com_

ESCROW HOLDER ACKNOWLEDGMENT:
Escrow Holder acknowledges receipt of a Copy of this Agreement, (if checked, ☐ a deposit in the amount of $ _____), counter offer numbers _____ and _____, and agrees to act as Escrow Holder subject to paragraph 28 of this Agreement, any supplemental escrow instructions and the terms of Escrow Holder's general provisions.

Escrow Holder is advised that the date of Confirmation of Acceptance of the Agreement as between Buyer and Seller is _____

Escrow Holder _____ Escrow # _____
By _____ Date _____
Address _____
Phone/Fax/E-mail _____
Escrow Holder is licensed by the California Department of ☐ Corporations, ☐ Insurance, ☐ Real Estate. License # _____

C. Brokers Signature Section – In this paragraph the listing and selling brokers acknowledge, that:

    A. The brokers are not parties to the agreement.
    B. The agency relationships stated in paragraph 27 are confirmed.
    C. The Buyer's agent's receipt of the deposit if he is designated in paragraph 2A.
    D. Listing broker's agreement to pay cooperating broker compensation.

D. Escrow Holder Acknowledgement – The escrow holder acknowledges receipt of the contract and agrees to act as escrow holder.

III. CHAPTER SUMMARY

Most transactions for the purchase and sale of real state in California involve the sellers and buyers entering into a contractual arrangement. Commonly referred to as the "Deposit Receipt," or the "Purchase Contract," the most frequently used contract is the CAR form entitled "California Residential Purchase Agreement and Joint Escrow Instructions." Intended to be a legally binding contract (not just a preliminary agreement), it's imperative that it is filled out accurately, read carefully, and signed by both parties.

Written or typed in instructions supersede (take precedence over) the preprinted terms of the form. Specific provisions ordinarily qualify the meaning of general provisions, should inconsistencies arise.

When filling out the form, write out dates rather than using numbers. Strive for simplicity in language, as both buyer and seller must clearly understand the terms of the contract.

Liquidated damages are agreed to in advance and stated in the contract, determining how much money will be paid for not fulfilling a clause or condition in the contract.

Seller financing, secondary financing, and assumption require an addendum that must be attached to the agreement.

If the appraisal doesn't come in at or above the specified purchase price, a buyer applying for an 80% loan is usually released from further obligation.

It's possible that a tenant with a valid lease may remain in possession after the sale of a property.

To avoid a buyer's right to cancel, all disclosures must be acknowledged as promptly as possible.

Agents must never offer advice concerning how title should be taken.

Indicate that the seller is to provide for the termite clearance report under Article 25 of the purchase contract, otherwise, the broker may end up paying for termite eradication.

IV. KEY TERMS

Allocation of Costs
Buyer Indemnity
Buyer Occupancy
California Residential Purchase Agreement and Joint Escrow Instructions
Cancellation Rights
CE+3
Contingency Rights
Date of Final Acceptance
Deposit Receipt
Dispute Resolution
Financing
Initial Deposit
Liquidated Damages
Loan Contingency Removal
Natural and Environmental Hazards
Offer
Purchase Agreement
Purchase Contract
Seller-Financing Addendum
Statutory Disclosures
Title and Vesting
Verification of Down Payment and Closing Costs

V. CHAPTER 6 QUIZ

1. In a typical residential real estate transaction, what types of questions must be addressed?
    a. Financing
    b. Possession
    c. Condition of title
    d. All of the above

2. In California, who customarily conducts the title search, prepares preliminary reports, and issues policies of title insurance?
    a. Title insurance company
    b. Escrow company
    c. Real estate agent
    d. None of the above

3. The California Residential Purchase Agreement and Joint Escrow Instructions is also commonly referred to as the:
    a. deposit receipt.
    b. purchase contract.
    c. listing agreement.
    d. both a and b.

4. When interpreting the completed Purchase Agreement:
    a. the written word takes precedence over the preprinted words.
    b. the preprinted words take precedence over the written words.
    c. a lawyer must fill in the written words to be legal.
    d. none of the above.

5. When there are inconsistencies between general provisions and specific provisions:
    a. the general provisions ordinarily qualify the meaning of the specific provisions.
    b. the specific provisions ordinarily qualify the meaning of the general provisions.
    c. specific provisions will be ignored.
    d. a new contract must be written to be valid.

6. When filling out the date at the top of the Purchase Agreement, it's important to:
    a. use digits, like 02/04/05.
    b. use words and full dates, like February 2, 2005.
    c. Postdate the form to cover any oversights.
    d. none of the above.

7. The sum of money, agreed to in advance and stated in the contract, that will be paid for not fulfilling a clause or condition in the contract, is called:
    a. solid damages.
    b. soft damages.
    c. liquidated damages.
    d. none of the above.

8. If a buyer applies for an 80% loan and the appraisal does not come at or above the specified purchase price:
    a. the buyer will still have to go through with the purchase.
    b. the buyer will probably be released from further obligation.
    c. the seller must get a new appraisal.
    d. none of the above.

9. In the closing and occupancy section of the Purchase Contract, the words "CE+3" means:
    a. the buyer will take possession 3 days after the close of escrow.
    b. the seller will make a counter offer 3 days after the creation of escrow.
    c. the buyer will take possession 3 years after the close of escrow.
    d. none of the above.

10. Which of the following is true concerning wood-destroying pest inspection?
    a. Termite clearance is not mandated by law, it's a lender's requirement.
    b. Who pays for the inspection is negotiable.
    c. Section one refers to actual termite infestations and section two, to conditions that may allow for termite infestation.
    d. All of the above.

ANSWERS: 1. d; 2. a; 3. d; 4. a; 5. b; 6. b; 7. c; 8. b; 9. a; 10. d

CHAPTER 7
Additional Forms for the Purchase Contract
How to Complete the Process

I. Forms Supplied to the Buyer

Congratulations! Your buyer and seller have agreed on the price and terms of the property and the Purchase Agreement has been completed, accepted by the parties, and communicated back to the buyer. Still, you do not yet have a binding transaction until all the seller's disclosures have been approved by the buyer! Even then, no legally binding contract exists until all contingencies have been removed (like getting financing, buyer is unconditionally qualified, physical inspections, and requested repairs complied with).

The following is a list of CAR forms you will supply your buyer:

1. Disclosure Regarding Real Estate Agency Relationships (**Figure 7-1**)

2. California Residential Purchase Agreement and Joint Escrow Instructions (RPA-CA) (See Chapter 6, **Figure 6-1**)

3. Estimated Buyer's Costs (EBC) (**Figure 7-2**)

4. Contingency for Sale or Purchase of Other Property (COP) (**Figure 7-3**)

5. Buyer's Inspection Advisory (Attached RPA-CA - **Figure 7-4**)

CHAPTER 7 OUTLINE

I. FORMS SUPPLIED TO THE BUYER (p. 255)
  A. Disclosure Regarding Real Estate Agency Relationships (p. 258)
  B. Estimated Buyer's Costs (p. 259)
  C. Contingency for Sale or Purchase of Other Property (p. 260)
  D. Buyer's Inspection Advisory (p. 261)
  E. Professional Physical Inspection (p. 263)
  F. Wood Destroying Pest Inspection and Allocation of Cost Addendum (p. 264)
  G. Cooperating Broker Compensation Agreement and Escrow Instruction (p. 265)
  H. Counter Offer (p. 266)
  I. Buyer's Affidavit (p. 267)
  J. Request for Repair (p. 268)
  K. Receipt for Reports and Contingency Removal (p. 269)
  L. Notice to Seller to Perform (p. 270)
  M. Notice to Buyer to Perform (p. 271)
  N. Verification of Property Condition (p. 272)
II. CAR® REAL ESTATE DISCLOSURE SUMMARY CHART (p. 273)
III. CHAPTER SUMMARY (p. 286)
IV. KEY TERMS (p. 287)
V. CHAPTER 7 QUIZ (p. 288)

6. Professional Physical Inspection Waiver (**Figure 7-5**)

7. Wood Destroying Pest Inspection and Allocation of Cost Addendum (WPA) (**Figure 7-6**)

8. Cooperating Broker Compensation Agreement and Escrow Instruction (CBC) (**Figure 7-7**) (This form is provided by the selling agent to the listing agent. Buyers and sellers are not involved.)

9. Counter Offer (CO) (**Figure 7-8**)

10. Listing Kit (See Chapter 4)

Buyers to receive and approve all the seller's disclosures in the listing kit except Seller's Advisory (SA) which is attached to the Listing Agreement (LA). You should do this as quickly as possible to insure a binding contract.

11. Buyer's Affidavit (FIRPTA Compliance) (**Figure 7-9**)

12. Request for Repair (RR) (**Figure 7-10**)

13. Receipt for Reports and Contingency Removal (RRCR) (**Figure 7-11**)

14. Notice to Seller to Perform (NSP) (**Figure 7-12**)

15. Notice to Buyer to Perform (NBP) (**Figure 7-13**)

16. Verification of Property Condition (VP) (**Figure 7-14**)

17. Home Warranty Waiver (See Chapter 4, **Figure 4-13**)

A few days prior to closing, listing and selling agents should call the escrow officer and request an Estimate of Closing Costs Statement for their individual clients. This avoids many errors in fees to be paid and there are no unhappy surprises on closing day. It has been reported that three out of ten escrows have serious errors such as misspelled names, wrong calculations for monthly payments, etc. Remind your buyer to have a certified or cashier's check for the remainder of the down payment and closing costs.

Remind the sellers that any payments (such as mortgage payments and taxes) that are due near the closing date should be made through escrow with verified funds. Otherwise, the Title Company will withhold a sufficient amount from the seller's proceeds to cover more then the estimated costs of these items. Of course, this will eventually be released to the seller after the checks clear. Also remind the sellers that their bank will probably put a hold for a few days on their closing check when it is deposited. The seller should cancel the home insurance policy; escrow officers usually do not do this.

Figure 7-1

CALIFORNIA ASSOCIATION OF REALTORS®

DISCLOSURE REGARDING REAL ESTATE AGENCY RELATIONSHIPS
(As required by the Civil Code)
(C.A.R. Form AD-11, Revised 10/01)

When you enter into a discussion with a real estate agent regarding a real estate transaction, you should from the outset understand what type of agency relationship or representation you wish to have with the agent in the transaction.

SELLER'S AGENT

A Seller's agent under a listing agreement with the Seller acts as the agent for the Seller only. A Seller's agent or a subagent of that agent has the following affirmative obligations:
To the Seller:
    A Fiduciary duty of utmost care, integrity, honesty, and loyalty in dealings with the Seller.
To the Buyer and the Seller:
    (a) Diligent exercise of reasonable skill and care in performance of the agent's duties.
    (b) A duty of honest and fair dealing and good faith.
    (c) A duty to disclose all facts known to the agent materially affecting the value or desirability of the property that are not known to, or within the diligent attention and observation of, the parties.

An agent is not obligated to reveal to either party any confidential information obtained from the other party that does not involve the affirmative duties set forth above.

BUYER'S AGENT

A selling agent can, with a Buyer's consent, agree to act as agent for the Buyer only. In these situations, the agent is not the Seller's agent, even if by agreement the agent may receive compensation for services rendered, either in full or in part from the Seller. An agent acting only for a Buyer has the following affirmative obligations:
To the Buyer:
    A fiduciary duty of utmost care, integrity, honesty, and loyalty in dealings with the Buyer.
To the Buyer and the Seller:
    (a) Diligent exercise of reasonable skill and care in performance of the agent's duties.
    (b) A duty of honest and fair dealing and good faith.
    (c) A duty to disclose all facts known to the agent materially affecting the value or desirability of the property that are not known to, or within the diligent attention and observation of, the parties.

An agent is not obligated to reveal to either party any confidential information obtained from the other party that does not involve the affirmative duties set forth above.

AGENT REPRESENTING BOTH SELLER AND BUYER

A real estate agent, either acting directly or through one or more associate licensees, can legally be the agent of both the Seller and the Buyer in a transaction, but only with the knowledge and consent of both the Seller and the Buyer.

In a dual agency situation, the agent has the following affirmative obligations to both the Seller and the Buyer:
    (a) A fiduciary duty of utmost care, integrity, honesty and loyalty in the dealings with either the Seller or the Buyer.
    (b) Other duties to the Seller and the Buyer as stated above in their respective sections.

In representing both Seller and Buyer, the agent may not, without the express permission of the respective party, disclose to the other party that the Seller will accept a price less than the listing price or that the Buyer will pay a price greater than the price offered.

The above duties of the agent in a real estate transaction do not relieve a Seller or Buyer from the responsibility to protect his or her own interests. You should carefully read all agreements to assure that they adequately express your understanding of the transaction. A real estate agent is a person qualified to advise about real estate. If legal or tax advice is desired, consult a competent professional.

Throughout your real property transaction you may receive more than one disclosure form, depending upon the number of agents assisting in the transaction. The law requires each agent with whom you have more than a casual relationship to present you with this disclosure form. You should read its contents each time it is presented to you, considering the relationship between you and the real estate agent in your specific transaction.

This disclosure form includes the provisions of Sections 2079.13 to 2079.24, inclusive, of the Civil Code set forth on the reverse hereof. Read it carefully.

I/WE ACKNOWLEDGE RECEIPT OF A COPY OF THIS DISCLOSURE.

BUYER/SELLER _____ Date _____ Time _____ AM/PM

BUYER/SELLER _____ Date _____ Time _____ AM/PM

AGENT _____ By _____ Date _____
    (Please Print)   (Associate-Licensee or Broker Signature)

THIS FORM SHALL BE PROVIDED AND ACKNOWLEDGED AS FOLLOWS (Civil Code §2079.14):
•When the listing brokerage company also represents the Buyer, the Listing Agent shall give one AD-11 form to the Seller and one to the Buyer.
•When Buyer and Seller are represented by different brokerage companies, then the Listing Agent shall give one AD-11 form to the Seller and the Buyer's Agent shall give one AD-11 form to the Buyer and one AD-11 form to the Seller.

SEE REVERSE SIDE FOR FURTHER INFORMATION

Published and Distributed by:
REAL ESTATE BUSINESS SERVICES, INC.
a subsidiary of the CALIFORNIA ASSOCIATION OF REALTORS®
525 South Virgil Avenue, Los Angeles, California 90020

Reviewed by _____
Broker or Designee _____ Date _____

EQUAL HOUSING OPPORTUNITY

AD-11 REVISED 10/01 (PAGE 1 OF 1)   **Print Date**

DISCLOSURE REGARDING REAL ESTATE AGENCY RELATIONSHIPS (AD-11 PAGE 1 OF 1)

The Agency Disclosure is signed by both the agent and the buyer, explaining what agency relationship is being offered, prior to any contract being written; this disclosure is to accompany the Purchase Contract when first presented to the seller.

Figure 7-2

CALIFORNIA ASSOCIATION OF REALTORS®

ESTIMATED BUYER'S COSTS

BUYER _____ DATE _____

PROPERTY ADDRESS _____

This estimate is based on costs associated with _____ type of financing.

LOAN AMOUNT $ _____ INTEREST RATE _____ % ☐ FIXED ☐ ADJUSTABLE ☐ OTHER

PROPOSED PURCHASE PRICE $ _____ PROJECTED CLOSING DATE _____

ESTIMATED BUYER'S EXPENSE:

Loan Origination Fee	$ _____
Processing Fee	_____
Funding Fee	_____
Lender's Prepaid Interest: Days _____	_____
Appraisal Fee	_____
Credit Report	_____
PMI/MIP	_____
Other Lender Fees	_____
Tax Service	_____
Tax Impounds	_____
Prorated Taxes	_____
Documentary Transfer Tax:	
County	_____
City	_____
Hazard Insurance	_____
Prorated Insurance	_____
Insurance Impounds	_____
Title Insurance (Owners)	_____
Title Insurance (Lenders)	_____
Escrow Fee	_____
Sub-Escrow Fee	_____
Recording Fees	_____
Notary Fees	_____
Preparation of Documents	_____
Structural Pest Control Inspection	_____
Structural Pest Control Repairs	_____
Physical Inspection Fee	_____
Natural Hazard Disclosure Report	_____
Other Inspection Fees	_____
Home Protection Policy	_____
Homeowners' Association Transfer Fees	_____
Brokerage Fee	_____
Administrative/Transaction Fee	_____
Other:	_____
TOTAL ESTIMATED EXPENSES:	$ _____

ESTIMATED CREDITS:

Prorated Taxes	$ _____
Rent	_____
Security Deposits	_____
Other _____	_____
Other _____	_____
Other _____	_____
TOTAL CREDITS:	$ _____

ESTIMATED CASH REQUIRED:

Expenses	$ _____
Down Payment	_____
Less Credits	- _____

**ESTIMATED
TOTAL CASH REQUIRED:** $ _____

ESTIMATED MONTHLY PAYMENTS

Principal & Interest*	$ _____
(at origination)	
Taxes	_____
Insurance	_____
Other _____	_____
Other _____	_____
TOTAL MONTHLY PAYMENTS:	$ _____

*Buyer is aware that with regard to adjustable rate loans, the monthly payment may increase at various times over the life of the loan. Buyer should confirm directly with lender all terms and conditions of said loan.

This estimate, based upon the above proposed purchase price, type of financing and projected closing date, has been prepared to assist Buyer in computing his/her costs. Lender, title companies and escrow holders may vary in their charges. Expenses will also vary according to expenses for required repairs, if any, and other items. Therefore, these figures cannot be guaranteed by the Broker or his/her representatives. All estimates and information are from sources believed reliable but not guaranteed.

I have read the above figures and acknowledge receipt of a copy of this form.

Real Estate Broker (Firm) _____

Presented by _____

BUYER _____ Date _____   Address _____

BUYER _____ Date _____   Phone _____

Published and Distributed by:
REAL ESTATE BUSINESS SERVICES, INC.
a subsidiary of the CALIFORNIA ASSOCIATION OF REALTORS®
525 South Virgil Avenue, Los Angeles, California 90020

Reviewed by _____
Broker or Designee _____ Date _____

EQUAL HOUSING OPPORTUNITY

REVISION DATE 10/2000   Print Date
EBC-11 (PAGE 1 OF 1)

ESTIMATED BUYER'S COST (EBC-11 PAGE 1 OF 1)

The buyer needs to know the total costs of this purchase, including the monthly payments, prior to making the offer. This is an estimate you calculate working with the lender and various affiliates involved in the transaction, such as Home Owner's Insurance companies, Home Inspection providers, etc.

Figure 7-3

CALIFORNIA
ASSOCIATION
OF REALTORS®

**CONTINGENCY FOR SALE OR PURCHASE
OF OTHER PROPERTY**
(C.A.R. Form COP, Revised 10/02)

This is an addendum to the ☐ California Residential Purchase Agreement, ☐ Counter Offer, ☐ Other _____,
_____ ("Agreement"), dated _____
on property known as _____ ("Property"),
between _____ ("Buyer"),
and _____ ("Seller").

A. ☐ **SALE OF BUYER'S PROPERTY (if checked):**
1. The Agreement is contingent on the close of escrow of Buyer's property, described as: _____
    _____ ("Buyer's Property").
2. Buyer's Property is:
    (a) ☐ (if checked) not yet listed for sale,
    OR (b) ☐ (if checked) listed for sale with _____ company,
    and ☐ (if checked) offered for sale in the _____ MLS, # _____.
    OR (c) ☐ (if checked) in escrow no. _____ with
    _____ escrow holder, scheduled to close escrow on _____ (date).
3. Buyer shall deliver to Seller Copies of the contract for the sale of Buyer's Property, escrow instructions and all
    amendments and modifications thereto. Delivery to occur within **5 Days** After Acceptance if Buyer's Property is
    already in escrow or within **5 Days** After Buyer enters into an agreement to sell Buyer's Property. If Buyer fails
    to provide these documents within that time, Seller, after first giving Buyer a Notice to Buyer to Perform (C.A.R.
    Form NBP), may cancel the Agreement in writing.
4. If Buyer's Property does not close escrow by **(i)** the date specified in paragraph A2(c); or **(ii)** (if checked)
    ☐ _____), then: **(i)** Seller, after first giving Buyer a Notice to Buyer to Perform,
    may cancel this agreement in writing; or **(ii)** Buyer may cancel the Agreement in writing.
5. After Acceptance, Seller SHALL have the right to continue to offer the Property for sale:
    (a) Removal of Sale and Loan Contingency: If Seller accepts another written offer, Seller shall give written
    notice to Buyer to: **(i)** in writing remove this contingency; **(ii)** in writing remove the loan contingency, if any;
    and **(iii)** comply with the following additional requirement(s): _____
    _____
    If Buyer fails to complete these actions within **72 (or** ☐ _____**) hours** after receipt of such notice,
    Seller may immediately cancel the Agreement in writing.
    OR (b) ☐ (if checked) **Backup Offers Only.** Seller shall have the right to continue to offer the Property for
    sale for backup offers only and shall not invoke the notice provisions in paragraph 5a during the term
    of the Agreement.

B. ☐ **SELLER'S PURCHASE OF REPLACEMENT PROPERTY (if checked):**
1. The Agreement is contingent on Seller entering a contract to acquire replacement property.
2. Seller shall, within **17 (or** ☐ _____**) Days** After Acceptance, remove this contingency or cancel the Agreement. If
    Seller does not remove this contingency in writing within that time, Buyer may cancel the Agreement in writing.
3. **(a)** Time periods in the Agreement for inspections, contingencies, covenants and other obligations shall begin:
    (i) as specified in the Agreement; **(ii) (if checked)** ☐ the day after Seller delivers to Buyer a written notice
    removing the contingency for Seller's purchase of replacement property; or **(iii)** (if checked) _____).
    (b) Buyer and Seller agree that Seller may, by providing Buyer written notice at the time Seller removes this
    contingency, extend the Close Of Escrow date for a maximum of _____ additional Days or
    ☐ _____ (date).

By signing below, Buyer and Seller each acknowledge that they have read, understand, accept and have received a Copy
of this agreement.

Date _____   Date _____
Buyer _____   Seller _____
Buyer _____   Seller _____

SURE TRAC
The System for Success™

Published by the
California Association of REALTORS®

EQUAL HOUSING
OPPORTUNITY

COP REVISED 10/02 (PAGE 1 OF 1) Print Date

Reviewed by _____ Date _____

CONTINGENCY FOR SALE OR PURCHASE OF OTHER PROPERTY   (COP PAGE 1 OF 1)

*All contingencies about the sale of the buyer's property or the seller's
purchase of a replacement property should be noted in the appropriate
sections and become an addendum to the Purchase Agreement, or any counter
offer, thereof. Become familiar with this form as it contains several options
on how to remove this contingency and the remedy, if the prescribed time
constriction is not adhered to.*

Figure 7-4

Along with the Purchase Agreement, the buyer is required to read and approve this two-page broker's recommendations on the values of obtaining and paying for qualified inspections from the appropriate professionals prior to finalizing the transaction. You must provide the seller with a signed copy of the Buyer's Inspection Advisory, have it signed, and return a copy to the selling agent.

 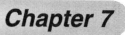

Property Address: _____ Date: _____

4. **SOIL STABILITY:** Existence of fill or compacted soil, expansive or contracting soil, susceptibility to slippage, settling or movement, and the adequacy of drainage. (Geotechnical engineers are best suited to determine such conditions, causes and remedies.)
5. **ROOF:** Present condition, age, leaks, and remaining useful life. (Roofing contractors are best suited to determine these conditions.)
6. **POOL/SPA:** Cracks, leaks or operational problems. (Pool contractors are best suited to determine these conditions.)
7. **WASTE DISPOSAL:** Type, size, adequacy, capacity and condition of sewer and septic systems and components, connection to sewer, and applicable fees.
8. **WATER AND UTILITIES; WELL SYSTEMS AND COMPONENTS:** Water and utility availability, use restrictions and costs. Water quality, adequacy, condition, and performance of well systems and components.
9. **ENVIRONMENTAL HAZARDS:** Potential environmental hazards, including, but not limited to, asbestos, lead-based paint and other lead contamination, radon, methane, other gases, fuel oil or chemical storage tanks, contaminated soil or water, hazardous waste, waste disposal sites, electromagnetic fields, nuclear sources, and other substances, materials, products, or conditions (including mold (airborne, toxic or otherwise), fungus or similar contaminants). (For more in formation on these items, you may consult an appropriate professional or read the booklets "Environmental Hazards: A Guide for Homeowners ,Buyers, Landlords and Tenants," "Protect Your Family From Lead in Your Home" or both.)
10. **EARTHQUAKES AND FLOODING:** Susceptibility of the Property to earthquake/seismic hazards and propensity of the Property to flood. (A Geologist or Geotechnical Engineer is best suited to provide information on these conditions.)
11. **FIRE, HAZARD AND OTHER INSURANCE:** The availability and cost of necessary or desired insurance may vary. The location of the Property in a seismic, flood or fire hazard zone, and other conditions, such as the age of the Property and the claims history of the Property and Buyer, may affect the availability and need for certain types of insurance. Buyer should explore insurance options early as this information may affect other decisions, including the removal of loan and inspection contingencies. (An insurance agent is best suited to provide information on these conditions.)
12. **BUILDING PERMITS, ZONING AND GOVERNMENTAL REQUIREMENTS:** Permits, inspections, certificates, zoning, other governmental limitations, restrictions, and requirements affecting the current or future use of the Property, its development or size. (Such information is available from appropriate governmental agencies and private information providers. Brokers are not qualified to review or interpret any such information.)
13. **RENTAL PROPERTY RESTRICTIONS:** Some cities and counties impose restrictions that limit the amount of rent that can be charged, the maximum number of occupants; and the right of a landlord to terminate a tenancy. Deadbolt or other locks and security systems for doors and windows, including window bars, should be examined to determine whether they satisfy legal requirements. (Government agencies can provide information about these restrictions and other requirements.)
14. **SECURITY AND SAFETY:** State and local Law may require the installation of barriers, access alarms, self-latching mechanisms and/or other measures to decrease the risk to children and other persons of existing swimming pools and hot tubs, as well as various fire safety and other measures concerning other features of the Property. Compliance requirements differ from city to city and county to county. Unless specifically agreed, the Property may not be in compliance with these requirements. (Local government agencies can provide information about these restrictions and other requirements.)
15. **NEIGHBORHOOD, AREA, SUBDIVISION CONDITIONS; PERSONAL FACTORS:** Neighborhood or area conditions, including schools, proximity and adequacy of law enforcement, crime statistics, the proximity of registered felons or offenders, fire protection, other government services, availability, adequacy and cost of any speed-wired, wireless internet connections or other telecommunications or other technology services and installations, proximity to commercial, industrial or agricultural activities, existing and proposed transportation, construction and development that may affect noise, view, or traffic, airport noise, noise or odor from any source, wild and domestic animals, other nuisances, hazards, or circumstances, protected species, wetland properties, botanical diseases, historic or other governmentally protected sites or improvements, cemeteries, facilities and condition of common areas of common interest subdivisions, and possible lack of compliance with any governing documents or Homeowners' Association requirements, conditions and influences of significance to certain cultures and/or religions, and personal needs, requirements and preferences of Buyer.

Buyer and Seller acknowledge and agree that Broker: **(i)** Does not decide what price Buyer should pay or Seller should accept; **(ii)** Does not guarantee the condition of the Property; **(iii)** Does not guarantee the performance, adequacy or completeness of inspections, services, products or repairs provided or made by Seller or others; **(iv)** Shall not be responsible for identifying defects that are not known to Broker and **(a)** are not visually observable in reasonably accessible areas of the Property; **(b)** are in common areas; or **(c)** are off the site of the Property; **(v)** Shall not be responsible for inspecting public records or permits concerning the title or use of Property; **(vi)** Shall not be responsible for identifying the location of boundary lines or other items affecting title; **(vii)** Shall not be responsible for verifying square footage, representations of others or information contained in Investigation reports, Multiple Listing Service, advertisements, flyers or other promotional material; **(viii)** Shall not be responsible for providing legal or tax advice regarding any aspect of a transaction entered into by Buyer or Seller; and **(ix)** Shall not be responsible for providing other advice or information that exceeds the knowledge, education and experience required to perform real estate licensed activity. Buyer and Seller agree to seek legal, tax, insurance, title and other desired assistance from appropriate professionals.

By signing below, Buyer and Seller each acknowledge that they have read, understand, accept and have received a Copy of this Advisory. Buyer is encouraged to read it carefully.

_____   _____
Buyer Signature   Date   Buyer Signature   Date

_____   _____
Seller Signature   Date   Seller Signature   Date

SURE TRAC
The System for Success™

Published by the
California Association of REALTORS®

Reviewed by _____ Date _____

EQUAL HOUSING OPPORTUNITY

BIA REVISED 10/02 (PAGE 2 OF 2)

BUYER'S INSPECTION ADVISORY (BIA PAGE 2 OF 2)

Figure 7-5

Lyons and Associates, Inc., Realtor

REAL ESTATE   EXCELLENCE

PROFESSIONAL PHYSICAL INSPECTION

WAIVER

BUYER/SELLER: _____

PROPERTY ADDRESS: _____

_____

I/We the Buyer(s)/Seller(s) of the above property have been informed that professional home inspection services are available for our protection and benefit. I/We are aware that the intent of a physical inspection by a professional inspector is to uncover any existing defects within the property.

I/We elected not to hire a professional property inspector and do hereby release the agents and the brokers from any liability for our decision to waive the right to same.

_____	_____
Signature	Date
_____	_____
Signature	Date
_____	_____
Buyer/Seller Agent Signature	Date
_____	
Real Estate Company Name	

2820 E. GARVEY AVENUE SOUTH, WEST COVINA, CA 91791 • (818) 331-0141 • FAX: (818) 331-9772

This is a broker-generated form, intended to reduce agent/broker liability should the buyer decline a (recommended) professional physical inspection.

Figure 7-6

CALIFORNIA
ASSOCIATION
OF REALTORS®

**WOOD DESTROYING PEST INSPECTION AND
ALLOCATION OF COST ADDENDUM**
(C.A.R. Form WPA, Revised 10/02)

This is an addendum to the ☐ California Residential Purchase Agreement or ☐ Other _____
_____ ("Agreement"), dated _____,
on property known as _____ ("Property"),
between _____ ("Buyer"),
and _____ ("Seller").

THE FOLLOWING SHALL REPLACE PARAGRAPH 4A IN THE AGREEMENT and shall supercede any conflicting terms
in any previously-generated agreement:

WOOD DESTROYING PESTS

A. ☐ Buyer ☐ Seller shall pay for a Pest Control Report for wood destroying pests and organisms only ("Report").
The Report shall be prepared by _____, a registered structural pest
control company, who shall separate the Report into sections for evident infestation or infection (Section 1) and for
conditions likely to lead to infestation or infection (Section 2). The Report shall cover the main building and
attached structures and, if checked: ☐ detached garages and carports, ☐ detached decks, ☐ the following other
structures on the Property:_____.
The Report shall not include roof coverings. If the Property is a unit in a condominium or other common interest
subdivision, the Report shall include only the separate interest and any exclusive-use areas being transferred, and
shall not include common areas. Water tests of shower pans on upper level units may not be performed unless the
owners of property below the shower consent. If Buyer requests inspection of inaccessible areas, Buyer shall pay
for the cost of entry, inspection and closing for those areas, unless otherwise agreed. A written Pest Control
Certification shall be issued prior to Close Of Escrow, unless otherwise agreed, only if no infestation or infection is
found or if required corrective work is completed.

B. **(Section 1)** ☐ Buyer ☐ Seller shall pay for work recommended to correct "Section 1" conditions described in the
Report and the cost of inspection, entry and closing of those inaccessible areas where active infestation or
infection is discovered.
(Section 2) ☐ Buyer ☐ Seller shall pay for work recommended to correct "Section 2" conditions described in the
Report if requested by Buyer.

**By signing below, the undersigned acknowledge that each has read, understands and has received a copy of
this Addendum.**

Date_____   Date _____

Buyer _____   Seller_____

Buyer _____   Seller_____

SURE TRAC
The System for Success™

Published by the
California Association of REALTORS®

WPA REVISED 10/02 (PAGE 1 OF 1)   Print Date

Reviewed by _____ Date _____

EQUAL HOUSING
OPPORTUNITY

WOOD DESTROYING PEST INSPECTION AND ALLOCATION OF COST ADDENDUM (WPA PAGE 1 OF 1)

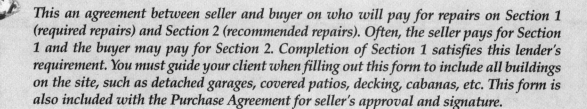

*This an agreement between seller and buyer on who will pay for repairs on Section 1
(required repairs) and Section 2 (recommended repairs). Often, the seller pays for Section
1 and the buyer may pay for Section 2. Completion of Section 1 satisfies this lender's
requirement. You must guide your client when filling out this form to include all buildings
on the site, such as detached garages, covered patios, decking, cabanas, etc. This form is
also included with the Purchase Agreement for seller's approval and signature.*

Figure 7-7

CALIFORNIA
ASSOCIATION
OF REALTORS®

**COOPERATING BROKER COMPENSATION
AGREEMENT AND ESCROW INSTRUCTION**
(C.A.R. Form CBC, Revised 10/02)

1. **IDENTITY OF LISTING BROKER, PROPERTY AND SELLER:**
   _____ ("Listing Broker") is a real estate broker who has entered into a written agreement for the marketing and sale or lease of the real property or manufactured home described as _____, Assessor's Parcel No. _____, situated in _____, County of _____, California ("Property") for _____ ("Seller").

2. **IDENTITY OF COOPERATING (SELLING) BROKER AND BUYER:**
   _____ ("Cooperating Broker") is a real estate broker licensed to practice real estate in California (or ☐ if checked _____) and represents _____ ("Buyer") who has offered, is contemplating making an offer, or has entered into a contract, to purchase or lease the Property.

3. **LISTING BROKER COMPENSATION TO COOPERATING BROKER:**
   Provided that: **(i)** the transaction between the principals closes, and **(ii)** Listing Broker receives compensation for the transaction, Listing Broker agrees to pay Cooperating Broker, and Cooperating Broker agrees to accept, compensation as follows:
   (check one)
   A. ☐ **Property is listed in the** _____ **Multiple Listing Service ("MLS"), Cooperating Broker is a participant in the MLS or reciprocal Multiple Listing Service and accepts the offer of compensation published in the MLS as:**
   _____% of the selling (or leasing) price or $_____.
   OR B. ☐ **Property is listed in the** _____ **Multiple Listing Service ("MLS"), Cooperating Broker is a participant in the MLS or reciprocal Multiple Listing Service and accepts the offer of compensation as modified below:**
   _____% of the selling (or leasing) price or $_____.
   OR C. ☐ **Property is listed in the** _____ **Multiple Listing Service ("MLS"), Cooperating Broker is NOT a Participant in the MLS or reciprocal Multiple Listing Service. Cooperating Broker compensation shall be:**
   _____% of the selling (or leasing) price or $_____.
   OR D. ☐ **Property is NOT listed with any Multiple Listing Service. Cooperating Broker compensation shall be:**
   _____% of the selling (or leasing) price or $_____.

4. **LISTING BROKER INSTRUCTION TO ESCROW HOLDER:**
   Listing Broker and Cooperating Broker instruct Escrow Holder to disburse to Cooperating Broker the amount specified in paragraph 3, out of Listing Broker's proceeds in escrow, and upon Close Of Escrow of the Property. This compensation instruction can be amended or revoked only with the written consent of both Brokers. Escrow Holder shall immediately notify Brokers if either Broker instructs Escrow Holder to change the terms of this instruction.

5. **ACKNOWLEDGMENT:**
   By signing below, the undersigned acknowledges that each has read, understands, accepts and has received a Copy of this Agreement.

Listing Broker (Firm) _____
By (Agent) _____ Date _____
Address _____ City _____ State _____ Zip _____
Telephone _____ Fax _____ E-mail _____

Cooperating Broker (Firm) _____
By (Agent) _____ Date _____
Address _____ City _____ State _____ Zip _____
Telephone _____ Fax _____ E-mail _____

SURE TRAC
The System for Success™

Published by the
California Association of REALTORS®

EQUAL HOUSING
OPPORTUNITY

CBC REVISED 10/02 (PAGE 1 OF 1) PRINT DATE

Reviewed by _____ Date _____

COOPERATING BROKER COMPENSATION AGREEMENT AND ESCROW INSTRUCTION (CBC PAGE 1 OF 1)

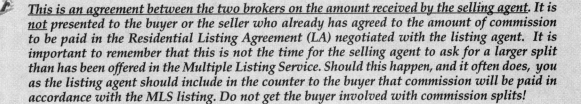

This is an agreement between the two brokers on the amount received by the selling agent. It is not presented to the buyer or the seller who already has agreed to the amount of commission to be paid in the Residential Listing Agreement (LA) negotiated with the listing agent. It is important to remember that this is not the time for the selling agent to ask for a larger split than has been offered in the Multiple Listing Service. Should this happen, and it often does, you as the listing agent should include in the counter to the buyer that commission will be paid in accordance with the MLS listing. Do not get the buyer involved with commission splits!

Figure 7-8

COUNTER OFFER No. _____

For use by Seller or Buyer. May be used for Multiple Counter Offer.

(C.A.R. Form CO, Revised 10/02)

Date _____, at _____, California.
This is a counter offer to the: ☐ California Residential Purchase Agreement, ☐ Counter Offer, or ☐ Other _____ ("Offer"),
dated _____, on property known as _____ ("Property"),
between _____ ("Buyer") and _____ ("Seller").

1. **TERMS:** The terms and conditions of the above referenced document are **accepted subject to the following:**
    A. Paragraphs in the Offer that require initials by all parties, but are not initialed by all parties, are excluded from the final agreement unless specifically referenced for inclusion in paragraph 1C of this or another Counter Offer.
    B. Unless otherwise agreed in writing, down payment and loan amount(s) will be adjusted in the same proportion as in the original Offer.
    C. _____
        _____
        _____
        _____
        _____
        _____
        _____
        _____
    D. The following attached supplements are incorporated in this Counter Offer: ☐ Addendum No. _____
        ☐ _____ ☐ _____

2. **RIGHT TO ACCEPT OTHER OFFERS:** Seller has the right to continue to offer the Property for sale or for other transaction, and to accept any other offer at any time prior to notification of acceptance, as described in paragraph 3. If this is a Seller Counter Offer, Seller's acceptance of another offer prior to Buyer's acceptance and communication of notification of this Counter Offer, shall revoke this Counter Offer.

3. **EXPIRATION:** This Counter Offer shall be deemed revoked and the deposits, if any, shall be returned unless this Counter Offer is Signed by the Buyer or Seller to whom it is sent and a Copy of the Signed Counter Offer is personally received by the person making this Counter Offer or _____
    who is authorized to receive it, by 5:00 PM on the third Day After this Counter Offer is made or, (if checked)
    by ☐ _____ (date), at _____ AM/PM. This Counter Offer may be executed in counterparts.

4. ☐ **(If checked:) MULTIPLE COUNTER OFFER:** Seller is making a Counter Offer(s) to another prospective buyer(s) on terms that may or may not be the same as in this Counter Offer. Acceptance of this Counter Offer by Buyer shall **not** be binding unless and until it is subsequently re-Signed by Seller in paragraph 7 below and a Copy of the Counter Offer Signed in paragraph 7 is personally received by Buyer or by _____, who is authorized to receive it. Prior to the completion of all of these events, Buyer and Seller shall have no duties or obligations for the purchase or sale of the Property.

5. **OFFER: BUYER OR SELLER MAKES THIS COUNTER OFFER ON THE TERMS ABOVE AND ACKNOWLEDGES RECEIPT OF A COPY.**
    _____ Date _____
    _____ Date _____

6. **ACCEPTANCE: I/WE** accept the above Counter Offer **(If checked ☐ SUBJECT TO THE ATTACHED COUNTER OFFER)** and acknowledge receipt of a Copy.
    _____ Date _____ Time _____ AM/PM
    _____ Date _____ Time _____ AM/PM

7. **MULTIPLE COUNTER OFFER SIGNATURE LINE:** By signing below, Seller accepts this Multiple Counter Offer.
    NOTE TO SELLER: Do NOT sign in this box until after Buyer signs in paragraph 6. (Paragraph 7 applies only if paragraph 4 is checked.)
    _____ Date _____ Time _____ AM/PM
    _____ Date _____ Time _____ AM/PM

8. (_____/_____) (Initials) **Confirmation of Acceptance:** A Copy of Signed Acceptance was personally received by the maker of the Counter Offer, or that person's authorized agent as specified in paragraph 3 (or, if this is a Multiple Counter Offer, the Buyer or Buyer's authorized agent as specified in paragraph 4) on (date) _____, at _____ AM/PM. **A binding Agreement is created when a Copy of Signed Acceptance** is personally received by the the maker of the Counter Offer, or that person's authorized agent (or, if this is a Multiple Counter Offer, the Buyer or Buyer's authorized agent) whether or not confirmed in this document. Completion of this confirmation is not legally required in order to create a binding Agreement; it is solely intended to evidence the date that Confirmation of Acceptance has occurred.

SURE TRAC
The System for Success™

Published by the
California Association of REALTORS®

Reviewed by _____ Date _____

EQUAL HOUSING OPPORTUNITY

CO REVISED 10/02 (PAGE 1 OF 1) Print Date

COUNTER OFFER (CO PAGE 1 OF 1)

When the offer is not accepted in its entirety, counter offers are made back and forth between the parties. If you have more than two counter offers, it is preferable to start from scratch and incorporate all the changes in one contract eliminating any confusion as to what terms were accepted and which ones were amended. When the counter is accepted by all parties, the listing agent usually faxes the counters and the original Purchase Agreement, as well as Cooperating Broker Compensation Agreement and Escrow Instruction (CBC), to the selected escrow company. The escrow company prepares the escrow instructions that are to represent the intention of the parties based on the original contract and all counters. The earnest money deposit is delivered to the escrow company by the buyer's agent within three days from acceptance. It is from the acceptance date that all time contingencies begin, as well as the escrow period. You and the other agent receive a receipt for this deposit from the escrow company as proof of timely deposit.

Figure 7-9

BUYER'S AFFIDAVIT

That Buyer is acquiring property for use as a residence
and that sales price does not exceed $300,000.
(FOREIGN INVESTMENT IN REAL PROPERTY TAX ACT)

1. I am the transferee (buyer) of real property located at _____
_____.

2. The sales price (total of all consideration in the sale) does not exceed $300,000.

3. I am acquiring the real property for use as a residence. I have definite plans that I or a member of my family will reside in it for at least 50 percent of the number of days it will be in use during each of the first two 12 month periods following the transfer of the property to me. I understand that the members of my family that are included in the last sentence are my brothers, sisters, ancestors, descendents, or spouse.

4. I am making this affidavit in order to establish an exemption from withholding a portion of the sales price of the property under Internal Revenue Code §1445.

5. I understand that if the information in this affidavit is not correct, I may be liable to the Internal Revenue Service for up to 10 percent of the sales price of the property, plus interest and penalties.

Under penalties of perjury, I declare that the statements above are true, correct and complete.

Date _____   Signature _____

     Typed or Printed Name _____

Date _____   Signature _____

     Typed or Printed Name _____

IMPORTANT NOTICE: An affidavit should be signed by each individual transferee to whom it applies. Before you sign, any questions relating to the legal sufficiency of this form, or to whether it applies to a particular transaction, or to the definition of any of the terms used, should be referred to an attorney, certified public accountant, other professional tax advisor, or the Internal Revenue Service.

Published and Distributed by:
REAL ESTATE BUSINESS SERVICES, INC.
a subsidiary of the CALIFORNIA ASSOCIATION OF REALTORS®
525 South Virgil Avenue, Los Angeles, California 90020

PRINT DATE

OFFICE USE ONLY
Reviewed by Broker
or Designee _____
Date _____

FORM AB-11 REVISED 2/91

This should be signed by the buyer when appropriate; it involves the Foreign Investment in Real Property Tax Act (FRPTA). There are exemptions from the withholding portion of the sales price of the property being purchased, such as the price being no more than $300,000, and that the property will be the buyer's principal residence. If the buyer has any questions about this form, refer him or her to an attorney, certified public accountant, other professional tax advisor, or the Internal Revenue Service.

Figure 7-10

CALIFORNIA
ASSOCIATION
OF REALTORS®

REQUEST for REPAIR No. _____
(Or Other Corrective Action)
(C.A.R. Form RR, Revised 10/02)

In accordance with the terms and conditions of the: ☐ California Residential Purchase Agreement or ☐ Other _____
_____ ("Agreement"), dated _____,
on property known as _____ ("Property"),
between _____ ("Buyer"),
and _____ ("Seller").

1. BUYER'S REQUEST:
   A. Buyer requests that Seller repair the following items or take the specified action prior to final verification of condition:
      ☐ See attached list dated _____ for requests.

   B. A copy of the following inspection or other report is attached.
      ☐ _____ ☐
      ☐ _____ ☐

Buyer _____ Date _____
Buyer _____ Date _____

2. SELLER'S RESPONSE TO BUYER'S REQUEST:
   A. If Buyer agrees to remove in writing the following contingency(ies), _____
      (i) ☐ Seller agrees to repair or take the other specified action with respect to all of the items in 1A above.
   OR (ii) ☐ Seller agrees to repair or take the other specified action with respect to all of the items in 1A above, with the following
      exception(s): _____

   B. ☐ Seller does not agree to any of Buyer's requests.

Seller _____ Date _____
Seller _____ Date _____

3. BUYER'S REPLY TO SELLER'S RESPONSE:
   A. ☐ Buyer accepts Seller's response, withdraws all requests for items that Seller has not agreed to, and removes the
      contingency(ies) identified in 2A
   B. ☐ Buyer withdraws the request in 1A above, and makes a new request as specified in the attached Request for Repair No. _____.

Buyer _____ Date _____
Buyer _____ Date _____

SURE TRAC
The System for Success™

Published by the
California Association of REALTORS®

RR REVISED 10/02 (PAGE 1 OF 1) Print Date

Reviewed by _____ Date _____

EQUAL HOUSING OPPORTUNITY

REQUEST FOR REPAIR (RR PAGE 1 OF 1)

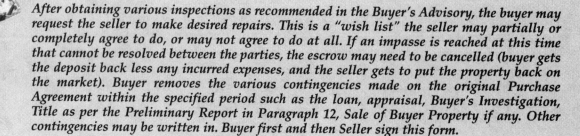

After obtaining various inspections as recommended in the Buyer's Advisory, the buyer may request the seller to make desired repairs. This is a "wish list" the seller may partially or completely agree to do, or may not agree to do at all. If an impasse is reached at this time that cannot be resolved between the parties, the escrow may need to be cancelled (buyer gets the deposit back less any incurred expenses, and the seller gets to put the property back on the market). Buyer removes the various contingencies made on the original Purchase Agreement within the specified period such as the loan, appraisal, Buyer's Investigation, Title as per the Preliminary Report in Paragraph 12, Sale of Buyer Property if any. Other contingencies may be written in. Buyer first and then Seller sign this form.

Figure 7-11

CALIFORNIA ASSOCIATION OF REALTORS®

RECEIPT FOR REPORTS AND CONTINGENCY REMOVAL   No. _____
(C.A.R. Form RRCR, Revised 10/02)

In accordance with the terms and conditions of the: ☐ California Residential Purchase Agreement or ☐ Other _____
_____ ("Agreement"), dated _____,
on property known as _____ ("Property"),
between _____ ("Buyer"),
and _____ ("Seller").

1. RECEIPT FOR REPORTS:
Buyer acknowledges receipt of the following written report(s) or disclosure(s) checked below:

Report	Prepared By	Date	# of Pages
A. ☐ Wood Destroying Pest Inspection (Paragraph 4A)	_____	_____	_____
B. ☐ Inspection or Report (Paragraph 4_____)	_____	_____	_____
C. ☐ Lead Disclosures (Paragraph 5A)	_____	_____	_____
D. ☐ Statutory Disclosures (Paragraph 5A)	_____	_____	_____
E. ☐ Common Interest Disclosures (Paragraph 6B)	_____	_____	_____
F. ☐ Property Insurance Claims (Paragraph 7B)	_____	_____	_____
G. ☐ Preliminary Title Report (Paragraph 12A)	_____	_____	_____
H. ☐ _____	_____	_____	_____
I. ☐ _____	_____	_____	_____

Buyer _____ Date _____

Buyer _____ Date _____

2. CONTINGENCY REMOVAL:
Buyer removes only those contingencies that are checked below:

EFFECT OF REMOVAL: With respect to any contingency and applicable cancellation right that Buyer removes below, Buyer shall conclusively be deemed to have: **(i)** completed all Buyer Inspections, investigations and review of reports and other applicable information and disclosures; **(ii)** elected to proceed with the transaction; and **(iii)** assumed all liability, responsibility and, if any, expense for repairs or corrections, unless, pursuant to the Agreement or another written agreement (C.A.R. Form RR), Seller has agreed to make Repairs or take other specified action.

Contingency

☐ **ALL CONTINGENCIES**

OR A. ☐ Loan (Paragraph 2I)
    B. ☐ Appraisal (Paragraph 2J)
    C. ☐ Tenant Occupied Property (Paragraph 3C (iii))
    D. ☐ Disclosures/Reports (Paragraphs 4 and 5)
    E ☐ Common Interest Disclosures (Paragraph 6B)
    F. ☐ Buyer Investigation, including insurability (Paragraph 9)
    G. ☐ Title: Preliminary Report (Paragraph 12)
    H. ☐ Sale of Buyer's Property (Paragraph 13)
    I. ☐ _____
    J. ☐ _____
    K. ☐ _____

NOTE: Paragraph numbers refer to the California Residential Purchase Agreement (C.A.R. Form RPA-CA)

Buyer _____ Date _____

Buyer _____ Date _____

(____/____) (Initials) **CONFIRMATION OF RECEIPT:** A Copy of this Signed Receipt for Reports and Contingency Removal was personally received by Seller or Seller's authorized agent on _____ (date), at _____ AM/PM.

SURE TRAC
The System for Success™

Published by the California Association of REALTORS®

EQUAL HOUSING OPPORTUNITY

Reviewed by _____ Date _____

RRCR REVISED 10/02 (PAGE 1 OF 1)   Print Date

RECEIPT FOR REPORTS AND CONTINGENCY REMOVAL   (RRCR   PAGE 1 OF 1)

The buyer acknowledges which reports and disclosures he or she received and checks the appropriate contingency removals.

Figure 7-12

CALIFORNIA ASSOCIATION OF REALTORS®

NOTICE TO SELLER TO PERFORM
No. _____
(C.A.R. Form NSP, Revised 10/02)

In accordance with the terms and conditions of the ☐ California Residential Purchase Agreement or ☐ Other
_____
_____ ("Agreement"), dated _____,
on property known as _____ ("Property"),
between _____ ("Buyer"),
and _____ ("Seller").

Buyer hereby gives Seller notice that Buyer has not yet received from Seller the items checked below. If Seller does not provide Buyer with these items, Buyer may be entitled to cancel the Agreement or delay removing an applicable contingency:

<u>Contractual Action</u>

A. ☐ Delivery of Wood Destroying Pest Inspection (Paragraph 4A)
B. ☐ Delivery of the following Inspection or Report (Paragraph 4_____):
   _____
C. ☐ Delivery of Lead Disclosures (Paragraph 5A)
D. ☐ Delivery of the following Statutory Disclosures (Paragraph 5A): _____
   _____
E. ☐ Delivery of the following booklets/guides (Paragraph 5B): _____
   _____
F. ☐ Disclosure of Property in Common Interest Development (Paragraph 6A)
G. ☐ Delivery of Common Interest Disclosures (Paragraph 6B)
H. ☐ Disclosure of Known Property Insurance Claims (Paragraph 7B)
I. ☐ Delivery of Preliminary Title Report (Paragraph 12A)
J. ☐ Approval of verification of down payment and closing costs (Paragraph 14C(3))
K. ☐ Approval of verification of cash (Paragraph 14C(3))
L. ☐ _____
M. ☐ _____

NOTE: Paragraph numbers refer to the California Residential Purchase Agreement (C.A.R. Form RPA-CA)

SELLER: If you do not take the specified contractual action indicated above, Buyer may cancel the Agreement.

_____   _____   _____ AM/PM
Buyer   Date   Time

_____   _____   _____ AM/PM
Buyer   Date   Time

(_____/_____) (Initials) **CONFIRMATION OF RECEIPT:** A Copy of this Signed Notice to Seller to Perform was personally received by Seller or authorized agent on _____ (date), at _____ AM/PM.

SURE TRAC
The System for Success™

Published by the
California Association of REALTORS®

NSP REVISED 10/02 (PAGE 1 OF 1)   Print Date

Reviewed by _____ Date _____

EQUAL HOUSING OPPORTUNITY

NOTICE TO SELLER TO PERFORM (NSP PAGE 1 OF 1)

If the seller is not able or willing to perform the terms and conditions agreed upon in the original Purchase Agreement, the buyer's agent forwards this form to the selling agent advising that the buyer may cancel his or her offer if this request is not complied with in a timely fashion.

Figure 7-13

CALIFORNIA
ASSOCIATION
OF REALTORS®

NOTICE TO BUYER TO PERFORM
No. _____
(C.A.R. Form NBP, Revised 10/02)

In accordance with the terms and conditions of the: ☐ California Residential Purchase Agreement or ☐ Other _____
_____ ("Agreement"), dated _____,
on property known as _____ ("Property"),
between _____ ("Buyer"),
and _____ ("Seller").

SELLER hereby gives Buyer notice to remove the following contingencies or take the specified contractual action:

Contingency

☐ **ALL CONTINGENCIES**

A. ☐ Loan (Paragraph 2I)
B. ☐ Appraisal (Paragraph 2J)
C. ☐ Tenant-Occupied Property (Paragraph 3C(iii))
D. ☐ Disclosures/Reports (Paragraphs 4 and 5)
E ☐ Common Interest Disclosures (Paragraph 6B)
F. ☐ Buyer Investigation, including insurability (Paragraph 9)
G. ☐ Title: Preliminary Report (Paragraph 12)
H. ☐ Sale of Buyer's Property (Paragraph 13)
I. ☐ _____
J. ☐ _____
K. ☐ _____

Contractual Action

L. ☐ Initial Deposit (Paragraph 2A)
M. ☐ Increased Deposit (Paragraph 2B)
N. ☐ Loan Application Letter (Paragraph 2G)
O. ☐ Down Payment Verification (Paragraph 2H)
P. ☐ All Cash Verification (Paragraph 2L)
Q. ☐ Return of Statutory Disclosures (Paragraph 5A(2))
R. ☐ Return of Lead Disclosures (Paragraph 5A(2))
S. ☐ Receipt for Increased Deposit (Paragraph 16)
T. ☐ _____
U. ☐ _____
V. ☐ _____

NOTE: Paragraph numbers refer to the California Residential Purchase Agreement (C.A.R. Form RPA-CA)

BUYER: If you do not remove the contingency(ies) (C.A.R. Form RRCR) or take the contractual actions specified above within 24 (or ☐ _____) hours (but no less than the time specified in the Agreement) of receipt of this Notice to Buyer to Perform, Seller may cancel the Agreement.

_____ _____ _____ AM/PM
Seller   Date   Time

_____ _____ _____ AM/PM
Seller   Date   Time

(_____ / _____) (Initials) **CONFIRMATION OF RECEIPT:** A Copy of this Signed Notice to Buyer to Perform was personally received by Buyer or authorized agent on _____ (date), at _____ AM/PM.

SURE TRAC
The System for Success™

Published by the
California Association of REALTORS®

Reviewed by _____ Date _____

EQUAL HOUSING
OPPORTUNITY

NBP REVISED 10/02 (PAGE 1 OF 1) Print Date

NOTICE TO BUYER TO PERFORM (NBP PAGE 1 OF 1)

This form is more specific than the Notice to Seller to Perform (NSP), as this gives the right to the seller to cancel the escrow within 24 hours if the buyer does not take the contractual actions specified within and remove the contingencies. It is important to remember that this must not be less than the times specified in the Purchase Agreement or any pertinent counter offer.

Figure 7-14

CALIFORNIA ASSOCIATION OF REALTORS®

VERIFICATION OF PROPERTY CONDITION
(BUYER FINAL INSPECTION)
(C.A.R. Form VP, Revised 4/02)

Property Address _____

The purpose of this inspection is to satisfy the Buyer regarding the condition of the Property. Buyer and Seller understand and agree that this inspection is not a contingency of the purchase and sale, unless it was expressly made a contingency of the prior contractual agreement between Buyer and Seller.

Buyer acknowledges that: (1) Property is in substantially the same condition as on the date of acceptance of the offer to purchase/sell and (2) Seller has completed any repairs, alterations, replacements, or modifications as agreed to by the Buyer and Seller with the following exceptions:

_____
_____
_____
_____
_____
_____
_____
_____
_____
_____
_____
_____
_____
_____
_____
_____
_____
_____

The evaluation of the condition of the Property, including any items listed above, is based upon a personal inspection by Buyer and/or tests, surveys, inspections, or other studies performed by inspector(s) selected by Buyer.

This acknowledgement and evaluation is not based upon any statement or representation by the Broker(s), Associate-Licensee(s) or brokerage employees. We agree to hold Broker(s) and brokerage employees harmless from any liability, claims, demands, damages, or costs arising out of the contractual obligations of the Buyer and Seller concerning the condition of Property. Buyer and Seller understand that this inspection is not intended in any way to alter the contractual obligations of Seller regarding the condition of Property to be delivered to the Buyer at possession date.

Receipt of a copy is hereby acknowledged.

Date _____ Buyer _____

Date _____ Buyer _____

Date _____ Seller _____

Date _____ Seller _____

Reviewed by
Broker or Designee _____ Date _____

VP-11 REVISED 4/02 (PAGE 1 OF 1) **Print Date**

EQUAL HOUSING OPPORTUNITY

VERIFICATION OF PROPERTY CONDITION (VP-11 PAGE 1 OF 1)

This is used as a final walk-through, a few days prior to closing the sale, confirming that the property is basically in the same condition as when the offer was made and that the agreed upon repairs and/or alteration have been satisfactorily performed. Remember, this is not the time to test switches, and check for leaks—your buyer has already had the physical inspections. If the buyer declines to have a final inspection, it must be so noted on this form and signed by the buyer.

II. C.A.R.® Real Estate Disclosure Summary Chart

The **REAL ESTATE DISCLOSURE SUMMARY CHART** is designed to provide REALTORS® and their clients with an easy-to-use reference guide for determining the applicability of the state and federal laws to real estate transactions most commonly handled by real estate licensees.

The *Real Estate Disclosure Summary Chart* (**Figure 7-15**) provides a disclosure "trigger" as well as a brief summary of the disclosure requirement, but does not cover all disclosures required by law. Some of the disclosures addressed in this chart, though generally applicable to a particular type of transaction, may be subject to exceptions which, unless otherwise noted, are not addressed in this publication. More detailed information regarding disclosure and other legal topics is available to C.A.R. members at *C.A.R. Online*.

www.car.org
California Association of Realtors®

Figure 7-15

REAL ESTATE DISCLOSURE SUMMARY CHART

SUBJECT	DISCLOSURE TRIGGER	DISCLOSURE REQUIREMENT (Brief Summary) FORM	C.A.R. INFORMATION SOURCE LAW CITATION
Advisability of Title Insurance	An escrow transaction for the purchase or simultaneous exchange of real property where a policy of title insurance will not be issued to the buyer.	The buyer must receive the statutory notice. The law does not specify who is responsible for providing this notice.	Cal. Civ. Code § 1057.6.
Agency Relationship Disclosure and Confirmation	Sale of residential real property of 1-4 units and mobilehomes; lease for a term of over one year of residential real property of 1-4 units.	The buyer must receive the agency disclosure form (AD) from the buyer's agent prior to signing the offer. The seller must receive the agency disclosure form (AD) from the seller's agent prior to signing the listing contract and	**Agency Disclosure and Confirmation** **Summary of How to Comply With the Agency Legislation**

Reprinted with permission, CALIFORNIA ASSOCIATION OF REALTORS®. Endorsement not implied.

SUBJECT	DISCLOSURE TRIGGER	DISCLOSURE REQUIREMENT (Brief Summary) FORM	C.A.R. INFORMATION SOURCE LAW CITATION
Agency Relationship Disclosure and Confirmation (cont'd.)		must receive another agency disclosure form (AD) from the buyer's agent prior to accepting the buyer's offer. The agency confirmation form must be given to the buyer and seller "as soon as practicable." This can be accomplished either by having the language in the purchase agreement or by using a separate form (AC-6). C.A.R. forms AD (disclosure) and AC-6 (confirmation) may be used.	Cal. Civ. Code §§ 2079.13 *et seq.*
Area of Potential Flooding (in the event of dam or reservoir failure)	Sale of all real property if the seller or the seller's agent has actual knowledge or a list has been compiled <u>by parcel</u> and the notice posted at a local county recorder, assessor and planning agency. Also applies to Manufactured Homes (as defined in H&S §18007, which includes personal property Mobilehomes) offered for resale.	The seller's <u>agent</u> or the seller without an agent must disclose to the buyer <u>if the property is in</u> this Area of Potential Flooding as designated on an inundation map, if a parcel list has been prepared by the county and a notice identifying the location of the list is available at the county assessor's, county recorder's or county planning commission office, or if the seller or seller's agent has actual knowledge that the property is in an area. If a TDS is required in the transaction, either C.A.R. Form NHD, "Natural Hazard Disclosure Statement" or an updated Local Option disclosure form must be used to make this disclosure.	**Natural Hazard Disclosure Statement** Cal. Gov't Code §§ 8589.4, 8589.5; Cal. Civ. Code § 1103.
Brokers Statutory Duty to Inspect Property	Sale of all residential real property of 1-4 units (No exemptions except for never occupied properties where a public report is required or properties exempt from a public report pursuant to Business & Professions Code §11010.4) Also applies to Manufactured Homes (as defined in H&S § 18007, which includes personal property Mobilehomes).	A real estate licensee must conduct a reasonably competent and diligent visual inspection of the property; this inspection duty does not include areas which are reasonably and normally inaccessible, off the site, or public records or permits concerning the title or use of the property; this inspection duty includes only the unit for sale and not the common areas of a condo or other common interest development. There is no requirement that the inspection report be in writing; however, it is recommended that all licensees put it in writing.	**Real Estate Licensee's Duty to Inspect Residential Property** Cal. Civ. Code §§ 2079.13 *et seq.*

SUBJECT	DISCLOSURE TRIGGER	DISCLOSURE REQUIREMENT (Brief Summary) FORM	C.A.R. INFORMATION SOURCE LAW CITATION
Brokers Statutory Duty to Inspect Property (cont'd.)		C.A.R. Form TDS (or for mobilehomes and manufactured housing, C.A.R. Form MHTDS) may be used. If the seller is exempt from the TDS, then C.A.R. Form AID may be used by the agent.	
Commercial Property Owner's Guide to Earthquake Safety	<u>Mandatory delivery:</u> Sale, transfer, or exchange of any real property or manufactured home or mobilehome if built of precast concrete or reinforced/unreinforced masonry with wood frame floors or roofs and built before January 1, 1975, located within a county or city, if not exempt. Same exemptions as for Homeowner's Guide below. <u>Voluntary delivery:</u> Transfer of <u>any</u> real property.	<u>Mandatory delivery:</u> The transferor/transferor's agent must give the transferee a copy of "The Commercial Property Owner's Guide to Earthquake Safety." <u>Voluntary delivery:</u> If the Guide is delivered to the transferee, then the transferor or broker is not required to provide additional information concerning general earthquake hazards. Known earthquake hazards must be disclosed, whether delivery is mandatory or voluntary.	Cal. Bus. & Prof. Code § 10147; Cal. Gov't Code §§ 8875.6, 8875.9, 8893.2, 8893.3; Cal. Civ. Code § 2079.9.
Death and/or AIDS	Sale, lease, or rental of <u>all</u> real property.	The transferor/agent has no liability for not disclosing the fact of any death which occurred more than 3 years prior to the date the transferee offers to buy, lease, or rent the property. Any death which has occurred within a 3-year period should be disclosed if deemed to be "material." Affliction with AIDS or death from AIDS, no matter when it occurred, need not be voluntarily disclosed. However, neither a seller nor seller's agent may make an intentional misrepresentation in response to a direct question concerning AIDS/death from AIDS on the property. An agent may simply respond that discussing such information is an invasion of privacy.	**Disclosure of Aids and Death: The Legislative Solution** Cal. Civ. Code § 1710.2.

SUBJECT	DISCLOSURE TRIGGER	DISCLOSURE REQUIREMENT (Brief Summary) FORM	C.A.R. INFORMATION SOURCE LAW CITATION
"Drug Lab" (Release of Illegal Controlled Substance)	Transfer or exchange of residential real property of 1-4 units and lease of any residential dwelling unit. Same exemptions as for the Transfer Disclosure Statement.	In the event that toxic contamination by an illegal controlled substance has occurred on a property and upon receipt of a notice from the Dept. of Toxic Substances Control (DTSC) or other agency—or if the seller has actual knowledge of the toxic contamination—the seller must disclose this information to the buyer by checking item II.C.1 of the TDS form and attaching the DTSC notice, if there is one. In the case of rental property, the landlord must give a prospective tenant written notice of the toxic contamination. Providing the tenant with a copy of the DTSC notice will suffice if there is such a notice. C.A.R. Form TDS may be used.	Cal. Civ. Code §§ 1102.18, 1940.7.5.
Earthquake Fault Zone	Sale of all real property which does contain or will eventually contain a structure for human occupancy and which is located in an earthquake fault zone (special studies zone) as indicated on maps created by the California Geological Survey. Also applies to Manufactured Homes (as defined in H&S § 18007, which includes personal property Mobilehomes) offered for resale.	The seller's agent or the seller without an agent must disclose to the buyer the fact that the property is in an earthquake fault zone (special studies zone), if maps are available at the county assessor's, county recorder's, or county planning commission office, or if the seller or seller's agent has actual knowledge that the property is in the zone. If the map is not of sufficient accuracy or scale to determine whether the property is in the zone, then either the agent indicates "yes" that the property is in the zone or the agent may write "no" that the property is not in this zone, but then a report prepared by an expert verifying that fact must be attached to C.A.R. Form NHD. If a TDS is required in the transaction, either C.A.R. Form NHD, "Natural Hazard Disclosure Statement," or an updated local option disclosure form must be used to make this disclosure.	**Natural Hazard Disclosure Statement** Cal. Pub. Res. Code §§ 2621 et seq.; Cal. Civ. Code § 1103.

SUBJECT	DISCLOSURE TRIGGER	DISCLOSURE REQUIREMENT (Brief Summary) FORM	C.A.R. INFORMATION SOURCE LAW CITATION
Energy Ratings Booklet (Optional Disclosure) (Not Yet Available)	Transfer or exchange of <u>all</u> real property. Also applies to Manufactured Homes (as defined in H&S § 18007, which includes personal property Mobilehomes)	If an energy ratings booklet is delivered to the transferee, then a seller or broker is not required to provide additional information concerning the existence of a statewide energy rating program. NEITHER THIS PROGRAM NOR THE BOOKLET IS AVAILABLE AT THIS TIME.	Cal. Civ. Code § 2079.10; Cal. Pub. Res. Code §§ 25402.9, 25942.
FHA/HUD Inspection Notice	Sale of residential real property of 1-4 units, including mobilehomes on a permanent foundation, which involve FHA loans or HUD-owned properties.	For all properties regardless of when they were built, the borrower must sign the notice entitled, "The Importance of a Home Inspection." C.A.R. Form HID may be used for this purpose.	**FHA Inspection Disclosure Form** HUD Mortgagee Letters 99-18, 99-32.
FIRPTA (Federal Withholding Tax) and California Withholding Tax	FIRPTA: All sales, including installment sales, exchanges, foreclosures, deeds in lieu of foreclosure and other transactions by a "foreign person" – See the legal memorandum for the exemptions. CAL Withholding: Any "disposition of a California real property interest" (includes sales, exchanges, foreclosures, installment sales, and other types of transfers).	FIRPTA: Buyers must withhold 10% of the gross sales price and send it to the IRS. See the legal memorandum for all the details. If the seller is not a "foreign person," he or she may complete the affidavit of non-foreign status. CAL Withholding: Buyers must withhold 3 1/3 percent of the gross sales price on sales of California real property interests, unless an exemption applies, and send it to the FTB. See the legal memorandum for all the details. C.A.R. form AS may be used.	**Federal Withholding: The Foreign Investment in Real Property Tax Act (FIRPTA)** **California Withholding on the Sale of Real Property** 42 U.S.C. §5154a; Cal Rev. & Tax Code §§18662(e)(f).
Flood Disaster Insurance Requirements (Applicable for any flood disaster declared after September 23, 1994)	Any transfer of personal (e.g., mobilehomes), residential, or commercial property where the owner received federal flood disaster assistance conditioned on the owner subsequently obtaining and maintaining flood insurance.	The transferor must notify the transferee in writing on a document "evidencing the transfer of ownership of the property" about the requirement to obtain and maintain flood insurance in accordance with applicable Federal law. Failure to notify the transferee means that in the event the transferee fails to maintain the required flood insurance and the property is damaged by a flood disaster requiring Federal disaster relief, the transferor will be required to reimburse the Federal government.	**Federal Flood Insurance Disclosure** 42 U.S.C. § 5154a.

SUBJECT	DISCLOSURE TRIGGER	DISCLOSURE REQUIREMENT (Brief Summary) FORM	C.A.R. INFORMATION SOURCE LAW CITATION
Flood Disaster Insurance Requirements (cont'd.)		The law is unclear as to what document(s) should contain this notice. C.A.R. Forms RPA-CA and NHD may be acceptable, but technically are not. documents that "evidence the transfer of ownership." Clearly, a grant deed is such a document.	
Homeowner's Guide to Earthquake Safety	<u>Mandatory delivery:</u> Transfer of residential real property of 1-4 units, manufactured homes, and mobilehomes, of conventional light frame construction, and built prior to January 1, 1960, if not exempt (almost same exemptions as for the Transfer Disclosure Statement). Additional exemption if the buyer agrees, in writing, to demolish the property within one year from date of transfer. <u>Voluntary delivery:</u> Transfer of <u>any</u> real property.	<u>Mandatory delivery:</u> The licensee must give the transferor the booklet "The Homeowner's Guide to Earthquake Safety" and the transferor must give this booklet to the transferee. Known structural deficiencies must be disclosed by the transferor to the transferee and the form in the booklet entitled "Residential Earthquake Hazards Report" may be used to make this disclosure. <u>Voluntary delivery:</u> If the Guide is delivered to the transferee, then the transferor or broker is not required to provide additional information concerning general earthquake hazards. Known earthquake hazards must be disclosed whether delivery is mandatory or voluntary.	Cal. Bus. & Prof. Code § 10149; Cal. Gov't Code §§ 8897.1, 8897.2, 8897.5; Cal. Civ. Code § 2079.8.
Industrial Use Zone Location	Transfer or exchange of residential real property of 1-4 units.	The seller of real property subject to the TDS law must disclose "actual knowledge" that the property is affected by or zoned to allow an industrial use of property (manufacturing, commercial, or airport use) as soon as possible before transfer of title. C.A.R. Form TDS may be used.	Cal. Civ. Code § 1102.17; Cal. Code Civ. Proc. § 731a.

SUBJECT	DISCLOSURE TRIGGER	DISCLOSURE REQUIREMENT (Brief Summary) FORM	C.A.R. INFORMATION SOURCE LAW CITATION
Lead-Based Paint Pamphlet and Form	Sale or lease of <u>all</u> residential property, <u>built before 1978,</u> except as indicated below. Mobilehomes are also subject to this law. <u>Exemptions:</u> ?? foreclosure or trustee's sale transfer (REO properties and deed in lieu of foreclosure are NOT exempt!) ?? zero-bedroom dwelling (loft, efficiency unit, dorm, or studio) ?? short-term rental (100 or fewer days) ?? housing for elderly or handicapped (unless children live there) ?? rental housing certified free of lead paint	The seller/lessor must provide the buyer/lessee with a lead hazard information pamphlet, disclose the presence of any known lead-based paint and provide a statement signed by the buyer that the buyer has read the warning statement, has received the pamphlet, and has a 10-day opportunity to inspect before becoming obligated under the contract. The purchaser (not lessee) is permitted a 10-day period to conduct an inspection unless the parties mutually agree upon a different time period. The agent, on behalf of the seller/lessor, must ensure compliance with the requirements of this law. C.A.R. pamphlet, "Protect Your Family From Lead in Your Home," and C.A.R. form FLD satisfy these requirements (except for sales of HUD properties—HUD forms required). The C.A.R. revised home environmental hazards booklet may be used in lieu of the pamphlet mentioned above.	**Federal Lead-Based Paint and Lead-Based Paint Hazards Disclosures** **Federal Pre-Renovation Lead Information Rule** Residential Lead-Based Paint Hazard Reduction Act of 1992, 42 U.S.C. § 4852d.
Material Facts	Any transfer of real property or manufactured homes (including mobilehomes). No exemptions.	A seller (transferor) or real estate agent involved in the transaction must disclose any <u>known "material facts"</u> that affect the value or desirability of the property. Whether or not something is deemed material is determined by case law.	Case law; Cal. Civ. Code § 2079 *et seq.*
Megan's Law Disclosure (Registered Sex Offender Database)	Sale or lease/rental of all residential real property of 1-4 units (No exemptions except for never-occupied properties where a public report is required or properties exempted from a public report pursuant to Business & Professions Code.)	Every lease or rental agreement and every sales contract is required to include a statutorily-defined notice regarding the existence of public access to database information regarding sex offenders. The following C.A.R. forms contain this statutory notice: LR, LR-S, RIPA, RPA-CA	**Megan's Law: Notifying the Public About Registered Sex Offenders** Cal. Civ. Code § 2079.10a.

SUBJECT	DISCLOSURE TRIGGER	DISCLOSURE REQUIREMENT (Brief Summary) FORM	C.A.R. INFORMATION SOURCE LAW CITATION
Mello-Roos and 1915 Bond Act Assessments	Transfer or exchange of residential real property of 1-4 units subject to a continuing lien securing the levy of special taxes pursuant to the Mello-Roos Community Facilities Act or the 1915 Bond Act. Same exemptions as for the Transfer Disclosure Statement, except that new subdivisions are not exempt.	The transferor must make a good faith effort to obtain a disclosure notice concerning the special tax or assessment from each local agency that levies a special tax or assessment and deliver the notice(s) to the prospective transferee. Transferors may comply with this law by using a third-party disclosure company. Transferors may comply with the bond assessment disclosure requirement by using a recent tax bill or an itemization from a title report. The transferee has a 3 or 5-day right of rescission. There is no affirmative duty by an agent to discover a special tax or district or assessment not actually known to the agent.	**Mello-Roos District Disclosure Requirements** Cal. Civ. Code § 1102.6b; Cal. Gov't Code §§ 53340.2, 53341.5, 53754.
Military Ordnance Location (former military munitions site)	Transfer or exchange of residential real property of 1-4 units and lease of <u>any</u> residential dwelling unit. Same exemptions as for the Transfer Disclosure Statement.	Disclosure is required when the transferor/lessor has actual knowledge that a former military ordnance location (military training grounds which may contain explosives) is within one mile of the property. The transferor/lessor must disclose in writing to the transferee/lessee, that these former federal or state military ordnance locations may contain potentially explosive munitions. The transferee has a 3 or 5-day right of rescission. C.A.R. Form TDS may be used.	Cal. Civ. Code §§ 1102.15, 1940.7.

SUBJECT	DISCLOSURE TRIGGER	DISCLOSURE REQUIREMENT (Brief Summary) FORM	C.A.R. INFORMATION SOURCE LAW CITATION
Mold (Disclosure of Excessive Mold or Health Threat)	Sale, lease, rental, or other transfer of any commercial, industrial or residential property	There are no current disclosure requirements until after the Dept. of Health Services (DHS) develops permissible exposure limits for mold and a consumer booklet. The TDS has been modified to include the word "mold" in paragraph II.C.1. As always, any transferor must disclose actual knowledge of toxic mold on the property.	**Mold and Its Impact on Real Estate Transactions** Cal. Health & Safety Code §§ 26100 et seq. , §§ 26140, 26141, 26147, 26148.
Natural Hazard Disclosure Statement (Form)	Transfer of residential real property of 1-4 units if the property is located in one or more of the following hazard zones: Special Flood Hazard Area, Area of Potential Flooding, Very High Fire Severity Zone, Earthquake Fault Zone, Seismic Hazard Zone, or State Responsibility Area. Also applies to Manufactured Homes (as defined in H&S § 18007, which includes personal property Mobilehomes) offered for resale. See the legal memorandum for the list of exemptions.	The seller and the listing agent must sign the statutory form or a substantially equivalent form (provided by a disclosure company or other) to be provided to the buyer.	**Natural Hazard Disclosure Statement** Cal. Civ. Code §§ 1103 et seq.
Residential Environmental Hazards Booklet (Optional Disclosure)	Transfer or exchange of all real property. Also applies to Manufactured Homes (as defined in H&S § 18007, which includes personal property Mobilehomes)	If a consumer information booklet is delivered to the transferee, then a seller or broker is not required to provide additional information concerning common environmental hazards. Although highly recommended, delivery is voluntary. However, known hazards on the property must be disclosed to the transferee.	Cal. Civ. Code § 2079.7.
Seismic Hazard Zones	Sale of all real property which does contain or will eventually contain a structure for human habitation and which is located in a seismic hazard zone as indicated on maps created by the California	The seller's agent, or the seller without an agent, must disclose to the buyer the fact that the property is in a seismic hazard zone if maps are available at the county assessor's, county recorder's, or county planning commission office, or if the seller or seller's agent has	**Seismic Hazard Zone Maps Update**

SUBJECT	DISCLOSURE TRIGGER	DISCLOSURE REQUIREMENT (Brief Summary) FORM	C.A.R. INFORMATION SOURCE LAW CITATION
Seismic Hazard Zones (cont.d)	Division of Mines and Geology. Also applies to Manufactured Homes (as defined in H&S § 18007, which includes personal property Mobilehomes) offered for resale.	actual knowledge that the property is in the zone. If the map is not of sufficient accuracy or scale to determine whether the property is in the zone, then either the agent indicates "yes" that the property is in the zone or the agent may write "no" that the property is not in this zone, but then a report prepared by an expert verifying that fact must be attached to C.A.R. Form NHD. If a TDS is required in the transaction, either C.A.R. Form NHD, "Natural Hazard Disclosure Statement" or an updated local option disclosure form must be used to make this disclosure.	**Natural Hazard Disclosure Statement** Cal. Pub. Res. Code § 2690 et seq., § 2694; Cal. Civ. Code § 1103.
Smoke Detectors Must Be In Compliance	All existing dwelling units must have a smoke detector centrally located outside each sleeping area (bedroom or group of bedrooms). In addition, new construction (with a permit after August 14, 1992) must have a hard-wired smoke detector in each bedroom. Any additions, modifications, or repairs (after August 14, 1992) exceeding $1,000 for which a permit is required or the addition of any bedroom will also trigger the requirement of a smoke detector in each bedroom. (These may be battery operated.)	Same exemptions from the Transfer Disclosure Statement but only for single family homes and factory-built housing, not other types of dwellings. However, transfers to or from any governmental entity, and transfers by a beneficiary or mortgagee after foreclosure sale or trustee's sale or transfers by deed in lieu of foreclosure, which are exempt under the TDS law, are <u>not</u> exempt from this law. LOCAL LAW MAY BE MORE RESTRICTIVE! Check with the local City or County Department of Building and Safety.	**Smoke Detector Requirements** Cal. Health & Safety Code §§ 13113.7, 13113.8, 18029.6.
Smoke Detector Written Statement of Compliance	The seller of a <u>single family home or factory-built housing</u> must provide the buyer with a written statement indicating that the property is in compliance with current California law.	Same exemptions as from the TDS law. However, transfers to or from any governmental entity, and transfers by a beneficiary or mortgagee after foreclosure sale or trustee's sale or transfers by deed in lieu of foreclosure, which are exempt under the TDS law, are <u>not</u> exempt from this law. C.A.R. Form SDS may be used.	**Smoke Detector Requirements** Cal. Health & Safety Code § 13113.8.

SUBJECT	DISCLOSURE TRIGGER	DISCLOSURE REQUIREMENT (Brief Summary) FORM	C.A.R. INFORMATION SOURCE LAW CITATION
Special Flood Hazard Area	Sale of real property located in Zone "A" or " V" as designated by FEMA and if the seller or the seller's agent has actual knowledge or a list has been compiled <u>by parcel</u> and the notice posted at a local county recorder, assessor, and planning agency. Also applies to Manufactured Homes (as defined in H&S § 18007, which includes personal property Mobilehomes) offered for resale.	The seller's <u>agent</u> or the seller without an agent must disclose to the buyer if the property is in this Special Flood Hazard Area, if a parcel list has been prepared by the county and a notice identifying the location of the list is available at the county assessor's, county recorder's or county planning commission office, or if the seller or seller's agent has actual knowledge that the property is in an area. If a TDS is required in the transaction, either C.A.R. Form NHD, "Natural Hazard Disclosure Statement" or an updated Local Option disclosure form must be used to make this disclosure.	**Natural Hazard Disclosure Statement** Cal. Civ. Code § 1103; Cal. Gov't Code § 8589.3.
State Responsibility Area (Fire Hazard Area)	Sale of <u>any</u> real property located in a designated state responsibility area (generally a "wildland area") where the state not local or federal govt. has the primary financial responsibility for fire prevention. The California Department of Forestry provides maps to the county assessor of each affected county. Also applies to Manufactured Homes (as defined in H&S § 18007, which includes personal property Mobilehomes) offered for resale.	The seller must disclose to the buyer the fact that the property is located in this zone, the risk of fire, state-imposed additional duties such as maintaining fire breaks, and the fact that the state may not provide fire protection services. The disclosure must be made if maps are available at the county assessor, county recorder or county planning commission office, or if the seller has actual knowledge that the property is in the zone. If the map is not of sufficient accuracy or scale to determine whether the property is in this Area, then either the agent indicates "yes" that the property is in this Area or the agent may write "no" that the property is <u>not</u> in this Area, but then a report prepared by an expert verifying that fact must be attached to C.A.R. Form NHD. If a TDS is required in the transaction, either C.A.R. Form NHD, "Natural Hazard Disclosure Statement" or an updated local option disclosure form must be used to make this disclosure.	**Natural Hazard Disclosure Statement** Cal. Pub. Res. Code §§ 4125, 4136; Cal. Civ. Code § 1103.

SUBJECT	DISCLOSURE TRIGGER	DISCLOSURE REQUIREMENT (Brief Summary) FORM	C.A.R. INFORMATION SOURCE LAW CITATION
Subdivided Lands Law	Sale, leasing, or financing of new developments (condos, PUDs) or conversions consisting of 5 or more lots, parcels, or interests.However, a transfer of a single property to 5 or more unrelated people (unless exempt) may also trigger this law. There are exemptions too numerous to discuss in this chart.	The owner, subdivider, or agent, prior to the execution of the purchase contract or lease, must give the buyer/lessee a copy of the final public report (FPR), preliminary public report (PPR), or the conditional public report (CPR) issued by the DRE. No offers may be solicited until the DRE has issued one of these three reports. If the DRE has issued a CPR or PPR, then offers may be solicited, but close of escrow is contingent upon issuance of the FPR. Contracts entered into pursuant to a PPR may be rescinded by either party; contracts entered into pursuant to a CPR are contingent upon satisfaction of certain specified conditions.	**Subdivided Lands Law** Cal. Bus. & Prof. Code §§ 11018.1, 11018.12; Cal. Code Regs., tit. 10, § 2795. See generally, Cal. Bus. & Prof. Code §§ 11000 *et seq.*; Cal. Code Regs., tit. 10, §§ 2790 *et seq.*
Subdivision Map Act	Any division of real property into 2 or more lots or parcels for the purpose of sale, lease, or financing. There are exemptions too numerous to discuss in this chart.	The owner/subdivider must record either a tentative and final map, or a parcel map (depending on the type of subdivision). Escrow on the transfer cannot close until the appropriate map has been recorded.	Cal. Gov't Code §§ 66426, 66428. See generally, Cal. Gov't Code §§ 66410 *et seq*.
Transfer Disclosure Statement	Transfer of residential real property of 1-4 units. Also applies to Manufactured Homes (as defined in H&S § 18007, which includes personal property Mobilehomes) offered for resale. See the legal memorandum for all the exemptions.	Sellers and real estate agents must complete a statutory disclosure form. C.A.R. form TDS (for real property); C.A.R. form MHTDS (for personal property mobilehomes)	**Transfer Disclosure Statement Law** Cal. Civ. Code §§ 1102 *et seq.*
Very High Fire Hazard Severity Zone	Sale of any real property. Also applies to Manufactured Homes (as defined in H&S § 18007, which includes personal property Mobilehomes) offered for resale.	The seller must disclose the fact that the property is located within this zone and whether it is subject to the requirements of Gov't Code Section 51182 (e.g., clear brush, maintain fire breaks). The disclosure must be made if maps are available at the county assessor, county recorder or county planning commission office, or if the seller has actual	**Natural Hazard Disclosure Statement** Cal. Gov't Code §§ 51178, 51183.5; Cal. Civ. Code § 1103.

SUBJECT	DISCLOSURE TRIGGER	DISCLOSURE REQUIREMENT (Brief Summary) FORM	C.A.R. INFORMATION SOURCE LAW CITATION
Very High Fire Hazard Severity Zone (cont'd.)		knowledge that the property is in the zone. If the map is not of sufficient accuracy or scale to determine whether the property is in this zone, then either the agent indicates "yes" that the property is in this zone or the agent may write "no" that the property is not in this zone, but then a report prepared by an expert verifying that fact must be attached to C.A.R. Form NHD. If a TDS is required in the transaction, either C.A.R. Form NHD, "Natural Hazard Disclosure Statement" or an updated local option disclosure form must be used to make this disclosure.	
Water Heater Bracing Statement of Compliance	All properties with any standard water heater with a capacity of not more than 120 gallons for which a pre-engineered strapping kit is readily available. Legislative intent suggests this law applies only to residential properties, but the language of the statute does not limit the requirement to residential properties.	All owners of new or replacement water heaters and all owners of existing residential water heaters must brace, anchor or strap water heaters to resist falling or horizontal displacement due to earthquake motion. Water heaters located in closets are also subject to this law. The seller of real property must certify in writing to a prospective purchaser that he has complied with this section and applicable local code requirements. This certification may be done in existing transactional documents, including but not limited to, the Homeowner's Guide to Earthquake Safety, a real estate purchase contract, a transfer disclosure statement, or a local option disclosure of compliance. C.A.R. Form WHS may be used.	**Water Heater Bracing and Disclosure Requirements** Cal. Health & Safety Code § 19211.

III. CHAPTER SUMMARY

Once the buyer and seller have agreed on a price and terms, and the Purchase Contract has been completed, you will need to supply your buyer with an additional set of forms (currently there are 17 listed).

The **Disclosure Regarding Real Estate Agency Relationships** is signed by both agent and buyer, explaining what agency relationship is being offered prior to any contract being written. It accompanies the Purchase Contract when first presented to the seller.

The buyer needs to know the total costs of purchasing a property. Working with the lender and various affiliates involved, you can calculate these costs on the form entitled Estimated Buyer's Costs.

All contingencies about the sale of a the buyer's property or the seller's purchase of a replacement property are noted in the **Contingency For Sale or Purchase of Other Property** form. There are several options for removing this contingency and remedies for noncompliance with time restrictions.

The **Buyer's Inspection Advisory** must be read and approved by the buyer. It recommends obtaining and paying for qualified inspections before finalizing the transaction. The seller receives a copy signed by the buyer, signs it, and returns a copy to the selling agent.

The **Wood Destroying Pest Inspection and Allocation of Cost Addendum** is an agreement between seller and buyer covering who will pay for required repairs (section 1) and recommended repairs (section 2). Often, the seller pays for section 1 and the buyer for section 2. You should guide your clients to be sure all buildings on the sight are included, such as detached garages, covered patios, decking, cabanas, etc.

The **Cooperating Broker Compensation Agreement and Escrow Instruction** form is an agreement between two brokers on the amount received by the selling agent. This is <u>not</u> presented to the seller, who has already agreed to the amount of commission to be paid to the listing agent. Do not get your buyer involved in commission splits.

When an offer is not accepted in its entirety, counter offers are made back and forth between the buyer and seller using a **Counter Offer** form. Escrow instructions are drawn up based on the intention of the parties as reflected in the original contract and any following counter offers. As such, if more than two counter offers are made, it's best to start over with a new purchase offer to eliminate confusion.

The **Foreign Investment in Real Property Tax Act (FRPTA)** requires a buyer to sign a **Buyer's Affidavit** if the property is to be used as a principal residence and the price does not exceed $300,000.

Based on various inspections, the **Request for Repairs** is a buyer's wish list of repairs he or she would like the seller to make. The seller then indicates whether he or she agrees to make all of the repairs, some of the repairs, or none of the repairs. Based on the seller's response, the buyer either agrees to remove contingencies and follow through on the sale or opts to cancel the escrow. If escrow is cancelled, the buyer gets the deposit back, minus incurred expenses, and the seller can put the property back on the market. (The buyer may write in contingencies other than repairs that he or she wants the seller to address in this form.) Both buyer and seller sign.

The **Receipt for Reports and Contingency Removal** is signed by the buyer, acknowledging which reports and disclosures he or she received, and whether those contingencies are removed. If the buyer has not received the appropriate reports and disclosures from the seller, or other terms and conditions agreed upon in the purchase contract have not been met by the seller, the buyer's agent forwards a **Notice to Seller to Perform** to the seller's agent. If this request isn't met in a timely fashion, the buyer may cancel the offer.

The **Notice to Buyer to Perform** gives the seller the right to cancel escrow within 24 hours (unless otherwise specified in the offer or counter offer) if the buyer doesn't take specific contractual actions and remove contingencies. Buyer signs form to indicate receipt.

A few days prior to closing the sale, the buyer makes a final walk-through of the property. He or she fills out a **Verification of Property Condition** confirming that the property is in basically the same condition as when the offer was made, and that the agreed-upon repairs or alterations have been satisfactorily performed. If the buyer declines a final inspection, it must be noted on the form and signed by the buyer.

If the buyers or sellers decline to have a professional inspection, it would be wise to have them sign a waiver attesting to this. There is no CAR® form specifically waiving this option, so many brokers create their own **Professional Waiver Inspection**. The waiver should indicate that, by signing, the parties relieve the broker of any liability that may result from declining the inspection. A **Real Estate Disclosure Summary Chart** is available online to active CAR® members through their website (www.car.org).

IV. KEY TERMS

Buyer's Affidavit
Buyer's Inspection Advisory
Contingencies
Contingency Removal
Cooperating Broker Compensation Agreement

Counter Offer
Deposit Receipt
Disclosure Regarding Agency Relationships
Estimated Buyer's Costs
Home Warranty Waiver
Listing Kit
Notice to Buyer to Perform
Notice to Seller to Perform
Physical Inspection Waiver
Purchase Contract
Receipt for Reports
Request for Repair
Verification of Property Condition
Walk-Through
Wood Destroying Pest Inspection and Allocation of Cost Addendum

V. CHAPTER 7 QUIZ

1. Which of the following (seller's) listing forms does the buyer not receive a copy of?
    a. Residential Listing Agreement
    b. Estimated Seller's Proceeds
    c. Both "a" and "b" are for seller's eyes only
    d. The buyer gets a copy of <u>all</u> listing documents

2. Which of the following is TRUE concerning a Competitive Market Analysis (CMA)?
    a. A CMA is required before an offer can be written.
    b. It's a good practice to offer a CMA as this informs the buyer about the price range in a particular neighborhood.
    c. Although not required, it is a helpful tool to write a "reasonable" offer.
    d. Both b and c are correct.

3. When making an offer contingent on the sale of the buyer's home:
    a. The buyer and agent need not inform the seller of this contingency.
    b. The buyer is still obligated to consummate the sale, regardless of whether his or her house sells.
    c. The buyer is offering to trade properties with the seller in a 1031 exchange.
    d. Always use the Contingency for Sale or Purchase of Other Property (COP) form, and make this an amendment to the Purchase Agreement.

4. Which of the following is TRUE concerning a selling agent's commission?
    a. The selling agent can ask for any acceptable commission split prior to close of escrow.
    b. The selling agent must abide by the commission details placed on the MLS by the listing agent.
    c. The selling agent can renegotiate his or her percentage of the commission with the seller regardless of the MLS information.
    d. All of the above.

5. After the physical inspection, the buyer requests the seller to repair the defects noted in the report. Which of the following is correct?
   a. The seller must comply and do all the work.
   b. The seller is responsible for making the repairs, but the buyer has to pay for them.
   c. The seller may do some, all, or none of the repairs.
   d. None of the above are correct.

6. With regard to contingencies, the buyer must deliver designated documents to the seller within five days. If the buyer fails to do so, the seller:
   a. may send the buyer a Notice to Buyer to Perform.
   b. may cancel the Agreement in writing.
   c. cannot cancel, even if the buyer does not remove the contingencies.
   d. both a and b are correct.

7. The home warranty:
   a. is always paid by the seller.
   b. is always paid by the buyer.
   c. can be paid by anybody.
   d. is not a valuable option.

8. The Agency Relationship Disclosure:
   a. can be signed at any time prior to close of escrow.
   b. is a requirement for the seller only.
   c. is a requirement for buyer only.
   d. is a requirement for both parties prior to entering into any real estate contract.

9. Wood Destroying Pest Inspection and Allocation of Cost Addendum (WPA):
   a. states whether the seller or the buyer will be responsible for the costs of the required work.
   b. states that inspection and repairs are usually paid by the agents.
   c. states that the seller always pays for Section 1 and Section 2.
   d. none of the above is correct.

10. When doing the final walk-through:
    a. the buyer and seller sign the Verification of Property Condition, after noting that the requested repairs have been performed and the property is in the same condition as when the offer was made.
    b. the buyer checks for the first time for leaks, electrical outlets and switches, checks all the windows.
    c. the seller must be accompanied by his or her attorney.
    d. all of the above.

ANSWERS: 1. c; 2. d; 3. d; 4. b; 5. c; 6. d; 7. c; 8. d; 9. a; 10. a

Finance

How to Choose the Right Loan

I. Nature of Financing

A. INTRODUCTION TO THE FINANCING PROCESS

Financing is the key to most real estate transactions.

The buying and selling of real estate would grind to a halt without trust deed and mortgage funds. And you, as a real estate professional, can play a big part in your clients obtaining their mortgages. Although you will have a lender qualify your buyers and provide them with a pre-approval letter prior to showing them properties, it's important for you to familiarize yourself with the various types of loans presently available.

1. California Calls Trust Deeds "Mortgages"

Although mortgages are rarely used in California, the term "mortgage" is so ingrained in the tradition of lending that often trust deeds and other loans are referred to as "mortgages." However, adjustable rate mortgages and fixed rate mortgages are actually deeds of trust in California.

291

CHAPTER 8 OUTLINE

I. NATURE OF FINANCING (p. 291)
 A. Introduction to the Financing Process (p. 291)
  1. California Calls Trust Deeds "Mortgages" (p. 291)
   a. Parties to a Trust Deed (p. 294)
 B. The Cost of Borrowing Money (p. 294)
  1. Interest Rates (p. 294)
  2. Origination Fees (p. 294)
  3. Points (p. 294)
  4. Annual Percentage Rate (APR) (p. 295)
  5. Prepayment Penalties (p. 295)
  6. Impound Accounts (Reserves) (p. 295)

II. INSTITUTIONAL (CONVENTIONAL) FINANCING (p. 296)
 A. Mortgage Bankers (p. 296)
  1. Mortgage Bankers vs. Mortgage Brokers (p. 296)
 B. Savings Banks (p. 296)
 C. Commercial Banks (p. 298)
 D. Life Insurance Companies (p. 299)
 E. Private Mortgage Insurance (PMI) (Provide a Valuable Service) (p. 299)
  1. Credit Requirements (p. 300)
 F. Fixed Rate Mortgages (p. 300)
 G. Adjustable Rate Mortgages (ARMs) (p. 300)
 H. Special Purpose Loans (p. 301)
  1. Graduated Payment Mortgage (GPM) (For First-Time Buyers) (p. 301)

III. THE SECONDARY MORTGAGE MARKET (p. 303)
 A. Secondary Mortgage (Trust Deed) Market (p. 303)
  1. Federal National Mortgage Association (Fannie Mae - Private) (p. 303)
  2. Government National Mortgage Association (Ginnie Mae) (p. 303)
  3. Federal Home Loan Mortgage Corporation (Freddie Mac) (p. 304)
 B. Final Word on Conventional Loans (Risk—Without Government Backing) (p. 304)

IV. GOVERNMENT FINANCING (GOVERNMENT-BACKED LOANS) (p. 304)
 A. Federal Housing Administration (FHA) (p. 305)
  1. Purchase Requirements (p. 305)
  2. Loan Discount Fee (p. 308)
  3. Calculating the Maximum Loan (p. 308)
  4. FHA Section 245—Graduated Payment Mortgage (GPM) (p. 308)
 B. Veterans Administration (VA) (p. 309)
  1. Certificate of Reasonable Value (CRV) (p. 309)
  2. Secondary Financing (p. 309)
  3. Eligibility and Entitlement (p. 310)
  4. Reinstatement of Veteran's Loan Entitlement (p. 310)

C. California Department of Veterans Affairs (Cal-Vet) (p. 311)
  1. Insurance Requirements (p. 311)
  2. Maximum Loans (p. 312)
V. QUALIFYING THE BORROWER (p. 312)
  A. The Loan Application (p. 312)
    1. Credit Scoring (Access to Credit Profile) (p. 315)
    2. Equal Credit Opportunity Act (ECOA) (p. 315)
    3. Fair Credit Reporting Act (p. 317)
    4. Truth in Lending Act (p. 317)
VI. NONINSTITUTIONAL FINANCING (p. 317)
  A. Junior Loans (Secondary Financing) (p. 317)
    1. Acceleration Clause (p. 318)
    2. Discounting Second Trust Deeds (p. 318)
    3. Balloon Payments (p. 319)
  B. All-Inclusive Trust Deed (AITD) (p. 319)
  C. Contract of Sale (Land Contract) (p. 319)
  D. All-Cash Transactions (p. 320)
VII. LOAN TAKEOVERS (p. 321)
  A. "Assumption" vs. "Subject To" (p. 321)
    1. FHA Loan Assumption (p. 321)
    2. VA Loan Assumption (p. 321)
    3. Cal-Vet Loan Assumption (p. 321)
    4. Conventional Loan Assumption (p. 321)
    5. Seller-Carryback Assumption (p. 322)
VIII. LOAN BROKERAGE (p. 322)
  A. Mortgage Loan Disclosure Statement (p. 322)
  B. Business and Professions Code (Commissions and Other Requirements) (p. 326)
    1. Article 7 - Loan Broker Laws (p. 326)
  C. Usury Limitations (p. 326)
IX. CHAPTER SUMMARY (p. 327)
X. KEY TERMS (p. 329)
XI. CHAPTER 8 QUIZ (p. 331)

The banking industry, as well as many government agencies, use the term mortgage rather than trust deed. In California, the term mortgage usually refers to trust deed.

We will use the general words "mortgage" and "deed of trust" interchangeably. But remember, "mortgagee" or "mortgagor" refer only to mortgages. "Trustee," "trustor," and "beneficiary" refer only to trust deeds.

a. Parties to a Trust Deed

In a trust deed there are three parties. The *TRUSTOR is usually the party that is borrowing the money.* This is usually the buyer, but may also be the owner if the property is being refinanced. The *BENEFICIARY is the lender who is lending money for the purchase of real property.* Home lenders in California are usually savings banks, but may also be commercial banks. The *TRUSTEE is the third, disinterested party (usually a corporation) who holds naked legal title to the property, but only in so far as the trustee may have to sell the property for the beneficiary, should the trustor default.* This is normally a title insurance company. **Figure 8-1** illustrates this three-party relationship.

Figure 8-1

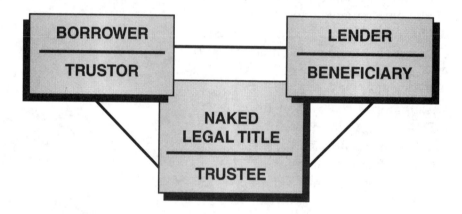

A. THE COST OF BORROWING MONEY

1. Interest Rates

INTEREST is the charge for borrowing money. In real estate, we use simple interest, not compound interest. Interest can be thought of as a rental charge for the use of money.

The "Nominal Interest Rate" is the rate stated in the note. The "Effective Interest Rate" is the rate the borrower is actually paying (including interest, points, and loan fees).

2. Origination Fees

A *LOAN ORIGINATION FEE is based on the loan amount and is collected as compensation for processing the loan and setting it up on the books.*

3. Points

Discounts (or points) paid to lenders are, in effect, prepaid interest.

They are used by lenders to adjust the effective interest rate so that it is equal to, or nearly equal to, the *PREVAILING MARKET RATE (the rate charged on conventional loans)*. The discounts (points) are sometimes absorbed by the sellers, depending on the terms of the loan. On FHA-insured and VA-guaranteed loans, buyers may be charged only one percent. This restriction, however, does not apply to conventional loans.

The charge for making a loan at most institutions is usually called a loan fee, service charge, commitment fee, or points. These charges vary considerably. Whether called points, discounts, loan brokerage fee, or new loan fee, they're all the same.

Points are used in over half the home sales in California.

How are points figured? One point is 1 percent of the new loan amount. For example, if the current market is "5 points," it means that the cost for a $100,000 loan is 5 percent x $100,000, or $5,000.

Points are figured on the amount of the new loan, not the selling price of the property.

4. Annual Percentage Rate (APR)

The *ANNUAL PERCENTAGE RATE (APR) represents the relationship between the total of the finance charges (interest rate, points, and the loan fee) and the total amount financed, expressed as a percentage.* It is the actual cost of borrowing money. It must be computed to the nearest one-quarter of one percent and must be printed on the loan form more conspicuously than the rest of the printed material.

When shopping for a loan, advise your buyers to look at the APR rather than just the advertised interest rate.

5. Prepayment Penalties

A *PREPAYMENT PENALTY is a charge to the borrower for paying off all or part of a loan balance before the due date.*

A prepayment penalty is only enforceable during the first five years of a one-to-four unit home loan.

6. Impound Accounts (Reserves)

IMPOUND ACCOUNTS are prepaid items consisting of taxes, insurance, and mutual mortgage insurance reserves. Some programs require a buyer to invest a down payment and establish an impound account, while others may require only an impound account to be paid in cash by the buyer. The account is often referred to as a "trust fund" or "trust account" and, once established, it is maintained by being included in the regular monthly loan payments disbursed when taxes and insurance are paid.

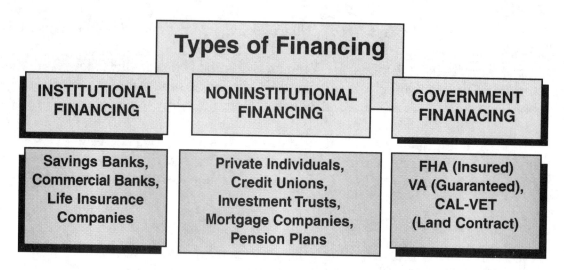

II. Institutional (Conventional) Financing

These loans are not backed—guaranteed or insured—by any government agency. The three primary sources of such conventional loans are referred to as *INSTITUTIONAL LENDERS, namely, savings banks, commercial banks, and life insurance companies.* These three institutional giants account for approximately 80 percent of all home loans nationwide. Many of them rely on mortgage bankers and mortgage loan brokers.

A. MORTGAGE BANKERS

MORTGAGE BANKING companies are direct lenders that underwrite for usually hundreds of investors such as Countrywide, Washington Mutual, Chase Manhattan and so on. They actually fund the loan themselves under one of their investor's guidelines, and then sell the loan to that investor.

1. Mortgage Bankers vs. Mortgage Brokers

Mortgage companies can be both. Mortgage bankers lend their own money. They can either keep the loan in their portfolio or sell the loan to another lender. *MORTGAGE BROKERS shop for a lender for the borrowers and earn a fee by putting lender and borrower together.*

B. SAVINGS BANKS

Savings Banks are one source for conventional real estate loans, since their operational charters normally restrict them to investments connected with real estate financing. Conversely, commercial banks and life insurance companies may have varied investments and frequently withdraw from the normal real estate investment market as interest rates change.

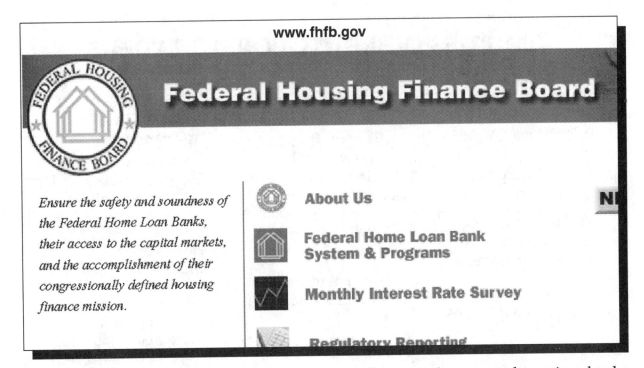

Federal Housing Finance Board

Ensure the safety and soundness of the Federal Home Loan Banks, their access to the capital markets, and the accomplishment of their congressionally defined housing finance mission.

About Us

Federal Home Loan Bank System & Programs

Monthly Interest Rate Survey

Regulatory Reporting

Certain circumstances permit up to 95 percent financing, but, as a rule, savings banks are restricted to originating loans in an amount equal to 80 percent of the sale price or appraisal value, whichever is less. A 10 percent second loan (on top of the first loan) may be permitted when the buyer makes a 10 percent down payment.

State and federal laws, and the bank's charter, govern the general mode of operation. Federal and state-chartered associations operate under different rules and regulations. For instance, savings banks may also make personal, consumer, and commercial loans and have no limit on the amount of home loans. However, the association's board of directors determines its lending policies according to the current money market, the amount of deposits, and the amount of outstanding loans.

Loans on well-located properties to borrowers with good income and credit are referred to as **PRIME LOANS** *and will carry an interest rate from at least 2 percent to 7 percent above the rate of interest an association pays to its depositors. The interest charged on a prime loan is apt to be 4 percent to 6 percent. Any change from this rule is determined by the element of risk involved with the property and the buyer.*

Savings rates are generally determined by the Federal Housing Finance Board (see website above), while lending rates are determined almost entirely by market conditions.

Savings banks often allow the buyer to put as little as 10 percent cash down payment on a property, if the seller or someone else will carry 10 percent of the purchase price on a note and second deed of trust. The savings bank will then provide an 80 percent loan on the purchase price.

PRIORITIES OF INSTITUTIONAL LENDERS

SAVINGS BANKS (Residential Lenders)	COMMERCIAL BANKS (General Purpose Lenders)	LIFE INSURANCE COMPANIES (Big Money Lenders)
1. Single family homes and condos	1. Business and auto loans	1. Large shopping centers and office buildings
2. Apartment buildings	2. Conventional home loans	2. Hotels and industrial properties
3. Home improvement loans	3. Government-backed FHA and VA home loans	3. FHA and VA home loans through mortgage companies (Government-backed loans)
4. Manufactured homes	4. Credit cards	
	5. Construction loans	

Loans may be approved on poorly located property, with less stringent qualifications required of the buyer. But, to offset the added risk, a higher-than-normal interest rate and loan origination fee will usually be demanded. Down payment requirements may also be increased and the loan amortization period decreased on loans with greater risk.

Banking regulators consider you to be a **SUBPRIME BORROWER** *if you have a FICO score of 620 or lower; two (or more) 30-day late payments in the past 12 months, or one 60-day late payment in the past 24 months; a foreclosure or charge-off in the past 24 months; any bankruptcy in the last 60 months (FHA - 24 months); qualifying debt-to-income ratios of 50% or higher; or "limited ability to cover family living expenses each month."*

C. COMMERCIAL BANKS

Commercial banks are usually more selective about both properties and buyers than savings banks when making loans.

Commercial banks make their own appraisals and, by law, may not generally exceed loans over 80 percent of appraised value. At the present time, conventional bank loans are normally limited to a period of 30 years.

The Federal Reserve (our nation's central bank) Board plays an important role in the loan policies of national banks, that is, banks that are members of the Federal Reserve

System. When the Federal Reserve Board raises or lowers prime interest rates on money the bank may borrow or requires an adjustment in the ratio of loans to deposits, the consumer-borrower is directly affected.

D. LIFE INSURANCE COMPANIES

Generally considered the third most important source of conventional real estate loans, lending policies of life insurance companies are governed by the laws of the state in which the company is chartered, the laws of the state in which the loan is originated, as well as the policies of management and the availability of loan funds.

Insurance companies are normally even more selective about properties and borrowers than commercial banks and savings banks.

They are usually interested only in prime loans with very little risk involved. The law generally prohibits a loan in excess of 75 percent of the appraisal.

Interest rates are often lower than those of savings banks and commercial banks, due to their prime requirements for the property and the buyer. Loan origination fees (cost to obtain loan) are comparatively small and the loan amortization period varies from 25 to 30 years, with a normal period of 25 years.

A qualified buyer often uses this type of conventional loan because of the lower interest rates and costs.

Mortgage brokers are usually correspondents for insurance companies, and, as a general rule, loans are processed by the correspondent.

Insurance companies are heavily involved in the **secondary market** (after the loan is made), buying vast quantities of already existing home loans from banks and other institutional lenders.

The secondary mortgage (trust deed) market provides an opportunity for financial institutions to buy and sell first mortgages (trust deeds) for a profit, from one another.

E. PRIVATE MORTGAGE INSURANCE (PMI) (PROVIDE A VALUABLE SERVICE)

PRIVATE MORTGAGE INSURANCE companies insure conventional loans that have less than 20 percent down. These private insurers are similar to the Federal Housing Administration (FHA) in that they insure the lender against loss in the event of foreclosure. However, rather than insuring the lender for the full amount of the loan, the private insurers generally cover only the top 10 to 20 percent of the loan and leave the lender exposed for approximately 80 to 90 percent of the loan.

The cost of private mortgage insurance varies with the type of contract coverage the lender requires.

The PMI commonly used for 90 percent loans costs the buyer (in addition to the interest rate already being paid) approximately 0.5 percent of the loan amount for the first year premium and 0.25 percent thereafter. Private mortgage insurance is not a deductible item for income tax purposes like interest is.

Private mortgage insurance allows institutional lenders (savings banks, commercial banks, and insurance companies) to make loans above the usual 75% to 80% of the sale's price. Remember that a private mortgage insurance premium is not a deductible item from the borrower's income tax return.

1. Credit Requirements

Credit requirements for the 90 and 95 percent, privately insured loan plans vary from institution to institution. In general, however, the verified income, employment, and credit analysis of the borrower must be favorable in relation to family obligations. The borrower's total mortgage payments generally should not exceed 25 to 30 percent of gross income (3.5 to 1 ratio); total obligations to income should not exceed 33 percent (3 to 1 ratio). A co-borrower's income will be given consideration, given an adequate employment history. Part-time jobs, overtime, bonuses, and other income sources must be substantiated by W-2 statements to be accepted as stable income. Because of the high price of housing in California, there is a trend toward more liberal ratios in qualifying buyers.

A high net worth, insurance, and guaranteed retirement income indicate the ability to continue making payments in spite of illness, unemployment, or retirement. Paying habits indicate an individual's stability and probability of performance on the contract. When the borrower is self-employed, recent financial statements and income tax reports for previous years are necessary to substantiate income.

F. FIXED RATE MORTGAGES

A **FIXED RATE MORTGAGE** *is a loan for which the payments are usually the same each month for the life of the loan.* The equal monthly payment includes both the principal and the interest. A loan with this kind of fixed rate of interest is said to be a "fully amortized, fixed rate loan."

G. ADJUSTABLE RATE MORTGAGES (ARMS)

The *variable rate mortgage is more popularly referred to as an ADJUSTABLE RATE MORTGAGE, or ARM.* About 100 different types of ARMs are used in California, with no standardized ARM. Before recommending an ARM to a client, you should ask the following questions of the lender:

1. What is the initial interest rate and how long will it be used?

2. What causes the interest rate to change? (The index to which the rate is tied may be six-month Treasury bill rates, lender's cost of funds, and so on.)

3. How often can the interest rate change? (This may be anywhere from every month to once a year.)

4. How much can the rate change? (This is usually 0.5%, but again it may vary.)

5. Is there a ceiling, or cap, on the total adjustment rate? (A 5% cap is the most common.)

6. Can the payments be changed? (Rate increases are normally accompanied by payment increases, within given limits. Lenders do try to keep a reasonable ratio between a borrower's income and the monthly payments.)

As a licensee, you owe the duty of full disclosure in any loan arrangement, especially in cases in which rates, payments, or both may increase.

After all, borrowers may lose their homes if surprise increases occur and they are unable to meet the heavier obligation. (See **Figure 8-2** to see how ARMs work.)

H. SPECIAL PURPOSE LOANS

1. Graduated Payment Mortgage (GPM) (For First-Time Buyers)

With a *GRADUATED PAYMENT MORTGAGE (GPM), the rate and term are fixed, but monthly payments are smaller at the beginning of the term and increase over time.*

The GPM is just one instrument that attacks the problem of borrowers who cannot afford housing with current income. With a GPM, a family is expected to raise its average income over the term of the loan.

The instrument has drawbacks for both lender and borrower. In the early years, the low monthly payments are not sufficient to cover interest owed, so the loan balance actually increases for the first few years. This results in negative amortization. Since under most conditions the increase in property value is greater than the increase in principal, the buyer retains a positive equity, but the risk to the lender increases.

"Negative Amortization" occurs when monthly installment payments are insufficient to pay the interest accruing on the principal balance, so that the unpaid interest must be added to the principal due. Your borrower may choose, whenever possible, to make larger monthly payments, thereby greatly reducing the unpaid balance.

Figure 8-2

How ARMs Work

THE INDEX

The **INDEX** *is the starting interest rate used as the indicator so that changes from it can be calculated.* If the index rises 1%, the ARM interest rate you pay goes up 1%. The index must be: 1) beyond the control of the lender, and 2) available and verifiable by the public. Examples of indexes used are the Cost of Living Index, the 11th District Cost of Funds Index, the One Year T-Bill, and the London Interbank Offered Rate (LIBOR).

THE ADJUSTABLE INTERVAL

The **ADJUSTABLE INTERVAL** *is the frequency with which interest rates are reset.* This period can be monthly, quarterly, every six months, or even once a year. If the index has risen .3% by the end of the interval period, the interest rate you pay goes up .3%.

THE CAP

The **CAP** *is a percentage rate ceiling or restriction on the 1) periodic (adjustable) interval; and 2) lifetime change in interest rates or payments.* An adjustable interval cap limits the percentage of change upward to, or downward to, for example, 1/2% every quarter. The lifetime cap is often around a maximum of 5% above or below the initial agreed-to contract rate.

You may find the Cap being refigured every five years!

THE MARGIN

The **MARGIN** *is the spread between the index rate and the initial contract rate from which the lender will make a profit and cover its costs.* It is the amount of profit for the lender, agreed to in advance. If the index rate is 4% and the margin is 3%, then the current interest rate paid by the borrower is 7%. Even if the index rate moves up to 5%, the margin will always remain at 3% and the new interest rate will be 8%. Some adjustables have **teaser rates** that are even below the starting rate to entice the borrower into the transaction. The borrower is qualified based on the teaser rate, which only lasts for a short period of time and then goes up to the agreed upon rate.

ADVANTAGES OF ARMS

The main advantage of an ARM is a lower interest rate than can be found with a fixed rate loan because the lender is protected if interest rates rise over the loan period. This makes an ARM more affordable, thus more people can qualify for it. Generally there are no prepayment penalties, and an assumption is usually permitted if the new buyer meets credit standards. ARMs benefit first-time buyers and short-term investors who just want a lower interest rate, because interest rates are initially lower.

ARMs often start out with unusually low (teaser) interest rates, causing negative amortization, which could lead to a foreclosure. Warn your clients of this possibility!

III. The Secondary Mortgage Market

Savings banks, commercial banks, life insurance companies, and others can easily resell their first trust deed loans if they conform to secondary market loan standards.

A. SECONDARY MORTGAGE (TRUST DEED) MARKET

Lenders in the secondary market are concerned with the "liquidity and marketability" of loans.

The **SECONDARY MORTGAGE (TRUST DEED) MARKET** *provides an opportunity for financial institutions to buy and sell first mortgages (trust deeds) to and from, other financial institutions.* California has a growing real estate market that will pay higher interest rates than other parts of the country. Therefore, California's financial institutions will make trust deed loans and sell them to other institutions for a profit. The secondary mortgage market enables lenders to keep an adequate supply of money for new loans.

The secondary mortgage (trust deed) market is the market where lenders buy and sell mortgages. Anytime lenders need cash, they can sell their first trust deeds for a profit.

1. Federal National Mortgage Association (Fannie Mae - Private)

The FNMA was created to increase the amount of funds available to finance housing.

The Federal National Mortgage Association (FNMA), which is commonly referred to as Fannie Mae, dominates the secondary mortgage market. Originally, it bought and sold only FHA and VA trust deeds. In 1968 it became a private corporation and now sells securities over the stock exchange to get money so that it can buy and sell conventional loans in addition to government-backed notes.

"Fannie Mae," the Federal National Mortgage Association (FNMA), helps set loan standards and helps to maintain the secondary mortgage market. The FNMA is not a demand source to borrow money.

www.fanniemaefoundation.org
Fannie Mae

2. Government National Mortgage Association (Ginnie Mae)

The **GOVERNMENT NATIONAL MORTGAGE ASSOCIATION (GNMA)** *is a government corporation referred to as Ginnie Mae. It sells secondary mortgages to the public and provides the federal government with cash.* These trust deeds are grouped

together in pools, and shares are sold on the stock market exchange. All shares are federally guaranteed, making this one of the safest investments available.

www.ginniemae.gov
Ginnie Mae

3. Federal Home Loan Mortgage Corporation (Freddie Mac)

The *FEDERAL HOME LOAN MORTGAGE CORPORATION (FHLMC), commonly known as Freddie Mac, is a government corporation that issues preferred stock to the public.* It is supervised by the Federal Home Loan Bank Board. It helps savings banks maintain a stable and adequate money supply by purchasing their home loan mortgages and repackaging them for sale to investors. The savings banks use the money obtained to make new loans available for home buyers.

The Federal Home Loan Mortgage Corporation, commonly called "Freddie Mac," increases the availability of funds through its involvement in the maintenance of the secondary mortgage market.

www.freddiemac.com
Freddie Mac

B. FINAL WORD ON CONVENTIONAL LOANS
(Risk—Loans Without Government Backing)

Since conventional loans are loans made without government backing or guarantees, they are riskier. Even if conventional loans have lower loan-to-value (LTV) ratios, which make them safer, government-backed loans are the safest. Because the government will then pay off if there is a foreclosure, Fannie Mae and Freddie Mac currently have loan limits of $333,700 for a house or condo. *If the requested loan amount is higher than the Fannie Mae and Freddie Mac loan limit, it is called a **JUMBO LOAN**.*

IV. Government Financing
(Government-Backed Loans)

The three primary sources of government financing are the Federal Housing Administration (FHA), the Veterans Administration (VA), and California Department of Veterans Affairs (Cal-Vet).

Only the California Department of Veteran's Affairs is a direct lender of funds, the FHA and VA being insurers and guarantors of loans otherwise made by approved institutional lenders. **Figure 8-3** summarizes the various government backed loans, comparing FHA, VA, and Cal-Vet financing—each of which is discussed in the following sections.

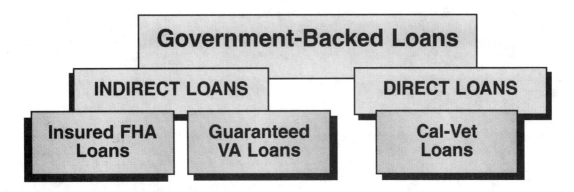

Government-Backed Loans

INDIRECT LOANS		DIRECT LOANS
Insured FHA Loans	Guaranteed VA Loans	Cal-Vet Loans

A. FEDERAL HOUSING ADMINISTRATION (FHA)

The primary purpose of FHA Section 203b is to encourage and assist people to become homeowners.

FHA is not a lender; it merely insures lenders against loss after an approved loan is processed in accordance with FHA regulations. In the event of foreclosures, FHA reimburses the lender for the loan balance. In order to reduce the possibilities of a foreclosure, the buyer's income and credit history must measure up to certain standards.

Points or discount points may be charged to either the buyer or the seller under either FHA or VA financing.

1. Purchaser Requirements

The FHA requires the purchaser to have some financial interest in the (one-to-four unit) property on which a loan is to be insured.

Cash investment requirements vary in each of the numerous programs offered, depending on price and buyer's qualifications. For example, some FHA programs require the buyer to invest a down payment and establish an impound account, while others may require only an impound account to be paid in cash.

Give consideration to the client's financial qualifications before shopping for a home.

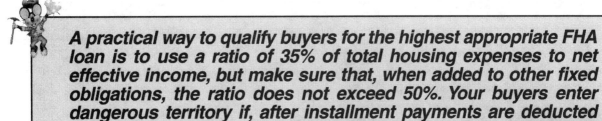

A practical way to qualify buyers for the highest appropriate FHA loan is to use a ratio of 35% of total housing expenses to net effective income, but make sure that, when added to other fixed obligations, the ratio does not exceed 50%. Your buyers enter dangerous territory if, after installment payments are deducted from gross monthly income, their net effective income is dropped below three times their monthly house payments.

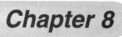

Figure 8-3	**Federal Housing Administration** **(FHA 203b "basic")**
ELIGIBILITY	Anyone residing in the United States
SOURCE OF FUNDS	Approved Lenders
LOAN INSTRUMENT	**Trust Deed or Mortgage**
TERM	30 years
INTEREST RATE	Current interest rates plus mortgage insurance premiums paid up front, prior to close of escrow
MAXIMUM PURCHASE	**No Maximum**
MAXIMUM LOAN AMOUNT **(For high cost areas)** **(Alaska & Hawaii up to** **150% higher)**	97% of the maximum for the county average: house-condo $290,319; duplex $371,621; tri-plex $449,181; and 4-unit $558,236
DOWN PAYMENT	3% minimum cash investment; 100% over appraisal
SECONDARY FINANCING	**Allowed**
PREPAYMENT PENALTY	None (30 days' notice)
ASSUMABLE	After 2 years, if owner-occupant
POINTS PAID BY	**Buyers or Sellers**
BORROWER'S MONTHLY **PAYMENTS**	Monthly principal and interest 29% to 41% of annual gross income
MONTHLY SALARY **(AFTER FEDERAL TAXES)**	Approximately 3 times total monthly payment

Veterans Administration VA	State of California CAL-VET
W.W. II, Korean Conflict, Vietnam Era, Persian Gulf War, or continuous active duty for 90 days (181 Peacetime)	W.W. II, Korean Conflict, Vietnam Era, Persian Gulf War, or certain medal winners
Approved Lenders	California Bond Issues
Trust Deed or Mortgage	**Conditional Sales Contract**
30-year maximum	30-year maximum
Set by Veterans Administration	Set by State of California, but may increase later
No Maximum by DVA (restricted by guarantee)	**None**
1-to-4 units, owner occupied, up to CRV. No loan maximum but usually under $240,000; Guaranty Maximum is $60,000	Manufactured Home - $125,000 (in Mobile Park) (on owned lot - $250,000) House - $333,700
None required, lender may require down payment	Manufactured Home - 3% to 20% House - 3% to 20%
Only up to amount of CRV	
None	None
Subject to VA approval of assumer's credit	To a Cal-Vet, YES
Buyer or Seller	**Buyer**
Monthly principal and interest: 29% to 41% of annual gross income	Monthly principal and interest: 28% to 50% of annual gross income
Approximately 3 times total monthly payment	Approximately 2 times total monthly payment

The borrower must meet standard FHA credit qualifications. He or she is eligible for approximately 97% financing and may finance the up-front mortgage insurance premium into the mortgage.

From the standpoint of income, FHA may consider the applicant's base salary plus all of the usual overtime and bonuses verified by the employer. A VA school allotment or any other verified income may be included. Net income from rental properties may also be considered when substantiated by tax returns.

2. Loan Discount Fee

Buyers are allowed to pay part or all of the loan discount fee or points. Buyers may also be charged a 1 percent loan origination fee. The discount fee is not collected; it is withheld by the lender to equalize the yield. For example, a mortgage broker collects the 1 percent loan origination fee for processing the loan, but the lender, for whom the broker is a correspondent, withholds the discount fee from the seller's proceeds when funds are placed in escrow.

3. Calculating the Maximum Loan

The maximum insurable FHA loan amounts vary, depending on the median priced home in a particular area, including basic areas, high-cost areas, and ceiling limits set for Hawaii and Alaska (see **Figure 8-4**).

Figure 8-4

Maximum Loan Amounts
(These amounts change fairly frequently)

Nationwide Basic Limits (the floor)		Statutory Ceilings (high-cost areas)		Statutory Ceilings (Hawaii and Alaska)	
One Unit	$160,176	One Unit	$290,319	One Unit	$435,479
Two Unit	$205,032	Two Unit	$371,621	Two Unit	$557,431
Three Unit	$247,824	Three Unit	$449,181	Three Unit	$673,772
Four Unit	$307,992	Four Unit	$558,236	Four Unit	$837,353

4. FHA Section 245—Graduated Payment Mortgage (GPM)

FHA has several graduated payment plans to choose from, providing lower payments in earlier years.

The outstanding principal amount due on a Graduated Payment Mortgage increases during the initial years as unpaid interest is added to the principal balance and negative amortization is created.

Home buyers may choose the GPM plan that suits their needs. The five plans vary the rate at which the monthly payments increase—from approximately 2 to 7.5 percent per year, depending on interest rate fluctuations. Borrowers also have the option of choosing the number of years (either five or ten) over which the payments increase before levelling off for the remainder of the loan.

The greater the rate of increase or the longer the period of increase, the lower the mortgage payments in early years.

B. VETERANS ADMINISTRATION (VA)

A "VA Loan" is not a loan, but rather a guarantee to an approved lender.

In 1944, the Servicemen's Readjustment Act was passed. It contained a great many special benefits for the returning veterans of World War II to help them adjust to civilian life. The Veterans Home Loan Guarantee program was initiated within the framework of the Readjustment Act. Since that time, additional laws and regulations have created changes in the loan guaranty program.

Federal funds are not used except in isolated areas where private lenders are not available. However, the Veterans Administration guarantees (in high cost areas) a maximum of $60,000. There's no loan maximum, but it's usually under $240,000.

1. Certificate of Reasonable Value (CRV)

A CERTIFICATE OF REASONABLE VALUE (CRV) is an appraisal of the property a veteran wishes to buy. The Veterans Administration appoints accredited "fee" appraisers to submit appraisal reports, from which a Certificate of Reasonable Value (CRV) is issued. A CRV is effective for 129 days and specifies the maximum amount to be loaned on the property in connection with the loan guarantee. It also indicates the economic life estimated to remain on the property, which is the limit of the loan amortization period. Some lenders limit VA loans to 29.5 years but consider them 30-year loans.

The amount of down payment needed for a VA loan is determined by the CRV.

2. Secondary Financing

There can be secondary (junior) financing on the subject property to help obtain the new loan if the terms of the second, lower priority loan, runs concurrently with the first trust deed.

Borrowers in such cases must be able to qualify for both the first and second loans. Once the loan has been established, junior financing may also be utilized if

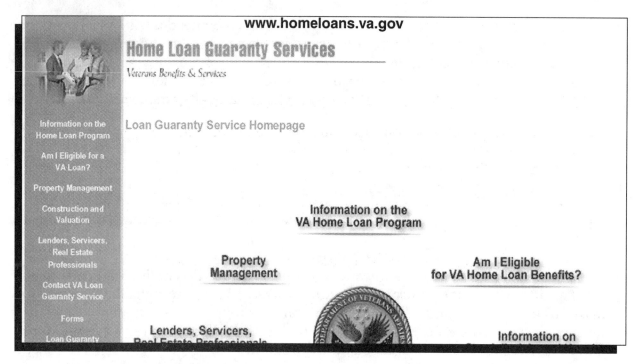

the veteran should resell the home, or borrow on it for any reason. Secondary financing is discussed in more detail later in the chapter.

3. Eligibility and Entitlement

Any eligible veteran may obtain a VA loan on the purchase of residential property with from one-to-four units, provided he or she is going to occupy one of the units.

World War II veterans with other than a dishonorable discharge are eligible, provided they served 90 days or more or as little as one day if discharged because of a service-connected injury or disability.

Korean conflict veterans must have served in active military service between June 27, 1950 and January 31, 1955, and are under the same program as World War II veterans. Cold war veterans are also eligible if they served on active military duty for more than 180 days between July 26, 1947 and June 26, 1950 and after January 31, 1955.

Vietnam Era veterans who served between August 5, 1964 and May 7, 1975 and Persian Gulf War veterans who served from August 2, 1990 to a date yet to be determined are also eligible. Veterans of the more recent conflicts will no doubt be eligible as well, but information is not currently available.

4. Reinstatement of Veterans Loan Entitlement

Eligibility for another VA loan under the same entitlement is restored for the veteran when the Veterans Administration is no longer liable to the lender (loan has been paid off).

If the veteran has not fully used the current guaranty, he or she is eligible for an additional entitlement of the difference between the current guaranty and the amount actually used.

C. CALIFORNIA DEPARTMENT OF VETERANS AFFAIRS (CAL-VET)

Along with other benefits to qualified wartime veterans, California provides a special assistance program for farm and home purchases. Laws pertaining to the program are governed by the Military and Veterans' Code.

The California Department of Veterans Affairs, Division of Farm and Home Loans, administers the program. Operating budgets must be approved by the legislature.

Loan funds are obtained through the sale of **general obligation bonds**. Repayment of the bonds is guaranteed by the state from the general fund. The bond issues, when needed, must be approved by popular vote on a proposition included on the general election ballots.

Operating costs of the program, plus retirement of the bonds and interest thereon, are reflected in the interest rates charged on Cal-Vet loans. The state has never been forced to repay any portion of a bond issue, as the program is self-sustaining.

Interest rates may vary on a fluctuating or "floating" basis. Amortization periods may fluctuate between 25 and 40 years. Whenever the interest rate is increased, the increased interest merely extends the amortization period for outstanding loans and does not increase the original loan interest and principal payments paid each month.

When a farm or a home and the veteran are approved for a Cal-Vet loan, the property is purchased by the state and in turn is resold to the veteran on an agreement of sale, in reality a **sales contract** popularly referred to as a **land contract of sale**. Title to the property remains with the state until the loan is paid in full, after which a grant deed is issued to the veteran.

With the exception of establishing a loan trust account and paying for tax prorations, the costs of obtaining a new Cal-Vet loan are practically nil. There are no discount points, and loan origination fees are low.

All veterans are eligible for the Cal-Vet program. The same person could be eligible for a FHA, a VA, and a Cal-Vet loan.

1. Insurance Requirements

A low-cost group term life insurance policy on the veteran is purchased by the state and paid for by the veteran along with regular monthly loan payments. In

case the veteran should die, the loan balance is paid off through the life insurance policy. A fire and extended coverage insurance policy is also purchased by the state and paid for by the veteran as a part of regular monthly payments. Should the veteran desire more extensive insurance coverage, the vet purchases it from his own agent with separate billing and payment.

2. Maximum Loans

The maximum Cal-Vet home loan is $333, 700 and $125,000 for manufactured homes in parks. The veteran must pay to the seller the difference between the sales price and the Cal-Vet loan.

V. Qualifying the Borrower

Shopping for a loan is like shopping for any other commodity that is to be purchased (or rented) on time payments. The borrower-purchaser must be able to qualify, based on the risks involved.

A. THE LOAN APPLICATION

In the purchase of a home, all prospective lenders ask for a completed application that contains personal and financial data, such as that shown in **Figure 8-5**. Among the items are employment history of the borrowers, other income, bank references, legal actions, current and past creditors, and a summary of assets and liabilities.

Figure 8-5

Uniform Residential Loan Application

This application is designed to be completed by the applicant(s) with the lender's assistance. Applicants should complete this form as "Borrower" or "Co-Borrower", as applicable. Co-Borrower information must also be provided (and the appropriate box checked) when ☐ the income or assets of a person other than the "Borrower" (including the Borrower's spouse) will be used as a basis for loan qualification or ☐ the income or assets of the Borrower's spouse will not be used as a basis for loan qualification, but his or her liabilities must be considered because the Borrower resides in a community property state, the security property is located in a community property state, or the Borrower is relying on other property located in a community property state as a basis for repayment of the loan.

I. TYPE OF MORTGAGE AND TERMS OF LOAN

Mortgage Applied for:	☐ VA ☐ FHA	☐ Conventional ☐ FmHA	☐ Other:	Agency Case Number	Lender Case No.

Amount	Interest Rate	No. of Months	Amortization Type:	☐ Fixed Rate ☐ GPM	☐ Other (explain): ☐ ARM (type):
$	%				

II. PROPERTY INFORMATION AND PURPOSE OF LOAN

Subject Property Address (street, city, state, & ZIP) — No. of Units

Legal Description of Subject Property (attach description if necessary) — Year Built

Purpose of Loan	☐ Purchase ☐ Refinance	☐ Construction ☐ Construction-Permanent	☐ Other (explain):	Property will be: ☐ Primary Residence ☐ Secondary Residence ☐ Investment

Complete this line if construction or construction-permanent loan.

Year Lot Acquired	Original Cost $	Amount Existing Liens $	(a) Present Value of Lot $	(b) Cost of Improvements $	Total (a + b) $

Complete this line if this is a refinance loan.

Year Acquired	Original Cost $	Amount Existing Liens $	Purpose of Refinance	Describe Improvements ☐ made ☐ to be made Cost: $

Title will be held in what Name(s)	Manner in which Title will be held	Estate will be held in: ☐ Fee Simple ☐ Leasehold (show expiration date)

Source of Down Payment, Settlement Charges and/or Subordinate Financing (explain)

III. BORROWER INFORMATION

Borrower	Co-Borrower
Borrower's Name (include Jr. or Sr. if applicable)	Co-Borrower's Name (include Jr. or Sr. if applicable)

Social Security Number	Home Phone (incl. area code)	Age	Yrs. School	Social Security Number	Home Phone (incl. area code)	Age	Yrs. School

☐ Married ☐ Separated ☐ Unmarried (include single, divorced, widowed)	Dependents (not listed by Co-Borrower) no. ages	☐ Married ☐ Separated ☐ Unmarried (include single, divorced, widowed)	Dependents (not listed by Borrower) no. ages

Present Address (street, city, state, ZIP) ☐ Own ☐ Rent No. Yrs.	Present Address (street, city, state, ZIP) ☐ Own ☐ Rent No. Yrs.

If residing at present address for less than two years, complete the following:

Former Address (street, city, state, ZIP) ☐ Own ☐ Rent No. Yrs.	Former Address (street, city, state, ZIP) ☐ Own ☐ Rent No. Yrs.

Former Address (street, city, state, ZIP) ☐ Own ☐ Rent No. Yrs.	Former Address (street, city, state, ZIP) ☐ Own ☐ Rent No. Yrs.

IV. EMPLOYMENT INFORMATION

Borrower	Co-Borrower

Name & Address of Employer ☐ Self Employed	Yrs. on this job Yrs. employed in this line of work/profession	Name & Address of Employer ☐ Self Employed	Yrs. on this job Yrs. employed in this line of work/profession

Position/Title/Type of Business	Business Phone (incl. area code)	Position/Title/Type of Business	Business Phone (incl. area code)

If employed in current position for less than two years or if currently employed in more than one position, complete the following:

Name & Address of Employer ☐ Self Employed	Dates (from - to) Monthly Income $	Name & Address of Employer ☐ Self Employed	Dates (from - to) Monthly Income $

Position/Title/Type of Business	Business Phone (incl. area code)	Position/Title/Type of Business	Business Phone (incl. area code)

Name & Address of Employer ☐ Self Employed	Dates (from - to) Monthly Income $	Name & Address of Employer ☐ Self Employed	Dates (from - to) Monthly Income $

Position/Title/Type of Business	Business Phone (incl. area code)	Position/Title/Type of Business	Business Phone (incl. area code)

Freddie Mac Form 65

Fannie Mae Form 1003

313

V. MONTHLY INCOME AND COMBINED HOUSING EXPENSE INFORMATION

Gross Monthly Income	Borrower	Co-Borrower	Total	Combined Monthly Housing Expense	Present	Proposed
Base Empl. Income *	$	$	$	Rent	$	▓▓▓▓▓▓
Overtime				First Mortgage (P&I)		$
Bonuses				Other Financing (P&I)		
Commissions				Hazard Insurance		
Dividends/Interest				Real Estate Taxes		
Net Rental Income				Mortgage Insurance		
Other (before completing, see the notice in "describe other income," below)				Homeowner Assn. Dues		
				Other:		
Total	$	$	$	Total	$	$

* Self Employed Borrower(s) may be required to provide additional documentation such as tax returns and financial statements.

Describe Other Income *Notice:* Alimony, child support, or separate maintenance income need not be revealed if the Borrower (B) or Co-Borrower (C) does not choose to have it considered for repaying this loan.

B/C		Monthly Amount
		$

VI. ASSETS AND LIABILITIES

This Statement and any applicable supporting schedules may be completed jointly by both married and unmarried Co-Borrowers if their assets and liabilities are sufficiently joined so that the Statement can be meaningfully and fairly presented on a combined basis; otherwise separate Statements and Schedules are required. If the Co-Borrower section was completed about a spouse, this Statement and supporting schedules must be completed about that spouse also.

Completed [ ] Jointly [ ] Not Jointly

ASSETS — Description	Cash or Market Value	Liabilities and Pledged Assets. List the creditor's name, address and account number for all outstanding debts, including automobile loans, revolving charge accounts, real estate loans, alimony, child support, stock pledges, etc. Use continuation sheet, if necessary. Indicate by (*) those liabilities which will be satisfied upon sale of real estate owned or upon refinancing of the subject property.	Monthly Payt. & Mos. Left to Pay	Unpaid Balance
Cash deposit toward purchase held by:	$	**LIABILITIES**		
		Name and address of Company	$ Payt./Mos.	$
List checking and savings accounts below				
Name and address of Bank, S&L, or Credit Union				
		Acct. no.		
		Name and address of Company	$ Payt./Mos.	$
Acct. no.	$			
Name and address of Bank, S&L, or Credit Union				
		Acct. no.		
		Name and address of Company	$ Payt./Mos.	$
Acct. no.	$			
Name and address of Bank, S&L, or Credit Union				
		Acct. no.		
		Name and address of Company	$ Payt./Mos.	$
Acct. no.	$			
Name and address of Bank, S&L, or Credit Union				
		Acct. no.		
		Name and address of Company	$ Payt./Mos.	$
Acct. no.	$			
Stocks & Bonds (Company name/number & description)	$			
		Acct. no.		
		Name and address of Company	$ Payt./Mos.	$
Life insurance net cash value	$			
Face amount: $				
Subtotal Liquid Assets	$			
Real estate owned (enter market value from schedule of real estate owned)	$	Acct. no.		
Vested interest in retirement fund	$	Name and address of Company	$ Payt./Mos.	$
Net worth of business(es) owned (attach financial statement)	$			
Automobiles owned (make and year)	$			
		Acct. no.		
		Alimony/Child Support/Separate Maintenance Payments Owed to:	$	▓▓▓▓▓
Other Assets (itemize)	$	Job Related Expense (child care, union dues, etc.)	$	▓▓▓▓▓
		Total Monthly Payments	$	▓▓▓▓▓
Total Assets a.	$	Net Worth ▶ $	**Total Liabilities b.**	$

Freddie Mac Form 65

Fannie Mae Form 1003

1. Credit Scoring (Access to Credit Profile)

CREDIT SCORING gives lenders a fast, objective measurement of your ability to repay a loan or make timely credit payments. It is based solely on information in consumer credit reports maintained at one of the credit reporting agencies. Factors comprising a credit score include:

1. Payment History - What is your track record?
2. Amounts Owed - How much is too much?
3. Length of Credit History - How established is yours?
4. New Credit - Are you taking on more debt?
5. Types of Credit Use - Is it a "healthy" mix?

The most widely used credit bureau scores are developed by Fair, Isaac and Company. These are known as FICO SCORES. If a credit agency refuses to provide a copy of a credit report to an applicant who is denied credit, the applicant can:

1. file civil action against the credit agency;
2. negotiate a settlement; or
3. require the credit agency to pay all legal fees.

See **Figure 8-6** for a more complete description of credit scoring, which is often difficult to explain.

2. Equal Credit Opportunity Act (ECOA)

This law requires that financial institutions and other persons engaged in the extension of credit make that credit equally available to all creditworthy customers without regard to sex, marital status, race, color, religion, national origin, age (provided that the applicant has the capacity to enter into a binding contract), or receipt of income from public assistance programs. The law strictly prohibits any lender from discriminating in the extension of credit based on any of the above, or from discounting income such as alimony, child support, or public assistance, if the applicant desires this income to be considered and it can be established that such income will continue in the foreseeable future.

Lenders may ask information regarding the applicant's race, national origin, sex, marital status, and age, but are prohibited from requiring this information.

Information is requested only for the use of federal agencies for monitoring purposes, and any applicant may decline to divulge this information.

Figure 8-6

CREDIT SCORING

Over the past several years, lenders have increased their use of "credit scores," derived from information in a consumer's credit report, using a mathematical model to develop a three-digit score and determine whether or not to make a loan, and at what interest rate. The enactment of SB 1607 (Figueroa), CAR's landmark credit-scoring legislation, gives consumers access to their credit scores. In addition to providing consumers with their specific credit score and key reasons why a score was not better, the legislation also gives consumers the right to receive a copy of their credit scores, when they request copies of their credit file.

WHAT IS CREDIT SCORING?

Credit scores are assigned numbers used by lenders to determine whether a consumer will get a loan and at what interest rate. Individual lenders often contract with a credit reporting agency such as Trans Union, Experian, or Equifax who compile consumer credit information. These companies then contract with a credit scoring company (more often than not, Fair, Isaacs and Company [www.fairisaac.com], who own the mathematical model used to create the score). They provide the lender with a list of "reason codes" that the lender can choose from when receiving scores for consumers applying for mortgages. The reason codes can include things like, "too few bank card accounts," "too many sub-prime accounts," etc. The credit scoring company uses information from a consumer's credit report, together with these reason codes and the mathematical formulas to create an individual's credit score.

This law:

1. requires lenders to provide consumers with their specific credit score, what credit information went into making up the score, and an explanation of how credit scores work in the loan approval process;

2. compels credit reporting agencies to correct inaccurate information in a timely manner; and

3. requires credit reporting agencies to correct inaccurate information more quickly and provide consumers with additional legal recourse if an agency continues to report inaccurate information once they become aware that a mistake has been made.

www.transunion.com
TransUnion
www.experian.com/experian us.html
Experian
Equifax- www.equifax_com
Equifax

3. Fair Credit Reporting Act

The *FAIR CREDIT REPORTING ACT allows loan applicants who have data collected on them to see their files.* Incorrect information may be gathered because of confusion about names or faulty reporting, or a revenging party may furnish half-truths and even outright lies. The law states that the credit bureau must quickly correct mistakes found in its records. If there is a dispute over debts, the credit agency is supposed to insert the aggrieved party's explanation into the file. This federal law offers some relief to potential borrowers who might not otherwise qualify.

4. Truth in Lending Act

The *TRUTH IN LENDING ACT ("Regulation Z") lets borrowers and customers know the cost of credit so that they can compare costs with those of other credit sources and thereby avoid the uninformed use of credit.* This Act is regulated by the Federal Reserve Board. It does not fix maximum, minimum, or any charges for credit. Rather, it requires disclosure of fees charged for arranging the loan, prepaid interest amount, buyer's escrow fee, application fee, mortgage inspection fee, VA funding fee, prepaid mortgage insurance premiums on FHA loans, finder's fees, costs of termite inspection, tax service fee, disclosure statement fee, origination or closing fee, loan discount fee and points paid by the seller, and any other costs that increase the effective interest rate. Through the use of tables available at any Federal Reserve Board office, these finance costs, when added to the total interest charged, show the effective yield, or **annual percentage rate (APR)**. Of course, if there are no charges connected with the granting of a loan, the APR equals the stated or nominal rate.

VI. Noninstitutional Financing

There are many sources of private, noninstitutional financing. *NONINSTITUTIONAL FINANCING is financing by parties who are not governed or controlled by federal and state agencies in the stringent manner in which the savings banks, commercial banks, and life insurance companies are.* A list of such noninstitutional lenders includes pension funds, stocks, credit unions, mortgage companies, real estate investment trusts (REITs), private and public syndications, and individuals. In this section, we focus strictly on the financing obtained from individuals or private parties. For a complete treatment of these and other forms of financing, consult *Real Estate Finance*, by Walt Huber and Levin P. Messick (see order form in back of book).

A. JUNIOR LOANS (Secondary Financing)

JUNIOR LOANS (also referred to as "secondary financing") are secured by a second trust deed or mortgage, and any other loans on a property that come after the first, or prime, security. Except where a subordination clause is agreed to in a loan, a second trust deed loan is second in the order of priority—not because of any label on the

document that calls it a second, but because it was recorded subsequent to another trust deed loan, the first or senior loan.

A junior loan is best illustrated by an example. When the owner sells property for $100,000, with a down payment of $10,000, representing 10 percent of the selling price, the buyers will be short of the purchase price if they are unable to obtain financing for $90,000, or 90 percent of the purchase price. In actual practice, most conventional loans are made for 80 percent of the selling price or appraised value, whichever is lower. It can be seen, then, that the buyer will be deficient by $10,000. Solution? The seller "carries back" the 10 percent balance of the price as a purchase money second trust deed loan. Thus, the seller carries back a loan, the paper, as it is called, for the difference between the first loan plus down payment and the selling price.

The seller "carrying back" is a junior mortgage holder ("lendlord").

In addition to the seller carrying back a loan to supplement the first trust deed, junior financing originates in three other ways:

1. Home improvement loans provide direct injection of secondary funds.

2. Direct loans to the home owner for other uses—debt consolidation or payoff, personal emergencies, cash for investment opportunities, and so on—are another way.

3. A trust deed note can be given to a broker for part or all of the commission in lieu of cash, notably under circumstances in which insufficient cash is generated from the proceeds of a sale. By deferring your cash commission, you provide the seller with an opportunity for purchasing a replacement home, thus generating another commission from the second sale.

1. Acceleration Clause

Frequently, a trust deed contains an *ACCELERATION (ALIENATION) CLAUSE, which states that, should the property be subsequently sold (or default occur), the entire note is now due and payable.* This clause may be objectionable to purchasers who feel that when they in turn sell at a later date, they would like to afford the new buyer the opportunity to assume the note. In other words, owners would like the flexibility of additional built-in financing to help sell. To assure enforceability of the alienation provisions, separate and specific consideration ought to be given by the seller to the buyers at the time of sale.

2. Discounting Second Trust Deeds

Many purchase money trust deeds are written under terms that call for 1 percent of the loan balance as a monthly payment, which may include interest of 10 percent or more per annum, all due and payable at the end of three-to-five years. Because of the need for cash and because of the relatively low yield in relation to the risk, sellers very often do not want to keep the second trust loan for the full term. Brokers are frequently called upon to sell such notes, almost always at a discount.

A trust deed note is "discounted" when it sells for less than the principal amount or less than the unpaid balance.

3. Balloon Payments

Secondary financing usually involves **BALLOON PAYMENTS**, *that is, junior trust deed loans that are not self-amortizing, will require a large payment to pay off the remainder of the loan.* Where there is a payment schedule of 1 percent of the original loan per month, for example, the payments may not be sufficient to pay off the loan in full by the end of the term, and therefore, will require a balloon payment.

B. ALL-INCLUSIVE TRUST DEED (AITD)

The *ALL-INCLUSIVE TRUST DEED (AITD) is a purchase money encumbrance that includes, yet is subject to, the existing loans.* The installments received by the seller from the buyer are used first to pay the underlying liens, the balance going to the sellers as recovery of their remaining equity. Also referred to as a **wraparound deed of trust**, overriding, overlapping, or hold harmless, the AITD is especially useful in tight money markets or when mortgage money is expensive.

A sales contract financed through an AITD should include the following statement:

BUYER AND SELLER ARE AWARE THAT THE UNDERLYING NOTES SECURED BY TRUST DEEDS MAY CONTAIN A "DUE-ON-SALE" CLAUSE WHICH MAY GIVE THE LENDER THE ELECTION TO CALL THE LOAN DUE UPON RECORDATION OF THE DEED AND A.I.T.D. BUYER AND SELLER ARE ADVISED TO SEEK LEGAL COUNSEL TO EXPLAIN THEIR RIGHTS AND/OR LIABILITIES IN SUCH EVENT.

C. CONTRACT OF SALE (LAND CONTRACT)

The "contract of sale," also referred to as a "land contract," is sometimes used in real estate transactions, but it is not always advisable to do so.

A land contract is generally employed when a buyer invests little or no cash in the purchase. In a *LAND CONTRACT, the seller, as owner of record, retains legal title to the property until a certain point in time, which is generally after the buyer has paid in a substantial amount of cash toward the seller's equity, if not all of it.* Meanwhile, the buyer obtains what is referred to as "equitable title," that is, a buildup of ownership in increments, through payments on the principal indebtedness, in addition to appreciation arising outside the principal reduction itself.

A land contract is like a car loan—you may be driving the car, but you don't own the title until it's paid off.

When the agreed amount is paid, the seller transfers legal title to the buyer, who might, in turn, assume the existing loan. Until that time, however, the principal payments, interest on the unpaid balance of the contract, and the monthly tax and insurance payments are paid to the seller, who in turn makes the monthly payments on the underlying trust deed. This, of course, is the seller's assurance that the loan payments are kept current. On the other hand, the buyer has no assurance that the seller is making the existing loan payments.

To overcome the problems of the simple two-party (vendor-vendee) land contract, the parties may agree to a three-party instrument in which the rights of the parties are insured by a policy of title insurance.

In the typical insured transaction, a title company is designated as trustee "with power of sale" in the same way as trustees are vested in the normal trust deed. The vendor conveys legal title to the trustee, while the vendee conveys equitable title to the trustee, thus facilitating the insurer's role as trustee.

The contract should be drawn by a competent real estate attorney to assure a complete meeting of the minds, with no details omitted. Repossession of the property often requires court action; if the court ruled that both parties be restored to their original positions, the repercussions could be disastrous.

D. ALL-CASH TRANSACTIONS

Very few buyers pay all cash for property, but occasionally, someone who is reluctant to pay interest on a loan will do so. The seller is, of course, expected to deliver the property free and clear to the buyer in an all-cash transaction. In instances in which an existing loan must be paid off, the seller is expected to pay any prepayment penalties, reconveyance fees, and other expenses involved in paying off existing loans. From the standpoint of expenses, it is not as economical for the seller as a loan assumption, but it is considerably less expensive than paying discount points for a new FHA or VA loan.

Paying off an existing loan is often inadvisable when the interest rate is low.

VII. Loan Takeovers

A. "ASSUMPTION" VS. "SUBJECT TO"

A *LOAN ASSUMPTION* *occurs when a buyer pays a seller for part or all of the equity in a property and assumes the responsibility for payment of the existing loans.* From then on, the buyer makes the necessary payments until the existing loans are paid in full or until such time another disposition of the loans is made. *EQUITY* *is the difference between market value and existing loans against the property.* Taking title *SUBJECT TO* *a prior loan constitutes an agreement to take over and make the loan payments or lose the property.*

This method of purchasing is normally more desirable, from the standpoint of saving buyer's and seller's expenses, provided the buyer has sufficient funds to complete the transaction. There are no discount points, prepayment penalties, origination fees, ALTA (American Land Title Association) policies, tax service, trustee's fees, or unearned interest penalties involved in assuming FHA and VA loans, nor with many conventional types of loans.

If the loan interest rate on an older loan is lower than the current loan market, the remaining years of payment are reduced.

1. FHA Loan Assumption

Anyone may assume an FHA or VA loan, once it is established, without regard to the rules and regulations involving buyer's qualifications prior to obtaining a new loan.

2. VA Loan Assumption

The Veterans Administration (VA) holds the original maker of the loan responsible for any losses resulting from foreclosure on a GI loan. However, liability may be eliminated from the original veteran by obtaining a release from the VA and transferring responsibility for the loan to the buyer.

3. Cal-Vet Loan Assumption

A Cal-Vet loan may be assumed by another qualified California veteran at the prevailing interest rate.

Non-vets may not assume a Cal-Vet loan.

In all instances, prior approval must be obtained from the California Department of Veterans Affairs.

4. Conventional Loan Assumption

Conventional fixed loans may not usually be assumed.

If the lender's note and deed of trust contains an alienation clause, it permits the lender to approve the buyers before allowing them to assume the loan. A conventional lender may require a favorable credit report and a higher-than-normal assumption fee and may also have the option of increasing the rate of interest to a new owner. Therefore, it is advisable to determine in advance of a sale what the lender's requirements are going to be with respect to the assumption of the subject loan.

5. Seller Carryback Assumption

Buyers frequently do not have sufficient cash to pay the difference between the purchase price and the existing loan and, for one reason or another, prefer not to refinance with a new loan.

Circumstances may make it more beneficial for the seller not to receive all the equity in cash because of adverse income tax consequences. If the seller has no immediate need for all the cash, he or she could carry a part of the equity on a second deed of trust and receive a greater yield than a savings account would provide.

VIII. Loan Brokerage

Being a broker or salesperson, as part of most real estate transactions, you may help your buyer fill out a loan application for a financial institution or arrange financing for your buyer. In either case, there are certain restrictions that apply to a real estate licensee acting as a loan broker in buying, selling, or exchanging loans. Most of these loans are in the form of a trust deed since it is the usual financing instrument in California.

California law allows real estate licensees who negotiate mortgage loans to receive compensation for their services (as arrangers, managers of loans, middlemen, or intermediaries).

A. MORTGAGE LOAN DISCLOSURE STATEMENT

As a real estate licensee negotiating a loan for a prospective borrower, you (or the lender) must present to that person a completed loan disclosure statement. This statement must be given to the borrower prior to his or her signing the loan documents. It is usually referred to as the Mortgage Loan Disclosure Statement.

A **MORTGAGE LOAN DISCLOSURE STATEMENT** *is a form that completely and clearly states all the information and charges connected with a particular loan.* It must be kept on file for three years. (See **Figure 8-8**.)

As a loan broker, you must keep the Mortgage Loan Disclosure Statement (disclosure given to borrower) on file for three years for the Commissioner's inspection.

Figure 8-8

CALIFORNIA
ASSOCIATION
OF REALTORS®

MORTGAGE LOAN DISCLOSURE STATEMENT
(BORROWER)

(As required by the Business and Professions Code §10241
and Title 10, California Administrative Code, §2840)

_____
(Name of Broker/Arranger of Credit)

_____
(Business Address of Broker)

I. SUMMARY OF LOAN TERMS

   A. PRINCIPAL AMOUNT . . . . $ _____

   B. ESTIMATED DEDUCTIONS FROM PRINCIPAL AMOUNT

      1. Costs and Expenses (See Paragraph III-A) . . . . $ _____

      *2. Broker Commission/Organization Fee (See Paragraph III-B) . . . . $ _____

      3. Lender Origination Fee/Discounts (See Paragraph III-B) . . . . $ _____

      4. Additional compensation will/may be received from lender not deducted from loan proceeds.

         ☐ YES $ _____ (if known) or ☐ NO

      5. Amount to be Paid on Authorization of Borrower (See Paragraph III) . . . . $ _____

   C. ESTIMATED CASH PAYABLE TO BORROWER (A less B) . . . . $ _____

II. GENERAL INFORMATION ABOUT LOAN

   A. If this loan is made, Borrower will be required to pay the principal and interest at _____% per year, payable
as follows: _____ payments of $ _____
          (number of payments)   (monthly/quarterly/annually)
and a **FINAL/BALLOON** payment of $ _____ to pay off the loan in full.

   NOTICE TO BORROWER: IF YOU DO NOT HAVE THE FUNDS TO PAY THE BALLOON PAYMENT WHEN IT COMES DUE, YOU MAY HAVE TO OBTAIN A NEW LOAN AGAINST YOUR PROPERTY TO MAKE THE BALLOON PAYMENT. IN THAT CASE, YOU MAY AGAIN HAVE TO PAY COMMISSIONS, FEES AND EXPENSES FOR THE ARRANGING OF THE NEW LOAN. IN ADDITION, IF YOU ARE UNABLE TO MAKE THE MONTHLY PAYMENTS OR THE BALLOON PAYMENT, YOU MAY LOSE THE PROPERTY AND ALL OF YOUR EQUITY THROUGH FORECLOSURE. KEEP THIS IN MIND IN DECIDING UPON THE AMOUNT AND TERMS OF THIS LOAN.

   B. This loan will be evidenced by a promissory note and secured by a deed of trust on property identified as (street
address or legal description):

   _____

   _____

   C. 1. Liens presently against this property (do not include loan being applied for):

Nature of Lien	Priority	Lienholder's Name	Amount Owing
_____	_____	_____	_____
_____	_____	_____	_____
_____	_____	_____	_____

      2. Liens that will remain against this property after the loan being applied for is made or arranged (include loan
being applied for):

Nature of Lien	Priority	Lienholder's Name	Amount Owing
_____	_____	_____	_____
_____	_____	_____	_____
_____	_____	_____	_____

   NOTICE TO BORROWER: Be sure that you state the amount of all liens as accurately as possible. If you contract with the broker to arrange this loan, but it cannot be arranged because you did not state these liens correctly, you may be liable to pay commissions, fees and expenses even though you do not obtain the loan.

REVISION DATE 10/2000 Print Date
MS-11 (PAGE 1 OF 3)

Borrower acknowledges receipt of copy of this page.

Borrower's Initials (_____)(_____)

EQUAL HOUSING OPPORTUNITY

Reviewed by
Broker or Designee _____ Date _____

MORTGAGE LOAN DISCLOSURE STATEMENT (MS-11 PAGE 1 OF 3)

Property Address: _____ Date: _____

D. If Borrower pays all or part of the loan principal before it is due, a PREPAYMENT PENALTY computed as follows may be charged:

_____
_____
_____

E. Late Charges: ☐ YES, see loan documents   or   ☐ NO
F. The purchase of credit life or credit disability insurance by a borrower is not required as a condition of making this loan.
G. Is the real property which will secure the requested loan an "owner-occupied dwelling?" ☐ YES____ or ☐ NO____
   (Borrower initial opposite YES or NO)

An "owner-occupied dwelling" means a single dwelling unit in a condominium or cooperative or residential building of four or fewer separate dwelling units, one of which will be owned and occupied by a signatory to the mortgage or deed of trust for this loan within 90 days of the signing of the mortgage or deed of trust.

III. DEDUCTIONS FROM LOAN PROCEEDS

A. Estimated Maximum Costs and Expenses of Arranging the Loan to be Paid Out of Loan Principal:

	PAYABLE TO	
	Broker	Others
1. Appraisal fee	_____	_____
2. Escrow fee	_____	_____
3. Title insurance policy	_____	_____
4. Notary fees	_____	_____
5. Recording fees	_____	_____
6. Credit investigation fees	_____	_____
7. Other costs and expenses:		
_____	_____	_____
_____	_____	_____
Total Costs and Expenses	$ _____	

*B. Compensation . . . . $ _____
   1. Brokerage Commission/Origination Fee . . . . $ _____
   2. Lender Origination Fee/Discounts . . . . $ _____

C. Estimated Payment to be Made out of Loan Principal on Authorization of Borrower

	PAYABLE TO	
	Broker	Others
1. Fire or other hazard insurance premiums	_____	_____
2. Credit life or disability insurance premiums (see Paragraph II-F)	_____	_____
3. Beneficiary statement fees	_____	_____
4. Reconveyance and similar fees	_____	_____
5. Discharge of existing liens against property:		
_____	_____	_____
_____	_____	_____
6. Other:		
_____	_____	_____
_____	_____	_____
_____	_____	_____
Total to be Paid on Authorization of Borrower	$ _____	

If this loan is secured by a first deed of trust on dwellings in a principal amount of less than $30,000 or secured by a junior lien on dwellings in a principal amount of less than $20,000, the undersigned licensee certifies that the loan will be made in compliance with Article 7 of Chapter 3 of the Real Estate Law.

*This loan **may / will / will not** (delete two) be made wholly or in part from broker-controlled funds as defined in Section 10241(j) of the Business and Professions Code.

Borrower acknowledges receipt of copy of this page.
Borrower's Initials (_____)(_____)

EQUAL HOUSING OPPORTUNITY

Reviewed by _____
Broker or Designee _____ Date _____

MORTGAGE LOAN DISCLOSURE STATEMENT (MS-11 PAGE 2 OF 3)

Property Address: _____ Date: _____

*NOTICE TO BORROWER: This disclosure statement may be used if the Broker is acting as an agent in arranging the loan by a third person or if the loan will be made with funds owned or controlled by the broker. If the Broker indicates in the above statement that the loan "may" be made out of Broker-controlled funds, the Broker must notify the borrower prior to the close of escrow if the funds to be received by the Borrower are in fact Broker-controlled funds.

_____   _____
Name of Broker   Broker Representative

_____   _____
License Number   OR   License Number

_____   _____
Signature of Broker   Signature

The Department of Real Estate License Information phone number is _____.

NOTICE TO BORROWER:

DO NOT SIGN THIS STATEMENT UNTIL YOU HAVE READ AND UNDERSTAND ALL OF THE INFORMATION IN IT. ALL PARTS OF THE FORM MUST BE COMPLETED BEFORE YOU SIGN.

Borrower hereby acknowledges the receipt of a copy of this statement.

DATED _____   _____
                                                     (Borrower)

                                                        _____
                                                        (Borrower)

<u>Broker Review</u>: Signature of Real Estate Broker after review of this statement.

                                                        _____

DATED _____

                                                       Real Estate Broker or Assistant Pursuant to Section 2725

REBS INC   Published and Distributed by:
REAL ESTATE BUSINESS SERVICES, INC.
a subsidiary of the CALIFORNIA ASSOCIATION OF REALTORS®
525 South Virgil Avenue, Los Angeles, California 90020

Reviewed by
Broker or Designee _____ Date _____

EQUAL HOUSING OPPORTUNITY

REVISION DATE 10/2000   **Print Date**
MS-11 (PAGE 3 OF 3)

MORTGAGE LOAN DISCLOSURE STATEMENT (MS-11 PAGE 3 OF 3)

B. BUSINESS AND PROFESSIONS CODE
(Commissions and Other Requirements)

1. Article 7 - Loan Broker Laws

Brokers negotiating trust deed loans are subject to certain limitations regarding commissions and expenses and must meet other requirements set out by the Real Estate Commissioner (see **Figure 8-9**). Legislation also requires that brokers provide both the borrower and the lender, on property for first trust deed loans under $30,000 and seconds under $20,000, with copies of the appraisal report. Anyone performing these services, whether soliciting borrowers or lenders in home loans secured by real property, must have a real estate license. This restriction applies even if no advance fee is paid.

Figure 8-9

Loan Broker Commission Limits

	Loans for Less Than 2 Years	Loans for 2 Years and Less Than 3 Years	Loans for 3 Years and Over	Transactions That are Exempt
First Trust Deeds	5 %	5 %	10 %	Loans of $30,000 and over
Junior Trust Deeds	5 %	10 %	15 %	Loans of $30,000 and over

On hard money loans (cash) of $30,000 and over for first trust deeds, and $20,000 and over for junior deeds of trust, the broker may charge as much as the borrower will agree to pay.

Loans on owner-occupied homes negotiated by brokers for a term of six years or less may not have a balloon payment. If nonowner occupied, loans are exempt from balloon payments when the term is less than three years. Neither of these restrictions apply to transactions where the seller extends credit to the buyer. When such transactions have balloon payments, the seller is obligated to notify the buyer 60 to 150 days before the payment is due. Also, the broker is obligated to inform the buyer regarding the likelihood of obtaining new financing.

C. USURY LIMITATIONS

USURY is charging more than the legally allowed percentage of interest. In California, the maximum interest rate charged for various loans is set by law. Anyone charging more than the designated rate is committing usury and is breaking the law. In determining whether an interest charge is usurious or not, all loan fees and points are added to the interest rate. Prepayment penalties are not included in the usury law test.

The constitutional usury rate in California is ten percent, or five percent above the discount rate charged by the Federal Reserve Bank of San Francisco, whichever is higher. This limit only applies to lenders who are not exempt from the law. Nearly every conventional source of real estate financing, however, has been exempted from the usury limit. Banks, savings banks, and other institutional lenders are all exempt. Sellers carrying back a purchase money trust deed as part of their equity in a real estate sale are exempt. **Any transaction made through a licensed broker is also exempt from usury laws.** The problem arises when a private individual lends money to another private individual. Check with an attorney first.

 www.frbsf.org (Federal Reserve Bank of San Francisco, 12th District)
www.fdic.gov (Federal Deposit Insurance Corporation - FDIC)

IX. CHAPTER SUMMARY

In California, the commonly used term "mortgage" usually refers to a **trust deed**. The parties to a trust deed include the **trustor** (borrower), **beneficiary** (lender), and **trustee** (disinterested third party who holds title).

The cost of borrowing money includes **interest rates, origination fees**, and **points**, which are included in the **annual percentage rate (APR)**, as well as prepayment penalties and impound accounts.

Institutional (or **conventional loans)** are not guaranteed by any government agency, and include **savings banks, commercial banks**, and **insurance companies**. Mortgage bankers are direct lenders that underwrite for larger investors and often act as **correspondents** for those loans. Life insurance companies are usually the most selective about the properties and borrowers to whom they will lend money, but also offer the best rates. **Private mortgage insurance (PMI)** insures these conventional loans when they have less than 20 percent down.

The loan payments on a **fixed rate mortgage** are the same each month for the life of the loan, and the loan is payed off at the end of the term, making it "**fully amortized**." With an **adjustable rate mortgage (or ARM)** the rates are variable. With a **graduated payment mortgage (GPM)**, the rate and term are fixed, but monthly payments are smaller at the beginning of the term and increase over time. This may result in **negative amortization**, and borrowers need to know in advance of this possibility.

The **secondary mortgage market** is where lenders buy and sell mortgages (trust deeds). The **FNMA (Fannie Mae), GNMA (Ginnie Mae)**, and **FHLMC (Freddie Mac)** are all involved in the secondary mortgage market.

The three primary sources of government-backed financing are the **Federal Housing Administration (FHA)**, the **Veterans Administration (VA)**, and the **California Department of Veterans Affairs (Cal-Vet)**. Only the Cal Vet is a direct lender of funds, the FHA and Va insure or guarantee loans made by approved institutional lenders.

A **certificate of reasonable value (CRV)** is the appraisal necessary for a veteran to buy a property. Operating expenses of the Cal-Vet program come from the sale of general obligation bonds, with the state guaranteeing the repayment of the bonds from the general fund.

A **credit score** gives lenders an idea of a borrower's ability to repay a loan and make timely credit payments. A **FICO score** is used most often (developed by Fair. Isaac and Company).

The **Equal Credit Opportunity Act** protects against discrimination in lending practices. The **Fair Credit Reporting Act** allows loan applicants to see their files, and the Truth in Lending Act (also known as **Regulation Z**) lets borrowers know the true cost of credit.

Noninstitutional financing is by parties who are not as strictly governed or controlled by federal and state agencies. Some of these parties include pension funds, public syndications and individuals. **Junior loans** (secondary financing) are secured by a second deed of trust, meaning they are secondary to any first or primary trust deeds.

An **acceleration clause** states that the loan is due and payable if the property is sold or something else occurs. A **balloon payment** is a large payment due at the end of the loan term, in order to pay off the balance of the loan.

With a **land contract**, sometimes known as a **contract of sale**, the seller retains the legal title to the property until the buyer has paid off the loan (like a car loan).

A **loan assumption** occurs when a buyer pays a seller for part or all of the equity in a property and assumes the responsibility for payment of the existing loans. **Equity** is the difference between market value and existing loans against the property. Taking title **"subject to"** a prior loan substitutes an agreement to take over and make the loan payments, or lose the property. The seller remains liable in case of default or foreclosure.

California allows real estate licensees to negotiate mortgage loans, and receive compensation for their services as managers, arrangers of loans, middlemen or intermediaries. A **mortgage loan disclosure statement** must be given to the borrower and kept on file for three years for the Real Estate Commissioner's inspection.

Usury is the illegal charging of too much interest on a loan.

X. KEY TERMS

Acceleration Clause
Adjustable Interval
Adjustable Rate Mortgages (ARMs)
Annual Percentage Rate (APR)
Article 7 Broker Laws
Assumption
Balloon Payments
Beneficiary Interest
Cal-Vet
Cap
Certificate of Reasonable Value
Commercial Banks
Credit Scoring
Discounting
Equal Credit Opportunity Act (ECOA)
Fair Credit Reporting Act
Fannie Mae
FHA
Fixed Rate Mortgages
Freddie Mac
Ginnie Mae
Government-Backed Financing
Graduated Payment Mortgage (GPM)
Impound Accounts
Index
Institutional Financing
Junior Loans
Land Contract
Life Insurance Companies
Margin
Mortgage Loan Disclosure Statement
Mortgages Trust Deeds
Negative Amortization
Noninstitutional Financing
Origination Fees
Points
Prime Loans
Private Mortgage Insurance (PMI)
Regulation Z
Savings Banks
Secondary Mortgage Market
Subprime Borrower

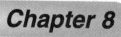

Trustee
Trustor
Truth in Lending Act
Usury Laws
VA

XI. CHAPTER 8 QUIZ

1. Which of the following is NOT a party to a trust deed?
    a. Beneficiary
    b. Executor
    c. Trustor
    d. Trustee

2. Loans that are neither insured nor guaranteed by an agency of the government are termed:
    a. prime loans.
    b. fixed interest loans.
    c. institutional loans.
    d. noninstitutional loans.

3. In addition to the amount financed, the annual percentage rate (APR) includes:
    a. interests rates.
    b. points.
    c. loan fees.
    d. all of the above.

4. Which institutional lender usually charges the lowest interest rates and requires repayment in 25 years or less?
    a. Savings banks
    b. Commercial banks
    c. Life insurance companies
    d. None of the above

5. Which type of loan is repayed in equal monthly payments for the life of the loan?
    a. Fixed rate
    b. Adjustable rate
    c. Graduated payment
    d. None of the above

6. A drawback of the graduated payment mortgage is its:
    a. negative amortization.
    b. positive amortization.
    c. fluctuating interest rate.
    d. none of the above.

7. Which of the following is involved in the secondary mortgage market?
    a. Fannie Mae
    b. Ginnie Mae
    c. Freddie Mac
    d. All of the above

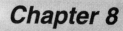

8. The maximum number of origination points which can be charged to buyers under either FHA or VA loans is/are:

    a. one.

    b. seven.

    c. ten.

    d. none of the above.

9. A seller who retains legal title to a property until the buyer has paid off the loan has a(n):

    a. junior trust deed.

    b. land contract.

    c. first trust deed.

    d. all of the above.

10. Brokers must keep a Mortgage Loan Disclosure Statement on file for:

    a. one year.

    b. two years.

    c. three years.

    d. seven years

ANSWERS: 1. b; 2. d; 3. d; 4. c; 5. a; 6. a; 7. d; 8. d; 9. a; 9. b; 10. c

CHAPTER 9
Escrow
How to Navigate the Journey

I. The Escrow Procedure

An escrow is the processing, by a neutral party, of the paperwork and money involved in a sale or other real estate transaction. The purpose of an escrow is to assure that the appropriate parties perform the terms of the contract.

An **ESCROW** *is created when a new written agreement instructs a neutral third party to hold funds and proceed only when all the agreed to conditions have been performed.* This information is usually taken from the California Residential Purchase Agreement and Joint Escrow Instructions. In California, an escrow is usually a requirement for the sale of a home or any other real estate. Although it is not always required by law, it is an indispensable process by which an independent third party handles the legal paperwork of a real estate sale. An escrow is not only an effective tool for handling normal real estate transactions ,like sales or refinancing, but is also for the sale of trust deeds, exchanges and transfer of liquor licenses, businesses, securities, and court-required transfers. The legally required and recommended uses of an escrow are illustrated in **Figure 9-1**.

335

CHAPTER 9 OUTLINE

I. THE ESCROW PROCEDURE (p. 335)
A. Requirements of a Valid Escrow (p. 337)
B. Escrow Holder (p. 337)
C. Real Estate Brokers Can Conduct Escrows (p. 339)

II. HOW ESCROWS WORK (p. 339)
A. Fax Purchase Agreement to Escrow (p. 339)
B. Follow-Through Checklist (p. 339)
C. Opening Escrow (p. 343)
D. Escrow Rules (p. 343)
E. Who Selects the Escrow Company? (p. 344)
F. Escrow Instructions (p. 344)
G. Financing is an Important Aspect of the Escrow (p. 345)
H. Escrow Example (p. 345)
I. Closing Date is the Date of Recordation (p. 346)

III. PRORATION (p. 346)
A. 30 Days is the Basis for Proration (p. 349)

IV. TERMITES AND OTHER PROBLEMS (p. 349)
A. Structural Pest Control Certification Report (Report and Clearance) (p. 349)
B. Broker Maintains Pest Control Documentation (p. 350)

V. FIRE INSURANCE (p. 351)
A. Fire Insurance... A Must! (p. 351)
B. Fire Insurance Proration (p. 352)

VI. TITLE INSURANCE (p. 352)
A. Chain of Title (Recorded Public History) (p. 352)
B. Title Insurance (Has Four Functions) (p. 352)
C. Preliminary Title Report (Ordered First) (p. 353)

VII. TYPES OF TITLE INSURANCE POLICIES (p. 355)
A. California Land Title Association (CLTA) (Standard Coverage Policy) (p. 355)
B. American Land Title Association (ALTA)
   (Extended Coverage Policy - Survey Included) (p. 360)
C. ALTA-R (One-to-Four Residential Units) (p. 361)
D. Who Pays Title Insurance Fees? (p. 362)
E. Title Insurance Disclosure (p. 362)

VIII. REAL ESTATE SETTLEMENT PROCEDURES ACT (RESPA) (p. 362)
IX. CALIFORNIA ESCROW ASSOCIATION (p. 363)
X. CHAPTER SUMMARY (p. 368)
XI. KEY TERMS (p. 370)
XII. CHAPTER 9 QUIZ (p. 371)

Figure 9-1

Highly Recommended	Required By Law
1. Sales of Real Property	1. Liquor License Transfers
2. Loans	2. Security Sales (Impound Accounts)
3. Exchanges	3. Court Ordered Transfers (Probate Sales)

A. REQUIREMENTS FOR A VALID ESCROW

The Escrow Act is found in the Financial Code.

The three requirements for a valid escrow are:

1. Signed escrow instructions (found in the Joint Escrow section of the deposit receipt), forming a binding contract between two or more parties: usually a buyer and seller.
2. A neutral party, which is the escrow company, acting as a dual agent of the buyer and seller.
3. Conditional delivery of funds and documents, after all the conditions in the escrow are met.

When escrow closes, dual agency (representing both parties, usually buyers and sellers, at once) changes to separate agency (handling each party's separate paperwork requirements).

An escrow is usually initiated with the California Residential Purchase Agreement and Escrow Instructions (deposit receipt), or rarely through oral instructions. It is important to have agreed upon the written instructions drawn by the escrow company. Since this may be a new experience for most people, the escrow agent will, when necessary, explain each step to a buyer or seller. A helpful escrow officer can point out possible problems, and suggest alternatives, but cannot give legal advice.

B. ESCROW HOLDER

An escrow holder can be: 1) a corporation, 2) an attorney, or 3) a real estate broker who acts as a real estate agent in the transaction.

A **NEUTRAL DEPOSITORY** *is an escrow business conducted by a licensed escrow holder. An* **ESCROW OFFICER, HOLDER, OR AGENT**, *though not licensed by the state, is an employee of a licensed escrow company who acts as the agent.* Escrow law is found in the California Financial Code. An independent escrow corporation must be licensed by the Department of Corporations to handle escrows. Corporations that are exempt from the escrow law, but can handle escrows, include: banks, savings banks, and title insurance companies, because they are under the supervision of their respective authorizing agencies.

In Northern California, the majority of escrows are handled by escrow departments of title insurance companies, which are governed by the Insurance Commissioner. In Southern California, many escrows are handled by independent escrow companies which, by law, must be incorporated and are governed by the Commissioner of Corporations.

There are two other types of escrow holders. They are attorneys who perform escrow duties as a part of their practice, and real estate brokers who handle their own escrows (must be the broker in the transaction). Regardless of the type of escrow company, the functions of an escrow may be summarized in four broad categories. (See **Figure 9-2**.)

Figure 9-2

Four Functions of Escrow

| Provide a custodian of funds and documents who can deliver them concurrently | Provide a clearing house for payments of liens and for refinancing | Compute all prorations for Statements | Prepare documents, then record |

The complete sequence of events in an escrow is:

1. Preliminary title search and report
2. Lender's demand (amount owed, pay-off statement)
3. Request for new loan documents
4. Completion of conditions and depositing of funds
5. Adjustments and prorations
6. Transfer of existing fire policies, or creation of new ones
7. Recording and issuing of title policy
8. Disbursement of funds
9. Escrow statement sent to each party

After these steps have been completed and all other escrow conditions have been met, the closing of an escrow is usually routine. **See Figure 9-3**.

The escrow agent is authorized to call for a buyer's documents and funds.

C. REAL ESTATE BROKERS CAN CONDUCT ESCROWS

A broker can handle escrows for a fee only if the broker is acting as a real estate agent or principal in that transaction.

As a licensed broker, you can handle an escrow for a fee only if you are acting as a broker in that real estate transaction. This right is personal to the broker, and the broker shall not delegate any duties other than escrow duties normally performed under the direct supervision of the broker.

All written escrow instructions executed by a buyer or seller must contain a statement, in not less than 10-point type, that includes the licensee's name and the fact that he or she is licensed by the Department of Real Estate.

II. How Escrows Work

The basis for the escrow instructions is the Residential Purchase Agreement and Joint Escrow Instructions. Of course, its terms can be modified by mutual agreement.

A. FAX PURCHASE AGREEMENT TO ESCROW

The last page of the Purchase Agreement contains an acknowledgement for receipt of the completed agreement (see **Figure 9-4**). Escrow companies often write a disclaimer regarding any discrepancies between the Purchase Agreement and the escrow instructions, stating that it's not their intention to supersede the original terms of the Purchase Agreement. To avoid any discrepancies, always double check for mistakes and file addendums for changes.

Once the California Residential Purchase Agreement and Joint Escrow Instructions form has been filled out and executed properly, you will fax it to the escrow company for their signature.

B. FOLLOW-THROUGH CHECKLIST

Follow-through services are the responsibility of both the listing and selling agents. These services include ordering a structural pest control report, getting loan applications to the borrower and arranging all necessary financing, ordering the preliminary title report, followed by the ultimate issuance of the title insurance policy,

Figure 9-3

California Customs (North vs. South) for Escrow Services and Title Insurance

When are signed escrow instructions delivered?

Customarily in Southern California, the (bilateral) escrow instructions are signed by both the buyer and seller just after the **start of escrow**.

Customarily in Northern California, the (unilateral) escrow instructions are given to the escrow officer just before the **close of escrow**.

Who performs the escrow services?

Escrow services in Southern California are traditionally performed by **independent escrow companies (corporations) or financial institutions**.

Escrow services in Northern California are traditionally performed by **title insurance companies**.

Who pays the escrow fees?

Escrow service fees in Southern California are usually **split 50-50 between the buyer and the seller**.

Escrow service fees in Northern California are usually **paid for by the buyer**.

Who traditionally pays title insurance fees?

Customarily in Southern California, the **seller pays for the California Land Title Association (CLTA) policy (standard policy)**.

Customarily in Northern California, the **buyer pays for the California Land Title Association (CLTA) policy (standard policy)**.

In both the North and the South, the buyers pay for any coverage above the California Standard Title Insurance (CLTA) policy.

Figure 9-4

ESCROW HOLDER ACKNOWLEDGMENT:

Escrow Holder acknowledges receipt of a Copy of this Agreement, (if checked, ☐ a deposit in the amount of $ _____),
counter offer numbers _____ and _____
_____, and agrees to act as Escrow Holder subject to paragraph 28 of this Agreement, any
supplemental escrow instructions and the terms of Escrow Holder's general provisions.

Escrow Holder is advised that the date of Confirmation of Acceptance of the Agreement as between Buyer and Seller is _____

Escrow Holder _____   Escrow # _____
By _____   Date _____
Address _____
Phone/Fax/E-mail _____
Escrow Holder is licensed by the California Department of ☐ Corporations, ☐ Insurance, ☐ Real Estate. License # _____

---

securing property insurance, getting the various documents in order, and all other things necessary to carry out the terms of the purchase and sale agreement. Although a large part of these services are performed by others, it's your job to assist the escrow company and keep a record of progress to see that the sale is properly consummated.

As a conscientious agent, you won't simply put the contract in the lap of the escrow company and hope that "everything will be taken care of." Your follow-up is so important that if you do not continue your service through escrow, you may find yourself confronted with many problems, and even a falling-out in the escrow. Too often the salesperson who does not follow through on the escrow winds up losing the sale. You can end up with disgruntled buyers and sellers on your hands, or worse, a lawsuit.

Always follow up on your escrows—it's much better for you to call the escrow officer and check the status of the process, than to hope the officer calls you.

To keep track of the escrow process, you'll want to use an agent/broker escrow checklist (see **Figure 9-5**). Servicing includes tasks before and during escrow, and post-escrow activities as well. You should check everything on your progress chart as completely as possible to assure a smooth and consummated transaction.

After the escrow has closed and the buyers have moved in, you can visit them to determine what else can be done—introduce them to their new neighbors or show them the nearby shopping facilities. This is bound to earn good will—and referrals!

It's a good idea to drop your former buyers an occasional note— reminding them to follow through on updating insurance for example—or simply telling them you like what they've done with the landscaping, paint job. etc.

Figure 9-5

Escrow Checklist

Contracts & Disclosures	Seller	Buyer	Broker Initials
Agency - Seller and Buyer (both should be in file) **(AD)**	/	/	/
Listing w/Termite and Title Clauses stated on 2nd page. & Sellers Advisory **(LA & SA)**			
Transfer Disclosure (Do not qualify problems) **(TDS)**			
FRPTA/Fed. & Calif. Law (Seller/Buyer) **(SA)**	/	/	/
Smoke Detector and Water Heater **(SDS & WHS)**			
Horizontal Defective Furnaces (if applicable)			
Lead Base Paint Disclosure (housing blt. prior to 1978) **(FLD)**			
Res. Earthquake Booklet and receipt of same	/	/	/
Zone Disclosures appropriately signed: Natural Hazard, Mold, Database, Airport, etc.			
Supplemental Tax Disclosure			
Supplemental Statutory Contractual Disclosure. **(SSD)**			
Order sign up and send mail outs to neighborhood			
Sellers/Buyers Estimate Costs **(ESP/EBC)**			
Res. Purchase Agreement (All pages initialed including buyer's agency & Advisory) **(RPA-CA,AD & BIA)**			
Prequalification letter & Copy of Check			
Counters to Purchase Agreement & Multiple Offer (Item 7) **(CO)**			
Compensation to cooperating broker **(CCB)**			
Receipt from Escrow of Buyers' earnest money deposit within 3 days of acceptance			
Escrow Inst. & Prelim (Read both carefully)			
Appraisal (ordered and appointment made); provide comps			
Physical Inspection or Waiver (Do not Meddle)			
Termite Inspection and clearance to be **signed by buyers**			
Request for Repairs From Buyers **(RRI)**			
Response to Request for Repairs from Sellers			
Removal of Contingencies or Cancellation			
Home Warranty/Waiver (Watch the amount to be paid by seller)			
Walk Through or Waiver **(VP)**			
Check closing costs (Have escrow give you estimated proceed two days prior to close of escrow)			
Remove lock box and have sign taken down			
Report Sale to Association (otherwise you will be fined by the Board)			
Send mail outs to the neighbors and follow up			

C. OPENING ESCROW

When opening escrow, always double-check the spelling of names and the addresses. This helps keep the loan documents and deed from being drawn wrong.

You can call the escrow company with instructions, and then fax the Purchase Agreement. As a broker, your instructions should set forth clear communications as to who will open escrow and where, the date escrow is opened, length of escrow, terms of the loans being sought, contingencies that may have been incorporated into the deposit receipt, the way in which title is to be taken, commissions (not shown on the buyers' copy), termite report instructions, personal property that may be included, legal description, earnest money deposit, and any other information that went into the terms.

If it's available, provide escrow with the property profile—obtained from the title company—when you open escrow.

After typing the escrow instructions, the escrow holder sends them to the agents of both the buyers and sellers with a copy to the broker. The escrow officer then calls the parties into his or her office for signatures, or sends the instructions to the broker for follow-up, depending upon what the broker instructs the escrow officer to do. At the time of mailing, he or she encloses the grant deed and a statement of information for the seller. Included with the buyers' papers is a statement of information for them to complete as well.

D. ESCROW RULES

Once the escrow instructions have been drawn from the original contract (deposit receipt) and signed by each party, neither party may change the escrow instructions without the written agreement of the other. (All time frames commence from the time the contract became binding; usually the deposit receipt has a provision for escrow to acknowledge receipt of this document.) The escrow is complete when: 1) all conditions of the escrow have been met; 2) all conditions of the parties have been met; and 3) the parties have received an accounting of the procedure. If both parties mutually agree to change the instructions, the change can be put into effect at any time. However, if a dispute should arise, the escrow company will not proceed until both parties come to terms. If the parties cannot agree to terms, an escrow company will bring an interpleader action (court action) to determine where the money or consideration goes. **Figure 9-6** illustrates the three ways in which an escrow can be terminated.

If the seller thinks he or she can obtain more money and wants to rescind an escrow, remember: the seller cannot rescind an escrow without the consent of the buyer.

Figure 9-6

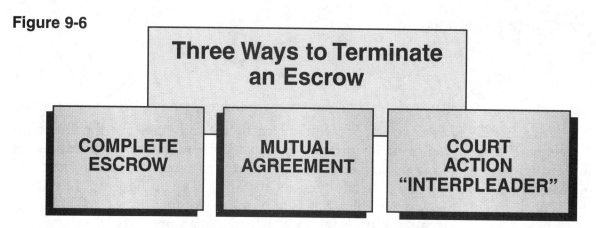

Three Ways to Terminate an Escrow

| COMPLETE ESCROW | MUTUAL AGREEMENT | COURT ACTION "INTERPLEADER" |

E. WHO SELECTS THE ESCROW COMPANY?

A real estate licensee is prohibited by law from receiving any "kickback" for solicitation of escrow business.

Selection of an escrow company and an escrow officer are part of the negotiation between buyer and seller. Like any other item in a real estate transaction, it is part of the negotiated agreement. Either one of the parties may choose the escrow company, which should be explained when completing the deposit receipt. As a salesperson, you may certainly make suggestions as to a preferred escrow company for both the buyer and seller. When the escrow company is named in the listing agreement, you cannot change the escrow company without the consent of the seller or the seller's agent. If the buyer and seller each desire a different escrow company, then the salesperson must work for a mutual agreement before there can be an offer and acceptance of the sale.

Death does not cancel an escrow; it is binding on the heirs (estate) because of the prior, agreed-to contract.

It is imperative that you, the salesperson, disclose in writing any shared interest that you or your broker has with the selected escrow company. This disclosure must be made either at the time of listing or whenever the escrow company is selected. Disciplinary action will be taken against any salesperson or broker who, in bad faith and against the wishes of the buyer and seller, attempts to force the use of a particular escrow company. Furthermore, a real estate licensee is prohibited by law from receiving any "kickback" for solicitation of escrow business.

F. ESCROW INSTRUCTIONS

ESCROW INSTRUCTIONS are formal instructions drawn from the information contained in the original agreement, usually the signed deposit receipt (California Residential Purchase Agreement and Joint Escrow Instructions). When these instructions are drawn and signed, they become an enforceable contract binding on all parties.

Escrow instructions and the deposit receipt are interpreted together, but if a conflict arises, the latest signed document will prevail (unless otherwise specified).

Since the escrow instructions supplement the original contract, both are interpreted together whenever possible. Escrow companies often use a disclaimer stating that it's not their intention to supersede the original intent of the Purchase Agreement.

All parties to the escrow should read the escrow instructions very carefully, and sign them only after every detail is absolutely correct and the terms meet with their approval.

G. FINANCING IS AN IMPORTANT ASPECT OF THE ESCROW

Most escrows for the sale of a home include obtaining a new loan and the payoff or assumption of an old loan. As an agent/broker, you can be helpful to the buyer obtaining new financing by providing the necessary loan documentation to the escrow company in a timely manner. Keeping the buyer and seller informed about the progress of the financing and escrow helps to maintain good client-agent communication and trust.

The *PAYOFF DEMAND STATEMENT is a formal demand statement from the lender that details the amounts owed, as calculated by the lender, for the purpose of **paying off the loan in full**.* The failure to obtain a payoff or beneficiary statement in a timely manner could hold up the escrow. A payoff demand statement is different from a beneficiary's statement. A *BENEFICIARY'S (LENDER'S) STATEMENT is a demand statement by a lender, under a deed of trust, that provides information, such as the unpaid balance, monthly payment, and interest rate, necessary **if the loan is to be assumed**.* The lender may charge up to $100 for furnishing the payoff or beneficiary statement, except when the loan is insured by the FHA or guaranteed by the VA.

During escrow, if a buyer receives loan approval and requests to move into the property before escrow closes, he or she must obtain permission from the seller, with written authorization.

H. ESCROW EXAMPLE

To help illustrate the closing statements used in a simple escrow, let's assume the following facts:

Figure 9-7 illustrates the buyer's escrow statement, and **Figure 9-8** illustrates the seller's statement. These statements include many other miscellaneous costs that are a usual part of the escrow.

An Escrow Example

BUYER	John Buyer and Jane Buyer	
SELLER	John Seller and Jane Seller	
SALES PRICE		$800,000
1ST TRUST DEED		$640,000
2ND TRUST DEED		$ 80,000
DOWN PAYMENT		$ 80,000
BROKER	J.Q. Smart	$ 48,000
EXISTING LIENS		
1) 1ST TRUST DEED		$290,000
2) STREET ASSESSMENT BOND		$ 1,300
CLTA TITLE POLICY PAID BY SELLER		$ 2,165

Date of Closing is June 1, 2020

I. CLOSING DATE IS THE DATE OF RECORDATION

Closing is the process of signing, transfer of documents, and distribution of funds. When time is not specified, the escrow will close by mutual consent or within a reasonable period.

The **CLOSING DATE** *is the date that the documents are recorded.* Escrow usually approximates the closing date, but the actual date is when all the conditions of the escrow have been completed, the buyer's remaining money (cashier's checks) is received, and when all the documents are recorded. Most escrows are for handling the paperwork of property sale and loan financing, but escrows can be for almost any purpose.

At the close of escrow, if a seller decides not to pay the commission, the broker/agent can file civil action in court.

Note: In closing statements, the buyer's and seller's totals are different. However, each closing statement must balance within itself. In the buyer's closing statement, the purchase price is debited.

III. Proration

Property taxes, interest, fire insurance, and rents are prorated, but not title insurance or non-recurring fees.

PRORATION *is the process of proportionately dividing expenses or income to the precise date that escrow closes, or any other date previously agreed upon.* It enables the buyer and seller to

Figure 9-7

601 East Glenoaks Blvd. Suite 210
Glendale, CA 91207
P.O. Box 433 Glendale, CA 91209-0433
Tel: (818) 500-1633
Fax: (818) 500-0862

SELLER FINAL SETTLEMENT STATEMENT

PROPERTY: 123 Purchase Lane   CLOSING DATE: 06/01/20
          Glendale, CA   ESCROW NO.:   1-10533
SELLER: John Seller and Jane Seller

	DEBITS	CREDITS
FINANCIAL		
Total Consideration	$	$ 800,000.00
New 2nd Trust Deed	80,000.00	
PRORATIONS AND ADJUSTMENTS		
Taxes at 4000.00/6 mo. from 06/01/20 to 07/01/20		666.67
PAYOFF CHARGES TO MOST SUPERIOR		
SAVINGS AND LOAN		
Principal Balance	490,000.00	
Interest on Principal Balance at 10.0000% from 05/01/20 to 06/01/20	4,161.64	
Forwarding Fee	50.00	
Reconveyance Fee	60.00	
OTHER DISBURSEMENTS		
Pest Control, Inc. for Termite Report/Work	1,000.00	
Home Warranty, Inc. for Home Protection Policy	400.00	
COMMISSION		
Listing Broker: J. Q. Smart	48,000.00	
TITLE CHARGES TO AMERICAN COAST		
TITLE		
Title Policy Premium	2,165.00	
Sub Escrow Fee	75.00	
Documentary Transfer Tax	880.00	
Recording Reconveyance	5.00	
Street Assessment Bond	1,300.00	
ESCROW CHARGES TO COLONIAL ESCROW, INC.		
Escrow Fee	900.00	
Processing Demands	35.00	
Document Fee	85.00	
NET PROCEEDS	171,550.03	
TOTALS	800,666.67	800,666.67

SAVE FOR INCOME TAX PURPOSES

Figure 9-8

601 East Glenoaks Blvd. Suite 210
Glendale, CA 91207
P.O. Box 433 Glendale, CA 91209-0433
Tel: (818) 500-1633
Fax: (818) 500-0862

BUYER FINAL SETTLEMENT STATEMENT

PROPERTY: 123 Purchase Lane
           Glendale, CA
BUYER: John Buyer and Jane Buyer

CLOSING DATE: 06/01/20
ESCROW NO.: 1-10533

	DEBITS	CREDITS
FINANCIAL		
Total Consideration	$ 800,000.00	$
Cash Deposit		5,000.00
Cash Deposit		86,000.00
New 1st Trust Deed		640,000.00
New 2nd Trust Deed		80,000.00
PRORATIONS AND ADJUSTMENTS		
Taxes at 4000.00/6 mo. from 06/01/20 to 07/01/20	666.67	
OTHER DISBURSEMENTS		
Property Insurance, Inc. for Fire Insurance	1,000.00	
TITLE CHARGES TO AMERICAN COAST TITLE		
Title Policy Premium	628.50	
Sub Escrow Fee	75.00	
Recording Grant Deed	8.00	
Recording Trust Deed(s)	20.00	
Title Endorsement Fee(s)	50.00	
ESCROW CHARGES TO COLONIAL ESCROW, INC.		
Escrow Fee	900.00	
Messenger Fee	50.00	
Loan Tie In Fee	125.00	
NEW 1ST TRUST DEED TO GET SMART SAVINGS AND LOAN		
Loan Fees	6,400.00	
Credit Report	45.00	
Appraisal	350.00	
Tax Service	89.00	
Document Fee	250.00	
Interest at 7.5000% from 05/31/20 to 06/01/20	131.51	
REFUND	211.32	
TOTALS	811,000.00	811,000.00

SAVE FOR INCOME TAX PURPOSES

348

pay or receive their proportionate share of expenses or income. Items that are commonly prorated include:

1. property taxes;
2. fire insurance;
3. interest; and
4. rents.

A. 30 DAYS IS THE BASIS FOR PRORATION

All escrow companies use 30 days as a base month. For example, if an escrow closes on the 10th day of the month, all prepaid rents for that month would constitute 9/30 of the rent left for the seller, and 21/30 of the rent would go to the buyer. If the rent is $2,000, the seller's portion would be 9/30 of $2,000, or $600, and the buyer's portion would be 21/30 of $2,000 or $1,400. (Rents belong to the buyer as of the closing date.)

The two rules of proration are: (1) date escrow closes; and (2) date item is paid.

The date used in calculating proration is usually assumed to be the date of closing, but any date may be used if agreed upon by all parties. This is the case when the possession date differs from the closing date.

Property tax prorations are based on the amount the seller is paying. Escrow uses the old assessed valuation when prorating.

Taxes are prorated either from July 1, which marks the beginning of the county fiscal year, or January 1, the middle of the fiscal year. If the property taxes on a home, amounting to $2,400 per year, have been paid up to July 1, what is the proration if escrow is to be closed on June 1? In this case, the buyer would reimburse the seller for one month's taxes (or $2,400 divided by twelve months, equaling $200 per month). The seller would then be credited for the $200 in property taxes that he or she had already paid in advance.

IV. Termites and Other Problems

A. STRUCTURAL PEST CONTROL CERTIFICATION REPORT (Report and Clearance)

A Structural Pest Control Report is usually a condition of the escrow.

Pest control inspection reports are not required by law in California, but many lenders will require this report. A *STRUCTURAL PEST CONTROL CERTIFICATION REPORT is a written report given by a licensed pest control company, identifying any wood-*

ESCROW COMPANY REPORTS INFORMATION TO THE I.R.S.

All real estate transactions must be reported to the Internal Revenue Service. This is done by the escrow company or whoever handles the closing. A 1099 Form is required for any sale or exchange.

Escrow reports real estate transactions to the I.R.S. using the seller's social security number.

---

destroying pests or conditions likely to cause pest infestation. The report states the condition and correction cost of any pest, dry rot, excessive moisture, earth-wood contacts, or fungus damage in accessible areas of a structure. Who pays for the (1) pest control inspection report and (2) any required or recommended repair work is up to the buyer and seller, although they are usually paid for by the seller. There may sometimes be a local custom that dictates who will pay, while in other instances financial institutions or financing agencies will decide which one of the parties will pay.

Under the Business and Professions Code, any person, whether or not a party to a real property transaction, has a right to request and, upon payment of the required fee, to obtain directly from the Structural Pest Control Board in Sacramento, a certified copy of all inspection reports and completion notices filed during the preceding two years. As a real estate agent, you have a duty to disclose structural defects and wood-destroying organisms, if you know of any. This requirement is also written into the Commissioner's Regulations under Section 2903, which requires agents' full disclosure to buyers and sellers of any knowledge or information they may have concerning any infestations or structural defects caused by termites or other wood-destroying organisms. If there is more than one inspection, the buyer must approve, in writing, all inspections, and agree to the selected trades people.

The best time for a seller to have a termite report issued is before putting the home on the market.

California law requires that the buyer must receive a copy of the pest control certificate before the close of escrow.

B. BROKER MAINTAINS PEST CONTROL DOCUMENTATION

The Civil Code requires that the broker shall deliver a copy of the Structural Pest Control Certification Report and Notice of Work Completed to the buyer, if such a report is a condition of the deposit receipt or is a requirement imposed as a condition of financing. If more than one broker is acting as an agent in the transaction, the broker who obtained the offer (selling broker) made by the buyer, shall deliver the required documents to the buyer.

www.pestboard.ca.gov

Welcome to *California*

About the SPCB
Board Actions
Board Meetings
Committees
Education
Forms
Laws and Rules
License Lookup
Live Scan
Publications
Regulation Update

Contact Us:
SPCB

search

GOVERNOR
Schwarzenegger
Click To Visit His
Home Page

Links to Other Affiliates
- Department of Consumer Affairs
- Department of Pesticide Regulation
- Pest Control Operators of California (PCOC)
- National Pest Management Association

STRUCTURAL PEST CONTROL BOARD
'Improve and Assure the Protection of the Public in the Rendering of Structural Pest Control Service'

Welcome To Our Website!

RATE THIS SITE!

➤ What is Structural Pest Control
Click here to find out the definition of Structural Pest Control

V. Fire Insurance

When one party agrees to indemnify another for loss in return for periodic premium payments, it is called "insurance."

A. FIRE INSURANCE . . . A MUST!

Fire insurance is very inexpensive compared to the possible dollar loss due to fire, and all property owners should have this financial protection. A lending institution will require coverage for the amount of its loan. However, it is in the owner's best interest to carry sufficient fire insurance to replace the structure if it is totally destroyed. It is only necessary to insure the current replacement value of the dwelling, since the land itself cannot be destroyed by fire.

The *CALIFORNIA STANDARD FORM FIRE INSURANCE POLICY* insures the dwelling against (1) fire and (2) lightning. If your clients so desire, they may procure an *EXTENDED COVERAGE ENDORSEMENT* that will insure them against the additional perils of windstorm, explosion, hail, aircraft, smoke, riot, and vehicles not attributed to a strike or civil commotion. Other types of endorsements may insure against vandalism, malicious mischief, floods, and other damage. Coverage depends on your buyer's needs and the perils common to that area.

B. FIRE INSURANCE PRORATION

If the old policy is canceled, the buyer is charged a higher rate. It is said to be "short-rated."

When purchasing property, a buyer usually obtains a new policy. **If the seller/owner has filed an insurance claim during the previous five years, he or she must disclose this to the buyer in writing.** This may cause some hardship to the new owner/buyer in obtaining his or her own insurance. Cancellation of the seller's insurance must be initiated by the seller after close of escrow, with any unused premium to be prorated and reimbursed to the seller. It is always the buyer's choice to select his or her own house insurance. Condo insurance is chosen by the association.

Recommend to your clients who are buying insurance that they review the policy carefully to determine if they have the correct type of coverage and are carrying an adequate amount of insurance, particularly when their property value has increased.

VI. Title Insurance

A. CHAIN OF TITLE (Recorded Public History)

Abstract of title: a written summary of a property's documents that evidences title.

If one person sells a property to another person, *a recorded public history of a specific property called the* **CHAIN OF TITLE** is compiled. These public records include files at the county recorder's office, various tax agencies, federal court clerk, and the Secretary of State. *All such information about people and their real property is stored in computers (within a grantor-grantee index) and is referred to as a* **TITLE PLANT**.

A title insurance company is primarily concerned with a search of the public records, which includes: the Federal Lands Office, the County Clerk's Office, the County Recorder's Office and other sources. This search establishes what is called the "chain of title."

B. TITLE INSURANCE (Has Four Functions)

Title insurance companies are regulated by the California Insurance Commissioner. Fee schedules must be available to the general public upon request. To guarantee solvency, each title insurance company must set aside reserves.

Because many things outside the public record can affect the legality of title, title insurance functions to protect the insured.

Figure 9-9

TITLE INSURANCE also insures a lender (and property owner for an additional fee) against losses that result from imperfections in title. Title insurance companies examine the records documenting chain of title, review any risks that might not be found in the public records, interpret legality, help the seller correct any defects, and insure marketable title to the property. Title insurance is only paid once, unlike auto or fire insurance, which must be paid annually. **Figure 9-9** emphasizes the four most important functions of title insurance.

C. PRELIMINARY TITLE REPORT (Ordered First)

The first step in a title search is the ordering of the preliminary title report by the escrow officer. After the buyer or borrower completes a statement of information, a title search can begin. **See Figure 9-10.** A *PRELIMINARY TITLE REPORT is a report showing the condition of title before a sale or loan transaction.* After completion of the transaction, a title insurance policy is issued.

State law requires that buyers acknowledge receipt of the preliminary title report.

The preliminary title report consists of the following items:

1. The name of the owner and a description of the property.
2. A list of any outstanding taxes, bonds, or other assessments.
3. The identity of any covenants, conditions or restrictions.
4. Any recorded liens or other encumbrances that must be eliminated before any loan is made.

A "preliminary title report" gives the current status of items from the county records that affect the property's title.

Figure 9-10

Complete, Sign and Return
STATEMENT OF INFORMATION

Order No. 5278

To expedite the completion of your escrow, please fill out and return this form at your earliest convenience. This information is for confidential use by North American Title Company in searching the land records in connection with the order number shown above. Further explanation of the need for this information is printed on the reverse side of this form.

Please Print all information

PERSONAL IDENTIFICATION

Name

_____
FIRST NAME   FULL MIDDLE NAME—IF NONE, INDICATE   LAST NAME

Year of Birth _____ Birthplace _____ Social Security No. _____

Full name of Wife/Husband _____
FIRST NAME   FULL MIDDLE NAME—IF NONE, INDICATE   LAST NAME

Year of Birth _____ Birthplace _____ Social Security No. _____

We were married on _____ at _____
DATE   CITY AND STATE

Wife's maiden name _____

RESIDENCES DURING PAST 10 YEARS

NUMBER AND STREET	CITY	FROM (DATE)	TO (DATE)
NUMBER AND STREET	CITY	FROM (DATE)	TO (DATE)
NUMBER AND STREET	CITY	FROM (DATE)	TO (DATE)

(If more space is needed, use reverse side of form)

OCCUPATIONS DURING PAST 10 YEARS

Husband's

OCCUPATION	FIRM NAME	STREET AND CITY	FROM (DATE) TO (DATE)
OCCUPATION	FIRM NAME	STREET AND CITY	FROM (DATE) TO (DATE)
OCCUPATION	FIRM NAME	STREET AND CITY	FROM (DATE) TO (DATE)

Wife's

OCCUPATION	FIRM NAME	STREET AND CITY	FROM (DATE) TO (DATE)
OCCUPATION	FIRM NAME	STREET AND CITY	FROM (DATE) TO (DATE)

(If more space is needed, use reverse side of form)

FORMER MARRIAGE(S), IF ANY

If no former marriages, write "None" _____ Otherwise, please complete the following:

Name of former wife _____

Deceased ☐   Divorced ☐   When _____ Where _____

Name of former husband _____

Deceased ☐   Divorced ☐   When _____ Where _____

(If more space is needed, use reverse side of form)

Buyer intends to reside on the property in this transaction   Yes ☐   No ☐

THIS PORTION IS TO BE COMPLETED BY THE SELLER

The Street Address of the property in this transaction is _____
(LEAVE BLANK IF NONE)

The land is unimproved ☐ or improved with a structure of the following type;

IMPROVEMENTS: ☐ SINGLE RESIDENCE OR 1–4 FAMILY   ☐ MULTIPLE RESIDENCE   ☐ COMMERCIAL

OCCUPIED BY: ☐ OWNER   ☐ LESSEE   ☐ TENANTS

ANY PORTION OF NEW LOAN FUNDS TO BE USED FOR CONSTRUCTION

IMPROVEMENTS, REMODELING OR REPAIRS TO THIS PROPERTY HAVE BEEN MADE WITHIN THE PAST SIX MONTHS   ☐ YES   ☐ NO
IF YES,

HAVE ALL COSTS FOR LABOR AND MATERIALS ARISING IN CONNECTION THEREWITH BEEN PAID IN FULL?   ☐ YES   ☐ NO

The undersigned declare, under penalty of perjury, that the foregoing is true and correct.

DATE _____   _____

HOME PHONE _____   BUSINESS PHONE _____   _____
(IF MARRIED, BOTH HUSBAND AND WIFE SHOULD SIGN)

NAT 44 (5/88)

VII. Types of Title Insurance Policies

All title insurance policies in California cover policyholders as of the date of the policy.

A. CALIFORNIA LAND TITLE ASSOCIATION (CLTA)
(Standard Coverage Policy)

In California, the standard title insurance policy is the CLTA. The *CALIFORNIA LAND TITLE ASSOCIATION (CLTA) policy is the basic title insurance policy.* It may be issued to insure a lender only, or an owner only, or it may insure both the lender and the owner (a joint-protection standard coverage policy). This standard policy insures the lender only, unless the owner requests and pays for owner coverage.

CLTA is the acronym for the state trade association, California Land Title Association®.

Figure 9-11 is a sample of a standard CLTA policy form.

Besides insuring against all items of record, the CLTA policy offers protection against many off-record risks. Some of these off-record risks include forgeries, acts of minors and incompetents, acts of an agent whose authority has terminated, invalid deed delivery, unrecorded federal estate tax liens, undisclosed rights of husband and wife when the chain of title states "unmarried," and the expenses (including attorneys' fees) incurred in defending title.

The "standard" and most common title insurance policy in California is the CLTA policy (no survey). The CLTA policy protects against:

1) someone else who owns a recorded interest in your title; 2) a document not properly signed; 3) forgery, fraud, duress, incompetency; 4) defective recording of a document; 5) unmarketability of title; 6) restrictive covenants; and 7) lack of a right of access to and from the land.

It is very important to note those items not included in the standard policy. The items not included are:

1. Easements, encumbrances, and liens that are not shown by the public record.
2. Rights or claims of persons in physical possession of the land.
3. Unrecorded claims not shown by the public record that could be ascertained by physical inspection or correct survey.
4. Mining claims, reservations in patents, water rights, and government actions, such as zoning ordinances.

Figure 9-11

POLICY OF TITLE INSURANCE

ISSUED BY

SUBJECT TO THE EXCLUSIONS FROM COVERAGE, THE EXCEPTIONS FROM COVERAGE CONTAINED IN SCHEDULE B AND THE CONDITIONS AND STIPULATIONS, NORTH AMERICAN TITLE INSURANCE COMPANY, a California corporation, herein called the Company, insures, as of Date of Policy shown in Schedule A, against loss or damage, not exceeding the Amount of Insurance stated in Schedule A, sustained or incurred by the insured by reason of:

1. Title to the estate or interest described in Schedule A being vested otherwise than as stated therein;
2. Any defect in or lien or encumbrance on such title;
3. Unmarketability of the title;
4. Lack of a right of access to and from the land;
5. The invalidity or unenforceability of the lien of the insured mortgage upon the title;
6. The priority of any lien or encumbrance over the lien of the insured mortgage;
7. Lack of priority of the lien of the insured mortgage over any statutory lien for services, labor or material:
    (a) arising from an improvement or work related to the land which is contracted for or commenced prior to Date of Policy; or
    (b) arising from an improvement or work related to the land which is contracted for or commenced subsequent to Date of Policy and which is financed in whole or in part by proceeds of the indebtedness secured by the insured mortgage which at Date of Policy the insured has advanced or is obligated to advance.
8. Any assessments for street improvements under construction or completed at Date of Policy which now have gained or hereafter may gain priority over the insured mortgage; or
9. The invalidity or unenforceability of any assignment of the insured mortgage, provided the assignment is shown in Schedule A, or the failure of the assignment shown in Schedule A to vest title to the insured mortgage in the named insured assignee free and clear of all liens.

The Company will also pay the costs, attorneys' fees and expenses incurred in defense of the title or the lien of the insured mortgage, as insured, but only to the extent provided in the Conditions and Stipulations.

NORTH AMERICAN TITLE INSURANCE COMPANY

BY _Gerald B Beery_ PRESIDENT

ATTEST _____ SECRETARY

SCHEDULE A

POLICY NO. 116823   FILE NO.: 14-15360-63

AMOUNT OF INSURANCE: $296,800.00   PREMIUM: $1,161.75

DATE OF POLICY: JULY 22, 1992 AT 8:00 A.M.

1. **NAME OF INSURED:**

SYCAMORE FINANCIAL GROUP, INC., A CALIFORNIA CORPORATION

2. **THE ESTATE OR INTEREST IN THE LAND WHICH IS ENCUMBERED BY THE INSURED MORTGAGE IS:**

A CONDOMINIUM, AS DEFINED IN SECTION 783 OF THE CALIFORNIA CIVIL CODE, IN FEE

3. **TITLE TO THE ESTATE OR INTEREST IN THE LAND IS VESTED IN:**

WALTER ROY HUBER AND DEBBIE R. HUBER, HUSBAND AND WIFE AS COMMUNITY PROPERTY

4. **THE INSURED MORTGAGE AND ASSIGNMENTS THEREOF, IF ANY, ARE DESCRIBED AS FOLLOWS:**

A DEED OF TRUST TO SECURE AN INDEBTEDNESS IN THE AMOUNT SHOWN BELOW AND ANY OTHER OBLIGATIONS SECURED THEREBY:

RECORDED: JULY 22, 1992 AS INSTRUMENT NO. 92-1329290 OF
                OFFICIAL RECORDS
AMOUNT: $296,800.00
DATED: JULY 13, 1992
TRUSTOR: WALTER ROY HUBER AND DEBBIE R. HUBER, HUSBAND AND
                WIFE AS COMMUNITY PROPERTY
TRUSTEE: UTICA ESCROW INC., A CALIFORNIA CORPORATION
BENEFICIARY: SYCAMORE FINANCIAL GROUP, INC., A CALIFORNIA
                CORPORATION

5. **THE LAND REFERRED TO IN THIS POLICY IS DESCRIBED AS FOLLOWS:**

PARCEL 1:

THAT PORTION OF PARCEL A OF PARCEL MAP L.A. NO. 3111, IN THE CITY OF LOS ANGELES, COUNTY OF LOS ANGELES, STATE OF CALIFORNIA, AS PER MAP FILED IN BOOK 72 PAGE 26 OF PARCEL MAPS, IN THE OFFICE OF THE COUNTY RECORDER OF SAID COUNTY, SHOWN AND DEFINED AS UNIT 1 AND AIR SPACE A ON THE CONDOMINIUM PLAN, RECORDED DECEMBER 17, 1976 AS INSTRUMENT NO. 5334, OF OFFICIAL RECORDS OF SAID COUNTY.

PARCEL 2:

AN UNDIVIDED 1/4 INTEREST IN AND TO PARCEL A OF SAID PARCEL MAP LOS ANGELES NO. 3111.

EXCEPT THEREFROM THOSE PORTIONS SHOWN AND DEFINED AS UNITS 1 TO 4 AND AIR SPACE A AND B ON SAID CONDOMINIUM PLAN.

EXCLUSIONS FROM COVERAGE

The following matters are expressly excluded from the coverage of this policy and the Company will not pay loss or damage, costs, attorneys' fees or expenses which arise by reason of:

1. (a) Any law, ordinance or governmental regulation (including but not limited to building and zoning laws, ordinances, or regulations) restricting, regulating, prohibiting or relating to (i) the occupancy, use, or enjoyment of the land; (ii) the character, dimensions or location of any improvement now or hereafter erected on the land; (iii) a separation in ownership or a change in the dimensions or area of the land or any parcel of which the land is or was a part; or (iv) environmental protection, or the effect of any violation of these laws, ordinances or governmental regulations, except to the extent that a notice of the enforcement thereof or a notice of a defect, lien or encumbrance resulting from a violation or alleged violation affecting the land has been recorded in the public records at Date of Policy.
   (b) Any governmental police power not excluded by (a) above, except to the extent that a notice of the exercise thereof or a notice of a defect, lien or encumbrance resulting from a violation or alleged violation affecting the land has been recorded in the public records at Date of Policy.
2. Rights of eminent domain unless notice of the exercise thereof has been recorded in the public records at Date of Policy, but not excluding from coverage any taking which has occurred prior to Date of Policy which would be binding on the rights of a purchaser for value without knowledge.
3. Defects, liens, encumbrances, adverse claims or other matters:
   (a) created, suffered, assumed or agreed to by the insured claimant;
   (b) not known to the Company, not recorded in the public records at Date of Policy, but known to the insured claimant and not disclosed in writing to the Company by the insured claimant prior to the date the insured claimant became an insured under this policy;
   (c) resulting in no loss or damage to the insured claimant;
   (d) attaching or created subsequent to Date of Policy (except to the extent that this policy insures the priority of the lien of the insured mortgage over any statutory lien for services, labor or material or the extent insurance is afforded herein as to assessments for street improvements under construction or completed at Date of Policy); or
   (e) resulting in loss or damage which would not have been sustained if the insured claimant had paid value for the insured mortgage.
4. Unenforceability of the lien of the insured mortgage because of the inability or failure of the insured at Date of Policy, or the inability or failure of any subsequent owner of the indebtedness, to comply with applicable doing business laws of the state in which the land is situated.
5. Invalidity or unenforceability of the lien of the insured mortgage, or claim thereof, which arises out of the transaction evidenced by the insured mortgage and is based upon usury or any consumer credit protection or truth in lending law.
6. Any statutory lien for services, labor or materials (or the claim of priority of any statutory lien for services, labor or materials over the lien of the insured mortgage) arising from an improvement or work related to the land which is contracted for and commenced subsequent to Date of Policy and is not financed in whole or in part by proceeds of the indebtedness secured by the insured mortgage which at Date of Policy the insured has advanced or is obligated to advance.
7. Any claim, which arises out of the transaction creating the interest of the mortgagee insured by this policy, by reason of the operation of federal bankruptcy, state insolvency, or similar creditors' rights laws.

CONDITIONS AND STIPULATIONS

1. DEFINITION OF TERMS.
The following terms when used in this policy mean:

(a) "insured": the insured named in Schedule A. The term "insured" also includes

(i) the owner of the indebtedness secured by the insured mortgage and each successor in ownership of the indebtedness except a successor who is an obligor under the provisions of Section 12(c) of these Conditions and Stipulations (reserving, however, all rights and defenses as to any successor that the Company would have had against any predecessor insured, unless the successor acquired the indebtedness as a purchaser for value without knowledge of the asserted defect, lien, encumbrance, adverse claim or other matter insured against by this policy as affecting title to the estate or interest in the land);

(ii) any governmental agency or governmental instrumentality which is an insurer or guarantor under an insurance contract or guaranty insuring or guaranteeing the indebtedness secured by the insured mortgage, or any part thereof, whether named as an insured herein or not;

(iii) the parties designated in Section 2(a) of these Conditions and Stipulations.

(b) "insured claimant": an insured claiming loss or damage.

(c) "knowledge" or "known": actual knowledge, not constructive knowledge or notice which may be imputed to an insured by reason of the public records as defined in this policy or any other records which impart constructive notice of matters affecting the land.

(d) "land": the land described or referred to in Schedule (A), and improvements affixed thereto which by law constitute real property. The term "land" does not include any property beyond the lines of the area described or referred to in Schedule (A), nor any right, title, interest, estate or easement in abutting streets, roads, avenues, alleys, lanes, ways or waterways, but nothing herein shall modify or limit the extent to which a right of access to and from the land is insured by this policy.

(e) "mortgage": mortgage, deed of trust, trust deed, or other security instrument.

(f) "public records": records established under state statutes at Date of Policy for the purpose of imparting constructive notice of matters relating to real property to purchasers for value and without knowledge. With respect to Section 1(a)(iv) of the Exclusions From Coverage, "public records" shall also include environmental protection liens filed in the records of the clerk of the United States district court for the district in which the land is located.

(g) "unmarketability of the title": an alleged or apparent matter affecting the title to the land, not excluded or excepted from coverage, which would entitle a purchaser of the estate or interest described in Schedule A or the insured mortgage to be released from the obligation to purchase by virtue of a contractual condition requiring the delivery of marketable title.

2. CONTINUATION OF INSURANCE.

(a) **After Acquisition of Title.** The coverage of this policy shall continue in force as of Date of Policy in favor of (i) an insured who acquires all or any part of the estate or interest in the land by foreclosure, trustee's sale, conveyance in lieu of foreclosure, or other legal manner which discharges the lien of the insured mortgage; (ii) a transferee of the estate or interest so acquired from an insured corporation, provided the transferee is the parent or wholly-owned subsidiary of the insured corporation, and their corporate successors by operation of law and not by purchase, subject to any rights or defenses the Company may have against any predecessor insureds; and (iii) any governmental agency or governmental instrumentality which acquires all or any part of the estate or interest pursuant to a contract of insurance or guaranty insuring or guaranteeing the indebtedness secured by the insured mortgage.

settlement, and (ii) in any other lawful act which in the opinion of the Company may be necessary or desirable to establish the title to the estate or interest or the lien of the insured mortgage, as insured. If the Company is prejudiced by the failure of the insured to furnish the required cooperation, the Company's obligations to the insured under the policy shall terminate, including any liability or obligation to defend, prosecute, or continue any litigation, with regard to the matter or matters requiring such cooperation.

5. PROOF OF LOSS OR DAMAGE.

In addition to and after the notices required under Section 3 of these Conditions and Stipulations have been provided the Company, a proof of loss or damage signed and sworn to by the insured claimant shall be furnished to the Company within 90 days after the insured claimant shall ascertain the facts giving rise to the loss or damage. The proof of loss or damage shall describe the defect in, or lien or encumbrance on the title, or other matter insured against by this policy which constitutes the basis of loss or damage and shall state, to the extent possible, the basis of calculating the amount of the loss or damage. If the Company is prejudiced by the failure of the insured claimant to provide the required proof of loss or damage, the Company's obligations to the insured under the policy shall terminate, including any liability or obligation to defend, prosecute, or continue any litigation, with regard to the matter or matters requiring such proof of loss or damage.

In addition, the insured claimant may reasonably be required to submit to examination under oath by any authorized representative of the Company and shall produce for examination, inspection and copying, at such reasonable times and places as may be designated by any authorized representative of the Company, all records, books, ledgers, checks, correspondence and memoranda, whether bearing a date before or after Date of Policy, which reasonably pertain to the loss or damage. Further, if requested by any authorized representative of the Company, the insured claimant shall grant its permission, in writing, for any authorized representative of the Company to examine, inspect and copy all records, books, ledgers, checks, correspondence and memoranda in the custody or control of a third party, which reasonably pertain to the loss or damage. All information designated as confidential by the insured claimant provided to the Company pursuant to this Section shall not be disclosed to others unless, in the reasonable judgment of the Company, it is necessary in the administration of the claim. Failure of the insured claimant to submit for examination under oath, produce other reasonably requested information or grant permission to secure reasonably necessary information from third parties as required in this paragraph, unless prohibited by law or governmental regulation, shall terminate any liability of the Company under this policy as to that claim.

the insured was and continued to be obligated to advance at and after Date of Policy.

9. REDUCTION OF INSURANCE; REDUCTION OR TERMINATION OF LIABILITY.

(a) All payments under this policy, except payments made for costs, attorneys' fees and expenses, shall reduce the amount of the insurance pro tanto. However, any payments made prior to the acquisition of title to the estate or interest as provided in Section 2(a) of these Conditions and Stipulations shall not reduce pro tanto the amount of the insurance afforded under this policy except to the extent that the payments reduce the amount of the indebtedness secured by the insured mortgage.

(b) Payment in part by any person of the principal of the indebtedness, or any other obligation secured by the insured mortgage, or any voluntary partial satisfaction or release of the insured mortgage, to the extent of the payment, satisfaction or release, shall reduce the amount of insurance pro tanto. The amount of insurance may thereafter be increased by accruing interest and advances made to protect the lien of the insured mortgage and secured thereby, with interest thereon, provided in no event shall the amount of insurance be greater than the amount of insurance stated in Schedule A.

(c) Payment in full by any person or the voluntary satisfaction or release of the insured mortgage shall terminate all liability of the Company except as provided in Section 2(a) of these Conditions and Stipulations.

10. LIABILITY NONCUMULATIVE.

If the insured acquires title to the estate or interest in satisfaction of the indebtedness secured by the insured mortgage, or any part thereof, it is expressly understood that the amount of insurance under this policy shall be reduced by any amount the Company may pay under any policy insuring a mortgage to which exception is taken in Schedule B or to which the insured has agreed, assumed, or taken subject, or which is hereafter executed by an insured and which is a charge or lien on the estate or interest described or referred to in Schedule A, and the amount so paid shall be deemed a payment under this policy.

11. PAYMENT OF LOSS.

(a) No payment shall be made without producing this policy for endorsement of the payment unless the policy has been lost or destroyed, in which case proof of loss or destruction shall be furnished to the satisfaction of the Company.

(b) When liability and the extent of loss or damage has been definitely fixed in accordance with these Conditions and Stipulations, the loss or damage shall be payable within 30 days thereafter.

(b) After Conveyance of Title. The coverage of this policy shall continue in force as of Date of Policy in favor of an insured only so long as the insured retains an estate or interest in the land, or holds an indebtedness secured by a purchase money mortgage given by a purchaser from the insured, or only so long as the insured shall have liability by reason of covenants of warranty made by the insured in any transfer or conveyance of the estate or interest. This policy shall not continue in force in favor of any purchaser from the insured of either (i) an estate or interest in the land, or (ii) an indebtedness secured by a purchase money mortgage given to the insured.

(c) Amount of Insurance: The amount of insurance after the acquisition or after the conveyance shall in neither event exceed the least of:

(i) the amount of insurance stated in Schedule A;

(ii) the amount of the principal of the indebtedness secured by the insured mortgage as of Date of Policy, interest thereon, expenses of foreclosure, amounts advanced pursuant to the insured mortgage to assure compliance with laws or to protect the lien of the insured mortgage prior to the time of acquisition of the estate or interest in the land and secured thereby and reasonable amounts expended to prevent deterioration of improvements, but reduced by the amount of all payments made; or

(iii) the amount paid by any governmental agency or governmental instrumentality, if the agency or instrumentality is the insured claimant, in the acquisition of the estate or interest in satisfaction of its insurance contract or guaranty.

3. NOTICE OF CLAIM TO BE GIVEN BY INSURED CLAIMANT.

The insured shall notify the Company promptly in writing (i) in case of any litigation as set forth in Section 4(a) below, (ii) in case knowledge shall come to an insured hereunder of any claim of title or interest which is adverse to the title to the estate or interest or the lien of the insured mortgage, as insured, and which might cause loss or damage for which the Company may be liable by virtue of this policy, or (iii) if title to the estate or interest or the lien of the insured mortgage, as insured, is rejected as unmarketable. If prompt notice shall not be given to the Company, then as to the insured all liability of the Company shall terminate with regard to the matter or matters for which prompt notice is required; provided, however, that failure to notify the Company shall in no case prejudice the rights of any insured under this policy unless the Company shall be prejudiced by the failure and then only to the extent of the prejudice.

4. DEFENSE AND PROSECUTION OF ACTIONS; DUTY OF INSURED CLAIMANT TO COOPERATE.

(a) Upon written request by the insured and subject to the options contained in Section 6 of these Conditions and Stipulations, the Company, at its own cost and without unreasonable delay, shall provide for the defense of an insured in litigation in which any third party asserts a claim adverse to the title or interest as insured, but only as to those stated causes of action alleging a defect, lien or encumbrance or other matter insured against by this policy. The Company shall have the right to select counsel of its choice (subject to the right of the insured to object for reasonable cause) to represent the insured as to those stated causes of action and shall not be liable for and will not pay the fees of any other counsel. The Company will not pay any fees, costs or expenses incurred by the insured in the defense of those causes of action which allege matters not insured against by this policy.

(b) The Company shall have the right, at its own cost, to institute and prosecute any action or proceeding or to do any other act which in its opinion may be necessary or desirable to establish the title to the estate or interest or the lien of the insured mortgage, as insured, or to prevent or reduce loss or damage to the insured. The Company may take any appropriate action under the terms of this policy, whether or not it shall be liable hereunder, and shall not thereby concede liability or waive any provision of this policy. If the Company shall exercise its rights under this paragraph, it shall do so diligently.

(c) Whenever the Company shall have brought an action or interposed a defense as required or permitted by the provisions of this policy, the Company may pursue any litigation to final determination by a court of competent jurisdiction and expressly reserves the right, in its sole discretion, to appeal from any adverse judgment or order.

(d) In all cases where this policy permits or requires the Company to prosecute or provide for the defense of any action or proceeding, the insured shall secure to the Company the right to so prosecute or provide defense in the action or proceeding, and all appeals therein, and permit the Company to use, at its option, the name of the insured for this purpose. Whenever requested by the Company, the insured, at the Company's expense, shall give the Company all reasonable aid (i) in any action or proceeding, securing evidence, obtaining witnesses, prosecuting or defending the action or proceeding, or effecting

6. OPTIONS TO PAY OR OTHERWISE SETTLE CLAIMS; TERMINATION OF LIABILITY.

In case of a claim under this policy, the Company shall have the following options:

(a) To Pay or Tender Payment of the Amount of Insurance or to Purchase the Indebtedness.

(i) to pay or tender payment of the amount of insurance under this policy together with any costs, attorneys' fees and expenses incurred by the insured claimant, which were authorized by the Company, up to the time of payment or tender of payment and which the Company is obligated to pay; or

(ii) to purchase the indebtedness secured by the insured mortgage for the amount owing thereon together with any costs, attorneys' fees and expenses incurred by the insured claimant which were authorized by the Company up to the time of purchase and which the Company is obligated to pay.

If the Company offers to purchase the indebtedness as herein provided, the owner of the indebtedness shall transfer, assign, and convey the indebtedness and the insured mortgage, together with any collateral security, to the Company upon payment therefor.

Upon the exercise by the Company of either of the options provided for in paragraphs a(i) or (ii), all liability and obligations to the insured under this policy, other than to make the payment required in those paragraphs, shall terminate, including any liability or obligation to defend, prosecute, or continue any litigation, and the policy shall be surrendered to the Company for cancellation.

(b) To Pay or Otherwise Settle With Parties Other than the Insured or With the Insured Claimant.

(i) to pay or otherwise settle with other parties for or in the name of an insured claimant any claim insured against under this policy, together with any costs, attorneys' fees and expenses incurred by the insured claimant which were authorized by the Company up to the time of payment and which the Company is obligated to pay; or

(ii) to pay or otherwise settle with the insured claimant the loss or damage provided for under this policy, together with any costs, attorneys' fees and expenses incurred by the insured claimant which were authorized by the Company up to the time of payment and which the Company is obligated to pay.

Upon the exercise by the Company of either of the options provided for in paragraphs b(i) or (ii), the Company's obligations to the insured under this policy for the claimed loss or damage, other than the payments required to be made, shall terminate, including any liability or obligation to defend, prosecute or continue any litigation.

7. DETERMINATION AND EXTENT OF LIABILITY.

This policy is a contract of indemnity against actual monetary loss or damage sustained or incurred by the insured claimant who has suffered loss or damage by reason of matters insured against by this policy and only to the extent herein described.

(a) The liability of the Company under this policy shall not exceed the least of:

(i) the amount of insurance stated in Schedule A, or, if applicable, the amount of insurance as defined in Section 2 (c) of these Conditions and Stipulations;

(ii) the amount of the unpaid principal indebtedness secured by the insured mortgage as limited or provided under Section 8 of these Conditions and Stipulations or as reduced under Section 9 of these Conditions and Stipulations, at the time the loss or damage insured against by this policy occurs, together with interest thereon; or

(iii) the difference between the value of the insured estate or interest as insured and the value of the insured estate or interest subject to the defect, lien or encumbrance insured against by this policy.

(b) In the event the insured has acquired the estate or interest in the manner described in Section 2(a) of these Conditions and Stipulations or has conveyed the title, then the liability of the Company shall continue as set forth in Section 7(a) of these Conditions and Stipulations.

(c) The Company will pay only those costs, attorneys' fees and expenses incurred in accordance with Section 4 of these Conditions and Stipulations.

8. LIMITATION OF LIABILITY.

(a) If the Company establishes the title, or removes the alleged defect, lien or encumbrance, or cures the lack of a right of access to or from the land, or cures the claim of unmarketability of title, or otherwise establishes the lien of the insured mortgage, all as insured, in a reasonably diligent manner by any method, including litigation and the completion of any appeals therefrom, it shall have fully performed its obligations with respect to that matter and shall not be liable for any loss or damage caused thereby.

(b) In the event of any litigation, including litigation by the Company or with the Company's consent, the Company shall have no liability for loss or damage until there has been a final determination by a court of competent jurisdiction, and disposition of all appeals therefrom, adverse to the title or to the lien of the insured mortgage, as insured.

(c) The Company shall not be liable for loss or damage to any insured for liability voluntarily assumed by the insured in settling any claim or suit without the prior written consent of the Company.

(d) The Company shall not be liable for:

(i) any indebtedness created subsequent to Date of Policy except for advances made to protect the lien of the insured mortgage and secured thereby and reasonable amounts expended to prevent deterioration of improvements; or

(ii) construction loan advances made subsequent to Date of Policy, except construction loan advances made subsequent to Date of Policy for the purpose of financing in whole or in part the construction of an improvement to the land which at Date of Policy were secured by the insured mortgage and which

12. SUBROGATION UPON PAYMENT OR SETTLEMENT.

(a) The Company's Right of Subrogation.

Whenever the Company shall have settled and paid a claim under this policy, all right of subrogation shall vest in the Company unaffected by any act of the insured claimant.

The Company shall be subrogated to and be entitled to all rights and remedies which the insured claimant would have had against any person or property in respect to the claim had this policy not been issued. If requested by the Company, the insured claimant shall transfer to the Company all rights and remedies against any person or property necessary in order to perfect this right of subrogation. The insured claimant shall permit the Company to sue, compromise or settle in the name of the insured claimant and to use the name of the insured claimant in any transaction or litigation involving these rights or remedies.

If a payment on account of a claim does not fully cover the loss of the insured claimant, the Company shall be subrogated to all rights and remedies of the insured claimant after the insured claimant shall have recovered its principal, interest, and costs of collection.

(b) The Insured's Rights and Limitations.

Notwithstanding the foregoing, the owner of the indebtedness secured by the insured mortgage, provided the priority of the lien of the insured mortgage or its enforceability is not affected, may release or substitute the personal liability of any debtor or guarantor, or extend or otherwise modify the terms of payment, or release a portion of the estate or interest from the lien of the insured mortgage, or release any collateral security for the indebtedness.

When the permitted acts of the insured claimant occur and the insured has knowledge of any claim of title or interest adverse to the title to the estate or interest or the priority or enforceability of the lien of the insured mortgage, as insured, the Company shall be required to pay only that part of any losses insured against by this policy which shall exceed the amount, if any, lost to the Company by reason of the impairment by the insured claimant of the Company's right of subrogation.

(c) The Company's Rights Against Non-insured Obligors.

The Company's right of subrogation against non-insured obligors shall exist and shall include, without limitation, the rights of the insured to indemnities, guaranties, other policies of insurance or bonds, notwithstanding any terms or conditions contained in those instruments which provide for subrogation rights by reason of this policy.

The Company's right of subrogation shall not be avoided by acquisition of the insured mortgage by an obligor (except an obligor described in Section 1(a)(ii) of these Conditions and Stipulations) who acquires the insured mortgage as a result of an indemnity, guarantee, other policy of insurance, or bond and the obligor will not be an insured under this policy, notwithstanding Section 1(a)(i) of these Conditions and Stipulations.

13. ARBITRATION.

Unless prohibited by applicable law, either the Company or the insured may demand arbitration pursuant to the Title Insurance Arbitration Rules of the American Arbitration Association. Arbitrable matters may include, but are not limited to, any controversy or claim between the Company and the insured arising out of or relating to this policy, any service of the Company in connection with its issuance or the breach of a policy provision or other obligation. All arbitrable matters when the Amount of Insurance is $1,000,000 or less shall be arbitrated at the option of either the Company or the insured. All arbitrable matters when the Amount of Insurance is in excess of $1,000,000 shall be arbitrated only when agreed to by both the Company and the insured. Arbitration pursuant to this policy and under the Rules in effect on the date the demand for arbitration is made or, at the option of the insured, the Rules in effect at Date of Policy shall be binding upon the parties. The award may include attorneys' fees only if the laws of the state in which the land is located permit a court to award attorneys' fees to a prevailing party. Judgment upon the award rendered by the Arbitrator(s) may be entered in any court having jurisdiction thereof.

The law of the situs of the land shall apply to an arbitration under the Title Insurance Arbitration Rules.

A copy of the Rules may be obtained from the Company upon request.

14. LIABILITY LIMITED TO THIS POLICY; POLICY ENTIRE CONTRACT.

(a) This policy together with all endorsements, if any, attached hereto by the Company is the entire policy and contract between the insured and the Company. In interpreting any provision of this policy, this policy shall be construed as a whole.

(b) Any claim of loss or damage, whether or not based on negligence, and which arises out of the status of the lien of the insured mortgage or of the title to the estate or interest covered hereby or by any action asserting such claim, shall be restricted to this policy.

(c) No amendment of or endorsement to this policy can be made except by a writing endorsed hereon or attached hereto signed by either the President, a Vice President, the Secretary, an Assistant Secretary, or validating officer or authorized signatory of the Company.

15. SEVERABILITY.

In the event any provision of this policy is held invalid or unenforceable under applicable law, the policy shall be deemed not to include that provision and all other provisions shall remain in full force and effect.

16. NOTICES, WHERE SENT.

All notices required to be given the Company and any statement in writing required to be furnished the Company shall include the number of this policy and shall be addressed to the Company at 114 East Fifth Street, Santa Ana, California 92701, or to the office which issued this policy.

Standard title insurance (CLTA) does NOT insure against undisclosed liens placed on a property by a grantor (although it is warranted in a grant deed). NO title insurance policy covers everything.

B. AMERICAN LAND TITLE ASSOCIATION (ALTA)
(Extended Coverage Policy - Survey Included)

Most lenders require more protection than provided for by the standard coverage (CLTA) policy. They require the extended coverage (ALTA) policy.

The *AMERICAN LAND TITLE ASSOCIATION (ALTA) policy is an extended coverage policy that insures against many exclusions in the standard coverage (CLTA) policy.* The ALTA policy (which includes a competent survey or physical inspection) is usually required by California lenders and by out-of-state lenders who are not able to make a personal physical inspection of the property.

An extended ALTA title insurance policy is a lender's policy. It protects only the lender. If an owner wants this kind of protection, he or she should request the extended ALTA Owner's Policy.

Purchasers should note that there are still certain exceptions to the CLTA standard policy and even to the ALTA extended policy. There is no insurance coverage for the following:

1. Defects known to the insured at the time the policy was issued, but not designated in writing.

2. Government regulations regarding occupancy and use (zoning).

No title insurance protects against governmental regulations (zoning changes) or defects known to the insured.

There are three different kinds of standard coverage title insurance: 1) an owner's policy; 2) a lender's policy; and 3) a joint protection policy. A smart agent makes sure the buyer and lender get the kind they want and understand the kind they have!

C. ALTA-R (One-to-Four Residential Units)

The **ALTA-R POLICY** *is recommended by title companies for one-to-four unit owner-occupied residential dwellings*. It doesn't include a survey because the property lines are already established by a recorded subdivision map. Since the title company does not have to do a survey, it gives the buyer more coverage for the same price. The CAR® deposit receipt includes the ALTA-R as the preferred residential title policy choice.

D. WHO PAYS TITLE INSURANCE FEES?

Title insurance fees are a part of the escrow closing costs. Title insurance companies are required to publish rate schedules and charge according to the published rates. Who assumes payment of the fees, however, varies depending upon the area in which one lives.

In Southern California it is customary for the seller to pay the title fees, whereas in Northern California it is usually the buyer who assumes the cost. Because there is no law determining who must pay, it should be stated in the deposit receipt to prevent any misunderstanding. This, however, covers only the standard CLTA policy. The additional cost of the ALTA extended policy is usually charged to the party purchasing the property (the buyer).

E. TITLE INSURANCE DISCLOSURE

In any escrow transaction for the purchase or exchange of real property where a title insurance policy will not be issued to the buyer (or exchanger), the buyer (or exchanger) must sign and acknowledge a disclosure statement stating that it may be advisable to obtain title insurance.

VIII. Real Estate Settlement Procedures Act (RESPA)

RESPA allows borrowers to shop for settlement services. The law covers first loans on one-to-four unit residential dwellings.

The **REAL ESTATE SETTLEMENT PROCEDURES ACT (RESPA)** *is a law for the sale or transfer of one-to-four residential units requiring: 1) specific procedures and 2) forms for settlements (closing costs) involving most home loans from financial institutions with federally insured deposits, including FHA and VA loans.*

This law, although amended several times, states that the closing settlement cost of a real estate transaction must be made known to the borrower, on or before the settlement date, although, at the buyer's request, it must be provided one business day before escrow closes. Before this law was passed, buyers were unaware of the exact amount needed until the actual escrow closing day. Sometimes the buyers were surprised to find that more money than expected was needed to complete the procedure. The current law alleviates this problem.

RESPA disclosure requirements are for federally related lenders. This means almost all lenders.

Other provisions required by the Real Estate Settlement Procedures Act include the following:

1. At the time of loan application, or within three business days, the lender must give a good faith estimate of the total closing charges to the borrower.

2. At the same time, the lender must furnish the buyer with an information booklet.

3. The escrow agent must give a uniform settlement statement to the borrower, the seller, and the lender. **Figure 9-12** illustrates the settlement statement. It must be furnished by the time of settlement, except when the borrower waives it, or in areas where the HUD (Department of Housing and Urban Development) permits a later date for supplying it.

The settlement statement must be delivered on or before the date of settlement, at no charge. The buyer can request it one business day before closing.

4. Individuals are prohibited from receiving kickbacks and unearned fees. Payments to cooperating brokerages and referral agreements between brokers are exempt.

5. No seller may require a buyer to purchase title insurance from any particular company as a condition of sale.

There are penalties for "kickbacks" and unearned fees. The seller may request a specific title insurer, but only the buyer can require a specific insurance company.

IX. California Escrow Association

The California Escrow Association has developed a statewide program to promote professional service and educational opportunities for its members. Many community colleges have also adopted certificate courses for escrow personnel and real estate brokers to provide a better understanding of the highly technical escrow field.

Figure 9-12

A.	B. TYPE OF LOAN	
U.S. DEPARTMENT OF HOUSING AND URBAN DEVELOPMENT	1. [ ] FHA 2. [ ] FmHA 3. [X] Conv. unis 4. [ ] VA 5. [ ] Conv. ins	
SETTLEMENT STATEMENT	6. ESCROW NUMBER: 1-10533	7. LOAN NUMBER:
	8. MORTGAGE INSURANCE NUMBER:	

THIS NOTE IS FURNISHED TO GIVE YOU A STATEMENT OF THE ACTUAL SETTLEMENT COSTS. AMOUNTS PAID TO AND BY THE SETTLEMENT AGENT ARE SHOWN. ITEMS MARKED "(P.O.C.)" WERE PAID OUTSIDE OF THE CLOSING; THEY ARE SHOWN HERE FOR INFORMATIONAL PURPOSES AND ARE NOT INCLUDED IN THE TOTALS.

D. NAME OF BORROWER:	E. NAME OF SELLER:	F. NAME OF LENDER:
JOHN BUYER JANE BUYER 123 Purchase Lane Glendale, CA	JOHN SELLER JANE SELLER	GET SMART SAVINGS AND LOAN 123 Lending Lane Beverly Hills, CA 91020

G. PROPERTY LOCATION:	H. SETTLEMENT AGENT: COLONIAL ESCROW, INC.	I. SETTLEMENT DATE:
123 PURCHASE LANE GLENDALE, CA	PLACE OF SETTLEMENT: 601 EAST GLENOAKS BLVD. SUITE 210 GLENDALE, CA 91207 P.O. BOX 433 GLENDALE, CA 91209-0433	06/01/20

J. SUMMARY OF BORROWER'S TRANSACTIONS		K. SUMMARY OF SELLER'S TRANSACTIONS	
100. GROSS AMOUNT DUE FROM BORROWER		**400. GROSS AMOUNT DUE TO SELLER**	
101. CONTRACT SALES PRICE	800,000.00	401. CONTRACT SALES PRICE	800,000.00
102. PERSONAL PROPERTY		402. PERSONAL PROPERTY	
103. SETTL. CHRGS. TO BORROWER (LINE 1400)	10,122.01	403. DEPOSITS	
104.		404.	
105.		405.	
Adjustments: items paid by seller in advance		Adjustments: items paid by seller in advance	
106. CITY/TOWN TAXES		406. CITY/TOWN TAXES	
107. COUNTY TAXES		407. COUNTY TAXES	
108. ASSESSMENTS		408. ASSESSMENTS	
109. TAXES : 06/01/20 TO 07/01/20	666.67	409. TAXES : 06/01/20 TO 07/01/20	666.67
110.		410.	
111.		411.	
112.		412.	
120. GROSS AMOUNT DUE FROM BORROWER	810,788.68	420. GROSS AMOUNT DUE TO SELLER	800,666.67
200. AMOUNTS PAID BY OR IN BEHALF OF BORROWER		**500. REDUCTIONS IN AMOUNT DUE TO SELLER**	
201. DEPOSITS	91,000.00	501. EXCESS DEPOSIT	
202. PRINCIPAL AMOUNT OF NEW LOAN(S)	640,000.00	502. SETTL. CHRGS. TO SELLER (LINE 1400)	54,845.00
203. EXISTING LOAN(S) TAKEN SUBJECT TO		503. EXISTING LOAN(S) TAKEN SUBJECT TO	
204. NEW 2ND TRUST DEED	80,000.00	504. PAYOFF TO MOST SUPERIOR SAVINGS AND L	490,000.00
205.		505. INTEREST FROM 05/01/20 TO 06/01/20	4,161.64
206.		506. FORWARDING FEE	50.00
207.		507. RECONVEYANCE FEE	60.00
208.		508. NEW 2ND TRUST DEED	80,000.00
209.		509.	
Adjustments: Items unpaid by seller		Adjustments: Items unpaid by seller	
210. CITY/TOWN TAXES		510. CITY/TOWN TAXES	
211. COUNTY TAXES		511. COUNTY TAXES	
212. ASSESSMENTS		512. ASSESSMENTS	
213.		513.	
214.		514.	
215.		515.	
216.		516.	
217.		517.	
218.		518.	
219.		519.	
220. TOTAL PAID BY/FOR BORROWER	811,000.00	520. TOTAL REDUCTION AMOUNT DUE SELLER	629,116.64
300. CASH AT SETTLEMENT FROM/TO BORROWER		**600. CASH AT SETTLEMENT TO/FROM SELLER**	
301. Gross amounts due from borrower (line 120)	810,788.68	601. Gross amount due to seller (line 420)	800,666.67
302. Less amounts paid by/for borrower (line 220)	811,000.00	602. Less reductions in amount due seller (line 520)	629,116.64
303. CASH FROM[ ] TO[X] BORROWER	211.32	603. CASH FROM[ ] TO[X] SELLER	171,550.03

L. SETTLEMENT STATEMENT

	PAID FROM BORROWER'S FUNDS AT SETTLEMENT	PAID FROM SELLER'S FUNDS AT SETTLEMENT
700. TOTAL SALES/BROKER'S COMMISSION		
BASED ON PRICE $ 800,000.00 @ 6.00%		
701. BROKER: J. Q. SMART 48,000.00		
702.		
703.		
704. COMMISSIONS PAID AT SETTLEMENT		48,000.00
800. ITEMS PAYABLE IN CONNECTION WITH LOAN		
801. LOAN FEE	6,400.00	
802. LOAN DISCOUNT		
803. APPRAISAL	350.00	
804. CREDIT REPORT	45.00	
805. LENDER'S INSPECTION FEE		
806. MORTGAGE INSURANCE APPLICATION FEE		
807. ASSUMPTION FEE		
808. TAX SERVICE	89.00	
809. DOCUMENT FEE	250.00	
810.		
811.		
900. ITEMS REQUIRED BY LENDER TO BE PAID IN ADVANCE		
901. INTEREST AT 7.5000% FROM 05/31/20 TO 06/01/20	131.51	
902. MORTGAGE INSURANCE		
903. PROPERTY INSURANCE, INC. FOR FIRE INSURANCE	1,000.00	
904.		
905.		
1000. RESERVES DEPOSITED WITH LENDER		
1001. HAZARD INSURANCE		
1002. MORTGAGE INSURANCE		
1003. CITY PROPERTY TAXES		
1004. COUNTY PROPERTY TAXES		
1005. ANNUAL ASSESSMENTS		
1006.		
1007.		
1008.		
1100. ESCROW AND TITLE CHARGES		
1101. ESCROW FEE TO COLONIAL ESCROW, INC.	900.00	900.00
1102. ABSTRACT OR TITLE SEARCH		
1103. TITLE EXAMINATION		
1104. TITLE INSURANCE BINDER		
1105. DOCUMENT PREPARATION TO COLONIAL ESCROW, INC.		
1106. MESSENGER FEE TO COLONIAL ESCROW, INC.	50.00	
1107. ATTORNEY'S FEES		
1108. TITLE POLICY TO AMERICAN COAST TITLE	628.50	2,165.00
1109. LENDERS COVERAGE $ 640,000.00		
1110. OWNERS COVERAGE $ 800,000.00		
1111. PROCESSING DEMANDS TO COLONIAL ESCROW, INC.		35.00
1112. DOCUMENT FEE TO COLONIAL ESCROW, INC.		85.00
1113. LOAN TIE IN FEE TO COLONIAL ESCROW, INC.	125.00	
1200. GOVERNMENT RECORDING AND TRANSFER CHARGES		
1201. RECORDING FEES: DEED $8.00; MORTGAGE $20.00; RELEASES $5.00	28.00	5.00
1202. DOCUMENTARY TRANSFER TAX		880.00
1203. STATE TAX/STAMPS		
1204.		
1205.		
1300. ADDITIONAL SETTLEMENT CHARGES		
1301. SURVEY		
1302. PEST CONTROL, INC. FOR TERMITE REPORT/WORK		1,000.00
1303. SUB ESCROW FEE TO AMERICAN COAST TITLE	75.00	75.00
1304. TITLE ENDORSEMENT FEE(S) TO AMERICAN COAST TITLE	50.00	
1305. STREET ASSESSMENT BOND TO AMERICAN COAST TITLE		1,300.00
1306. HOME WARRANTY, INC. FOR HOME PROTECTION POLICY		400.00
1307.		
1400. TOTAL SETTLEMENT CHARGES (ENTER ON LINES 102 SECTION J AND 501, SECTION K)	10,122.01	54,845.00

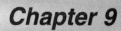

California Escrow Association
530 Bercut Drive, Suite G
Sacramento, CA 95814

Vesting Chart - Methods of Holding Title

	Tenancy in Common	Joint Tenancy	Community Property	Community Property w/Right of Survivorship
Parties	Any number of persons (can be husband and wife).	Any number of persons (can be husband and wife).	Only husband and wife.	Only husband and wife, and only when interest is created on or after 7/1/2002.
Division	Ownership can be divided into any number of interests equal or unequal.	Ownership interests must be equal and cannot be divided.	Ownership interests are equal.	Ownership interests are equal.
Title	Each co-owner has a separate legal title to the individual's undivided interest in the whole property.	There is only one title for the whole property.	Title in "community," similar to title of being in partnership.	Title in "community," similar to title of being in partnership.
Possession	Equal right of possession.	Equal right of possession.	Equal right of possession.	Equal right of possession.
Conveyance	Each co-owner's interest may be conveyed separately by its owner.	Conveyance by one co-owner w/o others breaks joint tenancy— owners become tenants in common.	Both co-owners must join in conveyance of real property. Separate interests cannot be conveyed.	Both co-owners must join in conveyance of real property. Separate interests cannot be conveyed.
Purchaser's Status	Purchaser becomes a tenant in common w/the other co-owners.	Purchaser becomes a tenant in common w/the other co-owners.	Purchaser can only acquire whole title of community, not part of it.	Purchaser can only acquire whole title of community, not part of it.
Death	On co-owners death, interest passes by will to the devisees or heirs. No survivorship right.	On co-owner's death, his/her interest ends & cannot be willed. Survivor(s) owns property by survivorship.	On co-owner's death, it goes to survivor in severalty (by will to devisee, or by succession to survivor).	On co-owner's death, it goes to survivor in severalty (by will to devisee, or by succession to survivor).
Successor's Status	Devisees or heirs become tenants in common.	Last survivor(s) owns property in severalty.	If passing by will, tenancy in common between devisee and survivor results.	Each survivor owns property in severalty.
Creditor's Rights	Co-owner's interest may be sold on execution sale to satisfy a creditor, who becomes a tenant in common.	Co-owner's interest may be sold on execution sale to satisfy a creditor. Joint tenancy is broken. Creditor becomes a tenant in common.	Co-owner's interest cannot be seized and sold separately. The whole property may be sold to satisfy debts of either spouse.	Co-owner's interest cannot be seized and sold separately. The whole property may be sold to satisfy debts of either spouse.
Presumption	Favored in doubtful cases except husband and wife (community property).	Must be expressly stated and properly formed. Not favored.	Strong presumption that property acquired by spouses is community.	Strong presumption that property acquired by spouses is community.

X. CHAPTER SUMMARY

An **escrow** is created when a written agreement (usually from a **Deposit Receipt**) instructs a neutral third party to hold funds and proceed only when all the agreed to conditions have been completed. An escrow is strongly recommended in connection with real estate sales, loan agreements, or exchanges made in California. But escrows are required for liquor license transfers, security sales, and court ordered transfers (**probate sales**).

A valid escrow requires: 1) signed escrow instructions (a written escrow contract) between the buying and selling parties; 2) a neutral escrow company acting as a dual agent for the buyer and the seller; and 3) conditional delivery of funds until the escrow conditions are completed.

An **escrow holder** can be a corporation, an attorney, or a real estate broker acting as a real estate agent in the transaction. An escrow officer, holder, or agent, though not licensed by the state, must be an employee of a licensed escrow company acting as agent. The duties of an escrow company include conditional delivery of funds until escrow conditions are met, confidentiality of escrow instructions, and acting as a deposit holder until funds are disbursed when escrow closes.

A real estate broker can handle escrow for a fee, but only if the broker acts as a real estate agent in that transaction, or if the broker is a principal (buyer or seller).

The escrow is complete when: 1) all escrow conditions of the parties have been met; and 2) the parties have received an accounting of the procedure. Escrows can be terminated in three ways: by **completion**, **mutual agreement**, or court action **interpleader**.

Amendments changing escrow instructions must be signed by both parties. The seller cannot rescind escrow without consent of the buyer, but the salesperson may recommend an escrow company. **Selection of an escrow company and officer is negotiated between buyer and seller.** It is illegal for a real estate licensee to receive a kickback for solicitation of escrow business.

Escrow instructions for the sale of a house are formal instructions drawn from the information contained in the Deposit Receipt. They are usually interpreted together, but if a conflict arises, the latest signed document will usually prevail. Most escrows for home sales include getting a new loan and the payoff or assumption of an old one. The **payoff demand statement** details the lender's calculations of the amounts owed for the purpose of paying off the loan in full. If a loan is to be assumed, a **beneficiary's (lender's) statement** under a deed of trust provides information, such as the unpaid balance, monthly payment and interest rate.

Closing escrow is the process of signing various documents, transfer of documents, recordation of deed and trust deeds, and distribution of funds. The **closing date** is the date that the documents are recorded.

Proration is the process of dividing expenses or income proportionately between buyer and seller to the precise date that escrow closes, or an agreed upon date. Items commonly prorated include: **property taxes**, **fire insurance**, **interest** and **rents**. All escrow companies use 30 days as a "base month." The two important dates in determining proration amounts are the dates escrow closes and when the item is paid.

A **Structural Pest Control Report** (termite report) is usually a condition of the escrow. This report is given by a licensed pest control company to identify any wood-destroying pests or conditions likely to cause pest infestation. It also states the conditions and correction costs of any pest, dry rot, excessive moisture, earth-wood contacts, or fungus damage in accessible areas of a structure. Payment for the report is negotiated between parties, but is usually made by the seller, as indicated in the allocation of costs signed by both parties. **Required repairs** are usually paid for by the seller, then a notice of work completed is obtained. But **recommended repairs** are negotiated between the parties.

Most lenders require a pest control inspection before making a loan. Every VA and FHA loan application requires one. A copy of the pest control report and notice of work completed must be delivered to the buyer if it's a condition of the deposit receipt or financing.

Fire insurance is a necessity. A lending institution requires fire coverage for the amount of its loan. **California Standard Form Fire Insurance Policy** insures the dwelling **only against fire and lightning**. An **Extended Coverage Endorsement** insures against windstorms, explosions, hail, aircraft, smoke, riot, and vehicles not attributed to a strike or civil commotion. Buyers can assume existing fire insurance policies or obtain new ones. When assuming fire insurance policies, the premium amount will be prorated in escrow. A coinsurance clause in a policy requires that 80% of the value of a commercial dwelling be insured, or only a percentage of the insurance value will be payable.

Chain of title is the recorded public history of a specific property. Information about people and their real property is stored in computers in a grantor-grantee index and referred to as a **title plant**. Title insurance companies examine chain of title records, review any risks not found in public records, seek legal interpretation of deeds or other real estate documents, help the seller correct any defects, and insure marketable title to the property.

A **preliminary title report** is the first step in a title search. It shows the condition of title before a sale or loan transaction.

Title insurance policies in California include the **California Land Title Association (CLTA) Policy**, the more comprehensive **American Land Title Association (ALTA) Policy**, or the **ALTA-R Policy**.

The **CLTA policy** is the most common and basic title insurance policy. The standard CLTA policy insures only the lender, unless the owner pays for "owner" coverage. It protects against lack of capacity of a party in a the chain of title, deeds not properly delivered, and forgery.

The **ATLA policy** is an extended coverage policy that insures against many exclusions in the standard coverage (CTLA) policy. The ALTA policy (which includes a competent survey or physical inspection) is usually required by California lenders and out of state lenders unable to make personal inspections of the property. Neither ALTA or CTLA covers unwritten **title defects known** to the insured at the time of policy issuance or **zoning changes**.

The **ALTA-R policy** is recommended by title companies for one-to-four owner-occupied residential dwellings. It offers more coverage for less money because no survey is necessary.

Payment for the CTLA policy insurance fees is negotiable, but the deposit receipt must state who pays the insurance fees to prevent any misunderstanding. In Southern California, the seller customarily pays for the CTLA policy. In Northern California, the buyer pays. The fees to upgrade the coverage from a CTLA to an ALTA policy are paid by the buyer in either part of the state.

Escrow service fees are usually split 50-50 in Southern California. The buyer usually pays in Northern California.

The **Real Estate Settlement Procedures Act (RESPA)** involves most federally insured home loans. It is a Federal law relating to the sale or transfer of one-to-four residential units requiring specific procedures and forms for settlements closing costs. All settlement closing costs must be disclosed to the borrower one business day before escrow closes.

XI. KEY TERMS

ALTA
Chain of Title
CLTA
Coinsurance
Commissioner of Corporations
Date of Closing
Escrow
Escrow Instructions
Escrow Officer
Payoff Demand Statement
Pest Control Report
Preliminary Title Report
Proration
RESPA
Title Insurance
Title Plant

XII. CHAPTER 9 QUIZ

1. The processing of paperwork and money involved in a sale or other real estate transaction is called:

    a. property transfer.
    b. acknowledgment.
    c. escrow.
    d. none of the above.

2. Which of the following is a requirement of a valid escrow?

    a. Signed instructions
    b. Neutral third party
    c. Conditional delivery
    d. All the above

3. Of the following, which would be the last function in an escrow sequence of events?

    a. Recording and issuing of title policy
    b. Request of new loan documents
    c. Adjustments and prorations
    d. None of the above

4. An independent escrow company:

    a. must be a corporation.
    b. is governed by the Commissioner of Corporations.
    c. both A & B.
    d. none of the above.

5. The only way that escrow instructions can be changed, once they have been drawn and signed by each party, is by:

    a. the escrow officer.
    b. mutual consent of the parties.
    c. the listing broker.
    d. operation of law.

6. Escrow information is usually taken from the:

    a. California Residential Purchase Agreement and Joint Escrow Instructions.
    b. Title policy.
    c. Transfer disclosure Statement.
    d. All of the above.

7. When calculating prorations how many days are in the standard base period?

    a. 31 days
    b. 30 days
    c. 28 days
    d. Depends on the month being prorated.

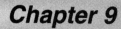

8. What title policy would cover most of the exclusions of a standard policy?

    a. ALTA

    b. MLTA

    c. CLTA

    d. All of the above

9. Escrow companies are selected by:

    a. broker

    b. buyer and seller

    c. seller only

    d. agent only

10. Which of the following is an annual recurring charge?

    a. County recording fees

    b. Title insurance fees

    c. Escrow fees

    d. Property tax fees

ANSWERS: 1. c; 2. d; 3. a; 4. c; 5. b; 6. a; 7. b; 8. a; 9. b; 10. d

CHAPTER 10
Taxation
How to Satisfy Uncle Sam

Taxes are an important aspect of all real estate transactions. Property owners are taxed annually on the property they own. In addition, there are other state and federal taxes that must be paid in order to buy, sell, or give away real property. **Figure 10-1** illustrates the five taxes with which every taxpayer, investor, and salesperson should be familiar. The amount of tax and who must pay the tax are often major factors to consider in the transfer of real estate.

I. Property Taxes

A city or county receives most of its operating revenue from the assessment and collection of real property taxes. *REAL PROPERTY TAXES are determined according to the value of the real property, and are paid annually or semi-annually.* These taxes are called ad valorem taxes. An *AD VALOREM TAX is a tax that is charged in proportion to the value of the property.* Property taxes are based on the concept that taxes should be assessed in accordance with a person's ability to pay. In the case of real estate, the higher the value of the property, the higher the property taxes.

"Ad valorem" means taxed "according to value." Real property is reassessed each time it is transferred (sold). The property tax is set at one percent of its selling price (or market value, if it is higher).

375

CHAPTER 10 OUTLINE

I. PROPERTY TAXES (p. 375)
　A. Proposition 13 (p. 378)
　　1. Transfers Can Trigger Reassessment (Under Prop 13) (p. 380)
　　2. Propositions Altering Prop 13 (Propositions 58/60/90) (p. 380)
　B. Property Taxes Become a Specific Lien (p. 382)
　C. Property Tax Time Table (p. 382)
　D. Property Tax Proration Problem (p. 383)
　E. Homeowner's Property Tax Exemption (p. 385)
　F. Disabled and Senior Citizen's Property Tax Postponement (p. 386)
　G. Veteran's Exemption (p. 386)
　H. Tax Exempt Property (p. 386)

II. SPECIAL ASSESSMENT TAX (p. 387)
　A. Improvement Bond Act of 1915 (p. 387)
　B. Mello-Roos Community Facilities Act (p. 388)

III. DOCUMENTARY TRANSFER TAX (p. 388)

IV. GIFT AND ESTATE TAXES (p. 388)
　A. Federal Gift Taxes (p. 388)
　B. Federal Estate Tax (p. 390)
　C. No State Gift and Inheritance Taxes (p. 390)

V. FEDERAL AND STATE INCOME TAXES (p. 390)

VI. INCOME TAX ASPECTS OF REAL ESTATE TRANSACTIONS (p. 391)

VII. TAXES ON PERSONAL RESIDENCE (p. 392)
　A. Deduction of Interest (p. 393)
　B. Deduction of Property Taxes (p. 393)
　C. Deduction of Prepayment Penalties (p. 393)
　D. Sale of a Residence (p. 394)

VIII. TAXES FOR INCOME PRODUCING PROPERTIES (p. 394)
　A. Depreciation of Business Property (Federal and State) (p. 395)
　B. Advantages of "Sale-Leaseback" (Buyer Gets to Depreciate New Building Cost) (p. 395)

IX. SALE OF REAL PROPERTY (p. 396)
　A. Capital Assets (Gains and Losses) (p. 396)
　B. Federal Income Tax Rates (p. 396)
　C. Alternative Minimum Tax (AMT) (Must Calculate Taxes Twice) (p. 397)
　D. Accounting for the Sale of Real Estate (Investment/Commercial) (p. 398)

X. INSTALLMENT SALES AND EXCHANGES (p. 398)
　A. Installment Sales of Real Estate (p. 398)
　B. Exchanges Tax-Deferred (Federal and State) (Section 1031 of the IRS Code) (p. 399)
　　1. Simultaneous 1031 Exchanges (Clients' Investment Properties) (p. 399)
　　　a. Like-Kind Property (p. 400)
　　2. Starker Delayed Exchange (p. 400)

        3. Reverse 1031 Exchanges (p. 400)

        4. Accounting for Exchanges (p. 400)

XI. DEALER PROPERTY (p. 401)

XII. WE ARE NOW TAX COLLECTORS
    (FEDERAL AND STATE INCOME TAX LAWS) (p. 402)

    A. Federal Tax Collection Requirements and Exemptions (If a Foreigner) (p. 402)

    B. State Tax Collection Requirements and Exemptions
       (If a Foreigner or Resident of Another State) (p. 403)

XIII. OTHER TAXES PAID BY BROKERS (p. 405)

    A. Business License Taxes (City Taxes) (p. 405)

XIV. CHAPTER SUMMARY (p. 405)

XV. KEY TERMS (p. 406)

XVI. CHAPTER 10 QUIZ (p. 407)

Figure 10-1

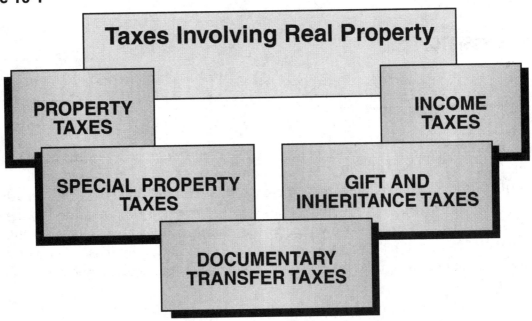

The **COUNTY ASSESSOR** *is the county officer who has the responsibility of determining the assessed valuation of land, improvements, and personal property used in business.* The county assessor determines the value of both county and city properties, except in a few cities that use their own assessors. In Los Angeles County, the City of Pasadena has its own assessor who assesses the property in that city. San Francisco is unique because the city and county are combined, so the city and county assessor's functions are combined.

www.co.la.ca.us/assessor
L. A. County Assessor

In general, all real property, except that owned by the government, and all tangible personal property except inventory used in a business, is subject to property tax assessment in California. **Intangible personal property, such as shares of stock, goodwill of a business opportunity, and promissory notes, as well as tangible property, such as household furnishings and personal effects of individuals, are not assessed or taxed.**

County Assessor assesses; County Board of Supervisors sets tax rate; County Tax Collector collects.

The **COUNTY TAX COLLECTOR** *is the county officer who collects the real property taxes.* He or she only collects taxes; the county tax collector has nothing to do with determining how much tax is levied. If the real property taxes are not paid, the county tax collector will eventually require that the property be sold at a tax sale.

www.cacttc.org/start.html
List of Assessors

A. PROPOSITION 13

Prop 13 (Jarvis-Gann Initiative) sent shock waves through the nation by rolling back the California property tax to 1% of the seller's price, making it the lowest rate in the country.

PROPOSITION 13 *limits the amount of taxes to a maximum of 1% of the March 1, 1975, market value of the property plus the cumulative increase of 2% in market value each year thereafter.* Voted indebtedness may increase this rate beyond 1% from area-to-area with voter approval. Improvements made after March 1, 1975, are added to the value in the year they are made. If ownership has changed after March 1, 1975, the tax is limited to 1% of the market value plus the 2% cumulative increase each succeeding year. Any state-allowed exemptions are deducted after figuring the basic tax. (See **Figure 10-2.**)

A "rough" estimate of property tax is approximately 1.25% of the sales price. (1% of sales price + .25% for other voter-approved indebtedness.)

Property tax assessment is subject to an adjustment in the event that a purchase, new construction, or a change in ownership has taken place after the 1975 lien date. If the property has undergone such a change, it is subject to a new assessor's appraisal. If the new value is higher, the tax will be increased. If the new value is lower, the tax will be decreased. Due to rising property values, Prop 13 can be a burden for new buyers, especially when similar properties in the neighborhood, which haven't changed ownership in several years, are taxed considerably lower.

Figure 10-2   **PROPOSITION 13**

That Article XII A is added to the Constitution to read:

Section 1.

(a) The maximum amount of any ad valorem tax on real property shall not exceed one percent (1%)* of the full cash value of such property. The one percent (1%)* tax to be collected by the counties and apportioned according to law to the districts within the counties.

(b) The limitation provided for in subdivision (a) shall not apply to ad valorem taxes or special assessments to pay the interest and redemption charges on any indebtedness approved by the voters prior to the time this section becomes effective.

Section 2.

(a) The full cash value means the county assessors valuation of real property as shown on the 1975-76 tax bill under "full cash value," or thereafter, the appraised value of real property when purchased, newly constructed, or a change in ownership has occurred after the 1975 assessment. All real property not already assessed up to the 1975-76 tax levels may be reassessed to reflect that valuation.

(b) The fair market value base may reflect, from year to year, the inflationary rate, not to exceed two percent (2%) for any given year or reduction as shown in the consumer price index or comparable data for the area under taxing jurisdiction.

Section 3.

From and after the effective date of this article, any changes in state taxes enacted for the purpose of increasing revenues collected pursuant thereto whether by increased rates or changes in methods of computation must be imposed by an Act passed by not less than two-thirds of all members elected to each of the two houses of the Legislature, except that no new ad valorem taxes on real property, or sales or transaction taxes on the sales of real property may be imposed.

Section 4.

Cities, counties, and special districts, by a two-thirds vote of the qualified electors of such district, may impose special taxes on such district, except ad valorem taxes on real property or a transaction tax or sales tax on the sale of real property within such city, county, or special district.

Section 5.

This article shall take effect for the tax year beginning on July 1 following the passage of this Amendment, except Section 3 which shall become effective upon the passage of this article.

Section 6.

If any section, part, clause, or phrase hereof is for any reason held to be invalid or unconstitutional, the remaining sections shall not be affected but will remain in full force and effect.

* Voted indebtedness may increase this rate beyond 1% from local area to area, with voter approval.

NEW CONSTRUCTION means any addition or improvement to land, including alterations of existing improvements if the alterations result in conversion to another use or an extension of the economic life of the improvement. An example of a TAXABLE ALTERATION would be anything that increases the usefulness of the structure, such as the addition of a bedroom or bathroom.

Construction, reconstruction, or alteration performed for the purpose of routine or normal maintenance and repair would not trigger Proposition 13. Thus, interior or exterior painting, replacement of roof coverings, or the addition of aluminum siding would not be taxable. An example of an alteration that does not result in an increased usefulness of existing facilities is the modernization of a kitchen.

Escrow agents fill out property tax information forms to help the county recorder facilitate the distribution of the forms, but they are not statutorily required to prepare the form or to file it. Hence, as a real estate agent, you need to be aware of your responsibility to draw your clientele's attention to the statement and assure compliance.

1. Transfers Can Trigger Reassessment (Under Prop 13)

As stated above, Prop 13 determines property tax rates when a property "changes" ownership. What constitutes a change, for purposes of establishing a new valuation, is not always easy to define. **Figure 10-3** shows which transfers (changes) do and do not require reassessment.

2. Propositions Altering Prop 13 (Propositions 58/60/90)

Californian's have voted for several changes to alter Proposition 13.

Proposition 58 allows real property transfers from one spouse to another or to children without property tax reassessment. Because tax laws change, call a tax advisor regarding possible forgiveness of property tax increases when alterations are made in real estate ownership.

Under the following conditions (based on Propositions 60 and 90), homeowners may be permitted to transfer their current Proposition 13 tax base with them when they buy a new home:

1. Homeowners over the age of 55; and
2. Home purchased within two years of original sale; and
3. Replacement home of equal or lesser value; and
4. New home must be in the same county; or another participating county (check first).

Figure 10-3

Summary of Real Property Transfers

DO Require Reassessment

1. Purchase or change in ownership for consideration.

2. Transfer of property to a joint tenant, other than to the person who created the joint tenancy.

3. Creation, transfer, or termination of a tenancy in common where proportional ownership interests are changed.

4. Transfers of interests in real property between a corporation, partnership, or any other person, except mere changes in method of holding title.

5. Acquisition of control of a corporation or partnership which owns the property (except as the result of a reorganization).

6. Foreclosures on any lien.

7. Creation, transfer, or termination of a leasehold interest in taxable real property for a term of 35 years or more.

8. Exchanges of real estate.

9. Transfer by gift or inheritance, except transfers between spouses.

DO NOT Require Reassessment

1. Transfers between husband and wife.

2. Transfer of property into joint tenancy where original owner is one of the joint tenants.

3. Return of property to person who created the joint tenancy.

4. Transfer of property to or from a trust which is revocable, for the benefit of the grantor or spouse or which reverts back to the grantor or spouse after less than 12 years.

5. A change in the method of holding title between co-owners without changing the proportional interests of the co-owners.

6. Recording of a deed of trust giving security for a loan.

7. Transfers of a minority interests in a corporation.

8. Transfers of a minority partnership interest.

9. Any transfer of a lessor's interest in taxable real property subject to a lease with a remaining term of less than 35 years.

10. Replacement of property taken by condemnation.

Thanks to Prop 13, a homeowner who bought a house for $100,000 in 1980 would have started out paying $1,000 a year in property taxes. Due to increasing property values, that house may now sell for $500,000, meaning your new buyer will have to start out paying $5,000 a year in property taxes.

Propositions 60 and 90 allow "empty-nesters" to purchase new homes (one at a time) while holding on to their low tax base, thus freeing up larger multiple bedroom homes for younger families.

ASSESSED VALUATION is set at 100% of the property's selling price or fair market value, whichever is higher, plus a 2% increase for every year the property has been owned, but only as far back as March 1, 1975. The tax rate is set at 1% of fair market value (or selling price, whichever is higher) plus any voter-approved indebtedness. Properties that are transferred and new construction are subject to a new appraisal based upon the current market value or selling price, whichever is higher. Existing structures are given a new assessment each year as of January 1. New construction and transfers are assessed immediately upon the first day of the next month. **See Figures 10-4 and 10-5** for an example of a property tax bill.

B. PROPERTY TAXES BECOME A SPECIFIC LIEN

Property taxes are, in effect, liens against that specific property. Business personal property taxes also become liens against that specific real property on the same tax bill. For example, the furniture in furnished apartments is taxed as business personal property, and is usually included on the property tax bill.

Property taxes for the following fiscal year become a lien against the real property on January 1 of the current year. Officially, the first installment for half of the taxes becomes due on November 1, and is delinquent after 5pm on December 10. The second installment is due on February 1, and is delinquent if not paid by 5pm on April 10. If either December 10 or April 10 falls on a Saturday, Sunday, or legal holiday, the delinquency date is extended to the close of the next business day.

C. PROPERTY TAX TIME TABLE

The city or county fiscal year starts on July 1 and ends on June 30. All revenues and expenditures are planned for this period of time. **Figure 10-6** illustrates all the important dates that are associated with property taxes. Assessable property is evaluated by the assessor on January 1 for the upcoming year in the name of the property's legal owner on that date. Most cities allow the county assessor to evaluate the property in both the county and the incorporated parts of the county (which are the cities). In a few rare cases, as stated earlier, cities may use their own assessors. County assessors complete their assessment rolls by July 1, the beginning of the government (fiscal) year.

Important tax dates can be remembered "**No Darn Fooling Around**" as follows:

N November 1 (first installment due)
D December 10 (first installment is delinquent)
F February 1 (second installment due)
A April 10 (second installment is delinquent)

Figure 10-4

2003	**ANNUAL PROPERTY TAX BILL**	**2003**

CITIES, COUNTY, SCHOOLS AND ALL OTHER TAXING AGENCIES IN LOS ANGELES COUNTY

SECURED PROPERTY TAX FOR FISCAL YEAR JULY 1, 2003 TO JUNE 30, 2004

MARK J. SALADINO, TREASURER AND TAX COLLECTOR

FOR ASSISTANCE CALL (213) 974-2111 OR (888) 807-2111

ASSESSOR'S ID. NO. CK
DETAIL OF TAXES DUE FOR 4225 007 032 03 000 87

AGENCY	AGENCY PHONE NO.	RATE		AMOUNT
GENERAL TAX LEVY				
ALL AGENCIES		1.000000	$	829.18
VOTED INDEBTEDNESS				
COUNTY		.000992	$	.82
CITY-LOS ANGELES		.050574		41.93
METRO WATER DIST		.006100		5.06
FLOOD CONTROL		.000462		.38
COMMNTY COLLEGE		.019857		16.47
UNIFIED SCHOOLS		.077145		63.97
DIRECT ASSESSMENTS				
CITY LND/LT 96-1	(213) 847-9579		$	14.59
LA STORMWATER	(213) 473-8098			5.03
CITY 911 FUND	(213) 978-1099			7.58
FLOOD CONTROL	(626) 458-3945			6.31
COUNTY PARK DIST	(213) 738-2983			15.03
CITY LT MTC	(213) 847-5507			.69
TRAUMA/EMERG SRV	(866) 587-2862			27.60
LA WEST MOSQ AB	(310) 915-7370			3.97

PROPERTY IDENTIFICATION
ASSESSOR'S ID.NO.: 4225 007 032 03 000
OWNER OF RECORD AS OF JANUARY 1, 2003
SAME AS BELOW

MAILING ADDRESS

Wolfgang Hubie
100 Internet Highway
Culver City, CA 90230

ELECTRONIC FUND TRANSFER (EFT) NUMBER
ID#:19 4225 007 032 7 YEAR:03 SEQUENCE:000 7
PN: 7095

For American Express, Mastercard and Visa payments call (888) 473-0835 and have available the EFT number listed above. Service fees will be charged.
For check payments, please write the EFT number above on your check.

SPECIAL INFORMATION

PROPERTY LOCATION AND/OR PROPERTY DESCRIPTION
100 Internet Highway   Culver City
TRACT NO 31507 CONDOMINIUM UNIT 2

ASSESSOR'S REGIONAL OFFICE
REGION #07 INDEX: TRA:00067
WEST DISTRICT OFFICE
6120 BRISTOL PARKWAY
CULVER CITY CA 90230
(310)665-5300

ACCT. NO.:   PRINT NO.: 565806 BILL ID.:

TOTAL TAXES DUE	**$1,038.61**
FIRST INSTALLMENT TAXES DUE NOV. 1, 2003	**$519.31**
SECOND INSTALLMENT TAXES DUE FEB. 1, 2004	**$519.30**

VALUATION INFORMATION

ROLL YEAR 03-04	CURRENT ASSESSED VALUE	TAXABLE VALUE
LAND	43,828	43,828
IMPROVEMENTS	39,090	39,090
TOTAL		82,918
LESS EXEMPTION:		
NET TAXABLE VALUE		82,918

THERE WILL BE A $50.00 CHARGE FOR ANY CHECK RETURNED BY THE BANK.
KEEP THIS UPPER PORTION FOR YOUR RECORDS. YOUR CANCELLED CHECK IS YOUR RECEIPT.

The government fiscal tax year is July 1 through June 30.

D. PROPERTY TAX PRORATION PROBLEM

Proration question: Who owes how much to whom ?

Figure 10-5

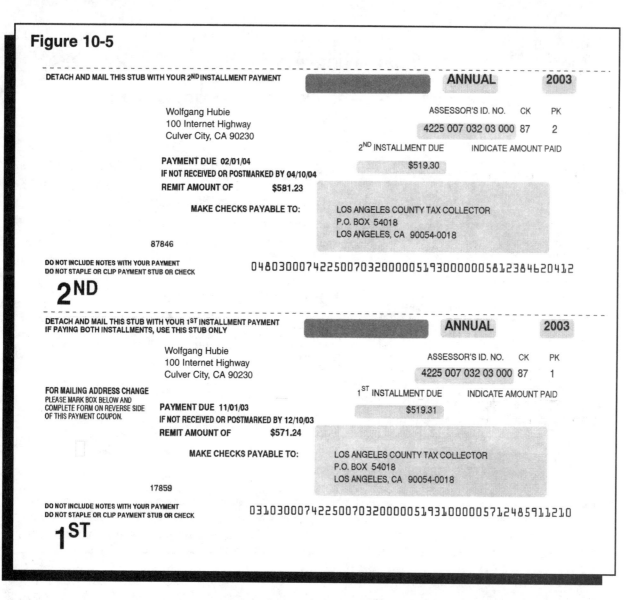

Figure 10-6   **PROPERTY TAX TIME TABLE**

January 1	July 1	November 1	February 1
Property tax becomes a lien on real property	Fiscal year starts	1st installment is due November 1, and delinquent after December 10 at 5:00 P.M.	2nd installment is due February 1, and delinquent after April 10 at 5:00 P.M.

If the seller of the subject property has paid both the 1st and 2nd installments of the property taxes for a total annual bill of $2,760, what is the proration of property taxes for both the seller and buyer if the buyer takes possession on May 1?

Remember: Escrow prorates property taxes using old (seller's) assessed value (tax bill).

The first step is to determine the amount of taxes per month. The annual tax bill of $2,760 is divided by 12 months to determine that the monthly tax is $230. Since the seller paid the property taxes through the month of June (the end of the fiscal tax year, which is July 1 through June 30), and the buyer took possession on May 1, two months of paid property taxes are owed the seller. The buyer would owe the seller for two months (May and June) that were already paid by the seller. This amount would be $460 (2 x $230).

When a property is sold, the buyer will receive one new property tax bill, but it may be followed by other updated property tax bills referred to as supplemental property tax bills. **See Figure 10-7**.

Figure 10-7

SUPPLEMENTAL PROPERTY TAX BILLS

The law requires reassessment of property **immediately** after it changes ownership or after new construction is completed. While the amount of the supplemental assessment is still determined in accordance with Proposition 13, the actual effect is to "speed up" reassessment of property.

The Office of Assessor enters the new property value onto the assessment roll as of the first of the month following the month in which the property changes ownership, or new construction is completed.

Depending upon the date your client purchased property or the date construction is completed, he or she will receive **one or more** supplemental tax bills in addition to his or her regular tax bill. Taxes on the supplemental tax roll become a lien against the real property on the date of change in ownership or the date new construction is completed.

E. HOMEOWNER'S PROPERTY TAX EXEMPTION

Homeowner's property tax exemption is $7,000 of assessed valuation.

The *HOMEOWNER'S PROPERTY TAX EXEMPTION is a deduction on the property tax bill of the first $7,000 of assessed value of an owner-occupied property.*

A homeowner's exemption on a home does the following:

1. All personal property of the homeowner is exempt from property taxes.
2. A resident owner receives a $7,000 homeowner's exemption in assessed value if the property is the principal residence on the 1st of March.

Advise your buyers to file immediately for homeowner exemption.

The time to file for the homeowner's exemption is from January 1 to February 15 in order to receive the full exemption. Once the exemption is filed, it remains on the property until the homeowner terminates it. If the exemption is terminated, a new claim form must be obtained from, and filed with, the assessor to regain eligibility.

Qualifying owner-occupied residential property receives a $7,000 homeowner's exemption. For example, an assessed value of $500,000 minus the homeowner's exemption of $7,000 is $493,000. (Prop 13 tax rate is 1% of the $7,000 exemption, so your buyer's tax savings, in reality, is only $70 per year.)

F. DISABLED AND SENIOR CITIZEN'S PROPERTY TAX POSTPONEMENT

Seniors who are 62 years of age or older and have a household income of $24,000 or less may qualify for this tax postponement assistance program. This program offers them the option of having the state pay all or part of the taxes on their homes. In return, a lien is placed on the property for the amount that the state has to pay. This specific lien becomes payable when the taxpayer moves or dies. In effect, the homeowner is relieved of his or her tax burden in exchange for a lien on his or her home to be paid upon death. California has extended this program to include persons under the age of 62 who are legally disabled. **Further information is available from the State Controller.**

G. VETERAN'S EXEMPTION

Any California resident who served in the military during a time of war is entitled to an annual $4,000 property tax exemption against the assessed value of one property. This exemption also applies to the widow, widowed mother, or pensioned father of a deceased veteran. For disabled California veterans who qualify, however, the assessment limit can be raised up to $100,000.

A veteran cannot have a veteran's exemption and a homeowner's property tax exemption on the same property.

H. TAX EXEMPT PROPERTY

In California there are some properties that are partially or totally tax exempt. All real property that is owned by the federal, state, county, or city government is automatically tax exempt. This is a huge benefit to the federal government (and detriment to the state), as the federal government owns 45% of California land.

Eastern states benefit because only about 10% of their land is owned by the federal government. **A lessee with possessory interest in oil and gas rights on government owned property is not exempt from property taxes.**

Since California has many national and state parks, the majority of land in this state is tax exempt.

Any property that is used exclusively by non-profit organizations for religious, charitable, medical, or educational purposes is also tax exempt. In addition, 50 percent of all growing crops, young orchard trees, immature timber, and young grapevines are tax exempt.

Property of non-profit organizations used for religious, charitable, medical, or educational purposes is tax exempt.

II. Special Assessment Tax

A *SPECIAL ASSESSMENT TAX is levied by a city council or a county board of supervisors, with the voters' approval, for the cost of specific local improvements such as streets, sewers, irrigation, or drainage.* **Assessments differ from property taxes in that property taxes finance the general functions of government and go into the general fund, whereas a special assessment is levied once (usually) by the city, county, or "improvement district" for a particular work or improvement.**

The official body that levies a special assessment is called a SPECIAL ASSESSMENT DISTRICT BOARD. According to state law, any self-governing area, such as a city or county, may establish a special assessment district for the purpose of levying a special assessment.

As a rule, a district issues its own bonds to finance particular improvements, such as water distribution systems, parking facilities, street lighting, and many other types of developments. To repay the funds borrowed through the bonds issued, these districts have the power to assess all lands included in the district. Such loans constitute liens on the land until paid. These liens can be foreclosed by sale similar to a tax sale and have priority over private property interests.

A. IMPROVEMENT BOND ACT OF 1915

The *IMPROVEMENT BOND ACT OF 1915 finances street and highway improvements through an assessment to property owners based upon the frontage of the property facing the improved street.* Through the issuance of municipal bonds, it allows property owners up to 30 years to pay off their portion of the improvement assessment. As the broker, you and the seller must give the buyer a disclosure notice of assessment amount and the amount applicable to the property.

B. MELLO-ROOS COMMUNITY FACILITIES ACT

The Mello-Roos Community Facilities Act is another type of improvement bond. **Figure 10-8** explains Mello-Roos in detail.

III. Documentary Transfer Tax

Documentary transfer taxes are paid only on the new amount of money (cash down and new financing), not on any assumed financing.

The **DOCUMENTARY TRANSFER TAX** *is a tax that is applied to the consideration paid or money borrowed when transferring property, except for any remaining loans or liens on the property.* This tax is computed at the rate of 55 cents for each $500 or $1.10 per $1,000 of consideration or any fraction thereof. The consideration is any amount of cash payment plus any new loans. However, this tax does not apply to any liens or encumbrances that remain on the property as part of the transfer. If a house were sold for $230,000 and a buyer assumed the old loan of $30,000, the documentary transfer tax would be $220.

$$\frac{\$200,000}{\$500} \times \$.55 = \$220$$

The documentary transfer tax is handled as part of the escrow. According to state law, the county is allowed to charge this tax. However, a city within a county can charge that county for one-half of this tax. Therefore, in most cities, the county collects the documentary transfer tax and gives half of it to the city. Based on the information found at the county recorder's office, the documentary transfer tax can be used, in many cases, to determine a previous sale price of a property. Simply divide 55 cents into the amount of the documentary transfer tax and multiply by $500. If any loans have been assumed by the new owner, also add that amount to arrive at the total prior sale price of the property.

IV. Gift and Estate Taxes

For federal purposes, the transfer of property by a gift or inheritance is taxed. Exemptions may reduce the taxes and sometimes eliminate them. **Figure 10-9** illustrates the federal taxes encountered by transferring property as a gift or by inheritance.

A. FEDERAL GIFT TAXES

Both a husband and wife may now give away $1 million each over a lifetime without paying any gift tax.

Frequently, as an individual family matures, the value of the real property owned by the family increases, and the owning family may consider bestowing it as a gift. When a

Figure 10-8

Mello-Roos Liens
DISCLOSURE REQUIRED

As an agent, if you fail to disclose a Mello-Roos lien, the buyer has a three-day right of rescission, and it may result in disciplinary action against you.

MELLO-ROOS LIENS *are municipal bonds issued to fund streets, sewers, and other infrastructure needs before a housing development is built.* This financial device allows developers to raise money to complete off-site improvements in a house or condo subdivision. The developer is usually responsible for making payments on the bond until the home is sold. The homeowner then becomes responsible for payment via a special tax.

The Mello-Roos Community Facilities Act is a way that a city or governmental district can skirt the property tax limitations of Proposition 13. The city can include the cost and maintenance of infrastructure items in the property tax bill as a special tax, which is allowed to go above the limits of Proposition 13.

This has been a boon for developers who need help financing their projects and for municipalities anxious to upgrade new developments under the restrictions of Proposition 13. The downside is that, if something goes wrong with the economy or the project, the municipality may have to foreclose on the developer.

The primary responsibility for disclosure of any Mello-Roos bonds lies with the seller.

A broker must disclose to property buyers that a project is subject to a Mello-Roos special tax levy. If the agent fails to provide this disclosure, he or she is subject to discipline by the Real Estate Commissioner. A disclosure notice of the amount assessed and the amount of special tax applicable to the property is required on the sale or lease (for more than five years) of property subject to this lien. Failure to give notice before signing the sales contract permits the buyer or tenant a three-day right of rescission, after receipt of the notice.

Warning: Whereas property taxes are totally deductible from state and federal income taxes, Mello-Roos taxes may only be partially deductible depending upon whether they are for maintenance or improvements. Consult with your C.P.A. before claiming such a deduction.

Figure 10-9

family gives property, whether real or personal, to another individual, there may be federal gift taxes that must be paid. If the value of the property is higher than an exempt amount, the donor is responsible for a gift tax. A **DONOR** *is the person or persons giving the property as a gift. Generally, people give their property away to relatives on a systematic basis so that taxes are avoided. The* **DONEE** *is the person or persons who receive the property as a gift.* The federal gift tax law also provides for an $11,000 annual exemption per donee.

B. FEDERAL ESTATE TAX

A **FEDERAL ESTATE TAX** *return must be filed for the estate of every resident of the United States whose gross estate exceeds $1,000,000 ($1,500,000 in 2004, $2,000,000 in 2006) in value at the date of death.* Estate tax exemptions will gradually increase the size of estates that are exempt from $1,000,000, to being repealed in 2010. However, the estate tax can be restored in 2011.

C. NO STATE GIFT AND INHERITANCE TAXES

California State Inheritance Tax
   None (Repealed June 8, 1982)

California State Gift Tax
   None (Repealed June 8, 1982)

V. Federal and State Income Taxes

The annual Federal Income Tax Form 1040 and the State Income Tax Form 540 are bookkeeping or accounting summaries of the prior year's financial facts. These facts are a history and cannot be altered at the time of filing the income tax return.

www.irs.ustreas.gov
Internal Revenue Service (IRS)
www.ftb.ca.gov
Franchise Tax Board (FTB)

California has both state and federal income taxes. (See **Figure 10-10**). That's right! California residents pay both income taxes, which ranks us among the most taxed people in the United States. It is no wonder that Californians are very interested in understanding the effects of income taxes on both their personal residence and income-producing property.

Figure 10-10

CALIFORNIA vs. FEDERAL INCOME TAX:
Emphasis is on the Federal

California state income tax laws tend to conform with federal laws in most respects. There are, however, several important income tax exceptions listed below:

1. State does not tax Social Security benefits.
2. State has no capital gains rates; just ordinary income rates.
3. State does not allow tax breaks for IRA plans (simple).
4. State does not tax lottery winnings.

The state taxes at a lower rate (a maximum of 9.3 percent) but tends to be more restrictive on deductions. State taxes paid are themselves deductible from the federal return.

Most state and local tax laws are considered by many insiders to be antiquated. Tax reform on these levels has become a much slower process than that by the federal government. Focus is on the federal government, which taxes at higher rates and sets the tone for state and local taxes. For more detailed information on preparing personal income taxes, a tax attorney or CPA should be consulted.

VI. Income Tax Aspects of Real Estate Transactions

Because of the complexity and vast scope of income taxation, we can offer here only a basic primer on some income tax aspects of real estate. You cannot be expected to become expert in taxation, but you should have a working acquaintance with some basics. After all, you will often be consulted when a prospect or client wants guidance in the purchase, sale, exchange, or transfer of real property, and with investment decisions.

> **Never give legal or tax advice to your clients. Always refer them to professionals. This applies to this text as well—don't rely on this information as legal or tax advice, but use it as a general guide only.**

As a real estate professional, you need to recognize opportunities and drawbacks with respect to clients' holdings and understand that tax liabilities differ according to the specific transaction. You should also know when to call a CPA or attorney, and to advise your client to consult with either or both when significant tax and legal implications are involved. Property tax laws change frequently. For example, the 2001 community property laws changed to include a spouse's right to survivorship, allowing surviving spouses to maintain previous tax basis without being penalized for inheriting the deceased spouses' portions of the properties.

We will discuss only the most basic concepts of reducing the income tax bite for the average citizen. A basic knowledge of the requirements necessary to take advantage of federal and state income tax incentives is helpful. Arranging the purchase of real estate in a manner that reduces your personal income taxes is the purpose of tax planning. This may allow you to reduce the income taxes you pay, or at least postpone such taxes.

Tax shelters are the reduction in income taxes. Advise your clients that now is the time to start tax planning for their future income tax returns.

Figure 10-11 shows the five main areas of the federal and state income tax laws that are incentives to owning real estate. Each area will be explained only to give the general concepts or ideas behind the laws. To obtain the exact meaning and clauses of the law, an owner or investor should seek the help of a Certified Public Accountant for advice on the accounting, or an attorney who is familiar with tax problems. Remember, these are only generalizations, and our income tax laws are more complex than the basic concepts presented here.

VII. Taxes on Personal Residence

Homeowners can annually deduct these three items from their income taxes based on their personal residence:

1. Mortgage Interest on Loan (Trust Deeds)
2. Property Taxes
3. Prepayment Penalties

Figure 10-11

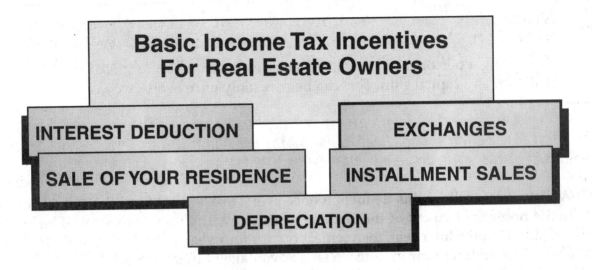

A. DEDUCTION OF INTEREST

Deduction of interest on your client's home loan from their income taxes is one of the major tax advantages of owning real estate.

Buying a first and second home provides the average family with the biggest buffer against income taxes that they are likely to enjoy. Federal tax laws provide incentives to those who purchase a first and even a second home. When buying these homes your clients may finance up to $1 million ($1,000,000) with all the interest paid out during the year fully tax deductible. An additional deduction is available on the interest from home equity loans, taken for any purpose, even buying a second home, of up to $100,000 in principal. The $1,000,000 and $100,000 debit limit is a total applied against both first and second homes together or one owner-occupied home taken separately.

B. DEDUCTION OF PROPERTY TAXES

Property taxes on your 1st and 2nd homes are deductible from your income taxes. This makes us feel better about paying local property taxes.

C. DEDUCTION OF PREPAYMENT PENALTIES

Prepayment penalties are also deductible from your clients' income taxes. If they pay off, or drastically reduce their home loan balance, there may be a prepayment penalty.

Interest, property taxes, and prepayment penalties paid on a personal residence can be deducted from income taxes.

D. SALE OF A RESIDENCE

This selling deduction is by far your clients best tax benefit of home ownership.

When selling a personal residence, the seller can exclude up to $250,000 ($500,000 if married) of any capital gain. This can be used only once every two years.

Federal income tax laws allow a taxpayer to exclude up to $250,000 of gain for each individual ($500,000 if married and on the title). This benefit may only be used once every two years for a residence.

While the law allows this deduction once every two years, **your client must reside in the home for two out of the last five years to qualify.** In other words, if he or she lives in the home for a year, then rents it out for four years, they would have to move back in for another year in order to take advantage of this tax break.

Your clients can deduct a loss on sale of a personal residence, if they have turned it into income producing property by renting it.

The only way to deduct a loss on a personal residence is to turn that property into income-producing property first by renting it. Then any loss based on its sale is deductible because it is income-producing property, not a personal residence.

VIII. Taxes for Income Producing Properties

Investors of income producing properties can annually deduct these items from their income taxes:

1. Mortgage Interest on Loans (no maximum)
2. Property Taxes
3. Prepayment Penalties

In addition they can deduct:

4. Operating Expenses
5. Depreciation of Improvements

In addition to deducting mortgage interest (no maximum), property taxes, and prepayment penalties, income property owners can deduct operating expenses and depreciation. Owners cannot deduct losses due to vacancies.

A. DEPRECIATION OF BUSINESS PROPERTY (Federal and State)

DEPRECIATION FOR TAX PURPOSES *is a yearly tax deduction for wear and tear on investment property that is deducted from the taxpayer's income on his or her income tax form.* This deduction applies only to investment property or property used in a business, not on a taxpayer's personal residence. Apartment buildings, commercial buildings, and any building improvements to investment property, can be depreciated. The land itself cannot be depreciated.

Only the buildings and other improvements on income, trade, or business property can be depreciated, not the land.

One can only depreciate property that is improved. Since land cannot be usually depreciated, only the improvements can be depreciated. Currently, the straight-line method is the accepted way to depreciate buildings and other improvements.

Residential (homes and apartments) property depreciation schedule:
Minimum 27.5 years (Straight-line)

Commercial improvements depreciation schedule:
Minimum 39 years (Straight-line).

The amount of depreciation must be spread uniformly over the useful life of the property, with the same amount deducted each year (straight-line depreciation). Since most buildings in these inflationary times actually increase in value, depreciation is usually just a technique for postponing income taxes until the property is sold.

Example: If you own a cabin in the desert that you rent to vacationers and the cabin cost $100,000 and the land value is $25,000, this leaves improvements of $75,000. Divide this $75,000 by 30 years giving you a depreciation of $2,500 for each year of the 30 years. If we had used a 27.5 year formula, the yearly depreciation amount would be slightly higher.

Remember: A property owner can deduct depreciation on income, trade, or business real property, not on a residence.

B. ADVANTAGES OF "SALE-LEASEBACK" (Buyer Gets to Depreciate New Building Cost)

If the owner of a business sells his or her building for cash, and then leases it back, the seller becomes a lessee and the buyer the lessor.

The advantage to the seller: all lease payments can be deducted from income taxes and he or she receives cash for the building.

The advantage to the buyer: he or she can use the purchase price as the new basis for depreciation and establish a new depreciation schedule.

Your seller, now a renter, deducts 100% of future rents paid. Your buyer can depreciate new cost of buildings (even if they have been depreciated previously).

IX. Sale of Real Property

A. CAPITAL ASSETS (Gains and Losses)

In real estate a capital asset includes a personal residence (including a second home) and any other real estate, because they are long-term investments. When your client sells a home or other real estate (for more than $250,000 as a single or $500,000 as a couple), there is probably a capital gain or loss. *CAPITAL GAINS are taxed at a lower rate than is ordinary income,* but *CAPITAL LOSSES can be deducted from capital gains.*

It is in the public interest to foster investment in land and buildings and other long-term assets so that businesses are encouraged to expand. This in turn creates more job opportunities for everyone.

Congress and the President have established four capital gains tax rates that are subject to change. The current rates are:

1. 20% maximum capital gains tax rate if held for more than 18 months
2. 15% maximum capital gains tax rate if held for more than 7 years
3. 10% capital gains tax rate if net income is less than $50,000
4. 5% capital gains tax rate (over 7 years) if net income is less than $50,000

Gains are taxed at the lower capital gains tax rates (lower than ordinary income tax rates).

Lower tax rates on capital gains encourage entrepreneurs to risk investing long-term in things such as equipment, stocks, bonds, and real estate in order to obtain capital gains or losses. Other countries, like Japan and Germany, have very low capital gain tax rates which encourage investment in companies so that more career opportunities are generated for their employees. The size of the nation's "economic pie," which everyone enjoys, increases.

B. FEDERAL INCOME TAX RATES

As the old saying goes, "Nothing in life is certain, except death and taxes." One other certainty is the constant change in federal tax rates. Income tax rates are progressive.

PROGRESSIVE TAXES *are taxes where the rates (percentage paid) increase as the amount to be taxed increases.* So as you make more money, not only does the amount increase, but the rate at which income is taxed also increases. The end effect is that higher income families (the exact ones who usually own businesses and can expand job opportunities) pay most of the income taxes.

MARGINAL TAX RATE *is the rate that the next dollar earned puts you into.*

REGRESSIVE TAXES *use the same rate no matter how much is earned. Sales tax is an example of a regressive tax.* The rate is the same, so in effect the poor pay a higher percent of their income.

Income tax rates are progressive. Sales taxes are regressive.

C. ALTERNATIVE MINIMUM TAX (AMT) (Must Calculate Taxes Twice)

The **ALTERNATIVE MINIMUM TAX (AMT)** *requires taxpayers, who make above a certain amount of gross income, to figure their taxes twice.* First, they have to calculate their tax liability, using the actual itemized deductions method. They then have to refigure it, by limiting their itemized deductions and using the Alternative Minimum Tax rate, paying whichever is higher.

The seven itemized deductions that must be limited with the AMT are:

1. Sizable state income taxes deducted on your federal return.
2. An unusually large number of personal exemptions.
3. Deductible medical and dental expenses.
4. A home equity loan that was used not to improve your property but to buy other items.
5. Incentive stock options.
6. Substantial miscellaneous itemized deductions.
7. Depreciation of a business or investment property.

The alternative minimum tax was instituted to ensure that wealthy people (in the upper 10% tax brackets) actually paid some tax, regardless of how they sheltered their income.

Unfortunately, AMT tax provisions have not changed along with income tax rates. With inflation, upper middle-income taxpayers (a single, head-of-household, making $40,000 a year) is subject to this tax as well.

The number of taxpayers subject to the AMT has more than quadrupled in the last decade, and it's only expected to get worse. By

2009, the AMT is expected to affect nine million Americans, whose tax bills will increase by $19.8 billion.

D. ACCOUNTING FOR THE SALE OF REAL ESTATE (Investment/Commercial)

The method of determining a profit or loss on the sale of real property is spelled out by the Internal Revenue Service. Steps 1 and 2 must be completed before determining the profit or loss on a sale (Step 3).

"Adjusted cost basis" is the base cost, plus capital improvements, minus depreciation and sale expenses. As a broker, your commission is an expense of the sale.

(1) Cost Basis (Purchase price)	**$500,000**
+ Improvements	**200,000**
	$700,000
- Depreciation (tax records)	**30,200**
= Adjusted Cost Basis	**$669,800**
(2) Sale price	**$1,000,000**
- Sale Expenses	**32,500**
= Adjusted Sale Price	**$967,500**
(3) Adjusted Sale Price	**$967,500**
- Adjusted Cost Basis	**669,800**
= Gain	**$297,700**

X. Installment Sales and Exchanges

A. INSTALLMENT SALES OF REAL ESTATE

An **INSTALLMENT SALE** *is the sale of real estate in which the payments for the property extend over more than one calendar year.* Installment sales are used to spread a gain over two or more calendar years so that the entire gain is not taxed all in the first year. Our income tax system has progressive rates, which means that the higher the income, the higher the income tax rate for that year. If a person can spread a gain over more than one calendar year, the same income may be taxed at a lower rate.

By doing this, your seller avoids the disadvantages of paying for his or her entire gain in one year and thereby has a substantial savings on his or her income taxes. This method is usually used when selling large tracts of land held for a period of time or large buildings owned by one individual.

Installment sales are used because a gain is only taxed in the year that it is received. Spreading the gain over several years may drop you into a lower tax bracket (marginal tax rate).

A sale of a lot for $400,000 all at once might force your seller into a higher tax bracket. So by having an installment sale of $100,000 for each of the next four years, he or she may substantially reduce the total income taxes paid. An installment sale may be a good way to defer income taxes if your seller's income varies from year-to-year; they can just arrange to get larger installment payments in years when their ordinary income is low.

B. EXCHANGES TAX-DEFERRED (Federal and State) (Section 1031 of the IRS Code)

1. Simultaneous 1031 Exchanges (Clients' Investment Properties)

Appreciated real estate investment property, when sold, creates a capital gain. The capital gain is usually taxed by the state up to 9.3%, plus federal income taxes up to 39.6%, in the year sold.

A simple explanation of **EXCHANGING** *is the trading of one property for another.*

Exchanging may allow your client to save a lot on income taxes now, yet obtain the same desired result as selling a property and buying a new investment property later.

Under IRS Section 1031, property held for productive use in a trade or business, is exchanged for like-kind property. Some of the reasons your clients may want to exchange property include the following:

1. Difficulty refinancing to improve property.
2. Trade a highly appreciated property for a property that generates a good cash flow income.
3. Trade non-productive land for a property that generates cash flow income.
4. Exchange to change lifestyle. (An older owner may want less management worries.)
5. Trade many properties for one big property.
6. Trade high-debt property for low debt and interest payments.

1031 Exchanges can be complex. It is advisable to talk to a professional intermediary who acts as a middleman or facilitator in the exchange of a property.

a. Like-Kind Property

*A **LIKE-KIND PROPERTY** is any real property held for investment that can be exchanged for other investment property, under IRC Section 1031. They include:*

1. apartments and residential rentals,
2. commercial property,
3. industrial property, and
4. farms or land.

2. Starker Delayed Exchange

The Starker Court Case was the first court decision to allow a delayed exchange (up to 180 days). Simultaneous Exchanges were common until Starker Delayed Exchanges came into existence.

A "delayed exchange" takes place (a day up to 180 days) in between the initial sale of the (relinquished) property and subsequent acquisitions of the new (replacement) property.

3. Reverse 1031 Exchanges

The newest version of a 1031 exchange is the "Reverse" exchange.

A "reverse exchange" takes place (a day up to 180 days) in between the initial purchase of the new (replacement) property and subsequent sale of the old (relinquished) property.

4. Accounting for Exchanges

An exchange may be a straight trade (tax-free) or one party may receive cash in addition to the property (partially tax-free). An exchange can be income tax free, partially taxed, or fully taxed, depending on the cash received and amount of mortgage loan relief in each particular exchange. Exchanges are too detailed to fully explain here, but it is a way of deferring, or possibly eliminating, income taxes on the transfer of real estate.

To defer all current taxes, a party in an exchange needs to receive a more valuable building with a larger loan on it than the current property, and pay compensation to the other party for any difference in the equities. *Any net cash or net mortgage relief that a participant in an exchange might receive, in addition to the actual property, is known as **BOOT**.* All boot is taxable to the extent of the gain in this partially tax-free exchange. **See Figure 10-12.**

"Boot" is cash or debt relief where the receiver has recognized gain. If there is no boot in an exchange, the old basis is the new basis.

Figure 10-12

Tax-Deferred Exchanges

Boot is defined as cash or mortgage relief.

In a "tax-free" exchange, boot is defined as cash or mortgage relief given in addition to the property. Boot is the amount received to balance the equities in the exchange. As a broker, you will often encounter the term "boot" when talking with a client about income taxes.

The person receiving boot has a net gain and has to pay taxes on it. When no boot is given or received, then the basis remains the same.

In an exchange, the adjusted cost basis of the old property becomes the basis of the new property.

In a tax-free exchange, properties must be of a "like kind" in nature or character, not in use, quality or grade. "Tax free" merely means to DEFER the payment of taxes until a later time. Since your clients can move their equity to another property, it is almost like buying and selling without paying income taxes.

The actual techniques used to exchange are too complex to be explained here, but many six-hour seminars and exchange clubs are available to interested investors.

Exchanges are popular among apartment owners and commercial property investors. This is because these owners are usually in high-income tax brackets, and exchanging enables them to move up to a more valuable property without paying taxes on the gain. People in higher income tax brackets often keep their money invested in real estate, and they find exchanges to be a way of selling and buying simultaneously.

XI. Dealer Property

DEALER PROPERTY *is the inventory of properties held primarily for sale to customers.* Hence, it is frequently called "inventory property," as it is held as the dealer's stock in trade like the merchandise on the shelves of a retail store. What constitutes dealer property is often the subject of much controversy; profits on the sale of such property are taxed as ordinary income (highest tax rate), and losses are treated as ordinary losses. During the holding period, the dealer is entitled to deductions for all expenses incurred on the property, except for depreciation allowances, unless the property also produces income or is held for such purposes.

Unlike investment, income, or business property, dealer property does not qualify for tax-free exchange.

To be classed as a dealer, a number of factors are applied. Among these factors are: 1) frequency of sales; 2) dollar volume; 3) extent to which the property represents the taxpayer's major source of income; 4) listing and selling activities; 5) maintenance of a sales office; 6) reinvestment of sales proceeds into more real estate; 7) evidence that the property was purchased for immediate resale; 8) real estate licensee status; 9) subdivision activity; and 10) amount of income generated from the property.

Brokers have to be careful or they may be classified as "dealers," which has few tax advantages.

The taxpayer's entire background in real estate is evaluated before a property sale is labeled a "dealer sale of inventory." Each case is judged on the facts. Real estate licensees, subdividers, developers, and builders are naturally suspect, but the fact that they are more knowledgeable in real estate matters does not conclusively place them in the dealer category. Indeed, they may be considered investors in some transactions and dealers in others. Each sale should be explained in terms of economic justification or overriding consideration, and not judged solely on the fact of its quick turnover.

XII. We Are Now Tax Collectors (Federal and State Income Tax Laws)

A. FEDERAL TAX COLLECTION REQUIREMENTS AND EXEMPTIONS (If a Foreigner)

If your client is buying property from foreign investors (sellers), your buyer is required to set aside 10% of the purchase price for the Internal Revenue Service. This 10% withholding is kept by the IRS to ensure that property capital gains taxes are paid on the transaction. Both the buyer and broker share liability.

If this amount is not withheld, you, as the broker, may be liable for the full amount of the tax not paid.

This law holds brokers responsible to check the citizenship of all sellers and see to it that the buyer retains either a 10% deposit, an affidavit from the seller stating that he or she is not a foreigner, or a waiver from the IRS. Residential property, purchased for under $300,000 and to be used as the buyer's residence, is exempted from this withholding.

The key points for licensees to remember are these:

1. **Inquire** into the citizenship of all sellers of **residential** properties priced at **$300,000 or more**, even if a foreigner holds only partial or syndicate interest.

2. **Require** a statement of citizenship as part of the listing agreement and then follow up in escrow by having the seller or sellers sign a sworn affidavit.

3. **Do not discriminate.** Require this information of all sellers in transactions of $300,000 or more. Even if someone does not appear to be an alien, they might hold foreign citizenship.

The CAR® Seller's Affidavit of Nonforeign Status and/or California Withholding Exemption is a form for the seller to sign (**Figure 10-13**) swearing that he or she is not a nonresident alien. If the seller completes the lower portion of this sworn statement, the buyer and broker may no longer be liable for any portions of unpaid taxes.

A Buyer's Affidavit form is available from CAR®. This form states that the sales price is less than $300,000 and that the property will be used as a residence. It is signed by the buyer under penalty of perjury. If these two considerations can be met, the buyer is immediately exempted from the withholding requirement. If neither of these forms can truthfully be completed, then the broker should see to it that 10% of the sales price is withheld in escrow, or that the proper waiver is obtained from the IRS. The escrow officer will help you with this matter.

B. STATE TAX COLLECTION REQUIREMENTS AND EXEMPTIONS
(If a Foreigner or Resident of Another State)

If your client is buying property from foreign or out-of-state investors, or non-owner occupied properties, he or she may be required to set aside 3.3% of the sales price for the Franchise Tax Board. If this amount is not withheld, you, as the broker, and the buyer may be liable for the full amount of income taxes not paid. Escrow usually handles this, but the buyer and broker are responsible.

The exemptions from the buyer withholding 3.3% of the sales price for the Franchise Tax Board are:

1. Sales price is $100,000 or less.
2. Property is seller's principal residence, under certain conditions.
3. Seller signs California Residency Declaration.
4. Seller receives a waiver—Franchise Tax Board Form 593-C.

These laws put the burden on the buyer, not the seller. Escrow officers will help with these requirements. Buyer and broker must retain the documentation for 5 years.

Figure 10-13

CALIFORNIA
ASSOCIATION
OF REALTORS®

SELLER'S AFFIDAVIT OF NONFOREIGN STATUS
AND/OR CALIFORNIA WITHHOLDING EXEMPTION
FOREIGN INVESTMENT IN REAL PROPERTY TAX ACT (FIRPTA)
AND CALIFORNIA WITHHOLDING LAW
(Use a separate form for each Transferor)
(C.A.R. Form AS, Revised 1/03)

USE ONLY FOR ESCROWS CLOSING ON OR AFTER JANUARY 1, 2003

Internal Revenue Code ("IRC") Section 1445 provides that a transferee of a U.S. real property interest must withhold tax if the transferor is a "foreign person." California Revenue and Taxation Code Section 18662 provides that a transferee of a California real property interest must withhold tax if the transferor: **(i)** is an individual (unless certain exemptions apply); or **(ii)** is any entity other than an individual ("Entity") if the transferor's proceeds will be disbursed to a financial intermediary of the transferor, or to the transferor with a last known street address outside of California. California Revenue and Taxation Code Section 18662 includes additional provisions for corporations.

I understand that this affidavit may be disclosed to the Internal Revenue Service and to the California Franchise Tax Board by the transferee, and that any false statement I have made herein (if an Entity Transferor, on behalf of the Transferor) may result in a fine, imprisonment or both.

1. **PROPERTY ADDRESS** (the address of the property being transferred): _____

2. **TRANSFEROR'S INFORMATION:**
   Full Name _____
   Telephone No. _____
   Address _____
   (Use HOME address for individual transferors. Use OFFICE address for Entities: corporations, partnerships, limited liability companies, trusts and estates.)
   Social Security No., Federal Employer Identification No., or California Corporation No. _____

3. **AUTHORITY TO SIGN:** If this document is signed on behalf of an Entity Transferor, THE UNDERSIGNED INDIVIDUAL DECLARES THAT HE/SHE HAS AUTHORITY TO SIGN THIS DOCUMENT ON BEHALF OF THE TRANSFEROR.

4. **FEDERAL LAW:** I, the undersigned individual, declare under penalty of perjury that, for the reason checked below, if any, I am exempt (or if signed on behalf of an Entity Transferor, the Entity is exempt) from the federal withholding law (FIRPTA):
   ☐ (For individual Transferors) I am not a nonresident alien for purposes of U.S. income taxation.
   ☐ (For corporation, partnership, limited liability company, trust, and estate Transferors) The Transferor is not a foreign corporation, foreign partnership, foreign limited liability company, foreign trust, or foreign estate, as those term are defined in the Internal Revenue Code and Income Tax Regulations.

5. **CALIFORNIA LAW:** I, the undersigned individual, declare under penalty of perjury that, for the reason checked below, if any, I am exempt (or if signed on behalf of an Entity Transferor, the Entity is exempt) from the California withholding law:
   ☐ The total sale price for the property is $100,000 or less.
   For individual or revocable/grantor trust Transferors only:
   ☐ The property being transferred is in California and was my principal residence within the meaning of IRC Section 121.
   ☐ The property is being, or will be, exchanged for property of like kind within the meaning of IRC Section 1031.
   ☐ The property has been compulsorily or involuntarily converted (within the meaning of IRC1033) and I intend to acquire property similar or related in service or use to be eligible for non-recognition of gain for California income tax purposes under IRC Section 1033.
   ☐ The transaction will result in a loss for California income tax purposes.
   For Entity Transferors only:
   ☐ (For corporation Transferors) The Transferor is a corporation qualified to do business in California, or has a permanent place of business in California at the address shown in paragraph 2 ("Transferor's Information").
   ☐ (For limited liability company ("LLC") or partnership Transferors) The Transferor is an LLC or partnership and recorded title to the property being transferred is in the name of the LLC or partnership and the LLC or partnership will file a California tax return to report the sale and withhold on foreign and domestic nonresident partners as required.
   ☐ (For irrevocable trust Transferors) The Transferor is an irrevocable trust with at least one trustee who is a California resident and the trust will file a California tax return to report the sale and withhold when distributing California source taxable income to nonresident beneficiaries as required.
   ☐ (For estate Transferors) The Transferor is an estate of a decedent who was a California resident at the time of his/her death and the estate will file a California tax return to report the sale and withhold when distributing California source taxable income to nonresident beneficiaries as required.
   ☐ (For tax-exempt Entity and nonprofit organization Transferors) The Transferor is exempt from tax under California or federal law.

By _____ Date _____
(Transferor's Signature) (Indicate if you are signing as the grantor of a revocable/grantor trust.)

_____   _____
Typed or printed name   Title (If signed on behalf of entity Transferor)

SURE TRAC
The System for Success™

Published by the
California Association of REALTORS®

AS REVISED 1/03 (PAGE 1 OF 1) Print Date

Reviewed by _____ Date _____

EQUAL HOUSING OPPORTUNITY

SELLER'S AFFIDAVIT OF NONFOREIGN STATUS AND/OR CALIFORNIA WITHHOLDING EXEMPTION (AS PAGE 1 OF 1)

XIII. Other Taxes Paid by Brokers

A. BUSINESS LICENSE TAXES (City Taxes)

A city may levy a tax against real estate brokerage firms, which is based upon the gross receipts, through a BUSINESS LICENSE TAX. In most areas of California, this annual city business license tax is a nominal amount that usually starts at about $100. Other city taxes may also include employee payroll taxes.

A city tax on a real estate brokerage firm's gross receipts is called a business license tax.

XIV. CHAPTER SUMMARY

Real property taxes are determined by the value of the real property (ad valorem), and the property is reassessed each time a property is sold at 1% of its selling price. The **County Assessor** assesses property, the **County Tax Collector** collects taxes, and the **County Board of Supervisors** sets the rates. **Proposition 13** limits the amount of taxes to 1% of the 1975 market value of the property plus a cumulative increase of 2% in assessed value each year thereafter, called **assessed valuation**.

Property taxes due are liens against that specific property. Important tax dates include **November 1** (first installment), **December 10** (first installment is delinquent), **February 1** (second installment) and **April 10** (second installment is delinquent), or No Darn Fooling Around.

The **homeowner's property tax exemption** is $7000 of assessed valuation. And, although California has no exemption for low income families, it does have senior citizen and disabled person postponements, as well as veterans' and non-profit organizations' tax exemptions.

Local improvement taxes for off-site improvements like streets, sewers, irrigation, etc. are called **special assessment taxes**. Additional taxes may be incurred, including: **documentary transfer taxes, Mello-Roos liens** (for which disclosure is required), **federal gift taxes,** and **federal estate taxes.**

Interest, property taxes and prepayment penalties paid on a personal residence can be deducted from income taxes. Federal income tax allows a taxpayer to exclude up to $250,000 of gain for each individual ($500,000 if married and on title). When you sell your home (capital asset), a capital gain or loss may result. **Capital gains** are taxed at a lower rate than ordinary income tax rates.

A loss on a sale of a personal residence can also be deducted if it is turned into **income producing property** by renting it. Income property owners can deduct **mortgage interest, property taxes,** and **prepayment penalties,** as well as **operating expenses** and **depreciation,**

but not losses due to vacancies. If a business owner sells a building for cash, then leases it back (a **sale-leaseback**), the seller becomes the lessee and the buyer the lessor, and the seller can deduct 100% of future rents paid.

Federal taxes are **progressive**, meaning the percentage paid increases as the amount to be taxed increases, which is the opposite of sales taxes which are regressive. The **alternative minimum tax (AMT)** may be applicable to a single, head of household individual making $40,000.

In addition to depreciation, two major tax benefits of owning income producing property are **installment sales** (gain is only taxed in the year it is received) and **1031 tax-deferred exchanges** (a means of deferring or eliminating income taxes on property transfers). Cash or debt relief gained in a tax deferred exchange is known as **boot**.

Persons buying property from foreign investors are required to set aside 10% of the purchase price for the IRS, to insure the property capital gains taxes are paid on the transaction. An additional 3.3% of the sales price for the Franchise Tax Board may also have to be withheld. In both cases, the burden is on the buyer and broker, not the seller. Brokers may also have to pay a business license tax, which is a city tax based on gross receipts.

XV. KEY TERMS

$250,000 Homeowner Exemption
Ad Valorem
Assessed Valuation
Boot
County Assessor
County Collector
Depreciation for Tax Purposes
Documentary Transfer Tax
Donee
Donor
Exchange
Federal and State Income Tax
Federal Estate Tax
Federal Gift Tax
Homeowners Property Tax Exemption
Installment Sale
Proposition 13
Real Property Taxes
Renter's Credit
Special Assessment
Two Out of the Last 5 Years Residency Requirement

XVI. CHAPTER 10 QUIZ

1. The first installment on property taxes would be considered delinquent after 5:00pm on:
   a. July 10.
   b. April 10.
   c. December 10.
   d. March 10.

2. The second installment on property taxes becomes due on:
   a. June 30.
   b. February 1.
   c. March 1.
   d. November 1.

3. Of the following, which one is a progressive tax?
   a. Gas Tax
   b. Income Tax
   c. Sales Tax
   d. All of the above

4. A tax that is charged in proportion to the value of the property is referred to as a(n):
   a. progressive tax.
   b. progression tax.
   c. ad valorem tax.
   d. excise tax.

5. Proposition 13 set the maximum amount property taxes can increase each year at:
   a. 1%.
   b. 2%.
   c. 5%.
   d. 10%.

6. How much gain can one person (who lived in his or her house for two of the last five years) exclude from income taxes on the sale of that home?
   a. $100,000
   b. $200,000
   c. $250,000
   d. $500,000

7. Which of the following is TRUE concerning capital gains?
   a. Capital gains are taxed at a lower rate than ordinary income tax rates.
   b. Captial gains are taxed at a higher rate than ordinary income tax rates.
   c. Captial gains are taxed at the same rate as ordinary income tax rates.
   d. Capital gains are not taxed.

 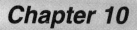

8. The documentary transfer tax is how much per $1,000 of new loans and considerations?

    a. 6%

    b. $1.10

    c. $.55

    d. None of the above

9. Another word for cash or debt relief is:

    a. boot.

    b. shoe.

    c. pocket money.

    d. none of the above.

10. The person who receives a gift is called a:

    a. trustor.

    b. donee.

    c. donor.

    d. none of the above.

ANSWERS: 1. c; 2. b; 3. b; 4. c; 5. b; 6. c; 7. a; 8. b; 9. a; 10. b

REAL ESTATE
INVESTMENTS
IN THE CENTER
OF
MEXICO
The Real Estate Book
La Revista de Bienes R
Se Publica cada 4 Semanas
MÉXICO
CUSTOM H
30 YEA
NOTE: THE 30
s Raíc

CHAPTER 11
Investing
How to Approach Real Estate as an Investment

This chapter deals with real estate investments from both the investors' and the real estate practitioners' perspectives. It includes a variety of investment factors that should be considered: the benefits and rewards of investing, the risks associated with investing, the financing of income properties, and the role you, as a licensee, play in the investment process. A thorough analysis of an apartment house follows thereafter. Then the rental market is discussed from an analysis point of view, followed by a treatment of syndication and an introduction to estate planning.

I. Why Invest in Real Estate?

People invest in property for a variety of reasons. In general, these can be reduced to three: to meet their personal goals and objectives, to give them a means to meet their other financial commitments, and because of the economic soundness of the real property—in other words, to make money.

A. OBJECTIVES

Investors may be seeking additional income through well-chosen properties or a tax shelter to help reduce the bite on otherwise taxable income. Other considerations may be prestige, personal enjoyment in the properties or activities, and the creation

CHAPTER 11 OUTLINE

I. WHY INVEST IN REAL ESTATE? (p. 411)
   A. Objectives (p. 411)
   B. Capacity (p. 413)
   C. Soundness (p. 413)
II. BENEFITS OF INVESTING (p. 414)
   A. Tax Shelter (Ways to Reduce Gains) (p. 414)
   B. Other Tax Benefits (p. 414)
   C. Appreciation Potential (p. 414)
   D. Hedge Against Inflation (p. 415)
   E. Income (p. 415)
   F. Interim Use (p. 415)
   G. Stability (p. 415)
   H. Control and Use (p. 416)
   I. Refinancing (To Buy More Property) (p. 416)
   J. Amenities (p. 416)
III. CHALLENGES TO REAL ESTATE INVESTING (p. 416)
   A. Large Capital Outlay (p. 416)
   B. Lack of Liquidity (p. 417)
   C. Professional Property Management Needed (p. 417)
   D. Potentially Unfavorable Financing (p. 417)
   E. Personal Attachment (Affecting Profitability) (p. 418)
   F. Miscellaneous Negative Factors (p. 418)
IV. FINANCING INCOME PROPERTIES (p. 418)
   A. Sources of Financing (p. 418)
      1. Savings Banks (Limited Investment Financing) (p. 419)
      2. Commercial Banks (No Long-Term Loans, No Apartment Projects) (p. 419)
      3. Life Insurance Companies (Favor Large Investment Properties) (p. 420)
   B. Available Funds (p. 420)
V. YOUR ROLE IN THE INVESTMENT PROCESS (p. 420)
   A. Apartment Prospecting and Marketing (p. 420)
      1. Qualifying the Potential Buyers (p. 421)
      2. Getting the Listing (p. 422)
   B. Investment Planning and Counseling (p. 422)
VI. RESIDENTIAL INCOME PROPERTIES (p. 423)
   A. Property Analysis (Appraisal) (p. 423)
      1. Potential Gross Income (p. 423)
      2. Effective Gross Income (p. 425)
      3. Net Operating Income (p. 425)
      4. Times Gross (Estimation) (p. 427)
      5. Capitalization of Net Income (p. 427)
   B. Analyzing the Rental Market (p. 428)

C. Study Area Characteristics (p. 429)
1. Population Analysis (p. 429)
2. Dwelling Unit Trends (p. 429)
3. Projected Demand for Multiple Units in the Area (p. 430)
D. Characteristics of the Rental Market (p. 430)
1. Income Characteristics (p. 430)
2. Rent-to-Income Relationships (p. 430)
3. Current Rental Ranges (p. 430)
4. Current Vacancy Rates (p. 430)
5. Rent Control (p. 431)
6. Desirable Distribution of Units by Type and Price Class (p. 431)
VII. SYNDICATION (PURCHASE GROUP) (p. 431)
A. Definition (p. 431)
B. Brokerage Opportunities (p. 432)
C. Forms of Legal Organization (p. 432)
1. Limited Partnership (Most Preferred) (p. 433)
2. General Partnership (Not Recommended) (p. 434)
3. Corporation (Can Be Double-Taxed) (p. 434)
a. Subchapter S Corporations (p. 435)
4. Real Estate Investment Trust (REIT) (p. 435)
VIII. CHAPTER SUMMARY (p. 436)
IX. KEY TERMS (p. 438)
X. CHAPTER 11 QUIZ (p. 439)

of an estate. The investor needs to decide which of these, or which combination, is important in order to select the property most likely to accomplish those objectives.

The number one objective for investing in real estate is to make money.

B. CAPACITY

The investor in real estate should have the financial ability to handle carrying the costs of the investment—such as debt service (loan payments) and taxes—and still retain a cash reserve for emergencies.

The costs of operating expenses continue to escalate.

C. SOUNDNESS

After deciding on objectives and analyzing your financial investor's capacity to carry a given amount of debt, the economic health of the property must be considered. This includes the economic trends of the surrounding area, growth trends in the community, zoning (both current and planned), and income projections.

The investment should be sound from an economic point of view, that is, investors ought to look beyond projected figures. Projected figures should reflect financial reality. Paper figures could include market and economic analysis. The market for the property should be properly and objectively analyzed. There should be a real need for the services (rents, sales, and fees) the property is expected to produce. All too often, only income tax consequences are presented to the buyer, without regard to the basic financial soundness of the venture.

II. Benefits of Investing

Income properties are generally high-ticket items, therefore you can expect larger commissions than you would earn selling single-unit properties.

Whether investment factors are beneficial or not depends on the degree to which they meet or exceed your investor's specific objectives. In the following discussions, you'll discover how rewarding real estate investing can be, and be made aware of some cautionary factors as well.

A. TAX SHELTER (Ways to Reduce Gains)

Your clients in high income tax brackets may benefit from "sheltering," or conserving, part of their ordinary income through wise planning, selection, and operation of an income-producing property. Depreciation expenses on both real and personal property may account for a portion of the cash flow generated from the operation of the property, particularly in the earlier years. The level of your investor's income subject to ordinary tax rates can be reduced through proper deductions for operating expenses from the rental income generated from the investment. Many highly taxed investors seek ways to protect all of their income from taxation. They may also attempt to reduce their tax liability on their regular (job) income from wages and salary.

B. OTHER TAX BENEFITS

As demonstrated in Chapter 10, gains can be deferred through one of several devices, mainly through: 1) a tax-free exchange, 2) a deferred sale, or 3) an installment sale. As a side benefit, the proceeds from a profitable sale could be reinvested into another profitable venture.

C. APPRECIATION POTENTIAL

"The Good Lord stopped making land a long time ago, but He's making more people than ever before."

Growth through appreciation is a function of supply and demand, economic conditions, influx of population, inflation, and scarcity. Since land is fixed in relation to the demand, prices tend to be driven upward over a given period of time. One trait of real estate, especially urban property, is the ability to plot its growth potential, within reasonable limits. Basically, real estate value relates to "utility" (usefulness), which can often be predicted. Once the nature and extent of utility is determined, it's possible to anticipate income and, therefore, value.

D. HEDGE AGAINST INFLATION

Even following the worst of recessions, California's real estate is worth more now than ever!

Real estate tends to keep abreast with the fluctuations of the purchasing power of the U.S. Dollar. During inflationary periods the cost of everything rises, including real estate. However, real estate historically outpaces inflation, although during a recession, housing prices may dip. This is only temporary, and the market is usually quick to bounce back.

E. INCOME

"Cash flow" (either positive or negative) is the difference between the income generated from a property and the expenses associated with it, including taxes, mortgage payments, and operating expenses.

Many investors purchase property with the objective of providing an annuity for themselves. How much this monthly cash income will be is dependent upon many variables, the most important of which are the size of the investment and the amount of leverage (debt) involved. For example, a well-managed apartment house containing, say, 30 units will provide the investor with a very high monthly cash income, while a smaller parallel property encumbered with a large trust deed loan will net little, if any, cash flow. Properly structured, the property could well provide the investor with an independent, or supplemental source, of retirement funds.

F. INTERIM USE

Real property ownership offers the purchaser of a ranch, farm, or other investment the opportunity to use the property to make some income while waiting for appreciation of value to take place. This future increase in value may come from a zoning change and/or inflation. In a big city, vacant land might be used for some interim use, like a parking lot, until it is slated for development.

G. STABILITY

Many types of real estate, particularly commercial and industrial properties, enjoy long-term leases with top corporations, producing a dependable, stable investment for as long

as twenty years or more. In the case of apartments, strong neighborhood patterns can produce the same kind of effect as long-term leases, based upon such things as favorable zoning and community planning, shopping conveniences, and transportation routes.

Trends can often be charted in such a way that investors can see the benefits of owning. These trends require careful analysis and the assistance of well-informed brokers and other trained individuals.

H. CONTROL AND USE

As a real estate professional, you have the opportunity to assist your investors to thoroughly study the environment and economic background of their investments, before buying, by analyzing them for tax benefits, inflation hedge, financing opportunities, income and cash flow, and stability. All of these can be changed from time-to-time to serve the goal of improving the investment. Rezoning of a property, for example, can enhance it's highest and best use, which could increase its value. A new leasing pattern to different lessees, at higher rents, can also produce dramatic results in terms of improving gross income.

I. REFINANCING (To Buy More Property)

Let's take the case of one of your clients who has an investment property with a large equity. If your owner decides to refinance the property in order to purchase more income property, three things can be accomplished. First, the cash proceeds from refinancing are tax-free. Second, the interest paid on the new debt is fully tax deductible. Third, your investor is acquiring another investment property, adding to his or her worth.

J. AMENITIES

Other benefits to the investor include pride of ownership, security, status, achievement, estate building, and the opportunity to improve profits.

III. Challenges to Real Estate Investing

Now that you are familiar with the benefits of real estate investments, it's important to be aware of some of the potential downfalls, as well. When counseling investment clients, it's your responsibility to make sure they have the capacity to meet their financial objectives. In order to ensure that your clients have realistic expectations, you should be aware of the following limitations.

A. LARGE CAPITAL OUTLAY

The amount of capital (cash) required for down payment and periodic monetary outlay is large when compared to alternate forms of investments. Unless a substantial amount is involved in the purchase, the investment may not be as profitable as it could be otherwise. For example, a $700,000 investment in apartment units may not provide the economy of scale that could be effected through a $4 million project.

The more apartment units purchased, the larger the number over which your investor will have to spread fixed operating expenses. A gardener, for example, doesn't charge twice as much to care for twice as many units.

B. LACK OF LIQUIDITY

LIQUIDITY is the ease and rate with which an asset can be converted into a medium of exchange. Because real estate usually takes between two to nine months to sell, depending on the market, with more unique properties taking even longer, investment property is not considered a very liquid asset. While it may be true that there is a buyer for everything, finding the right buyer may be time consuming. Conditions of the market, size of the market, location, financing opportunities, and many other variables will affect the length of time required to sell the property and turn it into cash.

C. PROFESSIONAL PROPERTY MANAGEMENT NEEDED

As generals must delegate authority to their officers in the field, so too must investors delegate duties to their property managers.

In any real estate venture, a high degree of investment know-how and continuous management skill and care are required if it is to be profitable. The more time and effort your investor is prepared to put into a property, the more he or she can expect to gain in satisfaction, including a higher rate of return. Unfortunately for them, most real estate investors lack the time, knowledge, or inclination to properly manage their properties. (In this case, you should recommend that your client have a professional property manager.) Fortunately, as a broker, you have the option of offering property management as part of your real estate services, and can expect to earn approximately seven percent of total rents collected. See Chapter 13 for more information on property management as a career.

In California, an apartment complex with 16 or more units requires an on-site property manager, meaning he or she must actually live on the premises, but does not need a real estate license.

D. POTENTIALLY UNFAVORABLE FINANCING

The amount and terms of current financing may not meet the goals and objectives of your investor. For example, if short-term loans with high interest rates are the only loans currently available, your investor's cash flow potential will be greatly diminished. Additional restrictive and unappealing financing terms include acceleration clauses, lock-in provisions, prepayment penalties, and more.

E. PERSONAL ATTACHMENT (Affecting Profitability)

While pride of ownership may be a significant reason for the purchase of a particular investment, it can be all too easy to become emotionally attached to a property and tenants. As a result, an investor may fail to take advantage of the rental market. To "fall in love" with an investment property reduces flexibility in its operation, may seriously diminish its capacity to produce the highest possible return by increasing rents for example, and may otherwise work counter to the objectives of the individual investor.

Owners of rental property often become emotionally involved with their tenants, making wise financial decisions difficult. A property manager may be a necessity to keep all transactions at "arm's length."

F. MISCELLANEOUS NEGATIVE FACTORS

Other disadvantages to investing in real estate include vulnerability to high local taxation and support of local government, social welfare, schools, and other services. Immobility is another disadvantage. Your investor can't just pick up and leave with his or her investment as with movable assets.

Restrictions may render a property less useful and, therefore, less valuable than would otherwise be the case. These restrictions include zoning (government restriction) and private covenants, conditions, and restrictions created by deed. The possibility of loss due to excess actual depreciation, obsolescence, poor management, and softening of the market are also possible negatives.

IV. Financing Income Properties

One of the outstanding advantages of real estate is the special financing and refinancing opportunities available to the investor. The type of leverage he or she is seeking should be readily available through a variety of lenders.

A. SOURCES OF FINANCING

Miscellaneous sources of funds for investment properties include syndicates and trusts (to be discussed in a separate section), real estate bonds and debentures, bank-administered pension trust funds, sellers under purchase money transactions and land contracts, and a variety of others to a lesser degree. Real estate syndicates and REITs (real estate investment trusts) have proved to be useful devices for higher-income investors as well as small investors who pool their resources to develop and operate residential income and commercial properties. Seller carryback purchase money trust deeds and contracts of sales are, perhaps, the most important sources of financing for raw land and many special purpose projects.

During tight money periods in particular, sellers frequently become the only source of financing for raw land and special purpose projects, wherein the seller effectively operates as a bank, actually supplying the financing, which the buyer agrees to replace when, and if, outside financing can be secured.

In Chapter 8 we covered, in depth, the three main lending sources for residential property. At least two of these large institutional lenders are also active, to varying degrees, in financing investment properties. As such, a summary of these lending sources bears repeating here.

1. Savings Banks (Limited Investment Financing)

SAVINGS BANKS specialize in housing loans, particularly for single-family dwellings. However, increasingly, they are expanding into the apartment market. They are not active in special purpose properties, such as individual and commercial buildings.

2. Commercial Banks (No Long-Term Loans, No Apartment Projects)

COMMERCIAL BANKS are very active in the urban mortgage market. Banks are short-term lenders, so an investor who is seeking a high-leverage position or low payments over a long period will find the commercial bank inadequate. In the field of real estate, they specialize in interim financing. *INTERIM FINANCING is a loan for the construction period only, generally repaid within a year from the sale of the individual units constructed.* Commercial banks are also interested in making "takeout" or standard (30-year) home loans to the buyers of these units. They are also active in single-family dwellings, both conventional and FHA-VA. Apartment projects are virtually dormant, since large funds would be tied up for too long.

Commercial banks make the majority of their funds available for high interest, short-term loans, like credit cards, automobile, and construction loans.

3. Life Insurance Companies (Favor Large Investment Properties)

LIFE INSURANCE COMPANIES, along with their correspondents, show a different pattern of lending than the other institutions. They invest in large commercial projects, like shopping malls, and serve markets far away from their home offices. Because their lending radius is not restricted by legislation, and because they have created elaborate and far-flung channels for the acquisition of very large loans, insurance companies have been comparatively free to allocate their funds regionally. Most do so through local representatives called mortgage correspondents or mortgage bankers.

Life insurance companies (as distinguished from other types of insurance companies) are heavily involved in takeout (30-year) loans on prime homes and large income projects, and well-located single-family dwellings with high down payments. They

also prefer large apartment complexes, shopping centers, office buildings, prime industrial buildings, and sale-leaseback arrangements with top-rated lessees.

B. AVAILABLE FUNDS

The amount of financing available depends upon its source. High debt ratio financing can be achieved from some sources, while a relatively low ratio is required of others. In any event, how much is attainable is dependent upon the type of property, the credit of the individual, market conditions, the relationship of the borrower with the lender, and other variables.

V. Your Role in the Investment Process

What follows is a discussion of selling investment real property. Naturally, different salespeople have different approaches to selling. The following suggestions are, in the authors' opinions, the best approach to marketing.

A. APARTMENT PROSPECTING AND MARKETING

Sources of prospects for listing and buying investment properties include many of the same as those for residential properties. While it may be true that the sale of a home appeals more to your prospect's emotions, and that the sale of investments relies more on an economic and rational approach, similarities do exist. It was pointed out previously that the reasons for investing include providing supplemental income or building an estate. Why not approach the sellers of a home with the idea that they replace their home with a fourplex, occupy one of the units, and rent out the other three? This could well be the start of a happy, long-term broker/client relationship as the client increase his or her investments.

Suppose that you were the listing agent on a ten-unit apartment house. You would advertise in the newspapers, by direct mailing to your prospect list, through the multiple listing services so that other brokers will become aware of the new offering, and so on. Whether you get permission to place a "for sale" sign on the property will depend upon persuading the owners that tenants will not leave en masse, a fear not without merit. Occasionally, occupants will terminate their tenancy because of the uncertainty surrounding impending change. They may fear a rise in rents, a less concerned owner/landlord, or worry they may be ousted by the new owners. On the other side of the fence are tenants who, seeing that the property is going to be sold anyway, may take advantage of the changeover by withholding one or more rent payments, and even leave before the new management has the chance to catch up with them.

Don't overlook the current tenants as potential prospects.

After all, tenants very likely are satisfied with the property, location, and so on, or they would not be living there. Many tenants with no children and a working spouse will have more money saved than single occupants. These tenants may consequently need more shelter from taxes and are, in many ways, logical candidates for the property. It might be noted that commercial tenants are even more likely prospects than residential tenants. You should consider sending a letter to the tenants which might be framed somewhat as shown in **Figure 11-1**.

Figure 11-1

CBA Realtors
6515 Van Nuys Boulevard
Van Nuys, California 91411
(818)786-2663

January 25, 2005

Dear Tenants:

We wish to inform you that the property in which you reside is being offered for sale.

It occurred to us that you may be seeking an investment in order to obtain some of the many advantages which buyers of such properties are accorded.

CBA Realtors specializes in all types of real estate. Should you wish to learn about the many benefits of this or any other properties, we shall be happy to be of service. Call or write to us at the above address. No obligation, of course.

---

1. Qualifying the Potential Buyers

To assist in the qualifying prospects, you need to obtain certain information. The names and ages of family members, occupation and income, sources of other income, assets and encumbrances, investment needs, and additional remarks should be gathered. You should also know how to assess the prospect's ability to buy and be able to determine what kind of property and how much he or she should invest. The process of qualifying the purchaser of investment property is not much different from that of qualifying home buyers, only you should understand financial analysis better and take into account and weigh the investment objectives of your prospects.

Include a lender with whom you have a relationship in the qualifying process.

2. Getting the Listing

Listing an apartment house is not unlike listing a house. You meet the owners, ask searching questions, come prepared with valuation data, and create opportunities for the sellers by showing them how the proceeds can be reinvested, and so on.

In buying income-producing property, greater emphasis is placed on financial benefits than on sentimental attachments.

When gathering information, you'll also need to get detailed facts about the property, such as:

1. needed repairs;
2. condition of units;
3. quality of tenants;
4. rent schedules;
5. lease terms;
6. vacancy factors; and
7. evaluation of income and expenses.

Showing the owners how they can improve their estate or income, through selling and buying or exchanging for more profitable property, will help you secure a saleable listing. Point out, for example, how the owners' objectives are no longer being met if their property is fully depreciated or has a low book value. This will promote a listing at a price that will sell.

The owner of a fully depreciated property is an excellent listing prospect!

B. INVESTMENT PLANNING AND COUNSELING

As a broker who expects to build up a following in the field of real estate investments, you will need to do more than the typical agent. To pick up repeat business, you will have to earn the respect and confidence of your clients. This can come only with a thorough understanding of your client's total financial and family picture. A confidential file should be maintained for each of your clients. By integrating all of the data and information about the client, you're in a better position to render superior service.

Investment planning may be thought of as the integration of a number of steps, starting with a thorough analysis of your client's investment requirements.

Conferring with your client's attorney, accountant, or business advisor may be advisable somewhere along the way.

Researching and selecting properties to meet the objectives of your client is the second step. A decision to buy a particular property is then made, and you negotiate its acquisition, followed by title search and escrow. Management of the property is next, to safeguard the investment, to minimize expenses, and to maximize profits. Along every step of the way, you must be aware of change, offering suggestions and making recommendations as the circumstances warrant.

VI. Residential Income Properties

The factors to be considered before your client purchases an apartment house, and the advantages and disadvantages of such a purchase, are about the same as in any income producing real estate investment. In this section, analysis, valuation, management, and the rental market will be explained in detail.

A. PROPERTY ANALYSIS (Appraisal)

The preparation of a comprehensive income and expense analysis on a given apartment project is a complicated and difficult process. The income and expense analysis should be focused on the future operating income of the building.

Because most apartments are held for long-term investment, the third year, the seventh year, and the tenth year can all be as important to the investor as the first year.

To understand the analysis of an income producing property, an Income Property—Residential Statement is shown in **Figure 11-2**. A four-unit apartment house listed at $468,000 is illustrated, along with all the pertinent data. You should study the form in order to understand the financial details of the rental property.

PRICE *is the listing price, the proposed sale price.* **LOANS** *include all first and junior trust deeds that comprise the financing (loans) for the purchaser.* **DOWN PAYMENT** *is the amount the buyer is to pay towards the purchase price.* **SCHEDULED INCOME** *is that gross income which the property would generate if there were no vacancies.*

The steps listed below are arranged in the order you will need to follow to complete a property analysis.

1. Potential Gross Income

POTENTIAL GROSS INCOME *is the total income that the property is capable of producing at full occupancy, without any deductions for expenses.* For example, if the rental rate for a two-bedroom unit is $1,410 per month, an apartment with ten two-bedroom units would have a potential gross income of $14,100 per month (10 x $1,410).

Figure 11-2

Income Property - Residential

PRESENTED BY CBA Realtors

6515 Van Nuys Blvd.

Van Nuys, CA 91411

Tele: 818-786-2663

IMPROVEMENT 4 unit apartment building

ADDRESS 12548 Compton Ave.

CITY Compton

(3) BLOCKS N (S) OF Broadview Blvd.

(1) BLOCKS E (W) OF Watts Ave.

SALES REPRESENTATIVE L. Galivez

TELEPHONE 818-781-5937

SHOWING INSTRUCTIONS Call Mr. F. Topik

OWNER (MANAGER) TENANT

TELEPHONE 818-769-2929 ___ KEY _____

(Picture of property or business card may be placed in above space)

SPECIAL FEATURES

GENERAL INFORMATION

LOT SIZE 90 x 150 _____ ZONE R-3 ___ AGE 11 __ CONST La & Stucco ___ ELEVATOR No __ STYLE English Tudor

LEGAL Lot 14, Tract 16829 _____ PARKING 10 stalls ___ STORIES 2 __ SEWER Y __ HEAT F/A __ AIR COND Y

EXISTING INFORMATION	NO YEARS	INVESTMENT INFORMATION BASED ON

FIRST LOAN 225,000 __ PYMT 2,124 __ INT 9 __ ORIG 25 TO GO 14 | FIRST LOAN 300,000 __ PAYMENT 3,000 __ INT 11 NO YRS 5

LENDER Housing Savings Bank __ LOCKED IN YES __ NO X | LENDER Seller

SECOND LOAN 24,000 __ PYMT 360 __ INT 9 DUE 2010 ACCEL NO | SECOND LOAN _____ PAYMENT _____ INT __ DUE ___

LENDER Private party | LENDER

OTHER LOANS None __ PYMT _____ INT ___ DUE _____ ACCEL ___ | SELLER WILL CARRY Above PAYMENT _____ INT __ DUE ___

SCHEDULED INCOME

#	DESC	RENT
1	3 bd - 2 ba	$ 1,590
2	2 bd - 1.5 ba	$ 1,410
3	2 bd - 1.5 ba	$ 1,410
4	3 bd - 2 ba	$ 1,590
		$
		$
		$
		$
		$
		$
		$
		$

TOTAL SCHEDULED
MONTHLY INCOME $ 4,730

Above information is from sources believed reliable but not guaranteed.

ETC Form 100
© 2005

PROJECTED OPERATING EXPENSES:

Taxes	$ 5,850
Insurance F&L	$ 3,600
License & Fees	$ 195
Utilities	
Water	$ 1,050
Electricity	$ 2,487
Gas	$ 1,440
Management	$ 3,600
	$
Trash	$ 1,440
Gardener	$ 1,080
Maintenance (Est.) ___%	$ 7,200
Other	$
TOTAL	$ 27,942

ASSESSED VALUE

	Amount	Percent
Land	$ 93,600	20 %
Improvement	$ 369,720	79 %
Pers Prop	$ 4,680	1 %
TOTAL	$ 468,000	100%

PROJECTED INVESTMENT INFORMATION:

Price	$ 468,000
Loan (1)	$ 300,000
Down Payment	$ 168,000
Scheduled Income	$ 72,000
Vacancy Factor (Est.) 2 %	$ 1,440
Gross Operating Income	$ 70,560
Projected Operating Expenses	$ 27,942
Net Operating Income (Est.)	$ 42,618
Loan Payments	$ 36,000
Gross Spendable (Est.)	$ 6,618
Furniture Reserve (Est.)	$ 750
Carpet Reserve (Est.)	$ 600
Adj. Gross Spendable (Est.)	$ 5,268
Paid on Principal	$ 3,048
Projected Total Return	$ 8,316

Earns 9.11 _____ % on Sale Price

Spendable at 3.13 __ % on Down Payment

Earns 4.95 _____ % on Down Payment

Purchase Price is 6.5 _____ Times Gross

VACANCY FACTOR is an allowance for vacancies and uncollectible rents. Few, if any, properties will maintain a fully occupied building year after year. The amount of allowance will vary from one apartment building to another, depending on the location, rent schedule, amenities, management, and other factors. Ordinarily, a five percent minimum vacancy should be shown even if there are no present or recent vacancies. An exception might be for rental homes or very small apartment buildings in well-located areas, where high occupancy can be demonstrated on a continuous basis.

Vacancies can be calculated in one of three ways: 1) actual current vacancy as shown by the records; 2) an average percentage of historical vacancies for the subject property; or 3) by checking out vacancies for comparable properties in the area. This last method can be accomplished by determining the number of idle electric meters, periodic post office surveys, statistical data revealed by institutional lenders and some governmental agencies, and personal interviews with apartment house owners, landlords, and tenants.

As a knowledgeable professional, you should counsel your apartment building investor to estimate at least a five percent vacancy factor, even if it is actually lower now.

2. Effective Gross Income

EFFECTIVE GROSS INCOME is the scheduled gross income adjusted (subtracting) for vacancy. It represents the amount of money the owner will receive from rent collections before deductions for expenses and debts. *OPERATING EXPENSES include fixed and variable expenses, as detailed in the bottom half of the Income Property Statement.* You can remember the largest of these expenditures, which are found in every statement, by an acronym *MITUM. The initials stand for Maintenance, Insurance (not interest), Taxes (not trust deed), Utilities, and Management (not mortgage).* These are items which are operational in nature, and are encountered whether the property is fully encumbered or free and clear. Therefore, loan payments are not included, nor are depreciation allowances or provision for income taxes.

Operating expenses do not include loan payments, depreciation allowances, or income tax provisions.

3. Net Operating Income

NET OPERATING INCOME (NOI) is the form of income that is most often used in direct capitalization. Operating expenses are subtracted from effective gross income. Net operating income is a more reliable indicator of value than potential or effective gross income, because it represents the amount of income (after all net operating expenses) that is available as a return to the investor. Properties with similar gross incomes may have widely different net operating incomes, due to differences in operating expenses.

Example: Two properties each have effective gross incomes of $300,000 each per year. Property A has operating expenses of $180,000 per year, while Property B has annual operating expenses of $240,000. In this case, Property A has twice as much net operating income as Property B, even though their effective gross incomes are the same.

Property A: $300,000 - $180,000 = $120,000 NOI

Property B: $300,000 - $240,000 = $60,000 NOI

To determine net operating income, all the operating expenses for the property are subtracted from the effective gross income. Payments on principal and interest are NOT deducted. Depreciation is not a cash expense and is NOT deducted.

OPERATING EXPENSES are any ongoing expenses that are necessary to maintain the flow of income from the property. For appraisal purposes, operating expenses fall into three categories:

1. fixed expenses;
2. variable expenses; and
3. reserves for replacement.

FIXED EXPENSES are operating expenses that do not vary depending on the occupancy of the property. They must be paid regardless of whether the property is leased or vacant. The most common examples of fixed expenses are property taxes and hazard insurance premiums.

VARIABLE EXPENSES are operating expenses that do vary depending on occupancy. They may include a wide variety of expenses, such as utility costs, property management fees, cleaning and maintenance expenses, and leasing commissions.

RESERVES FOR REPLACEMENT are funds that are set aside for replacing short-lived components of the property. A SHORT-LIVED COMPONENT is an item that has a life span that is less than the expected life of the building, such as carpeting, paint, roofing, or mechanical equipment. Normally, the amount of the reserves is calculated by dividing the replacement cost of the item by its remaining useful life.

Example: The cost to replace the roofing on a building is $24,000. If the existing roof has a remaining useful life of 10 years, the annual amount to be set aside for replacement would be $2,400.

$24,000 ÷ 10 years = $2,400

Note that some items that are often listed as expenses for accounting or tax purposes are not included as operating expenses when calculating net operating income. The most notable of these are mortgage principal and interest, depreciation (book depreciation), and income taxes.

4. Times Gross (Estimation)

Real estate agents often refer to the gross income multiplier as the "times gross." *TIMES GROSS is simply the proposed selling price divided by the scheduled gross income, with the multiple used as a ballpark figure to weigh the prospective value of the investment.*

Example: The subject property has potential gross income of $108,000 per year. The appraiser has determined that the annual potential gross income multiplier for this type of property is "11." The value of the property, therefore, is estimated to be:

$1,188,000 ($108,000 x 11)

Multipliers are most often used to convert gross income to value. The use of gross income multipliers is limited almost exclusively to appraisers of single-family and small multi-family residences.

While times gross is a useful tool to screen out properties, it measures only the quantity of income and, therefore, should be considered along with other tests to determine its value as an acceptable investment. All too often, however, brokers misuse it by ignoring other factors that measure the quality and durability of the income, like the age of the property.

Investors are looking for a low (or at least reasonable) times gross of eight or less. The higher the gross multiplier, the higher the price.

5. Capitalization of Net Income

There are a number of techniques that are employed in the determination of the capitalization approach. However, all have a simple common denominator. The net operating income is divided by the selling price to determine the appropriate capitalization rate (cap rate). As a simple example of its application, the worksheet in Figure 11-2 shows the breakdown of a property listed at $468,000, whose net operating income (N.O.I.) is $42,618. This represents a 9.1 percent capitalization rate, or yield, arrived at as follows:

$$\frac{\text{Net Operating Income}}{\text{Sales Price}} = \frac{\$42,618}{\$468,000} = 9.1\% \text{ Capitalization Rate}$$

Stated differently, if four-unit apartment buildings of this grade and quality attract investors only if they offer a 9.1 percent rate of return, the cap rate or yield is 9.1 percent. Thus, if records reveal that a certain income-producing property is producing a net operating income of $42,618, and the prospective purchaser

wants at least a 9.1 percent return on his or her total investment, he or she will not pay more than $468,000. The capitalized value as indicated by the net income, computed as follows:

$$\frac{\text{Net Operating Income}}{\text{Cap Rate}} = \frac{\$42,618}{9.1\%} = \$468,000 \quad \textbf{Selling Price}$$

Simple substitution of other numbers for those shown in the denominator will reveal larger or smaller amounts of value, assuming the purchaser requires at least a 9.1 percent return. For instance, if the annual net operating income was $91,000, the capitalized value ($91,000 ÷ 9.1%) would indicate the value of $1 million. In contrast, if the income after allowance for all operating expenses was, say, only $18,200, then the investor could afford to pay only as much as $200,000 ($18,200 ÷ 9.1%) and still get a return of 9.1 percent.

While it's important to know how cap rates are determined, in actual practice, most agents will just make a phone call to a friendly appraiser and ask what the cap rate is for such an improvement.

B. ANALYZING THE RENTAL MARKET

A significant characteristic of all real estate, but one that is overlooked many times because it is so obvious, is that the investment is physically fixed in its location. This fact produces a finality about the decision to purchase an existing apartment project or to acquire property for construction of such a project.

Each site has its own advantages and disadvantages. Some unfavorable factors may be modified by the actions you take as a property manager, while some are totally out of your reach, such as traffic congestion, aircraft noise, or unfavorable climate. These factors, especially those that are not favorable to human habitation, can develop or increase in intensity with the passage of time. If a trend such as this should set in, there is usually little effective action that you or your property owner can take to offset it.

To some extent, the favorable and unfavorable aspects of the location are in a state of constant change. For example, improved transportation systems can "move" property nearer to the places people go by reducing both distance and time spent traveling. Therefore, you, your investor, and your appraiser need the greatest possible foresight in selecting a location for an apartment property or in acquiring an already existing project. Foresight is also needed in acquiring an enterprise located in the midst of an established matrix of transportation arteries and service facilities, existing and unfolding patterns of urban growth, and adjoining or authorized future land uses. Investigation of these in some detail will help to protect your client's investment by providing data on the basis of which logical and successful plans may be made.

You should provide market studies for your investor to help decide when and how to purchase or produce a project in terms of size of units, furnishings and decor, location, architectural plan and room layout, and population concentration. Properly combined, all these ingredients should create demand for space that will produce a satisfactory experience for your potential owner. This section identifies some of the most significant ingredients of a market study, alerting your potential investor to important factors that he or she must take into consideration.

C. STUDY AREA CHARACTERISTICS

Any useful market analysis must, to one extent or another, include the following information.

1. Population Analysis

The number and type of people within the area determined to be the logical marketing area of the proposed project should be defined and analyzed. The increase or decrease of population should be stated and explained, together with a rational projection of any likely increase or decrease. A comparison of such population increase or decrease with other subareas of the metropolitan community in which the project is to be located would also be useful for comparison purposes.

Checking rental vacancies is another way of establishing the desirability of an investment. This can be done through the MLS and newspaper advertisements.

2. Dwelling Unit Trends

The feasibility of the proposed project depends, in large measure, upon the market conditions for the housing offered in terms of demand (the number of families seeking apartment housing in the particular price class) and supply (the number of apartments in the area that will satisfy the demand). Population pressures would have already been defined, and now it is the responsibility of the analyst to define the market by price class and to state the likelihood of oversupply or undersupply in the market area. Useful, in this instance, is a dwelling unit inventory in the study area, both quantitative and qualitative, with reference to the relationship between single-family and multiple-family dwelling units, and the relationship between numbers of bedrooms and baths within the multiple-family category.

In projecting future housing demand, it is important to consider the reasons for the shifting demands for single-family into multiple-family units, such as substantial increase in the cost of home ownership, increasing land values, higher

construction costs, higher property taxes, and increasing consumer demands. Access to and from the area to major sources of employment is also a significant consideration. Numbers of family formations, numbers of people in certain age categories in the area, and similar demographic information is invaluable, as it helps to identify the size and extent of the market.

3. Projected Demand for Multiple Units in the Area

All of the foregoing data, and a considerable body of additional data, must then be related to the proposed project and stated in terms of the projected demand for multiple units in the community. This is the total demand, an uncritical listing of numbers that constitutes the total market available to the project. It is from this market that the investor must draw support for his or her project.

D. CHARACTERISTICS OF THE RENTAL MARKET

1. Income Characteristics

The success of an apartment project depends to a considerable extent upon the income characteristics of families attracted to the area. The changing distribution of income should be analyzed with an eye toward future possibilities for increasing rent in the project or future necessities to decrease rent.

2. Rent-to-Income Relationships

In California, it is generally held that across the income range a family can, or will, pay about 25 to 40 percent of its income for shelter.

This varies somewhat, however, from income range to income range, and this variance is a critical matter that requires refined definition.

3. Current Rental Ranges

In this part of the study, an attempt is made to analyze competition in a particular study area. The percentage of families prepared to pay a certain amount of money for shelter is a theoretical one, while the number of families actually paying certain rates for certain types of facilities is a matter of practical experience and it must be investigated. The theoretical ability to pay is balanced against practical ability to pay, and related specifically to services (utilities and parking) and facilities (number of bedrooms, number of baths, furnishings, etc.).

4. Current Vacancy Rates

Vacancy rate data is quite reliable in most areas of California and is of maximum importance in determining the amount of new space an area can absorb.

Vacancy by type of facility is more significant than the overall vacancy rate in the area and should be analyzed carefully.

5. Rent Control

Communities and municipalities that impose rent control or rent stabilization adversely impact the potential earnings of a project. Rent control looms large as an important negative consideration in the maximization of rents and, therefore, capitalized values.

Rent control diminishes an investor's income potential. As such, it discourages new construction.

6. Desirable Distribution of Units by Type and Price Class

With any project, it's important to determine the amount of emphasis to place on single units versus one-, two-, or even three- and four-bedroom units. Additional consideration must be given to the requirements for furnishing each unit and demands for amenities by size of unit. The square footage involved in each type of unit is also important and must be considered in light of the kind of tenant your investor wants to appeal to. For example, units that are appealing to families with children or high-income tenants will require more space than units designed for singles or marrieds without children.

VII. Syndication (Purchase Group)

Syndications are based on complex legal concepts, so advise your clients to seek advice from an attorney.

Another area open to you, as a licensee, is the marketing and financing of real estate through syndication. Opportunities for syndication abound because of increasing demand for a shrinking supply of land, population influx, relatively small outlays required of investors, and the solution which the syndication vehicle provides to the problem of tight money.

A. DEFINITION

A **SYNDICATION** *is an association of two or more people who combine their financial resources for the purpose of achieving one or more investment objectives.* It is the process whereby investment capital is pooled or combined for the purpose of acquiring real estate, which ordinarily could not be bought by individuals alone. The rights, responsibilities, benefits, and obligations of the syndicator or promoter toward the investment group, and the investors toward each other, are governed by the legal form of business organization adopted by the participants.

> *As a broker/syndicator, it's possible to make more money in different ways than in any other single real estate endeavor. By taking the initiative to bring together a group of investors, you can expect to earn the following:*
>
> *1. Commission from purchase of large property: 3% - 6%*
> *2. Management fees on rents collected: 5% - 8%*
> *3. Percentage of ownership for creating syndicate: 10% - 20%*
> *4. Commission on resale of syndicated property: 3% - 6%*

B. BROKERAGE OPPORTUNITIES

Creating a real estate syndication can be creative, challenging, and profitable for the enterprising broker. The market for group investing is likely to continue growing and is bound to seriously challenge other investment media for the dollars of the typical investor.

The many benefits available to you as the organizer/promoter of a syndicate include the commissions earned from the sale of the property to the investment group, management fees, a percentage of ownership in exchange for organizational and promotional skills, resale commissions, opportunities for creation of new syndications, and options to acquire one or more interests through right of first refusal provisions. If you are a syndicator who is a licensed contractor, there is the additional opportunity to develop a site through a separate entity and earn the usual contractor's profit, which is customarily a percentage of the cost of development.

Aside from all of the monetary rewards, there is also the satisfaction derived from developing your creative skills and from making it possible for the small investor, by joining a group of investors, to reap the benefits of real estate ownership without the liabilities and problems associated with sole ownership.

C. FORMS OF LEGAL ORGANIZATION

Syndications may assume a number of different legal forms of business organizations, depending upon the specific objectives of the individual participants. You'll find the first three forms of ownership are identical to those we discussed in the brokerage section of Chapter One. They bear repeating here, however, as the pros and cons of each may be different for investment syndicates than for those of a brokerage.

1. Limited Partnership (Most Preferred)

LIMITED PARTNERSHIP consists of two or more persons who have joined together for their mutual investment benefit to share profits and losses. It consists of at least one general partner, plus up to 35 limited partners. It's so-named because the limited partners have limited liabilities—only up to the extent of their capital investment in the venture. This means they can only lose as much as they have invested. The general partner, however, has unlimited liability for the debts and obligations of the undertaking. For this reason, the general partner should be an expert in real estate, such as a knowledgeable attorney, a real estate broker, or a syndicator richly experienced in all phases of real estate.

Advantages of the Limited Partnership Format

The limited partnership is the most popular form of ownership, and is favored over the corporate and other business organizational forms. In California, this form of ownership is preferred for the following reasons.

1. The limited partnership entity is considered separate and distinct from its partners just like the corporation, but is not separately taxed, thus avoiding being taxed twice.

2. Each limited partner is allowed proportionate deductions for expenses of administration, interest, property taxes, depreciation, and operating expenses.

3. The participants are taxed as individuals.

4. Each limited partner enjoys limited liability, not exceeding his or her capital contributions.

5. Neither death, retirement, nor disability of any of the limited partners will dissolve the entity, as would occur under a general partnership.

6. There is a right to sell, transfer, or assign individual interests, subject to restrictions contained in the agreement, without affecting continuity.

7. There is a right of majority to remove and replace the general partner.

8. There is improved bargaining power, leverage, and investment diversification; professional management; and often wholesale purchasing power through pooling of resources.

General partners are financially responsible for more than just the amount of their investment and risk losing everything they own—including their homes. If a limited partner invests $10,000, he or she can only lose $10,000.

Because of their limited liability, limited partners cannot actively engage in the operation of the enterprise. Their activities are limited to those rights set out in the agreement, such as voting on the purchase and sale of partnership property, hiring and firing the general partner, sharing in profits and losses, inspecting the books, amending the agreement, and so on. If the limited partner participates in daily operations, he or she may lose his or her limited status and be treated as a general partner.

2. General Partnership (Not Recommended)

GENERAL PARTNERSHIP is defined as an "association of two or more persons doing business as co-owners for profit." It is perhaps the simplest form of co-ownership to create, but it carries the disadvantage of unlimited personal liability for partnership debts and obligations. Each partner has an equal voice in the daily operation and management of the venture. Each is liable for all of the partnership debts, since, as an agent for the partnership, each partner can bind the other in promoting the business. Because of this and other disadvantages, the general partnership form of ownership is not favored by investors in a syndicate.

3. Corporation (Can Be Double-Taxed)

CORPORATION is legally defined as "an artificial being, intangible, invisible, and existing only in contemplation of law." It is recognized as having an existence separate and apart from its owners, whose interests are evidenced by certificates of stock.

The corporate form of ownership provides for centralized management in a board of directors and officers of the corporation. Like the limited partnership, the stockholders enjoy limited liability to the extent of their capital investment.

Unlike the partnership form of ownership, the corporation has the disadvantage of being taxed twice: the first time on its earnings, and again to the shareholders who share in these earnings through dividend distributions at a 15% tax rate.

At the same time, if there is a tax loss through depreciation allowance, only the corporation may take the deduction; the deduction cannot pass through directly to the owners, as in the limited partnership.

a. Subchapter S Corporations

Under prescribed conditions, where there are fewer than eleven stockholders and where no more than 20 percent of the corporate income is derived from rents, interest, and dividends, the investors may elect to have their corporation taxed as a subchapter S corporation. This is the small business corporation which is taxed like the partnership forms, thus avoiding being taxed twice.

A Subchapter S Corporation income is taxed only once—on an individual income tax return.

4. Real Estate Investment Trust (REIT)

A *REAL ESTATE INVESTMENT TRUST (REIT) is a type of real estate investment company that sells ownership shares.* Ownership in such investments is evidenced by "shares of equity." Because of very stringent tests that must be met to qualify for the trust's favored tax status, this form of organization is rarely used in the typical syndication. It is commonly used to raise mortgage funds. *When the main function of the trust is lending money, it is referred to as a REAL ESTATE MORTGAGE TRUST (REMT). Another form of trust actually purchases property, and is referred to as a REAL ESTATE EQUITY TRUST (REET). If it is used for investments in both mortgages and real property, it would be labeled a HYBRID TRUST.* The requirements that must be met to establish this form of unincorporated trust or association relate to the number of shareholders allowed, management, receipt and distribution of income, tax consequences, transferability of interests, sources of revenue, and other factors.

The principal benefit from the REIT form of ownership is that the qualified trust itself pays no income taxes.

Since at least 90 percent of its income must be distributed to the participants (subject to some exemption), the income tax is imposed on the individual recipients to the extent of the distributions, similar to the partnership.

VIII. CHAPTER SUMMARY

The number one objective of investing in real estate is to make money. An investor's capacity to handle the cost of the investment, as well as the soundness of the investment, should be determined first.

Because of higher selling prices, salespeople generally make more money in commissions selling income properties than single-unit properties.

Some of the benefits of real estate investment are: the potential for tax sheltering and deferment, appreciation in value, and as a hedge against inflation. The rewards also include a monthly income, stability, the potential for change in control and use, and added tax advantages for refinancing.

There are also potential drawbacks to real estate investing. They include the large amount of money (capital) required to buy and maintain multiple units, slow turnaround for sales resulting in a lack of liquidity, and the necessity to hire professional managers. Additionally, cash flow can be diminished due to unfavorable financing conditions and personal attachment to a property affecting productivity.

The three main sources of financing include **savings banks, commercial banks,** and **life insurance companies**. Savings banks generally specialize in single-family housing loans, but are expanding into the apartment market. Commercial banks are short-term lenders, specializing in interim financing for individual unit construction, so apartment financing is virtually nonexistent. Most life insurance companies allocate funds through mortgage bankers and finance large income projects (like apartment complexes).

Financing may also be obtained from real estate syndicates and trusts, as well as sellers themselves. During tight money periods, sellers often become the only source of financing for raw land and special purpose projects through **seller carrybacks** and contracts of sales (**land contracts**).

Good sources of potential investment property buyers are the current tenants of the property, especially commercial tenants.

Qualifying investment buyers is similar to that of home buyers, but additional consideration must be given to their financial objectives. As such, details on the property's condition, tenants, rent schedules, vacancy factors, and more need to be gathered and analyzed.

Investment planning includes: 1) analyzing clients' investment requirements; 2) researching and selecting appropriate properties; 3) negotiating the purchase of a property followed by title search and escrow; and 4) property management.

An **Income Property Statement** is used to prepare a comprehensive income and expense analysis of an apartment building. The analysis is based on future operating income of the building. **Scheduled income** is the gross income a property would generate if there were no vacancies.

The steps involved in completing a property analysis include:

1. **Potential Gross Income** – total income possible at full occupancy, no deductions for expenses. **Vacancy factor** is an allowance for vacancies and uncollectible rent.

2. **Effective Gross Income** – Gross income adjusted for vacancies. No deductions for expenses.

3. **Net Operating Income (NOI)** – Operating expenses are subtracted from effective gross income. Represents income available as a return to the investor. Value indicator most often used in direct capitalization.

   Operating expenses include fixed and variable expenses and replacement reserves. **MITUM** stands for maintenance, insurance, taxes, utilities, and management, which are all operating expenses. Loan payments, depreciation, and income taxes are not considered operating expenses.

4. **Times Gross** – (Gross rent multiplier) Proposed selling price divided by scheduled gross income. Result is a multiple (number) used to find rough estimate of prospective value. The higher the gross multiplier, the higher the price. Most investors are looking for a times gross of eight or less.

5. **Capitalization of Net Income** – Divide net operating income by selling price to find **Cap Rate**. The higher the cap rate, the lower the price.

A **market analysis** should include a population analysis, dwelling unit trends, and the projected demand for multiple units in the area.

The characteristics of a particular rental market are comprised of: 1) income characteristics; 2) rent to income relationships; 3) current rental ranges; 4) current vacancy rates; 5) rent control; and 6) desired distribution of unit type and price class.

A **real estate syndication** is an association of two or more people combining their financial resources to purchase property. Syndication offers numerous money-making opportunities for a broker/syndicator. Syndicates can be limited partnerships, general partnerships, corporations (including S corps), or real estate investment trusts (REITs). A **REIT** is a type of real estate investment company that sells ownership shares. Because the trust pays no income taxes, REITs are stringently regulated.

IX. KEY TERMS

Appreciation
Capitalization of Net Income
Cap Rate
Commercial Banks
Corporation
Down Payment
Effective Gross Income
General Partnership
Gross Income Multiplier
Hybrid Trust
Interim Financing
Interim Use
Life Insurance Companies
Limited Partnership
Liquidity
MITUM
Net Operating Income (NOI)
Operating Expenses
Potential Gross Income
Property Analysis
Real Estate Equity Trust (REET)
Real Estate Investment Trust (REIT)
Real Estate Mortgage Trust (REMT)
Reserves for Replacement
Savings Banks
Scheduled Income
Short-Lived Components
Subchapter S Corporation
Syndication
Tax Shelter
Times Gross
Vacancy Factor
Valuable Expenses

X. CHAPTER 11 QUIZ

1. Which of the following is considered a benefit of real estate investment?
    a. Tax sheltering
    b. Appreciation potential
    c. Monthly income
    d. All of the above

2. The difference between income generated from a property and the expenses associated with that property:
    a. is called cash flow.
    b. can be negative or positive.
    c. both "a" and "b" are correct.
    d. neither "a" nor "b" is correct.

3. Which of the following is NOT a potential negative factor for real estate investors?
    a. Size of capital required.
    b. Fast and easy liquidation.
    c. Unfavorable financing conditions.
    d. Personal attachment.

4. Which of the following lenders is the most likely to finance the purchase of a large apartment complex?
    a. Savings bank
    b. Commercial bank
    c. Life insurance company
    d. None of the above

5. What type of income is most commonly used in determining the capitalization of net income?
    a. Net operating income
    b. Potential gross income
    c. Effective gross income
    d. Times gross

6. In reference to operating expenses, the acronym MITUM does NOT include:
    a. maintenance.
    b. interest.
    c. taxes.
    d. utilities.

7. Which of the following is true concerning the cap rate?
    a. The higher the cap rate, the lower the price.
    b. The higher the cap rate, the higher the price.
    c. The lower the cap rate, the lower the price.
    d. None of the above.

8. When determining the characteristics of a rental market, the percentage of income a family can, or will, pay for shelter is:

    a. 5 to 10 percent.

    b. 10 to 20 percent.

    c. 25 to 40 percent.

    d. 50 to 60 percent.

9. An association of two or more people who combine their financial resources to acquire real estate is:

    a. illegal in California.

    b. called a syndication.

    c. an unlikely source of income for the organizing broker.

    d. none of the above.

10. A real estate investment trust (REIT) is a form of ownership:

    a. that's easy to qualify for.

    b. that sells shares of equity.

    c. where the trust itself pays no income taxes.

    d. both "b" and "c" are correct.

ANSWERS: 1. d; 2. c; 3. b; 4. c; 5. a; 6. b; 7. a; 8. c; 9. b; 10. d

大 平 洋 食 界

PACIFIC PLAZA

東湖 EAST LAKE 海鮮館	美食世界 FOOD COURT
真善美 禮品 PERFECT GIFTS	燕京飯店 YEN CHING RESTAURANT
綠豆苗 Little Bean	舒美被品
天仁茗茶 TEA GINSENG	素之根 健康素食 VEGE KENCO
綺儷精品	視聽坊 MULTI VIDEO
金石堂書局 Kingstone Books	DENTISTRY 牙科
今韻珠寶	ROYALE Bakery 聖璃琍 蛋糕

CHAPTER 12
Sale of a Business
How to Expand Into Other Broker-Related Fields

I. Small Business Opportunities

As a broker, you may wish to engage in a variety of activities that complement your basic real estate brokerage operation. Not only can each activity supplement income from real estate sales, but they can also provide you with additional sources of prospects. The satisfied client who has bought or sold a business through you, for instance, may become a buyer or seller of a home or income-producing property. Also, you can ask the client for referrals.

A client may purchase a security interest, such as a trust deed note, through the same broker whom he or she considers a financial adviser. A client may seek your counsel on hazard insurance for his or her property. Notary services are a convenience for your daily operations and can provide an additional source of income and prospects. Exchanging and broker specialization are other activities, for which no specialized license is required.

You should be aware of the value of informing all your clients about other services offered by your company, such as property management.

CHAPTER 12 OUTLINE

I. SMALL BUSINESS OPPORTUNITIES (p. 443)

II. SELLING A BUSINESS (p. 445)

    A. Listing Agreement (p. 445)

    B. Uniform Commercial Code (UCC) (p. 446)

    C. Security Agreement and Financing Statement (p. 448)

    D. Sales and Use Taxes (p. 450)

    E. Bill of Sale (p. 451)

    F. Assignment of Lease (p. 451)

III. VALUATION OF BUSINESS OPPORTUNITIES (p. 451)

IV. TAX CONSEQUENCES ON THE SALE OF BUSINESS OPPORTUNITIES (p. 453)

V. ALCOHOLIC BEVERAGE CONTROL ACT (p. 453)

VI. ANCILLARY ACTIVITIES AND SPECIALTY ROLES (p. 455)

    A. Real Properties Securities Dealer (RPSD) (p. 455)

    B. Notary Public Services (p. 456)

VII. PROPERTY MANAGEMENT ACTIVITIES (p. 457)

VIII. ESCROW ACTIVITIES (p. 457)

IX. LOAN BROKERAGE ACTIVITIES (p. 458)

X. SYNDICATION (p. 459)

XI. BROKERAGE OPPORTUNITIES IN PROBATE SALES (p. 459)

    A. Mechanics of the Probate Sale (p. 460)

        1. Right to Sell (p. 463)

        2. Term (p. 463)

XII. STATE OF CALIFORNIA SALES OPPORTUNITIES (p. 463)

    A. Board of Education Real Estate Sales (p. 463)

    B. CALTRANS (p. 463)

        1. Background (p. 463)

        2. Procedure (p. 464)

    C. Subdivision Sales Opportunities (p. 464)

        1. Intrastate Sales (p. 464)

        2. Interstate Sales (p. 465)

    D. Real Estate Investment Counselor (p. 466)

        1. Investment Planning and Counseling (p. 467)

XIII. REAL ESTATE BROKERAGE—GENERAL VS. SPECIALIZATION (p. 467)

XIV. MANUFACTURED HOUSING AND THE LICENSEE (p. 469)

    A. Mobile Home Parks (p. 469)

    B. Opportunities (p. 470)

    C. Mobile Home Dealer vs. Real Estate Broker (p. 470)

    D. Marketing (p. 470)

    E. Listing Manufactured Homes (p. 470)

F. Selling Manufactured Homes (p. 471)
    1. Buyer Profile (p. 471)
    2. Financing (p. 471)
XV. CHAPTER SUMMARY (p. 475)
XVI. KEY TERMS (p. 477)
XVII. CHAPTER 12 QUIZ (p. 478)

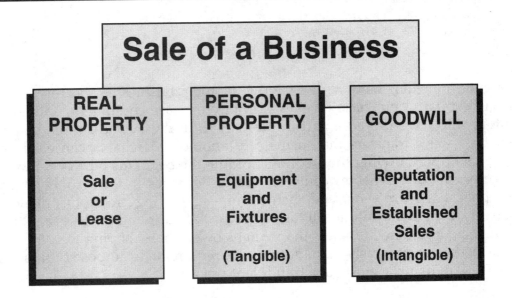

II. Selling a Business

Section 10030 of the Real Estate Law defines a **BUSINESS OPPORTUNITY** *as a "sale or lease of the business and goodwill of an existing business enterprise or opportunity."* Since this transaction consists of the sale of personal property, the rules and laws governing the transfer of chattels (personal property) apply. Usually the transaction involves very few assets and is comparatively small in size. Examples of this kind of business opportunity are drug stores, service stations, cocktail bars, restaurants, auto parts stores, floral shops, bakeries, garages, photo stores, hardware stores, beauty shops, delicatessens, dress shops, laundromats, liquor stores, dry cleaning establishments, and others. The principal assets that are transferred in these sales are stock-in-trade or inventory, fixtures, equipment, and *GOODWILL, defined as the expectation of continued public patronage.* Real property seldom is involved in the transaction; instead, the existing lease, or leasehold interest, is normally transferred to the purchaser.

A. LISTING AGREEMENT

In the first step, an agency is created by securing a listing on the business, just as in real estate.

B. UNIFORM COMMERCIAL CODE (UCC)

The **UNIFORM COMMERCIAL CODE (UCC)** *is a body of law adopted throughout the United States that standardizes a number of practices commonly found in commerce and business.*

Article 6 covers the subject of bulk transfers. It stipulates that whenever there is a sale or transfer in bulk, and not in the ordinary course of the transferor's business, certain requirements must be met in order to protect creditors of the business being transferred.

In real estate talk, the expression "bulk transfer" means the same thing as a business opportunity—an extraordinary sale of more than half of a seller's inventory and equipment.

Most entrepreneurs, who wish to grow in their businesses, borrow money for working capital to purchase inventory, to buy or lease equipment, and so on. The creditors who have played a part in the growth of the business must be protected when the owner transfers the business to another. Merchants can easily commit commercial fraud, leaving the creditors holding the bag. This type of fraud can take two forms: the owner-debtor could sell his or her stock in trade to anyone for any price, pocket the proceeds, and then disappear, leaving creditors unpaid; or the merchant owing debts might sell his or her stock to a friend for less than it's worth and pay his or her creditors less than what's owed them, hoping to come back into the business surreptitiously in the future. The requirements imposed under Article 6 of the UCC mitigate against such fraudulent practices.

Whenever a bulk sale or transfer is made, the transferee must give public notice to the transferor's creditors by recording a Notice to Creditors of Bulk Sale (Figure 12-1) at least twelve days before the bulk transfer is consummated.

Moreover, the notice to creditors must be delivered to the county tax collector before the transfer is to be consummated. This procedure must be followed in the office of the county recorder in which the property is located. In addition, at least twelve days before the bulk transfer, the notice of its intended sale must be published, at least once, in a newspaper of general circulation in the judicial district in which the property is located.

Accurate completion of the **Notice to Creditors of Bulk Sale** form assures that the specific requirements of the UCC are met. These requirements include:

1. information that a bulk transfer is to be made;

2. location and general description of the property to be transferred;

3. the name and business address of the transferor, and all other names and addresses used by him within the previous three years, so far as is known to the intended transferee; and

Figure 12-1

RECORDING REQUESTED BY AND
WHEN RECORDED, MAIL TO

ESCROW NO.   SPACE ABOVE THIS LINE FOR RECORDER USE

NOTICE TO CREDITORS OF BULK SALE
(Notice pursuant to UCC Sec. 6105)

NOTICE IS HEREBY GIVEN that a bulk sale is about to be made.
The name(s) and business address of the seller are:

Doing business as:

All other business name(s) and address(es) used by the seller(s) within the past three years, as stated by the seller(s), are:
(if none, so state):

The location in California of the chief executive office of the seller is:

The name(s) and business address of the buyer(s) are:

The assets being sold are generally described as:

and are located at:

The bulk sale is intended to be consummated at the office of:

          and the anticipated sale date is _____

The bulk sale _____ subject to California Uniform Commercial Code Section 6106.2.
   is/is not

     [If the sale is subject to Sec. 6106.2, the following information must be provided.]

The name and address of the person with whom claims may be filed is:

      and the last day for filing claims by any creditor shall be _____
which is the business day before the anticipated sale date specified above.

_____
_____
_____
_____
Buyer(s)

MET-LGL 1024

447

4. the place and date on or after which the bulk transfer is to be consummated.

Noncompliance with the notice requirements renders the transfer fraudulent and void against those creditors of the transferor whose claims are based on credit transactions prior to the bulk transfer. With compliance, on the other hand, the creditors' recourse is against sellers only, not against the business or buyers.

C. SECURITY AGREEMENT AND FINANCING STATEMENT

Under **Article 9** of the Uniform Commercial Code, titled "Secured Transactions; Sales of Accounts, Contract Rights and Chattel Paper," a filing system is established as additional protection for creditors and for purchasers. It regulates security transactions in personal property, replacing a variety of previously used security instruments (conditional sales contracts, chattel mortgages, trust receipts, assignment of accounts receivable) with a uniform and comprehensive Security Agreement and Financing Statement. The *SECURITY AGREEMENT AND FINANCING STATEMENT shows the debtor's name and address (cosigners and trade names would be included); the secured party's name and address (assignee); description and nature of the property used as collateral; and other items.* (The Financing Statement is shown in **Figure 12-2**.)

Although the **Financing Statement** is subject to a Security Agreement, only the former is **filed with the Secretary of State** in California. Since California is a leader in the volume of credit transactions secured by personal property (and the Security Agreement may run many pages), to require the filing of the agreement would create a massive space and storage problem. Only the brief, one-page Financing Statement, executed in quadruplicate is required on file. Moreover, security transactions which involve consumer goods—personal, family, or household purchases—do not have to be filed. That leaves commercial transactions, the subject that you, as a broker, will be concerned with in the sale of a business opportunity.

The purposes for filing a Financing Statement with the state are similar to those for recording real property interests with the county—to protect innocent purchasers and encumbrancers for value.

ENCUMBRANCERS are those who have an interest in the property by virtue of having placed a lien on the property, acquired an easement against the property, imposed restrictions against it, or acquired any other interest which might be said to encumber the subject property. Just as local records establish priorities for lien claimants on real estate matters, state records establish priorities for claimants on debts secured by personal property. Thus, if a financing statement is not filed, subsequent purchasers without actual knowledge take that property free of the prior security interest, that is, they would not be liable for the pre-existing debt.

By taking advantage of the UCC filing provisions, secured parties protect their interests against those of subsequent purchasers.

Figure 12-2

UCC FINANCING STATEMENT

FOLLOW INSTRUCTIONS (front and back) CAREFULLY

A. NAME & PHONE OF CONTACT AT FILER [optional]

B. SEND ACKNOWLEDGMENT TO: (Name and Address)

THE ABOVE SPACE IS FOR FILING OFFICE USE ONLY

1. DEBTOR'S EXACT FULL LEGAL NAME - insert only <u>one</u> debtor name (1a or 1b) - do not abbreviate or combine names

1a. ORGANIZATION'S NAME				
OR 1b. INDIVIDUAL'S LAST NAME	FIRST NAME		MIDDLE NAME	SUFFIX
1c. MAILING ADDRESS	CITY		STATE / POSTAL CODE	COUNTRY

| 1d. TAX ID #: SSN OR FIN | ADD'L INFO RE ORGANIZATION DEBTOR | 1e. TYPE OF ORGANIZATION | 1f. JURISDICTION OF ORGANIZATION | 1g. ORGANIZATIONAL ID #, if any ☐ NONE |

2. ADDITIONAL DEBTOR'S EXACT FULL LEGAL NAME - insert only <u>one</u> debtor name (2a or 2b) - do not abbreviate or combine names

2a. ORGANIZATION'S NAME				
OR 2b. INDIVIDUAL'S LAST NAME	FIRST NAME		MIDDLE NAME	SUFFIX
2c. MAILING ADDRESS	CITY		STATE / POSTAL CODE	COUNTRY

| 2d. TAX ID #: SSN OR EIN | ADD'L INFO RE ORGANIZATION DEBTOR | 2e. TYPE OF ORGANIZATION | 2f. JURISDICTION OF ORGANIZATION | 2g. ORGANIZATIONAL ID #, if any ☐ NONE |

3. SECURED PARTY'S NAME (or NAME of TOTAL ASSIGNEE of ASSIGNOR S/P) - insert only <u>one</u> secured party name (3a or 3b)

3a. ORGANIZATION'S NAME				
OR 3b. INDIVIDUAL'S LAST NAME	FIRST NAME		MIDDLE NAME	SUFFIX
3c. MAILING ADDRESS	CITY		STATE / POSTAL CODE	COUNTRY

4. This FINANCING STATEMENT covers the following collateral:

5. ALTERNATIVE DESIGNATION [if applicable]:	☐ LESSEE/LESSOR	☐ CONSIGNEE/CONSIGNOR	☐ BAILEE/BAILOR	☐ SELLER/BUYER	☐ AG. LIEN	☐ NON-UCC FILING

6. ☐ This FINANCING STATEMENT is to be filed [for record] (or recorded) in the REAL ESTATE RECORDS. Attach Addendum [if applicable]	7. Check to REQUEST SEARCH REPORT(S) on Debtor(s) [ADDITIONAL FEE] [optional]	☐ All Debtors	☐ Debtor 1	☐ Debtor 2

8. OPTIONAL FILER REFERENCE DATA

FILING OFFICE COPY — NATIONAL UCC FINANCING STATEMENT (FORM UCC1) (REV. 07/29/98)

In any transaction handled by an escrow agent, the transferee must deposit with the escrow the full amount of purchase price or consideration. No funds can be drawn from escrow prior to the actual closing and completion of the escrow for payment of any commission, fee, or other consideration as compensation for a service that is contingent upon the performance of any act, condition, or instruction set forth in the escrow.

Not all escrow companies handle the sale of business opportunities.

D. SALES AND USE TAXES

Whenever a merchant engages in a business where sales of personal property at retail are made, he or she must secure a seller's permit from the State Board of Equalization.

The sale of a business opportunity is also subject to sales tax. Taxes are payable on the tangible personal property items only, and not on goodwill, patents, closes in action (a personal right not reduced to possession, but recoverable by court suit), and other intangibles. Thus, when a Business Opportunity (BO) is sold, sales tax must be charged on the furniture, trade fixtures, and equipment that are transferred. Until these taxes are paid, together with sales and use taxes owed by the seller to the state Board of Equalization, that agency will not issue its **CERTIFICATE OF PAYMENT OF SALES AND USE TAX**. *The issuance of this certificate releases the buyer from liability for the seller's unpaid sales and use taxes.* Without it, buyers will find themselves responsible for their payment, popularly referred to as **successor's liability**.

To guard against the possibility of unpaid taxes, the escrow agent is required to withhold from the purchase price a sufficient amount to cover any liability.

Similar withholdings of funds are also applicable to certain other state agencies to which contributions are due, such as unemployment taxes and disability insurance premiums owed the state Employment Development Department (EDD). Through such safeguards, the transferee is able to acquire the business free of taxes that are otherwise due and payable, and that might not be discovered until months after the close of escrow. This concept is just like the bulk transfer notice under Article 6 of the UCC.

By filing and publishing the required notices of intent to sell, the buyer takes the business free of unfiled claims, and creditors who fail to file claims must look solely to the seller for payment.

As for taxation, the sovereign powers of the state are affected, and the successor to the business will still be liable until released.

E. BILL OF SALE

The *BILL OF SALE serves the same function in the transfer of personal property as the grant deed does for real property.*

F. ASSIGNMENT OF LEASE

Because few BOs transfer the underlying fee title to the land and improvements, one of the major reasons why businesses sell for comparatively less (in contrast to real property) is that only the personal property is being purchased, accompanied by an assignment of the lessee's interest in the realty.

Obviously, a going concern is not as valuable without continued operation from a given location, particularly if a major reason for its success is its location. Many factors account for goodwill, not the least of which is the value of the location. Therefore, it may be critical that the business continue from the same site under the new owner. Securing a lease assignment from the transferor, along with consent to such assignment from the lessor, is the only way to insure goodwill.

You should make sure that the business lease is assignable.

After all the foregoing have been met, prorations are made for insurance, rents, taxes, licenses, receivables, loan payments, and other applicable items; closing statements are prepared and delivered along with the fully executed documents to the respective parties, and escrow is closed.

III. Valuation of Business Opportunities

You should learn how to determine the value of a business—before you embark on your first listing. There is no magic formula to calculate the value of a BO, any more than there is for the valuation of real property. However, there are some guidelines to follow, though generalities apply to BOs less reliably than they do to realty. More variables are involved, especially in pegging a true appraisal on the leasehold.

A business opportunity may have one value to the lessor, but an altogether different value to the lessee.

Many differences of opinion inevitably exist because of the varying degrees of knowledge and skill of the appraisers and the approaches they utilize. When the business is large and involved, advise your seller to bear the expense of having it appraised by a trained specialist.

There are tables that show rules of thumb as price guides, but these tables do not include inventory value, age, appearance and usefulness of the furnishings, fixtures, equipment, the

exterior and interior physical appearance of the improvements, specific location, and terms and conditions of the lease. For example, new furniture and fixtures depreciate half of their value as they are used. After a few years of service, they're not worth much more than a third of the original cost. If they're not used in the operation of the business, but rather are sold on the open market, they bring hardly more than 15 percent of cost. Equipment is somewhat more stable, and value depends on age, utility, and condition. The value of used or rebuilt equipment can best be determined by wholesale equipment suppliers.

As might be expected, the value of goodwill is the most difficult to measure.

In establishing valuation for this intangible asset, consideration is given to the length of time the business has been in existence, location, customer traffic, vehicle count, adaptability to change (if desired), present and future competition, continued use of a well-established and respected business name, the quality of service and dependability, provision for a noncompetition clause included in the sale, customer habits, personalities and abilities of key personnel who will remain, and a variety of other factors.

You should visit an establishment on different days and at various times to determine business activities.

Based upon collection of data over many years, guidelines have been established to compute the value of a particular business. These guidelines may be said to be *NET MULTIPLIERS, that is, the amount that a business would sell for, based upon the multiplication of its annual net income by some standardized number, or multiplier. GROSS MULTIPLIERS are commonly used in valuations of income-producing real estate; multipliers are also applied to the annual net income of businesses.* These multipliers are based on the annual net prior to allowance for depreciation, owner's salary or withdrawals, and interest. In the table *Guidelines for Selling a Business,* only general guides are set up and figures must be adjusted for these factors. For instance, if an auto parts store has net annual earnings of $50,000, it should sell for from 100 percent to 150 percent of that income.

As the broker, you must be careful to obtain an accurate breakdown of income and expenses, as well as a correct count of the stock in trade. Assisting the transferor in the physical inventory may avoid misunderstandings.

Much more can be said about business opportunities. Only the limitations of space preclude discussion of the use of options occasionally employed in BO transactions; procedures for bulk transfers at public auction; the detailed provisions of the California Sales and Use Tax Law; the Alcoholic Beverage Control Act; lease analysis; and analysis of financial statements, especially the balance sheet and profit and loss statement.

Any agent who hopes to deal in business opportunities would be wise to take at least a basic course in accounting.

IV. Tax Consequences on the Sale of Business Opportunities

The tax implications and applications in the sale of businesses differ from those in the sale of real property. The method of allocation of the various business assets has tax consequences to both seller/transferor and buyer/transferee.

A covenant not to compete is valid in California. Under the terms of a **COVENANT NOT TO COMPETE**, *the seller agrees that he or she will not open a competing business for a period of time within a specified geographical area.* The amount paid for the covenant not to compete is ordinary income to the seller and is a deductible item to the buyer over the period of the covenant, that is, the buyer amortizes or spreads out that portion of the price that is allocated to the covenant.

The amount paid for leasehold improvements is deductible by the buyer over the remaining term of the lease. It is a capital transaction to the seller, with long- or short-term capital gain consequences dependent upon the holding period.

The amount paid for goodwill is not deductible by the buyer and is a capital item to the seller.

Amounts paid for fixtures and equipment are depreciable by the buyer and subject to special tax treatment to the seller, which goes beyond the scope of this discussion. Finally, inventory is generally priced at the seller's cost and does not have any immediate tax consequence to the buyers.

V. Alcoholic Beverage Control Act

The **CALIFORNIA DEPARTMENT OF ALCOHOLIC BEVERAGE CONTROL (ABC)** *is charged with administration and enforcement of the Alcoholic Beverage Control Act, which regulates the issuance of liquor licenses* (See **Figure 12-3**).

As a broker negotiating the sale of a business involving the sale and distribution of alcoholic beverages, you should be familiar with the legal controls and procedures for transfer of the liquor license or permit. In addition to federal statutes, many laws govern the manufacture, sale, and possession of alcoholic beverages in California. A detailed discussion of the subject is not essential for our purposes, but the reader who is interested in pursuing the matter is advised to consult the DRE Reference Book to obtain more information. Among the topics in this volume are the requirements for obtaining and transferring a license, classifications of liquor licenses, filing and escrow procedures, original and renewal license fees, limitations on use, and excerpts from the Alcoholic Beverage Control Act.

Figure 12-3

(ABC)
ALCOHOLIC BEVERAGE CONTROL

Any California real estate licensee who is interested in negotiating business opportunity transactions should be familiar with the legal controls on the transfer of licenses for the sale of alcoholic beverages.

The Department of Alcoholic Beverage Control (ABC) administers the Alcoholic Beverage Control Act and issues all licenses there under.

Alcoholic beverage licenses are issued to qualified adults, partnerships, fiduciaries, and corporations for use at a particular premises, which also has to be approved by the ABC. The ABC may refuse to issue a license to any person who has a criminal record or has violated the ABC Act. The premises may be disapproved for various reasons, including over concentration of alcoholic beverage licenses in the area, the creation of a police problem, or the proximity to a school, playground, or church.

With the sale of a business opportunity involving a liquor license, you cannot automatically assume that the ABC will permit the transfer. An escrow is legally required and no consideration may be paid out before the license and the sale of the business is approved. Each application and transfer is subject to protest by local officials and private parties within 30 days of the posted notice of intention to sell alcoholic beverages.

New licenses for bars (on-sale) and liquor stores (off-sale) are usually obtained through a lottery type system in each county. The maximum sales price for a new license is $6,000, but after a period of five years from the date of the original issuance, this restriction is lifted for resale, and the purchase price is usually considerably more.

DEPARTMENT OF ALCOHOLIC BEVERAGE CONTROL
1901 BROADWAY
SACRAMENTO, CALIFORNIA

www.abc.ca.gov
(Alcoholic Beverage Control)

VI. Ancillary Activities and Specialty Roles

Inevitably, as a broker, you will be engaged in many activities which complement that of your main concern, general brokerage. A review of some of these activities follows.

A. REAL PROPERTY SECURITIES DEALER (RPSD)

Closely associated with loan brokerage is the activity of the real property securities dealer, who is regulated under Chapter 3, Article 6 of the Real Estate Law.

The essential difference between the real property securities dealer and the real property loan broker is that the loan broker is dealing with new loans in the primary mortgage (or money) market, while the **REAL PROPERTY SECURITIES DEALER (RPSD)** *is engaged in the secondary market, in addition to a host of activities that come under the definition of real property securities.*

The statutes that regulate this area of real estate activity cover bulk transactions in trust deeds, real property sales contracts and investment plans dealing with them.

To secure endorsement as a real property securities dealer, you must first have a real estate broker license.

A real property securities dealer is defined as "any person, acting as principal or agent, who engages in the business of: (A) Selling real property securities to the public. . . ." These are defined by Section 10237.1, subdivision (a) of the Business and Professions Code as investment contracts made in connection with the sale of a secured promissory note, or a property sales contract, wherein the dealer or his principal expresses or implies agreement to any kind of guarantee, payment, or repurchase of such investment contracts. The dealer might, for instance, guarantee the note or contract against loss or nonpayment of either principal or interest, guarantee a specific yield or return on the note or contract, agree to assume one or more payments in order to protect the security, or even to repurchase the note or contract.

The Real Estate Law continues the definition:

"(b) Offering to accept or accepting funds for continual reinvestment in real property securities, or from placement in an account, plan, or program whereby the dealer implies that a return will be derived from a specific real property sales contract or promissory note secured directly or collaterally by a lien on real property which is not specifically stated to be based upon the contractual payments thereon."

The statute adds, however, that the phrase "sale to the public" is interpreted as excluding sales to corporations; pension, retirement or similar trust funds; to

institutional lending agencies; or to real estate brokers, attorneys, or licensed general building contractors.

A generalized definition of real property securities as set forth in Section 10237.1 holds them to be deeds of trust sold under an investment contract where the dealer guarantees the deed of trust in any one of several ways, or makes advances to or on behalf of the investor. Also included in the definition is the sale of one of a series of promotional notes or sales contracts. Promotional, as used here, refers to a note secured by a trust deed on unimproved real property in a subdivision; or a note executed after construction of an improvement on the property, but before the first sale; or executed as a means of financing the first purchase of property so improved, and which is subordinate to another trust deed, such as a purchase money second deed of trust on a new house in a subdivision.

Before selling real property securities to the public, the broker must obtain a permit from the Real Estate Commissioner.

This permit may be for selling existing securities, or the permit may authorize the applicant to acquire and sell securities under a proposed plan or program. In the latter case, the permit is obtained prior to the acquisition of the securities. Before issuing a permit, the Commissioner evaluates the application to determine whether the proposed plan and sale are equitable.

All advertising material that will be used must be filed with the Commissioner ten days prior to its use. No dealer shall use any advertising material after receiving notice in writing that such material contains any false or misleading statement or omits necessary information to make the statement complete and accurate.

A Real Property Security Statement must be furnished to the purchaser of a real property security.

This disclosure statement is to the real property securities dealer and his client what the Broker's Loan Statement is to the loan broker and his client. Both statements are designed to protect the investing public by prescribing disclosures of certain pertinent data. In certain situations (described in Sections 10239 et seq. of the Business and Professions Code), the Real Estate Commissioner is empowered to take possession of the records, business, and assets of the real property securities dealer and, when necessary, liquidate these assets in the interest of investors.

B. NOTARY PUBLIC SERVICES

A very significant part of every real estate transaction is the acknowledgement of a variety of documents used in the sale and purchase of real property. As you should be aware, such an *ACKNOWLEDGEMENT is a formal declaration before a duly authorized officer, by a person executing an instrument (that is, a formal document) that such execution is his or her act and deed.* Its purpose is to entitle the document to be recorded so as to impart constructive notice of its contents, and, in most cases, to entitle the instrument to be used as evidence of its existence and validity. Often such notarial service is performed for a nominal fee by a broker who is also a notary. Those who do not charge for such services perform them as an accommodation to the transaction.

Additional benefits from obtaining a notary commission may be monetary in nature, but the principal benefits are the conveniences for the broker and his or her clients—being a notary expedites real estate and business opportunity transactions. Indeed, a substantial number of the over 100,000 notaries public in this state are real estate licensees, most of whom presumably went through the expense and effort to obtain the appointment in order to better service their clientele. All documents, before recorded, must first be acknowledged before a notary public or qualified public officer.

As a notary public, you can notarize your clients' documents, but many successful brokers rely on assistants to take care of this detail. See Chapter 14 on Real Estate Assistants for more details on Notary Public.

VII. Property Management Activities

As with the insurance aspects, the managing of properties for others is a natural adjunct to your general practice as a broker. Usually this is done on the basis of a percentage of gross rentals or for a flat fee. You are guided by the same principle here: as agent for the owner, you are obligated to obtain the most competitive prices for your client when, for example, purchasing supplies and equipment for the property.

Specific functions and duties of the property manager are discussed in Chapter 13.

VIII. Escrow Activities

Another supporting service, which a large number of brokers offer, is that of escrow, discussed in detail in Chapter 9.

An *ESCROW is an impartial third party whose functions are to:*

1. *act as a depository of funds and documents placed with it;*

2. *prorate those charges and expenses between the parties to the escrow as instructed under the terms of the agreement for the sale and purchase; and*

3. *act as a clearinghouse for the exchange of monies and documents when the escrow is ready to close, that is, at the time when all the terms and conditions have been met.*

Under the Real Estate Law, an individual cannot be licensed as an escrow company; however, a broker may act as an escrow agent in those transactions in which he or she represents the buyer or seller or both.

Remember: Only the seller and buyer may select the escrow they wish to use.

Any real estate licensee who acts as an escrow agent (or escrow holder) must maintain all escrow funds in a trust account subject to inspection by the Real Estate Commissioner, and keep proper records.

Licensed escrow companies are prohibited by law from paying referral fees to anyone except a regular employee of the company. This prohibits the giving of commissions to real estate brokers and other outsiders for sending business to a particular escrow company. Such fees include gifts of merchandise or other things of value. Further, no commission payments can be made prior to actual closing and completion of the escrow.

Escrow companies are prohibited by law from soliciting or accepting escrow instructions or amended or supplemental instructions containing any blank to be filled in after the signing or initialing of the instructions, amendments or supplemental instructions.

They may not permit any person to make any addition to, deletion from, or alteration of an escrow instruction or amended or supplemental escrow instruction unless it is signed or initialed by all persons who had signed or initialed the original instructions or amendments thereto. Escrow companies are charged by law with delivering, at the time of execution, copies of any escrow instruction or amended or supplemental instruction to all parties executing it. However, escrow instructions, being confidential, may not be disclosed to non-parties. Limited disclosure to parties is permissible where the instructions form a part of the contract to which the person desiring disclosure has become a party.

The escrow holder is the agent for both the buyer and seller.

When the conditions are performed, the escrow holder usually becomes the agent of each of the parties, that is, of the grantor to deliver the deed and of the grantee to pay over the purchase money. The agency, however, is considered a limited one, and the only obligations to be fulfilled by the escrow holder are those set forth in the instructions.

IX. Loan Brokerage Activities

To compliment their business activities, an increasing number of real estate brokers are getting involved in the field of financing.

In playing the role of a negotiator, as the broker, you have considerable influence on the size of the down payment and balance of payment due the seller. As explained in an earlier chapter, the seller, instead of waiting for the buyer to obtain institutional financing, may accept a purchase money mortgage or trust deed and finance the buyer personally. If the purchaser has little cash, the seller may be willing to take a second trust deed behind the loan of an outside financing agency. In cases where the seller desires the full purchase price in cash, a buyer must be found with ample down payment funds of his or her own, possibly with an assist of a new loan on the property, if it is free and clear, or a buyer willing to assume an existing obligation acceptable to the existing lenders.

The volume of loan applications originating in your real estate office may become so great that you may wish to set up a loan division or subsidiary mortgage company and become a loan representative or agent of an insurance company, or a commercial or savings bank, usually situated in other locales. A loan representative or mortgage company can bring idle money to an area where it is in demand, thus aiding in creating a fluid market for loanable funds on a long-term basis. Also, you may wish to lend your own funds or funds of large private investors who prefer this form of investment to bonds and stocks.

In the normal course of your brokerage operation, you may perform only the single function of aiding the purchaser in making application for a loan from a financial institution. However, if so inclined, you may go a step further and become a representative, agent, or correspondent for a mortgage lending institution.

X. Syndication

Another area opening up to licensees on a very broad scale is syndication. Here, you have an opportunity to capitalize on the marketing and financing of real estate. Opportunities for syndication abound because of the increasing demand for land, population influx, relatively small outlays required of investors, and the solution which the syndication vehicle provides for the problem of tight money.

A "Syndicate" is an association formed to operate an investment business. It can be a corporation, partnership, or trust.

Readers who may want to specialize in the exciting field of syndication should plan to attend specialized seminars on this subject. See Chapter 11 for more information on syndication.

XI. Brokerage Opportunities in Probate Sales

An executor possessing a power of sale under the terms of a will may sell directly or through one or more brokers.

If you are the broker, but don't have such power of sale, or you're a court-appointed administrator, you may also seek offers, providing you publish a legal notice advising that the property is to be sold on specified terms and conditions, and that offers from interested parties are invited.

Information concerning a sale is usually obtained from the attorney handling the estate or from a bank or trust company that is acting as executor or administrator. When the public administrator is in charge of the administration of an estate, inquiry is directed to that office.

Written offers to purchase must conform to statutory requirements and to the rules of the local superior court governing probate sales.

They must be for at least 90 percent of the inheritance tax appraisal value and should conform to the terms stated in any public notice. The personal representative may accept an offer, subject to court confirmation. The court sets the matter for a hearing and, at that time, anyone may bid more in open court, provided he or she increases the offer by at least 10 percent of the first $10,000, and 5 percent of the remaining portion of the original bid price. At the discretion of the court, the bidding may proceed on lesser raises, until the court declares a bid to be the highest and best obtainable, and thereby confirms the sale to the successful bidder.

If you are the broker representing a bidder, you should attend the confirmation hearing and should be familiar with local court rules governing advance bidding, deposits required, and other matters. Normal escrow procedures are used to consummate the transaction, under terms and conditions approved by court.

Of course, as the broker, you should have a written agreement with the personal representative for payment of compensation. Commissions (5%) paid to participating brokers are governed by statute, and discretion is vested in the court as to distribution. **Generally, if more than one bid is made, half the commission goes to the broker representing the original bidder on the original amount, and the balance goes to the broker whose bidder submitted the higher bid, based on the higher amount.**

If the successful bidder is not produced by a bona fide agent, then the agent holding the contract is allowed a full commission on the amount of the original bid.

A. MECHANICS OF THE PROBATE SALE

Figure 12-5 is the CAR Probate Listing Agreement form that may be used to accomplish the marketing of probate property.

Figure 12-5

CALIFORNIA
ASSOCIATION
OF REALTORS®

PROBATE LISTING AGREEMENT
Under Authority of the Probate Code

1. **EXCLUSIVE RIGHT TO SELL:** _____,
   the court-appointed representative of the ☐ estate, ☐ conservatorship or ☐ guardianship identified by Superior Court case
   name as_____, case # _____ ("Seller"),
   hereby employs and grants _____ ("Broker") the
   exclusive and irrevocable right, commencing on (date) _____ and expiring at 11:59 P.M. on (date)
   _____ ("Listing Period") (not to exceed 90 days), to sell or exchange the real property in the City of
   _____, County of _____, California,
   described as follows: _____
   _____ ("Property").

2. **COURT CONFIRMATION** of any sale ☐ **is required** (limited authority), ☐ **may not be required** (full authority).

3. **TERMS OF SALE:**

   A. **LIST PRICE:** The listing price shall be _____
   _____ ($_____).

   B. **PERSONAL PROPERTY:** The following items of personal property are included in the above price: _____
   _____
   _____

   C. **ADDITIONAL TERMS:** _____
   _____
   _____

4. **MULTIPLE LISTING SERVICE:** Information about this listing ☐ will, ☐ will not, be provided to a multiple listing service ("MLS")
   of Broker's selection and all terms of the transaction will be provided to the MLS for publication, dissemination and use by persons
   and entities on terms approved by the MLS. Seller authorizes Broker to comply with all applicable MLS rules.

5. **TITLE:** Seller warrants that title to the Property is as follows: _____
   _____.

6. **COMPENSATION TO BROKER:**

   **Notice: The amount or rate of real estate commissions is not fixed by law. They are set by each Broker
   individually and may be negotiable between Seller and Broker.** (Local court rules may establish maximum
   permissible amounts.)

   A. Seller agrees to pay to Broker from the proceeds of the sale, as compensation for services, irrespective of agency relationships,
   and subject to California Probate Code, or an amount determined by the court, either ☐ _____ percent of the sales price,
   OR ☐ $ _____, AND _____ if Broker, cooperating broker, Seller, or any
   other person, produces a buyer who purchases the Property on the above price and terms or any other terms and conditions
   acceptable to Seller during the Listing Period or any extension.

   B. Broker is authorized to cooperate with other brokers, and divide with other brokers the above compensation in any manner
   acceptable to Broker, or as allowed or determined by the Court.

   C. Seller warrants that Seller has no obligation to pay compensation to any other Broker regarding the transfer of the Property
   except: _____.
   If the Property is sold to anyone listed above during the time Seller is obligated to compensate another broker: (a) Broker is not
   entitled to compensation under this Agreement; and (b) Broker is not obligated to represent Seller with respect to such
   transaction.

   Seller and Broker acknowledge receipt of copy of this page, which constitutes Page 1 of _____ Pages.
   Seller's Initials (_____) (_____)   Broker's Initials (_____) (_____)

Published and Distributed by:
REAL ESTATE BUSINESS SERVICES, INC.
a subsidiary of the CALIFORNIA ASSOCIATION OF REALTORS®
525 South Virgil Avenue, Los Angeles, California 90020
PRINT DATE

REVISED 10/99

OFFICE USE ONLY
Reviewed by Broker
or Designee _____
Date _____

EQUAL HOUSING
OPPORTUNITY

EXCLUSIVE AUTHORIZATION AND RIGHT TO SELL PROBATE (PL-11 PAGE 1 OF 2)

Property Address: _____ Date: _____

7. **BROKER'S AND SELLER'S DUTIES:** Broker agrees to exercise reasonable effort and due diligence to achieve the purposes of this Agreement, and is authorized to advertise and market the Property in any medium selected by Broker. Seller agrees to consider offers presented by Broker, and to act in good faith toward accomplishing the sale of the Property. Seller further agrees, regardless of responsibility, to indemnify, defend and hold Broker harmless from all claims, disputes, litigation, judgments and attorney's fees arising from any incorrect information supplied by Seller, whether contained in any document, omitted therefrom, or otherwise, or from any material facts which Seller knows but fails to disclose.

8. **AGENCY RELATIONSHIPS:** Broker shall act as the agent for Seller in any resulting transaction. Depending upon the circumstances, it may be necessary or appropriate for Broker to act as an agent for both Seller and buyer, exchange party, or one or more additional parties ("Buyer"). Broker shall, as soon as practicable, disclose to Seller any election to act as a dual agent representing both Seller and Buyer. If a Buyer is procured directly by Broker or an associate licensee in Broker's firm, Seller hereby consents to Broker acting as a dual agent for Seller and such Buyer. In the event of an exchange, Seller hereby consents to Broker collecting compensation from additional parties for services rendered, provided there is disclosure to all parties of such agency and compensation. Seller understands that Broker may have or obtain listings on other properties, and that potential buyers may consider, make offers on, or purchase through Broker, property the same as or similar to Seller's Property. Seller consents to Broker's representation of sellers and buyers of other properties before, during, and after the expiration of this Agreement.

9. **DEPOSIT:** Broker is authorized to accept and hold on Seller's behalf a deposit to be applied toward the sales price.

10. **LOCKBOX:**
    A. A lockbox is designed to hold a key to the Property to permit access to the Property by Broker, cooperating brokers, MLS participants, their authorized licensees and representatives, and accompanied prospective buyers.
    B. Broker, cooperating brokers, MLS and Associations/Boards of REALTORS® are **not** insurers against theft, loss, vandalism or damage attributed to the use of a lockbox. Seller is advised to verify the existence of, or obtain, appropriate insurance through Seller's own insurance broker.
    C. (If checked:) ☐ Seller authorizes Broker to install a lockbox. If Seller does not occupy the Property, Seller shall be responsible for obtaining occupant(s)' written permission for use of a lockbox.

11. **SIGN:** (If checked:) ☐ Seller authorizes Broker to install a FOR SALE/SOLD sign on the Property.

12. **EQUAL HOUSING OPPORTUNITY:** The Property is offered in compliance with federal, state, and local anti-discrimination laws.

13. **ADDITIONAL TERMS:** _____
    ☑ Probate Advisory (C.A.R. Form PAL-11)
    _____
    _____
    _____
    _____

14. **ENTIRE CONTRACT:** All prior discussions, negotiations, and agreements between the parties concerning the subject matter of this Agreement are superseded by this Agreement, which constitutes the entire contract and a complete and exclusive expression of their agreement, and may not be contradicted by evidence of any prior agreement or contemporaneous oral agreement. This Agreement and any supplement, addendum, or modification, including any photocopy or facsimile, may be executed in counterparts.

Seller warrants that Seller has the authority to execute this agreement.
Seller acknowledges that Seller has read and understands this Agreement, and has received a copy.

Date _____ at _____, California   Date _____ at _____, California

By _____   By _____

Court-Appointed Representative(s) of _____

Address _____   Address _____

City, State, Zip _____   City, State, Zip _____

Phone/Fax/Email _____   Phone/Fax/Email _____

Real Estate Broker (Firm) _____   By (Agent) _____ Date _____

Address _____   Phone _____

City _____ State _____ Zip _____   Fax/Email _____

REVISED 10/99
Page 2 of _____ Pages.

OFFICE USE ONLY
Reviewed by Broker
or Designee _____
Date _____

EQUAL HOUSING OPPORTUNITY

EXCLUSIVE AUTHORIZATION AND RIGHT TO SELL PROBATE (PL-11 PAGE 2 OF 2)

1. Right to Sell

The full and correct name of the decedent is inserted here, along with the agent's. The description of the property or properties (since more than one property may be involved) follows.

2. Term

An exclusive right to sell for a period not in excess of 90 days may be entered if, prior to the execution of the agreement, the executor or administrator of the estate has obtained court permission.

XII. State of California Sales Opportunities

Occasionally, the state has real property for disposal, such as excess land acquired for easements that is no longer needed. The Department of Finance may authorize employment of a broker to effect sales when, after proper advertising, bids offered for such properties do not equal the appraised value.

A. BOARD OF EDUCATION REAL ESTATE SALES

The Education Code provides that the governing body of any school district may pay a commission to a broker who procures a buyer for real estate sold by the board.

The sealed bid must be accompanied by the name of the broker to whom the compensation is to be paid, and by a statement of the rate or amount of the commission. In the event of an oral overbid submitted through another broker, half the commission based on the highest written bid is payable to the submitting broker, and the balance is paid to the broker who procured the purchaser to whom the sale is confirmed.

B. CALTRANS

Under the ***AIRSPACE DEVELOPMENT PROGRAM****, licensees are permitted to negotiate airspace leases through the California Division of Highways, and receive commissions for such services.*

1. Background

California law prescribes that airspace multiple-use parcels are in the state's right of way and can be over, under, or adjacent to a state highway.

The state has entered into an active program to lease many sites for long-term development proposals for such uses as parking facilities, warehouses, office buildings, and stores. The uses for airspace are virtually unlimited. Rather than being

http://www.caltrans.ca.gov/hq/row/

| California | Caltrans | Right-of-Way

Right of Way Online Manual

The purpose of this online Right of Way Manual is to give users a tool that will lead them through the Right of Way processes.

Online Manual Archives

Caltrans Home
Publications
Functions
Contact Us
About Us
Search

Related Links

State of California
► Business, Transportation and Housing Agency
► Governor Homepage
► State Senate
► State Assembly
► Legislative Homepage
L State All Codes
► Department of Justice

U.S. Government

search

○ My CA ○ This Site

GOVERN
Schwarzeneg
Click To Visit
Home P

Featured Links
• Caltrans Transportation Planning Home
• Caltrans Project Management
• Caltrans TEA Program
• Caltrans Local Programs Home

NEWS
Legal Expert Witness Consultants

Doing Business with Caltrans

Decent, Safe and Sanitary Inspections performed for other agencies
If your agency displaces a residential family due to a federal or federally funded project, and that family relocates to California, the Department of Transportation's Right of Way office can conduct the Decent, Safe and Sanitary (DS&S) inspection for you
► more...

a drain on tax monies for maintenance and upkeep, the properties should return money to the taxpayer in the form of local real estate, sales, and business taxes. This is intended to ease the burden of local taxes as well as bring a return to the state.

2. Procedure

Each State Highway District Office has an inventory of available airspace sites for the broker to review. Once you secure a specific potential tenant for a specific airspace site, you will sign a Broker's Commission Agreement that obligates the state to pay a commission, under prescribed conditions, based upon a schedule made a part of the agreement. The commission is paid when the lease is consummated and the state begins receiving payment.

If you are interested in entering the program, you should contact the Division of Highways, Right of Way Department, Airspace Development, at one of the eleven district offices located throughout the state.

C. SUBDIVISION SALES OPPORTUNITIES

1. Intrastate Sales

The division and subsequent sale of real property are governed by the Subdivision Map Act and the Subdivided Lands Act.

Under these two laws, the regulation of new subdivisions is administered by the Real Estate Commissioner's office, and the county or municipal authorities responsible for review of new maps proposing the division of land for development or sale.

Property may be divided in several manners, such as a record of survey or parcel maps. The most common division of property is through the use of a subdivision map.

The subdivision engineer usually processes the map through the various agencies for such matters as public schools, public utility availability, public roads, environmental impact reports, and involvement with the coastal commission, if required. This is merely a brief description of a complex process. The basic objective is to create a map where the yet-to-be completed lot improvements are in conformance with the general plan, and the proposed densities can be adequately served by available resources, or resources to be created as part of the project. A good example is the requirement that the subdivider provide a catch basin to alleviate water runoff during heavy rains.

Some brokerages specialize in the sale of new properties, which could fall in the following areas:

1. Home and condominium sales
2. Improved lot sales for custom construction
3. Sale and lease of industrial properties
4. Sale and lease of commercial properties
5. Time share sales

New Construction. In conjunction with improved lot sales, normally a buyer has the intent to improve the lot. In order to properly serve your client, you should be familiar with construction lenders in your area, their underwriting criteria, and their willingness to cooperate with brokers. As previously mentioned, loan placement is another commission opportunity to be explored.

2. Interstate Sales

As a California licensee, you also have the privilege to sell real estate to purchasers outside the state. With such opportunities also come responsibilities.

Because of the massive scale of land promotions and abuses, Congress passed the ***INTERSTATE LAND SALES FULL DISCLOSURE ACT***. *With certain exceptions, an offering for sale or lease of a subdivision of 25 lots or more through interstate commerce or by mail requires a permit from the Department of Housing and Urban Development. This permit is called a **PROPERTY REPORT**.*

A developer who has already complied with the state Subdivided Lands Act (California Real Estate Law) is required only to file a copy of the subdivision questionnaire with the Department of Real Estate, together with supporting documents and an abbreviated statement. Once submitted, the filing becomes effective immediately, instead of the 30-day wait in most other states. The prospective purchaser receives both the state **Public Report** and the federal **State Property Report Disclaimers**. Both are designed to protect purchasers by requiring full disclosure of all material facts that affect the subdivision. However, both reports contain disclaimers, stating in so many words that the agency has not passed upon the accuracy or adequacy of the report, or any of the advertising material.

A provision of the federal statute is that, with a contract for purchase or lease of a lot in a subdivision of this type, the purchaser has a right of rescission within a limited period. *In California, this type of remote subdivision is known as a LAND PROJECT.*

D. REAL ESTATE INVESTMENT COUNSELOR

For the real estate broker who has considerable experience and superior education, there is another specialized field of real estate activity. The *REAL ESTATE INVESTMENT COUNSELOR is the broker's broker or consultant, doing for other brokers what those brokers cannot do for themselves, until their own knowledge and experience is of such magnitude as to qualify them for similar status.*

Though you must be careful not to practice law without a license, the real estate counselor resembles the attorney: your only product is advice, for which you are paid a fee, whether or not the advice is taken. You will be concerned with diversified problems in the broad field of real estate involving all segments of the business. Your functions encompass analysis, interpretation, and recommendations. You will often be used by business firms which have become involved in real estate investing for profitable diversification, inflation hedge, tax advantages, and other benefits. The scope of such activities is reducible to four principal areas, namely:

1. firms that have organized real estate divisions or subsidiaries;

2. companies that have bought or merged with existing real estate firms;

3. companies that, by accident rather than design, got into real estate by involving themselves in buying and selling homes as a service for transferred employees;

4. corporations desiring the benefits of real estate investment without the concerns of staffing a department or acquiring an existing real estate firm.

As a consultant, you may wish to specialize in a limited area of real estate. You may choose subdividing land and assessment procedures, work primarily with retail leases, or confine your activities to mobile home parks or motels. Questions of land utilization—to buy, sell, rent or exchange, remodel or demolish, and many others—will confront you as a counselor. Accordingly, your background must cover not only a narrow and technical field for appraising or subdividing, but also at least a working knowledge of all fields of real estate. To counsel wisely and assist in making intelligent decisions based upon a number of possible alternatives, you should understand estate planning principles, and the advantages and disadvantages of the stock and bond market. You should also have a firm grasp of life insurance, and possess a wealth of knowledge in the fields of general business, law, income taxation, valuation, financing, economics, and research.

1. Investment Planning and Counseling

If you're a broker who expects to build up a following in the field of real estate investments, you will need to do more than the typical agent. To pick up repeat business, you will have to earn the respect and trust of the client. This trust can come only after you have gained a thorough knowledge and understanding of the client's total financial and family picture. A confidential file should be maintained for each client. By integrating all the data and information about the client, you're in a better position to render superior service. It goes without saying that education in this field is a must.

Investment planning may be thought of as the integration of a number of steps, starting with a thorough analysis of the client's investment requirements—income, appreciation, retirement, estate buildup, resale or exchange, tax shelter, diversification, leverage liquidity, funding of children's education years hence, or any combination of these. Conferring with the client's attorney, accountant, or business advisor is advisable somewhere along the way.

Researching and selecting properties to meet the objectives of the client is the second step. When a decision to buy a particular property is made, you will negotiate its acquisition, followed by title search and escrow. Management of the property is the next step, in order to safeguard the investment, to minimize expenses, and to maximize profits. You must be cognizant of change, along every step of the way, offering suggestions and making recommendations as the circumstances warrant.

XIII. Real Estate Brokerage— General vs. Specialization

The sale of residential property accounts for about three-fourths of sales made by the typical realty office.

After you've made a good start in general house selling, you may wish to specialize in a particular area of brokerage. You may become a specialist by turning to one of the following areas of sales activities:

1. Homes in a defined **geographical section** of the city, usually within a radius of five to ten miles of your office.

2. Homes within a certain **price range**.

3. **Types** of property: condominiums, cooperatives, and townhouses; residential income; commercial and industrial; farms and acreage; motels; hotels; or business opportunities.

4. **Exchanges** of real property.

Similarly, once exposed to general brokerage activities, you may, after extensive experience, choose to enter one of the following fields of specialization, generally non-selling in nature:

5. **Appraising**, with one or more of the professional designations: Certified Residential Appraiser (CRA), Certified Real Estate Appraiser (CREA), Member, Appraiser Institute (MAI), Member, Society of Real Estate Appraisers (SREA).

6. **Property manager**, ultimately as Certified Property Manager (CPM).

7. **Mortgage loan broker** or correspondent, representing one or more institutional (prime loans) and noninstitutional lenders (junior loans).

8. **Counselor**, Real Estate (CRE).

9. **Subdivider** and developer.

10. **Syndicator** of either or both improved and unimproved properties.

11. **Escrow**.

12. **Title insurance**.

13. **Government:** FHA, VA, Cal-Vet, HUD, FNMA (Federal National Mortgage Association), GNMA (Government National Mortgage Association), or one of the state or local agencies.

14. **Private:** industrial corporations, banks, railroad companies, savings and loan associations, insurance companies.

15. **Teaching**, research, law, franchise investments, or board administration.

Note that general brokerage is the block upon which to stand, or it can become the stepping stone to specialization. As an ambitious person entering the field of real estate, it would be wise to carefully examine your interests, aptitudes, and limitations, and then plan your career accordingly.

If you intend to make a career of the real estate business, you should strike a professional attitude early. You can gather information from the many courses offered at community colleges, state colleges and universities and various real estate seminars and workshops. Experience alone is not always enough to allow you to cope with conditions in a highly competitive market while, at the same time, rendering the best possible service to clients and customers.

The increasingly complex nature of real estate relationships requires more understanding of business conditions, architecture and construction, mathematics, engineering, taxation, planning, and trends in the economy.

The many available real estate courses give both the apprentice and the seasoned licensee opportunities to gain necessary knowledge and perspective.

XIV. Manufactured Housing and the Licensee

Although no longer referred to as "mobile homes," manufactured homes are what the original name implies, homes that can be moved. Like a vehicle, the *MANUFACTURED HOME is built on a steel chassis and equipped with wheels so that it can be pulled by truck from the factory to a dealer's lot and then to a site in a park or on private land. To be classed as a mobile home, a vehicle must be at least 8 feet wide and at least 32 feet long.*

Each *manufactured home unit is called a SINGLEWIDE; two or more manufactured home units together form a MULTISECTIONAL.* The multisectionals account for about one-third of all total manufactured home sales.

A manufactured home can be built in a matter of hours in factories that are models of modern assembly line technology. This technology allows manufacturers to control quality, improve product, reduce waste, and drastically cut labor costs.

A. MOBILE HOME PARKS

The mobile home park is an established form of residential development in California. These parks range from attractive, well-kept subdivisions with numerous amenities to the old, rundown parks that give this type of development a bad image.

Traditionally, spaces in mobile home parks have been rented, but with the high cost of traditional housing, the trend toward ownership continues unabated. It is very likely that the evolving interest in meeting the demand for decent, relatively low-cost housing will see an increasing number of developments planned to accommodate factory-built housing or mobile homes.

The majority of mobile home parks cater to retired and semi-retired residents, but greater attention is being devoted to the growing number of first-time buyers, unmarrieds, and singles. For "empty-nesters" who suddenly find themselves in a house which has become too large or too expensive to maintain, a mobile home park might provide a good alternative to condominium or apartment living.

Like all residential subdivisions, maps for own-your-own-lot mobile home parks are filed with the Department of Real Estate, but city and

county governments control the development of the parks through zoning laws.

Some counties, for example, do not permit own-your-own mobile home parks, while they may permit rental spaces.

B. OPPORTUNITIES

The manufactured housing industry represents to the licensee a source of additional revenue that for the most part has been ignored. Is the manufactured home buyer a bona fide prospect? Can the manufactured home be sold as real estate? Do zoning regulations restrict sales? What about depreciation, financing, sales, and service?

C. MOBILE HOME DEALER VS. REAL ESTATE BROKER

New manufactured homes cannot be sold by real estate licensees.

Real estate licensees are not allowed to act as agents in the sale of mobile homes that can be used as vehicles on the highway. To mitigate against such practice, licensees are not even permitted to maintain any place of business where two or more mobile homes are displayed and offered for sale by such person, unless the broker is also licensed as a vehicle dealer pursuant to the California Vehicle Code.

D. MARKETING

California specifically regulates manufactured home sales with a statute outlining rules and regulations permitting real estate brokers to sell the units.

Brokers may sell manufactured homes that have been registered with the Department of Motor Vehicles for at least one year and are greater than 8 feet in width and 40 feet in length.

Manufactured homes create greater title problems than ordinary real estate transactions. Before listing such property, you should demand and receive the owner's registration papers indicating the true owner and outstanding loans, if any.

The future of the manufactured home industry is tied to the industry's ability to get the real estate profession to realize that in manufactured home development lies an opportunity for great profit. The manufactured home industry is a natural business for licensees in both sales and resales.

E. LISTING MANUFACTURED HOMES

CAR's Manufactured Home Listing Agreement (for Real and Personal Property) is a form that may be used in the listing of manufactured homes (see **Figure 12-6**). In listing such properties, you must ascertain park rules to be sure you are not violating restrictions imposed by the park owners. Determination of ownership is vital at this stage, notwithstanding the owner's warranty to that effect in paragraph 2(e) of the listing form. As a licensee, you are liable for disciplinary action and criminal action if you knowingly participate in acquiring or disposing of a stolen mobile home. Further, you must be sure that the manufactured homes comply with the Department of Housing insignia and that no alterations have been done without complying with DOH regulations or local ordinances.

Where the purchase price includes manufactured home and lot, separate the transaction into two components: the manufactured home may be treated as the sale of a vehicle, unless it is taxed as real property because it rests on a permanent foundation; the land would, in any case, be treated as the sale of real property. If the manufactured home is located on a site other than an established park, you must check to determine that the installation is in accordance with local codes and zoning ordinances. Finally, anyone listing manufactured homes should fill in the agreement accurately and completely, leaving nothing to chance or possible disagreement.

F. SELLING MANUFACTURED HOMES

You owe your buyers duties beyond that of the sale of conventional housing. You must provide prospective park residents with information concerning the lot and available utilities. You must ascertain ownership of manufactured homes and other items in compliance with park rules and regulations, and they must explain the conditions contained in the lease, the state law, and the policies, rules and regulations of the park owners and resident association, if any. The purchase should be made subject to buyer and park owner agreeing on future occupancy. If the manufactured home is to be moved, you must be certain that the moving will conform to DMV requirements. Since manufactured home moving is expensive, it would be wise to counsel the buyer on costs and to make the purchase subject to approval by the buyer of expenses, DMV requirements, and anything else of a material nature.

1. Buyer Profile

Who is the typical manufactured home buyer? According to Manufactured Housing Industry statistics, more than 12 million persons live in mobile homes. Of this figure, 43 percent are 34 years of age and younger; 26 percent are between the age of 35 and 54; and 31 percent are 55 years of age and older. Nearly 75 percent are married and have an average family size of 2.3 persons.

2. Financing

Twenty-five percent of all manufactured home buyers pay cash for their units; the remaining 75 percent make large down payments. Only a small percentage are financed as real estate, and most units go on the books of commercial banks that are active installment lenders.

Figure 12-6

CALIFORNIA
ASSOCIATION
OF REALTORS®

MANUFACTURED HOME LISTING AGREEMENT
FOR REAL AND PERSONAL PROPERTY

1. **EXCLUSIVE RIGHT TO SELL:** _____ ("Seller") hereby employs and grants
    _____ ("Broker") the exclusive and irrevocable right, commencing on
    (date) _____ and expiring at 11:59 P.M. on (date) _____ ("Listing Period"), to sell or exchange
    the Manufactured Home Situated In _____, County Of _____,
    California, described as _____, and as further described below, ("Property").

2. **TYPE OF MANUFACTURED HOME:** (Check box below which applies: A(1), A(2) or B. Check ONLY one.):
    A.   PERSONAL PROPERTY MANUFACTURED HOME
        (1) ☐ **A Manufactured Home On Leased Or Rented Land** (complete paragraph 2A(3)).
            Space Number _____ Park Name _____
    OR   **(2)** ☐ **A Manufactured Home To Be Sold With Real Property** (complete paragraph 2A(3)) described as _____
            _____
            PURCHASE PRICE ALLOCATED AS FOLLOWS: Manufactured Home $_____ Land $_____
        (3) ADDITIONAL DESCRIPTION: (For personal property manufactured home only)
            Manufacturer's Name _____ Model _____ Date Of Manufacture_____ Date Of First Sale _____
            Property is: ☐ On Local Property Tax Roll, ☐ Department of Housing and Community Development ("HCD") registered (Use Tax Applies).
            Approximate Width _____ Approximate Length _____ (Without Hitch) Expando Size _____
            HCD/HUD License/Decal Number _____
            SERIAL NUMBERS: 1. _____ 2. _____ 3. _____
            HCD/HUD Label/Insignia: 1. _____ 2. _____ 3. _____
    OR B. ☐ **A REAL PROPERTY MANUFACTURED HOME** (A real property manufactured mobile home is one that meets the following requirements:
        (1) a building permit is obtained from local authorities pursuant to Health and Safety Code §18551, **(2)** the manufactured home is affixed to a
        foundation pursuant to Health & Safety Code §18551, **(3)** a certificate of occupancy is issued by local authorities, and **(4)** there is recordation
        with the local authorities of a form pursuant to Health and Safety Code §18551.)

3. **TERMS OF SALE:**
    A.   LIST PRICE: The listing price shall be _____ ($ _____).
    B.   PERSONAL PROPERTY: The following items of personal property (exclusive of the Property) are included in the above price: _____

    C.   ADDITIONAL TERMS: _____
        _____
        _____

4. **MULTIPLE LISTING SERVICE:** Information about this listing ☐ will, ☐ will not, be provided to a multiple listing service ("MLS") of Broker's selection
    and all terms of the transaction, including, if applicable, financing will be provided to the MLS for publication, dissemination and use by persons and
    entities on terms approved by the MLS. Seller authorizes Broker to comply with all applicable MLS rules.

5. **TITLE AND COMPLIANCE WITH MANUFACTURED HOME LAWS:**
    A. Seller warrants that Seller and no other persons have title to the Property, except as follows: _____
        _____
    B. Seller agrees Property shall be free of liens and encumbrances, recorded, filed, registered or known to Seller.
    C. Seller agrees that **(1)** evidence of title to the manufactured home, if personal property, shall be in the form of a duly endorsed, dated and
        delivered Certificate of Ownership; and **(2)** Seller shall deliver the current Registration Certificate of Title as required by law.
    D. Seller represents that Property, if personal property, is either: **(1)** Located within an established mobilehome park as defined in California Health
        and Safety Code §18214, and that advertising or offering it for sale is not contrary to any provision of any contract between Seller and
        mobilehome park ownership; OR **(2)** That Property is located pursuant to a local zoning ordinance or permit on a lot where its presence has
        been authorized or its continued presence and such use would be authorized for a total and uninterrupted period of at least one year.
    E. If applicable, Seller agrees to deliver as soon as possible to Broker, for submission to buyer, a copy of Seller's lease or rental agreement and
        all current park and/or Homeowners' Association rules and regulations, and to inform Broker of any changes to either during the Listing Period.

        Seller and Broker acknowledge receipt of copy of this page, which constitutes Page 1 of _____ Pages.
        Seller's Initials (_____) (_____)   Broker's Initials (_____) (_____)

REBS INC

Published and Distributed by:
REAL ESTATE BUSINESS SERVICES, INC.
a subsidary of the CALIFORNIA ASSOCIATION OF REALTORS®
525 South Virgil Avenue, Los Angeles, California 90020
PRINT DATE

REVISED 10/99

OFFICE USE ONLY
Reviewed by Broker
or Designee _____
Date _____

EQUAL HOUSING
OPPORTUNITY

MANUFACTURED HOME LISTING AGREEMENT (MHL-11 PAGE 1 OF 3)

Property Address: _____ Date: _____

6. **COMPENSATION TO BROKER:**

   Notice: The amount or rate of real estate commissions is not fixed by law. They are set by each Broker individually and may be negotiable between Seller and Broker.

   A. Seller agrees to pay to Broker as compensation for services irrespective of agency relationship(s), either ☐ _____ percent of the listing price (or if a sales contract is entered into, of the sales price), or ☐ $ _____, AND _____ as follows:

      (1) If Broker, Seller, cooperating broker, or any other person, produces a buyer(s) who offers to purchase the Property on the above price and terms, or on any price and terms acceptable to Seller during the Listing Period, or any extension;

      (2) If within _____ calendar days after expiration of the Listing Period or any extension, the Property is sold, conveyed, leased, or otherwise transferred to anyone with whom Broker or a cooperating broker has had negotiations, provided that Broker gives Seller, prior to or within **5 calendar days** after expiration of the Listing Period or any extension, a written notice with the name(s) of the prospective purchaser(s);

      (3) If, without Broker's prior written consent, the Property is withdrawn from sale, conveyed, leased, rented, otherwise transferred, or made unmarketable by a voluntary act of Seller during the Listing Period, or any extension.

   B. If completion of the sale is prevented by a party to the transaction other than Seller, then compensation due under paragraph 6A shall be payable only if and when Seller collects damages by suit, settlement, or otherwise, and then in an amount equal to the lesser of one-half of the damages recovered or the above compensation, after first deducting title and escrow expenses and the expenses of collection, if any.

   C. In addition, Seller agrees to pay: _____

   D. Broker is authorized to cooperate with other brokers and, provided the Property is or includes a personal property manufactured home, with HCD licensed dealers, and divide with other brokers and dealers the above compensation in any manner acceptable to Broker.

   E. Seller hereby irrevocably assigns to Broker the above compensation from Seller's funds and proceeds in escrow.

   F. Seller warrants that Seller has no obligation to pay compensation to any other broker or dealer regarding the transfer of the Property, except: _____

      If the Property is sold to anyone listed above during the time Seller is obligated to compensate another broker or dealer; (a) Broker is not entitled to compensation under this Agreement; and (b) Broker is not obligated to represent Seller with respect to such transaction.

7. **BROKER'S AND SELLER'S DUTIES:** Broker agrees to exercise reasonable effort and due diligence to achieve the purposes of this Agreement, and is authorized to advertise and market the Property in any medium selected by Broker. Seller agrees to consider offers presented by Broker, and to act in good faith toward accomplishing the sale of the Property. Seller further agrees, regardless of responsibility, to indemnify, defend and hold Broker harmless from all claims, disputes, litigation, judgments and attorney's fees arising from any incorrect information supplied by Seller, whether contained in any document, omitted therefrom, or otherwise, or from any material facts which Seller knows but fails to disclose.

8. **AGENCY RELATIONSHIPS:** Broker shall act as the agent for Seller in any resulting transaction. Depending upon the circumstances, it may be necessary or appropriate for Broker to act as an agent for both Seller and buyer, exchange party, or one or more additional parties ("Buyer"). Broker shall, as soon as practicable, disclose to Seller any election to act as a dual agent representing both Seller and Buyer. If a Buyer is procured directly by Broker or an associate licensee in Broker's firm, Seller hereby consents to Broker acting as a dual agent for Seller and such Buyer. In the event of an exchange, Seller hereby consents to Broker collecting compensation from additional parties for services rendered, provided there is disclosure to all parties of such agency and compensation.

      Seller understands that Broker may have or obtain listings on other properties, and that potential buyers may consider, make offers on, or purchase through Broker, property the same as or similar to Seller's Property. Seller consents to Broker's representation of sellers and buyers of other properties before, during, and after the expiration of this Agreement.

9. **DEPOSIT:** Broker is authorized to accept and hold on Seller's behalf a deposit to be applied toward the sales price.

10. **LOCKBOX:**

    A. A lockbox is designed to hold a key to the Property to permit access to the Property by Broker, cooperating brokers, MLS participants, their authorized licensees and representatives, and accompanied prospective buyers.

    B. Broker, cooperating brokers, MLS and Associations/Boards of REALTORS® are **not** insurers against theft, loss, vandalism, or damage attributed to the use of a lockbox. Seller is advised to verify the existence of, or obtain, appropriate insurance through Seller's own insurance broker.

    C. ☐ (If checked:) Seller authorizes Broker to install a lockbox. If Seller does not occupy the Property, Seller shall be responsible for obtaining occupant(s)' written permission for use of a lockbox.

11. **SIGN:** ☐ (If checked:) Seller authorizes Broker to install a FOR SALE/SOLD sign on the Property.

Seller and Broker acknowledge receipt of copy of this page, which constitutes Page 2 of _____ Pages.
Seller's Initials (_____) (_____)   Broker's Initials (_____) (_____)

REVISED 10/99

OFFICE USE ONLY
Reviewed by Broker
or Designee _____
Date _____

PRINT DATE

MANUFACTURED HOME LISTING AGREEMENT (MHL-11 PAGE 2 OF 3)

Property Address: _____ Date: _____

12. DISPUTE RESOLUTION:

    A. MEDIATION: Seller and Broker agree to mediate any dispute or claim arising between them out of this Agreement, or any resulting transaction, before resorting to arbitration or court action, subject to paragraph 12C below. Mediation fees, if any, shall be divided equally among the parties involved. If any party commences an action based on a dispute or claim to which this paragraph applies, without first attempting to resolve the matter through mediation, then that party shall not be entitled to recover attorney's fees, even if they would otherwise be available to that party in any such action. THIS MEDIATION PROVISION APPLIES WHETHER OR NOT THE ARBITRATION PROVISION IS INITIALED.

    B. ARBITRATION OF DISPUTES: Seller and Broker agree that any dispute or claim in Law or equity arising between them regarding the obligation to pay compensation under this Agreement, which is not settled through mediation, shall be decided by neutral, binding arbitration, subject to paragraph 12C below. The arbitrator shall be a retired judge or justice, or an attorney with at least five years of residential real estate experience, unless the parties mutually agree to a different arbitrator, who shall render an award in accordance with substantive California Law. In all other respects, the arbitration shall be conducted in accordance with Part III, Title 9 of the California Code of Civil Procedure. Judgment upon the award of the arbitrator(s) may be entered in any court having jurisdiction. The parties shall have the right to discovery in accordance with Code of Civil Procedure §1283.05.

        "NOTICE: BY INITIALING IN THE SPACE BELOW YOU ARE AGREEING TO HAVE ANY DISPUTE ARISING OUT OF THE MATTERS INCLUDED IN THE 'ARBITRATION OF DISPUTES' PROVISION DECIDED BY NEUTRAL ARBITRATION AS PROVIDED BY CALIFORNIA LAW AND YOU ARE GIVING UP ANY RIGHTS YOU MIGHT POSSESS TO HAVE THE DISPUTE LITIGATED IN A COURT OR JURY TRIAL. BY INITIALING IN THE SPACE BELOW YOU ARE GIVING UP YOUR JUDICIAL RIGHTS TO DISCOVERY AND APPEAL, UNLESS THOSE RIGHTS ARE SPECIFICALLY INCLUDED IN THE 'ARBITRATION OF DISPUTES' PROVISION. IF YOU REFUSE TO SUBMIT TO ARBITRATION AFTER AGREEING TO THIS PROVISION, YOU MAY BE COMPELLED TO ARBITRATE UNDER THE AUTHORITY OF THE CALIFORNIA CODE OF CIVIL PROCEDURE. YOUR AGREEMENT TO THIS ARBITRATION PROVISION IS VOLUNTARY."

        "WE HAVE READ AND UNDERSTAND THE FOREGOING AND AGREE TO SUBMIT DISPUTES ARISING OUT OF THE MATTERS INCLUDED IN THE 'ARBITRATION OF DISPUTES' PROVISION TO NEUTRAL ARBITRATION."   Seller's Initials ____/____   Broker's Initials ____/____

    C. EXCLUSIONS FROM MEDIATION AND ARBITRATION: The following matters are excluded from Mediation and Arbitration hereunder: (a) A judicial or non-judicial foreclosure or other action or proceeding to enforce a deed of trust, mortgage, or installment land sale contract as defined in Civil Code §2985; (b) An unlawful detainer action; (c) The filing or enforcement of a mechanic's lien; (d) Any matter which is within the jurisdiction of a probate, small claims, or bankruptcy court; and (e) An action for bodily injury or wrongful death, or for latent or patent defects to which Code of Civil Procedure §337.1 or §337.15 applies. The filing of a court action to enable the recording of a notice of pending action, for order of attachment, receivership, injunction, or other provisional remedies, shall not constitute a violation of the mediation and arbitration provisions.

13. EQUAL HOUSING OPPORTUNITY: The Property is sold in compliance with federal, state, and local anti-discrimination Laws.

14. ATTORNEY'S FEES: In any action, proceeding, or arbitration between Seller and Broker regarding the obligation to pay compensation under this Agreement, the prevailing Seller or Broker shall be entitled to reasonable attorney's fees and costs, except as provided in paragraph 12A.

15. ADDITIONAL TERMS: _____
_____
_____

16. ENTIRE CONTRACT: All prior discussions, negotiations, and agreements between the parties concerning the subject matter of this Agreement are superseded by this Agreement, which constitutes the entire contract and a complete and exclusive expression of their agreement, and may not be contradicted by evidence of any prior agreement or contemporaneous oral agreement. This Agreement and any supplement, addendum, or modification, including any photocopy or facsimile, may be executed in counterparts.

Seller warrants that Seller is the owner of the Property or has the authority to execute this contract. Seller acknowledges that Seller has read and understands this Agreement, and has received a copy.

Seller _____ Date _____
Address/City/State/Zip _____
Phone _____ Fax _____ E-mail _____

Seller _____ Date _____
Address/City/State/Zip _____
Phone _____ Fax _____ E-mail _____

Real Estate Broker (Firm Name) _____
By (Agent) _____ Date _____
Address/City/State/Zip _____
Phone _____ Fax _____ E-mail _____

REVISED 10/99

Page 3 of _____ Pages.

OFFICE USE ONLY
Reviewed by Broker
or Designee _____
Date _____

MANUFACTURED HOME LISTING AGREEMENT (MHL-11 PAGE 3 OF 3)

Financing opportunities in the manufactured housing field are becoming more attractive to mortgage banks because more manufactured homes are dealt with as real estate and financed by the familiar deed of trust.

One stimulus to manufactured home financing is federal legislation that authorizes savings banks to finance new manufactured home purchases, creates an FHA insurance guaranty program for manufactured home loans, and makes manufactured homes eligible for VA-guaranteed loans.

XV. CHAPTER SUMMARY

A **business opportunity (BO)** is the sale or lease of a business (inventory, fixtures, and equipment), as well as the goodwill of the existing business. **Goodwill** is the expectation of continued public patronage. Also known as a **bulk transfer**, the sale of a business is covered by the **Uniform Commercial Code (UCC)**. A **Notice to Creditors of Bulk Sale** must be given to a seller's creditors at least 12 days before the sale is consummated.

To protect buyers and creditors (**encumbrancers**), a **Security Agreement and Financing Statement** is also required for commercial transactions, although only the Financing Statement must be filed with the Secretary of State. The **State Board of Equalization** issues a **Certificate of Payment of Sales and Use Tax** to release the buyer from liability for the seller's unpaid sales and use tax.

As a sale of a business opportunity is considered the **transfer of personal property**, a **bill of sale** is used, which serves the same function as a grant deed for real property.

Net multipliers and **gross multipliers** are commonly used as guidelines to compute the value of a business.

A seller who agrees not to open a competing business for a period of time within a specific geographical area has entered into a **covenant not to compete**.

The issuance of liquor licenses is regulated by the **California Department of Alcoholic Beverage Control (ABC)**.

Real Property Security Dealers (RSPDs) are involved in the secondary mortgage (or money) market, and must have a broker's license as well as a **permit** issued by the Real Estate Commissioner.

In order to be recorded and give constructive notice, most real estate transaction documents require **acknowledgement** before a licensed **notary public**. Many brokers (or their assistants) acquire this assignation as a way to expedite and make transactions more convenient for clients.

In addition to notarial services, many brokers offer their clients property management and escrow services. An escrow is a neutral third party who acts as a depository of funds and documents, prorates charges and expenses detailed in the terms of an agreement, and serves as a clearinghouse for the exchange of monies and documents when all the terms and condition of escrow have been met. An individual cannot be licensed as an escrow company in California, but a broker may act as an escrow agent when he or she represents the buyer or seller or both. **Licensees acting as escrow agents** must keep proper records and maintain all escrow funds in a trust accounts subject to inspection by the Real Estate Commissioner.

Brokers can supplement their brokerage activities by lending their own money, or money of investors, as well as acting as representatives, agents, or correspondents for mortgage lending institutions. They can also organize or join a **syndication**, whereby funds are pooled by investors to purchase real estate.

Yet another avenue for business expansion is the marketing and sales of **probate property** (court-ordered sale of a deceased person's property or properties).

The Department of Finance may authorize a broker to earn a commission on the sale of state-owned property, including sales by the Board of Education. The California Division of Highways (Caltrans) permits licensees to negotiate the leasing of airspace under the Airspace Development Program.

Within California (intrastate), the Subdivision Map Act and the Subdivided Lands Act govern the division and subsequent sale of real property. The Real Estate Commissioner's office (and responsible county or municipal authorities) administer new subdivision regulations. Subdivision maps are the most commonly used method of property division.

When selling or leasing a subdivision of 25 lots or more (land project) through interstate commerce or by mail, a Property Report permit must be obtained from the Department of Housing and Urban Development (HUD). Potential buyers receive a (state) Public Report and (federal) State Property Report Disclaimers.

Superior knowledge is required for a broker involved in investment planning and counseling. Investment planning involves: 1) analyzing a client's investment requirements; 2) researching and selecting appropriate properties; 3) negotiating the purchase followed by title search and escrow; and 4) property management details.

Brokers may focus on general housing sales or may choose to specialize in one particular area of brokerage, such as commercial properties, exchanges, syndication, escrow, teaching, and many more.

Finally, brokers may sell manufactured (mobile) homes that have been registered with the Department of Motor Vehicles (DMV) for at least **one year**, and are greater than 8 feet wide and 40 feet long. A Manufactured Home Listing Agreement (for real and personal property) form is used for these types of sales. Brokers cannot sell mobile homes that can be used as vehicles on the highway, unless they are licensed vehicle dealers. Spaces in mobile home parks are no longer only available to rent, and ownership is on the rise. As residential subdivisions, these parks file subdivision maps with the DRE, although city and county zoning laws control their development.

XVI. TERMS

Airspace Development Program
Alcohol Beverage Control Act
Assignment of Lease
Bill of Sale
Board of Education Real Estate Sales
Bulk Transfer
Business Opportunity (BO)
CALTRANS
Certified Property Manager (CPM)
Certified Real Estate Appraiser (CREA)
Certified Residential Appraiser (CRA)
Counselor, Real Estate (CRE)
Covenant Not to Compete
Encumbrances
Escrow Activities
Goodwill
Gross Multipliers
Interstate Land Sales Full Disclosure Act
Interstate Sales
Intrastate Sales
Land Project
Listing Agreement
Loan Brokerage
Manufactured Home
Member, Appraiser Institute (MAI)
Member, Society of Real Estate Appraisers (SREA)
Multisectional
Net Multipliers
Notary Public
Notice of Intent to Sell
Notice to Creditors of Bulk Transfer
Probate Sales
Property Management

Property Report
Real Estate Investment Counselor
Real Property Securities Dealer (RPSD)
Security Agreement and Financing Statement
Seller's Permit
Singlewide
State Board of Equalization
Subdivision Sales Opportunities
Transferee
Transferor
Uniform Commercial Code (UCC)

XVII. CHAPTER QUIZ

1. A seller of a business agrees not to open a business establishment similar to that of the business being sold. Such an agreement is called a:

    a. closed business covenant.

    b. buy and sell agreement.

    c. covenant of allocation.

    d. covenant not to compete.

2. In a probate sale, the first acceptable bid must be:

    a. 90% or more of the court appraisal.

    b. same or more than the court appraisal.

    c. left to the discretion of the executor.

    d. none of the above.

3. A person with a CPM designation would most likely be engaged professionally in the field of:

    a. property management.

    b. property insurance.

    c. property appraisal.

    d. property financing.

4. Which of the following items would not be included in a bill of sale transferring title to a retail merchandising business?

    a. Inventory of stock

    b. Assignment of lease

    c. The trade name

    d. List of fixtures and equipment

5. Brokerage opportunities for syndication abound because of:

    a. increasing demand for land.
    b. increasing demand for lower-price properties.
    c. increasingly larger outlays required of individuals for higher-priced properties.
    d. population influx.

6. In a probate sale the second bid (that is, the first overbid) must be:

    a. 15 percent of the first $10,000 plus 5 percent of the remaining portion of the original amount of bid.
    b. 10 percent of the first $10,000 plus 5 percent of the remaining portion of the original bid.
    c. 10 percent of the first $15,000 plus 5 percent of the remaining portion of the the original bid.
    d. left up to the discretion of the court.

7. The essential difference between the real property securities dealer and the real property loan broker is that:

    a. loan brokers deal essentially with secondary loans.
    b. real property securities dealers operate in the so-called primary mortgage market.
    c. loan brokers operate mainly in the so-called money market.
    d. securities dealers are not regulated by the real estate law.

8. A real estate syndicate can be a:

    a. corporation.
    b. partnership.
    c. trust.
    d. all of the above.

9. Before an individual real estate broker gets into the field of loan brokerage, he must obtain which license?

    a. Loan broker
    b. Real estate investment counselor
    c. Real property securities dealer
    d. None

10. A real estate broker is going to expand his business to include negotiations of loans for prospective borrowers and for the sale of trust deeds secured by prime real property which shows a high rate of return. Since these are well seasoned, the broker also promises to buy back a trust deed in which there may be a default. His license will need to carry which of the following?

    a. A real property loan broker's endorsement
    b. A security and exchange commission endorsement
    c. A real property security dealer's endorsement
    d. Nothing, since his broker's license is sufficient

ANSWERS: 1. d.; 2. b.; 3. a.; 4. b.; 5. c.; 6. b.; 7. c.; 8. d.; 9. d.; 10. c.

Property Management
How to Manage Rental/Lease Properties

Before discussing your career in property management, it is extremely important to have a full understanding of the regulatory laws that govern the sensitive issues relating to **less-than-freehold estates**, also known as **leasehold estates**. If these laws are not closely adhered to, you (as the property manager) and the owner may be liable to high punitive fines and costly legal procedures.

A "leasehold estate" is a tenant's right to occupy real estate during the specific term of a lease.

I. Fair Housing Laws

California first passed the Unruh Civil Rights Act (no discrimination in business, including real estate agents' services) and then the Fair Employment and Housing Act (FEHA) (no discrimination in housing). These were later reinforced by the Federal Civil Rights Act of 1968 (expanded in 1988).

Figure 13-1 describes the different types of fair housing violations.

CHAPTER 13 OUTLINE

I. FAIR HOUSING LAWS (p. 481)

    A. State Law - Unruh Civil Rights Act (p. 484)

    B. State Law - California Fair Employment and Housing Act (FEHA) (p. 484)

    C. State Law - Housing Financial Discrimination Act of 1977 (No Redlining) (p. 484)

    D. Federal Law - Federal Civil Rights Act of 1968 (p. 485)

        1. Federal Civil Rights Act Expanded in 1988 (p. 487)

II. PROPERTY MANAGEMENT (p. 487)

    A. Types of Properties (p. 488)

    B. Types of Property Managers (p. 488)

        1. Outside Manager (Does Not Reside on Property) (p. 488)

        2. Resident Manager (Resides on Property) (p. 489)

        3. Institutional Manager (Works for Large Company) (p. 489)

    C. Duties and Responsibilities of Property Managers (p. 490)

        1. The Tenant's Responsibilities (p. 492)

    D. Landlord-Tenant Termination Laws (30- and 60-Day Notices) (p. 492)

    E. Selection of Property Managers (p. 493)

        1. Management Contract (p. 495)

        2. Compensation (p. 495)

    F. Leasing and Tenant Selection (p. 499)

        1. Lease Contracts (p. 502)

            a. Types of Leasehold Estates (p. 502)

        2. Establishing Rent Schedules (p. 507)

    G. Accurate Record Keeping (A Must for Property Managers) (p. 509)

        1. Cash Journal (p. 510)

        2. Activity Report (p. 510)

    H. Common Interest Development (CID) Management (p. 512)

        1. Duties of an HOA Manager (p. 514)

        2. Determining an HOA Budget (p. 514)

        3. Managing Agent (p. 515)

    I. Prepaid Rental Listing Service (PRLS) (p. 515)

    J. Improving Value Through Balanced Management (p. 516)

        1. To Spend or Not to Spend (Maintenance) (p. 517)

    K. Rent Control (p. 518)

    L. Low-Income Housing (p. 518)

    M. Professional Associations for Managers (p. 518)

III. CHAPTER SUMMARY (p. 519)

IV. KEY TERMS (p. 522)

 V. CHAPTER 13 QUIZ (p. 523)

Figure 13-1

FAIR HOUSING VIOLATIONS AND POSSIBLE REMEDIES

REDLINING — The refusal of a loan or insurance based upon a property's location (zip code).

STEERING — Showing a client property in only one type of neighborhood, such as a Caucasian buyer in a Caucasian neighborhood, and the refusal to communicate the availability of housing in other neighborhoods.

OWNER TELLS AGENT NOT TO SHOW PROPERTY TO MINORITY — The agent is relieved of the duty to show the property to ANYONE, including a minority who has requested to see the property.

CONTRACT REFUSED TO BUYER BECAUSE OF RACE — ADVISE BUYER of the right to complain to the Fair Employment and Housing (FEH) and WARN SELLER that he or she has violated fair housing laws.

RACE RESTRICTIONS — Any race restriction is UNENFORCEABLE.

PANIC SELLING OR BLOCK BUSTING AND PANIC PEDDLING — An agent intentionally incites existing homeowners to sell their properties by saying that property values will fall because persons of a different race or religion have targeted a move into their neighborhood.

SALE OF PROPERTY—AGENT ASKED TO DISCRIMINATE — Agent must REFUSE the listing.

As a real estate practitioner, you must be "color-blind" when it comes to selling and leasing properties.

Chapter 13

A. STATE LAW - UNRUH CIVIL RIGHTS ACT
(No Discrimination in Business)

The Unruh Civil Rights Act was the first civil rights act in California; it prohibits "steering" and "block busting" as a real estate business practice.

California first passed the Unruh Civil Rights Act that declares:

"All persons within the jurisdiction of this state are free and equal, and no matter what their race, color, religion, ancestry, or national origin, they are entitled to the full and equal accommodations, advantages, facilities, privileges, or services in all business establishments of every kind whatsoever. . ."

B. STATE LAW - CALIFORNIA FAIR EMPLOYMENT AND HOUSING ACT (FEHA)

The California Fair Employment and Housing Act (FEHA) outlaws discrimination in housing. It also established the Commission of Fair Employment and Housing to investigate and take action against property owners, financial institutions, and real estate licensees who engage in discriminatory practices.

FEHA clearly defines **DISCRIMINATION** *as the refusal to sell, rent, or lease housing accommodations, including misrepresentation as to availability, offering inferior terms, and cancellations on the basis of race, color, national origin, religion, sex, familial status, and handicap. It also outlaws sale or rental advertisements containing discriminatory information.*

Owners of three single-family homes and owner-occupied buildings that are four units or less are exempt from Fair Housing Laws under the "Mom and Pop" provision.

Not so many years ago, buyers of child-bearing age, applying for financing on a purchase loan, were questioned about their use of birth control. We've come a long way since then!

C. STATE LAW - HOUSING FINANCIAL DISCRIMINATION ACT OF 1977
(No Redlining)

The Housing Financial Discrimination Act of 1977 prohibits financial institutions from engaging in discriminatory loan practices called "redlining."

In remedying such violations, the state may force a landowner to proceed with the rental or sale in question, provide comparable housing accommodations if the original is no longer available, or pay punitive damages up to $1,000. Under the **Housing Financial Discrimination Act of 1977**, the practice of redlining is specifically outlawed. *REDLINING is the practice by financial institutions of denying loans or varying finance terms based on the location of a given property, regardless of the credit worthiness of the borrower.* This law explicitly forbids discrimination because of the race of the borrower or the racial composition of the neighborhood in which the borrower's prospective home is located.

The Housing Financial Discrimination Act (no redlining) covers 1-to-4 units (at least one owner-occupied) used for residential purposes, but an owner seeking a home improvement loan need not occupy the property.

A grievance under this Act is directed to the U.S. Department of Business, Transportation, and Housing. Lending institutions in violation of the Housing Financial Discrimination Act may be required to pay for damages, limited to $1,000 for each offense.

D. FEDERAL LAWS (Federal Civil Rights Act of 1968)

Federal law prohibits discrimination on the part of owners of property and their agents based on the **U.S. Supreme Court case *Jones v. Mayer*** (which upheld the Civil Rights Act of 1866) and Title VIII of the Civil Rights Act of 1968.

For all practical purposes, discrimination laws evolved from the U.S. Supreme Court Case Jones v. Mayer, Title VIII of the Civil Rights Act of 1968 and the 13th Amendment to the U.S. Constitution.

At the federal level, the Federal Civil Rights Act of 1968 reinforced the Unruh and Rumford Acts:

1. Any discrimination that the two acts did not prohibit was explicitly outlawed. **THERE ARE NO EXCEPTIONS.**

2. It makes it illegal for real estate licensees to engage in discriminatory practices, regardless of any instructions the agent may have received from the seller or landlord. If asked to discriminate in the sale of a property, the salesperson must refuse to accept the listing.

3. It bars real estate boards or multiple listing services from discriminating by denying participation or restricting terms and conditions of membership.

4. It requires a fair housing poster to be displayed at all real estate offices and subdivision model homes. **The poster (Figure 13-2) must also be displayed at all financial institutions or by mortgage lenders who make loans to the general public.**

Figure 13-2

Equal Housing Lender

We Do Business In Accordance With The Federal Fair Housing Law

(Title VIII of the Civil Rights Act of 1968, as Amended by the Housing and Community Development Act of 1974)

IT IS ILLEGAL TO DISCRIMINATE AGAINST ANY PERSON BECAUSE OF RACE, COLOR, NATIONAL ORIGIN, RELIGION, SEX, FAMILIAL STATUS (including children under the age of 18 living with parents or legal custodians, pregnant women, and people securing custody of children under the age of 18), AND HANDICAP, TO:

- Deny a loan for the purpose of purchasing, constructing, improving, repairing or maintaining a dwelling or

- Discriminate in fixing of the amount, interest rate, duration, application procedures or other terms or conditions of such a loan.

IF YOU BELIEVE YOU HAVE BEEN DISCRIMINATED AGAINST, YOU MAY SEND A COMPLAINT TO:

U.S. DEPARTMENT OF HOUSING AND URBAN DEVELOPMENT

Assistant Secretary for Fair Housing and Equal Opportunity Washington, D.C. 20410

or call your local HUD Area or Insuring Office.

The only time you, as an agent, can refuse to show a property to a buyer is when the owners have informed you that they will be out of town and, during their absence, have left instructions not to show the property to anyone.

A lender who charges an additional fee per annum for processing loans to non-English speaking applicants (because the lender must hire non-English speaking employees), is practicing discrimination.

1. Federal Civil Rights Act Expanded in 1988 (HUD Can Initiate Housing Discrimination Cases)

A 1988 federal law allows the U.S. Government to take court action if it believes discrimination exists in home sales or apartment rentals. Landlords are explicitly forbidden to discriminate against families with children under 18 years of age. The only exemptions from this would be in retirement communities where most of the residents are more than 55 years of age.

This federal law also extends protections to handicapped home buyers or tenants. As of 1991, builders of all new apartment buildings were required to include ground floor rooms suitable for use by residents in wheelchairs.

The 1988 Fair Housing Amendments Act extended protection in regard to familial status and the handicapped.

The Housing and Urban Development (HUD) Department is authorized to bring enforcement action against sellers and landlords who defy this law. Fines of up to $10,000 have been authorized for first time violators, up to $25,000 for a second offense within five years and up to $50,000 for a third offense within seven years. Those accused of violating this tough statute would face an administrative judge unless they specifically requested a jury trial.

Complaints should be filed with Housing and Urban Development (HUD). Fair Employment and Housing will enforce any action.

To sum up: Real estate licensees must not discriminate, and to that end should not accept restrictive listings or make, print, or publish any notice, statement or advertisement with respect to a sale or rental of a dwelling that suggests discrimination.

II. Property Management

Few people possess sufficient knowledge, skill, and time to manage their own properties, and therefore turn to property management specialists. Your reward for pursuing this specialty includes not only the additional revenue, but also the chance to meet your

owners' complete real estate needs. As a property manager, you are in a better position to assess your clients' insurance needs, handle financing, offer timely suggestions on exchanging or sale opportunities, recommend other investment properties, place them in a business, obtain more referrals, and offer them a wide variety of other financial and estate-planning services. In short, you become a financial counselor. You are also in a good position to assist tenants when they decide to purchase real estate.

A. TYPES OF PROPERTIES

The basic types of income-producing properties include: 1) residential; 2) office buildings; 3) retail property; and 4) industrial property.

Some types of property lend themselves especially well to the professional manager. Because **apartment buildings** are more common than other income-producing properties, they lead in the demand for management services.

Other properties requiring professional management are single-family houses, office buildings, retail stores and shopping centers, medical buildings, hotels, industrial parks, single-purpose structures, and even raw land. Included in the definition of single-purpose structure category are public buildings, hospitals, mortuaries, theaters, restaurants, garages and service stations, churches, loft buildings, and so on.

B. TYPES OF PROPERTY MANAGERS

The principal goal of any manager is to minimize expenses, maximize rents, and increase the long-term appreciation of the property.

Your prime objective as a professional property manager is to increase the net income of the property more than the amount of the fee charged by your real estate firm. Management, then, should not be a cost, but a completely recoverable fee, plus a profit to the property owner. In order to accomplish this objective, an owner may employ one or more managers. There are three classifications of real estate managers.

1. Outside Manager (Does Not Reside on Property)

The category that concerns us most is that of professional outside manager. As part of their general brokerage operations, or as exclusive property management firms, *OUTSIDE MANAGERS represent more than one owner in more than one property.* They depict themselves as property managers, taking the place of the owners in order to meet the objective of profitability. They require no specific license other than the real estate broker license.

Because they make themselves available for numerous properties, outside (off-site) managers are often called "general managers."

Real Estate Investments Trusts (REITs) also offer outside management opportunities for managers; these are handled much the same way as mutual funds. The REIT usually contracts with a management company. However, most REITs form separate management companies to perform the managerial tasks, thus keeping the management fees within the company.

2. Resident Manager (Resides on Property)

RESIDENT MANAGERS live on the premises and are directly employed by the property owner or his agent. Since they are treated as employees, resident managers do not need to be licensed. Of course, they cannot make themselves available to manage other properties without first obtaining a broker's or salesperson's license under a broker who engages in property management. They manage a single building and, therefore, may be referred to as **building superintendents**.

A resident (on-site) manager, as the title signifies, lives on the premises and does not need to be licensed.

For the protection and convenience of tenants, California law prescribes that when an owner does not reside in an apartment house containing **16 or more units**, a resident manager, agent, or other responsible person must be hired to live on the premises.

For fewer than 16 units, with an exemption for fewer than five, the owner is required to **post a notice stating the name and address of the owner or agent** in a conspicuous place on the premises. The law also provides protection against excessive working hours and prescribes minimum wages, as promulgated by the state Industrial Welfare Commission Order for the Public Housekeeping Industry and the Labor Code, and enforced by the Division of Industrial Welfare of the Department of Industrial Relations.

The California Apartment Association (CAA) offers the California Certified Residential Manager (CCRM) designation for qualified licensed real estate professionals and a certificate in residential management for qualified, on-site residential managers.

3. Institutional Manager (Works for Large Company)

The *INSTITUTIONAL MANAGER or BUILDING SUPERVISOR is also directly employed for a wage or salary, but by an institution* such as the real estate management department of a bank, insurance company, government agency, REIT, trust, or endowment fund.

C. DUTIES AND RESPONSIBILITIES OF PROPERTY MANAGERS

A list of the 25 most important duties and functions of the manager follows; **no attempt is made to specify the type of manager who usually performs each duty.** (For example, as a resident manager, you and an outside manager may have overlapping responsibilities in accounting for funds.) As a manager, you may be required to:

1. Establish the rent schedule that will bring the **highest yield** consistent with sound economics principles.

2. Rent vacant units. Tenants need to know what is expected of them and what they can expect from the owner.

3. Keep all plumbing, heating, and electrical in good working order.

4. Make sure roof is leak-free and that doors and windows are not broken and open and close properly.

5. Maintain the floors, stairways, and railings need to be in safe and good condition.

6. Keep the premises clean and free of pests.

7. Properly maintain the areas under lessor's control.

8. Qualify tenants through credit reports, eviction history, and character references.

The California Apartment Association (CAA) has many local associations to assist owners and managers with rental forms and credit checks.

As a property manager, it's a good practice to contact not only the tenant's last landlord, but the one prior to that for a fair portrayal of the renter's history. Too many moves should raise a red flag. A credit check should be used to determine a renter's ability to pay rent on time.

9. Prepare and renew leases and have them executed.

10. Collect rents and process them. Instigate eviction proceedings, if necessary, with the assistance of a real estate attorney.

11. Account for funds in a separate trust account and maintain accurate records.

12. Submit monthly and annual statements to the owner in a timely fashion.

13. Prepare budgets for each property managed, including appropriate statements for income, expenses, and the sources and application of funds.

14. Order, supervise, and check all maintenance and repair work deemed necessary after securing estimates.

15. Purchase all supplies and equipment necessary for operation of the building.

16. Advertise, prepare brochures, publicity releases, and correspondence.

17. Inspect properties periodically, particularly vacant space.

18. Interview, hire, fire, train and supervise personnel, including resident managers, maids, custodians, gardeners, pool maintenance crew, and others.

19. Maintain necessary insurance (and upgrades when property value increases), including the basic fire and windstorm, liability, workman's compensation, errors and omissions, and consequential loss policies.

20. Prepare, keep, and file social security reports; acquires health and other licenses.

21. Pay taxes and recommend tax appeals when warranted.

22. Pay bills, including payments for loans and insurance and all other authorized disbursements.

23. Estimate deferred maintenance, fixtures, and equipment and establish reserve accounts for their ultimate replacement.

24. Prepare plans and specifications for alteration, rehabilitation, and remodeling.

25. Act as an advisor; recommend appraisers to determine **highest and best use** of the property. Analyze market trends and leasing arrangements that will enlarge the owner's net income or favorable times to refinance, sell, or exchange the property.

"Highest and best use" is the most profitable, physically possible, and legally permissible use for the property.

Quite a few agents and brokers own their own investment properties. However, experience has taught them to hire property managers (even if they manage other people's properties). It's a good idea to hire an outsider because it's too easy to get attached and personally involved. It's always best to keep transactions at "arm's length."

1. The Tenant's Responsibilities

The tenant has the following responsibilities:

1. Keep the dwelling clean and sanitary.

2. Keep the property garbage-free and dispose of all waste properly.

3. Use all fixtures properly, keeping them clean.

4. Cause no damage to the property.

5. Use property as stated in the lease agreement.

6. Pay rent on time.

7. Give a 30-Day notice when vacating a month-to-month tenancy.

8. Return door and mailbox keys when vacating.

9. Leave unit in as clean a condition as taken at the start of the lease.

D. LANDLORD-TENANT TERMINATION LAWS (30- and 60-Day Notices)

A 60-Day Termination Notice must be given to a tenant who has been in possession of a rental unit for one year or more.

Effective through January 1, 2006, a landlord must provide a month-to-month periodic tenant with a 60-day notice to terminate the tenancy if the tenant has lived in the dwelling for one year or more.

The 60-Day Termination Notice applies to landlords, whereas a tenant who terminates a periodic tenancy may do so with a 30-day notice.

The following are situations where the 60-day notice is not required:

1. It does not apply if the landlord enters into a fixed-term lease, such as a one-year lease agreement.

2. A **30-day notice** is sufficient for tenants who have lived in the property for **less than one year**.

3. Landlords selling their properties may give a **30-day notice** if all of the following conditions are met:

    a. The owner has entered into a contract to sell the dwelling or unit to a bona fide purchaser for value.
    b. The buyer is a natural person(s).
    c. The buyer, in good faith, intends to live in the property for at least one year after termination of the tenancy.
    d. The termination notice is given within 120 days of opening escrow.
    e. Notice has not been previously given to the tenant under this law.
    f. The owner has established an escrow with a licensed escrow officer or a licensed real estate broker.
    g. The dwelling or unit is alienable separate from the title to any other dwelling unit.

> *As a representative of the landlord, you can use CAR's standard form entitled "Notice of Termination of Tenancy" (Figure 13-3). It is important to remember that it is unlawful for the landlord or property manager to lock out tenants, take the tenants' property, remove doors, shut off utilities, or trespass.*

The *THREE-DAY NOTICE TO QUIT* states that the tenant has three business days to pay all past due rent or vacate the property or face an **unlawful detainer**. The *30-DAY or 60-DAY NOTICE* is given when the landlord wants the tenant out of the property. No reason needs to be given, unless the property is in a rent controlled city. Naturally a 30-day or 60-day notice cannot be given to a tenant with a bona fide lease.

The Three-Day Notice is a legal document requesting either the rent or a return of the premises. The document must be properly (legally) served.

E. SELECTION OF PROPERTY MANAGERS

Many considerations go into the choice of the right manager. He or she should be selected on the same basis as a manager of a firm. As a manager, you should have

Figure 13-3

CALIFORNIA
ASSOCIATION
OF REALTORS®

NOTICE OF TERMINATION OF TENANCY
(C.A.R. Form NTT, Revised 10/02)
FOR USE BEGINNING JANUARY 1, 2003

To: _____

and all subtenants and any other occupant in possession of the premises located at (Street Address) _____

_____ (Unit/Apartment #) _____

(City) _____ (State) _____ (Zip Code) _____ ("Premises").

CHECK THE BOX THAT APPLIES. CHECK ONE BOX ONLY.

1. ☐ (If checked) Your tenancy, if any, in the Premises is terminated SIXTY days from service of this Notice, or on _____ (whichever is later).

2. **You have resided in the Premises for less than one year.**
    ☐ (If checked) Your tenancy, if any, in the Premises is terminated THIRTY days from service of this Notice, or on _____ (whichever is later).

3. **All of the following apply:**
    A. The landlord has entered into a contract to sell the Premises to a natural person(s);

AND **B.** The purchaser intends to occupy the Premises for at least one year following the termination of the tenancy in the Premises;

AND **C.** The landlord has established an escrow with a company licensed by the Department of Corporations or a licensed Real Estate Broker.

AND **D.** The escrow was opened less than 120 days prior to the delivery of this Notice;

AND **E.** The title to the Premises is separately alienable from any other dwelling unit (i.e., a single family unit or condominium);

AND **F.** The tenant has not previously been given a notice of termination of tenancy.

☐ (If checked) Your tenancy, if any, in the Premises is terminated THIRTY days from service of this Notice, or on _____ (whichever is later).

If you fail to give up possession by that date, a legal action will be filed seeking possession and damages which could result in a judgment being awarded against you.

Landlord (Owner or Agent) _____ Date _____

(Keep a copy for your records.)

SURE TRAC
The System for Success™

Published by the
California Association of REALTORS®

NTT REVISED 10/02 (PAGE 1 OF 1) Print Date

Reviewed by _____ Date _____

EQUAL HOUSING OPPORTUNITY

NOTICE OF TERMINATION OF TENANCY (NTT PAGE 1 OF 1)

skills and talent in handling people, money, and a diversity of other responsibilities. How much of these qualities are needed and to what degree depends on which level of the three types of management you work in.

In general, as a professional manager, you should have a mind for details and knowledge of construction and mechanics, enjoy supervisory work, and possess above-average education, especially in real estate, accounting, general business, and even engineering. You should be tactful, be able to make sound judgments, have experience in supervising maintenance personnel, understand how to identify and solve problems, have an affinity for people, possess good moral character, and know how to play the role of executive, operating the property as you would operate any important business.

1. Management Contract

Good business practice dictates that any agreement for the employment of a manager should be in writing. Standardized forms outlining the duties and responsibilities, as well as rights and benefits, are available through **apartment owners' associations**, realty boards, and stationery stores, or can be specially drafted by a lawyer. The California Association of Realtors® has a comprehensive three-page Property Management Agreement (**Figure 13-4**) that lists the broker's and owner's obligations, and can be adapted to typical situations. Included are provisions for marketing the space, leasing, collections, repairs and maintenance, fees to be paid when property is vacant, disbursements, periodic statements to owners, accounting for funds, and agent's compensation when renting and or leasing the property.

As with real estate sales, property management compensation is always negotiable. As a loose rule of thumb, when managing a single-family residence, many brokers charge from 6% to 10% of the monthly income. When managing multiple units, this fee is usually somewhat reduced.

2. Compensation

Resident and **institutional managers** are customarily paid a straight salary. As an apartment resident manager, you may also receive rent-free quarters in lieu of salary, in whole or in part. Bonuses for extra jobs or for extraordinary performance are also common.

Outside professional managers are usually paid a percentage of the gross revenues, depending on the type of services, size of property, and other compensation. Besides

Figure 13-4

CALIFORNIA
ASSOCIATION
OF REALTORS®

PROPERTY MANAGEMENT AGREEMENT

_____ ("Owner"), and
_____ ("Broker"), agree as follows:

1. **APPOINTMENT OF BROKER:** Owner hereby appoints and grants Broker the exclusive right to rent, lease, operate, and manage the property (ies)
   known as _____
   _____
   _____, and any additional property which may later be added to this Agreement, ("Property"),
   upon the terms below, for the period beginning on (date) _____ and ending on (date) _____, at 11:59 p.m.
   (If checked:) ☐ Either party may terminate this Agreement on at least 30 days written notice _____ months after the original commencement date
   of this Agreement. After the exclusive term expires, this Agreement shall continue as a Non-Exclusive Agreement which either party may terminate
   by giving at least 30 days written notice to the other.

2. **BROKER ACCEPTANCE:** Broker accepts the appointment and grant, and agrees to:
   A. Use due diligence in the performance of this Agreement.
   B. Furnish the services of its organization for the rental, leasing, operating, and management of the Property.

3. **AUTHORITY AND POWERS:** Owner grants Broker the authority and power, at Owner's expense, to:
   A. **ADVERTISING:** Display FOR RENT, FOR LEASE, and similar signs on the Property; advertise the availability for rental or lease of the Property, or
      any part of it.
   B. **RENTAL/LEASING:** Initiate, sign, renew, or cancel rental agreements and leases for the Property, or any part of it; collect and give receipts for
      rents, other charges, and security deposits. Any lease executed by Broker for Owner shall not exceed _____ year(s). Unless Owner
      authorizes a lower amount, rent shall: ☐ be a minimum of $ _____ per _____; OR ☐ see attachment.
   C. **TENANCY TERMINATION:** Sign and serve in Owner's name notices which are required or appropriate; commence and prosecute actions to
      evict tenants; recover possession of the Property in Owner's name; recover rents and other sums due; and when expedient, settle, compromise,
      and release claims, actions and suits, and/or reinstate tenancies.
   D. **REPAIR/MAINTENANCE:** Make, cause to be made, and/or supervise repairs, improvements, alterations, and decorations to the Property;
      purchase and pay bills for services and supplies. Broker shall obtain prior approval of Owner on all expenditures over $ _____ for
      any one item. Prior approval shall not be required for monthly or recurring operating charges, or, if in Broker's opinion, emergency expenditures
      over the maximum are needed to protect the Property or other property(ies) from damage, prevent injury to persons, avoid suspension of
      necessary services, avoid penalties or fines, or suspension of services to tenants required by a lease or rental agreement or by law. Broker shall
      not advance Broker's own funds in connection with the Property or this Agreement.
   E. **CONTRACTS/SERVICES:** Contract, hire, supervise and/or discharge firms and persons, including utilities, required for the operation and
      maintenance of the Property. Broker may perform any of Broker's duties through attorneys, agents, employees, or independent contractors, and,
      except for persons working in Broker's firm, shall not be responsible for their acts, omissions, defaults, negligence, and/or costs of same.
   F. **EXPENSE PAYMENTS:** Pay expenses and costs for the Property from Owner's funds held by Broker, unless otherwise directed by Owner.
      Expenses and costs may include, but are not limited to, property management fees and charges, expenses for goods and services, property
      taxes and other taxes, Owner's Association dues, assessments, loan payments, and insurance premiums.
   G. **SECURITY DEPOSITS:** Receive security deposits from tenants, which deposits shall be ☐ given to Owner, or ☐ placed in Broker's trust
      account. Owner shall be responsible to tenants for return of security deposits held by Owner.
   H. **TRUST FUNDS:** Deposit all receipts collected for Owner, less any sums properly deducted or disbursed, in a financial institution whose deposits
      are insured by an agency of the United States government. The funds shall be held in a trust account separate from Broker's personal accounts.
      Broker shall not be liable in event of bankruptcy or failure of a financial institution.
   I. **RESERVES:** Maintain a reserve in Broker's trust account of: $ _____.
   J. **DISBURSEMENTS:** Disburse Owner's funds, held in Broker's trust account, in the following order:
      1. Compensation due Broker under paragraph 6.
      2. All other operating expenses, costs, and disbursements payable from Owner's funds held by Broker.
      3. Reserves and security deposits held by Broker.
      4. Balance to Owner.
   K. **OWNER DISTRIBUTION:** Remit funds monthly, (or ☐ _____), to Owner.
   L. **OWNER STATEMENTS:** Render monthly, (or ☐ _____), statements of receipts, expenses and charges for each
      Property.

Owner and Broker acknowledge receipt of copy of this page, which constitutes Page 1 of _____ Pages.
Owner's Initials (_____) (_____)   Broker's Initials (_____) (_____)

Published and Distributed by:
REAL ESTATE BUSINESS SERVICES, INC.
a subsidiary of the CALIFORNIA ASSOCIATION OF REALTORS®
525 South Virgil Avenue, Los Angeles, California 90020
PRINT DATE

REVISED 4/98

OFFICE USE ONLY
Reviewed by Broker
or Designee _____
Date _____

PROPERTY MANAGEMENT AGREEMENT (PMA-11 PAGE 1 OF 3)

Owner Name: _____ Date _____

4. OWNER RESPONSIBILITIES: Owner shall:
   A. Provide all documentation and records required by Broker to manage and operate the Property.
   B. Indemnify, defend and hold harmless Broker, and all persons in Broker's firm, regardless of responsibility, from all costs, expenses, suits, liabilities, damages, attorney's fees, and claims of every type, including but not limited to those arising out of injury or death of any person, or damage to any real or personal property of any person, including Owner, in any way relating to the management, rental, security deposits, or operation of the Property by Broker, or any person in Broker's firm, or the performance or exercise of any of the duties, powers, or authorities granted to Broker.
   C. Carry and pay for: (i) public and premises liability insurance in an amount of no less than $1,000,000; and (ii) property damage and worker's compensation insurance adequate to protect the interests of Owner and Broker. Broker shall be named as an additional insured party on Owner's policies.
   D. Pay any late charges, penalties, and/or interest imposed by lenders or other parties for failure to make payment to those parties, if the failure is due to the fact that there are insufficient funds in Broker's trust account available for such payment.

5. LEAD-BASED PAINT DISCLOSURE:
   A. ☐ The Property was constructed on or after January 1, 1978.
OR B. ☐ The Property was constructed prior to 1978.
     (1) Owner has no knowledge of lead-based paint or lead-based paint hazards in the housing except: _____
        _____

     (2) Owner has no reports or records pertaining to lead-based paint or lead-based paint hazards in the housing, except the following, which Owner shall provide to Broker: _____
        _____

6. COMPENSATION:
   A. Owner agrees to pay Broker fees in the amounts indicated below for:
     (1) Management: _____
     (2) Renting or Leasing: _____
     (3) Evictions: _____
     (4) Preparing Property for rental, lease, or sale: _____
     (5) Managing Property during extended periods of vacancy: _____
     (6) An overhead and service fee added to the cost of all work performed by, or at the direction of, Broker: _____
     (7) Other: _____

   B. This Property Management Agreement ("Agreement") does not include providing on-site management services, property sales, re-financing, preparing Property for sale or re-financing, modernization, fire or major damage restoration, rehabilitation, obtaining income tax, accounting, or legal advice, representation before public agencies, advising on proposed new construction, debt collection, counseling, attending Owner's Association meetings, or_____
     If Owner requests Broker to perform services not included in this Agreement, a fee shall be agreed upon before these services are performed.
   C. Broker may divide compensation, fees and charges due under this Agreement in any manner acceptable to Broker.
   D. Owner further agrees that:
     (1) Broker may receive fees and charges from tenants for (i) requesting an assignment of lease or sublease of the Property, (ii) processing credit applications, and (iii) any returned checks, and (iv) any other services that are not in conflict with this Agreement.
     (2) Broker may perform any of Broker's duties, and obtain necessary products and services, through affiliated companies or organizations in which Broker may own an interest. Broker may receive fees, commissions, and/or profits from these affiliated companies or organizations. Broker has an ownership interest in the following affiliated companies or organizations: _____
        _____
        Broker shall disclose to Owner any other such relationships as they occur. Broker shall not receive any fees, commissions, or profits from unaffiliated companies in the performance of this Agreement, without prior disclosure to Owner._____
     (3) Other: _____

7. AGENCY RELATIONSHIPS: Broker shall act as the agent for Owner in any resulting transaction. Depending upon the circumstances, it may be necessary or appropriate for Broker to act as agent for both Owner and tenant. Broker shall, as soon as practical, disclose to Owner any election to act as a dual agent representing both Owner and tenant. If tenant is procured directly by Broker or an associate licensee in Broker's firm, Owner hereby consents to Broker acting as dual agent for Owner and such tenant. Owner understands that Broker may have or obtain property management agreements on other property, and that potential tenants may consider, make offers on, or lease through Broker, property the same as or similar to Owner's Property. Owner consents to Broker's representation of other owners' properties before, during, and after the expiration of this Agreement.

8. NOTICES: Any written notice to Owner or Broker required under this Agreement shall be served by sending such notice by first class mail to that party at the address below, or at any different address which the parties may later designate for this purpose. Notice shall be deemed received three calendar days after deposit into the United States mail.

Owner and Broker acknowledge receipt of copy of this page, which constitutes Page 2 of _____ Pages.
     Owner's Initials (_____) (_____)   Broker's Initials (_____) (_____)

OFFICE USE ONLY
Reviewed by Broker
or Designee _____
Date _____

EQUAL HOUSING OPPORTUNITY

REVISED 4/98

PROPERTY MANAGEMENT AGREEMENT (PMA-11 PAGE 2 OF 3)

Owner Name: _____ Date _____

9. DISPUTE RESOLUTION

   A. MEDIATION: Owner and Broker agree to mediate any dispute or claim arising between them out of this Agreement, or any resulting transaction before resorting to arbitration or court action, subject to paragraph 9C below. Mediation fees, if any, shall be divided equally among the parties involved. If any party commences an action based on a dispute or claim to which this paragraph applies, without first attempting to resolve the matter through mediation, then that party shall not be entitled to recover attorney's fees, even if they would otherwise be available to that party in any such action. THIS MEDIATION PROVISION APPLIES WHETHER OR NOT THE ARBITRATION PROVISION IS INITIALED.

   B. ARBITRATION OF DISPUTES: Owner and Broker agree that any dispute or claim arising between them out of the obligation to pay compensation under this Agreement, which is not settled through mediation, shall be decided by neutral, binding arbitration, subject to paragraph 9C below. The arbitrator shall be a retired judge or justice, or an attorney with at least five years of residential income real estate transactional law experience, unless the parties mutually agree to a different arbitrator, who shall render an award in accordance with substantive California Law. In all other respects, the arbitration shall be conducted in accordance with Part III, Title 9 of the California Code of Civil Procedure. Judgment upon the award of the arbitrator(s) may be entered in any court having jurisdiction. The parties shall have the right to discovery in accordance with Code of Civil Procedure §1283.05.

      "NOTICE: BY INITIALING IN THE SPACE BELOW YOU ARE AGREEING TO HAVE ANY DISPUTE ARISING OUT OF THE MATTERS INCLUDED IN THE 'ARBITRATION OF DISPUTES' PROVISION DECIDED BY NEUTRAL ARBITRATION AS PROVIDED BY CALIFORNIA LAW AND YOU ARE GIVING UP ANY RIGHTS YOU MIGHT POSSESS TO HAVE THE DISPUTE LITIGATED IN A COURT OR JURY TRIAL. BY INITIALING IN THE SPACE BELOW YOU ARE GIVING UP YOUR JUDICIAL RIGHTS TO DISCOVERY AND APPEAL, UNLESS THOSE RIGHTS ARE SPECIFICALLY INCLUDED IN THE 'ARBITRATION OF DISPUTES' PROVISION. IF YOU REFUSE TO SUBMIT TO ARBITRATION AFTER AGREEING TO THIS PROVISION, YOU MAY BE COMPELLED TO ARBITRATE UNDER THE AUTHORITY OF THE CALIFORNIA CODE OF CIVIL PROCEDURE. YOUR AGREEMENT TO THIS ARBITRATION PROVISION IS VOLUNTARY." "WE HAVE READ AND UNDERSTAND THE FOREGOING AND AGREE TO SUBMIT DISPUTES ARISING OUT OF THE MATTERS INCLUDED IN THE 'ARBITRATION OF DISPUTES' PROVISION TO NEUTRAL ARBITRATION." Owner's Initials _____/_____ Broker's Initials _____/_____**

   C. EXCLUSIONS FROM MEDIATION AND ARBITRATION: The following matters are excluded from Mediation and Arbitration hereunder: (a) A judicial or non-judicial foreclosure or other action or proceeding to enforce a deed of trust, mortgage, or installment land sale contract as defined in Civil Code §2985; (b) An unlawful detainer action; (c) The filing or enforcement of a mechanic's lien; (d) Any matter which is within the jurisdiction of a probate, small claims, or bankruptcy court; and (e) An action for bodily injury or wrongful death, or for latent or patent defects to which Code of Civil Procedure §337.1 or §337.15 applies. The filing of a court action to enable the recording of a notice of pending action, for order of attachment, receivership, injunction, or other provisional remedies, shall not constitute a violation of the mediation and arbitration provisions.

10. EQUAL HOUSING OPPORTUNITY: The Property is offered in compliance with federal, state, and local anti-discrimination laws.

11. ATTORNEY'S FEES: In any action, proceeding, or arbitration between Owner and Broker regarding the obligation to pay compensation under this Agreement, the prevailing Owner or Broker shall be entitled to reasonable attorney's fees and costs, except as provided in paragraph 9A.

12. ADDITIONAL TERMS: _____

_____

_____

_____

13. ENTIRE CONTRACT: All prior discussions, negotiations, and agreements between the parties concerning the subject matter of this Agreement are superseded by this Agreement, which constitutes the entire contract and a complete and exclusive expression of their agreement, and may not be contradicted by evidence of any prior agreement or contemporaneous oral agreement. This Agreement and any supplement, addendum, or modification, including any photocopy or facsimile, may be executed in counterparts.

Owner warrants that Owner is the owner of the Property or has the authority to execute this contract. Owner acknowledges that Owner has read and understands this Agreement, and has received a copy.

Owner _____ Date _____   Owner _____ Date _____

Owner (Print Name) _____   Owner (Print Name) _____

Address _____   Address _____

City _____ State _____ Zip _____   City _____ State _____ Zip _____

Phone _____ Fax _____ E-mail _____   Phone _____ Fax _____ E-mail _____

social security/tax ID # (for tax reporting purposes)   social security/tax ID # (for tax reporting purposes)

Real Estate Broker _____   Address _____

By _____   _____

Phone _____   Fax _____

REVISED 4/98

Page 3 of _____ Pages.

OFFICE USE ONLY
Reviewed by Broker
or Designee _____
Date _____

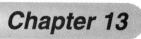
EQUAL HOUSING OPPORTUNITY

PROPERTY MANAGEMENT AGREEMENT (PMA-11 PAGE 3 OF 3)

the satisfaction of a job well done, a percentage of the gross rents should provide you with incentive to maintain high levels of occupancy, because the more space leased, the greater your income (as well as the owners').

F. LEASING AND TENANT SELECTION

As a property manager, you're really a merchandiser of space. The success of a project frequently rests squarely on your shoulders. Therefore, the sensible selection of worthy tenants is extremely important. Unless rental applicants are carefully screened and the proper and latest rental agreements are used, the owner's investment may be seriously impaired. At the least, the cash flow will be less than expected, thus defeating the owner's reason for making the investment.

Landlord and tenant laws change periodically. It's important for you to stay up-to-date with these changes and use the most current forms available.

While idealistic owners or managers may view the investment as brick and mortar on a piece of mother earth they call their own, in reality, the tenants are their principal assets. A proper balance must be maintained between viewing tenants' requests as always unrealistic and believing the tenants are always right. It is not the real property that may be developed to its highest and best use, but the human element. Without qualified tenants, the owner-landlord's economic position will be weakened.

As a property manager in California, you may charge up to $30.00 per applicant as a nonrefundable tenant screening fee.

As a property manager, it's good practice to make a copy of the prospective renter's driver's license, social security card, and other pertinent information, and then keep them in the rental file.

Many forms for qualifying tenants are available, including the CAR Application To Rent/Receipt For Deposit Screening Fee form shown in **Figure 13-5**. A copy is given to the applicant, who is less likely to falsify his or her credit and character references because the application is, after all, a contract that will be kept on file. Included in the application are employment data, bank references, address and telephone number, number of adults and children, and a stipulation against pets.

The application can easily be expanded to incorporate other questions, such as length of time at present address, reason(s) for leaving, auto, driver's license, and social security numbers, outstanding debts, and other credit data. It is of utmost importance

Figure 13-5

CALIFORNIA
ASSOCIATION
OF REALTORS®

APPLICATION TO RENT
RECEIPT FOR DEPOSIT/SCREENING FEE

(C.A.R. Form LRA, Revised 4/01)

I. APPLICATION TO RENT

THIS SECTION TO BE COMPLETED BY APPLICANT. A SEPARATE APPLICATION TO RENT IS REQUIRED FOR EACH OCCUPANT 18 YEARS OF AGE OR OVER.

Application to rent property at _____ ("Premises").

FULL NAME OF APPLICANT _____ Date of birth _____

Soc. Sec. No. _____ Driver's license no. _____ State _____ Expires _____

Phone Number: Home _____ Work _____ Other _____

Email _____

Current address _____ Previous address _____

City/State/Zip _____ City/State/Zip _____

Name of landlord/manager _____ Name of landlord/manager _____

Landlord/manager's phone _____ Landlord/manager's phone _____

How long at current address? _____ How long at this address? _____

Reason for leaving current address _____ Reason for leaving this address _____

Name(s) of all other proposed occupant(s) and relationship to applicant _____

_____

Proposed pet(s) (number and type) _____

Current employer _____ Supervisor _____ Length of employment _____

Employer's address _____ Phone _____

Position or title _____ Gross income $ _____ per _____

Previous employer _____ Supervisor _____ Length of employment _____

Employer's address _____ Phone _____

Position or title _____ Gross income $ _____ per _____

Other income $ _____ per _____ Source _____

Auto make _____ Model _____ Year _____ License no. _____ State _____ Color _____

In case of emergency, person to notify _____ Relationship _____

Address _____ Phone _____

Does applicant plan to use liquid filled furniture? ☐ No ☐ Yes   Type _____

Has applicant been a party to an unlawful detainer action or filed bankruptcy within the last seven years? ☐ No ☐ Yes

If yes, explain _____

Has applicant or any proposed occupant ever been convicted of or pleaded no contest to a felony? ☐ No ☐ Yes

If yes, explain _____

Name of creditor	Account number	Monthly payment	Balance due

Name of bank	Account Number	Address/branch	Type of account

Applicant represents the above information to be true and complete, and hereby authorizes Landlord or manager to **(I)** verify the information provided and **(II)** obtain credit report on applicant.

Date _____ Time _____

Applicant _____

Applicant and Landlord/Manager acknowledge receipt of a copy of this page.

Applicant's Initials (_____)(_____)

Landlord/Manager's Initials (_____)(_____)

EQUAL HOUSING OPPORTUNITY

LRA-11 (PAGE 1 OF 2)   Print Date

| Reviewed by |
| Broker or Designee _____ Date _____ |

APPLICATION TO RENT RECEIPT FOR DEPOSIT/SCREENING FEE (LRA-11 PAGE 1 OF 2)

Property Address: _____ Date: _____

II. RECEIPT FOR DEPOSIT

THIS SECTION TO BE COMPLETED BY AGENT, LANDLORD OR MANAGER.

Applicant has deposited the sum of $_____ as a deposit on the Premises. The deposit is evidenced by:

☐ Cashier's Check, ☐ Personal Check, or ☐ other _____, payable to _____, to be held uncashed until approval of the Application To Rent. If deposit is in cash, deposit shall be ☐ held in Broker's Trust Account or ☐ given to Owner. The executed lease or rental agreement may require additional sums to be paid, as a security deposit, or for other purposes. If the Application to Rent is approved, the deposited sum shall be applied to total sums due upon execution of a lease or rental agreement. If the Application to Rent is not approved within _____ days, the deposit shall be returned to Applicant.

III. SCREENING FEE

THIS SECTION TO BE COMPLETED BY AGENT, LANDLORD OR MANAGER.

In addition to the deposit, Applicant has paid a nonrefundable screening fee of $_____, applied as follows: (The screening fee may not exceed $30.00 (adjusted annually from 1-1-98 commensurate with the increase in the Consumer Price Index.))

$_____ for credit reports;

$_____ for _____ (other out-of-pocket expenses); and

$_____ for processing.

The undersigned has read the foregoing and acknowledges receipt of a copy.

_____ _____
Applicant Signature   Date

The undersigned has received the deposit and screening fee indicated above.

_____ _____
Landlord or Manager or Agent Signature   Date

Published and Distributed by:
REAL ESTATE BUSINESS SERVICES, INC.
a subsidiary of the CALIFORNIA ASSOCIATION OF REALTORS®
525 South Virgil Avenue, Los Angeles, California 90020

Reviewed by

Broker or Designee _____ Date _____

LRA-11 (PAGE 2 OF 2)

APPLICATION TO RENT RECEIPT FOR DEPOSIT/SCREENING FEE (LRA-11 PAGE 2 OF 2)

that you verify this information, particularly the applicant's reasons for vacating previous quarters. For instance, a quick check by telephone may reveal that he or she was asked to leave because of overdue rent, continued violations of house rules, or violations of other lease provisions. Remember that a landlord might confide things on the telephone that he or she would not disclose in a letter for fear of reprisal. A call to the tenant's landlord prior to the last reference quite often offers more information.

Remember: should the property owner decide to sell the property during an existing, valid lease, the lease stays in effect.

1. Lease Contracts

Lease contracts vary with the kind of property being let (leased) and the requirements and preferences of the owners.

The CAR Residential Lease or Month-To-Month Rental Agreement form (**Figure 13-6**) is designed primarily for the residential lease. There are innumerable forms used for different types of property. Select the lease that best fits the circumstances in each case.

Any rental agreement that ends over one year from the date of signing must be in writing. But it is a good idea to have all agreements in writing.

The standard form provides for the usual information, namely, the parties, date, property to be let, amount of rent and terms of payment, and where rent is to be remitted. The preprinted paragraphs contain provisions for assignment and subletting, default proceedings, condition of premises, usage and occupancy, compliance with applicable laws and ordinances, liability for insurance, renewal rights, and waiver stipulations. Additional space is provided for insertion of items not specifically covered. Both lessor and lessee sign the lease, although technically, the tenant is accepting the lease by taking possession of the property.

Not shown here, a very specific room-by-room inspection form (CAR's "Move In/Move Out Inspection"—MIMO) can be used if a more detailed description of the property condition is required by your owner or tenant. It would be filled out while walking your client through the property, before moving in and after moving out.

a. Types of Leasehold Estates

Prior to describing the five groups of leases, it is important to explain the four basic types of leasehold estates.

Figure 13-6

CALIFORNIA ASSOCIATION OF REALTORS®

RESIDENTIAL LEASE OR MONTH-TO-MONTH RENTAL AGREEMENT

(C.A.R. Form LR, Revised 1/03)

_____ ("Landlord") and
_____ ("Tenant") agree as follows:

1. **PROPERTY:**
   A. Landlord rents to Tenant and Tenant rents from Landlord, the real property and improvements described as: _____
   _____ ("Premises").
   B. The following personal property is included: _____
2. **TERM:** The term begins on (date) _____ ("Commencement Date"), (**Check A or B**):
   ☐ **A. Month-to-month:** and continues as a month-to-month tenancy. Tenant may terminate the tenancy by giving written notice at least 30 days prior to the intended termination date. Landlord may terminate the tenancy by giving written notice as provided by law. Such notice may be given on any date.
   ☐ **B. Lease:** and shall terminate on (date) _____ at
   _____ AM/PM. Any holding over after the term of this Agreement expires, with Landlord's consent, shall create a month-to-month tenancy which either party may terminate as specified in paragraph 2A. Rent shall be at a rate equal to the rent for the immediately preceding month, unless otherwise notified by Landlord, payable in advance. All other terms and conditions of this Agreement shall remain in full force and effect.
3. **RENT:** "Rent" shall mean all monetary obligations of tenant to landlord under the terms of this agreement, except security deposit.
   A. Tenant agrees to pay $ _____ per month for the term of the Agreement.
   B. Rent is payable in advance on the **1st (or** ☐ _____ **) day** of each calendar month, and is delinquent on the next day.
   C. If Commencement Date falls on any day other than the first day of the month, Rent shall be prorated based on a 30-day period. If Tenant has paid one full month's Rent in advance of Commencement Date, Rent for the second calendar month shall be prorated based on a 30-day period.
   D. PAYMENT: The Rent shall be paid by ☐ cash, ☐ personal check, ☐ money order, ☐ cashier check, ☐ other _____,
   to (name) _____ (phone) _____,
   at (address) _____,
   (or at any other location specified by Landlord in writing to Tenant) between the hours of _____ and _____,
   on the following days _____ .
4. **SECURITY DEPOSIT:**
   A. Tenant agrees to pay $ _____ as a security deposit. Security deposit will be ☐ transferred to and held by the Owner of the Premises; or ☐ held in Owner's Broker's trust account.
   B. All or any portion of the security deposit may be used, as reasonably necessary, to: (1) cure Tenant's default in payment of Rent, (which includes Late Charges, non-sufficient funds ("NSF") fees, or other sums due); (2) repair damage, excluding ordinary wear and tear, caused by Tenant or by a guest or licensee of Tenant; (3) clean Premises, if necessary, upon termination of tenancy; and (4) replace or return personal property or appurtenances. **SECURITY DEPOSIT SHALL NOT BE USED BY TENANT IN LIEU OF PAYMENT OF LAST MONTH'S RENT.** If all or any portion of the security deposit is used during tenancy, Tenant agrees to reinstate the total security deposit within five days after written notice is delivered to Tenant. Within three weeks after Tenant vacates the Premises, Landlord shall: (1) furnish Tenant an itemized statement indicating the amount of any security deposit received and the basis for its disposition; and (2) return any remaining portion of security deposit to Tenant.
   C. No interest will be paid on security deposit unless required by local ordinance.
   D. If security deposit is held by Owner, Tenant agrees not to hold Broker responsible for its return. If security deposit is held in Owner's Broker's trust account, **and** Broker's authority is terminated before expiration of this Agreement, **and** security deposits are released to someone other than Tenant, **then** Broker shall notify Tenant, in writing, where and to whom security deposit has been released. Once Tenant has been provided such notice, Tenant agrees not to hold Broker responsible for security deposit.
5. **MOVE-IN COSTS RECEIVED/DUE:**

Category	Total Due	Payment Received	Balance Due	Date Due
Rent from _____ to _____ (date)				
*Security Deposit				
Other _____				
Other _____				
Total				

*The maximum amount that Landlord may receive as security deposit, however designated, cannot exceed two month's Rent for an unfurnished Premises, or three month's Rent for a furnished premises.
6. **PARKING: (Check A or B)**
   ☐ **A.** Parking is permitted as follows: _____
   The right to parking ☐ is, ☐ is not, included in the Rent charged pursuant to paragraph 3. If not included in the Rent, the parking rental fee shall be an additional $ _____ per month. Parking space(s) are to be used for parking operable motor vehicles, except for trailers, boats, campers, buses or trucks (other than pick-up trucks). Tenant shall park in assigned space(s) only. Parking space(s) are to be kept clean. Vehicles leaking oil, gas or other motor vehicle fluids shall not be parked on the Premises. Mechanical work or storage of inoperable vehicles is not allowed in parking space(s) or elsewhere on the Premises.
   OR ☐ **B.** Parking is not permitted on the Premises.

LR REVISED 1/03 (PAGE 1 OF 4) Print Date

Landlord's Initials (_____)(_____)
Tenant's Initials (_____)(_____)

Reviewed by _____ Date _____

EQUAL HOUSING OPPORTUNITY

RESIDENTIAL LEASE OR MONTH-TO-MONTH RENTAL AGREEMENT (LR PAGE 1 OF 4)

Premises: _____   Date: _____

7. STORAGE: (Check A or B)
☐ **A.** Storage is permitted as follows:_____
The right to storage space ☐ is, ☐ is not, included in the Rent charged pursuant to paragraph 3. If not included in Rent, storage space shall be an additional $ _____ per month. Tenant shall store only personal property that Tenant owns, and shall not store property that is claimed by another or in which another has any right, title, or interest. Tenant shall not store any improperly packaged food or perishable goods, flammable materials, explosives, or other inherently dangerous material.
OR ☐ **B.** Storage is not permitted on the Premises.

8. LATE CHARGE/NSF CHECKS: Tenant acknowledges that either late payment of Rent or issuance of a NSF check may cause Landlord to incur costs and expenses, the exact amount of which are extremely difficult and impractical to determine. These costs may include, but are not limited to, processing, enforcement and accounting expenses, and late charges imposed on Landlord. If any installment of Rent due from Tenant is not received by Landlord within **5 (or ☐ _____) calendar days** after date due, or if a check is returned NSF, Tenant shall pay to Landlord, respectively, an additional sum of $ _____ as Late Charge and $25.00 as a NSF fee, either or both of which shall be deemed additional Rent. Landlord and Tenant agree that these charges represent a fair and reasonable estimate of the costs Landlord may incur by reason of Tenant's late or NSF payment. Any Late Charge or NSF fee due shall be paid with the current installment of Rent. Landlord's acceptance of any Late Charge or NSF fee shall not constitute a waiver as to any default of Tenant. Landlord's right to collect a Late Charge or NSF fee shall not be deemed an extension of the date Rent is due under paragraph 3, or prevent Landlord from exercising any other rights and remedies under this Agreement, and as provided by law.

9. CONDITION OF PREMISES: Tenant has examined Premises, all furniture, furnishings, appliances, landscaping, if any, and fixtures, including smoke detector(s).
(Check one:)
☐ **A.** Tenant acknowledges that these items are clean and in operative condition, with the following exceptions _____
_____
OR ☐ **B.** Tenant's acknowledgment of the condition of these items is contained in an attached statement of condition (C.A.R. Form MIMO).
OR ☐ **C.** Tenant will provide Landlord a list of items that are damaged or not in operable condition within **3 (or ☐ _____) days** after Commencement Date, not as a contingency of this Agreement but rather as an acknowledgment of the condition of the Premises.
OR ☐ **D.** Other: _____

10. NEIGHBORHOOD CONDITIONS: Tenant is advised to satisfy him or herself as to neighborhood or area conditions, including schools, proximity and adequacy of law enforcement, crime statistics, registered felons or offenders, fire protection, other governmental services, proximity to commercial, industrial or agricultural activities, existing and proposed transportation, construction and development that may affect noise, view, or traffic, airport noise, noise or odor from any source, wild and domestic animals, other nuisances, hazards, or circumstances, facilities and condition of common areas, conditions and influences of significance to certain cultures and/or religions, and personal needs, requirements and preferences of Tenant.

11. UTILITIES: Tenant agrees to pay for all utilities and services, and the following charges: _____
except _____, which shall be paid for by Landlord.
If any utilities are not separately metered, Tenant shall pay Tenant's proportional share, as reasonably determined by Landlord.

12. OCCUPANTS: The Premises are for the sole use as a personal residence by the following named persons **only:** _____
_____

13. PETS: No animal or pet shall be kept on or about the Premises without Landlord's prior written consent, except _____
_____

14. RULES/REGULATIONS: Tenant agrees to comply with all rules and regulations of Landlord, which are at any time posted on the Premises or delivered to Tenant. Tenant shall not, and shall ensure that guests and licensees of Tenant shall not, disturb, annoy, endanger, or interfere with other tenants of the building or neighbors, or use the Premises for any unlawful purposes, including, but not limited to, using, manufacturing, selling, storing, or transporting illicit drugs or other contraband, or violate any law or ordinance, or commit a waste or nuisance on or about the Premises.

15. CONDOMINIUM/PLANNED UNIT DEVELOPMENT ☐ (If checked) The Premises is a unit in a condominium, planned unit, or other development governed by a homeowners' association ("HOA"). The name of the HOA is _____
Tenant agrees to comply with all covenants, conditions and restrictions, bylaws, rules and regulations and decisions of HOA. Landlord shall provide Landlord copies of rules and regulations, if any. Tenant shall reimburse Landlord for any fines or charges imposed by HOA or other authorities, due to any violation by Tenant, or the guests or licensees of Tenant.

16. MAINTENANCE:
A. Tenant shall properly use, operate and safeguard Premises, including if applicable, any landscaping, furniture, furnishings, and appliances, and all mechanical, electrical, gas and plumbing fixtures, and keep them clean and sanitary. Tenant shall immediately notify Landlord, in writing, of any problem, malfunction or damage. Tenant shall pay for all repairs or replacements caused by Tenant, or guests of Tenant, excluding ordinary wear and tear. Tenant shall pay for all damage to Premises as a result of failure to report a problem in a timely manner. Tenant shall pay for repair of drain blockages or stoppages, unless caused by **defective** plumbing parts or tree roots invading sewer lines.
B. ☐ Landlord ☐ Tenant shall water the garden, landscaping, trees and shrubs, except _____
_____
C. ☐ Landlord ☐ Tenant shall maintain the garden, landscaping, trees and shrubs, except _____
_____

17. ALTERATIONS: Tenant shall not make any alterations in or about the Premises without Landlord's prior written consent, including: painting, wallpapering, adding or changing locks, installing antenna or satellite dish(es), placing signs, displays or exhibits, or using screws, fastening devices, large nails or adhesive materials.

18. KEYS/LOCKS:
A. Tenant acknowledges receipt of (or Tenant will receive ☐ prior to the Commencement Date, or ☐ _____):
☐ _____ key(s) to Premises,   ☐ _____ remote control device(s) for garage door/gate opener(s),
☐ _____ key(s) to mailbox,   ☐ _____
☐ _____ key(s) to common area(s),   ☐ _____.
B. Tenant acknowledges that locks to the Premises ☐ have, ☐ have not, been rekeyed.
C. If Tenant rekeys existing locks or opening devices, Tenant shall immediately deliver copies of all keys to Landlord. Tenant shall pay all costs and charges related to loss of any keys or opening devices. Tenant may not remove locks, even if installed by Tenant.

Landlord's Initials (_____)(_____)
Tenant's Initials (_____)(_____)

Reviewed by _____ Date _____

EQUAL HOUSING OPPORTUNITY

RESIDENTIAL LEASE OR MONTH-TO-MONTH RENTAL AGREEMENT (LR PAGE 2 OF 4)

Premises: _____ Date: _____

19. ENTRY: Tenant shall make Premises available to Landlord or representative for the purpose of entering to make necessary or agreed repairs, decorations, alterations, or improvements, or to supply necessary or agreed services, or to show Premises to prospective or actual purchasers, tenants, mortgagees, lenders, appraisers, or contractors. Landlord and Tenant agree that twenty-four (24) hours written notice shall be reasonable and sufficient notice. In an emergency, Landlord or representative may enter Premises at any time without prior notice.

20. SIGNS: Tenant authorizes Landlord to place For Sale/Lease signs on the Premises.

21. ASSIGNMENT/SUBLETTING: Tenant shall not sublet all or any part of Premises, or assign or transfer this Agreement or any interest in it, without prior written consent of Landlord. Unless such consent is obtained, any assignment, transfer or subletting of Premises or this Agreement or tenancy, by voluntary act of Tenant, operation of law, or otherwise, shall be null and void, and at the option of Landlord, terminate this Agreement. Any proposed assignee, transferee or sublessee shall submit to Landlord an application and credit information for Landlord's approval, and if approved, sign a separate written agreement with Landlord and Tenant. Landlord's consent to any one assignment, transfer or sublease, shall not be construed as consent to any subsequent assignment, transfer or sublease and does not release Tenant of Tenant's obligation under this Agreement.

22. ☐ LEAD PAINT (CHECK IF APPLICABLE): Premises was constructed prior to 1978. In accordance with federal law, Landlord gives and Tenant acknowledges receipt of the disclosures on the attached form (C.A.R. Form FLD) and a federally approved lead pamphlet.

23. POSSESSION: If Landlord is unable to deliver possession of Premises on Commencement Date, such Date shall be extended to date on which possession is made available to Tenant. If Landlord is unable to deliver possession within **5 (or ☐ _____) calendar days** after agreed Commencement Date, Tenant may terminate this Agreement by giving written notice to Landlord, and shall be refunded all Rent and security deposit paid.

24. TENANT'S OBLIGATIONS UPON VACATING PREMISES: Upon termination of Agreement, Tenant shall: **(a)** give Landlord all copies of all keys or opening devices to Premises, including any common areas; **(b)** vacate Premises and surrender it to Landlord empty of all persons; **(c)** vacate any/all parking and/or storage space; **(d)** deliver Premises to Landlord in the same condition as referenced in paragraph 9; **(e)** clean the Premises; **(f)** give written notice to Landlord of Tenant's forwarding address; and **(g)** _____
_____.
All improvements installed by Tenant, with or without Landlord's consent, become the property of Landlord upon termination.

25. BREACH OF CONTRACT/EARLY TERMINATION: In addition to any obligations established by paragraph 24, in event of termination by Tenant prior to completion of the original term of Agreement, Tenant shall also be responsible for lost Rent, rental commissions, advertising expenses and painting costs necessary to ready Premises for re-rental.

26. TEMPORARY RELOCATION: Tenant agrees, upon demand of Landlord, to temporarily vacate Premises for a reasonable period, to allow for fumigation, or other methods, to control wood destroying pests or organisms, or other repairs to Premises. Tenant agrees to comply with all instructions and requirements necessary to prepare Premises to accommodate pest control, fumigation or other work, including bagging or storage of food and medicine, and removal of perishables and valuables. Tenant shall only be entitled to a credit of Rent equal to the per diem Rent for the period of time Tenant is required to vacate Premises.

27. DAMAGE TO PREMISES: If, by no fault of Tenant, Premises are totally or partially damaged or destroyed by fire, earthquake, accident or other casualty, which render Premises uninhabitable, either Landlord or Tenant may terminate Agreement by giving the other written notice. Rent shall be abated as of date of damage. The abated amount shall be the current monthly Rent prorated on a 30-day basis. If Agreement is not terminated, Landlord shall promptly repair the damage, and Rent shall be reduced based on the extent to which the damage interferes with Tenant's reasonable use of Premises. If damage occurs as a result of an act of Tenant or Tenant's guests, only Landlord shall have the right of termination, and no reduction in Rent shall be made.

28. INSURANCE: Tenant's or guest's personal property and vehicles are not insured by Landlord or, if applicable, HOA, against loss or damage due to fire, theft, vandalism, rain, water, criminal or negligent acts of others, or any other cause. Tenant is to carry Tenant's own insurance (renter's insurance) to protect Tenant from any such loss.

29. WATERBEDS: Tenant shall not use or have waterbeds on the Premises unless: **(a)** Tenant obtains a valid waterbed insurance policy; **(b)** Tenant increases the security deposit in an amount equal to one-half of one month's Rent; and **(c)** the bed conforms to the floor load capacity of Premises.

30. WAIVER: The waiver of any breach shall not be construed as a continuing waiver of the same or any subsequent breach.

31. NOTICE: Notices may be served at the following address, or at any other location subsequently designated:
Landlord: _____ Tenant: _____
_____ _____

32. TENANT ESTOPPEL CERTIFICATE: Tenant shall execute and return a tenant estoppel certificate delivered to Tenant by Landlord or Landlord's agent within 3 days after its receipt. The tenant estoppel certificate acknowledges that this Agreement is unmodified and in full force, or in full force as modified, and states the modifications. Failure to comply with this requirement shall be deemed Tenant's acknowledgment that the tenant estoppel certificate is true and correct, and may be relied upon by a lender or purchaser.

33. JOINT AND INDIVIDUAL OBLIGATIONS: If there is more than one Tenant, each one shall be individually and completely responsible for the performance of all obligations of Tenant under this Agreement, jointly with every other Tenant, and individually, whether or not in possession.

34. ☐ MILITARY ORDNANCE DISCLOSURE: (If applicable and known to Landlord) Premises is located within one mile of an area once used for military training, and may contain potentially explosive munitions.

35. TENANT REPRESENTATIONS; CREDIT: Tenant warrants that all statements in Tenant's rental application are accurate. Tenant authorizes Landlord and Broker(s) to obtain Tenant's credit report at time of application and periodically during tenancy in connection with approval, modification, or enforcement of this Agreement. Landlord may cancel this Agreement: **(a)** before occupancy begins; **(b)** upon disapproval of the credit report(s); or **(c)** at any time, upon discovering that information in Tenant's application is false. A negative credit report reflecting on Tenant's record may be submitted to a credit reporting agency if Tenant fails to fulfill the terms of payment and other obligations under this Agreement.

36. PERIODIC PEST CONTROL: If Landlord has entered into a contract for periodic pest control treatment of the Premises, Landlord shall give tenant a copy of the notice originally given to Landlord by the pest control company.

Landlord's Initials (_____)(_____)
Tenant's Initials (_____)(_____)

Reviewed by _____ Date _____

EQUAL HOUSING OPPORTUNITY

RESIDENTIAL LEASE OR MONTH-TO-MONTH RENTAL AGREEMENT (LR PAGE 3 OF 4)

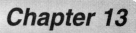

Premises: _____ Date: _____

37. DATA BASE DISCLOSURE: NOTICE: The California Department of Justice, sheriff's departments, police departments serving jurisdictions of 200,000 or more, and many other local law enforcement authorities maintain for public access a data base of the locations of persons required to register pursuant to paragraph (1) of subdivision (a) of Section 290.4 of the Penal Code. The data base is updated on a quarterly basis and a source of information about the presence of these individuals in any neighborhood. The Department of Justice also maintains a Sex Offender Identification Line through which inquiries about individuals may be made. This is a "900" telephone service. Callers must have specific information about individuals they are checking. Information regarding neighborhoods is not available through the "900" telephone service.

38. OTHER TERMS AND CONDITIONS/SUPPLEMENTS: _____
_____
The following ATTACHED supplements are incorporated in this Agreement: _____

39. ATTORNEY FEES: In any action or proceeding arising out of this Agreement, the prevailing party between Landlord and Tenant shall be entitled to reasonable attorney fees and costs.

40. ENTIRE CONTRACT: Time is of the essence. All prior agreements between Landlord and Tenant are incorporated in this Agreement, which constitutes the entire contract. It is intended as a final expression of the parties' agreement, and may not be contradicted by evidence of any prior agreement or contemporaneous oral agreement. The parties further intend that this Agreement constitutes the complete and exclusive statement of its terms, and that no extrinsic evidence whatsoever may be introduced in any judicial or other proceeding, if any, involving this Agreement. Any provision of this Agreement that is held to be invalid shall not affect the validity or enforceability of any other provision in this Agreement.

41. AGENCY:
  A. Confirmation: The following agency relationship(s) are hereby confirmed for this transaction:
  Listing Agent: (Print firm name) _____ is the agent of
  (check one): ☐ the Landlord exclusively; or ☐ both the Landlord and Tenant.
  Leasing Agent: (Print firm name) _____ (if not same as Listing Agent) is the agent of
  (check one): ☐ the Tenant exclusively; or ☐ the Landlord exclusively; or ☐ both the Tenant and Landlord.
  B. Disclosure: ☐ (If checked): The term of this lease exceeds one year. A disclosure regarding real estate agency relationships (such as C.A.R. Form AD), has been provided to Landlord and Tenant, who each acknowledge its receipt.

42. ☐ INTERPRETER/TRANSLATOR: The terms of this Agreement have been interpreted/translated for Tenant into the following language: _____. Interpretation/translation service has been provided by (print name) _____, who has the following Driver's License or other identification number: _____. Tenant has been advised to rely on, and has in fact solely relied on the interpretation/translation services of the above-named individual, and not on the Landlord or other person involved in negotiating the Agreement. If the Agreement has been negotiated primarily in Spanish, Tenant has been provided a Spanish language translation of this Agreement pursuant to the California Civil Code. (C.A.R. Form LR-S fulfills this requirement.)

Signature of interpreter/translator _____ Date _____

Landlord and Tenant acknowledge and agree that Brokers: **(a)** do not guarantee the condition of the Premises; **(b)** cannot verify representations made by others; **(c)** cannot provide legal or tax advice; **(d)** will not provide other advice or information that exceeds the knowledge, education or experience required to obtain a real estate license. Furthermore, if Brokers are not also acting as Landlord in this Agreement, Brokers: **(e)** do not decide what rental rate a Tenant should pay or Landlord should accept; and **(f)** do not decide upon the length or other terms of tenancy. Landlord and Tenant agree that they will seek legal, tax, insurance and other desired assistance from appropriate professionals.

Tenant _____ Date _____
Tenant _____ Date _____
Landlord _____ Date _____
(Owner or Agent with authority to enter into this lease)
Landlord _____ Date _____
(Owner or Agent with authority to enter into this lease)
Landlord Address _____ City _____ State ___ Zip ___
Telephone _____ Fax _____

Agency relationships are confirmed as above. Real estate brokers who are not also Landlord in this Agreement are not a party to the Agreement between Landlord and Tenant.

Real Estate Broker (Leasing Firm) _____
By (Agent) _____ Date _____
Address _____ City _____ State ___ Zip ___
Telephone _____ Fax _____
Real Estate Broker (Listing Firm) _____
By (Agent) _____ Date _____
Address _____ City _____ State ___ Zip ___
Telephone _____ Fax _____

SURE TRAC — The System for Success™

Published by the California Association of REALTORS®

Reviewed by _____ Date _____

LR REVISED 1/03 (PAGE 4 OF 4)

RESIDENTIAL LEASE OR MONTH-TO-MONTH RENTAL AGREEMENT (LR PAGE 4 OF 4)

1. **Estate for Years.** This estate is a right of occupancy for a definite fixed period of time. This time frame could be for any specified length measured in days, weeks, or months.

2. **Estate from Period-to-Period.** The most common periodic tenancy is a month-to-month lease.

3. **Estate at Sufferance.** This estate is created when a tenant obtains possession legally, but then remains on the property, without the owner's consent, after the expiration of the terms. The landlord has the choice of evicting the tenant through court action, or accepting the tenant on the same terms and conditions of the previous occupancy.

In non-emergency situations, the landlord must give the tenant a 24-hour advance notice, in writing, of his or her intent to enter the property. Entry must be during normal business hours, unless the tenant otherwise consents.

A court action called an "unlawful detainer" is used to evict a tenant who breaks the lease or stays past the expiration of a lease agreement.

4. **Estate at Will.** With this estate, possession is given with permission, but no agreement is made as to rent. Termination may be made by either party, at any time, with proper notice.

2. Establishing Rent Schedules

"Contract rent" is the current amount being paid, and "economic rent" is the amount the unit could make if available on the market today. As a good property manager, you should constantly work to bring contract rent up to economic rent.

Basic to the determination of a rental program is the market itself. As a property manager, you must assess the competition, which means determining how much space is available and the rents being charged—in short, the supply and demand factors. Other important considerations include terms of the lease and concessions allowed, the tenant's age, condition of the premises, amenities offered, distance to transportation and other conveniences, character of the neighborhood, including degree of economic and social obsolescence, and the form of lease.

Leases can be divided into five groups. Their names are derived from the way in which the rents are established. They include:

a. Flat Rental

A *FLAT RENTAL LEASE provides for a **fixed rate** applied uniformly to the spaces being let.* It is determined by a square foot rental, by cubic footage, or so much per room, and so on.

b. Net Leases

Under this type of lease the tenant agrees to pay a fixed rent plus the expenses of carrying the property, such as taxes, insurance, maintenance, and repairs. In the real estate practitioner's jargon, the net lease is distinguished from two others by the responsibilities the lessee assumes in carrying the property. In the *NET LEASE, the lessee pays for all maintenance and taxes only.* In the *NET NET LEASE, or double net, the lessee agrees to pay some, but not all, of the maintenance, taxes, and insurance.* Finally, in a *NET NET NET*, or *TRIPLE NET LEASE, the lessee agrees to pay for all taxes, insurance, maintenance, and repairs.*

Net leases are used in shopping centers as well as office and commercial buildings.

c. Gross Rental

Under the terms of a *GROSS LEASE, the lessee (tenant) pays a flat amount each month.* Out of this amount, the lessor (landlord) pays for all the expenses of carrying the property. Residential leases are usually rented this way. The prudent lessor will want to limit his or her liability to those repairs that, for example, might be classified as major or extraordinary.

d. Percentage Lease (Commercial)

A *PERCENTAGE LEASE commonly provides for a minimum fixed rental plus a percentage of the lessee's gross business income, above this minimum amount.* The percentage lease might also include prohibitions to protect the landlord against the lessee's conducting unethical off-site *WAREHOUSE SALES, whereby tenants declare other sites for their operation in order to minimize their percentage lease rents.*

Additionally, a percentage lease may have a *RECAPTURE CLAUSE which provides that, should the tenant not obtain a pre-set minimum of sales, then the lessor has the right to terminate the lease.*

Percentage leases are most often used in malls and shopping centers, where each business complements and aids other businesses in that center.

e. Graduated Lease

With a *GRADUATED LEASE, rents are increased at specified intervals, either for a fixed amount or at a fixed rate, which may be based on a percentage of the increased value of the leasehold.* Variations of this form include the *ESCALATOR LEASE, whereby the tenant agrees to pay for increases in taxes, insurance, and other operating expenses,* and the *COST OF LIVING LEASE, whereby the rents are adjusted up or down according to fluctuations in the purchasing power of the dollar, as determined by price indices, such as the one published monthly by the United States Bureau of Labor Statistics or the 11th District Cost of Funds.*

G. ACCURATE RECORD KEEPING (A Must for Property Managers)

Th following are some of the valid reasons for establishing and maintaining accurate records for the licensee who is engaged in the practice of property management.

1. The statutory requirements state that a **separate record must be kept for each managed property**.

2. The **fiduciary capacity** that requires you, as the agent, to operate with **full and complete disclosure** to your principal (owner).

The same agency disclosure forms used in a real estate sale are used in a lease agreement, as well as lead-based paint, water heater, and smoke detector disclosures.

3. Contractual obligations, such as the management agreement, will call for an accounting of all funds and financial data.

4. The client will need substantiating records in order to file **income tax** and other returns.

5. A fifth reason for keeping records is for control. Accurate records will aid you in **evaluating income and expenses**, analyzing costs, and preparing and forecasting budgets for each property.

6. Records should be kept for the **broker's files**, so that you, as a broker, or an agent of your employing broker, will have ready access to them whenever inquiries are made, problems arise, and so on.

7. The final reason for record keeping is to satisfy requirements of third parties (like tax assessors) who have an interest in the property. For example, if the rent schedule is the percentage lease, and you don't know how much the gross income was for a given period, a **correct rental charge** may be overlooked. Comparative records for similar periods help to disclose possible underreporting and shortages.

> **Specialized computer programs for property management are as varied as real property managers and the scope of their operations. Prices start at a few hundred dollars and go up from there. Many companies use a Microsoft Excel® program customized to their clients' needs, while others use professional software from Yardy Systems, Real Data, and other real estate software companies.**

1. Cash Journal

Figure 13-7 is a cash journal that can be used to report cash received from tenants. It includes the date when the rent was received and deposited in the bank, tenant's name, apartment number, period covered, amount received, overdue amounts, vacant rent schedule, and recapitulation. *RECAPITULATION is the cash report of the cash on hand (from the beginning of the period) and the cash received, from which all expenditures and the manager's compensation are subtracted.* The cash balance in the bank account is deposited into the broker's trust account or remitted directly to the owner, less the amount needed for petty cash expenditures, maintenance, and improvements for the ensuing period.

2. Activity Report

An activity report form for summarizing all revenues and expenses is shown in **Figure 13-8**. It is simple to read and understand, and it should be sent to the owner on a regular basis, at least monthly. It shows the bank balance for the owner, to which are added the rents that were detailed for each apartment in the cash journal.

Also added to the collections will be other items, such as **cleaning** and **security deposits**, washer and dryer receipts, capital contributions, and others. From this amount all the expenses and refunds are deducted, and the net cash on hand and in the bank at the end of the period is then computed by simple subtraction.

Note that the form also reflects new rentals secured during the period, those that were vacated, and the total number of apartments rented at the end of the month. This gives the owner and his agent a quick check of the vacancy rate for each month. If the occupancy ratio is down from one period to the next, corrective action may be in order. Also note that property expenses are not given in this form. As the manager, you should at least break down expenses into such categories as payroll, utilities, accounting, advertising, maintenance, repairs, supplies, capital expenditures, and capital replacements. Each of these broad groupings could also be further subdivided, depending upon the size of the operation.

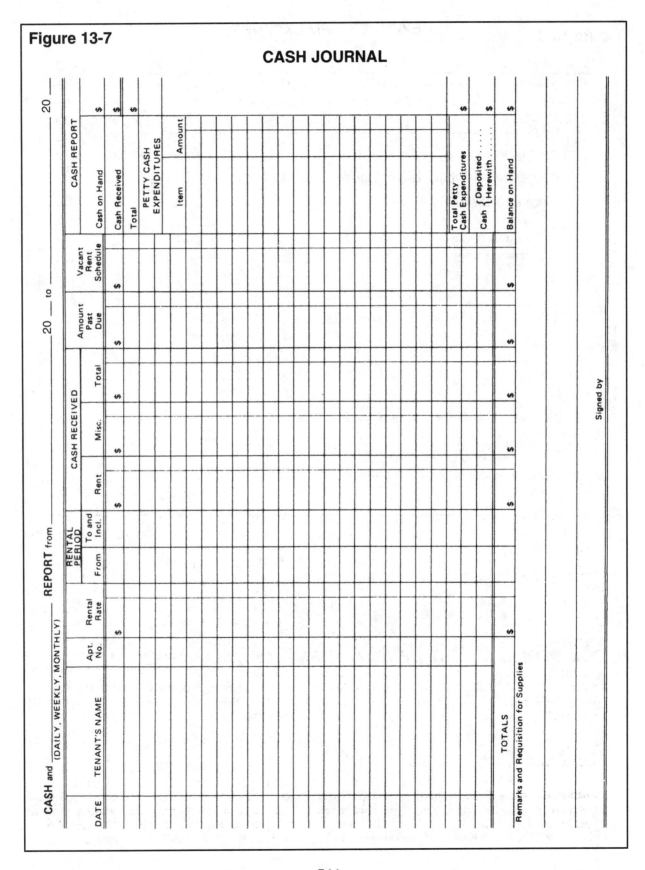

Figure 13-7

CASH JOURNAL

Figure 13-8   **REVENUES AND EXPENSES**

PROPERTY _____

ACTIVITY REPORT FOR _____ 20_____

    BANK BALANCE AT BEGINNING OF MONTH $ _____

    INCOME COLLECTED:

        Rent $ _____

        Cleaning Deposits $ _____

        Security Deposits $ _____

        Washer & Dryer Receipts $ _____

        Capital Contributions $ _____

        Other Income $ _____

    TOTAL INCOME PLUS BEGINNING BANK BALANCE $ _____

    LESS: Expenses $ _____

        Refunds $ _____

        Other $ _____ $ _____

    NET CASH ON HAND AND IN BANK AT END OF MONTH $ _____

New Rentals during Current Month _____

Apartments Vacated During Current Month _____

Total Number of Apartments Rented at End of Month _____ (____ %)

If you are hired to manage a single-family home or condo, the California Association of Realtors® form "Trust Bank Account Record for Each Property Managed (TAP)" accurately reflects income and expenses for each individual unit (see Figure 13-9).

H. COMMON INTEREST DEVELOPMENT (CID) MANAGEMENT

Common interest developments are not only a type of real estate and form of ownership, but often a lifestyle as well. In addition to condominiums and "shared wall" apartment-type complexes, a growing number of CIDs include golf course communities, retirement villages, resort properties, timeshares, and lakeside subdivisions.

Common interest developments in California (as well as many other states) are increasing dramatically every year. As such, the need for professionals specializing in Homeowner's Association Management is also on the rise. Recognizing this

Figure 13-9

CALIFORNIA
ASSOCIATION
OF REALTORS®

TRUST BANK ACCOUNT RECORD
FOR EACH PROPERTY MANAGED

Owner: _____
Address: _____
Property: _____
Units: _____
Remarks: _____

DATE	DEPOSIT (Received From)	OR	WITHDRAWAL (Paid To)	AMOUNT	BALANCE
	Name: _____ □ check □ cash □ ___ For: □ rent □ deposit □ ___		Name: _____ Check #_____ For: _____	$	$
	Name: _____ □ check □ cash □ ___ For: □ rent □ deposit □ ___		Name: _____ Check #_____ For: _____	$	$
	Name: _____ □ check □ cash □ ___ For: □ rent □ deposit □ ___		Name: _____ Check #_____ For: _____	$	$
	Name: _____ □ check □ cash □ ___ For: □ rent □ deposit □ ___		Name: _____ Check #_____ For: _____	$	$
	Name: _____ □ check □ cash □ ___ For: □ rent □ deposit □ ___		Name: _____ Check #_____ For: _____	$	$
	Name: _____ □ check □ cash □ ___ For: □ rent □ deposit □ ___		Name: _____ Check #_____ For: _____	$	$
	Name: _____ □ check □ cash □ ___ For: □ rent □ deposit □ ___		Name: _____ Check #_____ For: _____	$	$
	Name: _____ □ check □ cash □ ___ For: □ rent □ deposit □ ___		Name: _____ Check #_____ For: _____	$	$
	Name: _____ □ check □ cash □ ___ For: □ rent □ deposit □ ___		Name: _____ Check #_____ For: _____	$	$
	Name: _____ □ check □ cash □ ___ For: □ rent □ deposit □ ___		Name: _____ Check #_____ For: _____	$	$

explosive growth, the DRE now includes CID management in their required broker-related course options.

A *COMMON INTEREST DEVELOPMENT (CID) is a form of home ownership whereby individual owners are allowed the use of common property and facilities, the governing of which is controlled by a homeowner's association (HOA).* Membership in the association is automatic with the purchase of property in the CID. Members of the HOA usually elect a board of directors to operate the association and "preserve, enhance, and protect" the value of the common interest development.

1. Duties of an HOA Manager

It is increasingly common for boards of directors to contract professional management companies to run the day-to-day affairs of the association. A management company acts as an agent for the association, taking direction from the board of directors. Your duties as an HOA manager will normally include the following:

1. Collecting assessments.
2. Paying the association bills.
3. Enforcing rules and addressing infractions.
4. Hiring vendors to perform various services.

Additional responsibilities may include assisting with the budget process, preparing meeting agendas and minutes, and acting as a neutral third party in disputes.

Ultimately, the board of directors (not the management company) is responsible for the management of an HOA. These obligations are set forth in the CC&Rs, Bylaws, the Corporations Code and the Davis-Stirling Common Interest Development Act (California Civil Code Sections 1350-1376).

CC&Rs (COVENANTS, CONDITIONS, and RESTRICTIONS) are the limitations on land use made compulsory by a deed, usually at the time the land was subdivided. It regulates building restrictions, density, and use for the benefit of other property owners.

2. Determining an HOA Budget

The budget of an HOA is determined by the amount of money required to operate and maintain the common area obligations of the CID. The association has the right to bill members for their fair share of the budgeted amount, in the form of an assessment.

"Regular assessments" cover the day-to-day operation and long-term maintenance costs of the association. One time "special assessments" are levied to cover major repairs, replacement, or new construction of the common area.

3. Managing Agent

A *MANAGING AGENT* is a person or entity who, for compensation or in expectation of compensation, exercises control over the assets of a common interest development.

If you're interested in a career in HOA management, checkout *Common Interest Development Management* by Walt Huber and Kim Tyler, JD. This text covers the material required for the new broker course approved by the DRE.

I. PREPAID RENTAL LISTING SERVICE (PRLS)

You must pay for a Prepaid Rental Listing Service License (no exam required) for each location every two years, or have a real estate broker's license, in order to collect fees.

At one time, "advance fee rental agents" collected fees from prospective tenants before finding rental units for them, or handing them a list of homes for rent, most of which were usually already rented. Some of these "locators" were not licensed, in violation of state law. Many of them did not even have a listing for any rental properties or any targeted properties to show to prospective renters, and the renters paid for a service they did not actually receive. As a result of these abuses, advanced fee rental agents must register with the Department of Real Estate under the **Prepaid Rental Listing Service (PRLS)** licensing statutes, covered in the Business and Professions Code.

PRLS rules require, among other things, that licensees collecting fees from prospective tenants must have written or oral permission from owners to show the owners' properties, or to include such properties in a rental list.

There is no special examination or license, beyond a broker's license, required of advance fee agents, but they are required to register with the DRE and pay the required application and bonding fees for each location.

Many Prepaid Rental Listing Service companies get their information from active real estate brokers. Unfortunately, by the time their lists are sold to prospective tenants, the properties often are already rented.

J. IMPROVING VALUE THROUGH BALANCED MANAGEMENT

In this section the role of the manager in apartment house investments is discussed, with special emphasis on how you, as a manager, maximize the **return to the owner** while **remaining sensitive to tenants** and to the community at large.

All apartment properties require management, whether rendered by separate professional services or by the owner-investors themselves.

Any manager of this type of property is going to be faced with the performance of many different functions in many different areas. The relative importance of these functions depends upon the situation and nature of the given enterprise. Obviously, if the vacancy rate becomes excessive in the area, one of your main functions, as manager, will be to market the available space, while doing what's reasonable, under the circumstances, to minimize the possibility of present tenants leaving.

As the manager of large multiple-unit properties, you will have a **supervisory function** with regard to numbers of employees, and you must be familiar with at least the basics of personnel management. You must also be knowledgeable about the **physical side** of property management.

As a property manager, your responsibilities will include maintenance of the building, caring for mechanical equipment, and planning and implementing a "modernization" program. Especially in larger buildings, this can be a continuing process, requiring interaction with a variety of professionals.

This involves dealing not only with plumbers, carpenters, electricians, and other trades, but also with professionals such as engineers, architects, and hazardous material professionals.

From time to time, as a property manager, you must deal with **governmental bodies**. In most communities, government, at one level or another, involves itself directly with zoning regulations, health and safety codes, taxation of property, and the application of building codes. Certainly, changes in taxation and regulation of rental properties, under the police power of the taxing authority, are of definite and continuing interest for the property manager. This requires a current knowledge of these subjects. (Generally speaking, this knowledge is not adequate unless used in conjunction with competent legal counsel, especially when dealing with governmental agencies.)

Finally, the human relations aspects of your job as a manager are critical. In all activities relating to tenants, to professional, semiprofessional, and trades people, to governmental bodies, and to others within the real estate community, you will have to demonstrate a satisfactory level of **"reasonableness."**

Potential apartment owners must satisfy themselves that adequate plans are made and facilities available for various and competent management. This is usually one of the most neglected considerations at the time of purchase.

1. To Spend or Not to Spend (Maintenance)

"Deferred maintenance" is delaying the fixing of existing repairs considered necessary for the long-term rehabilitation of the property.

As a manager, you are usually trying to achieve **two objectives** for your investors that are, to a great degree, incompatible: continually striving to correct and relieve the deterioration of the buildings due to normal wear and tear, while at the same time trying to refrain from spending money. To maintain the condition of an apartment house at an acceptable level obviously costs money. If these periodic outlays are not made, the annual net income from the rental operation may increase over the short run. However, such a process will result in deferred maintenance, eventually causing extraordinary expenditures to halt and correct structural deterioration.

Spending a little to maintain a property saves the owner a lot in the long run.

Ideally, a structure should not be under maintained or over maintained, because either course will ultimately minimize the profitability of the property. You must balance this factor in the income and expense analysis if you're to properly reflect long-range performance satisfaction from the investment.

As the manger of a large property, you should consider hiring a professional real estate appraiser to advise you as to what improvements will be beneficial to increase the owner's net income in the long run. Part of your job description includes maximizing the resale value of a property.

Your careful analysis of the market, and flexibility in responding to changes in market conditions, should satisfy your owner that his or her property is a useful and profitable investment.

As a property manager, you must be acutely aware of **changing conditions** in the real estate market, generally, and the apartment house rental market, specifically. This is particularly true with regard to the care and handling of tenants, and the balancing of advertising to minimize vacancies. This is a matter relating to know-how, which is difficult to include in the income and expense statement, but you and the owner must make allowances for it.

You should be flexible enough to experiment with the rental schedule in order to test the analysis of present rental conditions every time you rent a space. This means that the property owner must allow you a reasonable degree of latitude in rental policies. One of the most common errors of ownership is to restrict the managers' area of decision making so that you're really not able to manage. This reduces you to the position of caretaker, and jeopardizes the total project.

Inflexible rental schedules are a prime cause of rent loss. It goes without saying that, once lost, rental income is gone forever, jeopardizing your investor's satisfaction.

K. RENT CONTROL

Rent control discourages the building of more apartments, causing existing rents to go even higher, further damaging a city's housing affordability.

If you decide to become a residential property manager, you should be knowledgeable of any local rent control ordinances to ensure that rents and increases charged are not in violation of the law. Currently, in a rent controlled area like Los Angeles, when a unit **becomes vacant** you can increase the rent without limitation, but laws change. Different communities have different laws concerning rent control.

By California law, no governmental agency can adopt any rent control restrictions on nonresidential property.

L. LOW-INCOME HOUSING

If you're hired to manage lower income housing, you should become familiar with *SECTION 8, which is a county rent subsidy for qualified tenants who meet the required criteria.* The property must be approved by county inspectors for eligibility, and is checked for its condition at least once a year. The tenants usually pay a very low portion of the rent based on their income and familial obligations.

M. PROFESSIONAL ASSOCIATIONS FOR MANAGERS

Property managers have professional associations of their own. Most notable among these is the **Institute of Real Estate Management (IREM)**, a division of the National Association of Realtors® (NAR). It was started by a group of Realtors® who felt the need for an organized body of practitioners to promote the professional growth of what was a comparatively new field during the Great Depression, but has become an ever more profitable field.

Through professional associations, knowledge and experience can be shared, ethical standards established and maintained, and other benefits derived that could not be achieved by individuals alone.

A Code of Professional Ethics for the Institute of Real Estate Management was adopted by the institute and must be adhered to by any Realtor® applying for membership. *Realtors® who qualify and are accepted into the institute are entitled to use the designation* **CPM (CERTIFIED PROPERTY MANAGER)** *after their names.* With the public's increasing awareness of the title, considerable prestige should be gained by the Realtor® CPM. Similarly, *the firm that specializes in this field and has qualified for membership is entitled to use the designation* **AMO, or ACCREDITED MANAGEMENT ORGANIZATION**. One key executive, at least, must be a CPM, but the firm cannot use the CPM label, which is restricted to individuals alone.

III. CHAPTER SUMMARY

Overlapping state and federal laws dealing with discrimination against prospective tenants govern the rental of income properties. Fair Housing Laws prohibit landlords from discriminating by reason of race, religion, national origin, ancestry, color, sex, physical handicap, or marital status.

The **Unruh Civil Rights Act** similarly bans discrimination, but is geared more toward "people in the business" of selling and renting properties.

The **California Fair Employment and Housing Act (FEHA)** provides an administrative remedy for the tenant who has been discriminated against; it applies to all housing accommodations. An injunction will prevent the rental or sale of a property when there is an issue of discrimination being investigated.

The law does not prohibit the use of **reasonable standards** in the selection of tenants or buyers. Economic factors, family size, age, and many other criteria may, in some cases, be used without breaking the law.

The state **Housing Financial Discrimination Act of 1977** prohibits financial institutions from engaging in discriminatory loan practices called "**redlining**," which is the practice by financial institutions of denying loans or varying finance terms based on the location of a given property, regardless of the credit worthiness of the borrower.

The federal **Civil Rights Act of 1968** similarly prohibits discrimination. **Blockbusting** is the practice of unscrupulous speculators or agents of inducing panic selling of homes below market value, especially by exploiting the prejudices of property owners in neighborhoods where the racial make-up is, or appears to be, changing.

Landlord/Tenant Law requires landlords to give a tenant a **60-day notice** (instead of a 30-day notice) if the tenant has been in possession of the unit for more than one year. The tenant still needs to give a 30-day notice to landlord.

There are several exceptions to the 60-day notice, for example, it does not apply to a fixed-term lease, and if the tenant has lived in the property for less than one year.

A **3-Day Notice** demands that the tenant pays the rent or vacates the property. It's unlawful to change locks, to shut of the utilities, etc. **Unlawful Detainer** is the name of the legal action to physically remove a tenant.

Additionally, the landlord must give the tenant a **24-hour notice to enter in writing**, and the entry must be performed during business hours, unless agreed to by the tenant.

Property Management. Owners often don't have the time, and need the expertise of a real estate practitioner, to properly manage their investment property by minimizing their expenses, maximizing their profits, and increasing resale value. This should be a benefit, rather than a cost, for the investor.

A multitude of properties require property management, including large apartment complexes, single-family residences, condos, homeowner associations, and shopping centers.

Types of Property Managers. Depending on the type of property to be managed, there are various classifications of property managers. **Outside managers** or **general managers** may manage as part of their general brokerage operations or as an exclusive management firm. They only require a real estate broker license, and they are usually paid a certain percentage of the monthly income they collect. **Resident managers** live on the premises. They do not need a license, and usually get a rent-free unit, with additional compensation for additional work. They are used when there are **16 or more units** and the owner does not reside on the property. **Institutional Managers** are employed by an institution, such as the real estate management department of a bank, and paid a salary.

Selection of Property Managers. Management Contracts should always be used in any agreement for the employment of a manager. There are varied contracts that can be used. One, 3-page **CAR Property Management Contract** is included in this chapter. This spells out the duties of the manager and the responsibilities of the owner. The compensation paid the manager is also addressed.

Tenant screening is very important. The manager should get proper identification, current credit report, references, and verify all information, including eviction history.

A **lease contract** should be signed by all parties and include the date, the property address, the amount of rent and the terms of payments, and where they should be made. It should have a clause regarding subletting, default proceedings, condition of premises, usage, and occupancy.

Flat Rental is a flat fee charged for a unit, depending on its size. In a **net lease**, the tenant agrees to pay a fixed rent plus some of the expenses incurred by the property, such as taxes, insurance, maintenance, and repairs. There are different types of net leases which vary with the responsibility and expenses the tenant is willing to take on. **With** a **net lease,** the tenant agrees to pay only for all maintenance and taxes. A **net net lease** requires a lessee to pay some, but not all, of the maintenance, taxes and insurance. Finally, the **net net net** or **triple-net lease** means the lessee has agreed to pay all of the above expenses.

A **percentage lease** is often used in shopping centers and includes a base rent plus a percentage of the tenant's gross receipts. With a **graduated lease**, rents are increased at specified intervals based on a various cost of funds indices.

Record keeping is an important duty of the property manager. Each property managed must have a separate record.

Condominium Management is another opportunity for property management firms. The Home Owner Associations (HOAs) often turn this task (consisting of a tremendous amount of paperwork) over to an outside property manager.

Prepaid Rental Listing Services (PRLS) charge prospective tenants for lists of rental properties. Due to abuses and complaints regarding these services, they now register with the Department of Real Estate under the **Prepaid Rental Listing Service licensing statutes**, covered under the Business and Professions code.

Proper maintenance of a property is a balancing act on the part of a manager. Under maintaining or over maintaining ultimately minimizes profitability for an owner/investor.

Rent Control is the government regulation of the amount of rent a landlord may charge tenants. In its usual form a city restricts, by percentage, annual increases in rental payments. Commercial, industrial, and luxury rentals are generally exempt from this control.

Low-Income Housing. Property managers of lower income housing should become familiar with **Section 8** (HUD), which is a county rent subsidy for qualified tenants who meet the required criteria.

IV. KEY TERMS

California Apartment Association (CAA)
California Fair Employment and Housing Act (FEHA)
California Fair Housing Laws
Certified Residential Manager (CRM)
Civil Rights Act
Cost of Living Lease
Escalator Lease
Federal Fair Housing Laws
Financial Statements
Flat Rental Lease
Graduated Lease
Gross Lease
Highest and Best Use
Housing Financial Discrimination Act
Institute of Real Estate Management (IREM)
Institutional Manager
Landlord/Tenant Laws (30- and 60-Day Notices)
Lease
Management Contract
Net Lease
Net Net Lease
Net Net Net, or Triple Net Lease
Outside Manager
Percentage Lease
Prepaid Rental Listing Service (PRLS)
Real Estate Investment Trust (REIT)
Recapture Clause
Redlining
Rent Control
Resident Manager
Section 8
Three-Day Notice to Quit
Trust Bank Account Record (TAP)
Unlawful Detainer
Unruh Civil Rights Act
Warehouse Sales

V. CHAPTER 13 QUIZ

1. One of the prime objectives of professional property management is:
    a. to minimize expenses and to maximize profits.
    b. to make sure the tenants are not taking advantage of the owner.
    c. to maximize the return to the professional property management firm.
    d. to help society through private rental subsidies.

2. A person or firm hired to manage property by banks, insurance companies, government agencies, trusts, etc., is referred to as a(n):
    a. resident manager.
    b. freelance manager.
    c. institutional manager.
    d. none of the above.

3. What form of lease is increased at specified intervals?
    a. Net lease
    b. Gross lease
    c. Percentage lease
    d. Graduated lease

4. Which of the following is a reason for managers to keep accurate records?
    a. Compliance with statutory requirements
    b. Meeting the agent's fiduciary obligation to client
    c. Substantiating records for filing income tax returns
    d. All of the above

5. With respect to balanced management, which of the following statements is correct?
    a. An effective manager tries to correct and relieve deterioration due to wear and tear, while trying to increase net income.
    b. If periodic outlays for materials and labor are not made, the annual income for the rental operation will be increased over the long run.
    c. It makes little difference whether a property is under maintained or over maintained, since either condition will maximize the profitability of the property.
    d. All of the above.

6. An on-site manager of an 18-unit apartment building:
    a. needs to have a real estate license.
    b. is directly employed by the property owner.
    c. usually manages several properties at once.
    d. all of the above.

7. Which of the following is an example blockbusting?
    a. Installing new streets within a city block.
    b. Persuading property owners to sell by telling them minorities are moving into the neighborhood.
    c. Offering incentives to renters, like free utilities.
    d. Denying a loan to a qualified borrower based on location of a property.

8. It is important to analyze prospective tenants' backgrounds before renting them space in an apartment project. Which of these is not a consideration in the tenant selection process?
    a. Number of jobs held by the applicant within the past ten years.
    b. Number of times an applicant has been married.
    c. Number and amount of installment debts owed by the prospect.
    d. Number of times the applicant has moved within last three years.

9. A property manager was instructed by his/her client to rent only to a married couple. Which is correct?
    a. The manager should screen the potential tenants to determine if they are married.
    b. The manager should rent to a couple and not tell the owner.
    c. The manager should inform the owner that he/she cannot violate Fair Housing Laws.
    d. None of the above is correct.

10. After two years, a landlord wants to get a month-to-month tenant out of his rental. He or she has to:
    a. give the tenant a 3-day notice to pay or quit.
    b. give the tenant a 30-Day notice.
    c. change the locks when the tenant is at work.
    d. give the tenant a 60-day notice.

ANSWERS: 1. a; 2. c; 3. d; 4. d; 5. a; 6. b; 7. b; 8. b; 9. c; 10. d

CHAPTER 14
Real Estate Assistants
How to Be the Best Assistant Possible

I. Assisting as a Career

There are only so many hours in the day to complete the necessary, time-consuming tasks required in real estate transactions. Therefore, having an assistant, licensed or not, comes in very handy and should be more than cost effective. An assistant can free the agent to perform activities that are more productive, such as getting listings and making sales.

Real estate licensees have numerous career options from which to choose, including specializing in single-family home sales, investment property sales, property management, loan brokering and more. One of the fastest growing opportunities in the field, however, is often overlooked in the majority of practice texts—that of the real estate assistant. As small independent real estate brokerages are disappearing, replaced by the ever-enlarging franchising firms (like ReMax and Century 21), the need for qualified assistants increases. After all, the bigger the company, the more need there is to free up time for their quota-driven, extremely busy agents. Moderately-sized brokerages may benefit from hiring assistants as well, by gaining a much needed competitive edge against those bigger companies.

CHAPTER 14 OUTLINE

I. ASSISTING AS A CAREER (p. 527)
A. What is a Real Estate Assistant? (p. 529)
   1. Licensed vs. Unlicensed (p. 529)
B. Why Become an Assistant? (p. 530)
   1. Shyness (p. 530)
   2. Inexperience (p. 530)
     a. Mentoring (p. 531)
   3. Finances (Salary Plus) (p. 532)
II. WHO HIRES ASSISTANTS? (p. 532)
A. When Does an Agent Need an Assistant? (p. 532)
   1. "Delegation" of Duties and "Authority" to Do Job (p. 533)
III. GETTING THE JOB DONE (p. 534)
A. Your Résumé (p. 534)
B. Interview Questions (p. 536)
C. The Job Offer (p. 537)
   1. Part-Time Employee (p. 537)
     a. Future Time and Workload Flexibility (p. 537)
     b. Assistant's Time Constraints May Change (p. 537)
   2. Full-Time Employee (p. 538)
     a. On Call (p. 538)
   3. Employee or Independent Contractor (p. 539)
IV. WHAT DO ASSISTANTS DO? (p. 542)
A. Office Administration (p. 542)
   1. Paperwork (p. 542)
     a. Alphabetical Filing Systems (p. 543)
     b. Separate Filing Systems (p. 543)
     c. Master Transaction File (p. 543)
     d. Cross Referencing (p. 544)
     e. Indexing (p. 544)
     f. Hybrid Filing Systems (p. 545)
B. Updating Data (p. 545)
C. Keeping and Assisting with Appointments (p. 546)
D. Staying in Touch with Your Agent's Clients (p. 546)
E. Technology (p. 547)
   1. Real Estate Software (p. 547)
     a. Unique Market Analysis (p. 548)
   2. Hand-Held Computers (PDAs) (p. 548)
F. Notary Public (p. 548)
   1. Functions of a Notary Public (Thumb Print Required) (p. 549)
   2. Purpose of Notarization (p. 549)
   3. Qualifications (p. 549)

        4. Official Seal of Notary (p. 550)
        5. Caveats (p. 551)
      G. Escrow Coordinator (p. 552)
      H. Follow-Up Details (p. 552)
    V. CHAPTER SUMMARY (p. 553)
    VI. KEY TERMS (p. 554)
    VII. CHAPTER 14 QUIZ (p. 556)

A. WHAT IS A REAL ESTATE ASSISTANT?

REAL ESTATE ASSISTANTS are helpmates and extensions of successful real estate agents. They are delegated a variety of duties that agents would normally be required to do in the course of a business day that takes them away from spending time in "the field." By definition, they may be licensed or unlicensed.

In this chapter we deal exclusively with the characteristics and duties of professional real estate assistants who have already passed their salespersons' examinations from the Department of Real Estate.

Real Estate Assistants may be expected to do several, if not all of the following duties:

1. Maintaining a filing system
2. Directing incoming calls
3. Soliciting and making listing appointments
4. Preparing documents
5. Updating client records
6. Writing correspondence
7. Communicating with clients
8. Inputting listings into the MLS
9. Maintaining company Website
10. Monitoring listings
11. Creating newsletters, brochures, and direct mail
12. Meeting with appraisers, home inspectors, and termite companies
13. Prospecting for buyers and sellers
14. Assisting and holding open houses
15. Database creation and management

1. Licensed vs. Unlicensed

There is a place for unlicensed assistants in the industry, but their duties are so limited by law that, in reality, they resemble glorified secretaries more than real estate agents. Hiring a licensed, rather than unlicensed assistant, eliminates many situations whereby agents risk exposing themselves to liability. The limitations

placed on unlicensed assistants are restrictive and difficult to avoid in the day-to-day operations of a busy office. As an assistant without a real estate license, for example, you would not be allowed to discuss many of the details about a listing. This is a difficult rule to adhere to, especially when you're expected to interact frequently with clients and have an in depth knowledge of the properties in which they may be interested.

Moreover, many of the time-consuming chores that bog down and hinder an agent's productivity are, by law, restricted to licensed agents. An agent, for example, may need to leave an open house in the hands of an assistant while he or she shows another house in the neighborhood to a potential buyer. If you were not licensed, you would be limited to handing out brochures and "hosting" guests as they tour the open house. This is because you're prohibited from discussing many of the "technical" aspects regarding the sale of the home, including the price.

B. WHY BECOME AN ASSISTANT?

You've worked very hard to get your real estate salesperson's license, so why would you choose to become an assistant rather than an agent? There are several valid reasons for this career choice. Some licensees discover that, although they enjoy the excitement of the profession, they experience problems they're not yet able to resolve.

1. Shyness

What happens if, after taking the Principles and the Practice courses and passing your state exam, you find that you're just not comfortable with the fast-paced, competitive elements of this field? An outgoing personality, the ability to meet and greet people easily, and competitiveness are invaluable traits of a successful agent. Many new licensees will discover that they're too shy to pursue potential sellers and buyers or nudge them toward the decision-making process. If you find this description fits, don't despair, assisting may be the perfect career for you! Successful agents who do possess the above-mentioned skills really appreciate a "go-to" man or woman who can tie up loose ends, do time-consuming paperwork, and otherwise free them up to spend more face-to-face (and therefore productive) time with clients.

If you discover that you're not the "people person" that you thought you were, but are more comfortable behind the scenes, assisting may be the perfect career option for you.

2. Inexperience

For some of you, shyness isn't the problem so much as a lack of confidence. It's normal to feel intimidated when you first start out in the business, observing experienced professionals multi-tasking and confidently carrying out the many complex details involved in acquiring listings and selling property. New licensees are often overwhelmed at first, particularly taking into consideration the enormous amount of money and emotional investment involved in the buying and selling of property. Assisting may allow you time to learn the ropes from the inside, until you feel comfortable in the role of agent and confident in your abilities. This may be a temporary career choice.

Different brokerages have different policies concerning the training of assistants to be agents. Some companies don't encourage using the position as a springboard to a career as a salesperson. Find out the brokerage policy towards grooming assistants to be agents before accepting a position.

Some agents and firms discourage hiring assistants who have aspirations of eventually moving into the role of salesperson. Inquire about this policy when applying for a job as assistant!

Under no circumstances should you cultivate and harvest your mentor's clients. It is important to determine your potential employer's policy towards using the position as a stepping stone in your career. If they frown on this career path, and you're looking for on-the-job training, you should find another place of employment. Taking the job anyway, without revealing your true intentions, is operating under false pretenses, and may lead to ill will and resentment in the industry. By being honest about your goals, you're a lot more likely to find an agent who is willing to nurture your aspirations and teach you the subtleties, as well as the technical aspects, of the trade.

Successful agents do not detract from another agents' performance. Rather, their productivity may be contagious.

a. Mentoring

Ultimately, if you're looking to use your experience as an assistant to give you the knowledge and confidence necessary to become a successful agent, nothing beats a mentor. The difference between a teacher and a mentor is the difference between reading an assembly manual and having someone show you how to put something together. *MENTORS are professionals who are willing to take novices under their wings and not only teach them the basics, but share their experience and secrets to success.* Finding someone willing to mentor you is the best of all possible worlds, but not always easy to come by. You may have to put yourself in the uncomfortable position of turning down job offers until you find the agent with the right attitude for mentoring.

3. Finances (Salary Plus)

Yet another drawback of inexperience may be financial in nature. In Chapter One we discussed the need for six months or more of savings when you first start out, and even then, there's no guarantee that market conditions or other influences won't prolong that period. Because real estate is basically a commission-based profession, you may not be able to support yourself or your family on your earnings for some time. In this case, assisting may be an option. Most assistants are paid a weekly salary, allowing you to make a living while you're establishing contacts in the business as well as the community.

Some agents will start you out at a salary and then graduate to sharing a percentage of the sales commissions they earn, based on the degree of your participation in the sale. This type of arrangement is a win-win situation for both you and your agent. He or she benefits from your efforts to bring in new clients or handle time-consuming details, and you benefit by gaining invaluable experience without the pressures of depending solely on commissions for your livelihood. There's no greater motivator than potential financial reward to encourage your efforts to hone your agenting skills.

II. Who Hires Assistants?

The National Association of Realtors® (NAR) conducted a survey among the most successful real estate brokerage firms in the country, and found that ten percent of the top producers hired real estate assistants. Over 70 percent of those who employed assistants felt that hiring those assistants contributed to their firms' increased profits. On average, the brokerages with over 50 agents employed seven assistants or more, and the most successful smaller firms employed at least one or two.

Agents who employed assistants listed more than twice as many properties and sold 60 percent more of their listings than agents working without the benefits of an assistant.

A. WHEN DOES AN AGENT NEED AN ASSISTANT?

The more successful an agent becomes, the less time he or she has to spend with buyers and sellers. The more time an agent has to spend dealing one-on-one with clients, the more successful he or she will be. Unfortunately, the business an agent generates is directly proportionate to the amount of "busy work" he or she also generates. The very thing that makes agents successful can get in the way of making them even more successful.

Every agent has to decide when he or she needs an assistant, but generally, the decision comes with the recognition that his or her professional and personal life would benefit from more free time. For some, it's a monetary threshold, like making over two million dollars a year in sales. For others, it's sales volume; an agent selling four or more properties a month is bound to be bogged down in paperwork and follow up responsibilities.

Another motivating factor in the decision to hire an assistant comes when agents realize that their time would be better spent on the profitable part, marketing themselves and their services, than doing office busy work.

The most ambitious agents strive to be more than merely "successful," aiming for becoming the "most successful." Very few "mega agents" get to that position without recognizing their need to delegate some of their responsibilities to a qualified helper or assistant.

1. "Delegation" of Duties and "Authority" to Do Job

A competent agent has the ability to deal with clients as well as to attend to the details of a complicated legal process, including detailed contractual obligations. It's a delicate art to balance the personal and professional expectations of a high volume salesperson. Any agent who has demonstrated his or her ability to maintain the focus necessary to be considered "exceptional," may also have a hard time delegating some of those responsibilities to an assistant.

The characteristics that make an agent successful enough to need an assistant are often the same traits that make it difficult for him or her to relinquish control.

Your job is to relieve your agent of as many of those responsibilities as possible. Be alert to the signals your agent sends you. Some employers will gladly hand over the paperwork, but resent an intrusion into what they may consider their "personal relationship" with their clients. Be prepared for the possibility that, in the beginning, your boss may double-check and second guess your work. Keep in mind that the tasks you have been hired to do were once done very well by the agent, and that it's his or her reputation on the line if you don't maintain the level of competence and service he or she has established.

> *Gradually, your competence and willingness to do the job "their way" will relax even the biggest control freaks.*

III. Getting the Job

Once you've decided to become a real estate assistant, you'll have to find the right brokerage or agent for you. As we discussed earlier, your long range goals and reasons for pursuing a career as an assistant should dictate where you intend to work. Before you're faced with the option of accepting or declining a job, you'll have to apply and interview for the position.

A. YOUR RÉSUMÉ

As in any profession, employees look for certain characteristics from a prospective employee. The following are all important aspects to include in your résumé:

1. **Consistency** - While a well-rounded background may be a plus in the real estate field, an employee who has jumped from job to job demonstrates unreliability. If you're a student, fresh from college, no one expects you to have an extensive employment history. If you're a more mature applicant, consider "trimming" your employment history to just those that reflect well on the type of experience that your position demands.

2. **People Skills** - The better you are at dealing with people, the better qualified you are to be involved in the real estate industry. This is particularly important if your goal is to eventually become an agent. Any experience you have with customer service or interpersonal skills should be accented. This is a people-business.

3. **Education** - Having a real estate license is always preferable to not having one. At the very least, your potential employer will know you possess the basic knowledge of the business, which means less training time and a lowered risk of liability. Your education level may also indicate your pay scale.

4. **Real Estate Background** - Any experience in the real estate field can be a plus. If you "got your feet wet" working as an agent, only to discover that you might be better suited to the role of assistant, don't be embarrassed to admit it! An agent looking for an assistant as a permanent employee, rather than an apprentice, will appreciate your decision-making process.

Retirees make exceptional assistants. All the knowledge and experience they've acquired can be hugely beneficial to an employer!

5. **Skills** - A variety of skills can enhance your value as a real estate assistant. Typing, dictation, and filing experience are always a plus. Computer and Internet skills, as well as a customer relations background are even more appealing to employers.

While any and all computer skills are valuable, familiarity with one or more real estate programs (like Top Producer®) give you an obvious advantage over other applicants.

If you're just starting out in the business, a knowledge of Microsoft Word® and Excel® are your most valuable program skills. Knowing how to use a spreadsheet program or financial management program (like Quicken®) are also beneficial.

Depending on your employer's needs, salary budget, and expertise expectations, a basic knowledge of computer and Internet skills may suffice. Understanding the computer as a tool indicates your ability to learn whatever program or programs your agent will need you to master. If, however, you're completely inexperienced with computers, you may severely limit your usefulness as an assistant and your employment potential.

Taking a community college course in computer basics can benefit real estate students as well as "old school" professionals who learned their craft before computer technology took over the business. Computers are here to stay! Real Estate Computer Applications by Donna Grogan and Walt Huber would be very helpful.

6. **Recommendations** - Former employers with positive things to say about you are important to any job applicant. Even if your past employment had nothing to do with real estate, your reliability, integrity, personality, and adaptability are assets any agent values. As a new licensee, a glowing recommendation from your real estate professor(s) may influence your prospective employer, both in terms of your knowledge and dedication, but also as evidence of your people skills.

7. **Presentation** - It goes without saying that your personal appearance should be professional and pulled together. Your resume should also be neat and orderly. Sentences should be well written, grammar and punctuation flawless, and the design attractive. All of these elements demonstrate your attention to details, and your ability to create an appealing and interesting written product—important skills if your job description includes writing newsletters and advertising copy.

The more articulate and persuasive you are with the written word, the more likely you are to be trusted with the creative aspects of your employing agent's responsibilities.

8. **Interests** - Any good résumé will include personal interests, like charity work club memberships, and social interests. You might consider taking this opportunity to mention something truly personal about yourself. Doing so will

not only allow your potential employer to know you a little better, but illustrates your willingness to share your life experiences—often a valuable asset when dealing with clients.

> *Hobbies count! If you like to surf, for example, you may have something in common with a client that your agent doesn't. He or she may be aware of the (surfing) client's request to be near the ocean, and therefore focus on finding homes with ocean views, or sandy beaches. This would be an opportunity for you to help steer your agent and his or her client toward a home that's not only within walking distance of a public beach, but one that has a "good break" to the waves.*

B. INTERVIEW QUESTIONS

You should expect to be asked a variety of questions by a prospective employer. The following is just a sampling of some typical interview questions.

1. Do you have your real estate license?
2. Why do you want to be an assistant?
3. What are your career goals?
4. How fast do you type?
5. What computer skills do you have?
6. What were your responsibilities at your last job?
7. What about the real estate business most interests you?
8. What do you consider your greatest strengths/weaknesses?
9. What kind of experience do you have in real estate? (Have you ever bought or sold a home? Worked for an agent, or as an agent?)
10. Where do you expect to be in five years?
11. Do you expect this to be a permanent position, or are you looking to advance?
12. Do you have any experience in escrow, title insurance, or lending?
13. Do you have a valid driver's license and a reliable car?
14. Do you have good organizational skills? Can you multi-task?
15. Do you have any experience in customer service, telemarketing, or advertising?
16. How flexible is your work schedule? Are you available full or part time? What about weekends or evenings?
17. Do you speak any other languages?
18. Are you related to or know anyone in the real estate industry?
19. Have you taken any additional courses, besides Principles, that might help you in this business? Do you intend to?
20. How would you handle an irate customer complaining on the phone?
21. Do you think of yourself as a problem-solver, or are you more comfortable behind the scenes, dealing with office details like filing, letter writing, etc?

In addition to the face-to-face interview, you may be asked to take one or more tests to demonstrate your typing speed, spelling accuracy, grammatical and punctuation skills, and letter writing talent.

Brushing up on your skills will only increase your chances of performing well under the pressure of the interview process.

C. THE JOB OFFER

You've impressed your future employer with your professional resume, charmed your way through the interview, passed the skills test with flying colors, and are offered the job as assistant. Now what?

1. Part-Time Employee

If you asked the right questions in the interview, you should know if your employer is looking for full or part-time help. It's not uncommon, however, for agents to be relatively flexible in terms of the commitment they're looking for, especially if they've never had an assistant before. Agents hiring their first assistants have obviously realized that they need help if they're going to maximize their potential, but may not know how much time that's going to require.

Your status as a full or part-time worker may be negotiable, depending on a variety of factors, including your employer's work load and willingness to delegate tasks, as well as your needs and expectations. After all, you may be pursuing this line of work because school or family obligations don't allow you to dedicate the long, unscheduled hours required to be a successful salesperson.

a. Future Time and Workload Flexibility

If either you, or your employer, is certain that part-time assisting is the way to go, it's best to express that requirement early in the interview process. That said, keep in mind that the needs and limitations of this position may, and probably will, change with time. Your employer, for example, may grow to depend more and more on you as you prove yourself reliable and your services invaluable. Therefore, if you'd prefer to work full-time, and the perfect job doesn't present itself, you may want to consider accepting a part-time position with a firm that has the potential for growth. Ultimately, if you make the effort to bring in new prospects, as well as free up your agent to increase his or her productivity, your employer's workload will grow, resulting in the need for full-time help too.

b. Assistant's Time Constraints May Change

Along the same lines, your time constraints may change too. Finishing your education, children entering or graduating from school, and a variety of time or

financial considerations may alter your desire to work part-time as well. As stated above, your investment in your job can directly affect your indispensability to your boss. If you know your present time constraints will be changing in the future, you may be able to convince a prospective employer looking for a full-time assistant that you'll both benefit from starting out part-time and working up to full-time, as your availability and his or her productivity increases.

As a part-time employee, you can expect to work 20 to 24 hours a week, and be paid either an hourly wage or a set weekly salary. As such, you shouldn't expect benefits like insurance, vacation pay, or retirement plans. You'll be more effective working several hours daily, rather than three eight-hour days a week.

2. Full-Time Employee

While the option of part-time work is one of the perks of a career as an assistant, we've focused so far on the assumption that you have earned your salesperson's license, and therefore, made a commitment to the real estate industry as a career rather than just a job. If you're only available to work part-time, a firm may justifiably relegate you to the position of secretary, receptionist, administrative assistant, closing coordinator or telemarketing assistant.

Armed with a license and the time to dedicate to your job, your desirability as an assistant will be dramatically improved.

As a licensed, full-time assistant, depending on your (negotiable) employment agreement, you can expect to work 35 to 40 hours a week, Monday through Friday, and be paid a weekly salary. If your employing agent or broker uses your licensed status to good advantage, he or she will probably expect you to be available some evenings and weekends, reflecting his or her own flexible hours. As such, the norm in the industry, by no means a guarantee, would be to pay you a base salary plus a percentage of commissions earned on transactions in which you're involved.

a. On Call

Occasionally, you'll find an employer who requires a full-time assistant with a totally flexible schedule. He or she may require your services day or night, weekday or weekend, depending on his or her unpredictable schedule. Many "high producers" work for large firms with efficient secretaries or office managers who are responsible for some of the tasks an assistant might be hired to do. Those agents may need assistants to help them in the field more than the office, showing homes, hosting open houses and so forth. In a situation such as this, they may require an "on call' assistant.

Don't be taken advantage of! The majority of licensed "on-call" assistants work for a salary plus commission. That way, you're assured of making a livable wage, even if sales are slow, and you'll be compensated for your hard work and overtime. An employer who suggests your pay will be based solely on the amount of time he or she uses your services may be looking to "save a buck" during lean times at your expense.

ON-CALL EMPLOYEES have no set working hours, but make their services available to their employers on a "need only" basis. In other words, you'd be working at the discretion of your employer. If he or she has a busy week, you could find yourself working 50 or 60 hours a week, and considerably less during slow times. Before considering an on-call position, you should evaluate your lifestyle and time flexibility carefully. If a lack of structure and an unpredictable schedule won't hurt your social or family life, this employment solution may suit you.

3. Employee or Independent Contractor

In terms of the employee versus independent contractor status, the relationship between assistant and agent is similar to that of salesperson and broker, An *EMPLOYEE works regular hours set by an employer, is paid a regular or hourly wage, and has a right to sick leave, insurance retirement and vacation benefits.* An employee works under the direct supervision of an employer, and his or her job definition is set by that employer.

An *INDEPENDENT CONTRACTOR pays his or her own taxes, works with a minimum of supervision, and, in general, sets his or her own schedule. He or she has some flexibility in determining the methods and procedures used to complete the job for which he or she was hired, and basically has more control over day-to-day activities than an employee.* (**Figure 14-1** shows CAR's Personal Assistant Contract.)

By labeling an assistant an independent contractor, an employer may be attempting to avoid paying payroll taxes; therefore the IRS has strict regulations concerning who is or is not an independent contractor.

It may be in your best interest to accept a position as an employee, rather than an independent contractor, particularly when you're first starting out as an assistant.

Figure 14-1

CALIFORNIA
ASSOCIATION
OF REALTORS®

PERSONAL ASSISTANT CONTRACT
(Between Associate-Licensee and Licensed or Unlicensed Assistant)

This Agreement, dated _____, is between _____
_____, ("Associate-Licensee") and
_____, ("Assistant")
Associate-Licensee is a California real estate licensee with a ☐ salesperson's, or ☐ broker's license, and is an associate licensee with _____, ("Broker"). Assistant desires to work for Associate-Licensee, and Associate-Licensee desires to use the services of Assistant. In consideration for the covenants and representations contained in this Agreement, Associate-Licensee and Assistant agree as follows:

1. **ASSISTANT REAL ESTATE LICENSE:** Assistant ☐ does, ☐ does not, hold a California real estate license. If Assistant does hold a real estate license, the license must be furnished to Broker immediately upon execution of this Agreement.

2. **EMPLOYEE OR INDEPENDENT CONTRACTOR STATUS:** Assistant shall be an employee (or ☐, if checked, independent contractor) of Associate-Licensee. Associate-Licensee shall be responsible for compliance with all local, state and federal laws applicable to the type of relationship defined, such as, but not limited to, minimum wage, tax and other withholdings, worker's compensation and anti-discrimination. **The type of relationship agreed to has significant tax and legal consequences. Associate-Licensee and Assistant are each advised to consult with an attorney, accountant, or any other appropriate professional regarding these matters.**

3. **DUTIES:** Assistant shall assist Associate-Licensee in fulfilling Associate-Licensee's obligations under the Independent Contractor agreement (attached) between Associate-Licensee and Broker. Assistant shall comply with all obligations of Associate-Licensee imposed under the terms of that agreement and any office policy established by Broker. Associate-Licensee shall monitor the work and results of Assistant. If Assistant does not have a real estate license, Assistant shall not engage in any activity for which a real estate license is required. (Assistant may become more familiar with these limitations by reading the "DRE Guidelines for Unlicensed Assistants.") In addition, and more specifically, Assistant shall perform the following activities: _____
_____
_____
_____
_____

4. **COMPENSATION:** Assistant shall be entitled to compensation as follows (or ☐, if checked, as specified in the attached addendum.) _____
_____
_____
_____
_____

5. **PROPRIETARY INFORMATION:** **(a)** Work Product: All files and documents pertaining to listings, leads and transactions are the property of Broker, and shall be submitted to Associate-Licensee immediately upon such request, or upon termination of this Agreement. None of Associate-Licensee's work product may be copied without the express consent of Associate-Licensee. **(b)** Trade Secrets: Assistant acknowledges that Associate-Licensee's and Broker's methods of conducting business are protected trade secrets. **(c)** Agreement Not To Compete: Assistant shall not use to his/her own advantage, or the advantage of any other person, business or entity, or reveal to any other person, business or entity, information gained for or from the business or files of Associate-Licensee or Broker (i) during the term of this Agreement and (ii) for the period of _____ months from the date of termination of this Agreement, within a radius of _____ miles from _____(address).

6. **ERRORS AND OMISSIONS INSURANCE:** Associate-Licensee represents that (check one):
   ☐ **A.** Assistant is covered by errors and omissions insurance obtained by Broker.
   ☐ **B.** Assistant is covered by errors and omissions insurance obtained by Associate-Licensee.
   ☐ **C.** Assistant is not covered by errors and omissions insurance.

Associate-Licensee and Assistant acknowledge receipt of copy of this page, which constitutes Page 1 of _____ Pages.
Associate-Licensee's Initials (_____) Assistant's Initials (_____)

Published and Distributed by:
REAL ESTATE BUSINESS SERVICES, INC.
a subsidiary of the CALIFORNIA ASSOCIATION OF REALTORS®
525 South Virgil Avenue, Los Angeles, California 90020

REVISED 10/98

OFFICE USE ONLY
Reviewed by Broker
or Designee _____
Date _____

EQUAL HOUSING OPPORTUNITY

PRINT DATE

PERSONAL ASSISTANT CONTRACT (PAC-11 PAGE 1 OF 2)

7. **AUTOMOBILE:** Assistant shall maintain automobile insurance coverage for liability and property damage in the following amounts $_____/$_____ respectively. Associate-Licensee and Broker shall be named as additional insured parties on Assistant's policies. A copy of the endorsement showing the additional insured parties shall be provided to Associate-Licensee.

8. **COMPLIANCE WITH APPLICABLE LAWS, RULES, REGULATIONS AND POLICIES:** Assistant agrees to comply with all local, state and federal laws and regulations, and any office policy and procedures to which Associate-Licensee is subject as a result of engaging in real estate brokerage activity.

9. **INDEMNIFICATION:** Assistant agrees to indemnify, defend and hold Associate-Licensee harmless from all claims, disputes, litigation, judgments, awards, costs and attorneys fees, arising from any action taken or omitted by Assistant in connection with services rendered or to be rendered pursuant to this Agreement. Payment for any such claims or costs is due from Assistant at the time Associate-Licensee makes payment, and, if not then paid, can be offset from any compensation due Assistant.

10. **DISPUTE RESOLUTION:**
    A. Mediation: Mediation is recommended as a method of resolving disputes arising out of this Agreement between Associate-Licensee and Assistant.
    B. Arbitration: All disputes or claims between Associate-Licensee and Assistant which cannot be otherwise resolved, shall be decided by neutral, binding arbitration in accordance with substantive California law. The Federal Arbitration Act, Title 9, U.S. Code Section 1, et seq., shall govern this Agreement to arbitrate.

11. **TERMINATION OF RELATIONSHIP:** Associate-Licensee or Assistant may terminate their relationship under this Agreement at any time, with or without cause. After termination, Assistant shall not solicit **(a)** prospective or existing clients or customers based upon company-generated leads obtained during the time Assistant was affiliated with Associate-Licensee, or **(b)** any principal with existing contractual obligations to Broker, or **(c)** any principal with a contractual transactional obligation for which Broker is entitled to be compensated. Even after termination, this Agreement shall govern all disputes and claims between Associate-Licensee and Assistant connected with their relationship under this Agreement, including obligations and liabilities arising from existing and completed listings, transactions, and services.

12. **OTHER TERMS AND CONDITIONS AND ATTACHED SUPPLEMENTS:**
    ☐ Broker and Associate-Licensee Independent Contractor Agreement, C.A.R. form ICA-11
    ☐ Broker/Associate-Licensee/Assistant Three Party Agreement, C.A.R. form TPA-11
    ☐ Broker Office Policy Manual (or, if checked, ☐ available in Broker's office)
    ☐ DRE Guidelines for Unlicensed Assistants
    ☐ California Association of REALTORS® Real Estate Licensing Chart
    _____
    _____
    _____
    _____
    _____

13. **ATTORNEY'S FEES:** In any action, proceeding, or arbitration between Associate-Licensee and Assistant arising from or related to this Agreement, the prevailing Associate-Licensee or Assistant shall be entitled to reasonable attorney fees and costs.

14. **ENTIRE AGREEMENT; CHANGES:** All prior agreements between the parties concerning their relationship as Associate-Licensee and Assistant are incorporated in this Agreement, which constitutes the entire contract. Its terms are intended by the parties as a final, complete, and exclusive expression of their agreement with respect to its subject matter, and may not be contradicted by evidence of any prior agreement or contemporaneous oral agreement. This Agreement may not be amended, modified, altered, or changed except in writing signed by Associate-Licensee and Assistant.

Associate-Licensee:

_____
(Signature)

_____
(Print name)

_____
(Address)

_____
(City, State, Zip)

_____
(Telephone)   (Fax)

_____
(e-mail)

Assistant:

_____
(Signature)

_____
(Print name)

_____
(Address)

_____
(City, State, Zip)

_____
(Telephone)   (Fax)

_____
(e-mail)

REVISED 10/98

Page 2 of _____ Pages

OFFICE USE ONLY
Reviewed by Broker
or Designee _____
Date _____

IV. What Do Assistants Do?

As we stated earlier in this chapter, many of the responsibilities of real estate assistants will depend on the needs of the agent or broker who hires them. Regardless of your original duties, your employer's needs may change and you should be prepared to step in and take over increasing responsibilities, as needed. In this section, we will discuss the broad variety of duties that may be required of a licensed real estate assistant.

A. OFFICE ADMINISTRATION

The most common duties assigned to assistants (particularly in the beginning) is office administration. It's important to familiarize yourself with your employer's office procedures, but once you've done so, the more ways you find to streamline or better organize your employer's (and your) personal office procedures, the more valuable you'll become.

While every office operates a little differently, some basics always apply. For example, a tremendous amount of paperwork and phone calls are generated in a real estate company.

1. Paperwork

All real estate transactions require paperwork, and plenty of it. The larger the office or more successful the broker/agent for whom you work, the more need they'll have to hire an assistant. Assistants can free agents from the avalanche of contracts, disclosures, market analysis, correspondence, appraisals, just to name a few. Basically, all the figures illustrated in this text, including forms, letters, ads and the like, need to be kept track of.

All documents generated in your office will require a certain amount of duplication and distribution. A listing, for example, requires several forms, including a listing contract, MLS disclosure forms, and information sheets which not only require signatures by the sellers and the agent/broker, but also need to be copied and distributed to sellers, and saved in the files of the selling agent.

PAPERFLOW is the the path a document travels within an office. Directing that flow may be one of your main responsibilities. A phone call from a prospective buyer or seller starts a paper trail that may include agency contracts, competitive market analysis, and loan prequalification documents. A completed transaction may also include caravan sheets, agent's commentaries, photographs of property, disclosures, purchase offers, appraisals, escrow papers and finally closing documents and copies of commission checks.

All of this paperwork needs to be organized and accessible to the appropriate parties, either immediately or in the future. Keeping track of all all these documents requires, above all, an organized filing system.

a. Alphabetical Filing Systems

One of the most often used filing systems is the *ALPHABETICAL FORM, where files are organized alphabetically by last name.* Typically, files will be arranged according to the last name of your agent's client, usually the seller's name. Buyers and sellers generate numerous documents and different information. *Any document that has both buyer and sellers signatures is referred to as a SHARED DOCUMENT,* and should go into the client's file. (See **Figure 14-2.**)

Figure 14-2

Example of Documents in Shared Document File

Sellers' Information	Purchase Agreement
Listings	Escrow Instructions
All Disclosures	Closing Statements
Buyers' Information	Lock Box Identification

b. Separate Filing Systems

To address the problem of oversized files, separate files may be kept under the names of both the buyer and the seller (see **Figures 14-3** and **14-4**). Any document having to do with a single client, such as the buyer, should go into that client's file (organized alphabetically, of course).

c. Master Transaction File

A MASTER TRANSACTION FILE contains all the documents a brokerage (broker) may require on a single completed transaction.

Figure 14-3

Example of Documents in a Buyer's File

1. Address and Telephone numbers, as well as e-mail address
2. Information on present home (size, amenities, value)
3. Information on buyer's family and income
4. Information on future home—desired price and size
5. Buyer's financial qualification*
6. Buyer's funds necessary to close sale*

(*Agents keep these in their own personal file cabinets,)

Figure 14-4

Example of Documents in a Seller's File

1. Agency disclosure
2. Listing, excluding terms
3. Disclosures, including FRPTA
4. Information on property
5. Estimate of seller's net proceed
6. Recommendation regarding property condition

The easier you make it for your agents to find documents, the more time you save them and the less risk of losing paperwork. Keeping different coding systems, like different color file folders for buyers and sellers, will help to simplify the filing system.

The longer a company or agent stays in business, the more clients will come back for repeat business, generating different transaction files. If all the client's paperwork were to be filed in just one master transaction file, it could quickly become enormous. Also, filing all document in one gigantic file makes if difficult for agents to access at later dates when they need to reference only specific details of one transaction.

d. Cross Referencing

When using a separate filing system, you'll need to include a cross reference to other files. *CROSS REFERENCING is a note or indication (a link) in a file to refer to another file that is connected to that transaction.* By keeping the files a manageable size and specific, agents who need to access information won't have to wade through a thick file containing all the documents generated by both buyers and sellers in the entire transaction.

Each agent keeps their clients' names in their own database. This includes the property address, date of sale, and the reference file number. With this information, whatever system the office uses, the file can be easily located.

e. Indexing

Once you've created an alphabetical and a cross-referencing system, you'll need to create an index. An **INDEX** *is an alphabetical list of topics.* If your office or agent produces lots of business, there are bound to be thousands of files to keep track of, including different filing cabinets and methods of keeping track of documents. An index is the only way to cross reference all those different files. Each agent should keep track of his or her clients' transactions in their databases.

f. Hybrid Filing Systems

An example of a hybrid system is to include a buyer's file, a seller's file, an agent's file, and a master transaction file. Each document would be filed according to that heading and cross referenced within (see **Figure 14-5**).

Figure 14-5   **Hybrid Filing System**

<u>Seller's Name - Buyer's Name</u> <u>Property Address</u> <u>10-03-R-105(*)</u> <u>Sales Price</u>

(*) The first number represents the month escrow opened.
The second number represents the year.
"R" stands for a residential sale; "C" represents a commercial sale.
"RL" is a residential lease and "CL" is a commercial lease.
The last number is the chronological number of the transaction for the office.

Agents hold their listing and master transaction folders in their personal file cabinets. After the transactions close, they are placed in the master file cabinet, by year. Naturally, the agents keep a record of their transactions in their own client data base. The files are kept for three years. Agents are not allowed to take the files out of the office, although they may make copies for their own use.

Perhaps the easiest hybrid system is one that contains all of the above information, but the transactions are filed alphabetically by property address and year of sale.

B. UPDATING DATA

The inventory of homes must be kept current. The agent may be so busy as to forget to report a pending or sold listing to the MLS. This infuriates other agents who, believing the property is still available, either call the office or show the property to their clients, thereby wasting valuable time. Additionally, most Association of Realtors® penalize the listing agents with hefty fines when they do not report a property either pending or sold in a timely fashion (which is usually 48 hours). You, as the assistant, can take on this task and report the listings' status to the MLS as well as updating the office inventory book for the benefit of the other agents. Your agent's website also needs to be updated regularly. Articles that are time sensitive if not updated make the web site lose its professional appearance.

Time is an extremely important commodity. No one can buy or rent any more of it!

C. KEEPING AND ASSISTING WITH APPOINTMENTS

Another important assistant's task is reminding your agent of all appointments in a timely fashion. As such, it's important to know where and how to reach your agent at all times. Most agents carry mobile phones, but if you both have hand-held computers (like Palm Pilot®), it will make this task even more efficient, as information is easily beamed from one device to another. We will discuss this handy real estate tool in more detail shortly.

A lost or delayed telephone call can result in missed opportunities in listing or selling. Showing up late or missing an appointment can be disastrous!

As a trusted employee and licensee, you may assist your agent further by keeping some of his or her appointments yourself. For example, you may be asked (or volunteer) to meet with appraisers with favorable comparables, or accompany buyers on walk-throughs prior to closing.

Determine which documents (forms, brochures, etc.) your agent prefers to take on listing or selling appointments. Prepare the appropriate packets in advance for your agent's appointments.

D. STAYING IN TOUCH WITH YOUR AGENT'S CLIENTS

Keeping your agent in constant contact with prospects is a very rewarding task for both of you. Seasonal cards and newsletters are an easy way to stay in touch with prospects and past clients. You can print your own cards with real estate computer software, but there are excellent and inexpensive professional cards being offered to the industry.

There are also many newsletter providers in the real estate business, and many agents subscribe to them. This service may cost a few hundred dollars per year. The agent gets several different masters on a monthly basis that need to be reproduced and, of course, mailed out regularly to the agent's prospects. Most of these newsletters are in color and have wonderful real estate-related articles about current interest rates and real estate trends. The reproduction and mailing of the newsletter can be done by the assistant. If bulk mail is used, then you'll be working with your agent's database, producing labels for each client, followed by a trip to the post office. If the agent subscribes to a real estate management software system, such as Top Producer®, this task is even easier.

Make friends with the person in charge of bulk mail or be prepared to spend a lot of time in the mail room. A valentine card or a thoughtful gift can go a long way in establishing a harmonious relationship.

E. TECHNOLOGY

You may be asked to take pictures, probably digital ones, of your agent's new listings.

Most Multiple List Services (MLS) have the capability of entering ten pictures for each listing, but the first picture MUST be of the front of the house or none of the pictures will be entered.

When taking pictures, be careful that the garage door is closed, and that there are no trash containers in front of the property. Take the pictures from different angles to insure some good shots; take inside shots of the best features of the home. Edit these to make sure they are centered and properly exposed; if you don't know how, take a class at a local association of Realtors, or a community college. You'll make your agent look good to his or her client, as well as to the real estate industry, when there are several beautiful pictures of the listing the agent just signed up. The pictures can be given to the advertising person in your office to be featured in the newspaper as the "house of the week." You'll also want to give copies of the pictures and advertising to your clients to show them what's being done on their behalf.

1. Real Estate Software

This is an excellent time to discuss real estate software. Most offices use Microsoft Word® for letter writing and Microsoft Excel® for spread sheets. Becoming proficient in these two programs is extremely important. A smart assistant will take some classes at a community college or adult education to perfect these skills. If your broker is involved in property management functions, WinForms® has a user-friendly form for entering monies received and disbursed, thereby giving the property owner an accurate accounting of his investment on a monthly basis.

A top-of-the-line sophisticated real estate software, Top Producer®, is an Internet-driven program well known in the industry. It keeps the agent's client databases on the Internet accessible to the agent, or to the assistant, from any location. So whether you are at the office, at home, or on a trip, searches for clients and leads can be performed by first name, last name, street name, or even by city. It can also set up a website for your sellers to check on the progress of their transaction. Although it takes time to set the system up, once it's done the rewards are great. Mass mail-outs are as easy as a couple of clicks of the mouse; brochures and flyers can be professionally produced in color with pictures of the property, the agent, and the logo; they can even be e-mailed. With the proper software, a text message can be sent to you or to your agent's mobile phone within seconds of a prospective client sending an inquiry from your website. Naturally, the assistant who can maintain this system for his or her agent will earn the respect and gratitude of that agent.

www.topproducer.com
Top Producer

a. Unique Market Analysis

With appropriate real estate software, you can also download MLS pictures and data into your system for a professional market analysis. Since sellers often interview more than one Realtor®, it is important that your agent distances himself or herself from the crowd by using a detailed and unique, thorough presentation. This sophisticated software has a large library of letters for various occasions and extensive follow up; these letters can even be customized further for a better personal communication. The software will even print post cards, place pictures on letters and envelopes, your agent's picture, electronic mail outs, and bulk mail information. This is not an easy program to learn because it is so comprehensive. But, when properly used, your agent will have a distinct advantage over the other presentations that are all probably very similar.

You may not access the MLS unless you are a Realtor® participant.

2. Hand-Held Computers (PDAs)

BlackBerry® is a PDA used in the industry that allows mobile users automatic delivery of messages. Real estate software (like Top Producer®) even interacts with mobile phones and hand-held computers that many agents presently own. These handy devices are synchronized nightly via a telephone line, and all information entered in the computer or the hand-held computer is simultaneously updated and transferred to the computer and to the hand-held computer, so that they both have identical data. Also, all listings in the MLS can be searched on the hand-held computer by either price, city, or address. There are also maps showing the location of each property. The listing agent's name, telephone number, and office is also displayed. Naturally, it also contains the agent's clients and personal database with all current addresses, telephone numbers, and notes. The hand-held computer, programmed with the appropriate real estate software, can double up as a calculator, a programmer that opens lock boxes, note pad, appointment book, and calendar. It can also alert the owner in advance of appointments and important dates. The contact records, notes, and digitized agent business cards can be easily beamed from your agent's hand-held computer to yours. The smart assistant will become proficient in the agent's marketing software of choice in order to assist in all of the above tasks.

The monthly cost for Top Producer® is around $30.00 to $35.00.

F. NOTARY PUBLIC

Being a notary public is extremely helpful in real estate and to your agent.

You, as an assistant, can perform this duty for your agent's clients. Just think, many buyers and sellers needing this mandatory service only have evenings and weekends to transact business, which makes it difficult to meet with escrow officers and lenders to have the necessary documents notarized. You can easily take care of this by becoming a notary.

1. Functions of a Notary Public (Thumb Print Required)

A **NOTARY PUBLIC** *is a person who is authorized to authenticate contracts, acknowledge deeds, take affidavits, and perform other official activities.* Official functions are limited to determining positively that the parties to a written agreement are the parties they claim to be; obtaining the acknowledgement of the parties that they have signed the agreement or taking oath that they are aware of the contents of the agreement; applying and affixing his or her official signature and seal to insure as fully as possible that the original agreement cannot later be altered, blanks filled in, or pages added or eliminated, whether intentionally or unintentionally, by the parties to the agreement or anyone else after the document has been notarized; and *maintaining an official written record of his or her notarial acts in a book kept for such purposes, called a* **NOTARY JOURNAL**.

2. Purpose of Notarization

A **NOTARIZATION** *is a written statement, also called a certification, to which a notary public has affixed his or her official signature, seal, title, jurisdiction, commission, expiration date, and address.* The certificate generally states that a person(s) voluntarily appeared before the notary, signed an agreement or took an oath, and acknowledged to the notary that they signed the agreement or took the oath. After the notary has affixed his or her signature and seal to his or her certification on the document, the instrument may be recorded in the county recorder's office, giving "notice to the world" of its existence. Proper identification (like a driver's license or passport) must be made available to the notary.

In California, the notary public does not exercise any legal or judicial acts.

The notary's acts are for the purpose of assisting the parties. Regardless of the notary's authorization and duty to perform such acts, if there is any doubt that he or she can competently perform them, he or she should either reject the task or seek legal advice from an attorney. California does not permit its notaries to practice law, unless, of course, the notary is also a licensed attorney-at-law. Thus, a notary cannot draw up agreements, prepare deeds, draft legal documents, or render legal advice.

3. Qualifications

An applicant must be at least 18 year years of age, a United States citizen, and a resident of California for at least 12 months preceding application for a notary public license.

In the application, the applicant must disclose arrests or convictions for violations of the law, whether he or she has ever had a professional license revoked, and if he or she has been bankrupt within the previous five years. The application includes 20 written questions on notarial law, which must be satisfactorily answered (75 percent correct), indicating that he or she has sufficient vision to read typewritten matter and that he or she understands, reads, speaks, and writes the English language.

The notary public examination and responsibility has increased in difficulty over the years.

We recommend taking a class on what is expected from a notary, and how to properly fill out the journal and forms.

After taking the test, you can go online to obtain your exam result. You must get an assigned password by calling 916-263-3520.

 www.ss.ca.gov/business/notary/notary.htm
California Business Portal - Notary Public

Due to fraud and forgeries, it is now necessary to have each person who signs the document place his or her right thumb print in the notary's journal on all real estate-related documents.

Any person signing a **grant deed**, **quitclaim deed** or **trust deed** is required to place a right thumb print on the notary's sequential journal. This is because of a high rate of fraud by the use of false deeds. Additionally, a notary must immediately notify the Secretary of State if the notary's sequential journal is stolen, lost, misplaced, destroyed, damaged or otherwise rendered unusable.

The applicant must obtain the appropriate notary bond. The commission is good for a term of four years, and the notary has power to act anywhere in the state.

4. Official Seal of Notary

Under Section 8207 of the Government Code, every notary public must use an official seal that shows clearly on the document and will photographically reproduce the name of the notary, state seal, the words Notary Public, the name of the county where he or she maintains a principal place of business, and the date his or her commission expires. The official seal may be a rubber stamp or a metal seal, rectangular in shape, no larger than 1" x 2.5" (if a circular shape, not over two inches in diameter) with a serrated or milled edge border (see **Figure 14-6**).

Figure 14-6

Documents may be rendered unacceptable for recordation if a seal is placed over an integral part of the text or a signature; if the seal obscures the decorative or colored symbols or borders so that the seal is not photographically reproducible; if the seal has been altered with ink, typewriter, pencil, or whatever; or if an impression is made of a metal seal that has been inked too heavily and is not reproducible. If the notary's name is clearly shown in the seal, the name need not be typed or printed under his signature.

5. Caveats

The Real Estate Commissioner and the Secretary of State often receive complaints concerning omissions or improper service on the part of notaries. The most frequent complaint concerns the certificate of acknowledgement, in which the notary claims, that on a specified date, the person who executed the document personally appeared before the notary and was known to him or her to be the person whose name is subscribed to the document and that he or she acknowledged execution of the document. The complainant often alleges that the person did not appear before the notary to acknowledge execution of the document and that his or her signature on the document is forged. These complaints often refer to grant deeds on real property, hence the thumb print requirement.

It is evident that notarization is a beneficial service, but like most things in life, there needs to be a caveat. You may be asked to notarize the signature of an agent's spouse. Naturally, you cannot legally do this without seeing the spouse sign the document. The agent may try to persuade you to do this by saying something like: "Don't you trust me when I tell you my significant other signed this document?"

If faced with this situation, the best answer may be: "Of course I trust you to tell me the truth, but I'm sure you don't realize that this is against the law, and I'm also certain that you would not want me to break it."

(continued)

> *Another problem with having your notary is that many agents will expect you to notarize their clients' signatures. This can be very time consuming and take you away from doing what makes you valuable—being an assistant to your agent. You can resolve this problem by informing the agents that if they need your notary services, you will gladly perform them and you would further appreciate a $10.00 per signature donation to your favorite charity from either their clients or themselves. This often encourages the agents to become notaries themselves, or look somewhere else for a notary that will not charge them anything.*

Agents and assistants may notarize their clients' documents, even though a commission will be earned. They can even notarize for their families, as long as they do not benefit from the transaction. Remember that only __original__ documents may be certified by the notary.

G. ESCROW COORDINATOR

Your agent may want you to assist with escrows. You need to have all the pertinent information on the transaction and a good understanding of the escrow process. Your agent should instruct you on what your responsibilities are. You can implement this information by talking to the escrow officer or his or her assistant. You need to find out if all documents have been returned to escrow and what is still needed to close. Find out if all contingencies have been removed. Are all conditions met, such as termite clearance, home warranty, disclosures, etc.? It may be a good idea to visit the escrow office at least once prior to opening escrow. When escrow closes, the listing needs to be removed from the MLS, the file complete with all chronological documents properly secured, and the file placed in the office master file cabinet after the office manager or broker has determined that all pertinent documents have been properly checked and initialed. At this time, the commission check is issued to the agent. Also, don't forget to order the "For Sale" sign or "Sold" rider down.

H. FOLLOW-UP DETAILS

After sending out at least 200 "Just Sold" cards to neighbors in the immediate area of the sold property and following up with telephone calls within a few days (if this does not conflict with "cold call" procedures), this may be a good time to review this transaction with your agent. You both may decide to make some adjustments in how to work your next transaction. This can be an ongoing endeavor to fine tune your cooperative association for the highest efficiency.

V. CHAPTER SUMMARY

A **real estate assistant** with a salesperson's license is not as limited as one who does not have a salesperson or broker license. **Assistants free up agents' time** to spend in the field, listing or selling. Their duties may include (among others) maintaining a filing system, soliciting appointments, preparing documents, maintaining the company website, meeting with appraisers and home inspectors as well as assisting and holding open houses.

Shyness, inexperience, and financial concerns are some of the reasons licensees become assistants. A **mentor** is a professional willing to train a novice, and share his or her professional experiences.

The more successful an agent becomes, the greater the need for an assistant. A NAR® survey found that **ten percent** of top producers hired real estate assistants, and were more successful as a result.

Finding the right broker for whom to work is an important decision. A **résumé** should include positive information concerning consistency, people skills, education, real estate background, skills, recommendations, and interests, presented in a professional manner. During the interview process, a prospective employer may ask about licensing, career goals, typing and computer skills, etc. Having a working car in good condition is important.

Employers hire both **part-time** and **full-time** assistants, and may request working on an **on-call** (or need only) basis. An **employee** works regular hours set by the employer, is paid a regular or hourly wage and has a right to sick leave, insurance, retirement and vacation benefits and possibly a commission. An **independent contractor** pays his or her own taxes, works with a minimum of supervision, and, in general, sets his or her own schedule, with more control over day-to-day activities. Most assistants work as employees rather than independent contractors.

Assistants are commonly asked to handle **office administration**, including a great deal of paperwork. An **efficient filing system** is necessary to keep track of shared documents, buyer's documents, seller's documents, and a **master transaction file**. This is frequently done alphabetically, with cross-referencing and an index of topics.

Updating data is another important function of a real estate assistant. This includes reporting listing status of properties to the agent's MLS, and updating websites with the latest information.

A busy agent needs to be reminded of upcoming appointments and set up with a **listing or selling packet** to take on those appointments. An assistant may be able to step in and take over some of those meetings, like taking buyers on a walk-through before closing. Keeping the agent updated may require some technological know-how, including hand-held computer devices known as PDAs. Software produced specifically for the real estate industry can make this job a lot easier.

Becoming a **notary public** is one more way an assistant can save his or her employer time. A notary authenticates contracts, acknowledges deeds, takes affidavits, among other things. A notary must keep an official record of all notarial acts, in a **notary journal.** The notarization includes an official signature, seal, title, jurisdiction, commission, expiration date and address. All parties who sign a notarized document must place a right thumb print in the notary journal on all real estate-related documents. The **official seal of notary** must be clearly legible to be acceptable.

Assistants may be asked to assist with escrows, as well, making sure all contingencies have been removed, all conditions met, etc. After escrow is closed, signs must come down and MLS notified. Finally, follow up cards and calls should be made within a few days of closing.

VI. KEY TERMS

Alphabetical Filing System
Buyer's File
Cross Referencing
Employees
Escrow Coordinator
Hand Held Computer Devices
Hybrid Filing System
Independent contractors
Index
Market Analysis
Master Transaction File
Mentor
Notarization
Notary public
Official Seal of Notary
On Call
Paperflow

PDA
Real Estate Assistant
Seller's file
Shared Document File

VII. CHAPTER 14 QUIZ

1. An assistant:
    a. needs to have an assistant license.
    b. must have a real estate license.
    c. should preferably hold a real estate license.
    d. none of the above are correct.

2. What are some of the reasons for choosing to be an assistant?
    a. Wants to make more money than a real estate agent.
    b. Lack of self-confidence.
    c. Wants to have a mentor teaching the in's and out's of the business.
    d. b and c are correct.

3. Who makes a good assistant?
    a. A retired person.
    b. A person with a real estate background.
    c. Licensed agents who prefer to work behind the front line.
    d. All of the above are correct.

4. What are some of the duties of a licensed assistant?
    a. Assist and hold open houses.
    b. Prepare listing packages for his or her agent.
    c. Make appointments for his or her agent.
    d. All of the above are correct.

5. How does an assistant get paid?
    a. Usually a salary plus a percentage of the commission earned
    b. Hourly
    c. Base pay
    d. All of the above can be correct

6. Closed transaction files:
    a. may be taken home by the assistant.
    b. should be filed by the assistant in the office file cabinet.
    c. may be discarded when escrow closes.
    d. must be kept in office for five years.

7. Computer skills are:
    a. very important for an assistant.
    b. not necessary.
    c. command a higher value to the assistant.
    d. both a and c are correct.

8. A licensed assistant:

    a. can communicate with buyers and sellers quoting price.

    b. prospect for his or her agent.

    c. monitor a listing progress.

    d. all of the above are correct.

9. An assistant's contract should:

    a. spell out how the assistant will be paid.

    b. spell out if the assistant is licensed or not.

    c. state who pays for the error and omission's insurance.

    d. all of the above are correct.

10. An assistant:

    a. may be an independent contractor.

    b. must be an independent contractor.

    c. always gets paid by the broker.

    d. does not need to know the office policies.

ANSWERS: 1. c; 2. d; 3. d; 4. d; 5. d; 6. b; 7. d; 8. d; 9. d; 10. a

CHAPTER 15
Licensing, Ethics, and Associations
How to Acquire and Maintain Your License

I. Department of Real Estate (DRE)

*Every state government regulates its own real estate brokerage activities by staff members who are collectively referred to as **REGULATORS**. In California, it is called the Department of Real Estate. The main purpose of the **DEPARTMENT OF REAL ESTATE (DRE)** is to protect the public by enactment and enforcement of the laws relating to real estate, and by establishing requirements for real estate brokers and salesperson's licenses.*

Any person advertising or participating in real estate transactions involving others must first be licensed.

The California Department of Real Estate is managed by the Real Estate Commissioner. He or she sets all of the rules and regulations for the DRE, and receives his or her power from the state legislature. The Commissioner's position arises out of *the **POLICE POWER** provisions of the California Constitution, under which laws beneficial to the health, safety, morals, and general welfare are enacted.*

CHAPTER 15 OUTLINE

I. DEPARTMENT OF REAL ESTATE (DRE) (p. 559)
II. REAL ESTATE LICENSE REQUIREMENTS (p. 561)
    A. Who Must Have a License (p. 561)
    B. When a License is Not Required (p. 562)
    C. Obtaining the Salesperson's License (p. 562)
        1. Conditional Salesperson's License (The 18-Month License) (p. 563)
        2. Four-Year Salesperson's License (Regular, Renewable License) (p. 563)
        3. Salesperson's Examination (p. 564)
        4. Notification of Examination Results (p. 564)
        5. Electronic Fingerprint Requirement (Salesperson and Broker) (p. 568)
    D. Obtaining the Broker's License (Renewable Four-Year License) (p. 569)
        1. Broker's Qualifying Experience (p. 569)
        2. Broker's Required Education (Eight Courses) (p. 570)
    E. Renewal of License - Every Four Years (Salesperson and Broker) (p. 570)
    F. Continuing Education (CE) Requirement
       (45 Hours Every Four Years to Renew Your License) (p. 570)
        1. "Six-Hour Continuing Education (CE) Survey" Course (p. 571)
    G. Prepaid Rental Listing Service (PRLS) License (p. 571)
III. REAL ESTATE LAW AND REGULATIONS (p. 572)
    A. Real Estate Commissioner (Appointed by the Governor) (p. 572)
    B. Enforcement of Real Estate Law (p. 573)
    C. Hearings for License Violations (p. 573)
    D. Licenses: Revoke, Restrict, Suspend (p. 574)
        1. Child Support Obligations (150-Day License) (p. 574)
    E. Real Estate Bulletin, and Other Bulletins (p. 574)
IV. COMMON REAL ESTATE LAW VIOLATIONS (p. 574)
    A. Section 10176: Licensee Acting in a Licensee Capacity (p. 576)
    B. Section 10177: Licensee Not Necessarily Acting as a Licensee (p. 576)
    C. Regulations of the Commissioner (Found in the Administrative Code) (p. 576)
        1. Broker Supervision (Regulation 2725) (p. 576)
V. REAL ESTATE GENERAL FUND (p. 580)
VI. TRADE AND PROFESSIONAL ASSOCIATIONS (p. 580)
    A. Local Real Estate Associations (p. 581)
    B. California Association of Realtors® (CAR) (p. 581)
    C. National Association of Realtors® (NAR) (p. 582)
        1. Trade Name (p. 582)
        2. Code of Ethics (p. 583)
           a. NAR Ethics Course Required (Every Four Years) (p. 583)
    D. Realtist Defined (p. 592)
    E. National Association of Hispanic Real Estate Professionals (NAHREP) (p. 594)

F. Asian Real Estate Association of America (AREAA) (p. 594)

G. Independent Associations (p. 595)

H. Other Associations (p. 595)

I. Real Estate Instructor and Licensing Associations (p. 595)

J. No Affiliation Necessary (p. 595)

VII. CHAPTER SUMMARY (p. 597)

VIII. KEY TERMS (p. 599)

IX. CHAPTER 15 QUIZ (p. 600)

II. Real Estate License Requirements

As mentioned in the preceding section, the Real Estate Commissioner's main purpose is the regulation of the real estate business in the state of California. This regulation is accomplished by imposing mandatory licenses on those individuals who choose to work in the field of real estate. Who is required to have these licenses?

In short, any person who is actively involved in a real estate transaction at the service of another, in the expectation of receiving a commission, must be licensed.

A. WHO MUST HAVE A LICENSE

A person is required to have a license if he or she:

1. sells or offers to sell, buys or offers to buy, and solicits buyers or sellers;

2. solicits or obtains listings;

3. negotiates the purchase, sale, or exchange of real property or business opportunities;

4. leases or rents, collects rents, or negotiates the sale, purchase, or exchange of leases;

5. assists in the purchase of leases on lands owned by the state or federal government; or

6. negotiates loans, collects payments, or performs services for borrowers or lenders.

Any person found to be involved in such actions without a license may be guilty of breaking the Real Estate Law, under which stiff penalties can be imposed.

B. WHEN A LICENSE IS NOT REQUIRED

It should be noted that there are a few exceptions to these regulations. The following people, because of the nature of their work, are exempt from the licensing regulations (NO LICENSE REQUIRED):

1. Employees of lending institutions.
2. Lenders making federally insured or guaranteed loans.
3. Certain agricultural associations.
4. Personal property brokers.
5. Cemetery authorities.
6. Collectors of loans made on real property.
7. Certain clerical help

An individual who is not a real estate salesperson or broker may solicit for the sale of real property as long as he or she is:

1. the owner;
2. holding power of attorney for the owner;
3. an attorney at law acting on behalf of the owner;
4. a receiver or court appointee; or
5. a trustee, selling under a deed of trust.

C. OBTAINING THE SALESPERSON'S LICENSE

The candidate for a real estate salesperson's license examination must:

1. be 18 years of age to apply for a license;

2. provide Proof of Legal Presence in the United States; if not a California resident, refer to "Out-of-State Applicants" on DRE Web site;

3. be honest and truthful;

4. complete a college-level Real Estate Principles course; and

5. pass the required examination. (Governmental Photo ID required)

Speeding Up the Licensing Process

You can dramatically shorten the amount of time it takes to get a salesperson's license by applying for an exam date as soon as you enroll in a real estate principles course. In addition to "self-certifying" that you're enrolled in a principles course, you can save time by supplying an electronic fingerprint scan with your exam application. You will, however, have to pass the exam and provide proof of having passed the principles course when you apply for your salesperson's license.

For further information, call or write any district office of the Department of Real Estate. Ask for the pamphlet, *Instructions to License Applicants* (See **Figure 15-1**). At the same time, ask for the examination application and a license application.

The salesperson exam takes "three hours, fifteen minutes," has 150 questions, and requires a 70% correct score to pass.

1. Conditional Salesperson's License (The 18-Month License)

To obtain a conditional salesperson's license (18-month), the applicant must: 1) complete a college-level Real Estate Principles course; 2) pass the DRE salesperson's exam; and 3) pay the necessary fees. A *CONDITIONAL SALESPERSON'S LICENSE is the license of a person who has only taken the Real Estate Principles course. This license expires 18 months after issuance unless the salesperson has submitted evidence to the DRE of the completion of one Real Estate Practice course and one other college-level (broker-required) real estate course.*

2. Four-Year Salesperson's License (Regular, Renewable License)

To obtain a regular four-year salesperson's license, the applicant must:

1. complete a college-level **Real Estate Principles course**, a college-level **Real Estate Practice course**, and one other approved college-level (broker-required) course;

2. pass the DRE salesperson's exam; and

3. pay the necessary fees.

With a conditional salesperson's license, the licensee must furnish, within 18 months, transcript evidence to the DRE that he or she has successfully completed Real Estate Practice and one other (broker-required) three semester-unit (or equivalent quarter-unit) course. See **Figures 15-2 and 15-3** for the salesperson's and broker's requirements.

Figure 15-1

DEPARTMENT OF REAL ESTATE

State of California
Department of Real Estate

Instructions to License Applicants

PRINCIPAL OFFICE

All offices open
8-5 weekdays

SACRAMENTO
2201 Broadway, Sacramento, CA 95818-2500
(916-227-0931)

 **www.dre.ca.gov**

DISTRICT OFFICES

LOS ANGELES **Suite 350** (213-620-2072)
320 W. 4th St. Los Angeles, CA 90013-1105

OAKLAND **Suite 702** (510-622-2552)
1515 Clay St. Oakland, CA 94612-1402

SAN DIEGO **Suite 3064** (619-525-4192)
1350 Front St., San Diego, CA 92101-3687

FRESNO **Rm. 3070** (559-445-5009)
2550 Mariposa Mall, Fresno, CA 93721-2273

3. Salesperson's Examination

To pass, an applicant must achieve a score of at least 70% in the three-hour, fifteen minute salesperson's exam, which has 150 multiple choice questions. Exams are usually scheduled during the morning or afternoon. A non-refundable fee is required to take the test. If you fail, you may take the exam as often as you wish, but you must pay for each exam application.

The use of silent, battery-operated, pocket-sized **electronic calculators,** that are non-programmable and do not have a printout capability, are permitted.

4. Notification of Examination Results

You will be notified of your examination results mail, normally within five working days after the examination. You can also check your examination results using the DRE exam Web site. (See **Figure 15-4** for elicensing).

Figure 15-2

EXAMINATION SUBJECT AREAS	SALESPERSON EXAM	BROKER EXAM
1. Property Ownership and Land Use Controls and Regulations	**18%**	15%
Classes of property; Property characteristics; Encumbrances; Types of ownership; Descriptions of property; Government rights in land; Public controls; Environmental hazards and regulations; Private controls; Water rights; Special categories of land		
2. Laws of Agency	**12%**	12%
Law, definition, and nature of agency relationships, types of agencies, and agents; Creation of agency and agency agreements; Responsibilities of agent to seller/buyer as principal; Disclosure of agency; Disclosure of acting as principal or other interest; Termination of agency; Commission and fees		
3. Valuation and Market Analysis	**12%**	11%
Value; Methods of estimating value		
4. Financing	**13%**	13%
General concepts; Types of loans; Sources of financing; How to deal with lenders; Government programs; Mortgages/deeds of trust/notes; Financing/credit laws; Loan brokerage		
5. Transfer of Property	**9%**	10%
Title insurance; Deeds; Escrow; Reports; Tax aspects; Special processes		
6. Practice of Real Estate and Mandated Disclosures	**24%**	27%
Trust account management; Fair housing laws; Truth in advertising; Record keeping requirements; Agent supervision; Permitted activities of unlicensed sales assistants; DRE jurisdiction and disciplinary actions; Licensing, continuing education requirements and procedures; California Real Estate Recovery Fund; General ethics; Technology; Property management/landlord-tenant rights; Commercial/industrial/income properties; Specialty areas; Transfer disclosure statement; Natural hazard disclosure statements; Material facts affecting property value; Need for inspection and obtaining/verifying information		
7. Contracts	**12%**	12%
General; Listing agreements; Buyer broker agreements; Offers/purchase contracts; Counter offers/multiple counter offers; Leases; Agreements; Promissory notes/securities		

Dept. of Real Estate % of Exam Questions Testing Emphasis

For more information:

www.dre.ca.gov
(Department of Real Estate Home Page)

www.dre.ca.gov/salesqs.htm
(Salesperson Examination Content and Test Questions)

Figure 15-3

SALESPERSON AND BROKER COURSES
(The statutory required college-level courses)

The statutory required college-level courses for people wishing to qualify for either the real estate salesperson or broker license examination are as follows:

APPLICANTS FOR THE SALESPERSON'S EXAM

1. To qualify to take an examination for a real estate **salesperson's** license, an applicant must have completed (or signed up for) the **REAL ESTATE PRINCIPLES** college-level course.

2. In order for the applicant to obtain the original four-year salesperson's license, he or she must also, either prior to the salesperson's exam or within 18 months after issuance of the conditional salesperson's license, complete the **REAL ESTATE PRACTICE** course and one additional basic real estate course selected from among the following:

Real Estate Appraisal	**Escrows**
Accounting	**Property Management**
Business Law	**Real Estate Office Administration**
Legal Aspects of Real Estate	**Mortgage Loan Brokering and Lending**
Real Estate Financing	**Computer Applications in Real Estate**
Real Estate Economics	**Common Interest Development (2005)**

3. **Salespeople** who qualify to take the examination by completing (or are in the process of completing) only the **Real Estate Principles** course shall have their licenses automatically suspended, effective 18 months after issuance of the conditional license, unless the **Real Estate Practice** course, and one additional course, have been completed within that time.

APPLICANTS FOR THE BROKER'S EXAM

1. An applicant for the broker's license examination must have completed eight courses in addition to the experience requirements. These eight courses must include the following five:

Real Estate Practice	**Real Estate Appraisal**
Legal Aspects of Real Estate	**Real Estate Economics (or Accounting)**
Real Estate Financing	

2. The remaining three courses are to be selected from the following:

Real Estate Principles	**Advanced Legal Aspects of R. E.**
Business Law	**Advanced Real Estate Finance**
Property Management	**Advanced R. E. Appraisal**
Escrows	**Computer Applications in Real Estate**
R. E. Office Administration	**Common Interest Development (2005)**
Mortgage Loan Brokering and Lending	

Figure 15-4

eLicensing by the Department of Real Estate (DRE)

*License information is now available online, using what the DRE refers to as **eLICENSING**.* The DRE continues to upgrade its website capabilities, making the process of scheduling an exam date and obtaining the results a lot easier. Using elicensing, look at the helpful Information available to you:

1. Find out which **tests are being scheduled**.
2. Look up your **new test date**.
3. Get your **exam results**.
4. Find out if your original **license has been issued** yet.

The DRE can also help licensees make changes online, including the following options:

1. Broker License Renewal.
2. Change Your Mailing Address Only.
3. Change Your Main Office Address Only.
4. Request a Duplicate License.
5. Change How You Receive the *Real Estate Bulletin*.
6. Status of Your Online Request.
7. Review Your License Application (requires Adobe Acrobat 5.0).
8. Change Your User Information.
9. Display Public License Information.

The general public can also obtain helpful information by accessing Internet DRE records, such as:

1. Licensee look up by **name or license identification number**.
2. Search for approved statutory **(pre-license) real estate courses**.
3. Search for approved real estate **continuing education offerings**.
4. Active prepaid rental listing service **(PRLS) licensees**.
5. Active Mineral, Oil, and Gas **(MOG) broker licensees**.

PROOF OF LEGAL PRESENCE IN THE UNITED STATES

The **Personal Responsibility and Work Opportunity Act** (the "Act") requires states to eliminate a broad array of public benefits for illegal immigrants. The definition of a public benefit includes professional and occupational licenses issued to individuals by state agencies. For purposes of the Department of Real Estate, the term "public benefit" applies to original and renewal real estate salesperson and broker licenses, prepaid rental listing service licenses, and a payment from the Real Estate Recovery Account.

To implement the provisions of the Act, the Department has adopted Regulation 2718. This regulation requires **proof of legal presence in the United States from all applicants for a license**, and from applicants for payment from the Real Estate Recovery Account. This requirement applies to applicants for both original and renewal licenses.

To pass the examination, you must correctly answer at least 70% of the questions. The examination is qualifying in nature; applicants who pass are not informed of their score. You will be notified of the actual score and the percentage of questions answered correctly in each of the seven subject areas only when unsuccessful. Those who pass will receive an application for a license. Those who do not receive a passing grade will automatically receive a reexamination form.

You may not apply for a reexamination until after notification of failure of a prior test. Another application fee payment will be required.

There is no limitation to the number of reexaminations you may take during the two-year period following the date of the filing of the original application. If you wish to take additional examinations after the two-year period, you must complete a new application.

5. Electronic Fingerprint Requirement (Salesperson and Broker)

Applicants for the salesperson's license must apply for a license within one year from the exam date.

If you have taken Principles and Practice, plus one other required course, and have passed the examination, you are qualified to apply for a four-year renewable license. You must pay for an active license and for the live scan set of your fingerprints (fee paid to the scan service provider—fee may vary). You must pay for the conditional 18-month license, if you have completed Principles, but not the other two required courses.

Upon completion of the real estate license exam, a copy of RE Form 237 (the Live Scan Service Request Form) will be mailed to all applicants. A list of providers of the live scan fingerprinting technique is available through the DRE website (**www.dre.ca.gov**).

D. OBTAINING THE BROKER'S LICENSE (Renewable Four-Year License)

A *BROKER'S LICENSE is required of any individual who wants to operate a real estate office.* The candidate for a real estate broker's license examination must:

1. be 18 years of age to apply for a license, although there is no age restriction for taking the exam;

2. provide Proof of Legal Presence in the United States;

3. if not a California resident, refer to "Out-of-State Applicants" on DRE Web site;

4. have had two year's previous experience or a bachelor's degree (or one year experience and an AA degree);

5. complete the required eight broker courses;

6. be honest and truthful; and

7. pass the required DRE examination (Governmental Photo ID required).

1. Broker's Qualifying Experience

A candidate must be able to prove that he or she has experience in real estate before applying for a broker's license. Generally, two years of full-time work (104 forty-hour weeks) as a salesperson is required. This two-year requirement may be replaced by an equivalent amount of part-time salesperson work. Such experience must have been completed within the five years immediately preceding the date of application.

Sometimes the State Real Estate Commissioner will accept experience in fields other than real estate sales. These fields include contract work, lease, escrow, title insurance, bonds, mortgage company, or experience in another area directly involved in real estate.

Besides direct experience in these fields, education may qualify as full or partial experience. For example, the Commissioner has ruled that any individual with a four-year college degree is exempt from the two-year experience requirement. But, all candidates **must** complete the eight required real estate courses, regardless of their educational degree. A community college graduate, with the required real estate courses, needs only one year of experience.

All students are encouraged to submit an equivalency request with the Department of Real Estate. All decisions made by the Commissioner are final.

B.S. or B.A. (four-year degree) = 2 years of experience
A.A. (two-year degree) = 1 year of experience

Most California colleges and universities offer courses and majors in real estate.

The broker's 200-question exam takes five hours to complete. The applicant must answer 75% of the questions correctly to pass.

2. Broker's Required Education (Eight Courses)

Applicants for the real estate broker's license examination must have successfully completed the eight statutory-required, college-level courses. The required salesperson's courses can be found on the list of required broker's courses, but the number of required courses is different: three for the regular salesperson's license, and eight for the broker's license. An applicant's choice of eight (broker-required) courses must be taken by all broker candidates. (Refer back to Figure 15-3.)

Once all of these requirements have been completed, a candidate may apply to take the broker's examination. By filing the examination fee, plus proof of 2 years' experience or the equivalent thereof, and transcripts showing that the eight statutory classes have been completed, the applicant will receive his or her admission card for the test.

E. RENEWAL OF LICENSE - EVERY FOUR YEARS
(Salesperson and Broker)

Broker's and salesperson's licenses can be renewed; a conditional (18-month) salesperson's license CANNOT.

Once the license has expired, no licensed activity can be performed by the salesperson until the license has been renewed. The late renewal period (often referred to as the "grace" period) simply allows the licensee to renew on a late basis without retaking the examination; it does not allow the licensee to conduct licensed activity during the late renewal period.

Whenever a real estate salesperson enters the employ of a real estate broker, or whenever the salesperson is terminated, the broker shall immediately notify the Department of Real Estate in writing.

F. CONTINUING EDUCATION (CE) REQUIREMENT
(45 Hours Every Four Years to Renew Your License)

The continuing education requirement (45 hours every 4 years for license renewal) is NOT the same as the requirement for statutory broker courses.

All real estate licensees are required to attend 45 clock hours of Commissioner-approved courses, seminars, or conferences during the four-year period preceding license renewal. Three of these hours must be in an Ethics course and three hours must be in Agency. On a salesperson's license first renewal, only the Ethics and Agency courses are required. Thereafter, however, the 45-clock-hour requirement continues indefinitely with every renewal. **Figure 15-5** shows distribution of continuing education courses.

Figure 15-5

45 Hours of Required Continuing Education

A three-hour continuing education course in Agency and a three-hour continuing education course in Ethics and Professional Conduct is a necessary part of the 45 hours. The required 45 hours of continuing education include:

3 hours of Ethics and Professional Conduct
3 hours of Agency
3 hours of Trust Fund Accounting and Handling
3 hours of Fair Housing
33 hours of Consumer Protection

45 TOTAL HOURS (Required)

1. "Six-Hour Continuing Education (CE) Survey" Course

The "Six-Hour CE Survey" course can replace the 12-hour combination of four separate 3-hour courses (in Ethics, Agency, Trust Fund Handling, and Fair Housing), starting with your second license renewal. So, if a licensee takes the *Six-hour CE Survey* course, he or she still needs an additional 39 hours of CE to complete the 45 total hours required every four years at license renewal time.

G. PREPAID RENTAL LISTING SERVICE (PRLS) LICENSE

A *PREPAID RENTAL LISTING SERVICE (PRLS) license is required when running a business that supplies prospective tenants with listings of residential real property for rent or lease while collecting a fee for such service.* Negotiation of the rental of property is not a part of this activity. An individual may obtain, without examination, a two-year license to conduct PRLS activities.

Prior to issuance of the PRLS license, the applicant must submit, and have approved by the DRE, a contract to be entered into between the licensee and client (prospective tenant). Fingerprints and a $2,500 surety bond are required for each business location.

III. Real Estate Law and Regulations

California laws affecting real estate are included in several different acts and codes. The *CALIFORNIA REAL ESTATE LAW is the portion of the Business and Professions Code that refers to licensing and subdivisions.* On the other hand, the *COMMISSIONER'S REGULATIONS are rules that form part of the California Administrative Code established and enforced by the Commissioner of Real Estate.* All licensees should be familiar with the Real Estate Law, the Commissioner's Regulations, and the Subdivided Lands Act administered by the Commissioner.

A. REAL ESTATE COMMISSIONER (Appointed by the Governor)

The Governor appoints the Real Estate Commissioner, who is defended by the state Attorney General. The Real Estate Commissioner issues rules and regulations that have the force and effect of law.

www.ca.gov
Welcome to California - Online Services

In addition to his or her position as chairperson of the State Real Estate Advisory Commission, the *REAL ESTATE COMMISSIONER is the chief executive of the Department of Real Estate.* It is the Commissioner's duty, therefore, to mold the department's policy, create regulations (California Administrative Code), and to enforce Real Estate Law (found in the Business and Professions Code) so that both real estate purchasers and real estate licensed agents benefit from his or her rulings. The Commissioner's other duties include:

1. Deciding the business policy of the State Department of Real Estate.

2. Informing the Governor and other state officials as to what services the department can render to the state and provide them with descriptions of the department's licenses.

3. Recommending changes in policy that may have been deemed necessary for the good of the public and the business of real estate in California.

4. Regulating the sales of subdivisions.

5. Deciding if applicants for real estate licenses have met all the experience and education requirements.

6. Investigating complaints against allegedly incompetent license holders.

7. Investigating complaints against those performing acts without the required license.

The Commissioner does not take the place of a court of law, does not give legal advice, and does not settle commission (payment for real estate services) disputes. Commission disputes are settled by arbitration or civil lawsuits in local courts.

The Real Estate Commissioner has the power to call formal hearings to discuss any issue concerning an applicant for a license, a current license holder, or a subdivider. The Commissioner may subsequently suspend, revoke or deny a license. He or she could also halt sales (desist and refrain order) in a subdivision. Remember: The Commissioner cannot take the place of a court of law.

A licensee can be disciplined by the Real Estate Commissioner, but the local District Attorney prosecutes for the Commissioner in a court of law.

B. ENFORCEMENT OF REAL ESTATE LAW

Licensing and regulatory law is effective only to the extent that it is enforced. The Commissioner, as the chief officer of the Department of Real Estate, is duty bound to enforce the provisions of the Real Estate Law. The Commissioner may, by his or her own choice, and must, upon a verified complaint in writing, investigate the actions of any person engaged in the real estate business or acting in the capacity of a licensee within this state. He or she has the power to suspend any real estate license, or to revoke it permanently. The Commissioner also has the authority to deny a license to an applicant if the applicant does not meet the full requirements of the law. If, through the screening process (including the fingerprint record) of an applicant for license, it is found that he or she has a criminal record or some other record that may adversely reflect on his or her character, an investigation is made by the Commissioner's staff. A formal hearing may be ordered to determine whether or not the applicant meets the requirements of honesty, truthfulness, and good reputation.

C. HEARINGS FOR LICENSE VIOLATIONS

One function of Real Estate Law is to hold a hearing when there is a question as to the rights of persons to obtain or keep their real estate licenses. The Department of Real Estate and other licensing agencies must conduct hearings with strict regard for the rules set forth in the **Administrative Procedure Act**. Before denying, suspending, or revoking any license, the licensee is served a statement, and the Commissioner acts as the complainant. The licensee, or respondent as he or she is known in the hearing procedures, may appear with or without counsel. The hearing is conducted according to rules of evidence in civil matters.

A decision is made by the hearing officer, based upon his or her findings. The Commissioner may reject or accept the proposed decision, or reduce the proposed penalty, and then make his or her official decision. The respondent has the right of appeal to the courts. If the testimony substantiates the charges and they appear to be sufficiently serious, the license of the respondent is suspended or revoked.

After a license is revoked, the person affected may not apply for reinstatement until one year has passed.

D. LICENSES: REVOKE, RESTRICT, SUSPEND

The Real Estate Commissioner can revoke, restrict, or suspend the license of any real estate agent for misconduct.

REVOKE — take away the license.
RESTRICT — to limit the use of the license.
SUSPEND — to take away the license for a period of time.

1. Child Support Obligations (150-Day License)

The Department of Child Protective Services regularly provides the DRE with a list of persons (obligors) who are over four month's delinquent in court-ordered child support payments.

Active licensees who appear on the list are given 150 days by the DRE to "get current," or have their licenses suspended. Furthermore, the DRE will not issue or renew full-term (four-year) licenses to otherwise qualified applicants who appear on the so-called "deadbeat" list. Instead, they will be issued temporary 150-day licenses. No license will be issued, or suspension revoked, until a release is furnished from the District Attorney's office.

E. REAL ESTATE BULLETIN, AND OTHER BULLETINS

The *REAL ESTATE BULLETIN alerts real estate licensees to necessary current information and also gives the names, plus details, of any license violations.* The bulletin is published quarterly by the Department of Real Estate (DRE), and is sent to each salesperson and broker as an educational service. It can be accessed online at the DRE website, where licensees and consumers alike may read the same version that is distributed in print. (See **Figure 15-6**.)

The other two bulletins made by the DRE are the Mortgage Loan Bulletin and the Subdivision Industry Bulletin. The *MORTGAGE LOAN BULLETIN is published biannually for those who use their license to make or underwrite loans.* This bulletin can be accessed online at the DRE website by brokers who are making loans. The *SUBDIVISION INDUSTRY BULLETIN is published annually and is designed for those interested in subdivisions.*

IV. Common Real Estate Law Violations

Section 10176 of the Business and Professions Code is the legal guideline for the licensee engaged in the practice and performance of any of the acts within the scope of the Real Estate Law. **Section 10177** of the Business and Professions Code applies to situations where the licensee involved was not necessarily acting as an agent or as a licensee.

Figure 15-6

REAL ESTATE BULLETIN

Arnold Schwarzenegger, *Governor*
Sunne Wright McPeak, *Secretary, Business, Transportation, & Housing Agency*
John R. Liberator, *Acting Real Estate Commissioner*

http://www.dre.ca.gov   **Department of Real Estate**   Spring 2004

Case study
C.E. Fraud

In a recent case, the Department received a tip from an anonymous source alleging that a continuing education provider was providing full continuing education credit for license renewal, as well as credit for real estate principles for individuals wishing to obtain licenses, without requiring completed coursework.

In responding to this tip, the DRE sent investigators to the provider's offices to purchase credit for completing these education requirements without completing the courses. In the first instance, a Deputy Commissioner posing as an individual wishing to obtain a real estate principles certificate paid $189 and received a certificate on the spot. The deputy was not offered any course materials, textbooks, or assignments. A few days later, a second Deputy went to the office of this provider posing as a real estate licensee wishing to obtain the necessary continuing education credits for license renewal. For a fee of $289, the Deputy left the office with a certificate reflecting that he had completed 51 hours of continuing education, including the mandatory course hours in agency, ethics, trust fund handling and fair housing. Again, there were no course materials offered.

In a separate case involving a different continuing education provider, a Deputy Commissioner went to an office posing as a licensee wishing to obtain the credits necessary for license renewal and was immediately given the final examination, together with the answer key so that he wouldn't miss any of the questions. Upon completing

eLicensing
Easy to use, paperless, & interactive

Licensees are encouraged to use the eLicensing online system for **expedited processing** of license renewal and change transactions. *It's easy to use, paperless, and interactive.*

Use eLicensing:

- To renew broker and salesperson licenses
- To request duplicate licenses (broker, salesperson, officer and branch offices)
- For salesperson requests to change employing broker
- For broker certification of salesperson employment
- For mailing address changes
- For broker main office address changes
- To receive the *Real Estate Bulletin* electronically

To use eLicensing for the first time, you need to **register** with the DRE to create a user name and password. Thereafter, you may simply click on the eLicensing graphic then enter your user name and password to sign in. A personalized menu of eLicensing options available to you will appear. 🏠

---

the examination, he was given a certificate for having completed the 45 hours of continuing education necessary for license renewal.

The DRE filed accusations against the course sponsors involved and disciplined the course offerings, as well as the individual real estate broker licenses of the school's owners. The story, however, goes beyond just one of unscrupulous course providers offering credit without education. The question remains open as to how many real estate licensees obtained credit for education that they did not complete and then submitted it to the DRE to either qualify for a license or renew an existing license. It is certain that any lic-

ensee who submitted fraudulent education credits to the DRE will face the possible revocation of their license.

In the future, the DRE will continue to monitor the offerings of education providers to weed out those that do not require licensees to complete education in order to receive credit. When these schools are discovered, the licensees who used the school will also be scrutinized and face disciplinary action if it is proven that they did not legitimately complete the education requirements. With this in mind, licensees should carefully assess the risk of possibly losing their license when attempting to avoid completing educational requirements. 🏠

All agents must adhere to the ethical and legal requirements of Section 10176 and Section 10177 of the Business and Professions Code, which include violations such as misrepresentation and failure to disclose hidden relationships.

A. SECTION 10176: LICENSEE ACTING IN A LICENSEE CAPACITY

This section of the Real Estate Law covers violations by those licensees who are acting within the scope of their licenses. (**See Figure 15-7.**)

B. SECTION 10177: LICENSEE NOT NECESSARILY ACTING AS A LICENSEE

Section 10177 applies to situations where the affected party was not necessarily acting in the capacity of an agent or as a real estate licensee. (**See Figure 15-8.**) The vast majority of brokers and salespeople are honest and perform their services in a straightforward manner. Occasionally, a section of the Real Estate Law may be violated inadvertently and without intent. In such cases, the Commissioner would most likely consider restriction of the real estate license. On the other hand, a flagrant violation would most likely cause a revocation of the license.

It is "blind advertising" if an agent falsely gives the impression that he or she is the owner of the property for sale. The Real Estate Commissioner does NOT approve of pocket listings (kept within real estate offices)—they are not part of the professional code and guidelines.

C. REGULATIONS OF THE COMMISSIONER
(Found in the Administrative Code)

The Regulations of the Real Estate Commissioner have the force and effect of the law itself.

Real Estate Law (California Administrative Code) empowers the Commissioner to issue regulations to aid in the administration and enforcement of the law. These regulations, which are known formally as the Regulations of the Real Estate Commissioner, have the force and effect of the law itself. Licensees, and prospective licensees, should be familiar with these regulations. The California Department of Real Estate produces a factual law book entitled *Real Estate Law* (Real Estate Law—Business and Professions Code—and Regulations of the Real Estate Commissioner), which can be obtained from their office.

1. Broker Supervision (Regulation 2725)

One of the most important regulations of the Real Estate Commissioner requires a broker to supervise their salespeople.

Figure 15-7

Business & Professions Code 10176
(Real Estate Licensee Acting As Licensee)

Grounds for Revocation or Suspension

Misrepresentation - 10176(a)

The licensee must disclose to his or her principal all material facts that the principal should know. Failure to do so or lying is cause for disciplinary action. A great majority of the complaints received by the commissioner allege misrepresentation on the part of the broker or his or her salespeople.

False Promise - 10176(b)

A false promise is a false statement about what the promisor is going to do in the future. Many times a false promise is provided by showing the promise was impossible to perform and that the person making the promise knew it was impossible.

Continued and Flagrant Misrepresentation by Agents - 10176(c)

This section gives the commissioner the right to discipline a licensee for a continued and flagrant course of misrepresentation or making of false promises through real estate agents or salespeople.

Divided Agency - 10176(d)

This section requires a licensee to inform all his or her principals if he or she is acting as agent for more than one party in a transaction.

Commingling - 10176(e)

Commingling takes place when a broker has mixed the funds of his or her principals with his or her own money. A broker should keep all funds separate.

Definite Termination Date - 10176(f)

A specified termination date, in writing, is required for all exclusive listing transactions.

Secret Profit - 10176(g)

Secret profit cases usually arise when the broker makes a low offer, usually through a "dummy" purchaser, when he or she already has a higher offer from another buyer. The difference is the secret profit.

Listing Option - 10176(h)

This section requires a licensee, when he or she has used a form which is both an option and a listing, to obtain the written consent of his or her principal approving the amount of such profit before the licensee may exercise the option. This does not apply where a licensee is using an option only.

Dishonest Dealing - 10176(i)

Dishonest dealing is a catch-all section used when the acts of the person required a license but he or she did not have a license.

Signatures of Prospective Purchasers - 10176(j)

Brokers must obtain a written (business opportunities) authorization to sell from an owner before securing the signature of a prospective purchaser to the agreement. This section strikes at what was once a common practice in some areas in the sale of business opportunities, where the prospective purchaser was forced to deal with the broker who furnished him or her the listing.

577

Figure 15-8

Business and Professions Code 10177
(R.E. Licensee Not Necessarily Acting as a Licensee)
Grounds for Revocation or Suspension

Obtaining License by Fraud - Section 10177(a)

This section gives the Commissioner the power to take action against a licensee for misstatements of fact in an application for a license and in those instances where licenses have been procured by fraud, misrepresentation, or deceit.

Convictions - Section 10177(b)

This section permits proceedings against a licensee after a criminal conviction for either a felony or a misdemeanor which involves moral turpitude (anything contrary to justice, honesty, modesty, or good morals).

False Advertising - Section 10177(c)

This section makes licensees who are parties to false advertising subject to disciplinary action. The ban extends to subdivision sales as well general property sales.

Violations of Other Sections - Section 10177(d)

This section gives the Department authority to proceed against the licensee for violation of any of the other sections of the Real Estate Law, the regulations of the commissioner, and the subdivision laws.

Misuse of Trade Name - Section 10177(e)

Only active members of the national association or local associations of real estate boards are permitted to use the term "Realtor." This is a term belonging exclusively to such members, and no licensee may advertise or hold himself or herself out as a "Realtor®" without proper entitlement.

Conduct Warranting Denial - Section 10177(f)

This is a general section of the Real Estate Law and almost any act involving crime or dishonesty will fall within it. An essential requirement for the issuance of a license is that the applicant be honest, truthful, and of good reputation.

Negligence or Incompetence - Section 10177(g)

Demonstrated negligence or incompetence, while acting as a licensee, is just cause for disciplinary action. The department proceeds in those cases where the licensee is so careless or unqualified that to allow him or her to handle a transaction would endanger the interests of his or her clients or customers.

Supervision of Salespersons - Section 10177(h)

A broker is subject to disciplinary action if he or she fails to exercise reasonable supervision over the activities of his or her salespersons.

Violating Government Trust - Section 10177(i)

Prescribes disciplinary liability for using government employment to violate the confidential nature of records thereby made available.

Other Dishonest Conduct - Section 10177(j)

Specifies that any other conduct which constitutes fraud or dishonest dealings may subject the ones involved to license suspension or revocation.

Restricted License Violation - Section 10177(k)

Makes violation of the terms, conditions, restrictions, and limitations contained in any order granting a restricted license grounds for disciplinary action.

(continued)

Inducement of Panic Selling (Blockbusting) - Section 10177(l)

It is a cause for disciplinary action to solicit or induce a sale, lease, or the listing for sale or lease, of residential property on the grounds of loss of value because of entry into the neighborhood of a person or persons of another race, color, religion, ancestry, or national origin.

Violation of Franchise Investment Law - Section 10177(m)

Violates any of the provisions of the Franchise Investment Law or any regulations of the Corporations Commissioner pertaining thereto.

Violation of Securities Law - Section 10177(n)

Violates any of the provisions of the Corporations Code or any regulations the Commissioner of Corporations relating to securities as specified.

Violation of Securities Law - Section 10177(o)

Failure to disclose to buyer the nature and extent of ownership interest licensee has in property in which the licensee is an agent for the buyer. Also, failure to disclose ownership on the part of licensee's relative or special acquaintance in which licensee has ownership interest.

Importance of Section 10176 and Section 10177
REGULATIONS OF THE COMMISSIONER

The Real Estate Commissioner is empowered to adopt Regulations for the administration and enforcement of the Real Estate Law and the Subdivided Lands Law. Duly adopted regulations become part of the California Code of Regulations and, in effect, have the force and authority of the law itself. Therefore, all licensees, prospective licensees, and subdividers should be thoroughly familiar with the Real Estate Commissioner's Regulations.

10176. The Commissioner may, upon his or her own motion, and shall, upon the verified complaint in writing of any person, investigate the actions of any person engaged in the business or acting in the capacity of a real estate licensee within this state, and he or she may temporarily suspend or permanently revoke a real estate license at any time where the licensee, while a real estate licensee, in performing or attempting to perform any of the acts within the scope of this chapter, has been guilty of any act listed in this Section.

10177. The Commissioner may suspend or revoke the license of any real estate licensee or may deny the issuance of a license to an applicant or may suspend or revoke the license of, or deny the issuance of a license to, a corporate applicant if an officer, director, or person owning or controlling 10 percent or more of the corporation's stock has done any of the acts listed in this section.

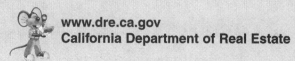

www.dre.ca.gov
California Department of Real Estate

A broker shall exercise reasonable supervision over the activities of his or her salespeople. Reasonable supervision includes, as appropriate, the establishment of policies, rules, procedures, and systems to review, oversee, inspect, and manage:

a. transactions requiring a real estate license;

b. documents which may have a material effect upon the rights or obligations of a party to the transaction;

c. filing, storage, and maintenance of such documents;

d. the handling of trust funds;

e. advertising of any service for which a license is required;

f. familiarizing salespeople with the requirement of federal and state laws relating to the prohibition of discrimination; and

g. regular and consistent reports of licensed activities of salespeople.

V. Real Estate General Fund

*All the money collected from license and exam fees goes into the **REAL ESTATE GENERAL FUND**.* Eighty percent of this money is used for the operating expenses of the Department of Real Estate. Twenty percent of the Real Estate General Fund is set aside as follows:

1. Eight percent to the Real Estate Education and Research Fund; and
2. Twelve percent to the Recovery Fund.

The ***RECOVERY FUND*** *was established for the payment of damages and arbitration awards to people who have suffered financial loss due to the wrongful act of a licensee in a real estate transaction.* To qualify for these funds, plaintiffs must first obtain a judgment in civil court (or through arbitration) against a licensee on the grounds of fraud, misrepresentation, deceit, or conversion of trust funds. If, after reasonable effort, the judgment remains uncollected, a claim may be filed with the Commissioner's office.

A license is suspended until the fund is reimbursed (plus interest). The total liability of the recovery fund in any one transaction is $20,000, and the total series of judgments against any individual licensee is limited to $100,000.

California is one of the few states that actively helps protect the public against fraudulent acts by real estate licensees.

VI. Trade and Professional Associations

A ***TRADE OR PROFESSIONAL ASSOCIATION*** *is a voluntary, non-profit organization made up of independent firms in the same industry.* It is formed to promote progress, aid in solving the industry's problems, and enhance its service to the community. We will discuss the role of local boards of Realtors®, the California Association of Realtors® (CAR), the National Association of Realtors® (NAR) and its Code of Ethics, and the term Realtist.

A "Realtor®" is a member of the National Association of Realtors® (NAR), a real estate trade association.

A. LOCAL REAL ESTATE ASSOCIATIONS

A *LOCAL ASSOCIATION OF REALTORS® is a voluntary organization of real estate licensees in a particular community.* A broker is entitled to full membership, a salesperson may be an associate member, and a non-Realtor® (who is in a real estate-related field) may be an affiliate member. For example, an affiliate member might work for a title insurance company, an escrow company, a lender, or any other business having an interest in local real estate activities.

Local associations usually provide multiple listing services for their members so that all members can be equally informed. Most local associations provide services such as distribution of educational material, seminars, library services, and other worthwhile services for the local Realtors®.

www.bhbr.com
(Beverly Hills, California, Board of Realtors)

B. CALIFORNIA ASSOCIATION OF REALTORS® (CAR)

The *CALIFORNIA ASSOCIATION OF REALTORS® is the state division of the National Association of Realtors®.* It is a voluntary organization whose membership includes local realty boards throughout the state and individual members who are not affiliated with any particular local board. With the exception of NAR, CAR is the largest Realtor® organization in the United States, with over 100,000 members in California.

The objectives of the California Association of Realtors® are:

1. to promote high standards and unite its members;
2. to safeguard the property-buying public;
3. to foster legislation for the benefit and protection of the real estate field; and
4. to cooperate in the economic growth and development of the state.

CAR has many standing committees that meet at director's meetings, seminars, and annual conventions. These committees specialize in specific areas such as education, ethics, legislation, political affairs, real property taxation, professional standards, and many other areas. There are also many divisions of CAR.

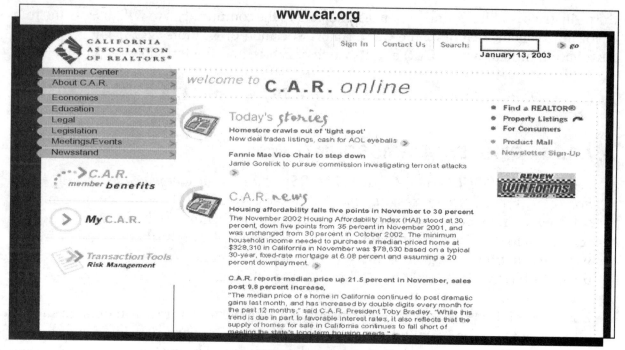

California Association of Realtors®
525 South Virgil Avenue
P. O. Box 76917
Los Angeles, California 90076

Most successful real estate salespeople in California are also members of the California Association of Realtors®. We suggest you become a member of this or some other trade association, if you are serious about selling real estate.

C. NATIONAL ASSOCIATION OF REALTORS® (NAR)

The *NATIONAL ASSOCIATION OF REALTORS® is the national trade association for all the state associations and local boards of Realtors® in the United States.* NAR unifies the real estate industry at the national level. It encourages legislation favorable to the real estate industry and enforces professional conduct standards on behalf of its members across the nation.

1. Trade Name

Only active members of the National Association of Realtors® (NAR) or the California Association of Realtors® (CAR), through their local real estate associations, are permitted to use the term Realtor®. This is a term belonging exclusively to such members, and no licensee may advertise or present himself or herself to be a Realtor® if not associated with such a group.

Use of the term "Realtor®," without proper group affiliation, is grounds for revocation of your license.

The National Association of Realtors® has affiliated institutes, societies, and councils that provide a wide-ranging menu of programs and services to assist members in increasing skills, productivity, and knowledge. (**See Figure 15-9.**)

2. Code of Ethics

See Figure 15-10 for the National Association of Realtors® Code of Ethics. These guidelines show not only how members should act, but how they must act.

Every Realtor® must swear to abide by the NAR Code of Ethics.

The National Association of Realtors® and its state and local divisions form a composite organization of brokers whose objective is to forward the interests of brokers, encourage education of practitioners and the public, raise the standard of real estate practice and increase the esteem in which brokers are held by their fellow citizens. To this end, a code of ethics has been formulated and adopted. It is the generally accepted code of ethics for real estate people.

"Under all is the land" are the beginning words of the NAR Code of Ethics.

a. NAR Ethics Course Required (Every Four Years)

The National Association of REALTORS® now requires all members to take a mandatory ethics course, or risk the loss of membership.

Figure 15-9

NAR Affiliates

1. American Society of Real Estate Counselors (ASREC)

This division of NAR offers the CRE (Counselor of Real Estate) designation.

2. Commercial Investment Real Estate Institute (CIREI)

CIREI enhances the professional development of those engaged in commercial investment real estate. Offers the CCIM (Certified Commercial Investment Member) designation.

3. Institute of Real Estate Management (IREM)

IREM is committed to enhancing the knowledge and professionalism of the real estate management industry.

 www.ccim.com

4. Realtors® National Marketing Institute (RNMI)

RNMI promotes professional competence in real estate sales and brokerage, and real estate brokerage management. It has two councils:

A. Council of Real Estate Brokerage Managers (CRB)

Recognized throughout the industry as the professional peer organization for managers of residential, commercial, industrial, relocation, appraising and property management companies. The CRB designation is available for members who meet experience requirements and complete a series of courses.

 www.crb.com

B. Counselors of Real Estate (CRE)

The Counselors of Real Estate is a professional membership organization established exclusively for leading real property advisors.

 www.cre.org

5. Certified Residential Specialists (CRS)

This designation is awarded to the top producing agents in the country who complete advanced training in selling and listing.

 www.crs.com

(continued)

6. Graduate Realtor® Institute (GRI)

The GRI symbol is recognized nationwide, showing buyers, sellers, and other real estate industry members that you are a true professional, and have a solid grasp of real estate fundamentals. It is the dominant real estate designation in California.

 www.edesignations.com

7. Real Estate Buyer's Agent Council (REBAC)

REBAC (Real Estate Buyer's Agent Council) serves Realtors® members who wish to devote all or part of their business to the practice of buyer's agency.

8. Society of Industrial and Office Realtors® (SIOR)

An international organization whose members specialize in a variety of commercial real estate activities. They offer the SIOR designation.

 www.sior.com

9. Women's Council of Realtors® (WCR)

WCR offers opportunities for developing leadership skills as well as a Referral and Relocation Certification (RRC). This is the only referral and relocation certification offered by NAR.

10. Professional Real Estate Executive (PRE)

The PRE designation is available for corporate real estate executives who meet experience and course completion criteria.

 www.realtor.org
NAR - All these affiliates can be accessed here

11. Senior Real Estate Specialist (SRES)

A Seniors Real Estate Specialist® (SRES) is experienced and knowledgeable in meeting the specific needs of clients 45 years or older. SRES has demonstrated requisite knowledge and expertise to counsel senior clients through major financial and lifestyle transitions involved in relocating, refinancing, or selling the family home.

 www.seniorsrealestate.com

12. The Institute of Real Estate Management (REM)

This is an organization, within NAR, of professional property managers. They offer a number of designations including:

A. Certified Property Manager (CPM)

B. Accredited Reside Manager (ARM)

C. Accredited Management Organization (AMO)

585

Figure 15-10

Code of Ethics and Standards of Practice of the National Association of REALTORS®
Effective January 1, 2004

Where the word REALTORS® is used in this Code and Preamble, it shall be deemed to include REALTOR-ASSOCIATE®s.

While the Code of Ethics establishes obligations that may be higher than those mandated by law, in any instance where the Code of Ethics and the law conflict, the obligations of the law must take precedence.

Preamble...

Under all is the land. Upon its wise utilization and widely allocated ownership depend the survival and growth of free institutions and of our civilization. REALTORS® should recognize that the interests of the nation and its citizens require the highest and best use of the land and the widest distribution of land ownership. They require the creation of adequate housing, the building of functioning cities, the development of productive industries and farms, and the preservation of a healthful environment.

Such interests impose obligations beyond those of ordinary commerce. They impose grave social responsibility and a patriotic duty to which REALTORS® should dedicate themselves, and for which they should be diligent in preparing themselves. REALTORS®, therefore, are zealous to maintain and improve the standards of their calling and share with their fellow REALTORS® a common responsibility for its integrity and honor.

In recognition and appreciation of their obligations to clients, customers, the public, and each other, REALTORS® continuously strive to become and remain informed on issues affecting real estate and, as knowledgeable professionals, they willingly share the fruit of their experience and study with others. They identify and take steps, through enforcement of this Code of Ethics and by assisting appropriate regulatory bodies, to eliminate practices which may damage the public or which might discredit or bring dishonor to the real estate profession. REALTORS® having direct personal knowledge of conduct that may violate the Code of Ethics involving misappropriation of client or customer funds or property, willful discrimination, or fraud resulting in substantial economic harm, bring such matters to the attention of the appropriate Board or Association of REALTORS®. (Amended 1/00)

Realizing that cooperation with other real estate professionals promotes the best interests of those who utilize their services, REALTORS® urge exclusive representation of clients; do not attempt to gain any unfair advantage over their competitors; and they refrain from making unsolicited comments about other practitioners. In instances where their opinion is sought, or where REALTORS® believe that comment is necessary, their opinion is offered in an objective, professional manner, uninfluenced by any personal motivation or potential advantage or gain.

The term REALTORS® has come to connote competency, fairness, and high integrity resulting from adherence to a lofty ideal of moral conduct in business relations. No inducement of profit and no instruction from clients ever can justify departure from this ideal.

In the interpretation of this obligation, REALTORS® can take no safer guide than that which has been handed down through the centuries, embodied in the Golden Rule, "Whatsoever ye would that others should do to you, do ye even so to them."

Accepting this standard as their own, REALTORS® pledge to observe its spirit in all of their activities and to conduct their business in accordance with the tenets set forth below.

Duties to Clients and Customers
Article 1

When representing a buyer, seller, landlord, tenant, or other client as an agent, REALTORS® pledge themselves to protect and promote the interests of their client. This obligation to the client is primary, but it does not relieve REALTORS® of their obligation to treat all parties honestly. When serving a buyer, seller, landlord, tenant or other party in a non-agency capacity, REALTORS® remain obligated to treat all parties honestly. (Amended 1/01)

Standard of Practice 1-1

REALTORS®, when acting as principals in a real estate transaction, remain obligated by the duties imposed by the Code of Ethics. (Amended 1/93)

Standard of Practice 1-2

The duties the Code of Ethics imposes are applicable whether REALTORS® are acting as agents or in legally recognized non-agency capacities except that any duty imposed exclusively on agents by law or regulation shall not be imposed by this Code of Ethics on REALTORS® acting in non-agency capacities. As used in this Code of Ethics, "client" means the person(s) or entity(ies) with whom a REALTOR® or a REALTOR®'s firm has an agency or legally recognized non-agency relationship; "customer" means a party to a real estate transaction who receives information, services, or benefits but has no contractual relationship with the REALTOR® or the REALTOR®'s firm; "agent" means a real estate licensee (including brokers and sales associates) acting in an agency relationship as defined by state law or regulation; and "broker" means a real estate licensee (including brokers and sales associates) acting as an agent or in a legally recognized non-agency capacity. (Adopted 1/95, Amended 1/99)

Standard of Practice 1-3

REALTORS®, in attempting to secure a listing, shall not deliberately mislead the owner as to market value.

Standard of Practice 1-4

REALTORS®, when seeking to become a buyer/tenant representative, shall not mislead buyers or tenants as to savings or other benefits that might be realized through use of the REALTOR®'s services. (Amended 1/93)

Standard of Practice 1-5

REALTORS® may represent the seller/landlord and buyer/tenant in the same transaction only after full disclosure to and with informed consent of both parties. (Adopted 1/93)

Standard of Practice 1-6

REALTORS® shall submit offers and counter-offers objectively and as quickly as possible. (Adopted 1/93, Amended 1/95)

NATIONAL ASSOCIATION OF REALTORS®

The Voice for Real Estate®

www.realtor.org/realtororg.nsf/pages/narcode
DRE Code of Ethics

Standard of Practice 1-7

When acting as listing brokers, REALTORS® shall continue to submit to the seller/landlord all offers and counter-offers until closing or execution of a lease unless the seller/landlord has waived this obligation in writing. REALTORS® shall not be obligated to continue to market the property after an offer has been accepted by the seller/landlord. REALTORS® shall recommend that sellers/landlords obtain the advice of legal counsel prior to acceptance of a subsequent offer except where the acceptance is contingent on the termination of the pre-existing purchase contract or lease. (Amended 1/93)

Standard of Practice 1-8

REALTORS® acting as agents or brokers of buyers/tenants shall submit to buyers/tenants all offers and counter-offers until acceptance but have no obligation to continue to show properties to their clients after an offer has been accepted unless otherwise agreed in writing. REALTORS® acting as agents or brokers of buyers/tenants shall recommend that buyers/tenants obtain the advice of legal counsel if there is a question as to whether a pre-existing contract has been terminated. (Adopted 1/93, Amended 1/99)

Standard of Practice 1-9

The obligation of REALTORS® to preserve confidential information (as defined by state law) provided by their clients in the course of any agency relationship or non-agency relationship recognized by law continues after termination of agency relationships or any non-agency relationships recognized by law. REALTORS® shall not knowingly, during or following the termination of professional relationships with their clients: 1) reveal confidential information of clients; or 2) use confidential information of clients to the disadvantage of clients; or 3) use confidential information of clients for the REALTOR®'s advantage or the advantage of third parties unless: a) clients consent after full disclosure; or b) REALTORS® are required by court order; or c) it is the intention of a client to commit a crime and the information is necessary to prevent the crime; or d) it is necessary to defend a REALTOR® or the REALTOR®'s employees or associates against an accusation of wrongful conduct. Information concerning latent material defects is not considered confidential information under this Code of Ethics. (Adopted 1/93, Amended 1/01)

Standard of Practice 1-10

REALTORS® shall, consistent with the terms and conditions of their real estate licensure and their property management agreement, competently manage the property of clients with due regard for the rights, safety and health of tenants and others lawfully on the premises. (Adopted 1/95, Amended 1/00)

Standard of Practice 1-11

REALTORS® who are employed to maintain or manage a client's property shall exercise due diligence and make reasonable efforts to protect it against reasonably foreseeable contingencies and losses. (Adopted 1/95)

Standard of Practice 1-12

When entering into listing contracts, REALTORS® must advise sellers/landlords of: 1) the REALTOR®'s general company policies regarding cooperation and the amount(s) of any compensation that will be offered to subagents, buyer/ tenant agents and/or brokers acting in legally recognized non-agency capacities; 2) the fact that buyer/tenant agents or brokers, even if compensated by listing brokers, or by sellers/landlords may represent the interests of buyers/tenants; and 3) any potential for listing brokers to act as disclosed dual agents, e.g. buyer/tenant agents. (Adopted 1/93, Renumbered 1/98, Amended 1/03)

Standard of Practice 1-13

When entering into buyer/tenant agreements, REALTORS® must advise potential clients of: 1) the REALTOR®'s general company policies regarding cooperation; 2) the amount of compensation to be paid by the client; 3) the potential for additional or offsetting compensation from other brokers, from the seller or landlord, or from other parties; and 4) any potential for the buyer/tenant representative to act as a disclosed dual agent, e.g. listing broker, subagent, landlord's agent, etc. (Adopted 1/93, Renumbered 1/98, Amended 1/04)

Standard of Practice 1-14

Fees for preparing appraisals or other valuations shall not be contingent upon the amount of the appraisal or valuation. (Adopted 1/02)

Standard of Practice 1-15

REALTORS®, in response to inquires from buyers or cooperating brokers shall, with the seller's approval, divulge the existence of offers on the property. (Adopted 1/03)

Article 2

REALTORS® shall avoid exaggeration, misrepresentation, or concealment of pertinent facts relating to the property or the transaction. REALTORS® shall not, however, be obligated to discover latent defects in the property, to advise on matters outside the scope of their real estate license, or to disclose facts which are confidential under the scope of agency or non-agency relationships as defined by state law. (Amended 1/00)

Standard of Practice 2-1

REALTORS® shall only be obligated to discover and disclose adverse factors reasonably apparent to someone with expertise in those areas required by their real estate licensing authority. Article 2 does not impose upon the REALTOR® the obligation of expertise in other professional or technical disciplines. (Amended 1/96)

Standard of Practice 2-2

(Renumbered as Standard of Practice 1-12 1/98)

Standard of Practice 2-3

Renumbered as Standard of Practice 1-13 1/98)

Standard of Practice 2-4

REALTORS® shall not be parties to the naming of a false consideration in any document, unless it be the naming of an obviously nominal consideration.

Standard of Practice 2-5

Factors defined as "non-material" by law or regulation or which are expressly referenced in law or regulation as not being subject to disclosure are considered not "pertinent" for purposes of Article 2. (Adopted 1/93)

Article 3

REALTORS® shall cooperate with other brokers except when cooperation is not in the client's best interest. The obligation to cooperate does not include the obligation to share commissions, fees, or to otherwise compensate another broker. (Amended 1/95)

Standard of Practice 3-1

REALTORS®, acting as exclusive agents or brokers of sellers/ landlords, establish the terms and conditions of offers to cooperate. Unless expressly indicated in offers to cooperate, cooperating brokers may not assume that the offer of cooperation includes an offer of compensation. Terms of compensation, if any, shall be ascertained by cooperating brokers before beginning efforts to accept the offer of cooperation. (Amended 1/99)

Standard of Practice 3-2

REALTORS® shall, with respect to offers of compensation to another REALTOR®, timely communicate any change of compensation for cooperative services to the other

REALTOR® prior to the time such REALTOR® produces an offer to purchase/lease the property. (Amended 1/94)

Standard of Practice 3-3

Standard of Practice 3-2 does not preclude the listing broker and cooperating broker from entering into an agreement to change cooperative compensation. (Adopted 1/94)

Standard of Practice 3-4

REALTORS®, acting as listing brokers, have an affirmative obligation to disclose the existence of dual or variable rate commission arrangements (i.e., listings where one amount of commission is payable if the listing broker's firm is the procuring cause of sale/lease and a different amount of commission is payable if the sale/lease results through the efforts of the seller/landlord or a cooperating broker). The listing broker shall, as soon as practical, disclose the existence of such arrangements to potential cooperating brokers and shall, in response to inquiries from cooperating brokers, disclose the differential that would result in a cooperative transaction or in a sale/lease that results through the efforts of the seller/landlord. If the cooperating broker is a buyer/tenant representative, the buyer/tenant representative must disclose such information to their client before the client makes an offer to purchase or lease. (Amended 1/02)

Standard of Practice 3-5

It is the obligation of subagents to promptly disclose all pertinent facts to the principal's agent prior to as well as after a purchase or lease agreement is executed. (Amended 1/93)

Standard of Practice 3-6

REALTORS® shall disclose the existence of accepted offer, including offers with unresloved contingencies, to any broker seeking cooperation. (Adopted 5/86, Amended 1/04)

Standard of Practice 3-7

When seeking information from another REALTOR® concerning property under a management or listing agreement, REALTORS® shall disclose their REALTOR® status and whether their interest is personal or on behalf of a client and, if on behalf of a client, their representational status. (Amended 1/95)

Standard of Practice 3-8

REALTORS® shall not misrepresent the availability of access to show or inspect a listed property. (Amended 11/87)

Article 4

REALTORS® shall not acquire an interest in or buy or present offers from themselves, any member of their immediate families, their firms or any member thereof, or any entities in which they have any ownership interest, any real property without making their true position known to the owner or the owner's agent or broker. In selling property they own, or in which they have any interest, REALTORS® shall reveal their ownership or interest in writing to the purchaser or the purchaser's representative. (Amended 1/00)

Standard of Practice 4-1

For the protection of all parties, the disclosures required by Article 4 shall be in writing and provided by REALTORS® prior to the signing of any contract. (Adopted 2/86)

Article 5

REALTORS® shall not undertake to provide professional services concerning a property or its value where they have a present or contemplated interest unless such interest is specifically disclosed to all affected parties.

Article 6

REALTORS® shall not accept any commission, rebate, or profit on expenditures made for their client, without the client's knowledge and consent. When recommending real estate products or services (e.g., homeowner's insurance, warranty programs, mortgage financing, title insurance, etc.), REALTORS® shall disclose to the client or customer to whom the recommendation is made any financial benefits or fees, other than real estate referral fees, the REALTOR® or REALTOR®'s firm may receive as a direct result of such recommendation. (Amended 1/99)

Standard of Practice 6-1

REALTORS® shall not recommend or suggest to a client or a customer the use of services of another organization or business entity in which they have a direct interest without disclosing such interest at the time of the recommendation or suggestion. (Amended 5/88)

Article 7

In a transaction, REALTORS® shall not accept compensation from more than one party, even if permitted by law, without disclosure to all parties and the informed consent of the REALTOR®'s client or clients. (Amended 1/93)

Article 8

REALTORS® shall keep in a special account in an appropriate financial institution, separated from their own funds, monies coming into their possession in trust for other persons, such as escrows, trust funds, clients' monies, and other like items.

Article 9

REALTORS®, for the protection of all parties, shall assure whenever possible that agreements related to real estate transactions including, but not limited to, listing and representaton agreements, purchase contracts, and leases are in writing in clear and understandable language expressing the specific terms, conditions, obligations and commitments of the parties. A copy of each agreement shall be furnished to each party to such agreements upon their signing or initialing. (Amended 1/04)

Standard of Practice 9-1

For the protection of all parties, REALTORS® shall use reasonable care to ensure that documents pertaining to the purchase, sale, or lease of real estate are kept current through the use of written extensions or amendments. (Amended 1/93)

Duties to the Public

Article 10

REALTORS® shall not deny equal professional services to any person for reasons of race, color, religion, sex, handicap, familial status, or national origin. REALTORS® shall not be parties to any plan or agreement to discriminate against a person or persons on the basis of race, color, religion, sex, handicap, familial status, or national origin. (Amended 1/90) REALTORS®, in their real estate employment practices, shall not discriminate against any person or persons on the basis of race, color, religion, sex, handicap, familial status, or national origin. (Amended 1/00)

Standard of Practice 10-1

REALTORS® shall not volunteer information regarding the racial, religious or ethnic composition of any neighborhood and shall not engage in any activity which may result in panic selling. REALTORS® shall not print, display or circulate any statement or advertisement with respect to the selling or renting of a property that indicates any preference, limitations or discrimination based on race, color, religion, sex, handicap, familial status, or national origin. (Adopted 1/94)

Standard of Practice 10-2

As used in Article 10 "real estate employment practices" relates to employees and independent contractors providing real-estate related services and the administrative and clerical staff directly supporting those individuals. (Adopted 1/00)

Article 11

The services which REALTORS® provide to their clients and customers shall conform to the standards of practice and competence which are reasonably expected in the specific real estate disciplines in which they engage; specifically, residential real estate brokerage, real property management, commercial and industrial real estate brokerage, real estate appraisal, real estate counseling, real estate syndication, real estate auction, and international real estate.

REALTORS® shall not undertake to provide specialized professional services concerning a type of property or service that is outside their field of competence unless they engage the assistance of one who is competent on such types of property or service, or unless the facts are fully disclosed to the client. Any persons engaged to provide such assistance shall be so identified to the client and their contribution to the assignment should be set forth. (Amended 1/95)

Standard of Practice 11-1

When REALTORS® prepare opinions of real property value or price, other than in pursuit of a listing or to assist a potential purchaser in formulating a purchase offer, such opinions shall include the following: 1) identification of the subject property 2) date prepared 3) defined value or price 4) limiting conditions, including statements of purpose(s) and intended user(s) 5) any present or contemplated interest, including the possibility of representing the seller/landlord or buyers/tenants 6) basis for the opinion, including applicable market data 7) if the opinion is not an appraisal, a statement to that effect. (Amended 1/01)

Standard of Practice 11-2

The obligations of the Code of Ethics in respect of real estate disciplines other than appraisal shall be interpreted and applied in accordance with the standards of competence and practice which clients and the public reasonably require to protect their rights and interests considering the complexity of the transaction, the availability of expert assistance, and, where the REALTOR® is an agent or subagent, the obligations of a fiduciary. (Adopted 1/95)

Standard of Practice 11-3

When REALTORS® provide consultive services to clients which involve advice or counsel for a fee (not a commission), such advice shall be rendered in an objective manner and the fee shall not be contingent on the substance of the advice or counsel given. If brokerage or transaction services are to be provided in addition to consultive services, a separate compensation may be paid with prior agreement between the client and REALTOR®. (Adopted 1/96)

Standard of Practice 11-4

The competency required by Article 11 relates to services contracted for between REALTORS® and their clients or customers; the duties expressly imposed by the Code of Ethics; and the duties imposed by law or regulation. (Adopted 1/02)

Article 12

REALTORS® shall be careful at all times to present a true picture in their advertising and representations to the public. REALTORS® shall also ensure that their professional status (e.g., broker, appraiser, property manager, etc.) or status as REALTORS® is clearly identifiable in any such advertising. (Amended 1/93)

Standard of Practice 12-1

REALTORS® may use the term "free" and similar terms in their advertising and in other representations provided that all terms governing availability of the offered product or service are clearly disclosed at the same time. (Amended 1/97)

Standard of Practice 12-2

REALTORS® may represent their services as "free" or without cost even if they expect to receive compensation from a source other than their client provided that the potential for the REALTOR® to obtain a benefit from a third party is clearly disclosed at the same time. (Amended 1/97)

Standard of Practice 12-3

The offering of premiums, prizes, merchandise discounts or other inducements to list, sell, purchase, or lease is not, in itself, unethical even if receipt of the benefit is contingent on listing, selling, purchasing, or leasing through the REALTOR® making the offer. However, REALTORS® must exercise care and candor in any such advertising or other public or private representations so that any party interested in receiving or otherwise benefiting from the REALTOR®'s offer will have clear, thorough, advance understanding of all the terms and conditions of the offer. The offering of any inducements to do business is subject to the limitations and restrictions of state law and the ethical obligations established by any applicable Standard of Practice. (Amended 1/95)

Standard of Practice 12-4

REALTORS® shall not offer for sale/lease or advertise property without authority. When acting as listing brokers or as subagents, REALTORS® shall not quote a price different from that agreed upon with the seller/landlord. (Amended 1/93)

Standard of Practice 12-5

REALTORS® shall not advertise nor permit any person employed by or affiliated with them to advertise listed property without disclosing the name of the firm. (Adopted 11/86)

Standard of Practice 12-6

REALTORS®, when advertising unlisted real property for sale/lease in which they have an ownership interest, shall disclose their status as both owners/landlords and as REALTORS® or real estate licensees. (Amended 1/93)

Standard of Practice 12-7

Only REALTORS® who participated in the transaction as the listing broker or cooperating broker (selling broker) may claim to have "sold" the property. Prior to closing, a cooperating broker may post a "sold" sign only with the consent of the listing broker. (Amended 1/96)

Article 13

REALTORS® shall not engage in activities that constitute the unauthorized practice of law and shall recommend that legal counsel be obtained when the interest of any party to the transaction requires it.

Article 14

If charged with unethical practice or asked to present evidence or to cooperate in any other way, in any professional standards proceeding or investigation, REALTORS® shall place all pertinent facts before the proper tribunals of the Member Board or affiliated institute, society, or council in which membership is held and shall take no action to disrupt or obstruct such processes. (Amended 1/99)

Standard of Practice 14-1

REALTORS® shall not be subject to disciplinary proceedings in more than one Board of REALTORS® or affiliated institute, society or council in which they hold membership with respect to alleged violations of the Code of Ethics relating to the same transaction or event. (Amended 1/95)

Standard of Practice 14-2

REALTORS® shall not make any unauthorized disclosure or dissemination of the allegations, findings, or decision developed in connection with an ethics hearing or appeal or in connection with an arbitration hearing or procedural review. (Amended 1/92)

Standard of Practice 14-3

REALTORS® shall not obstruct the Board's investigative or professional standards proceedings by instituting or threatening to institute actions for libel, slander or defamation against any party to a professional standards proceeding or their witnesses based on the filing of an arbitration request, an ethics complaint, or testimony given before any tribunal. (Adopted 11/87, Amended 1/99)

Standard of Practice 14-4

REALTORS® shall not intentionally impede the Board's investigative or disciplinary proceedings by filing multiple ethics complaints based on the same event or transaction. (Adopted 11/88)

Duties to REALTORS®

Article 15

REALTORS® shall not knowingly or recklessly make false or misleading statements about competitors, their businesses, or their business practices. (Amended 1/92)

Standard of Practice 15-1

REALTORS® shall not knowingly or recklessly file false or unfounded ethics complaints. (Adopted 1/00)

Article 16

REALTORS® shall not engage in any practice or take any action inconsistent with the exclusive representation or exclusive brokerage relationship agreements that other REALTORS® have with clients. (Amended 1/04)

Standard of Practice 16-1

Article 16 is not intended to prohibit aggressive or innovative business practices which are otherwise ethical and does not prohibit disagreements with other REALTORS® involving commission, fees, compensation or other forms of payment or expenses. (Adopted 1/93, Amended 1/95)

Standard of Practice 16-2

Article 16 does not preclude REALTORS® from making general announcements to prospects describing their services and the terms of their availability even though some recipients may have entered into agency agreements or other exclusive relationships with another REALTOR®. A general telephone canvass, general mailing or distribution addressed to all prospectives in a given geographical area or in a given profession, business, club, or organization, or other classification or group is deemed "general" for purposes of this standard. (Amended 1/04)

Article 16 is intended to recognize as unethical two basic types of solicitations:

First, telephone or personal solicitations of property owners who have been identified by a real estate sign, multiple listing compilation, or other information service as having exclusively listed their property with another REALTOR®; and Second, mail or other forms of written solicitations of prospects whose properties are exclusively listed with another REALTOR® when such solicitations are not part of a general mailing but are directed specifically to property owners identified through compilations of current listings, "for sale" or "for rent" signs, or other sources of information required by Article 3 and Multiple Listing Service rules to be made available to other REALTORS® under offers of subagency or cooperation. (Amended 1/04)

Standard of Practice 16-3

Article 16 does not preclude REALTORS® from contacting the client of another broker for the purpose of offering to provide, or entering into a contract to provide, a different type of real estate service unrelated to the type of service currently being provided (e.g., property management as opposed to brokerage) or from offering the same type of service for property not subject to other brokers' exclusive agreements. However, information received through a Multiple Listing Service or any other offer of cooperation may not be used to target clients of other REALTORS® to whom such offers to provide services may be made. (Amended 1/04)

Standard of Practice 16-4

REALTORS® shall not solicit a listing which is currently listed exclusively with another broker. However, if the listing broker, when asked by the REALTOR®, refuses to disclose the expiration date and nature of such listing; i.e., an exclusive right to sell, an exclusive agency, open listing, or other form of contractual agreement between the listing broker and the client, the REALTOR® may contact the owner to secure such information and may discuss the terms upon which the REALTOR® might take a future listing or, alternatively, may take a listing to become effective upon expiration of any existing exclusive listing. (Amended 1/94)

Standard of Practice 16-5

REALTORS® shall not solicit buyer/tenant agreements from buyers/tenants who are subject to exclusive buyer/tenant agreements. However, if asked by a REALTOR®, the broker refuses to disclose the expiration date of the exclusive buyer/tenant agreement, the REALTOR® may contact the buyer/tenant to secure such information and may discuss the terms upon which the REALTOR® might enter into a future buyer/tenant agreement or, alternatively, may enter into a buyer/tenant agreement to become effective upon the expiration of any existing exclusive buyer/tenant agreement. (Adopted 1/94, Amended 1/98)

Standard of Practice 16-6

When REALTORS® are contacted by the client of another REALTOR® regarding the creation of an exclusive relationship to provide the same type of service, and REALTORS® have not directly or indirectly initiated such discussions, they may discuss the terms upon which they might enter into a future agreement or, alternatively, may enter into an agreement which becomes effective upon expiration of any existing exclusive agreement. (Amended 1/98)

Standard of Practice 16-7

The fact that a client has retained a REALTOR® as an agent or in another exclusive relationship in one or more past transactions does not preclude other REALTORS® from seeking such former client's future business. (Amended 1/98)

Standard of Practice 16-8

The fact that an exclusive agreement has been entered into with a REALTOR® shall not preclude or inhibit any other REALTOR® from entering into a similar agreement after the expiration of the prior agreement. (Amended 1/98)

Standard of Practice 16-9

REALTORS®, prior to entering into a representation agreement, have an affirmative obligation to make reasonable efforts to determine whether the prospect is subject to a current, valid exclusive agreement to provide the same type of real estate service. (Amended 1/04)

Standard of Practice 16-10

REALTORS®, acting as buyer or tenant representatives or brokers, shall disclose that relationship to the seller/landlord's representative or broker at first contact and shall provide written confirmation of that disclosure to the seller/landlord's representative or broker not later than execution of a purchase agreement or lease. (Amended 1/04)

Standard of Practice 16-11

On unlisted property, REALTORS® acting as buyer/tenant agents or brokers shall disclose that relationship to the seller/landlord at first contact for that client and shall provide written confirmation of such disclosure to the seller/landlord not later than execution of any purchase or lease agreement.

REALTORS® shall make any request for anticipated compensation from the seller/landlord at first contact. (Amended 1/98)

Standard of Practice 16-12

REALTORS®, acting as representatives or brokers of sellers/landlords or as subagents of listing brokers, shall disclose that relationship to buyers/tenants as soon as practicable and shall provide written confirmation of such disclosure to buyers/tenants not later than execution of any purchase or lease agreement. (Amended 1/04)

Standard of Practice 16-13

All dealings concerning property exclusively listed, or with buyer/tenants who are subject to an exclusive agreement shall be carried on with the client's representative or broker, and not with the client, except with the consent of the client's representative or broker or except where such dealings are initiated by the client.

Before providing substantive services (such as writing a purchase offer or presenting a CMA) to prospects, REALTORS® shall ask prospects whether they are a party to any exclusive representation agreement. REALTORS® shall not knowingly provide substantive services concerning a prospective transaction to prospects who are parties to exclusive representation agreements, except with the consent of the prospects' exclusive representatives or at the direction of prospects. (Adopted 1/93, Amended 1/04)

Standard of Practice 16-14

REALTORS® are free to enter into contractual relationships or to negotiate with sellers/landlords, buyers/tenants or others who are not subject to an exclusive agreement but shall not knowingly obligate them to pay more than one commission except with their informed consent. (Amended 1/98)

Standard of Practice 16-15

In cooperative transactions REALTORS® shall compensate cooperating REALTORS® (principal brokers) and shall not compensate nor offer to compensate, directly or indirectly, any of the sales licensees employed by or affiliated with other REALTORS® without the prior express knowledge and consent of the cooperating broker.

Standard of Practice 16-16

REALTORS®, acting as subagents or buyer/tenant representatives or brokers, shall not use the terms of an offer to purchase/lease to attempt to modify the listing broker's offer of compensation to subagents or buyer/tenant representatives or brokers nor make the submission of an executed offer to purchase/lease contingent on the listing broker's agreement to modify the offer of compensation. (Amended 1/04)

Standard of Practice 16-17

REALTORS® acting as subagents or as buyer/tenant representatives or brokers, shall not attempt to extend a listing broker's offer of cooperation and/or compensation to other brokers without the consent of the listing broker. (Amended 1/04)

Standard of Practice 16-18

REALTORS® shall not use information obtained from listing brokers through offers to cooperate made through multiple listing services or through other offers of cooperation to refer listing brokers' clients to other brokers or to create buyer/ tenant relationships with listing brokers' clients, unless such use is authorized by listing brokers. (Amended 1/02)

Standard of Practice 16-19

Signs giving notice of property for sale, rent, lease, or exchange shall not be placed on property without consent of the seller/landlord. (Amended 1/93)

Standard of Practice 16-20

REALTORS®, prior to or after terminating their relationship with their current firm, shall not induce clients of their current firm to cancel exclusive contractual agreements between the client and that firm. This does not preclude REALTORS® (principals) from establishing agreements with their associated licensees governing assignability of exclusive agreements. (Adopted 1/98)

Article 17

In the event of contractual disputes or specific non-contractual disputes as defined in Standard of Practice 17-4 between REALTORS® (principals) associated with different firms, arising out of their relationship as REALTORS®, the REALTORS® shall submit the dispute to arbitration in accordance with the regulations of their Board or Boards rather than litigate the matter.

In the event clients of REALTORS® wish to arbitrate contractual disputes arising out of real estate transactions, REALTORS® shall arbitrate those disputes in accordance with the regulations of their Board, provided the clients agree to be bound by the decision. The obligation to participate in arbitration contemplated by this Article includes the obligation of REALTORS® (principals) to cause their firms to arbitrate and be bound by any award. (Amended 1/01)

Standard of Practice 17-1

The filing of litigation and refusal to withdraw from it by REALTORS® in an arbitrable matter constitutes a refusal to arbitrate. (Adopted 2/86)

Standard of Practice 17-2

Article 17 does not require REALTORS® to arbitrate in those circumstances when all parties to the dispute advise the Board in writing that they choose not to arbitrate before the Board. (Amended 1/93)

Standard of Practice 17-3

REALTORS®, when acting solely as principals in a real estate transaction, are not obligated to arbitrate disputes with other REALTORS® absent a specific written agreement to the contrary. (Adopted 1/96)

Standard of Practice 17-4

Specific non-contractual disputes that are subject to arbitration pursuant to Article 17 are:

1) Where a listing broker has compensated a cooperating broker and another cooperating broker subsequently claims to be the procuring cause of the sale or lease. In such cases the complainant may name the first cooperating broker as respondent and arbitration may proceed without the listing broker being named as a respondent. Alternatively, if the complaint is brought against the listing broker, the listing broker may name the first cooperating broker as a third-party respondent. In either instance the decision of the hearing panel as to procuring cause shall be conclusive with respect to all current or subsequent claims of the parties for compensation arising out of the underlying cooperative transaction. (Adopted 1/97)

2) Where a buyer or tenant representative is compensated by the seller or landlord, and not by the listing broker, and the listing broker, as a result, reduces the commission owed by the seller or landlord and, subsequent to such actions, another cooperating broker claims to be the procuring cause of sale or lease. In such cases the complainant may name the first cooperating broker as respondent and arbitration may proceed without the listing broker being named as a respondent. Alternatively, if the complaint is brought against the listing broker, the listing broker may name the first cooperating broker as a third-party respondent. In either instance the decision of the hearing panel as to procuring cause shall be conclusive with respect to all current or subsequent claims of the parties for compensation arising out of the underlying cooperative transaction. (Adopted 1/97)

3) Where a buyer or tenant representative is compensated by the buyer or tenant and, as a result, the listing broker reduces the commission owed by the seller or landlord and, subsequent to such actions, another cooperating broker claims to be the procuring cause of sale or lease. In such cases the complainant may name the first cooperating broker as respondent and arbitration may proceed without the listing broker being named as a respondent. Alternatively, if the complaint is brought against the listing broker, the listing broker may name the first cooperating broker as a third-party respondent. In either instance the decision of the hearing panel as to procuring cause shall be conclusive with respect to all current or subsequent claims of the parties for compensation arising out of the underlying cooperative transaction. (Adopted 1/97)

4) Where two or more listing brokers claim entitlement to compensation pursuant to open listings with a seller or landlord who agrees to participate in arbitration (or who requests arbitration) and who agrees to be bound by the decision. In cases where one of the listing brokers has been compensated by the seller or landlord, the other listing broker, as complainant, may name the first listing broker as respondent and arbitration may proceed between the brokers. (Adopted 1/97)

The Code of Ethics was adopted in 1913. Amended at the Annual Convention in 1924, 1928, 1950, 1951, 1952, 1955, 1956, 1961, 1962, 1974, 1982, 1986, 1987, 1989, 1990, 1991, 1992, 1993, 1994, 1995, 1996, 1997, 1998, 1999, 2000, 2001, 2002, and 2003.

Explanatory Notes

The reader should be aware of the following policies which have been approved by the Board of Directors of the National Association:

In filing a charge of an alleged violation of the Code of Ethics by a REALTOR®, the charge must read as an alleged violation of one or more Articles of the Code. Standards of Practice may be cited in support of the charge.

The Standards of Practice serve to clarify the ethical obligations imposed by the various Articles and supplement, and do not substitute for, the Case Interpretations in Interpretations of the Code of Ethics.

Modifications to existing Standards of Practice and additional new Standards of Practice are approved from time to time. Readers are cautioned to ensure that the most recent publications are utilized.

The *NAR ETHICS COURSE REQUIREMENT* is a mandatory course, taken every four years, studying the NAR Code of Ethics and Standards of Practice.

The NAR mandates that all REALTOR® members attend a training class on the Code of Ethics every four years. Failure to complete the required class results in suspension of membership until the training is completed. It is so important that NAR also requires new member applicants to complete an Ethics Orientation Class within 60 days of their application date, or face automatic denial of membership and forfeiture of application fees. In California, the required ethics class fulfills this requirement.

Remember, if you've taken an ethics course for licensing purposes, it may not apply to the NAR requirement, unless it specifically covered the NAR Code of Ethics and Standards of Practice.

D. REALTIST DEFINED

"Realtist" is the name for a member of the National Association of Real Estate Brokers (NAREB).

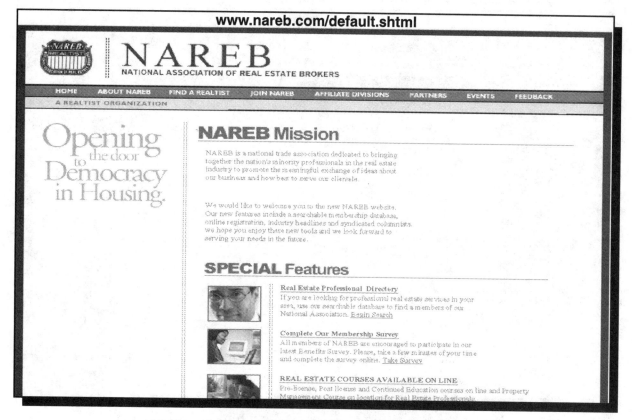

National Association of Real Estate Brokers
9831 Greenbelt Road
Lanham, Maryland 20706

The National Association of Real Estate Brokers is the oldest minority trade association in the United States. *Although composed principally of African Americans and other minority real estate professionals, the* **REALTIST** *organization is an integrated entity open to all practitioners who are committed to achieving "democracy in housing."*

The organization has local boards in the largest cities in most states. The organization in this state, called the California Association of Real Estate Brokers, has four board affiliations:

1. Associated Real Property Brokers, Oakland
2. Consolidated Real Estate Brokers, Sacramento
3. Consolidated Realty Board, Los Angeles
4. Logan Heights Realty Board, San Diego

A "Realtist" must be a member of a local board, as well as a member of the national organization. Both on the local and national levels, Realtists work for better housing in the communities they serve. In many instances, individuals are both Realtors® and Realtists by virtue of dual membership.

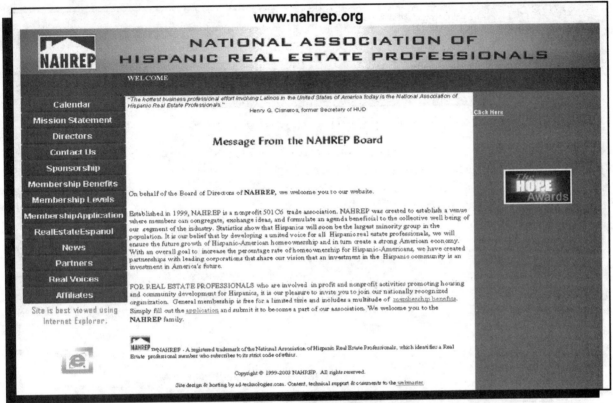

National Association of Hispanic Real Estate Professionals
1650 Hotel Circle North, Suite 215-A
San Diego, CA 92108

E. NATIONAL ASSOCIATION OF HISPANIC REAL ESTATE PROFESSIONALS (NAHREP)

The National Association of Hispanic Real Estate Professionals (NAHREP) is a national non-profit trade association made up primarily of Hispanic members. This association was created to establish a venue where members can congregate, exchange ideas, and formulate an agenda beneficial to the collective well-being of the Hispanic segment of the industry. The mission statement of NAHREP is "To increase the Hispanic homeownership rate by empowering the real estate professionals that serve Hispanic consumers."

F. ASIAN REAL ESTATE ASSOCIATION OF AMERICA (AREAA)

The Asian Real Estate Association of America is a national trade association committed to enhancing business opportunities and success of real estate professionals serving the Asian American community. AREAA is dedicated to promoting homeownership opportunities among the many Asian American communities throughout the nation.

G. INDEPENDENT ASSOCIATIONS

There are also several "independent" associations in California, some of which are large in membership and influential in their communities. Most of these boards are organized for some particular purpose, such as a multiple listing service. Many members of independent boards are also members of boards affiliated with CAR. Examples of independent boards are:

1. Chinese American Real Estate Professionals Association of Southern California
2. Chinese Real Estate Association of America
3. Korean Real Estate Brokers of Southern California
4. W.I.R.E. - Women in Real Estate

H. OTHER ASSOCIATIONS

In addition to the above-mentioned organizations, there are many trade associations and professional bodies that are related to the real estate business, such as:

1. American Bankers Association
2. American Savings and Loan Institute
3. Building Owners and Managers Association
4. Mortgage Bankers Association
5. National Association of Home Builders
6. National Association of Mutual Savings Banks
7. Prefabricated Home Manufacturers Institute

I. REAL ESTATE INSTRUCTOR AND LICENSING ASSOCIATIONS

Real estate instructor organizations and other professional bodies that are related to real estate education and licensing also play an important role in the real estate industry. See **Figure 15-11**.

J. NO AFFILIATION NECESSARY

A real estate licensee need not be a member of any trade or professional association. In this case, he or she is simply referred to as a salesperson or broker.

There is no compulsion for any licensee of the Department of Real Estate to join or affiliate with any local or state organization. That decision is strictly individual and personal.

Figure 15-11

REAL ESTATE TEACHERS' GROUPS

California Real Estate Educators Association (CREEA)

Real estate instructors from throughout the state have come together with the formation of CREEA, the California Real Estate Educators Association. This organization constitutes a chapter of REEA, the Real Estate Educators Association, a private trade association, which is international in scope. REEA has a reputation throughout the world for its comprehensive representation.

California Real Estate
Education Association
P.O. Box 1230
Costa Mesa, CA 92628
714-751-2787 Ext. 204

Real Estate Educators Association (REEA)
407 Wekiva Springs Road, Suite 241
Longwood, FL 32779
407-834-6688

 www.creea.org (CREEA)
www.reea.org (REEA)
www.ccsf.edu/Resources/Real_Estate_Education_Center/
(California Community Colleges Real Estate Education Center)
www.arello.org (Association of Real Estate License Law Officials - ARELLO)

CALIFORNIA COMMUNITY COLLEGES
REAL ESTATE EDUCATION CENTER

The California Community Colleges Real Estate Education Center is a real estate instructors group sponsored by the California Department of Real Estate. The Center publishes a quarterly newsletter and sponsors educators' conferences three times a year in cooperation with the California Community College Chancellor's office. The newsletter, called *The Informer*, is a useful reference source to keep educators up to date on new laws and real estate practices. The conferences are held in the San Francisco Bay area, the Los Angeles area, and the San Diego area. For information about *The Informer* and Endowment Fund contact:

Mario Yrun, Director
California Community Colleges
Real Estate Education Center
City College of San Francisco - Downtown Campus
800 Mission Street
San Francisco, California 94103
415-267-6550
mryun@ccsf.edu

Association of Real Estate
License Law Officials (ARELLO)
P. O. BOX 230159
Montgomery, AL 36123-0159

VII. CHAPTER SUMMARY

A person who is actively involved in a real estate transaction at the service of another, in the expectation of receiving a commission must be licensed by the **Department of Real Estate (DRE)**, which is the regulatory agency for real estate in California. The DRE is governed by the **Real Estate Commissioner**, who is appointed by the governor and defended by the state Attorney General. The Commissioner does not settle commission disputes, take the place of a court of law, nor give legal advice, but the rules and regulations he or she issues do have the force and effect of law.

To obtain a **salesperson's license**, a candidate must: be 18 or over, honest and truthful, complete college level Real Estate Principles course and pass the state exam. The salesperson exam takes 3 hours and 15 minutes, has 150 questions and requires a 70% or better to pass.

To take the salesperson's license exam as soon as possible, you can "self-certify" that you are currently taking a Principle's course, provide an **electronic fingerprint scan**, and apply to take the license exam before you have completed the course.

If you have a criminal record, you must disclose this information on your application, or you risk never getting you license.

A **conditional salesperson's license** can be obtained after taking the Real Estate Principles course. The license expires after 18 months, unless the salesperson completes the Real Estate Practice course and one other college-level (broker-required) real estate course. Once the two additional course are completed, the salesperson can apply for the (regular renewable) **four-year salesperson's license**. Applicants must apply for a license within one year from passing the exam date, at which time he or she will have to submit an electronic fingerprint scan.

A **broker's license** is required to operate a real estate office. A broker must be 18 years old, have had two years previous experience or college education, complete the required 8 broker courses, be honest and truthful, and pass the required examination. A four year degree (B.S. or B.A) = 2 years experience, and a two year degree (A.A.) = one year of experience.

The **continuing education requirement** of 45 hours every four years for a license renewal, includes three hours each of **Ethics**, **Agency**, **Trust Fund Handling**, and **Fair Housing**. After a second license renewal, these four three-hour courses can be replaced with a **six-hour CE survey course**.

California Real Estate Law is the portion of the **Business and Professions Code** that refers to licensing and subdivision. The **Commissioners' Regulations** are rules that form part of the **California Administrative Code** and are enforced by the Real Estate Commissioner. The Commissioner can revoke, restrict, or suspend the license of any real estate agent for misconduct.

All agents must adhere to **Section 10176** (acting in a licensee capacity) and **Section 10177** of the **Business and Professions Code**, which have the force and effect of the law itself.

The Real Estate General Fund provides for the **Recovery Fund**, which pays damages and arbitration awards to people due to the wrongful act of a licensee in a real estate transaction. There is a limit of $20,000 per transaction, and a total of $100,000 against an individual licensee in a lifetime.

A **Trade** or **Professional Association** is a voluntary, non-profit organization made up of independent firms in the same industry. A voluntary organization of real estate licensees in a particularly community is a **Local Association of Realtors®**. They usually provide a multiple listing service for their members.

The **California Association of Realtors® (CAR)** is the state division of the **National Association of Realtors® (NAR)**. Only active members of NAR or CAR are allowed to use the term "**Realtor®**." A realtor must swear to and abide by NAR's **Code of Ethics**, governing their behavior.

The term "**Realtists**" refers to members of the **National Association of Real Estate Brokers (NAREB)**. Although primarily African American and other minorities, all practitioners are welcome to join. Other associations include the **National Association of Hispanic Real Estate Professionals (NAHREP)** and the **Asian Real Estate Association of America (AREAA)**, as well as local and independent boards associations such as **The Chinese American Real Estate Professionals Association of Southern California** and **Women in Real Estate (W.I.R.E.)**.

Real estate instructor organizations include the **California Real Estate Educators Association (CREEA)**, the **Real Estate Educators Association (REEA)** and the **California Community Colleges Real Estate Education Center**, sponsored by the California Department of Real Estate. The **Association of Real Estate License Law Officials** is known as **(ARELLO)**.

Licensees are not required to be a member of any trade or professional association.

VIII. KEY TERMS

Asian Real Estate Association of America (AREAA)
Association of Real Estate License Law Officials (ARELLO)
Broker's License
Business
Business Opportunity and Bulk Sales
California Association of Realtors® (CAR)
Commissioner's Code of Ethics (2785)
Commissioner's Regulations
Continuing Education Requirements
Department of Real Estate (DRE)
elicensing
Local Board of Realtors®
Mortgage Loan Bulletin (DRE)
NARELLO
National Association of Hispanic Real Estate Professionals (NAHREP)
National Association of Real Estate Brokers (NAREB)
National Association of Realtors® (NAR)
NAR® Code of Ethics
Police Power
Real Estate Advisory Commission
Real Estate Bulletin (DRE)
Real Estate Law
Realtist
Realtor®
Recovery Fund
Subdivision Industry Bulletin (DRE)
Trade Association
Women in Real Estate (W.I.R.E.)

IX. CHAPTER 15 QUIZ

1. Who appoints the Real Estate Commissioner?
    a. The Governor
    b. The Legislature
    c. The Board of Governors
    d. Members of CAR

2. Who prosecutes for the Real Estate Commissioner?
    a. The Attorney General
    b. The District Attorney
    c. The Board of Governors
    d. The Real Estate Commissioner himself or herself

3. What is the minimum number of hours of Continuing Education required to renew a four-year license?
    a. 10
    b. 20
    c. 45
    d. 60

4. The broker's license examination process consists of:
    a. 200 multiple-choice question test.
    b. photo identification required for entry.
    c. two 2 1/2 hour exam periods.
    d. all of the above.

5. The Real Estate Commissioner has the right to:
    a. revoke licenses.
    b. restrict licenses.
    c. suspend licenses.
    d. all of the above.

6. The name NAHREP stands for:
    a. National Association of Happy Real Estate Professionals.
    b. National Asian Homeowners Representatives and Estate Planners.
    c. National Association of Hispanic Real Estate Professionals.
    d. none of the above.

7. What is the lifetime ceiling the Recovery Fund will pay out for one licensee?
    a. $20,000
    b. $100,000
    c. $200,000
    d. None of the above

8. To acquire a broker's license, person is NOT required to:
    a. be 18 years old.
    b. pass the exam.
    c. pass the salesperson's exam.
    d. file a set of fingerprints.

9. Every four years the National Association of Realtors® requires members to take a course covering the:
    a. Code of Ethics.
    b. NAR Commission Plan.
    c. NAR Fair Housing Guidelines.
    d. none of the above.

10. To call yourself a REALTOR®, you must:
    a. belong to NAIFA.
    b. belong to the NAR.
    c. be independent board member.
    d. be a member of ARELLO.

ANSWERS: 1. *a;* 2. *b;* 3. *c;* 4. *d;* 5. *d;* 6. *d;* 7. *b;* 8. *c;* 9. *a;* 10. *b*

Policy Manual

Hubie Real Estate

IMPORTANCE OF THE POLICY MANUAL

Please ask questions on any material you do not understand.

You are responsible for knowing everything in the policy book (and probably will remember nothing).

Everything in here is vital for group understanding, cooperation, and making money.

The terms of the relationship between the salespeople are guided by this Policy Manual.

Every real estate licensee associated with Hubie Real Estate is now, and desires to remain, an independent contractor. This manual is intended to be used as a guideline for our operation, and as a guideline to increase our incomes, compatibility, and social evolution. It is not intended that it shall be a mandatory document.

All licensees associated with Hubie Real Estate should read and acknowledge having read and understood the policy manual. It is to be available at all times for reference.

LEGAL PROBLEMS

In the event any transaction in which a salesperson is involved results in a dispute or legal expense, the salesperson shall cooperate fully with the broker. Broker and salesperson shall share all expenses connected therewith, in the same proportion as they would share the commission. It is the policy to avoid litigation wherever possible, and the broker reserves the right to determine whether or not litigation will be prosecuted, defended, or settled, and the terms of the settlement.

If at all possible, make every effort to avoid litigation! It cuts into the commission and your time!

ARBITRATION

Disputes between salespeople will be submitted to arbitration. After hearing both sides, the broker will decide the issue. The Policy Manual, common practice of the business, ethics, and the Golden Rule will be the bases of deciding the issue.

OFFICE RELATIONSHIP

Salespeople from the office should strive to show courtesy to each other.

Salespeople should keep noise at a minimum, especially when a salesperson has a client at his/her desk. No joking, laughing, or loud talking. Respect the salesperson's client. When a salesperson is talking on the telephone, respect his/her conversation and maintain sounds at a low decibel level.

We can make more *money* in a spirit of *harmony* and cooperation, than by cut-throat competition; we should always strive to show courtesy to each other.

There are to be *NO* discussions related to politics or religion. This is a big *NO! NO!*

PHONE MESSAGES

Every message taken by a salesperson for another salesperson *must* have the client's telephone number on the message. Do not take for granted that the salesperson knows the client's telephone number. All messages must be dated, timed, and signed with your name.

CODE OF ETHICS

The most important aspect of this business, and your primary concern, is to provide excellent service to our clients. Keep your focus on the effects of what *you* say and do, for if improper, it will reflect on you, the other salespeople, and your broker.

Take good care of your clients. The commissions will automatically follow!

The NAR® Code of Ethics is the basis of our business and is part of our policy.

To make it simple—just don't do to people what you wouldn't want other people to do to you.

EXPENDITURE OF OFFICE FUNDS

The office is not liable for any expenses incurred by salespeople without prior authorization of the company.

CLIENTS AND CUSTOMERS OF ALL RACES, FACTIONS, GROUPS, CULTURES, SUBCULTURES, ETC., ETC., ETC.

There will be no discrimination shown by salespeople in this office. In the event that you are a bigot (Neanderthal Flashback, Troglodyte, etc.) you shouldn't be in this office in the first place.

Regarding races, factions, etc., there are only two forms of human beings. There are *buyers*, and there are *sellers*. Each has a condition (e.g., disease) which you as the licensee must "cure" as quickly as possible. *Buyers are liars and sellers are yellers.*

When a buyer walks out of the office and you haven't written a contract, you've more than likely lost him or her.

CHANGING THE POLICY MANUAL

All changes in the office Policy Manual rules will be presented in an office bulletin, and the Policy Manual will then be changed accordingly.

Suggestions of changes are welcome.

The Policy Manual is also known as "The Big P.M."

All parties to this manual realize that it is, at best, as good an arrangement as those who participate in it! It is an effort toward an act of understanding, trust, creativity, mutual development, and finally friendship.

It is, like all things, subject to change and revision. If need be, we might once again conspire to remake these words and signatures closer to our hearts' desire.

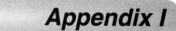

A

Abandonment. Giving up any further interest in a thing or a right.

Abatement of Nuisance. The extinction or termination of an offensive activity; such as pollution of the atmosphere.

ABC Law. Alcoholic Beverage Control Law. Regulates the sale of alcoholic beverages. Encountered in connection with escrows handling the sale of a liquor license.

Absolute Ownership. See **Fee Simple Estate**.

Abstract. A brief summary; an abridgment.

Abstract of Judgment. A summary or condensation of the essential provisions of a money judgment in a civil action. When recorded, it creates a general lien on real property of the judgment debtor in the county where the abstract is recorded.

Abstract of Title. A summary of the condition of title to real property based on an examination of public records. Includes a digest of the deeds or other transfers, encumbrances, and other instruments reflecting ownership of title or matters which may impair the title.

Abstraction. A method of valuing land. The indicated value of the improvement is deducted from the sale price.

Accelerated Cost Recovery System (ACRS). The system for figuring depreciation (cost recovery for depreciable real property acquired and placed into service after January 1, 1981 under the former federal income tax law).

Accelerated Depreciation. Allowing for a greater amount of depreciation of property in the earlier years of the life of the investment. Distinguished from Straight-line Depreciation (also see), which allows for equal amounts of depreciation each year.

Acceleration Clause. A provision in a note or deed of trust permitting the owner of the note to declare the entire unpaid balance due and payable earlier than the stated due date in the event of a default, such as failure to pay taxes or an installment when due, or in the event of the sale of the property.

Acceptance. Act indicating that the terms and provisions of a proposed contract are satisfactory and are agreed to; usually preceded by an *offer* by one contracting party, which is *accepted* by the other party. Evidences a "meeting of the minds" that is an essential element of a contract.

Access Right. The right of an owner to have ingress and egress (a means of entry and exit) to and from his or her property to a public street or way.

Accession. Acquisition of property by its incorporation or union (uniting) with other property. It may occur by the processes of **Accretion, Reliction,** or **Annexation**.

Accounts Payable. An aggregate or total of amounts *owed* to creditors; a liability.

Accounts Receivable. An aggregate or total of amounts *due* a creditor *from* his debtors; an asset.

Accretion. Increase of land on shore or bank of a river by the gradual deposit of sand or soil by natural action of the water.

Accrual Basis. Method of recording income and expenses in which each item is reported as earned or incurred without regard to when actual payments are received or made. Distinguished from **Cash Basis**.

Accrued. To be added or accumulated as a matter of periodic gain or advantage, as interest on money. Used variously, such as accrued dividends, accrued interest, or accrued depreciation.

Accrued Depreciation. The difference between the cost of replacement of a building new as of the date of a previous appraisal and the present appraised value.

Accrued Items of Expense. Those incurred expenses which are not yet payable. The seller's accrued expenses are credited to the purchaser in an escrow closing statement.

Acknowledgment. A form for authenticating instruments conveying property or otherwise conferring rights. A declaration before a notary public or other official by the party executing an instrument that it is his or her act and deed. Many instruments must be acknowledged before they are entitled to be recorded.

Acquisition. Act or process of acquiring or gaining title to or possession of property.

Acre. A measure of land equaling 160 square rods, or 4840 square yards, or 43,560 square feet. A football playing field (300 x 160 feet) contains a little more than an acre of land.

Acre Foot. A unit volume of water in irrigation; the amount covering one acre to a depth of 1 foot, equal to 43,560 cubic feet.

Action. A court proceeding to enforce a right or redress (obtain satisfaction for) a wrong.

Act of God. Any unavoidable disaster which is a the result of natural causes, rather then manmade, such as earthquakes, violent storms (cyclones or tornadoes), lightning, or flooding.

Actual Authority. Authority expressly given by the principal or given by the law and not denied by the principal.

Actual Fraud. An act meant to deceive another, such as making a promise without intending to keep it, suppressing the truth, or making a false statement.

Actual Notice. Having actual knowledge of a fact, as compared with implied or inferred notice.

Adjustable Rate Mortgage (ARM). A mortgage loan with an interest rate that is subject to change during the term of the loan.

Adjusted Cost Basis. The cost basis of property with certain additions, such as the cost of improvements, and certain subtractions, such as depreciation in value.

Adjustments. In appraising, a means by which characteristics of a residential property are reflected by dollar amount or percentage to conform to similar but not identical characteristics of another residential property.

Administrator. A person appointed by a probate court as the representative of a deceased peron's estate where the decedent left no will. A woman appointed as the representative is called the *administratrix*.

Ad Valorem. According to the value. Encountered in taxation of real property. An ad valorem tax assesses real property in relation to its value.

Advance Fee. A fee charged in advance for advertising or for preliminary expenses in connection with the sale of real estate or a business opportunity. Advance fees are regulated by statute.

Advances. Money advanced by the beneficiary under a trust deed to pay real estate taxes, hazard insurance premiums, or other items needed to protect the beneficiary's interest under the trust deed. Also refers to additional funds loaned under an open-end mortgage or trust deed.

Adverse Possession. A method of acquisition of title to property based on hostile use and occupation of another person's property for a continuous period of five years and payment of taxes.

Affidavit. A statement or declaration reduced to writing and sworn to or affirmed before some officer or official, such as a notary public, who has authority to administer an oath or affirmation.

Affidavit of Title. A written statement by a seller or grantor, made under oath and acknowledged before a Notary Public, in which seller or grantor identifies himself or herself and his or her marital status and certifies that, since the examination of title on the contract date, there are no judgments, bankruptcies, or divorces, no unrecorded deeds, contracts, unpaid repairs, or improvements, or defects of title known to sellor or grantor and that he or she is in possession of the property.

Affirm. To state or assert that a statement made is true, but without oath. Also, to confirm or ratify a judgment of a lower court by an appellate court. Also, to ratify and accept an otherwise voidable transaction.

Affirmation. The statement or assertion that something is true; similar to an affidavit, except that the person making the statement, due to religious beliefs, does not take an oath but merely affirms. Many affirmations are specificallly made under penalty of perjury.

Agency. The relationship between principal and agent, whereby the agent represents the principal in dealings with a third party.

Agent. A person who acts for another, who is called a principal.

Agreement. An expression of assent by two or more parties to the same object. The word actually ranges in meaning from a simple mutual understanding to a binding obligation, such as a formal contract.

Agreement of Sale. A written agreement or contract between a seller and purchaser of property in which they have reached a meeting of the minds on the terms and provisions of the sale.

Air Rights. The rights in real property to the reasonable use of the air space above the surface of the land.

Alien. An unnaturalized foreign resident; a foreigner; distinguished from citizen.

Alienate. To transfer or convey property to another.

Alienation. The voluntary parting with the ownership of real property; the transferring of property by the owner to another person; opposite of acquisition.

Alienation Clause. A clause in a note or trust deed permitting the payee or beneficiary to declare the entire unpaid balance immediately due and payable upon a subsequent transfer of the property. Also referred to as a *due-on-sale* clause.

All-Inclusive Deed of Trust. A trust deed that includes the amount due under another or other trust deed on the same property; also called a wraparound, or overriding deed of trust.

Allodial Tenure. A real property ownership system that can be complete ownership, except for rights held by the government. (For contrast, see *Feudal Tenure*.)

Alluvion. Soil or sand added by the process of accretion; i.e.; the gradual increase of land on the shore of a lake, sea, or ocean or on the bank of a river; also known as *alluvium*.

ALTA. American Land Title Association. the trade association of title insurance companies in the United States.

ALTA Owner's Policy. An extended policy that provides owners and buyers similar protection that lenders have with the ALTA policy.

ALTA Policy of Title Insurance. An extended coverage form of title insurance policy which extends the coverage of a standard coverage policy to include various off-record risks, such as matters disclosed by a survey, or by an inspection of the land, or by inquiry of persons in possession of the land.

Amenities. Intangible benefits in real property ownership arising from such factors as pride of ownership, desirable social or cultural environment, architectural excellence, etc.; conditions of agreeable living.

Amortization. The liquidation or payment of a principal debt or financial obligation either on an installment basis or by creating a sinking fund; also, recovery over a period of time of cost or value.

Amortized Loan. A loan to be repaid by a series of regular payments, which are equal or nearly equal, over the life of the loan.

Annexation. The addition to property by adding or attaching other property to it, such as a fixture. Also, the addition of unincorporated territory in a county to a city or town.

Annual Percentage Rate (APR). The actual cost of credit as determined under the Federal Truth in Lending Act.

Annuity. An amount of money payable yearly, or at other regular intervals, for a specified period of time.

Annul. To cancel or to make void and of no legal effect.

Anticipation, Principle of. Affirms that value is created by anticipated benefits to be derived in the future.

Appellant. The party appealing a court decision or ruling.

Appraisal. An opinion or estimate as to the fair market value of property; may be made for various purposes, such as sale, condemnation, assessment, taxation, etc.

Appraise. To estimate or render an opinion as to the value of property.

Appraiser. A person qualified by education, training, and experience to estimate the value or real or personal property.

Appropriation of Water. The taking of water flowing on the public domain from its natural course and the application of the water to some beneficial use to the appropriator.

Appurtenance. Something annexed to or made a part of another thing and transferred as an incident to it. This may be a dwelling or a garage or a barn or an orchard or other thing that becomes part of the land.

Appurtenant. Belonging to.

Architectural Style. Generally, the appearance and character of a building's design and construction.

ARM. Adjustable rate mortgage.

Articles of Incorporation. An instrument setting forth the basic rules and purposes under which a private corporation is formed.

Assess. To officially estimate the value of property as a basis for taxation.

Assessed Value. The value placed on property for the purpose of taxation.

Assessment. The valuation of property for the purpose of levying a tax; also, the amount of the tax levied. Assessments can also be imposed specially and locally upon property particularly benefited by a local work of improvement, such as sidewalks, curbs, lighting, sewers, etc.

Assessor. The official who has the responsibility for determining the assessed value of property. County tax assessors do not fix the amount of the property tax, nor do they collect the tax; these are responsibilities of other officials.

Assets. Items of ownership convertible into cash; things of value (opposed to liabilities).

Assign. To transfer one's interest in personal property, such as a contract or a leasehold estate.

Assignee. The person to whom property is assigned.

Assignment. A transfer by writing of a person's right, title, or interest in intangible property, usually of a chose in action (see **Choses**) such as a contract right.

Assignment of Rents. A usual provision in a mortgage or deed of trust that permits the lender, upon default, to collect the rents and apply them to the amount due.

Assignor. One who assigns or transfers his or her interest in property.

Assumption Agreement. Undertaking or adopting a debt or obligation primarily resting upon another person, such as the assumption by the purchaser of real property of a mortgage executed by the seller in favor of a third party lender. If the purchaser merely took *subject to* the mortgage, he or she would have no personal liability for the debt. By *assuming* the debt, he or she may become personally liable for payment.

Assumption Fee. A lender's charge for changing over and processing new records for a new owner who is assuming an existing loan.

Attachment. A seizure of property by judicial process while a court action is pending.

Attachment Lien. A lien on real property obtained prior to judgment in an action for money; obtained by levy of a writ of attachment.

Attest. To affirm or certify that a statement or document is true or genuine.

Attorney-in-Fact. An agent authorized to act for another person under a power of attorney.

Authorization to Sell. Formal name for a listing agreement under which a real estate broker is authorized to obtain a buyer for the owner's property.

Avulsion. The sudden removal of soil from an owner's property and its deposit on the property of another, as by a sudden change in the course of a river or other watercourse.

B

Backfill. The replacement of excavated earth into a hole or against a structure.

Balance. Used as a verb, this means to reconcile an account. Used as a noun, this represents the amount of loan still owed.

Balance Sheet. Statement showing assets, liabilities, and net worth as of a certain date.

Balloon Payment. The final installment payable on an installment note; it pays the note in full but is ordinarily considerably greater than the periodic installment payments called for by the note.

Bank. An institution for receiving, lending, exchanging, and safeguarding money and other things of value, and transacting other financial business. May be incorporated under state law or under federal law such as a national banking association.

Bankruptcy. A proceeding initiated under federal law whereby an insolvent debtor may obtain relief from payment of certain of his or her debts.

Bargain and Sale Deed. Any deed that recites a consideration and purports to convey the real estate.

Base and Meridian Lines. Imaginary lines used by surveyors to find and describe the location of land. A *base line* runs east and west, whereas a *meridian line* runs north and south. Their intersection forms a starting point for the measurement of land. There are three principal base and meridian lines in California, located on Mt. San Bernardino in San Bernardino County, Mt. Diablo in Contra Costa County, and Mt. Pierce in Humboldt County.

Base Price. See **Cost Basis**.

Basis. See **Cost Basis** and **Adjusted Cost Basis**.

Bearing Wall (or Partition). A wall or partition which supports a part of a building, usually a roof or floor above.

Bench Marks. A ground location indicated on a durable marker by surveyors and used to locate or describe real property.

Beneficiary. As used in a trust deed, the lender is designated as the beneficiary, i.e., the lender obtains the benefit of the security.

Beneficiary's Statement. Statement from a secured lender setting forth the unpaid principal balance and other information concerning the debt. Frequently obtained by an escrow agent during an escrow for the sale of real estate. Commonly referred to as a "Benny" statement.

Bequeath. To make a gift of *personal* property by will.

Bequest. A gift of *personal* property by will.

Betterment. An improvement upon property which increases the property's value; considered a capital asset, as distinguished from repairs or replacements where the original character or cost are unchanged.

Bid. An offer.

Bilateral Contract. A contract in which a promise is given by both parties; distinguished from a unilateral contract which calls for an act by one party in exchange for a promise by the other.

Bill of Sale. A written instrument evidencing the transfer of title to tangible personal property, such as furniture and furnishings, as distinguished from a chose in action (see **Choses**), such as contract right. The latter is transferred by an **Assignment**.

Binder. An agreement to consider a downpayment for the purchase of real estate as evidence of good faith on the part of the purchaser and binds the parties. Also, a notation of coverage on an insurance policy, issued by an agent, and given to the insured prior to the issuance of the policy.

Blanket Mortgage. A single mortgage or other encumbrance which covers more than one piece of real property; may describe "all real property" owned by the mortgagor in a designated county.

Blighted Area. A declining area in which real property values are seriously affected by destructive economic forces. May be caused by the infiltration of people from lower social and economic classes, by the rapid depreciation of the buildings, or by the inharmonious use of the property.

Blockbusting. The practice on the part of unscrupulous speculators or real estate agents of inducing panic selling of homes below market value, especially by exploiting the prejudices of property owners in neighborhoods in which the racial make-up is changing, or appears to be on the verge of changing. It is an actionable wrong.

Board of Equalization. A state or county board with the power and authority to adjust inequalities in tax assessements.

Bona Fide. In good faith; without fraud.

Bona Fide Purchaser. A person who buys property in good faith, for a fair value, and without notice of any adverse claims or rights of third parties.

Bond. A written promise of a surety, i.e., one who makes himself responsible for the faithful performance of an act by another person. Also, evidence of a debt or obligation owned by a governmental agency or other entity, such as a private corporation.

Book Value. Total cost of property minus total depreciation; the value of property as stated in a book of accounts (distinguished from market value).

Boot. In real estate exchange language, this represents cash, or something else of value, that is unlike the property in exchange. Applicable where the parcels being exchanged are not of the same value.

Boundary. Anything that indicates bounds or limits in the area or location of property.

Bounds. Boundaries. The word *bounds* is used with the word *metes* as **Metes and Bounds**, one of the principal methods for describing real property.

Breach. The violation of an obligation, or failure of duty, or the breaking of a law.

Broker. An agent who finds a buyer or seller of property for a principal on a commission basis; also may act as a loan broker in arranging loans on real property, or in other capacities. Licensed by DRE.

BTU. British thermal unit. The quantity of heat required to raise the temperature of one pound of water one degree Fahrenheit.

Building Code. A regulation of construction of buildings within a municipality established by ordinance or statute.

Building Line. Lines established by ordinance or statute, limiting how close an owner can build to the street; also referred to as setback lines (see **Setback Ordinance**).

Building, Market Value of. The amount of money a structure adds or subtracts from the value of the land it occupies. Land valued on the basis of highest and best use.

Building Restrictions. Zoning regulations or deed provisions limiting type, size and use of a building.

Built-In. Cabinets or similar features built as part of the house.

Bulk Sales Law. State law regulating the sale of business establishments, including stock in trade; enacted for the purpose of protecting the interest of creditors of the business.

Bundle of Rights. The various interests or rights that owners have in their property.

Bureau of Land Management. A federal bureau within the Department of the Interior which manages and controls certain lands owned by the United States.

Business Opportunity. As used in the Real Estate Law, refers to the sale or lease of the business and goodwill of an existing business enterprise or opportunity separate and apart from the real property.

Buyer's Market. The conditions which exist when a buyer is in a more commanding position as to the price and terms of sale, primarily because real property offered for sale is in plentiful supply compared to demand.

By-Laws. Rules governing the operation of the business and affairs of a corporation in addition to the rules set forth in its charter or articles of incorporation.

C

Cal-Vet Loan. A loan made under the California Veterans Farm and Home Purchase Program as an aid to veterans in purchasing a home or farm at low financing costs.

CCIM. Certified Commercial Investment Member.

CC&Rs. Covenants, conditions, and restrictions.

Capacity. Legal qualification for entering into a contract; being capable.

Capital. Any form of wealth, whether money or other property, employed or capable of being employed in the production of more wealth.

Capital Assets. Assets of a permanent nature used in the production of income, such as land, buildings, machinery, and equipment. Under income tax law, it is usually distinguishable from *inventory*, which comprises assets held for sale to customers in the ordinary course of trade or business.

Capital Gains. Gains on the sale of property; under the income tax law there are tax advantages in *long-term* capital gains, i.e., gains on the sale of certain property held longer than a prescribed period of time.

Capitalization. In appraising, to determine the value of property by considering net income and the percentage of reasonable return on the investment.

Capitalization Rate (Cap Rate). The rate of interest which is considered a reasonable return on the investment, and used in the process of determining value based upon net income.

CAR. California Association of Realtors®.

Cash Basis. Method of recording income and expenses in which each item is entered as received or paid. Distinguished from **Accrual Basis**.

Cash Flow. The measure of cash generated from income and depreciation after debt-servicing expenses.

Cause of Action. The basis for bringing a lawsuit; a ground for legal action; the matter over which a person goes to court. The party filing an action is the **Plaintiff**, who sets forth his or her cause of action in a pleading called a complaint.

Caveat Emptor. "Let the buyer beware." Usually, when a buyer examines the goods or property sold, he buys at his or her own risk, in the absence of misrepresentations.

Certificate of Eligibility. Certificate issued by the government evidencing an individual's eligibility to obtain a Veterans Administration (VA) loan.

Certificate of Reasonable Value. Certificate which informs a veteran under VA loan of the appraised value of the property and the maximum VA guaranteed loan a private lender may make.

Certificate of Sale. A certificate issued to the purchaser at a judicial sale, such as an execution sale. After the time for redemption has expired, the holder of the certificate is entitled to a deed.

Certificate of Taxes Due. A written statement in the form of a guaranty of the condition of the taxes on a particular property made by the County Treasurer of the County where the property is located.

Certificate of Title. A certification as to the ownership of land and the condition of title, based on an examination of the public records.

Chain. A unit of measurement used by surveyors. A chain consists of 100 links equal to 66 feet.

Chain of Title. A chronological list of recorded instruments affecting the title to land, commencing with the document under which title was transferred from the government to private ownership, and ending with the latest document transferring title. In order to have marketable title, there must be an unbroken chain of title.

Change, Principle of. Holds that it is the future, not the past, which is of prime importance in estimating value. Change is largely the result of cause and effect.

Chattel. Personal property.

Chattel Mortgage. A mortgage of personal property to secure payment of a debt. Since the adoption of the Uniform Commercial Code, chattel mortgages are referred to as Personal Property Security Agreements.

Chattel Real. An interest in real estate less than a freehold, such as an estate for years.

Circuit Breaker. (1) An electrical device which automatically interrupts an electrical circuit when an overload occurs; may be used instead of a fuse to protect each circuit and can be reset. (2) In property taxation, a method for granting property tax relief to the elderly and disadvantaged qualified taxpayers by rebate, tax credits, or cash payments. Usually limited to homeowners and renters.

Civil Action. A court action involving the civil law and private rights of parties, rather than the criminal law.

Civil Law. A body of law that is derived from the Roman system of law, rather than the common law of England. Often called **Statutory Law** in this country.

Civil Rights. Basic rights of freedom and liberty guaranteed to United States citizens by the 13th and 14th Amendments to the Federal Constitution and by later federal laws.

Closing. (1) Process by which all the parties to a real estate transaction conclude the datails of a sale or mortgage. The process includes the signing and transfer of documents and distribution of funds. (2) Condition in description of real property by courses and distances at the boundary lines where the lines meet to include all the tract of land.

Closing Costs. The numerous expenses buyers and sellers normally incur in the transfer of ownership of real property.

Closing Statement. Statement furnished by an escrow holder to the principals at the time of closing an escrow, setting forth the charges and costs.

Cloud on Title. Any conditions revealed by a search of title, such as an ancient pipeline easement, which affect the marketability of title to property. Although sometimes seemingly unimportant, there may be a need to remove them by either a quitclaim deed or a court decree.

CLTA. California Land Title Association, the trade association of title insurance companies in California.

Code. A system of law. In California most of the statutes have been codified in a series of codes, such as the Civil Code and the Business and Professions Code.

Code of Ethics. A set of rules and principles expressing a standard of accepted conduct for members of a professional group.

Collateral. Something additional, such as *collateral security*, i.e., a separate obligation attached to a contract to guarantee its performance. Also, the property subject to the security interest. Also, in estate matters, collateral means descended from the same stock but in different line, i.e., not lineal. For example, a cousin is a collateral relative.

Collateral Loan. A loan secured by collateral, i.e., something of value to give greater assurance of payment.

Collateral Security. A separate obligation attached to a contract to guarantee its performance; the transfer of something of value to insure the performance of a principal agreement.

Collusion. An agreement between two or more persons to defraud another of his or her rights by going through the forms of the law, or to obtain an object that is forbidden by law, such as obtaining the property of a client by devious means.

Color of Title. That which gives the appearance of good title but is not title, in fact, because of some defect, such as an erroneous or insufficient legal description.

Commercial Acre. A term applied to the remainder of an acre of subdivided land after the area devoted to streets, sidewalks, curbs, etc., has been deducted from the acre.

Commercial Loan. A personal loan from a commercial bank, usually unsecured and for a short term, for other than mortgage purposes.

Commercial Paper. Drafts, notes, and bills of exchange used in commercial transactions.

Commingling. Unauthorized mixing of funds of a customer or client with one's own personal funds.

Commission. An agent's compensation for performing the duties of his agency. In real estate practice, commission represents a percentage of the selling price of the property, such as 6 percent, or a percentage of rentals collected, etc.

Commissioner. The legislature has created various commissioners, such as the Real Estate Commissioner and the Corporations Commissioner, to carry out the responsibilities of various state agencies, including the enforcement of the law.

Commitment. A pledge or a promise or firm agreement to perform an act, such as commitment to make a loan.

Common Area. An entire common interest subdivision except the separate interests therein.

Common Interest Subdivision. Subdivided lands which include a separate interest in real property combined with an interest in common with other owners. The interest in common may be through membership in an association. Examples: condominiums and stock cooperatives.

Common Law. Body of unwritten law, founded upon general custom, usage, or common consent, that developed in England "since the memory of man runneth not to the contrary." Prevails in England and most of the United States. Sometimes referred to as **Case Law** in this country.

Common Stock. That class of corporate stock to which there is ordinarily attached no preference with respect to the receipt of dividends or the distribution of assets upon corporate dissolution.

Community Property. Property acquired by husband or wife or both during marriage when not acquired as separate property. Basically, property of a married person in California is either separate property or community property.

Compaction. Whenever extra soil is added to a lot to fill in low places or to raise the level of the lot, the added soil is often too loose and soft to sustain the weight of improvements. Accordingly, it is necessary to *compact* the added soil by pounding it with appropriate tools so that it will carry the added weight of buildings without the danger of their tilting, settling or cracking.

Comparable Sales. Sales which have similar characteristics as the subject property and are used for analysis in the appraisal process. Commonly called *comparables*, they are recent selling prices of properties similarly situated in a similar market.

Comparison Approach. A real estate comparison method which compares a given property with similar or comparable surrounding properties to determine value.

Competent. Legally qualified.

Competition, Principle of. Holds that profits tend to breed competition, and excess profits tend to breed ruinous competition. Component—One of the features making up the whole property.

Compound Interest. Interest paid on original principal and also on the accrued and unpaid interest which has accumulated.

Conclusion. The final estimate of value, realized from facts, data, experience, and judgment, set out in an appraisal. Appraiser's certified conclusion.

Condemnation. The exercise of the power of eminent domain, i.e., the taking of property for a public use upon payment of just compensation; also refers to condemnation of unsafe structures under the government's police power.

Condition. A qualification annexed to an estate upon the happening of which the estate is enlarged or defeated. It may be a *condition precedent*, which is a condition which must be fulfilled before an estate can vest. Or it may be a *condition subsequent*, which is a condition by the failure or nonperformance of which an estate already vested may be defeated.

Conditional. Not absolute, depending on a condition; made or allowed on certain terms.

Conditional Commitment. A commitment by an FHA lender of a definite loan amount on a specified property for some unknown purchaser of satisfactory credit standing.

Conditional Sales Contract. A contract for the sale of property where title remains in the seller until the conditions of the contract have been performed by the buyer.

Conditional Use Permit. Permitting a use of a parcel of property in contravention of zoning upon a finding that the permitted use is essential or desirable to the public convenience or welfare and is in harmony with the objectives of the master plan. Various conditions are imposed in granting such use permit.

Condominium. Ownership of a divided interest; i.e., an individually owned unit, in a multifamily or other structure, combined with joint ownership of the structure and the land. Sometimes referred to as a "horizontal" subdivision; involves both a vertical and a horizontal division.

Confirmation of Sale. Court approval of the sale of property by an executor, administrator, guardian, or conservator.

Conformity, Principle of. Holds that the maximum of value is realized when a reasonable degree of homogeneity of improvement is present.

Consent. To permit, approve, or agree.

Conservation. The process of utilizing resources in such a manner which minimizes their depletion.

Conservator. A person appointed by the probate court to take care of the person or property of an adult person needing such care. Similar to a guardian.

Consideration. The inducement for entering into a contract; it consists of either a benefit to the promisor, or a loss or detriment to the promisee. Anything of value given to induce entering into a contract. It may be money, personal services, or, in some cases, even love and affection.

Construction Loans. Loans, usually short term, made by a lender for the purpose of constructing homes or commercial buildings; funds are disbursed by the lender in stages after periodic inspections.

Constructive Notice. Notice given by the public records of a claim of ownership or interest in property. Generally, the law presumes that a person has the same knowledge of instruments properly recorded as if he or she were actually acquainted with them. The word constructive is frequently encountered in real estate. For instance, *constructive eviction* is applicable in the landlord-tenant relationship. *Constructive possession* may be involved in a claim of title based on adverse possession. And in the field of trusts, the courts may establish a *constructive trust* in property. **Fraud** also may be constructive or actual.

Consumer Goods. Goods used or bought for use primarily for personal, family, or household purposes. The term is used in the Commercial Code in connection with personal-property security agreements.

Contiguous. Adjoining or touching upon, such as contiguous parcels of land.

Contingent. Dependent upon an uncertain future event.

Constant. The percentage which, when applied directly to the face value of a debt, develops the annual amount of money necessary to pay a specified net rate of interest on the reducing balance and to liquidate the debt in a specified time period. For example, a 6% loan with a 20-year amortization has a constant of approximately 8.5%. Thus, a $10,000 loan amortized over 20 years requires an annual payment of approximately $850.00.

Constructive Fraud. A breach of duty, as by a person in a fiduciary capacity, without an actual fraudulent intent, which gains an advantage to the person at fault by misleading another to the other's prejudice. Any act of omission declared by law to be fraudulent, without respect to actual fraud.

Contract. An agreement by which a person undertakes or promises to do, or not to do, a certain thing. Must be supported by **Consideration** to be enforceable.

Contribution, Principle of. A component part of a property is valued in proportion to its contribution to the value of the whole. Holds that maximum values are achieved when the improvements on a site produce the highest (net) return, commensurate with the investment.

Conventional Loan. A mortgage loan which is not insured or guaranteed by a governmental agency, such as the FHA or VA.

Conversion. Change from one character or use to another. Also, the unauthorized appropriation by a person of property belonging to another.

Conveyance. A written instrument transferring the title to land or an interest therein from one person to another.

Co-op. Community apartment projects owned as "stock cooperatives," where individual owners each acquire a share of stock in the corporation which owns the title, with each person owning the exclusive right to occupy a particular apartment.

Corner Influence. The increase in value of a corner lot due to its location.

Corporation. An artificial being, created by law, and possessing certain rights, privileges, and duties of natural persons. A corporation may acquire title to real property in its corporate name.

Corporation Sole. A corporation consisting of one person only and his successors in office, and incorporated by law in order to give some legal capacity not otherwise owned, such as ownership of property in perpetuity. An example is the Roman Catholic Archbishop of Los Angeles, who may acquire title to real property on behalf of the church in his name as a corporation sole.

Correction Lines. A system for compensating inaccuracies in the Government Rectangular Survey System due to the curvature of the earth.

Correlation. A step in the appraisal process involving the interpretation of data derived from the three approaches to value, leading to a single determination of value. Also referred to as "reconciliation."

Correspondent. An abbreviated term meaning mortgage loan correspondent. A mortgage banker who services mortgage loans as agent for the owner of the mortgage or investor. Also applied to the mortgage banker in his or her role as originator of mortgage loans for the investor.

Co-signer. A second party who signs a promissory note together with the promissory obligor (borrower).

Cost Approach. One of three methods in the appraisal process. An analysis in which a value estimate of a property is derived by estimating the replacement cost of the improvements., deducting therefrom the estimated accrued depreciation, then adding the market value of the land.

Cost Basis. A property value determined at the time of acquisition. The amount is dependent upon the method of acquisition, and subsequently serves as a base figure in determining profit or loss for income tax purposes.

Cost, New. Represents the present construction costs of a new building, including labor, material, and other expenditures.

County. A political division of the state. There are 58 counties in California, each with a county recorder, tax collector, courthouse, and many other offices.

Covenants. Agreements contained in deeds and other instruments for the performance or nonperformance of certain acts, or the use or nonuse of property in a certain manner. Basically, a covenant is a promise to do or not do a certain thing.

CPM. Certified property manager. A member of the Institute of Real Property Management of the NAR®.

Crawl Hole. Exterior or interior opening permitting access underneath a building, ordinarily required by building codes.

CRE. Counselor of Real Estate. Member of American Society of Real Estate Counselors.

Credit. A bookkeeping entry on the right side of an account, recording the reduction or elimination of an asset or an expense, or the creation of or addition to a liability or item of equity or revenue.

Creditor. A person to whom a debt is owed. Any person extending credit to another person.

CREEA. California Real Estate Educators Association.

CRV. Certificate of reasonable value, used in connection with GI loans.

Cul-de-sac. A street, lane, or road closed at one end; a blind alley.

Curable Depreciation. Items of physical deterioration and functional obsolescence which are customarily repaired or replaced by a prudent property owner.

Current Index. With regard to an adjustable rate mortgage (ARM), the current value of a recognized index as calculated and published nationally or regionally. The current index value changes periodically and is used in calculating the new note rate as of each rate adjustment date.

Custodial Accounts. Bank accounts used for deposits of funds belonging to others.

Cyclical Movement. The sequential and recurring changes in economic activity of a business cycle, moving from prosperity through recession, depression, recovery, and back again to prosperity.

D

Damages. The amount recoverable by a victim of the wrongful or negligent act of another.

Data Plant. An appraiser's file of information on real estate.

DBA. "Doing business as." Applicable where a person engages in business under a fictitious name, such as "John Smith, doing business as the Acme Building Company."

Debenture. Bonds issued without security; an obligation not secured by a specific lien on property

Debit. A bookkeeping entry on the left side of an account; opposite of credit.

Debt. That which is due from one person to another; obligation; liability.

Debtor. A party owing money to another. Under the Uniform Commercial Code the debtor is the party who "owns" the property subject to a security agreement, where previously this person was referred to as the mortgagor or pledgor.

Declaration of Homestead. The document which is recorded in order to obtain an exemption from forced sale of a person's home in satisfaction of certain types of creditors' claims

Declining Balance Depreciation. A method of accelerated depreciation allowed by the IRS in certain circumstances. *Double Declining Balance Depreciation* is its most common form and is computed by using double the rate used for straight-line depreciation.

Decree of Distribution. An order of the probate court by which property of a decedent is distributed to his heirs or devisees.

Decree of Foreclosure. Decree by a court ordering the sale of mortgaged property and the payment of the debt owing to the lender out of the proceeds.

Dedication. A setting apart or donation of land by its owner for a public use. The dedication may be of the fee, perhaps for a park, or of an easement, such as a roadway.

Deed. Writen instrument by which the ownership of real property is transferred from one person to another.

Deed in Lieu of Foreclosure. A deed to real property accepted by a lender from a defaulting borrower to avoid the necessity of foreclosure proceedings by the lender.

Deed of Trust. Written instrument by which title to real property is transferred to a third party trustee as security for a debt or other obligation owed to another person. Used in place of mortgages in many states, including California. Also called *trust deed*.

Deed Restrictions. See **Restriction**.

Default. Failure to fulfill a duty or promise or to discharge an obligation; the omission or failure to perform any act.

Default Judgment. A judgment entered against a party who fails to make an appearance in the action.

Defeasance Clause. The clause in a mortgage that gives the mortgagor the right to redeem mortgagor's property upon the payment of mortgagor's obligations to the mortgagee.

Defeasance Fee. Sometimes called a base fee or qualified fee. A fee simple absolute interest in land that is capable of being defeated or terminated upon the happening of a specified event.

Defendant. The party against whom a court action is brought.

Deferred Maintenance. Existing but unfulfilled requirements for repairs and rehabilitation of property.

Deferred Payment Options. The privilege of deferring income payments to take advantage of statutes affording tax benefits.

Deficiency Judgment. A personal judgment in a lien foreclosure action for the amount of the debt still remaining due after a sale of the security.

Delegation of Powers. The conferring by an agent upon another of all or certain of the powers that have been conferred upon the agent by the principal.

Delivery. Giving possession of a document, such as a deed, by one party (the *grantor*) to the other (the *grantee*) with the intent to convey title.

Deposit Receipt. Document used when accepting "earnest money" to bind an offer for property by a prospective purchaser; when properly filled out and executed by both parties, it may result in a binding contract. In California, more commonly referred to as a **Purchase Contract** by real estate professionals.

Depreciation. Loss of value in real property brought about by age, physical deterioration, functional or economic obsolescence, or any other cause.

Depth Table. A statistical table that may be used to estimate the value of the added depth of a lot.

Desist and Refrain Order. An order, which the Real Estate Commissioner is empowered by law to issue, directing a person to desist and refrain from committing acts in violation of the Real Estate Law.

Deterioration. Impairment of the condition or utility of property, brought about by wear and tear, disintegration, use in service, or the action of the elements. One of the causes of depreciation and reflecting loss in value.

Determinable Fee. An estate which will end on the happening of an event, which may or may not occur.

Devise. A gift of real property by will.

Devisee. One who receives real property by will.

Devisor. One who disposes of real property by will.

Directional Growth. The location or direction toward which the residental sections of a city are destined, or determined, to go.

Disclosure Statement. Statement required under the federal Truth in Lending Act which sets forth the details of a loan transaction, including all finance charges.

Discount. To sell at a reduced price; to purchase or sell a note before maturity at a reduction based on the interest for the time it still has to run, or for market reasons.

Discount Points. The amount of money the borrower or seller must pay the lender to get a mortgage at a stated rate. This amount is equal to the difference between the principal balance on the note and the lesser amount which a purchaser of the note would pay the original lender for it under market conditions. A point equals one percent of the loan.

Divided Interest. Ownership of a particular piece or portion of a larger parcel of real property, such as a condominium; distinguished from an *undivided* interest.

Dividend. A sum of money paid to shareholders of a corporation out of earnings; also, anything received as a bonus or reward. In mathematics, the number divided by the *divisor*.

Document. An original or official paper relied upon as the basis, proof, or support of anything else. A more comprehensive word than *instrument*.

Documentary Transfer Tax. Counties are authorized to impose a documentary transfer tax to apply on transfers of real property located in the county; collected at the time of recording the document.

Dominant Tenement. The tenement (property) obtaining the benefit of an appurtenant easement.

Donee. A person to whom a gift is made.

Donor. A person who makes a gift to another.

Dual Agency. An agency relationship in which one agent acts concurrently for both of the principals in a transaction.

Due-on-Sale Clause. An acceleration clause granting the lender the right to demand full payment of the mortgage or trust deed upon a sale of the property, also called an **Alienation Clause**.

Duress. Unlawful constraint or coercion, such as a threat of bodily harm, exercised upon a person whereby he or she is persuaded to do some act against his or her will. Renders invalid a contract or other act entered into or performed under its influence.

DVA. Department of Veterans Affairs. The state agency that administers the California Veterans Farm and Home Purchase Program (*Cal-Vet* loans).

E

Earnest Money. Something given as a part of the purchase price to bind a bargain.

Easement. A right, privilege or interest in the land of another existing apart from the ownership of the land, such as a right of way (a right to cross over another person's property). (See **Prescriptive Easement**.)

Easement by Implication. An easement that is implied or inferred from conduct or circumstances rather than being expressed.

Economic Life. The period during which a property will yield a sufficient return on the investment to justify maintaining it.

Economic Obsolescence. A loss in value due to factors not part of the subject property but adversely affecting the value of the subject property.

Economic Rent. The reasonable rental expectancy if the property were available for renting at the time of its valuation.

Effective Age of Improvement. The number of years of age that is indicated by the condition of the structure. Distinct form *Chronological Age*.

Effective Date of Value. The specific day the conclusion of value applies.

Effective Interest Rate. The percentage of interest that is actually being paid by the borrower for the use of the money. Distinct from *Nominal Interest*.

Egress. A means, or place, of going out.

Emblements. Crops produced annually, by labor and industry, as distinguished from crops that grow naturally on the land.

Eminent Domain. The power of the government to take property for a public purpose upon payment of just compensation.

Encroachment. The extension of an improvement or branch of a tree or other vegetation onto the property of another person.

Encumbrance. A lien or charge or burden on land (also spelled *incumbrance*).

Endorsement. A writing on a negotiable instrument, such as a note, by which the instrument is transferred. Also, a provision or rider added to an insurance policy to alter or enlarge the terms of the insurance contract. (Sometimes spelled *indorsement*.)

Enjoin. To prohibit or restrain by an injunction.

Equitable Title. Title of the purchaser under a contract of sale.

Equity. Value of an owner's interest in property in excess of mortgages and other liens. Also, a system of jurisprudence or a body of doctrines and rules developed in England and followed in the United States which series to supplement and remedy the limitations or inflexibility of the common law.

Equity Buildup. The increase of an owner's equity in property due to mortgage principal reduction and to value appreciation.

Equity of Redemption. The right which the mortgagor has of redeeming his or her property for a limited period of time after a foreclosure sale.

Equity Participation. A mortgage transaction in which the lender, in addition to receiving a fixed rate of interest on the loan, acquires an interest in the borrower's real property, and shares in the profits derived from the real property.

Erosion. The gradual wearing away of land by the action of the elements, such as tidal water or winds.

Escalator Clause. A clause in a contract providing for the upward or downward adjustment of specified items, such as interest or rent, to cover certain contingencies, such as higher or lower costs of living.

Escheat. Reverting of property to the state of California when an owner dies without a will and without heirs.

Ecrow. The deposit of a deed or other instrument with a third party for delivery upon performance of a condition. Also, the transaction in which a third party acts as the agent for the buyer and seller or borrower and lender in carrying out the instructions of the parties and handling and disbursing the papers and funds. *Sales escrow* is one relating to the sale of a parcel of property, as distinguished from a loan or an exchange escrow.

Escrow Holder (Agent). The party who acts as the agent for the principals in an escrow transaction.

Estate. The degree, quantity, nature, and extent of the interest a person has in real estate, such as a fee or a life estate or lesser estate. Also refers to the property left by a decedent that is subject to probate administration, or the property of a bankrupt.

Estate at Sufferance. An estate arising when a tenant wrongfully holds over after the expiration of the term. The landlord has the choice of evicting the tenant (through court action) or accepting the tenant on the same terms and conditions of the previous occupancy.

Estate at Will. Occupation of lands and tenements by a tenant for an indefinite period of time; terminable by either party at any time on proper notice.

Estate for Life. An estate that continues for the duration of a person's natural life.

Estate for Years. An estate that continues for a specified period of time; usually created by a lease.

Estate from Period-to-Period. An interest in land where there is no definite termination date but the rental period is fixed at a certain sum per week, month, or year. Also called a **Periodic Tenancy**.

Estate of Inheritance. An estate which may descend to heirs, such as a fee estate.

Estimate. A preliminary opinion of value. Appraise, set a value.

Estimated Remaining Life. The period of time (usually years) it takes for the improvements to become valueless.

Estoppel. A doctrine which bars a person from asserting rights inconsistent with a previous position or representation.

Ethics. That branch of moral science, idealism, justness, and fairness concerned with the duties which a member of a profession or craft owes to the public, to his or her clients or patrons, and to fellow members of his or her profession or craft.

Eviction. Dispossession of a defaulting tenant or other person wrongfully in possession of property by bringing a court action.

Exception. In a deed, some part of a thing granted which is excluded from the conveyance and remains with the grantor. In zoning, it refers to an instance or case not conforming to the general rule.

Exchange. To transfer property for other property of equivalent value; to trade one parcel of property for another.

Exclusive Agency Listing. A written instrument giving one agent the right to sell property for a specified period of time but reserving the right of the owner to sell the property without payment of a commission.

Exclusive Right to Sell Listing. A written agreement between owner and agent giving the agent the right to collect a commission if the property is sold by anyone, including the owner, during the term of the agreement.

Execute. To sign a deed, or to perform or carry out a contract; to give effect or force to a law or decree of a court.

Executed. As used in contract law, this relates to a contract that has been fully performed.

Execution Sale. A sale of a judgment debtor's property by the sheriff to satisfy the judgment.

Executor. A person who is designated in a will as the representative of the decedent's estate.

Executory. As used in contract law, this relates to a contract that is yet to be performed.

Executrix. Feminine of executor.

Exemption. An immunity from some burden or obligation.

Expenses. Certain items which appear on a closing statement in connection with a real estate sale, chargeable to either buyer or seller.

Expressed. Something definitely stated rather than implied.

Extension Agreement. A grant of further time within which to pay an obligation.

F

Facade. Front of a building.

Fair Market Value. The highest price estimated in terms of money which a parcel of property will bring on the open market where neither buyer nor seller is under any compulsion to act.

False Pretenses. A deliberate misrepresentation of facts as a means of obtaining money or title to property.

Fannie Mae. See **Federal National Mortgage Association (FNMA)**.

Farmers Home Administration (FmHA). An agency of the Department of Agriculture. Primary responsibility is to provide financial assistance for farmers and others living in rural areas where financing is not available on reasonable terms from private sources.

Federal Deposit Insurance Corporation (FDIC). Agency of the federal government which insures deposits at commercial banks and savings banks.

Federal Home Loan Mortgage Coprporation (FHLMC) "Freddie Mac". An independent stock company which creates a secondary market in conventional residential loans and in FHA and VA loans by purchasing mortgages.

Federal Housing Administration. See **FHA**.

Federal Land Bank System. Federal government agency making long-term loans to farmers.

Federal National Mortgage Association (FNMA). Known as "Fannie Mae," a quasi-public agency converted into a private corporation whose primary function is to buy and sell FHA and VA mortgages in the secondary market.

Federal Reserve System. The federal banking system of the United States under the control of a central board of governors (*Federal Reserve Board*) involving a central bank in each of twelve geographical districts with broad powers in controlling credit and the amount of money in circulation.

Fee. A charge for services, such as attorney's fees. See also **Fee Estate**.

Fee Estate. An estate of inheritance in real property, often referred to as a *fee simple*.

Fee Simple Absolute. The highest type of estate or interest a person may have in property. In modern usage, it expressly establishes the title to real property in the owner, without limitation or end. The owner may dispose of it by sale or trade or will as he or she chooses.

Fee Simple Defeasible. A fee estate that is subject to a qualification, condition, or limitation.

Fee Title. Ownership of a fee estate.

Feudal Tenure. A real property ownership system in which ownership rests with a sovereign who may grant lesser interests in return for service or loyalty. Contrast *Allodial Tenure*.

FHA. Federal Housing Administration. A federal agency, created by the National Housing Act of 1934, for the purpose of expanding and strengthening home ownership by making private mortgage financing possible on a longterm, low-down-payment basis. The vehicle is a mortgage insurance program, with premiums paid by the homeowner to protect lenders against loss of these higher-risk loans. Since 1965, FHA has been part of the Department of Housing and Urban Development (HUD).

FHA Insurance. An undertaking by FHA to insure the lender against loss arising from a default by borrower.

Fictitious Name. An assumed name; a name used for business which does not include the actual name of the owner, such as "Ace Lumber Company."

Fidelity Bond. A security posted for the discharge of an obligation of personal responsibility.

Fiduciary. One who holds a thing in trust for another person, or who acts in a trust capacity, such as an escrow holder.

Fiduciary Duty. That duty owed by an agent to act in the highest good faith toward the principal and not to obtain any advantage over the latter by the slightest misrepresentation, concealment, duress, or pressure.

Financial Intermediary. Financial institutions such as commercial banks, savings banks, mutual savings banks, and life insurance companies which receive relatively small sums of money from the public and invest them in the form of large sums. A considerable portion of these funds are loaned on real estate.

Financing Process. The systematic five-step procedure followed by major institutional lenders in analyzing a proposed loan, which includes filing of application by a borrower, lender's analysis of borrower and property, processing of loan documentation, making the loan, and servicing (collection and record keeping).

Financing Statement. Evidence of a personal property security agreement that is filed or recorded to give public notice. Has replaced the term *chattel mortgage* (see **Security Agreement**).

First Mortgage. A legal document pledging collateral for a loan (See **Mortgage**) that has first priority over all other claims against the property except taxes and bonded indebtedness. A mortgage superior to any other.

First Trust Deed. A legal document pledging collateral for a loan (See **Trust Deed**) that has first priority over all other claims against the property, except taxes and bonded indebtedness. A trust deed superior to any other.

Fiscal Controls. Federal tax revenue and expenditure policies used to control the level of economic activity.

Fiscal Year. A business or accounting year as distinguished from a calendar year.

Fixity of Location. The physical characteristic of real estate that subjects it to the influence of its surroundings.

Fixture. A thing that was originally personal property but that has become attached to and is considered as part of the real property.

Flat Rental. Form of lease that provides a level or fixed amount of rent, as opposed to a variable amount.

FNMA. Federal National Mortgage Association . Popularly known as *Fannie Mae*.

Foreclosure. A proceeding to enforce a lien by a sale of the property in order to satisfy the debt.

Forfeiture. A loss of some right, title, estate, or interest in consequence of a default or failure to perform. Not readily enforceable, since the courts abhor a forfeiture. Liquidated damage clauses frequently have replaced forfeiture clauses in contracts of sale.

Franchise. A right or privilege conferred by law to carry on a business activity in a specified area, such as a franchise for a street railway; also, the permission granted by a manufacturer to a distributor or retailer to sell or service the manufacturer's product in a particular area or locale.

Fraud. The intentional and successful employment of any cunning, deception, collusion, or artifice, used to circumvent, cheat or deceive another person whereby that person acts upon it to the loss of property and to legal injury. (**Actual Fraud:** A deliberate misrepresentation or representation made in reckless disregard of its truth or its falsity, the suppression of truth, a promise made without the intention to perform it, or any other act intended to deceive.)

"Freddie Mac". See Federal Home Loan Mortgage Corporation (FHLMC).

Freehold. An estate of inheritance or for life.

Frontage. A term used to describe or identify that part of a parcel of land or an improvement on the land which faces a street. The term is also used to refer to the lineal extent of the land or improvement that is parallel to and facing the street, e.g., a 75-foot frontage.

Front Foot. A method of property measurement for purposes of sale or valuation, usually of commercial property. The property is measured by the front foot on its street line or boundary and valued at so much a front foot.

Front Money. The minimum amount of money necessary to initiate a real estate venture, to get the transaction underway.

Full Reconveyance. A release of all the property covered by a deed of trust.

Full Release. A complete release of liability under a contract or other obligation.

Fully Indexed Note Rate. As related to adjustable rate mortgages, the index value at the time of application plus the gross margin stated in the note.

Functional Obsolescence. Loss of value of a structure due to adverse factors from within it which affect its utility, such as old age, poor design, or faulty equipment.

Future Benefits. The anticipated benefits the present owner will receive from the property in the future.

G

Gain. A profit, benefit, or value increase.

Garnishment. A statutory proceeding whereby property, money, or credits of a debtor in possession of another are seized and applied to payment of the debt.

General Lien. A lien on all the property of a debtor.

General Plan Restrictions. Restrictions on the use of property imposed for the benefit of more than one parcel of property, usually a tract containing many lots.

GI Loan. Loans available to veterans of the armed services under a federal government program administered by the Veterans Administration.

Gift Deed. A deed where there is no material consideration; often given in consideration of "love and affection," especially between relatives.

GNMA. Government National Mortgage Association. Popularly known (for its initials) as Ginnie Mae. An agency of HUD, which functions in the secondary mortgage market, primarily in special housing programs.

Goodwill. An intangible, salable asset arising from the reputation of a business and its relations with its customers, distinct from the value of its stock in trade and other tangibles.

Government Survey. A method of specifying the location of parcels of land using prime meridians, base lines, standard parallels, guide meridians, townships and sections.

Grade. Ground level at the foundation of a building.

Graduated Lease. A lease which provides for a varying rental rate, often based upon future determination, such as periodical appraisals; used mostly in long-term leases.

Graduated Payment Mortgage. Provides for partially deferred payments of principal at start of loan. There are a variety of plans; usually after the first five years of the loan term the principal and interest payments are substantially higher, to make up the principal portion of payments lost at the beginning of the loan. (See **Variable Interest Rate.**)

Grant. A transfer of real property by deed.

Grant Deed. A form of deed used in the transfer of real property; distinguished from a quitclaim deed.

Grantee. The person to whom a grant is made.

Grantor. The person who makes a grant.

Gratuitous Agent. A person not paid by the principal for services on behalf of the principal, who cannot be forced to act as an agent, but who becomes bound to act in good faith and obey a principal's instructions once he or she undertakes to act as an agent.

GRI. Graduate, Realtors® Institute.

Gross Income. Total income from property before any expenses are deducted.

Gross Margin. With regard to an adjustable rate mortgage, an amount expressed as percentage points, stated in the note which is added to the current index value on the rate adjustment date to establish the new note rate.

Gross National Product (GNP). The total value of all goods and services produced in an economy during a given period of time.

Gross Profit. What is left after a business pays all its bills excluding taxes. See **Net Profit.**

Gross Rate. A method of collecting interest by adding total interest to the principal of the loan at the outset of the term.

Gross Rent Multiplier. A number which, times the gross income of a property, produces an estimate of value of the property. Example: The gross income from an unfurnished apartment building is $200,000 per annum. If an appraiser uses a gross multiplier of seven percent, then it is said that based on the gross multiplier the value of the building is $1,400,000.

Gross Rental. Form of lease or rental arrangement in which the lessor/landlord pays out all expenses.

Ground Lease. An agreement for the rental of the land only; sometimes secured by improvements placed on the land by the tenant.

Ground Rent. Earnings of improved property credited to earnings of the ground itself after allowance is made for earnings of the improvements; often termed economic rent.

Guarantee. An assurance or undertaking as to the performance or quality or accuracy of a product.

Guaranty. A promise to answer for the payment of another person's debt or obligation.

H

Habendum. That clause in a deed which states, "to have and to hold to said grantee, his heirs, successors, and assigns, forever." Not required in California.

Hard Money Loan. Loan from a private lender through an intermediary; actual money loaned, secured by a trust deed, as distinguished from a purchase money trust deed in favor of a seller.

Hazard Insurance. Insurance of property against such risks as fire, wind, floods, etc.

Heirs. The persons designated by law to succeed to the estate of a decedent who leaves no will.

Highest and Best Use. An appraisal term meaning that type of use which will produce the greatest return to the land and improvements over a given period of time.

Holder in Due Course. A phrase encountered under the Negotiable Instrument Law. Refers to a person who has taken a promissory note, check, or bill of exchange in due course before the due date, in good faith and for value, and without knowledge of any defects.

Holdover Tenant. Tenant who remains in possession of leased property after the expiration of the lease term.

Holographic Will. A will entirely written, dated, and signed by the testator in his own handwriting.

Homestead. A home upon which the owner has recorded a Declaration of Homestead under California law which affords protection from creditors' claims up to a specified amount. Exemption may also be claimed in an action for money without recording a Declaration of Homestead under prescribed conditions. Also, under federal law, the limited right to claim a small tract of the public domain by establishing residence or making improvement on the land. The latter is sometimes referred to as a *jackrabbit homestead*.

Housing Financial Discrimination Act of 1977. California Health and Safety Code Section 35800, et seq., designed primarily to eliminate discrimination in lending practices based upon the character of the neighborhood in which real property is located. (See **Redlining**).

HUD. Housing and Urban Development, an agency of the federal government.

Hundred Percent Location. A city retail business location which is considered the best available for attracting business.

Hypothecate. To give a thing as security without parting with possession.

I-J

Imperative Necessity. Circumstances under which an agent has expanded authority in an emergency, including the power to disobey instructions where it is clearly in the interests of the principal and where there is no time to obtain instructions from the principal.

Implied. Presumed or inferred, rather than expressed.

Impound Accounts. Funds retained in a special account by a secured lender to cover such items as taxes and hazard insurance on the property.

Improvement(s). Buildings and other structures on real property; a valuable addition made to the land.

Income Approach (Capitalization). One of the three methods of the appraisal process generally applied to income producing property. It involves a three-step process: (1) find net annual income, (2) set an appropriate capitalization rate or "present worth" factor, and (3) capitalize the income dividing the net income by the capitalization rate.

Income Tax. A tax imposed on gross income from a business or enterprise. Income tax laws (both federal and state) also apply to gains on real estate sales, and deductions are allowed for losses on such sales.

Incompetent. Unable to manage or incapable of managing one's own affairs, based on such factors as minority, illness, old age, insanity, etc.

Increment. An increase; most frequently used to refer to the increased value of land based on population growth and increasing wealth in the community. The term *unearned increment* is used in this connection, since values supposedly increase without effort on the part of the owner.

Incumbrance. See **Encumbrance**.

Indenture. Deeds or other instruments that are executed by both parties.

Independent Contractor. A person who acts for another but who sells final results and whose methods of achieving those results are not subject to the control of another.

Indorsement. See **Endorsement**.

Ingress. A means or way of entering onto property.

Inheritance. Property passing at the owner's death to his or her heirs; i.e., those entitled by law to succeed to the owner's estate.

Initial Note Rate. With regard to an adjustable rate mortgage, the note rate upon origination. This rate may differ from the fully indexed note rate.

Initial Rate Discount. as applies to an adjustable rate mortgage, the index value at the time of loan application, plus the margin, less the initial note rate.

Injunction. An order of a court of equity prohibiting some act, or compelling an act to be done.

In Propria Persona. "In his own person"; by himself, as in an action where the party acts as his or her own attorney (abbreviated as *pro per*).

Input. Data, information, etc., that is fed into a computer or other system.

Installment Note. A promissory note providing for payment of the principal in two or more certain amounts at stated or periodic times.

Installment Reporting. A method of reporting capital gains, by installments for successive tax years, to minimize the impact of the totality of the capital gains tax in the year of the sale.

Installment Sales Contract. Commonly called contract of sale or **Land Contract.** Purchase of real estate wherein the purchase price is paid in installments over a long period of time, title is retained by seller, and upon default by buyer (vendee) the payments may be forfeited.

Institutional Lenders. A financial intermediary or depository, such as a savings and loan association, commercial bank, or life insurance company, which pools money of its depositors and then invests funds in various ways, including trust deed and mortgage loans.

Instrument. A writing, such as a deed, made and executed as the expression of some act, contract, or proceeding.

Insurance. Coverage by contract in which one party (the insurer) agrees to indemnify or reimburse another (the insured) for any loss or damage that may occur under the terms of the contract.

Intangible. Incapable of being perceived by the senses, as incorporeal or immaterial things; also, existing only in connection with something else, such as an intangible asset in the form of the good will of a business.

Interest. A share, right, or title in the ownership of land or the degree thereof; also, a sum paid or charged for the use of money.

Interest Rate. The percentage of a sum of money charged for its use.

Interim Loan. A short-term, temporary loan used until permanent financing is available, e.g., a construction loan.

Intermediation. The process of pooling and supplying funds for investment by financial institutions called intermediaries. The process is dependent on individual savers placing their funds with these institutions and foregoing opportunities to directly invest in the investments selected.

Interpleader. An action brought by a third party (such as an escrow holder) in order to determine conflicting rights between two or more other parties (such as the principals to the escrow).

Interval Ownership. A form of timeshare ownership. (See *Timeshare Estate.*)

Intestate. Without a will; a person who died without leaving a will.

Involuntary Lien. A lien not voluntarily created by the debtor, such as a judgment lien.

Irrevocable. Incapable of being recalled, revoked, or withdrawn; unchangeable.

Jarvis-Gann Initiative. See **Proposition 13.**

Joint Note. A note signed by two or more persons who have equal liability for payment.

Joint Tenancy. Title held by two or more persons in equal shares with right of survivorship, i.e., when one joint tenant dies, his interest vests in the surviving joint tenant or tenants.

Joint Venture. Two or more individuals or firms joining together on a single project as partners.

Judgment. The final determination by a court having jurisdiction over the parties and subject matter of the action, of a matter presented to it for decision.

Judgment Lien. A statutory lien created by recording an abstract or certified copy of a judgment for money in the county recorder's office.

Junior Lien. A subordinate or inferior lien; behind another lien.

Junior Mortgage. A mortgage recorded subsequently to another mortgage on the same property or made subordinate by agreement to a later-recorded mortgage.

Jurisdiction. The power of a court to hear and determine a matter.

K-L

Key Lot. A lot so located that one side adjoins the rear of another lot; usually near a corner and considered less desirable.

Land. The solid material of the earth and anything affixed permanently to it, including buildings, trees, minerals, water flowing on the land or beneath it, and air space above it.

Land and Improvement Loan. A loan obtained by the builder-developer for the purchase of land and to cover expenses for subdividing.

Land Contract. A contract often used when property is sold on a small down payment where the seller does not choose to convey legal title until all or a certain portion of the purchase price has been paid by the buyer. Also referred to as a *land sales contract.*

Landlocked. Shut in completely by adjoining land without a means of access to or from a public highway or road.

Landlord. An owner of real property who leases it to a third party, called the *lessee* or *tenant.*

Late Charge. A charge assessed by a lender against a borrower failing to make loan installment payments when due.

Latent. Hidden from view; concealed, such as a latent ambiguity in a document; distinguished from **Patent**.

Lateral Support. The support which the soil of an adjoining owner gives to a neighbor's land.

Lawful Object. Allowed or permitted by law; one of the requisites of a valid contract.

Lease. A contract for the possession of land for a designated period of time in consideration of payment of rent.

Leasehold Estate. A tenant's right to occupy real estate during the term of the lease. This is a personal property interest.

Legacy. A gift of money or other personal property by will.

Legal Description. A description satisfactory in law, i.e., one by which property can be definitely located on the ground by reference to a recorded map or government survey.

Lessee. The tenant under a lease.

Lessor. The landlord under a lease, i.e., the person who transfers the right to occupy property to another person by a lease.

Level-Payment Mortgage. A loan on real estate that is paid off by making a series of equal (or nearly equal) regular payments. Part of the payment is usually interest on the loan and part of it reduces the amount of the unpaid principal balance of the loan. Also sometimes called an *amortized mortgage* or *installment mortgage*.

Leverage. Use of borrowed funds to purchase property in anticipation of substantial increase in value of the property; may produce a high return on a low down payment.

Levy. A seizure of property by judicial process, such as a levy under a writ of execution; a property tax is also a levy (collection of an assessment) under authority of law for governmental purposes.

Liability Insurance. Insurance covering the insured person against loss arising from injury or damage to another person or to property.

License. A personal privilege to enter upon or do some act on the land of another; also, authorization to engage in a business, an activity, or profession.

Licensee. A person to whom a license is issued or granted. In real estate, a person who has completed the requirements (including passing the examination) for a broker's or salesperson's license.

Lien. A charge upon property for the payment of a debt or performance of an obligation; a form of encumbrance. Liens include taxes, special assessments, and judgments, as well as mortgages. Additionally, there are mechanics' and material-men's liens for furnishing labor or materials to a work of improvement.

Life Estate. An estate in real property measured by the life of a natural person.

Limitations, Statute of. The commonly used identifying term for various statutes which require that a legal action be commenced with in a prescribed time after the accrual of the right to seek legal relief.

Limited Partnership. A partnership composed of one or more general partners and one or more limited partners. The contribution and liability of the latter are limited.

Lineal. In a direct line, such as a lineal descendant.

Linear. Involving measurement in one dimension only; pertaining to length, such as a *linear measure*, i.e., a foot, a yard, a meter, etc.

Liquidated Damages. Damages in an ascertained amount that may be recovered in a lawsuit.

Liquidated Damages Clause. A clause in a contract by which the parties, by agreement, fix the damages in advance for a breach of the contract.

Liquidity. Holdings in or the ability to convert assets to cash or its equivalent. The ease with which a person is able to pay maturing obligations.

Lis Pendens. A recorded notice of the filing of an action affecting real property.

Listing. An employment contract between a real estate broker (as agent) and a principal authorizing the broker to perform services in connection with the sale, purchase, exchange, or leasing of real property. There are various types of listing agreements, such as open, exclusive agency, option, etc.

Loan Administration. A general term encompassing those aspects of a mortgage lending operation that deal with the administration or servicing of loans after they have been put on the books, e.g., collection of monthly payments, accounting for payments, handling of real estate taxes and hazard insurance.

Loan Application. The loan application is a source of information on which the lender bases a decision to make the loan; defines the terms of the loan contract, gives the name of the borrower, place of employment, salary, bank accounts, and credit references, and describes the real estate that is to be mortgaged. It also stipulates the amount of loan being applied for and repayment terms.

Loan Closing. When all conditions have been met, the loan officer authorizes the recording of the trust deed or mortgage. The disbursal procedure of funds is similar to the closing of a real estate sales escrow.

The borrower can expect to receive less than the amount of the loan, as title, recording, service, and other fees may be withheld, or can expect to deposit the cost of these items into the loan escrow. This process is sometimes called "funding" the loan.

Loan Commitment. Lender's contractual commitment to make a loan on the appraisal and underwriting.

Loan Correspondent. One who acts as agent for lenders. Most often a large, incorporated mortgage banker representing institutional lenders such as eastern life insurance companies.

Loan Value. Value set on property to aid in determining the amount of a mortgage or trust deed loan to be made. Loan to value ratio is the percentage of a property's value that a lender can or may loan to a borrower. For example, if the ratio is 80 percent this means that a lender may loan 80 percent of the property's appraised value to a borrower.

Lot. A plot of ground.

M

MAI. Designates a person who is a member of the American Institute of Real Estate Appraisers of the National Association of Realtors® (NAR).

Margin of Security. The difference between the amount of the mortgage loan or loans and the appraised value of the property.

Marginal Land. Land which barely pays the cost of working or using it.

Marketable Title. The status of a title when viewed in the light of whether or not it is in such a condition as to attract a purchaser; a title that is free from reasonable doubt in law and in fact.

Market Data Approach. One of the three methods in the appraisal process. A means of comparing similar type properties, which have recently sold, to the subject property. Commonly used in comparing residential properties.

Market Price. The price actually paid for property on the open market.

Market Value. The highest price estimated in terms of money which a property will bring if exposed for sale in the open market, allowing a reasonable time to find a purchaser with knowledge of the property's use and capabilities for use.

Marketable Title. Title which a reasonable purchaser, informed as to the facts and their legal importance and acting with reasonable care, would be willing and ought to accept.

Material Fact. Significant fact; a fact which, for instance, an agent realizes is likely to affect the judgment of the principal in giving his or her consent to the agent to enter into a particular transaction of the specified terms. For example, the amount of income from rental property is a material fact.

Mechanic's Lien. A statutory lien in favor of laborers and material men who have contributed to a work of improvement.

Meridians. Imaginary north-south lines which intersect base (east-west) lines to form'a starting point for the measurement of land.

Metes. Measurements.

Metes and Bounds. Measurements and boundaries; a term used in describing the boundary lines of land, setting forth all the boundary lines together with their terminal points and angles.

Mile. 5,280 feet.

Minor. All persons under eighteen years of age. Prior to March 4, 1972, minors were persons under twenty-one years of age.

Misplaced Improvements. Improvements on land which do not conform to the most profitable use of the site.

Misrepresentation. A false or misleading statement or assertion.

Mobilehome (Manufactured Housing). As defined in Business and Professions Code Section 10131.6(c), "mobilehome" means a structure transportable in one or more sections, designed and equipped to contain not more than two dwelling units to be used with or without a foundation system. "Mobilehome" does not include a recreational vehicle, as defined in Section 18010.5 of the Health and Safety Code; a commercial coach, as defined in Section 18012 of the Health and Safety Code; or factory-built housing, as defined in Section 19971 of the Health and Safety Code.

Modular. A system for the construction of dwellings and other improvements to real property through the on-site assembly of component parts (modules) that have been mass produced away from the building site.

Monetary Controls. Federal Reserve tools for regulating the availability of money and credit to influence the level of economic activity, e.g., adjusting discount rates, reserve requirements, etc.

Monument. A fixed object or point designated by surveyors to establish land locations.

Moratorium. The temporary suspension, usually by statute, of the enforcement of liability for debts.

Mortgage. A written document executed by the owner of land by which the land is given as security for the payment of a debt or performance of an obligation.

Mortgage Banker. A company or individual engaged in the business of originating mortgage loans with its own funds, selling those loans to long-term investors, and servicing the loans for the investor until they are paid in full.

Mortgage Contracts with Warrants. Warrants make the mortgage more attractive to the lender by providing both the greater security that goes with a mortgage and the opportunity of a greater return through the right to buy either stock in the borrower's company or a portion of the income property itself.

Mortgage Guaranty Insurance. Insurance against financial loss available to mortgage lenders; in effect, guarantees payment of the debt; commonly referred to as *Private Mortgage Insurance (PMI)*.

Mortgage Investment Company. A company or group of private investors that buys mortgages for investment purposes.

Mortgage Loan Disclosure Statement. The statement on a form approved by the Real Estate Commissioner which is required by law to be furnished by a mortgage loan broker to the prospective borrower of loans of a statutorily prescribed amount before the borrower becomes obligated to complete the loan.

Mortgagee. The party who obtains the benefit of a mortgage; the lender.

Mortgagor. The party who executes a mortgage; the borrower.

Multiple Dwelling. A dwelling that is designed for occupancy by two or more families.

Multiple Listing. A listing, usually an exclusive right to sell, taken by a member of an organization composed of real estate brokers (*Multiple Listing Service - MLS*), with the provision that all members will have the opportunity to find an interested client, and the commission will be shared by the listing broker and the selling broker; a form of cooperative listing.

Mutual. Reciprocal; possessed, experienced, understood, or performed by each of two or more persons. One of the requisites of a valid contract is mutual consent. Also, mutual mistake, either of a fact or law, may be grounds for avoiding a contract.

Mutual Savings Banks. Financial institutions owned by depositors, each of whom has rights to net earnings of the bank in proportion to his or her deposits.

Mutual Water Company. A water company organized by or for water users in a given district or area with the object of securing an ample water supply at a reasonable rate for its members who are issued shares of water stock.

N

NAR. National Association of Realtors®.

NAREB. National Association of Real Estate Brokers.

Narrative Appraisal. A summary of all factual materials, techniques, and appraisal methods used by the appraiser in setting forth his or her value conclusion.

Natural Person. A person who is born and will die someday; distinguished from an artificial person, such as a corporation.

Naturalization. The conferring of the rights of citizenship upon a person who was an alien.

Negative Amortization. Occurs when monthly installment payments are insufficient to pay the interest accruing on the principal balance, so that the unpaid interest must be added to the principal due.

Negotiable. Capable of being negotiated; transferable in the ordinary course of business, usually by endorsement.

Negotiable Instrument. A promissory note or check or certificate of deposit or draft (bill of exchange) which under the Negotiable Instruments Law (now contained in the Commercial Code), entitles an endorsee to greater rights than an assignee, under certain prescribed conditions.

Net. Amount remaining after deduction of charges and expenses.

Net Income. Gross annual income less allowable expenses.

Net Lease. A lease requiring a lessee to pay certain charges against the property such as taxes, insurance and maintenance costs in addition to rental payments.

Net Listing. A listing agreement which provides that the broker may retain as compensation for his or her services all sums received over and above a net price to the owner.

Net, Net, Net. A term commonly used in connection with leases which means that all monies received by the lessor as rent are over and above all expenses of ownership, including taxes.

Net Profit. What is left after all bills and taxes are paid.

Net Worth. The difference between assets and liabilities.

Nominal Interest Rates. The percentage of interest that is stated in the loan documents.

Notary Public. A public officer or other person authorized to authenticate contracts, acknowledge deeds, take affidavits, etc.

Note. A signed written instrument acknowledging a debt and promising payment.

Note Rate. This rate determines the amount of interest charged on an annual basis to the borrower. Also called the *Accrual Rate, Contract Rate,* or *Coupon Rate.*

Notice. Being made aware. There are three types of notice: (1) *Actual Notice.* Express knowledge of a fact. (2)*Constructive Notice.* A fact, imputed to a person by law, which should have been discovered because of the person's actual notice of circumstances and the inquiry that a prudent person would have been expected to make, or implied or inferred from the public records. (3)*Legal Notice.* Information required to be given by law.

Notice of Cessation. A notice recorded under the mechanic's lien law after work has ceased for a period of time. Shortens the time for filing mechanics' liens.

Notice of Completion. A notice recorded under the mechanic's lien law after completion of the work of improvement. Shortens the time for filing mechanics' liens.

Notice of Default. Recorded notice that a default has occurred under a deed of trust and that the beneficiary intends to proceed with a trustee's sale.

Notice of Nonresponsibility. Notice recorded by an owner of real property to relieve the land from mechanics' liens which may result from an improvement on the property by a tenant or by a purchaser under a land sales contract.

Notice to Pay Rent or Quit. Notice to a tenant to either pay rent that is due or vacate the premises. Also known as a three-day notice to quit.

Novation. The substitution of a new obligation in place of an existing one.

Null. Without legal force and effect; not valid.

O

Obligatory. Mandatory, such as obligatory advances under a deed of trust; compared with *optional.*

Obligor. One who places himself or herself under a legal obligation, e.g., a mortgagor or trustor under a deed of trust.

Obsolescence. Impairment of desirability and usefulness of property; one of the causes of depreciation in value of property. Economic obsolescence is due to changes in the character of the neighborhood. Functional obsolescence relates to the declining usefulness of the structure itself.

Offer to Purchase. The proposal made to an owner of property by a potential buyer to purchase the property under stated terms.

Offset Statement. Statement furnished to an escrow from a tenant regarding his or her right of possession (payment of rent, security deposits, etc.); also, by an owner of land subject to an encumbrance as to the unpaid balance.

Open End Mortgage. A mortgage which secures additional advances which the lender may make to the mortgagor; permits the mortgagor to borrow additional money without rewriting the mortgage.

Open Housing Law. Congress passed a law in April, 1968 which prohibits descrimination in the sale of real estate because of race, color, or religion of buyers. California has enacted comparable laws.

Open Listing. A nonexclusive listing; provides that the broker is to receive a commission if he or she is the first one to obtain a buyer ready, willing, and able to purchase the property on the seller's terms. Open listings may be given to any number of agents.

Operating Expenses. Expenses incurred in the operation of a business.

Option. A right given for a consideration to acquire property upon specified terms within a specified period of time.

Optional. Not obligatory; discretionary. Optionee. The person who is given an option by the owner of property.

Option Listing. A type of listing which gives the broker the option to buy the property for a specified price.

Optionor. The person (owner) who gives an option to another person.

Oral. Spoken; verbal.

Oral Contract. A contract not in writing. Ordinance. A legislative enactment of a city or county.

Orientation. Placing a house on its lot with regard to its exposure to the rays of the sun, prevailing winds, privacy from the street, and protection from outside noises.

Original Contractor. Under the mechanic's lien law, a contractor who contracts directly with the owner of real property; others are designated as subcontractors.

Ostensible Authority. That authority which a third person reasonably believes an agent possesses because of the acts or omissions of the principal.

Overimprovement. An improvement which is not the highest and best use for the site on which it is placed by reason of excess size or cost.

Ownership. The right to the use and enjoyment of property to the exclusion of others.

Package Mortgage. A type of mortgage used in home financing covering real property, improvements, and movable equipment/appliances.

Paramount Title. Title which is superior or foremost to all others.

Partial Reconveyance. A release of a part only of the property described in a deed of trust.

Partial Release Clause. A clause in a deed of trust that requires the beneficiary, under prescribed conditions, to cause a designated portion of the property to be released prior to payment in full of the obligation.

Participation. Sharing of an interest in a property by a lender. In addition to base interest on mortgage loans on income properties, a percentage of gross income is required, sometimes predicated on certain conditions being fulfilled, such as a minimum occupancy or a percentage of net income after expenses, debt service and taxes. Also called *equity participation* or *revenue sharing.*

Parties. Persons who are involved in a lawsuit, designated as plaintiffs and defendants; also, those entities taking part in a transaction as a principal, e.g., seller, buyer, or lender in a real estate transaction.

Partition. An action which seeks to have property owned by two or more persons sold and the proceeds divided, or the property itself divided between the parties if physical division of the property is practical.

Partnership. A voluntary association of two or more persons to carry on as co-owners of a business for profit.

Party Wall. A wall for the common benefit and use of adjoining owners of property, their property being separated by the wall.

Par Value. Face value.

Patent. A conveyance of the title to public lands by the federal government. Also, when used as an adjective, it means something that is evident or obvious, such as a patent ambiguity in a document, and as such is distinguished from **latent** or hidden.

Payment Adjustment Date. With regard to an adjustable rate mortgage, the date the borrower's monthly principal and interest payment may change.

Payment Cap. With regard to an adjustable rate mortgage, this limits the amount of increase in the borrower's monthly principal and interest at the payment adjustment date, if the principal and interest increase called for by the interest rate increase exceeds the payment cap percentage. This limitation is often at the borrower's option and may result in negative amortization.

Payment Rate. With respect to an adjustable rate mortgage, the rate at which the borrower repays the loan—reflects buydowns or payment caps.

Penalty. A loss or forfeiture resulting from nonfulfillment of a contractual obligation, such as payment of an additional amount, called a late charge, if a note becomes delinquent.

Per Autre Vie. During the life of another. A life estate, for instance, may be measured by the life of a person other than the one who has the life estate, and would be referred to as a life estate *per autre vie.*

Per Capita. By the head. In the distribution of an estate, persons are said to take per capita when each one claims in his or her own right, based on an equal degree of kinship, an equal share of the estate. It is compared with the term *per stirpes*, which means by right of representation (according to the roots). In the latter situation the children of a deceased heir would all take but one share and would not share equally with the other heirs in their own right.

Percentage Lease. A lease under which the rent is computed as a percentage of the gross receipts from the business of the tenant, with provision (usually) for a minimum rental.

Periodic Interest Rate Cap. With respect to an adjustable rate mortgage, limits the increase or decrease in the note rate at each rate adjustment, thereby limiting the borrower's payment increase or decrease at the time of adjustment.

Periodic Tenancy. Tenancy for specified periods, such as month to month, which can be terminated at any time by either party on proper notice.

Personal Property. Movable property; all property consisting of chattels as contrasted with real estate, e.g., furniture, car, clothing, etc.

Physical Deterioration. Impairment of condition. Loss in value brought about by wear and tear, disintegration, use, and actions of the elements; termed *curable* and *incurable.*

Plaintiff. The party who brings a court action.

Planned Unit Development (PUD). A land-use design which provides intensive utilization of the land through a combination of private and common areas with prearranged sharing of responsibilities for the common areas. Individual lots are owned in fee with joint ownership of the open areas.

Planning Commission. The city or county agency that administers zoning regulations.

Plans and Specifications. Building plans with a detailed description of the requirements, dimensions, materials, etc., of the proposed structure.

Pledge. The depositing of personal property by a debtor with a creditor as security for a debt or other obligation.

Pledgee. One who is given a pledge as security.

Pledgor. One who gives a pledge as security.

Plottage Increment. The appreciation in unit value created by joining smaller ownerships into one large single ownership.

POB. Point of beginning; the commencement point in a good and sufficient legal description of land.

Points. Additional charges for obtaining a loan computed like interest; i.e., one point is comparable to one percent interest.

Police Power. The power to enact laws and regulations deemed necessary for the common welfare.

Power of Attorney. A written authorization to an agent to perform specified acts on behalf of his or her principal. May be a *general* power or a *limited* power. Also, may be a *durable* power or a springing power.

Power of Sale. As used in a will, authorizes the executor to sell estate property without the necessity of publishing a notice of sale.

PRD. Planned residential development. Used interchangeably with PUD, planned unit development.

Precedent. Used as an adjective, means going before, such as a *condition precedent*, i.e., a condition or event which must first occur before an estate can be terminated.

Pre-emption. Right to purchase before or in preference to others, such as a right of first refusal.

Prefabricated House. A house manufactured and sometimes partly assembled before delivery to a building site.

Preferred Stock. A class of corporate stock entitled to preferential treatment such as priority in distribution of dividends.

Prepaid Items of Expense. Prorations of prepaid items of expense which are credited to the seller in the closing escrow statement.

Prepayment. Provision made for loan payments to be larger than those specified in the note.

Prepayment Penalty. Penalty by way of an additional payment for the privilege of paying in full a mortgage or trust deed note prior to the due date.

Prescription. The obtaining of title to or a right in property by adverse possession, i.e., by occupying it openly, notoriously, and hostilely for a five-year period. By paying the real property taxes, the fee title can be claimed.

Present Value. The lump sum value today of an annuity. A $100 bill to be paid to someone in one year is worth less than if it were a $100 bill to be paid to someone today. This is due to several things, one of which is that the money has time value. How much the $100 bill to be paid in one year is worth today will depend on the interest rate that seems proper for the particular circumstances. For example, if 6% is the appropriate rate, the $100 to be paid one year from now would be worth $94.34 today.

Presumption. That which may be assumed as true without further proof. May be either a conclusive presumption or a rebuttable presumption.

Prima Facie. Presumptive on its face; assumed correct unless overcome by further proof.

Primary Money Market. A market where loans are made directly to borrowers by a lender who retains the loan in his portfolio rather than sell it to an investor.

Prime. Of the greatest commercial value, such as a prime building lot.

Principal. This term is used to mean the employer of an agent; or the amount of money borrowed, or the amount of the loan. Also, one of the main parties in a real estate transaction, such as a buyer, borrower, seller, lessor.

Principal Note. The promissory note which is secured by the mortgage or trust deed.

Principle. An accepted or professed rule of action or conduct.

Prior Lien. Earlier in point of time or right.

Priority of Lien. The state or quality of being earlier in point of time or right, as the priority of a first mortgage over a second mortgage.

Private Mortgage Insurance (PMI). Mortgage guaranty insurance available to conventional lenders on the first, high risk portion of a loan.

Probate Court. Department of the Superior Court which has authority over the estates of decedents, minors, incompetents, and missing persons.

Procuring Cause. The cause of originating a series of events that leads to the consummation of a real estate sale and normally entitles a broker to a commission.

Profit a Prendre. The right to take part of the soil or produce of land.

Progress Payments. Scheduled, periodic, and partial payment of construction loan funds to a builder as each construction stage is completed.

Progression, Principle of. The worth of a lesser valued residence tends to be enhanced by association with higher valued residences in the same area.

Promissory Note. A written obligation containing a promise to pay a definite amount of money at or prior to a specified time.

Property. Anything of which there may be ownership; classified as either real property or personal property.

Property Management. A branch of the real estate business involving the marketing, operation, maintenance and day-to-day financing of rental properties.

Proposition 13. A 1978 initiative limiting amount of property taxes that may be assessed to one percent of market value.

Pro Rata. In proportion; according to a certain rate.

Proration. A proportionate division or splitting of taxes and other expenses and income from real estate between buyer and seller in a sales escrow transaction; usually computed as of date escrow closes.

Proximate Cause. That cause of an event which, in a natural and continuous sequence unbroken by any new cause, produced that event, and without which the event would not have happened. Also, the *Procuring Cause*.

Public Records. As used in a title policy, those records which impart constructive notice of matters relating to the land described in the policy.

Public Report. Report of the Real Estate Commissioner containing information about subdivided property.

PUD. Planned unit development.

Purchase and Installment Saleback. Involves purchase of the property upon completion of construction and immediate saleback on a longterm installment contract.

Purchase of Land, Leaseback, and Leasehold Mortgages. An arrangement whereby land is purchased by the lender and leased back to the developer with a mortgage negotiated on the resulting leasehold of the income property constructed. The lender receives an annual ground rent, plus a percentage of income from the property.

Purchase and Leaseback. Involves the purchase of property by buyer and immediate leaseback to seller.

Purchase Money Mortgage. A mortgage (or trust deed) given as part or all of the purchase price of real estate.

Quiet Enjoyment. Right of an owner to the use of property without interference of possession.

Quiet Title. A court action to establish title to real property; similar in effect to an action to remove a cloud on title.

Quitclaim Deed. A deed which conveys whatever present right, title, or interest the party executing the deed may have.

R

Range. Part of a government survey; one of a series or divisions numbered east or west from the principal meridian of the survey and consisting of a row or tier of townships, each six miles square, which in turn are numbered north or south from a base line, e.g., Township 1 North, Range 3 East, SBBM (San Bernardino base and meridian).

Rate. The amount of a charge or payment, such as interest rate.

Rate Adjustment Date. With respect to an adjustable rate mortgage, the date the borrower's note rate may change.

Ratification. The adoption or approval of an act performed on behalf of a person without previous authorization.

Ready, Willing, and Able Buyer. One who is fully prepared to enter into the contract, really wants to buy, and unquestionably meets the financing requirements of purchase.

Real Estate. Real property; land and things affixed to land or appurtenant to land.

Real Estate Board. A local organization whose members consist primarily of real estate brokers and salespersons; affiliated with both the state association (CAR) and national board (NAR).

Real Estate Investment Trust (REIT). An association recognized under federal and state laws whereby investors may pool funds for investments in real estate and mortgages and avoid taxation as a corporation.

Real Estate Law. As codified in California, relates to the provisions of the Business and Professions Code creating the Department of Real Estate. Under this law, the Real Estate Commissioner has regulatory and disciplinary authority over real estate licenses, land sale transactions such as the sale of subdivided lands in or outside the state, and other related transactions.

Real Estate Settlement Procedures Act (RESPA). A federal law requiring the disclosure to borrowers of settlement (closing) procedures and costs by means of a pamphlet and forms prescribed by the United States Department of Housing and Urban Development.

Real Estate Syndicate. An organization of investors, usually in the form of a limited partnership, who have joined together for the purpose of pooling capital for the acquisition of real property interests.

Real Estate Trust. A special arrangement under Federal and State law whereby investors may pool funds for investments in real estate and mortgages and yet escape corporation taxes, profits being passed to investors who are taxed as individuals.

Real Property. Land and things attached to land or appurtenant to land; distinguished from personal property or chattels.

Real Property Loan Law. Article 7 of Chapter 3 of the Real Estate Law under which a real estate licensee negotiating loans secured by real property within a specified range is required to give the borrower a statement disclosing the costs and terms of the loan and which also limits the amount of expenses and charges that a borrower may pay with respect to the loan.

Real Property Sales Contract. An agreement to convey title to real property upon satisfaction of specified conditions which does not require conveyance within one year of formation of the contract.

Realtist. A member of the National Association of Real Estate Brokers.

Realtor®. A real estate broker holding active membership in a real estate board affiliated with the National Association of Realtors® (NAR).

Recapture. The rate of interest necessary to provide for the return of an investment (i.e., return of capital); distinguished from interest rate, which is the rate of interest on an investment (i.e., rate of return). May be more or less than the recapture amount.

Receipt. Written acknowledgment that money or other thing of value was received; as used in real estate practice, a deposit receipt when duly executed is also evidence of a contract between a buyer and seller.

Receiver. A person appointed by a court, such as a bankruptcy court, to take charge of a business or property of other persons, pending litigation.

Reconciliation. The act of bringing into harmony or agreement, such as reconciling an account, i.e., making it compatible or consistent.

Reconveyance. A conveyance to the landowner of the title held by a trustee under a deed of trust.

Record. An official writing or other document to be preserved; used as a verb, it means to make a public record of a document.

Recordation. Filing for record in the office of the county recorder.

Recovery Fund. A fund established by the Department of Real Estate from license fees to underwrite uncollectable court judgments against licensees based on fraud.

Redemption. Buying back one's property after a judicial sale, such as an execution or foreclosure sale.

Redemption Period. The time allowed by law during which the owner may redeem his or her property by paying, for instance, the amount of the sale on a foreclosed mortgage.

Redlining. A lending policy, illegal in California, of denying real estate loans on properties in older, changing urban areas, usually with large minority populations, because of alleged higher lending risks without due consideration being given by the lending institution to the creditworthiness of the individual loan applicant.

Refinancing. The paying-off of an existing obligation and assuming a new obligation in its place. To finance anew, or extend or renew existing financing.

Reformation. An action to correct a mistake in a deed or other document.

Regulate. To control or direct by a rule or law.

Regulation. A rule or direction prescribed under the authority of a statute, such as regulations of the Real Estate Commissioner.

Rehabilitation. The restoration of a property to satisfactory condition without drastically changing the plan, form or style of architecture.

Reinstate. To cure a default under a note secured by deed of trust.

Release Clause. A clause in a deed of trust providing for release of specified portions of the property upon compliance with certain conditions.

Reliction. Gradual recession of water from the usual water line or mark.

Remainder. A right to future possession after the expiration of a life estate.

Remainder Depreciation. The possible future loss in value of an improvement to real property.

Renegotiable Rate Mortgage. A loan secured by a long-term mortgage which provides for renegotiation, at pre-determined intervals, of the interest rate (for a maximum variation of five percent over the life of the mortgage).

Rent. Consideration paid for the use and possession of property under a rental agreement.

Replacement Cost. The cost to replace a structure with one having utility equivalent to that being appraised, but constructed with modern materials and according to current standards, design and layout.

Reproduction Cost. The cost of replacing the subject improvement with one that is the exact replica, having the same quality of workmanship, design and layout, or cost to duplicate an asset.

Rescission. An action to cancel or annul the effect of executing a contract or other document, based on fraud, mistake, etc.

Rescission of Contract. The abrogation or annulling of contract; the revocation or repealing of contract by mutual consent by parties to the contract, or for cause by either party to the contract.

Reservation. The creation on behalf of the grantor (in a deed) of a new right issuing out of the property granted, such as the reservation of a mineral interest.

Reserves. 1) In a common interest subdivision, an accumulation of funds collected from owners for future replacement and major maintenance of the common area and facilities. 2) With regard to mortgage loans, an accumulation of funds, collected by the lender from the borrower as part of each monthly mortgage payment; an amount allocated to pay property taxes and insurance when they are due.

Residual Cost. Accounting term for book value; the cost of a fixed asset, less any portion of the cost that has been treated as an expense, such as depreciation.

RESPA. (See **Real Estate Settlement Procedures Act**.)

Restriction. An encumbrance created by deed or agreement which limits the use and enjoyment of property; often created by a recorded Declaration of Covenants, Conditions and Restrictions (CC&R).

Return. A yield or profit from land or other property.

Return Premium. The refund of unearned advance premium resulting from cancellation of a hazard insurance policy prior to its expiration date or the date to which the premium has been paid.

Reversion. The residue of an estate remaining with a grantor after the expiration or termination of a lesser estate, such as an estate-for-years.

Reversionary Interest. The interest a person has in lands or other property upon the expiration or termination of a preceding estate.

Revocation. Nullification or cancellation or withdrawal, such as revocation of an offer to sell or an offer to buy a parcel of property.

Right of Redemption. The statutory right to buy back one's property after a judicial sale during a prescribed period of time, usually one year.

Right of Suvivorship. The distinguishing feature of joint tenancy, i.e., when one joint tenant dies, title vests automatically in the survivor without probate.

Right of Way. A right to cross or pass over, across, or under another person's land, for such purposes as ingress and egress, utility lines, sewer pipes, etc.

Right, Title, and Interest. A term used in deeds to denote that the grantor is conveying all of that to which the grantor held claim.

Riparian Rights. The right of a landowner to water located on, under, or adjacent to his or her land.

Risk Analysis. A study made, usually by a lender, of the various factors that might affect the repayment of a loan.

Risk Rating. A process used by the lender to decide on the soundness of making a loan and to reduce all the various factors affecting the repayment of the loan to a qualified rating of some kind.

S

Sale. Transfer of property for money or credit.

Sale-Leaseback. A transaction where the owner of a parcel of property sells it to another person (buyer) and retains physical possession by leasing it from the buyer.

Sales Contract. A contract by which a buyer and a seller of property agree to the terms of a sale. Sales Escrow. See **Escrow**.

Sales Tax. Tax on the sale of tangible personal property.

Salvage Value. In computing depreciation for tax purposes, the reasonably anticipated fair market value of the property at the end of its useful life, which must be considered with all but the declining balance methods of depreciation.

Sandwich Lease. A leasehold interest which lies between the primary lease and the operating lease; an in-between lease.

Satisfaction. Performance of the terms of an obligation.

Seal. An impression upon a document that lends authenticity to its execution.

Secondary Financing. A loan secured by a second mortgage or trust deed on real property.

Secondary Money (Mortgage) Market. A market in which existing mortgages are bought, sold or borrowed against, as distinguished from a *primary market*. The latter is made up of lenders who supply funds directly to borrowers and hold the mortgage until the debt is paid.

Section. One of the divisions employed in a government survey; measures one mile on each side and contains 640 acres of land.

Secured Party. The party having a security interest, such as a mortgagee, conditional seller, pledgee, etc.

Security. Something of value given or deposited to secure payment of a debt or performance of an obligation.

Security Agreement. Document now used in place of a chattel mortgage as evidence of a lien on personal property. A *financing statement* may be filed or recorded to give constructive notice of the security agreement.

Security Deposit. A deposit of money or other thing of value made to assure performance of an obligation; frequently required of lessees or tenants.

Security Interest. The interest of the creditor in the property of the debtor in all types of secured transactions.

Seisen. The possession of land under a claim of a freehold estate (also spelled *seizen*).

Seller's Market. The market condition which exists when a seller is in a more commanding position as to price and terms because demand exceeds supply.

Senior Lien. A lien that is ahead of or prior to or superior to another lien on the same property. Distinguished from *junior* lien.

Separate Property. Property of a married person acquired before marriage, and property acquired during marriage by gift, devise, descent, or bequest. Distinguished from *community* property.

Servicing Loans. Supervising and administering a loan after it has been made. This involves such things as: collecting the payments, keeping accounting records, computing the interest and principal, foreclosure of defaulted loans, and so on.

Servient Tenement. An estate burdened by an easement.

Servitude. A right in the nature of an easement in another person's property.

Setback Ordinance. An ordinance prohibiting the erection of a building or structure between the curb and the setback line.

Severalty Ownership. Sole ownership; owned by one person only, as compared with co-ownership, or ownership by two or more persons.

Shared Appreciation Mortgage. A loan having a fixed rate of interest set below the market rate for the term of the loan, which also provides for contingent interest to be paid to the lender on a certain percentage of appreciaton in the value of the property against which the loan is secured upon transfer or sale of the property or the replacement of the loan.

Sheriff's Deed. Deed given pursuant to an execution sale of real property to satisfy a judgment.

Simple Interest. Interest computed on the principal amount of a loan only, as distinguished from compound interest.

Sinking Fund. A fund created for the purpose of extinguishing an indebtedness, usually a bond issue; also, fund set aside from the income from property which, with accrued interest, will eventually pay for replacement of the improvements.

Slander of Title. False and malicious statements disparaging an owner's title to property and resulting in actual pecuniary damage to the owner.

Social and Economic Obsolescence. Reduction in value of property due to factors outside of the property; compared with **functional obsolescence**.

Sole Ownership. Ownership by one individual.

Special Assessments. Charges against real property imposed by a public authority to pay for the cost of local improvements, such as street lights, sidewalks, curbs, etc., as distinguished from taxes levied for the general support of the government (police and fire protection, etc.).

Special Power of Attorney. A written instrument whereby a principal confers limited authority upon an agent to perform certain prescribed acts on behalf of the principal.

Special Warranty Deed. A deed in which the grantor warrants or guarantees the title only against defects arising during grantor's ownership of the property and not against defects existing before the time of grantor's ownership.

Specifications. See **Plans** and **Specifications**.

Specific Performance. An action to compel performance of an agreement such as an agreement for the sale of purchase of land.

SREA. Designates a person who is a member of the Society of Real Estate Appraisers.

Standby Commitment. The mortgage banker frequently protects a builder by a *standby* agreement, under which banker agrees to make mortgage loans at an agreed price for many months into the future. The builder deposits a *standby fee* with the mortgage banker for this service. Frequently, the mortgage broker protects himself or herself by securing a standby from a long-term investor for the same period of time, paying a fee for this privilege.

State Contractors License Law. Law designed to protect the public against unqualified building contractors; establishes standards and requirements that must be met by contractors.

State Housing Law. State law which prescribes minimum building standards.

Statute. Federal laws enacted by Congress, and state laws enacted by the state legislature.

Statute of Frauds. State law which provides that certain contracts must be in writing to be enforceable, such as a contract for the sale of land, or a contract to pay a real estate broker a commission.

Statute of Limitations. Law which limits the time within which court action may be brought to enforce rights or claims.

Statutory Law. See **Civil Law.**

Statutory Warranty Deed. A short-term warranty deed which warrants by inference that the seller is the undisputed owner, has the right to convey the property, and will defend the title if necessary. This type of deed protects the purchaser in that the conveyor covenants to defend all claims against the property. If conveyor fails to do so, the new owner can defend said claims and sue the former owner.

Stock in Trade. Merchandise held by a business for sale to customers.

Straight-Line Depreciation. Definite sum of money set aside annually from income to pay cost of replacing improvements on property, without regard to interest it earns.

Straight Note. A promissory note that provides for repayment in a lump sum, as distinguished from installments.

Subagent. A person upon whom the powers of an agent have been conferred, not by the principal, but by an agent as authorized by the agent's principal.

Subcontractor. As used in the mechanic's lien law, a contractor hired by the general contractor rather than by the owner.

Subdivision. A parcel of property divided into lots for real estate development.

Subject to. The taking of real property subject to an encumbrance, such as a mortgage or deed of trust, is done without being personally liable to the holder of the note for payment of the debt; distinguished from *assuming*.

Sublease. A lease given by a lessee to another person for a term less than his or her own. The lessee retains a reversion. Distinguished from an *assignment*.

Subordinate. To make subject to, or junior to, another encumbrance.

Subordination Agreement. An agreement under which a prior lien is made inferior to an otherwise junior lien; changes the order of priority.

Subpoena. Court process for the summoning of witnesses.

Subrogation. Replacing one person with another in regard to a legal right or obligation. The substitution of another person in place of the creditor, to whose rights he or she succeeds in relation to the debt. The doctrine is used very often where one person agrees to stand surety for the performance of a contract by another person; also, an insurer is subrogated to the rights of the insured against a third party causing a loss.

Subsequent. Occurring or coming later in time.

Suburb. An area lying immediately outside a city or town.

Subsidy Buydown. Funds provided, usually by the builder or seller, to temporarily reduce the borrower's monthly principal and interest payment.

Substitution, Principle of. Affirms that the maximum value of a property tends to be set by the cost of acquiring an equally desirable and valuable substitute property, assuming no costly delay is encountered in making the substitution.

Succession. The taking of property by inheritance.

Successor. One who acquires or succeeds to the interest of another person.

Summons. Court process which directs a defendant to make an appearance in an action filed against him or her.

Supply and Demand, Principle of. In appraising, a valuation principle stating that market value is affected by interaction of supply and demand forces in the market as of the appraisal date.

Surety. A person who binds himself or herself with another, called the principal, for the performance of an obligation; a guarantor.

Surplus Funds. Money obtained at a foreclosure sale in excess of the amount to satisfy or pay the obligation in full.

Surplus Productivity, Principle of. The net income that remains after the proper costs of labor, organization and capital have been paid, which surplus is imputable to the land and tends to fix the value thereof.

Survey. A map or plat containing a statement of courses, distances, and quantity of land, and showing lines of possession.

Syndicate. A pooling arrangement or association of persons who invest in real property by buying shares in an organization in the form of a partnership, joint venture, corporation, or other entity.

Take-Out Loan. The loan arranged by the owner or builder developer for a buyer. The construction loan made for construction of the improvements is usually paid in full from the proceeds of this more permanent mortgage loan.

Tangible Assets. Anything of value having form or substance, such as real estate, chattels, etc.

Tax. A levy, under authority of law, for governmental purposes.

Tax Base. The value of property for determining the tax. For property taxes, it is the assessed value; for income taxes, it is the net taxable income.

Tax Deed. A deed issued to the purchaser at a tax sale of real property.

Tax-Free Exchange. The trade or exchange of one real property for another without the need to pay income taxes on the gain at the time of trade.

Tax Sale. Sale of property by the tax collector for nonpayment of taxes.

Tax Shelter. Under income tax law, a situation where cost and depreciation equal income from property, hence no income tax is payable.

Tenancy in Common. Ownership of property by any two or more persons in undivided interests (not necessarily equal), without right of survivorship.

Tenant. One who occupies property of another person under an agreement to pay rent.

Tenements. All rights in land which pass with a conveyance of the land.

Tentative Map. Under the Subdivision Map Act, a subdivider initially submits this map to the local planning commission for approval.

Tenure. The manner in which title to land is held.

Term. Used variously in the real estate field; denotes any provision of a contract, or the period or provisions of a loan, or the period of a lease.

Termites. Ant-like insects that feed on wood.

Testate. Having made a will (as an adjective, "a person died testate").

Testator. A man who makes a will.

Testatrix. Feminine of testator.

Third Party. Persons who are not parties to a contract which affects an interest they have in the object of the contract, such as a third-party beneficiary.

Thirty-Day Notice. Notice to tenant to vacate the premises within a thirty-day period. No reason required.

Tidelands. Lands that are covered and uncovered by the ebb and flow of the tide.

Tight Money Market. A market in which demand for the use of money exceeds the available supply.

Time is of the Essence. A clause in a contract that requires *strict compliance* with the stated time limitations (within which a contracting party may perform).

Timeshare Estate. A right of occupancy in a timeshare project (subdivision) which is coupled with an estate in the real property.

Timeshare Project. A form of subdivision of real property into rights to the recurrent, exclusive use or occupancy of a lot, parcel, unit, or segment of real property, on an annual or some other periodic basis, for a specified period of time. (See **Subdivision**.)

Timeshare Use. A license or contractual or membership right of occupancy in a time-share project which is not coupled with an estate in the real property.

Title. Evidence of a person's right or the extent of his or her interest in property.

Title Insurance. Assurances as to the condition of title; protects owner or other insured, such as a lender, against loss or impairment of title.

Title Plant. A physical collection of documents, maps, and other data which may be pertinent to future title searches. Maintained by title companies.

Title Report. A report which discloses condition of the title, made by a title company preliminarily to issuance of title insurance policy; usually called a preliminary report of title.

Topography. Nature of the surface of land, e.g., the topography may be level, rolling, mountainous, etc.

Tort. A wrongful act; violation of a person's legal right; a civil wrong not arising out of contract.

Townhouse. One of a row of houses usually of the same or similar design with common side walls or with a very narrow space between adjacent side walls.

Township. A part of a subdivision of the public lands of the United States; each township contains 36 sections.

Tract. A real estate development; an expanse or area of land.

Trade Fixtures. Articles of personal property, annexed to real property by a tenant, that are necessary to the carrying on of a trade and are removable by the owner of the fixtures upon termination of the tenancy.

Trade-in. A method of guaranteeing property owners a minimum amount of cash on sale of their present property to permit them to purchase other property. If the property is not sold within a specified time at the listed price, the broker agrees to arrange financing to purchase the property at an agreed-upon discount.

Trade Name. The name under which a firm does business.

Transaction. That which is conducted or processed as a business deal.

Transfer Fee. A charge made by a lending institution holding or collecting on a real estate mortgage to change its records to reflect a different ownership.

Transfer Tax. A tax payable upon the conveyance of property, measured by the consideration paid.

Trespass. An invasion of an owner's rights in his or her property; a wrongful entry upon the land of another person.

Trust. A fiduciary relationship in which one party (*trustee*) holds the title to property for the benefit of another party (*beneficiary*).

Trust Account. An account of property which is held in trust for another person; distinguished from personal account.

Trust Deed. See **Deed of Trust**.

Trustee. The person to whom property is conveyed in trust.

Trustee's Deed. Deed given by the trustee under a deed of trust when the property is sold under the power of sale.

Trustee's Sale. A foreclosure sale conducted by the trustee under a deed of trust after a default occurs.

Trust Funds. Money or other things of value received by a broker or salesperson to be held for the benefit of others.

Trustor. The person who conveys property in trust.

Truth-in-Lending. The name given to the federal statutes and regulations (*Regulation Z*) which are designed primarily to insure that prospective borrowers and purchasers on credit receive credit cost information before entering into a transaction.

Turnover. The number of times per year a given amount of inventory sells; change or movement of people, such as tenants, customers, etc.

U

UCC. See Uniform Commercial Code.

Underimprovement. An improvement which, because of its deficiency in size or cost, is not the highest and best use of the site.

Underwriting. Insuring something against loss; guaranteeing financially.

Undivided Interests. Nature of each owner's interest in property when owned as tenants in common or in joint tenancy.

Undue Influence. Taking fraudulent or unfair advantage of another person's weakness of mind or distress to induce him or her to do something he or she otherwise would not have done, such as disinheriting a close relative.

Unearned Increment. Increase in value of real estate due to no effort on the part of the owner; often due to increase in population.

Unenforceable. A claim or demand or agreement that cannot be sustained in court.

Uniform Commercial Code. Establishes a unified and comprehensive method for regulation of security transactions in personal property, superseding the existing statutes on chattel mortgages, conditional sales, trust receipts, assignment of accounts receivable and others in the field.

Unilateral Contract. A contract where one party makes a promise in exchange for an action on the part of the other contracting party; distinguished from a *bilateral* contract.

Unit-In-Place Method. The cost of erecting a building by estimating the cost of each component part, i.e., foundations, floors, walls, windows, ceilings, roofs, etc., (including labor and overhead).

Unities. As related to joint tenancy, there are four *unities* necessary to create a valid joint tenancy, namely, *time, title, interest,* and *possession*.

Unlawful Detainer. An action to recover possession of real property.

Unruh Act. A California act which, among other things, precludes discriminatory practices based on race, color, religion, national origin, or ancestry.

Unsecured. A loan that is not secured by a mortgage, pledge, or other security instrument.

Urban Property. City property; closely settled property.

Usury. Taking more interest than the law allows on a loan.

Utilities. Refers to services rendered by public utility companies, such as light, gas, water power, telephone, etc.

Utility. The ability to give satisfaction and/or excite desire for possession. An element of value.

V

VA. Veterans Administration; federal agency which administers GI loans. See **Veterans Administration**.

VA Guaranty. An undertaking by the federal government to guarantee the lender, subject to limitations, against loss arising from a default by the borrower under a GI loan.

Vacancy Factor. The percentage of a building's space that is unrented over a given period.

Valid. Sufficient in law; effective.

Valuation. The act or process of estimating value.

Value. The amount a property will command from a reasonable buyer in the open market.

Variable Interest Rate. (VIRs or VMRs, Variable Mortgage Rates). An interest rate in a real estate loan which by the terms of the note varies upward and downward over the term of the loan depending on money market conditions.

Variance. A departure from the general rule; an exception.

Vendee. The buyer or purchaser under a contract of sale.

Vendor. The seller under a contract of sale.

Verification. An affidavit attached to a pleading or other document which states that the matters set forth are true.

Vest. To give an immediate, fixed right, title, or interest in property, with either present or future enjoyment of possession; also denotes the manner in which title is held.

Vested Interest. An interest in property that is fixed or determined.

Veterans Administration. An independent agency of the federal government created by the Servicemen's Readjustment Act of 1944 to administer a variety of benefit programs designed to facilitate the adjustment of returning veterans to civilian life. Among the benefit programs is the Home Loan Guaranty program designed to encourage mortgage lenders to offer long-term low-down-payment financing to eligible veterans by guaranteeing the lender against loss on these higher-risk loans.

Void. Having no legal effect; null.

Voidable. An instrument that appears to be valid, but is in fact lacking in some essential requirement.

Voluntary Lien. A lien voluntarily created by the debtor, such as a mortgage or deed of trust as contrasted with a judgment lien.

W-Z

Waive. To relinquish or abandon; to forego a right to enforce or require something.

Waiver. A relinquishment or abandonment of a right.

Warranty. An assurance or understanding that certain defects do not exist.

Warranty Deed. A deed containing express warranties of title and quiet possession. Commonly used in other states, but not in California, since assurances are given by way of title insurance.

Warrenty of Authority. A representation by an agent to third persons that the agent has and is acting within the scope of authority conferred by the principal.

Water Table. Distance from surface of ground to a depth at which natural groundwater is found.

Wear and Tear. Depreciation of an asset due to ordinary usage.

Will. A disposition of property effective upon the owner's death; often referred to as "my last will and testament."

Witness. Used as a verb, means to see or know by personal presence and perception. As a noun, the person who sees or knows.

Wraparound Mortgage or Trust Deed. See **All-Inclusive Deed of Trust**.

Writ. A process of the court under which property may be seized or sold by the sheriff. A writ of execution is an example.

Yield. The interest earned by an investor on an investment (or by a bank on the money it has loaned). Also, called return or profit.

Yield Rate. The yield expressed as a percentage of the total investment. Also, called rate of return.

Zone. Area in a community set off by a zoning authority for specified uses, such as single-family residence.

Zoning. Governmental regulations by a city or county relating to the use of real property; imposes limitations regarding use.

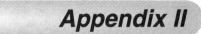

1031 Exchanges: 45
11th District Cost of Funds: 509
60-Day Termination Notice: 492

A

Absentee Owners: 45
Acceleration Clause: 318
Accredited Management Organization (AMO): 519
Acknowledgement: 456
Activity Report: 510
Ad Valorem Tax: 375
Adjustable Interval: 302
Adjustable Rate Mortgage (ARM): 300
   Advantages of ARMs: 302
   How ARMs Work: 302
      Adjustable Interval: 302
      Cap: 302
      Margin: 302
Advantages to Owning Real Estate: 57
Advertising and Promotion: 55
   Advertising Pointers: 62
   Billboards and Other Outdoor Advertising: 60
   Budgeting for Advertising: 64
      Guidelines: 65
   Bus, Car, Bench, and Taxi Signs: 61
   Club and Institutional Newsletters: 61
   Direct Mail: 60
   Evaluate Advertising Effectiveness: 66
   Giveaways: 61
   Internet Sites: 61
   Letterheads, Company Post Cards, Institutional
      Folders: 61
   Magazines: 59
   Newspapers: 57
   Radio and Television: 60
   Regulations of the Real Estate Commissioner: 67
   Shopping Guides: 60
   Signs: 60
   Telephone and City Directories: 59
   Window Displays: 60
   Writing Effective Ads (AIDA): 64
Agency: 73
   Agency Relationship Disclosure Act: 86
      Disclosure Regarding Real Estate Agency
       Relationships form: 88
      Dual Agency: 87
      Single Agency: 87
   Exclusive Authorization to Acquire Property: 85
Agency Relationship Disclosure Act: 86
Agent Comment Sheet: 179-180
AIDA: 64, 167

Airspace Development Program: 463
Alcoholic Beverage Control Act: 452-454
All-Inclusive Trust Deed (AITD): 319
Alphabetical Form: 543
ALTA-R Policy: 361
Alternative Minimum Tax (AMT): 397
American Land Title Association (ALTA): 360
Annual Percentage Rate (APR): 66, 295, 317
Application for Sales Associate: 41-42
Application To Rent/Receipt For Deposit
   Screening Fee: 499-500
Appraisal: 423
Appraisers: 149
Arbitration of Disputes: 239
Asian Real Estate Association of America
   (AREAA): 594
Assessed Valuation: 382
Assignment of Lease: 451
Association of Real Estate License Law Officials
   (ARELLO): 596
Assumption, Loan: 321
   Cal-Vet Loan Assumption: 321
   Conventional Loan Assumption: 321
   FHA Loan Assumption: 321
   Seller Carryback Assumption: 322
   VA Loan Assumption: 321

B

Balloon Payments: 319
Beneficiary's (Lender's) Statement: 345
Bill of Sale: 451
Block Busting: 483
Board of Education: 92
Boot: 400-401
Broker, Real Estate: 569
   Broker's Qualifying Experience: 569
   Broker's Required Education: 570
   Broker's License: 569
Brokerage Firm: 60
   Doing Business As (DBA): 61
   Forms of Business Ownership: 62
Building and Safety Department: 91
Bulk Transfer: 446
Bureau of Assessments: 92
Business and Professions Code: 326, 350, 577
Business License Tax: 405
Business Opportunities (Sale of a Business): 443
   Assignment of Lease: 451
   Bill of Sale: 451
   Bulk Transfer: 446
   Certificate of Payment of Sales and Use Tax: 450

Encumbrancers: 448
Goodwill: 445
Listing Agreement: 445
Notice to Creditors of Bulk Sale: 446-447
Security Agreement and Financing Statement: 448-449
Small Business Opportunities: 443
Tax Consequences: 453
Covenant Not to Compete: 453
Uniform Commercial Code (UCC): 446
Valuation of Business Opportunities: 451
Gross Multipliers: 452
Net Multipliers: 452
Buyer Comment Sheet: 188-189
Buyer's Affidavit: 257, 267
Buyer's Inspection Advisory: 242, 255, 261, 268
Buyer's Listing: 85

C

C.A.R.® Real Estate Disclosure
Summary Chart: 273
California Apartment Association (CAA): 489-490
California Association of Realtors®: 581-582
California Certified Residential Manager (CCRM): 489
California Community Colleges Real Estate
Education Center: 596
California Department of Veterans Affairs
(Cal-Vet): 307, 311-312
California Escrow Association: 363, 366
California Land Title Association (CLTA): 340, 355
California Real Estate Educators Association
(CREEA): 596
California Residential Purchase Agreement and
Joint Escrow Instructions: 208-209, 255, 339, 344
Evaluation and Analysis of the Purchase
Contract: 208
Filling Out the Form—a Breakdown: 217
Seller-Financing Addendum: 221
California Sales and Use Tax Law: 452
California Standard Form Fire Insurance Policy: 351
Caltrans: 463-464
Airspace Development Program: 463
Cal-Vet Loan Assumption: 321
Cap: 302
Cap Rate: 148, 427
Capital Gains: 396
Capital Losses: 396
Capitalization Approach (to valuation): 143, 148
Cap Rate: 148
Capitalization of Net Income: 427

Caravan: 179
Agent Comment Sheet: 179
Cash Journal: 510-511
Recapitulation: 510
CC&Rs: 514
Certificate of Payment of Sales and Use Tax: 450
Certificate of Reasonable Value (CRV): 309
Certified Property Manager (CPM): 468, 519
Certified Real Estate Appraiser (CREA: 468
Certified Residential Appraiser (CRA): 468
Certified Residential Specialist (CRS): 53
Chain of Title: 352
Child Support Obligations: 574
City or County Planning Departments: 91
Civil Rights Act of 1968: 485
Expanded in 1988: 487
Fair Housing Amendments Act: 487
Closing: 193
Closing Date: 346
Closing Techniques: 194
Assumptive Technique: 194
Call-Back Technique: 196
Minimize the Difference Technique: 195
Narrative Technique: 195
Negative-Yes Technique: 195
Opportunity Lost Technique: 195
Positive Choice Technique: 194
Want Technique: 194
Yes and No Itemizing Technique: 195
Yes-But Technique: 195
Cold Calls: 51
Color-Blind: 483
Combined Hazards Book: 124, 138
Commercial Banks: 298, 419
Interim Financing: 419
Commingling: 220
Commission: 40, 60, 75
100% Commission: 40
Right to a Commission: 75
Straight Commission: 40
Commission of Fair Employment and Housing: 484
Common Interest Development (CID): 512
CC&Rs: 514
Davis-Stirling Common Interest Development
Act: 514
Homeowner's Association (HOA): 514
Managing Agent: 515
Comparables: 91
Comparative Approach (to valuation): 143-144
Competitive Market Analysis (CMA): 144
Competitive Market Analysis (CMA: 41

Competitive Market Analysis (CMA): 92, 144
Conditional Salesperson's License: 563
Contingency for Sale or Purchase of Other
   Property: 255, 260
Continuing Education (CE) Requirement: 570
   45 Hours Every Four Years: 570-571
Contract Rent: 507
Conventional Loan Assumption: 321
Cooperating Broker: 80
Cooperating Broker Compensation Agreement and
   Escrow Instruction (CBC): 257, 265-266
Cooperative Sales: 57
Corporation: 63, 434
   Stock: 63
   Subchapter S Corporation: 63, 435
Cost Approach (to valuation): 143, 147
Cost of Living Lease: 509
Counselor, Real Estate (CRE): 468
Counter Offer: 257, 266
County Assessor: 377
County Tax Collector: 378
Covenant Not to Compete: 453
Credit Scoring: 315-316
   Equal Credit Opportunity Act (ECOA): 315
   Fair Credit Reporting Act: 317
   FICO Scores: 315
Cross Referencing: 544
Curb Appeal: 89, 188

D

Davis-Stirling Common Interest Development
   Act: 514
Dealer Property: 401
Deed of Trust: 293
   Beneficiary: 293-294
   Trustee: 293-294
   Trustor: 293-294
Deferred Maintenance: 517
Department of Housing and Urban Development
   (HUD): 363, 465, 487
Department of Motor Vehicles: 470
Department of Real Estate (DRE): 559, 564
Department of Real Estate Bulletins: 574
   Mortgage Loan Bulletin: 574
   Real Estate Bulletin: 574-575
   Subdivision Industry Bulletin: 574
Depreciation of Business Property: 395
   Advantages of "Sale-Leaseback": 395
   Straight-Line Depreciation: 395
Disabled and Senior Citizen's Property Tax
   Postponement: 386

Disclosure Regarding Agency Relationships: 124,
   127, 244, 255, 258
Disclosure Regarding Real Estate Agency
   Relationships form: 88
Discrimination: 484
Division of Highways: 92
Documentary Transfer Tax: 388
Doing Business As (DBA): 61
Down Payment: 423
Dual Agency: 56, 85, 87

E

Earthquake Fault Zone: 229
Economic Obsolescence : 161
Effective Gross Income: 425
Employee: 539
Employee-Employer Relationship: 44
   Employee: 44
   Independent Contractor: 44
      Independent Contractor Agreement: 45
Encumbrancers: 448
Engineering Departments: 92
Equal Credit Opportunity Act (ECOA): 315
Equity: 321
Escalator Lease: 509
Escrow: 335, 457
   Activities: 457
   California Escrow Association: 363
   Escrow and IRS Reports: 350
   Escrow Example: 345
      Closing Date: 346
   Escrow Holder: 337
      Escrow Officer: 338
      Neutral Depository: 338
   Escrow Services and Title Insurance: 340
   Fire Insurance: 351
   Four Functions of Escrow: 338
   How Escrows Work: 339
      Escrow Instructions: 344
      Escrow Rules: 343
      Financing: 345
         Beneficiary's (Lender's) Statement: 345
         Payoff Demand Statement: 345
      Opening Escrow: 343
      Who Selects the Escrow Company?: 344
   Proration: 346
   Requirements for a Valid Escrow: 337
      Escrow Act: 337
   Termites and Other Problems: 349
   Title Insurance: 352
Escrow Act: 337

Estate at Will: 507
Estimated Buyer's Costs: 255, 259
Estimated Seller's Proceeds: 124
Estimated Seller's Proceeds: 139
Exchanges: 398
    Accounting for Exchanges: 400
    Like-Kind Property: 400
    Reverse 1031 Exchanges: 400
    Simultaneous 1031 Exchanges: 399
    Starker Delayed Exchange: 400
    Tax-Deferred Exchanges: 401
Exclusive Agency Listing: 81
Exclusive Authorization to Acquire Property: 85
Exclusive Listing: 80
    Cooperating Broker: 80
Exclusive Right to Sell: 82, 113
    Safety Clause: 82
Expired Listings: 51, 46
Extended Listing Relationships: 46

F

Factors That Lead To Success: 54
Fair Credit Reporting Act: 317
Fair Employment and Housing Act (FEHA): 481, 484
    Discrimination: 484
Fair Housing Amendments Act: 487
Fair Housing Laws: 481
    Fair Employment and Housing Act (FEHA): 481
    Fair Housing Poster: 485
    Fair Housing Violations: 483
    Federal Laws: 485
    Unruh Civil Rights Act: 481
Fair Housing Poster: 485-486
Fair Housing Violations: 483
    Block Busting: 483
    Color-Blind: 483
    Panic Peddling: 483
    Panic Selling: 483
    Race Restrictions: 483
    Redling: 483
    Steering: 483
Farm: 49
Federal Emergency Management Agency
    (FEMA): 229
Federal Estate Tax: 390
Federal Gift Taxes: 388
Federal Home Loan Mortgage Corporation
    (FHLMC): 304
Federal Housing Administration (FHA): 305-306
    Graduated Payment Mortgage (GPM): 308
    Maximum Loan Amounts: 308

Federal National Mortgage Association
    (FNMA): 303
Feng Shui: 191, 192
FHA Loan Assumption: 321
FICO Scores: 315
Fiduciary Relationship: 56
Financing, Types of : 296
    Government Financing: 296
    Institutional Financing: 296
        Priorities of Institutional Lenders: 298
    Noninstitutional Financing: 296
    Qualifying the Borrower: 312
        Credit Scoring: 315
            Equal Credit Opportunity Act (ECOA): 315
            Fair Credit Reporting Act: 317
            Truth in Lending Act: 317
        Loan Application: 312
Fire Insurance: 351
    California Standard Form Fire Insurance
        Policy: 351
    Extended Coverage Endorsement: 351
    Fire Insurance Proration: 352
Fixed Expenses: 426
Fixed Rate Mortgage: 300
Fixer-Uppers: 160
Flat Rental Lease: 508
Floortime: 171
For Sale By Owners (FSBOs): 45, 48
    Guaranteed Sales Plan: 48
Foreign Investment in Real Property Tax Act
    (FIRPTA): 240
Foreign Investment in Real Property Tax Act
    (FRPTA): 267
Forms of Business Ownership: 62
    Corporation: 63
    Partnership: 62
    Sole Proprietorship: 62
Forms Supplied to the Buyer: 255
    Buyer's Affidavit: 257
    Buyer's Inspection Advisory: 255
    California Residential Purchase Agreement and
        Joint Escrow Instructions: 255
    Contingency for Sale or Purchase of Other
        Property: 255
    Cooperating Broker Compensation Agreement
        and Escrow Instruction: 257
    Counter Offer: 257
    Disclosure Regarding Agency Relationships: 255
    Estimated Buyer's Costs: 255
    Home Warranty Waiver: 257
    Listing Kit: 257

Notice to Buyer to Perform: 257
Notice to Seller to Perform: 257
Receipt for Reports and Contingency Removal: 257
Verification of Property Condition: 257
Wood Destroying Pest Inspection and Allocation of Cost Addendum: 257
FRPTA: 128
Functional Obsolescence: 161

G

General Partnership: 434
Geographical Farm: 43
Gift and Estate Taxes: 388
Federal Estate Tax: 390
Federal Gift Taxes: 388
No State Gift and Inheritance Taxes: 390
Goodwill: 51, 445, 452
Government Financing: 296, 304
California Department of Veterans Affairs (Cal-Vet): 307, 311-312
Federal Housing Administration (FHA): 305-306
Veterans Administration (VA): 307, 309-310
Government National Mortgage Association (GNMA): 303
Graduated Lease: 509
Cost of Living Lease: 509
Escalator Lease: 509
Graduated Payment Mortgage (GPM): 301, 308
Gross Lease: 508
Gross Multipliers: 452
Guaranteed Sales Plan: 48

H

Hand-Held Computers: 548
Highest and Best Use: 492
Home Warranty Application or Waiver: 124, 141
Home Warranty Waiver: 257
Homeowner's Association (HOA): 514
Regular Assessments: 514
Special Assessments: 514
Homeowner's Property Tax Exemption: 385
Homeowners Guide to Earthquake Safety: 137
Homeowner's Guide to Earthquake Safety: 229
Housing Financial Discrimination Act: 484-485
Hybrid Filing System: 545
Hybrid Trust: 435

I

Impound Accounts: 295
Improvement Bond Act of 1915: 228, 387

Income Properties, Financing: 418
Sources of Financing: 418
Commercial Banks: 419
Life Insurance Companies: 419
Savings Banks: 419
Income Tax Aspects of Real Estate Transactions: 391
Basic Income Tax Incentives: 393
Income Taxes: 390
Federal: 390-391, 402
Foreign Investors: 402
Income Tax Rates: 396
Income Tax Aspects of Real Estate Transactions: 391
State: 390-391, 402
Foreign Investors: 403
Incoming Call Register: 169
Independent Contractor: 44, 539
Independent Contractor Agreement: 44
Independent Contractor Agreement: 38, 44-45
Independent Real Estate Associations: 595
Index: 544
Installment Sales of Real Estate: 398
Institutional (Conventional) Financing: 296
Adjustable Rate Mortgage (ARM): 300
Commercial Banks: 298
Fixed Rate Mortgage: 300
Institutional Lenders: 296
Mortgage Banking: 296
Mortgage Bankers vs. Mortgage Brokers: 296
Jumbo Loan: 304
Life Insurance Companies: 299
Private Mortgage Insurance (PMI): 299
Savings Banks: 296
Subprime Borrower: 298
Institutional Lenders: 296
Interest: 294
Interim Financing: 419
Interstate Land Sales Full Disclosure Act: 465
Land Project: 466
Property Report: 465
Inundation Zones: 229
Investing: 411
Benefits of Investing: 414
Amenities: 416
Appreciation Potential: 414
Control and Use: 416
Hedge Against Inflation: 415
Income: 415
Interim Use: 415
Refinancing: 416
Stability: 415

Tax Shelter: 414
Challenges to Real Estate Investing: 416
  Lack of Liquidity: 417
  Large Capital Outlay: 416
  Miscellaneous Negative Factors: 418
  Personal Attachment (Affecting
    Profitability): 418
  Potentially Unfavorable Financing: 417
  Professional Property Management Needed: 417
Financing Income Properties: 418
Residential Income Properties: 423
Syndication: 431
Why Invest in Real Estate?: 411
Your Role in the Investment Process: 420
  Investing Planning and Counseling: 422
Investing Planning and Counseling: 422

J

Jones v. Mayer: 485
Jumbo Loan: 304
Junior Loans: 317
  Acceleration Clause: 318
  Balloon Payments: 319

L

Land Contract: 319
Land Project: 466
Landlord-Tenant Termination Laws: 492
Lead-Based Paint and Lead-Based Paint Hazards
  Disclosure: 124, 135
Life Insurance Companies: 299, 419
Like-Kind Property: 400
Limited Partnership: 433
  Advantages of the Limited Partnership Format: 433
Liquidated Damages: 220, 238
Liquidity: 417
Listing: 73, 149
  Buyer's Listing: 85
    Dual Agency: 85
  Closing the Seller: 92
    Competitive Market Analysis (CMA): 92
  Listing Interview: 89
  Multiple Listing Service (MLS): 83
  Office Exclusive: 85
  Overcoming Objections: 93
  Servicing Listings: 99
    Steps: 100
    Weekly Summary: 101
  Types of Listings: 79
    Exclusive Agency Listing: 81
    Exclusive Listing: 80

Exclusive Right to Sell: 82
Net Listing: 82
Open Listing: 79
  Pocket Buyer: 79
When to Reject a Listing: 149
Listing Agreement: 73, 111, 445
  Breakdown of: 111
  Residential Listing Agreement: 73
Listing Interview: 89
  Comparables: 91
  Curb Appeal: 89
  Seller's Proceeds: 89
Listing Kit: 124, 257
  Combined Hazards Book: 124
  Disclosure Regarding Real Estate Agency
    Relationships: 124
  Estimated Seller's Proceeds: 124
  Home Warranty Application or Waiver: 124
  Lead-Based Paint and Lead-Based Paint
    Hazards Disclosure: 124
  Natural Hazards Disclosure Statement: 124
  Notice to Buyers and Sellers - Defective
    Furnaces in California: 124
  Residential Listing Agreement: 124
  Seller's Advisory: 124
  Seller's Affidavit of Nonforeign Status: 124
  Smoke Detector Statement of Compliance: 124
  Supplemental Statutory and Contractual
    Disclosures: 124
  Transfer Disclosure Statement: 124
  Water Heater Statement of Compliance: 124
Listings: 66
Loan Application: 312
Loan Brokerage: 322, 458
  Activities: 458
  Business and Professions Code: 326
    Article 7 - Loan Broker Laws: 326
  Loan Broker Commission Limits: 326
  Mortgage Loan Disclosure Statement: 322-323
  Usury: 326
Loan Takeovers: 321
  Assumption, Loan: 321
  Subject To: 321
Loans: 423
Local Real Estate Associations: 581
Lock Box: 93, 100
Low-Income Housing: 518
  Section 8: 518

M

Managing Agent: 515

Manufactured Home Listing Agreement: 470, 472
Manufactured Housing: 469
   and the Licensee: 469
      Manufactured Home Listing Agreement:
      470, 472
      Marketing: 470
      Mobile Home Dealer vs. Real Estate Broker: 470
      Opportunities: 470
   Mobile Home Park: 469
   Multisectional: 469
   Singlewide: 469
Margin: 302
Marginal Tax Rate: 397
Market Value: 142
Master Transaction File: 543
Mediation: 238
Mello-Roos Community Facilities Act: 388-389
Mello-Roos District: 228
Member, Appraiser Institute (MAI): 468
Member, Society of Real Estate Appraisers
   (SREA): 468
Mentors: 531
MITUM: 425
Mobile Home Park: 469
Mortgage: 293
   Mortgagee: 293
   Mortgagor: 293
Mortgage Banking: 296
Mortgage Brokers: 296, 299
Mortgage Loan Bulletin: 574
Mortgage Loan Disclosure Statement: 322-323
Move In/Move Out Inspection (MIMO): 502
Moving Checklist: 53
Multiple Listing Service (MLS): 57, 83-84, 265
   MLS on the Internet: 84
Multisectional: 469

N

National Association of Independent Fee
   Appraisers (NAIFA): 142
National Association of Hispanic Real Estate
   Professionals (NAHREP): 594
National Association of Real Estate Brokers
   (NAREB): 592-593
National Association of Realtors®: 581-582
   Code of Ethics: 583, 586
   NAR Affiliates: 584-585
   NAR Ethics Course Requirement: 592
   Trade Name: 582
National Association of Realtors® (NAR: 532
National Association of Realtors® (NAR): 518

Natural Hazards Disclosure: 228
Natural Hazards Disclosure Statement: 124, 137
Net Lease: 508
   Net Net Lease: 508
   Triple Net Lease: 508
Net Listing: 82
Net Multipliers: 452
Net Operating Income: 425
Neutral Depository: 338
New Construction: 380
   Taxable Alteration: 380
Noninstitutional Financing: 296, 317
   All-Inclusive Trust Deed (AITD): 319
   Junior Loans: 317
      Acceleration Clause: 318
      Balloon Payments: 319
   Land Contract: 319
Notary Public: 548
   Functions of: 549
   Notarization: 549
   Notary Journal: 549
   Official Seal of Notary: 550
   Qualifications: 549
Notary Public Services: 456
   Acknowledgement: 456
Notice of Non-Responsibility: 233
Notice of Termination of Tenancy: 493
   Notice of Termination of Tenancy: 494
Notice to Buyer to Perform: 257, 271
Notice to Buyers and Sellers - Defective Furnaces
   in California: 124, 140
Notice to Creditors of Bulk Sale: 446-447
Notice to Seller to Perform: 257, 270-271

O

Office Exclusive: 85
On-Call Employees: 539
Open Houses: 45-46, 50
   Guidelines: 47
   Staging: 47
Open Listing: 79
Operating Expenses: 425-426
Ordnance: 132
Origination Fee: 294

P

Panic Peddling: 483
Panic Selling: 483
Paperflow: 542
Partnership: 62
Payoff Demand Statement: 345

Pending Listing: 147
Percentage Lease: 508
   Recapture Clause: 508
   Warehouse Sales: 508
Personal Assistant Contract: 539-540
Pocket Buyer: 79
Points: 294-295
Policy Manual: 57, 603
Potential Gross Income: 423
Preliminary Title Report: 353
Prepaid Rental Listing Service: 515
Prepaid Rental Listing Service (PRLS): 571
   License: 571
Prepayment Penalties: 393
Prepayment Penalty: 295
Prevailing Market Rate: 295
Price: 423
Prime Loans: 297
Private Mortgage Insurance (PMI): 299
   Credit Requirements: 300
Probate Attorneys: 45
Probate Listing Agreement: 460-461
Probate Sales: 459
   Brokerage Opportunities: 459
   Mechanics of the Probate Sale: 460
     Probate Listing Agreement: 460-461
     Right to Sell: 463
     Term: 463
Professional Physical Inspection Waiver: 263
Professional Property Management : 417
Property Management: 457, 481, 487
   Accurate Record Keeping: 509
   Activities: 457
   Activity Report: 510
   Application To Rent/Receipt For Deposit
     Screening Fee: 499-500
   California Apartment Association (CAA): 490
   California Certified Residential Manager
     (CCRM): 489
   Cash Journal: 510
   Common Interest Development (CID): 512
   Compensation: 495
   Establishing Rent Schedules: 507
     Contract Rent: 507
     Flat Rental Lease: 508
     Graduated Lease: 509
     Gross Lease: 508
     Net Lease: 508
     Percentage Lease: 508
   Fair Housing Laws: 481
   Highest and Best Use: 492

   Improving Value Through Balanced
     Management: 516
     Deferred Maintenance: 517
   Leasing and Tenant Selection: 499
   Low-Income Housing: 518
   Move In/Move Out Inspection (MIMO): 502
   Prepaid Rental Listing Service: 515
   Professional Associations for Managers: 518
     Accredited Management Organization
       (AMO): 519
     Certified Property Manager (CPM): 519
     Real Estate Management (IREM): 518
   Property Management Agreement: 495-496
   Rent Control: 518
   Residential Lease or Month-To-Month Rental
     Agreement: 502-503
   Selection of Property Managers: 493
   Trust Bank Account Record for Each Property
     Managed (TAP): 512
   Types of Properties: 488
   Types of Property Managers: 488
     Duties and Responsibilities: 490
       60-Day Termination Notice: 492
       Landlord-Tenant Termination Laws: 492
       Notice of Termination of Tenancy: 493
     General Managers: 488
     Institutional Manager: 489
     Outside Manager: 488
     Resident Manager: 489
Property Management Agreement: 495-496
Property Taxes: 375
   Ad Valorem Tax: 375
   Assessed Valuation: 382
   County Assessor: 377
   County Tax Collector: 378
   Disabled and Senior Citizen's Property Tax
     Postponement: 386
   Documentary Transfer Tax: 388
   Gift and Estate Taxes: 388
   Homeowner's Property Tax Exemption: 385
   New Construction: 380
   Property Tax Bill: 383-384
   Property Tax Time Table: 382, 384
   Proposition 13: 378
   Proposition 58: 380
   Proposition 60: 380
   Proposition 90: 380
   Proration Problem: 383
   Special Assessment Tax: 387
   Specific Lien: 382
   Summary of Real Property Transfers: 381

Supplemental Property Tax Bills: 385
Tax Exempt Property: 386
Taxable Alteration: 380
Taxes for Income Producing Properties: 394
Taxes Involving Real Property: 377
Taxes on Personal Residence: 392
Veteran's Exemption: 386
Proposition 13: 378-379
Proposition 58: 380
Proposition 60: 380
Proposition 90: 380
Proration: 346
30 Days Base Month: 349
Prospecting: 41
1031 Exchanges: 45
Absentee Owners: 45
Competitive Market Analysis (CMA): 41
Expired Listings: 46
Extended Listing Relationships: 46
Finding Buyers: 48
For Sale By Owners (FSBOs): 45
Geographical Farm: 43
Open Houses: 45
Probate Attorneys: 45
Referrals: 51
Reverse Phone Directory: 49
Sample Newsletter: 44
Statement of Identification: 43
Purchase Agreement Addendum: 242
Purchasing a Home: 160
Advantages to Owning a Home: 162
Budgeting for a Home: 163
Disadvantages to Owning a Home: 162
New Homes: 160
Older Homes: 160
Economic (Social) Obsolescence: 161
Functional Obsolescence: 161

Q

Qualifying the Buyer: 183

R

Race Restrictions: 483
Real Estate Appraisal, Broker's Role in: 142
Market Value: 142
National Association of Independent Fee
Appraisers (NAIFA): 142
Real Estate Assistants: 527
Getting the Job: 534
Interview Questions: 536
The Job Offer: 537

Employee or Independent Contractor: 539
Full-Time Employee: 538
On Call: 538
Part-Time Employee: 537
Personal Assistant Contract: 539-540
Your Resume: 534
Licensed vs. Unlicensed: 529
Mentors: 531
What Do Assistants Do?: 542
Escrow Coordinator: 552
Follow-Up Details: 552
Keeping and Assisting with Appointments: 546
Master Transaction File: 543
Notary Public: 548
Office Administration: 542
Staying in Touch with Your Agent's Clients: 546
Technology: 547
Hand-Held Computers: 548
Real Estate Software: 547
Unique Market Analysis: 548
Updating Data: 545
When Does an Agent Need an Assistant?: 532
Who Hires Assistants?: 532
Why Become an Assistant?: 530
Real Estate Brokerage—General vs.
Specialization: 467
Real Estate Bulletin: 574-575
Real Estate Commissioner: 456, 458, 464, 559, 561,
569, 572-573
Enforcement of Real Estate Law: 573
Hearings for License Violations: 573
Regulations of the Commissioner: 571, 576, 579
Broker Supervision (Regulation 2725): 576
Real Estate Educators Association (REEA): 596
Real Estate Equity Trust (REET): 435
Real Estate General Fund: 580
Recovery Fund: 580
Real Estate Investment Counselor: 466
Real Estate Investment Trust (REIT): 435
Real Estate Investments Trust (REIT): 489
Real Estate Law, California: 572
Common Violations: 574
Section 10176: 576-577
Section 10177: 576, 578
Revoke, Restrict, Suspend License: 574
Real Estate License Requirements: 561
Conditional Salesperson's License: 563
Electronic Fingerprint Requirement: 568
eLicensing: 567
Four-Year Salesperson's License: 563
Obtaining the Broker's License: 568

Proof of Legal Presence in the United States: 568
  Personal Responsibility and Work
    Opportunity Act: 568
Renewal of License: 570
Required Courses: 566
Salesperson's Examination: 564
  Examination Subject Areas (Salesperson and
    Broker): 565
  Notification of Examination Results: 564
Six-Hour CE Survey: 571
When a License is Not Required: 562
Real Estate License, Revoke, Restrict, Suspend : 574
Real Estate Management (IREM): 518
Real Estate Mortgage Trust (REMT): 435
Real Estate Settlement Procedures Act (RESPA): 362
  Department of Housing and Urban
    Development (HUD): 363
Real Estate Software: 547
Real Estate Transfer Disclosure Statement: 45
Real Property Securities Dealer (RPSD): 455
Real Property Transfers, Summary of: 381
Real Property, Sale of: 396
  Accounting for the Sale of Real Estate: 398
  Alternative Minimum Tax (AMT): 397
  Capital Assets: 396
    Capital Gains: 396
    Capital Losses: 396
  Federal Income Tax Rates: 396
Real Property, Types of
  Dealer Property: 401
Realtist: 592
Recapitulation: 510
Recapture Clause: 508
Receipt for Reports and Contingency Removal:
  257, 269
Record Keeping: 64
  Commingling: 64
  Sales Records: 64
  Trust Bank Account Record for All Trust Funds
  Deposited and Withdrawn: 64-65
Redling: 483, 485
Referrals: 51
  Sources: 52
Regressive Taxes: 397
Regular Assessments: 514
Regulation Z: 66
Rent Control: 431, 518
Request for Repair: 268
Re-Sales: 160
Reserves for Replacement: 426
Residential Income Properties: 423

Analyzing the Rental Market: 428
Characteristics of the Rental Market: 430
  Current Rental Ranges: 430
  Current Vacancy Rates: 430
  Desirable Distribution of Units by Type and
    Price Class: 431
  Income Characteristics: 430
  Rent Control: 431
  Rent-to-Income Relationships: 430
Property Analysis (Appraisal): 423
  Capitalization of Net Income: 427
  Down Payment: 423
  Effective Gross Income: 425
  Fixed Expenses: 426
  Loans: 423
  MITUM: 425
  Net Operating Income: 425
  Operating Expenses: 425-426
  Potential Gross Income: 423
  Price: 423
  Reserves for Replacement: 426
  Scheduled Income: 423
  Short-Lived Component: 426
  Times Gross: 427
  Vacancy Factor: 425
  Variable Expenses: 426
Studying Area Characteristics: 429
  Dwelling Unit Trends: 429
  Population Analysis: 429
  Projected Demand for Multiple Units in the
    Area: 430
Residential Lease or Month-To-Month Rental
  Agreement: 502-503
Residential Listing Agreement: 73, 76, 111, 124
Reverse 1031 Exchanges: 400
Reverse Phone Directory: 49
Riders: 100

S

Safety Clause: 82
Sale-Leaseback: 395
Sales Kit: 51-52, 185
Sales Opportunities, State of California: 463
  Board of Education Real Estate Sales: 463
  Caltrans: 463
  Interstate Land Sales Full Disclosure Act: 465
  Subdivision Sales Opportunities: 464
Savings Banks: 296, 419
  Prime Loans: 297
Scheduled Income: 423
Secondary Mortgage (Trust Deed) Market: 299, 303

Federal Home Loan Mortgage Corporation
(FHLMC): 304
Federal National Mortgage Association
(FNMA): 303
Government National Mortgage Association
(GNMA): 303
Section 10142 (Real Estate Law): 123
Section 10176: 576-577
Section 10177: 576, 578
Security Agreement and Financing Statement: 448-449
Seismic Hazard Zones: 229
Seller Advisory: 76
Seller's Affidavit of Nonforeign Status: 124
Seller-Financing Addendum: 221
Seller's Advisory: 124-125, 257
Seller's Affidavit of Nonforeign Status: 128
    FRPTA: 128
Seller's Proceeds: 89
Selling: 157
    Steps Involved in a Sale: 179
        Buyer Comment Sheet: 188
        Closing: 193
        Credit Rules of Thumb: 184
        Curb Appeal: 188
        Feng Shui: 190
        Planning the Showing: 188
        Qualifying the Buyer: 183
        Sales Kit: 185
        Showing: 190
        Types of Buyers: 185
    Techniques of Selling: 165
        AIDA: 167
        Caravan: 179
        Face-to-Face Communications: 165
        One-Way Communications: 167
        Two-Way Communications: 168
            Floortime: 171
            Incoming Call Register: 169
            Switch Sheet: 177
    The Sale: 193
        Closing Techniques: 194
        Overriding Objections: 196
Shared Document: 543
Short-Lived Component: 426
Showing: 190
Simultaneous 1031 Exchanges: 399
Singlewide: 469
Smoke Detector Statement of Compliance: 124, 133
Social Obsolescence : 161
Sole Proprietorship: 62
Soliciting: 51

Cold Calls: 51
Expired Listings: 51
Reverse Directory: 51
Warm Calls: 51
Special Assessment Tax: 387
    Improvement Bond Act of 1915: 387
    Mello-Roos Community Facilities Act: 388
    Special Assessment District Board: 387
Special Assessments: 514
Sphere of Influence: 35, 49-50
    Farm: 49
Staging: 47
Starker Delayed Exchange: 400
State Board of Equalization: 450
Statement of Identification: 43
Steering: 483
Stock: 63
Straight Commission: 40
Straight-Line Depreciation: 395
Structural Pest Control Certification Report: 349
Subchapter S Corporation: 63, 435
Subdivision Industry Bulletin: 574
Subject To: 321
Subprime Borrower: 298
Supplemental Statutory and Contractual
    Disclosures: 124, 132
Switch Sheet: 175, 177-178
Syndication: 431, 459
    Brokerage Opportunities: 432
    Forms of Legal Organization: 432
        Corporation: 434
        General Partnership: 434
        Limited Partnership: 433
        Real Estate Investment Trust (REIT): 435
            Hybrid Trust: 435
            Real Estate Equity Trust (REET): 435
            Real Estate Mortgage Trust (REMT): 435
        Subchapter S Corporation: 435

T

Tax Exempt Property: 386
Tax Shelter: 414
Taxable Alteration: 380
Tax-Deferred Exchanges: 401
    Boot: 401
Taxes for Income Producing Properties: 394
    Depreciation of Business Property: 395
Taxes on Personal Residence: 392
    Deduction of Interest: 393
    Deduction of Prepayment Penalties: 393
    Deduction of Property Taxes: 393

Sale of a Residence: 394
Termites and Other Problems: 349
   Structural Pest Control Certification Report: 349
Times Gross: 427
Title Insurance: 352
   Chain of Title: 352
   Four Functions of: 352
   Preliminary Title Report: 353
   Title Insurance Disclosure: 362
   Title Plant: 352
   Types of Title Insurance Policies: 355
      ALTA-R Policy: 361
      American Land Title Association (ALTA): 360
      California Land Title Association (CLTA): 355
   Who Pays Title Insurance Fees?: 362
Title Plant: 352
Trade and Professional Associations: 580
   California Association of Realtors®: 581
   National Association of Realtors®: 581
Traffic Sheet/Ad Call Log Book: 56
Transaction File: 57
Transfer Disclosure Statement: 124, 129, 228
Trust Bank Account Record for All Trust Funds
   Deposited and Withdrawn: 64-65
Trust Bank Account Record for Each Property
   Managed (TAP): 512-513
Truth in Lending Act: 317
   Annual Percentage Rate (APR): 317
Truth-in-Lending Act: 66

U

Uniform Commercial Code (UCC): 446
Unlawful Detainer: 507
Unruh Civil Rights Act: 481, 484
Usury: 326

V

VA Loan Assumption: 321
Vacancy Factor: 425
Valuation, Approaches to: 143
   Capitalization Approach: 143
   Comparative Approach: 143
   Cost Approach: 143
Variable Expenses: 426
Verification of Property Condition: 257, 272
Vesting Chart - Methods of Holding Title: 367
Veterans Administration (VA): 307, 309-310
   Certificate of Reasonable Value (CRV): 309
   Eligibility and Entitlement: 310
   Reinstatement of Veterans Loan Entitlement: 310
   Secondary Financing: 309

W

Warehouse Sales: 508
Warm Calls: 51
Water Heater Statement of Compliance: 124, 134
WINForms®: 38
Wood Destroying Pest Inspection and Allocation of
Cost Addendum: 257, 264

Order Department

Sometimes our textbooks are hard to find!

If your bookstore does not carry our textbooks, send us a check or money order and we'll mail them to you with our 30-day money back guarantee.

Other Great Books from Educational Textbook Company:

California Real Estate Principles, 10th ed., by Huber	$65.00 ____
How To Pass The Real Estate Exam (850 Exam Questions), by Huber	$40.00 ____
California Real Estate Law, by Huber & Tyler	$50.00 ____
Real Estate Finance, by Huber & Messick	$50.00 ____
Real Estate Economics, by Huber, Messick, & Pivar	$50.00 ____
Real Estate Appraisal, by Huber, Messick, & Pivar	$50.00 ____
Mortgage Loan Brokering, by Huber & Pivar	$50.00 ____
Property Management, by Huber & Pivar	$50.00 ____
Escrow I: An Introduction, by Huber	$50.00 ____
California Real Estate Practice, by Huber & Lyons	$50.00 ____
Real Estate Computer Applications, by Grogan & Huber	$50.00 ____
California Business Law, by Huber, Owens, & Tyler	$65.00 ____
Hubie's Power Prep CD – 100 Questions - Vol. 1, by Huber	$50.00 ____

Subtotal _____
Add shipping and handling @ $5.00 per book _____
Add California sales tax @ 8.25% _____
TOTAL _____

Allow 2-3 weeks for delivery

Name: _____

Address: _____

City, State, Zip: _____

Phone: _____

Check or money order: Educational Textbook Company, P.O. Box 3597, Covina, CA 91722

For faster results, order by credit card from the Glendale Community College Bookstore:

1-818-240-1000 x3024